Rising Tide

Rising Tide

LESSONS FROM 165 YEARS OF BRAND BUILDING AT PROCTER & GAMBLE

Davis Dyer

Frederick Dalzell

Rowena Olegario

Harvard Business School Press
Boston, Massachusetts

Printed in the United States of America
08 07 06 05 04 5 4 3 2 1

Library of Congress Cataloging-in-Publication Data
Dyer, Davis.
Rising tide : lessons from 165 years of brand building at Procter & Gamble / Davis Dyer, Frederick Dalzell, Rowena Olegario.
p. cm.
ISBN 1-59139-147-4
1. Procter & Gamble Company—History. 2. Brand name products—United States—Case studies. 3. Product management—United States—Case studies. 4. Soap trade—United States—History. I. Dalzell, Frederick. II. Olegario, Rowena. III. Title.
HD9999.S74P738 2004
338.7'67—dc22
2003019396

The paper used in this publication meets the requirements of the American National Standard for Permanence of Paper for Publications and Documents in Libraries and Archives Z39.48-1992.

CONTENTS

PART III Going Global, 1980–1990

PART IV Competing in a Shrinking World: Procter & Gamble Since 1990

PREFACE AND ACKNOWLEDGMENTS

THIS BOOK charts the rising tide of Procter & Gamble's fortunes from its beginning in Cincinnati, Ohio, 165 years ago to its present-day global leadership in branded consumer goods.

We have a dual purpose in telling this story. First, we seek to describe and explain P&G's evolution, which, some older books notwithstanding, has never received the attention it deserves. The company is one of the biggest and most influential in its industry worldwide, and its impact is felt broadly in modern consumer society and culture. Understanding where and how P&G became what it is today, helps to explain the development of the global consumer economy that shapes the way the vast majority of the Earth's peoples now live.

Our second purpose is to explain the company's success in its core business of building consumer brands. We accomplish this (we hope) by exploring key events and episodes that stimulated P&G's learning about brand building. In these moments of particular challenge and change—bringing new brands to market, penetrating new geographies, developing new capabilities and better ways to manage, and reviving flagging brands—the company learned how to build and sustain successful brands. By highlighting these moments and the lessons P&G drew from them, we hope to increase understanding of brand building as a management capability and a source of strategic strength.

The chronological narrative of P&G's history is broken into four parts and is tilted forward in time, focusing more on recent decades than on the company's earlier years. Part 1 describes the company's first one hundred years, from its founding in Cincinnati in 1837 through the development of its first major brand, Ivory, and its megabrand, Tide, in the middle of the twentieth century. Part 2 covers the period between 1945 and 1980, when P&G diversified into a broad range of branded consumer products—sometimes via acquisition—and began to penetrate markets in Latin America, Western Europe, and Japan. Part 3 deals with the 1980s, when the company greatly accelerated its global expansion, especially in the Far East, and developed its first global brands, including Always/Whisper feminine protection pads, Pringles Crisps, and Pantene shampoo. Part 4 considers the period since 1990, when the company addressed a host of opportunities and challenges, including the rise of mass merchandisers, the opening of markets in Central and Eastern Europe, Russia, and China, and the advent of the Internet and e-commerce.

The opening chapters in each of the four parts provide a narrative overview of P&G in the period covered. Chapters devoted to particular learning episodes—brands, geographical markets, and management innovations—follow. Each such chapter concludes with a brief summary, with observations about the lessons learned about brand building.

The prologue and epilogue frame the overall story by identifying the major themes that transcend the eras of P&G's history, as well as the high-order principles of brand building that P&G has formulated along the way.

This book originated at P&G in the 1990s when senior executives there recognized the need for a new company profile that would capture the story of its growth and change in recent decades. They wanted both to protect against the loss of institutional memory and to establish a shared knowledge of P&G's past as the company grew larger and more global.

In 2000, P&G retained The Winthrop Group, Inc. to undertake the research and writing and the three coauthors quickly formed as a working team. We are grateful to P&G's Chairman and Chief Executive, A. G. Lafley, as well as to his predecessors Durk Jager and John Pepper, for their sponsorship of the book. We wish also to thank Charlotte Otto, P&G's Global External Relations Officer, for her enthusiastic support and encouragement and for sharing her deep knowledge of the company and her fine skills as a critical reader.

Several past and present P&G employees, in addition to John and Charlotte, served as part of an informal advisory group to the project. Other participants included Gibby Carey, Gil Cloyd, Bob McDonald, Ed Rider, John Smale, and Chris Warmoth. They contributed in significant ways, pointing out important topics and themes to explore, saving us from wandering down blind alleys, and serving as first and last readers of the manuscript drafts. It has been a privilege and a pleasure to work with them.

The research underpinning this book was conducted in Cincinnati and at other P&G locations around the world, as well as in the public record. In Cincinnati, the P&G Corporate Archives are a treasure trove of historical information and a model of its kind. Our work entailed close cooperation with head archivist Ed Rider and his staff, including Dianne Brown, Amy Fischer, Barb Hemsath, Greg McCoy, Lisa Mulvany, Nancy Asman, and Diane Wagner, as well as Joe Singleton, an intern assigned to the project in its early months. We put innumerable requests and questions to these professionals and invariably received timely responses, typically backed up with sheaves of documents. If only doing research were always like this!

Many past and present P&G employees gave generously of their time for interviews, and furnished or referred us to key documents. The list of such people is too long to include here but many names are recorded in the notes at the end of the book. We thank these people for their manifold contributions. They taught us a lot and helped us to make sense of a complex, interconnected story.

A principal theme in this book is P&G's legendary discipline and thoroughness in carrying out its work. We saw this close-up and firsthand on numerous occasions as many past and present P&G employees, in addition to those already named, gave the manuscript or particular chapters close readings. We are grateful to Jeff Ansell, Dick Antoine, Sandy Argabrite, Ed Artzt, Wolfgang Berndt, Tom Blinn, Don Campbell, Mark Collar, Al Collins, Gary Cunningham, Steve David, Doug Dedeker, Jim Edwards, Rad Ewing, Chuck Fullgraf, Harald Einsmann, Stona Fitch, Bob Gill, Chris Hassall, Keith Harrison, Deb Henretta, Peter Hindle, Chris Holmes, Greg Icenhower, Mike Kehoe, Mark Ketchum, Keith Lawrence, Gary Martin, Rob Matteucci, Bob Miller, Shekhar Mitra, Jorge Montoya, Tom Muccio, Lisa Owens, Dimitri Panayotopoulos, Laurent Philippe, Paul Polman, Liz Ricci, Nabil Sakkab, Claude Salomon, Herbert Schmitz, Bob Seitz, Jim Sisson, Dave Swanson, John Tracey, Berenike Ullmann, and John Yam for their comments, corrections, and advice. The volume and quality of such input reminds us of another author's (or authors', we can't be certain) waggish comment after a similar list of acknowledgments: If any mistakes yet remain in the book, it's not our fault! Certainly, if any errors made it through this very fine sieve—and, alas, some probably did—it's not from lack of effort to stop them.

One of the pleasures in writing a book is the opportunity to discuss it as it is taking shape with friends and colleagues, whose questions and comments stimulate sharper thinking and open new avenues of inquiry. At Winthrop Group, we enjoyed many provocative discussions about P&G and the evolution of corporate institutions in general with Margaret B. W. Graham, Timothy Jacobson, and George Smith. Other friends with whom we discussed the book and/or some of its central ideas include Alfred D. Chandler, Jr., Alan Kantrow, Joshua Margolis, and Nitin Nohria.

Although P&G generously supported the book, its organization, themes, interpretations, and conclusions are solely the authors' responsibility. Procter & Gamble did not provide any kind of subvention to Harvard Business School Press, which followed its customary review procedures before agreeing to publish the manuscript; which prompts us to thank our editors at HBS Press, Jacque Murphy and Hollis Heimbouch, as well as the four anonymous reviewers who offered thought-provoking and thorough reviews of the manuscript.

Finally, we can never repay the debt of gratitude we owe our families and loved ones—Janice, Ricky, and Bella; Mary-Elise, Abby, and Molly; and Charles—for their love, understanding, support, and patience throughout this project.

—Davis Dyer, Cambridge, Massachusetts
Frederick Dalzell, Cambridge, Massachusetts
Rowena Olegario, Nashville, Tennessee
October 2003

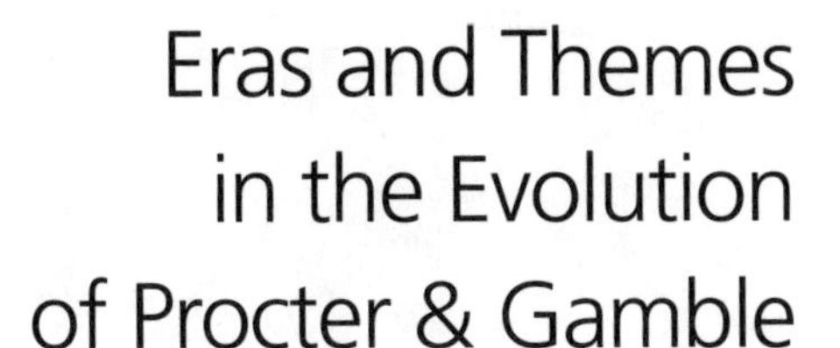

Eras and Themes in the Evolution of Procter & Gamble

ESTABLISHED as a soap and candle maker in Cincinnati in 1837, Procter & Gamble (P&G) has become one of the biggest and most visible consumer products companies in the world. In 2002, it posted approximately $40 billion in sales and employed 102,000 people in 80 countries. It sells dozens of the most popular branded consumer goods on the planet to more than 5 billion people living in more than 140 countries. Many P&G brands are, literally, household names all over the world: Tide, Ariel, Pampers, Crest, Always/Whisper, Pringles, Olay, and Pantene, to name but a few. The company has been the largest advertiser in the world for more than a century. Procter & Gamble is also widely recognized in the business community as a formidable and well-run institution. Perennially it ranks high on lists of the most admired companies in its industry and in business generally.[1]

Procter & Gamble's story is deeply intertwined with the growth of the modern consumer economy, first in the United States and then around the world. Along with a handful of its peers and other similar institutions, P&G has exerted a significant impact on how people live. Packaged P&G items find daily use in people's washing, grooming, cleaning, eating, and drinking; in the preservation of health and the treatment of minor ailments; in the care of infants; and in pet care. Procter & Gamble products crowd the cupboards and cabinets of homes everywhere. How the items got there, from their conception and development as merchandise, through the mass production and distribution that makes them ubiquitous, to the advertising that

Procter & Gamble boasted thirteen billion-dollar brands in 2003. Ranked by sales, these included Pampers, Tide, Ariel, Pantene, Always/Whisper, Charmin, Bounty, Crest, Iams/Eukanuba, Pringles, Downy/Lenor, Folgers, and Olay.

continuously invites consumers to buy and use them, is a central story, both in business history and in the evolution of material culture.

This book describes and explains the rising tide of P&G's fortunes as the company grew and expanded around the globe. The book aspires to be both a history of the company and a guide to the principles and practices of brand building as P&G has developed and learned them so far. These dual purposes are reflected in the book's hybrid architecture. First, there is a chronological frame to help portray P&G's overall evolution. Second, within that frame is a series of case studies that explore key episodes, moments of truth in which the company learned (or relearned) something important about building brands and developed new capabilities to carry forward. From these experiences, P&G derived the basic principles—summarized in the epilogue—by which it continues to navigate. This book, then, is not a conventional corporate history in narrative form; nor is it a management book about brand building. Rather, it is something of both: a learning history of a company that has prospered for more than a century and a half by getting better at building brands that satisfy consumers.

Three Eras

Procter & Gamble's history is one of constant change and adaptation, as it developed new products, discovered new markets, and responded to competitive threats and opportunities. Within a context of constant change, however, three distinct periods of common challenge stand out in P&G's case. In each of them, the company developed new capabilities or deepened existing ones.

1. FOUNDATIONS (part 1 of the book, covering the first 108 years, 1837–1945). Procter & Gamble underwent several transformative experiences as it took root and grew in this period. During the U.S. Civil War (1861–1865), for example, the company had thrived selling candles to the Union army. This business all but disappeared after the war. The search for a new source of stable growth eventually led to Ivory, the first differentiated and branded soap. Procter & Gamble built Ivory into a successful brand on a national scale by learning and mastering new capabilities in chemical control, large-scale manufacturing and distribution, and advertising and promotion. As it developed more products and brands, such as Crisco, Camay, and Oxydol, the company pioneered and mastered new capabilities in R&D, manufacturing, market research, and branding. These capabilities culminated in the development of the next blockbuster: Tide synthetic detergent.
2. ERA OF RELATED DIVERSIFICATION (part 2 of the book, covering the period between the end of World War II and about 1980). During this period, P&G grew rapidly and diversified from its base in soaps, fats, and oils into many new areas, including foods and beverages, oral care, and paper products. It also began to expand overseas. This era witnessed many defining moments for the company, from the rapid expansion of Tide and Ariel, to new businesses in foods and beverages (Jif, Duncan Hines, Folgers); paper products (Charmin, Bounty, and Puffs); disposable diapers (Pampers and Luvs); oral care (Crest); and the sudden, disappointing end to a promising start in feminine care (Rely). Along the way, P&G learned and enhanced still more capabilities. In R&D, it differentiated and improved existing brands and developed new ones while also innovating in process technology. In marketing and advertising, the company exploited the broadcast media and built long-standing partnerships with agencies. Procter & Gamble improved its human resource management to develop high-performance work systems in its factories. The company also

improved its general management capabilities to plan and control a sprawling, decentralized corporation with scores of brands and operations in multiple industries beginning to spread around the world.

3. ERA OF HEIGHTENED COMPETITION AND GLOBALIZATION (parts 3 and 4 of the book, covering from about 1980 to the present). In this era, P&G has been competing fiercely around the world with capable rivals such as Unilever, Kimberly-Clark, Colgate-Palmolive, Henkel, and Kao in its traditional businesses while continuing to expand into new industries such as health care, feminine care, beauty care, and pet nutrition—and encountering new global rivals along the way. The company learned—at times awkwardly—how to woo and win customers outside familiar markets in North America, Latin America, and Western Europe to penetrate Asia and capitalize on new opportunities in Central and Eastern Europe and China. During this era, P&G transformed many of its leading brands such as Tide, Ariel, Pampers, Always / Whisper, and Pantene into global powerhouses. Moreover, it revitalized sagging brands such as Crest, Bounty, and Charmin. By revamping its supply chain, the company operated in partnership with major trade customers such as Wal-Mart, Carrefour, Tesco, and METRO. Finally, P&G underwent a massive reorganization to sustain global leadership in the twenty-first century.

Five Overarching Themes

A danger in demarking the evolution of any institution is that the segments become too distinct and separate. Continuity, as well as change, marks P&G's development. Five important themes reach back nearly to its founding and span these chronological eras.

1. A FOCUS ON BRANDED CONSUMER PRODUCTS. Procter & Gamble's fundamental identity is that of a marketer of branded consumer products. Although it sells some intermediate chemicals and once sold by-products such as cotton oil and wood pulp for industrial uses, the company has never wandered far from its roots. Even the specialized pharmaceutical business the company is building relies heavily on P&G's expertise in consumer marketing. When many big U.S. manufacturing companies diversified into unrelated businesses in the 1960s, P&G was not tempted to follow suit. It always believed that its best opportunities lay in consumer products, a belief that remains vital today.

Much of P&G's growth has been self-generated and organic, as evidenced by the continuity of its business in soaps and cleaners, one of its original lines in the nineteenth century. The company has not only mastered the core chemistry of fats and oils at the base of this business but also followed this core into related science and its applications, a criss-crossing path of connections that opened up a wide array of consumer product opportunities. The move from soaps to shortening, for example, represented a new application of the company's expertise in oils. This expertise also led to bake mixes, peanut butter, and potato snacks.

Detergents, which have a different chemical base from soaps, are nonetheless an obvious and natural extension of the soap business—the next generation in technology, so to speak. Detergents also spawned opportunities in shampoos and dentifrices. Meanwhile, the manufacture of successful detergents required a deep understanding of the chemistry of wash water. One of the ingredients of wash water is calcium. Procter & Gamble's knowledge of calcium then enabled the company to develop a tartar-control dentifrice, calcium additives for beverages, and pharmaceutical drug treatments for osteoporosis and osteoarthritis.

And the list goes on. Although P&G has sometimes actively acquired other businesses, the acquisitions have always been in areas related to those it already understands: branded, packaged consumer goods sold primarily in grocery stores, drugstores, and mass merchandisers.

2. A BROAD APPROACH TO CREATING AND BUILDING BRANDS. Procter & Gamble has long been one of the world's biggest advertisers, and advertising clearly has been central to the company's success. But early on, P&G recognized that building brands is not exclusively or even primarily a marketing activity. Rather, it is a systems problem. Better brands are based on innovation and continuous improvement throughout the company's operations and activities, starting with developed or acquired products with performance features that consumers value. From there, the company competed successfully by promoting the brands, periodically refreshing and upgrading the products, and steadily lowering the costs of manufacturing and distribution. In organizational terms, this requires that every function, department, and facility—R&D, purchasing, manufacturing, logistics, finance, marketing, sales, human resources, public affairs—pulls together. The success of this approach, in turn, reflects widely shared values and the principles and practices that reinforce them.

3. A COMMITMENT TO RIGOROUS EXPERIMENTATION. The development of Ivory soap illustrates the beginning of a continuing story. James N. Gamble was on a quest to evaluate new ingredients that might give soap some distinctive properties. He combined an inquiring mind with a disciplined approach to experiments. Eventually he found new ingredients that produced a better soap—one, coincidentally, that also floated. Ivory was the result of rigorous experimental inquiry married to meticulous attention to detail and open-mindedness about where the experiments might lead.

   These factors converged again and again at significant moments in the company's history. Procter & Gamble researchers conducted thousands of experiments on the fundamental nature of ingredients and their interactions. This understanding, in turn, led to new opportunities, including some hardly anticipated at the outset, such as connections between detergent builders and bone chemistry, fabric softeners and hair conditioners, and papermaking and thermal pain relievers.

   The same emphasis on experimentation, rigorous analysis, and learning characterizes the company's general approach to marketing and management: Gather as much data before the fact as practicable, and analyze it. Test new ideas, approaches, and products repeatedly in trials of increasing scale, and make modifications before attempting a full-scale launch. Enter a new business or a new market via acquisition or joint venture on a small scale, and through trial and error learn the formula for success before making a major commitment. Evaluate high-performance work systems in one plant before spreading them elsewhere. Experiment with customer teams before reorganizing the sales force from a geographical base to a customer base. Set up a small-scale e-business initiative before rolling out a corporatewide effort.

   Procter & Gamble's patient, deliberate, and rigorous approach to management problems as opportunities to develop and apply new learning appears in virtually all the company's most successful new product initiatives, acquisitions, market entries, and organizational changes. Conversely, the absence of such an approach such as during occasional efforts to rush new brands to market, more often resulted in unhappy outcomes.

4. TENACITY IN EXECUTION. The company's objectives do not differ markedly from those of its competitors and other consumer products companies. Yet P&G is unusually effective in executing its strategy—a function of the disciplined approach to management just noted as well as of persistence and tenacity in execution.

These qualities are evident in the unusually long development cycles of some of P&G's major brands, as employees recognized good ideas and kept at them until these ideas could be commercialized. Tide, Pampers, and Pringles are noteworthy examples. Charmin, ultimately one of P&G's best acquisitions, did not pan out for years while P&G doggedly sought the formula for success. By refusing to let go on these occasions, the company later reaped significant benefits.

This tenacity, of course, has a downside, when the original idea is not robust or when changing circumstances alter its attractiveness. The disappointing development of olestra, the synthetic fat replacement, is a case in point. Generations of scientists and managers pinned high hopes on the compound before recognizing, reluctantly, that projections were excessively optimistic. Fortunately for P&G, such examples are the exceptions. And despite the recentness of the olestra experience, the pattern of persistence continues, as evidenced by the company's long-term commitments to carve places in the beauty care and pharmaceutical industries and to challenging business environments such as those in Russia and China.

Although P&G's tenacity is most visible whenever the company rose and met long-term challenges, this steadfast quality has also characterized the company's approach to short-term problems and everyday life. Be it next week's deadline, next month's volume forecast, a target margin for the quarter, or a readiness to launch in nine months—the company fights tenaciously to deliver on its commitments.

5. AN ABILITY TO BALANCE OPPOSING PRESSURES. To thrive over the long term as a brand builder, P&G has worked continually at balancing opposing pressures in every part of the business: long-term versus short-term orientations, central control versus unit autonomy, U.S. versus non-U.S. perspectives, developing new brands versus fortifying existing ones, a few big initiatives versus a larger number of smaller ones. Among the biggest of these balancing acts, as a former senior executive put it, is the tension between tradition and innovation: "The ongoing dilemma of how we effectively use our vast experience and learning, to perpetuate and build upon that which we perceive to be key to our success, while at the same time creating an environment where innovation, change, and challenges to the status quo are encouraged and rewarded . . . the way we go about choosing what to hang onto and what to change and let go of is absolutely fundamental to our success."[2]

Although it possesses a strong culture that reflects its rigorous recruiting criteria and its proven ways of competing in consumer products, P&G is far from the monochromatic, conformist, almost cultlike institution it is sometimes portrayed to be in the media. Rather, the company's history reveals an organization often in ferment, typified by strong opinions and vigorous internal debates about the merits and drawbacks of particular decisions and courses of action. Procter & Gamble's ability to tolerate this debate and dissent and to succeed in its balancing act generally may reflect a duality in its innermost core.

In 2001, the company underwent a self-examination to identify its most elemental qualities described as its corporate DNA. Employees from all over the world, at every level, with a variety of backgrounds, experiences, and tenures, participated in interviews and focus groups and contributed their stories, mostly about why they joined P&G and why they stay with the company. This information was distilled and common patterns and foundational stories were found. They uncovered a duality in the company's essence consistent globally, regardless of nationality.

At its core, P&G's identity has two dimensions that coexist in tension. The "best of the best" represents an elite community with high standards, rock-solid values, a quest for excellence, and a highly disciplined approach to business. The "caring cultivator" represents an inclusive community concerned about each of its members and inspired by the company's mission to make products that improve the lives of consumers.[3] Procter & Gamble is thus both a hard-headed, results-oriented company and a company that seeks to develop employees and help them maximize their potential.

This duality appears in numerous ways, notably in the significant investment the company makes in recruiting, training, and development combined with what has historically been an up-or-out culture for its brand managers. Another manifestation is the pattern of leadership as results-oriented executives and organization development-minded executives often complement and follow each other up the ranks. Maintaining the balance between the contrary poles is a constant tension in P&G's evolution and a source of difficulty when not sustained.

These eras and overarching themes provide windows into P&G's growing abilities in brand building, which began to emerge soon after the company's founding in Cincinnati well over a century and a half ago.

PART I

Foundations

1837–1945

CHAPTER ONE

Getting Started, 1837–1890

PROCTER & GAMBLE IN THE COMMODITY ERA

PROCTER & GAMBLE launched as an obscure start-up in a churning sea of ventures and failures. William Procter was an English storekeeper and candle maker, James A. Gamble an Irish soap maker. Both men had apprenticed in their respective trades, made their way separately to Cincinnati, and settled in to begin building businesses. Fatefully, they married sisters—Olivia and Elizabeth Ann Norris. When a banking crisis precipitated a sharp economic downturn several years later in 1837, their father-in-law, Alexander Norris (also a candle maker), suggested that the two entrepreneurs unite their operations. Calculating on the basis of roughly $3,000 in business assets that Procter had amassed, the partners fixed $7,192.24 as the firm's starting capital. Gamble managed to pay in his half on October 31, at which point the two founders signed a formal agreement launching the enterprise. By the end of their first year, the partners were advertising in the *Cincinnati Daily Gazette*.[1]

The venture would grow to become an industrial giant, producing some of the biggest brands in business history. But in 1837, William Procter and James Gamble were undertaking a very different business in a very different marketplace. There was no national market to speak of—the infrastructure to support one was not yet in place. The U.S. economy was still overwhelmingly rural, agrarian, and exchange based (as opposed to cash based). Pockets of urbanization and industrialization were forming, but the overwhelming majority of Americans still lived and worked on farms, produced most of what they consumed themselves or traded for it within local networks of production and distribution, went to the store once or twice a year, and bought no "brand" goods (as we know the term today) of any kind.[2]

SOAP AND CANDLE FACTORY,

Main street, second house north of Sixth street.

THE subscribers offer their manufactures, warranted full weight, correct tare, and marked as the late city Ordinance directs—

No 1 Palm Soap,
" 2 Rosin do,
Toilet and Shaving Soap,
Pure Tallow Candles, mould and dipped.

PROCTER & GAMBLE.

oct 26 99tf

One of Procter & Gamble's earliest advertisements appeared in the Cincinnati Daily Gazette *in 1838.*

Like nearly all the goods that moved through this economy, soap and candles were commodities, rendered (in their crudest forms) from readily obtainable raw materials. People living in farming communities had easy access to the lard and tallow (derived from livestock slaughter) and lye (derived from ashes) required to make serviceable soap and functional candles.

On the other hand, economic expansion was starting to transform the manufacture of goods like candles and soap, and Procter and Gamble were perfectly situated to capitalize on the opportunity. Cincinnati, their base of operation, was emerging as a western hub, strategically located at a nexus of infrastructure connections. The Ohio River linked Cincinnati to New Orleans, the biggest cotton port in the country when cotton was by far the country's largest export. This position was bolstered in 1840 by the completion of the Miami Canal, which hooked Cincinnati into the Great Lakes system and, via the Erie Canal, New York City, and the Atlantic seaboard. In an era when most commerce traveled by water, these were vital linkages, opening the largest markets in the country to Cincinnati's entrepreneurs.[3]

Various kinds of enterprises, most significantly Cincinnati's meat packers, plugged themselves into this network. By 1837 the packers of Porkopolis, as Cincinnati was becoming known, were "putting up" more than 100,000 hogs annually, or roughly a quarter of the total number of hogs slaughtered in the United States, along with comparable numbers of cattle. A city directory in 1841 counted sixty-two beef and pork butchers at work in Cincinnati, and another forty-eight pork packers.[4] For a few critical decades, as William Procter and James Gamble established their business, Cincinnati was by far the largest meatpacking center in the United States.

The proximity of this dynamic industrial activity was pivotal. Cincinnati's meat packers supplied a ring of related businesses. By 1841, 31 cooperages (barrel-making operations) were based in Porkopolis, along with 166 boot makers and shoemakers, 22 saddlery and harness "factories," 21 tanneries (which used the animals' hides), and 10 mattress makers and upholsterers (which used the animals' hair and bristles). Soap and candle makers also tapped into the steady, massive supply of animal by-products, specifically the lard and tallow that rolled from the packinghouses in barrels by the wagonful. No fewer than 17 soap- and candle-making businesses (including Procter & Gamble) were operating in Cincinnati by the early 1840s—firms generating total revenues of an estimated $332,940 annually.[5] By the standards of the era, this was big business. Close, reliable access to raw materials—especially problematic in this period, with railroads only beginning to spread across the continent—was key to making a business like soap making and candle making work smoothly.

Even more important, setting up shop among the meat packers exposed William Procter and James Gamble to pioneering methods of industrial production. Cincinnati's packers achieved impressive economies as they scaled up their operations. It was the nature of their product, however, to begin decaying rapidly and immediately, as soon as the manufacturing process (i.e., the slaughter) had begun. The packers were therefore forced to develop highly efficient new methods of processing meat and shipping it out before it was ruined. This relentless logic drove them to create what business historians have subsequently called disassembly lines—innovative, streamlined operations that anticipated later assembly lines like Henry Ford's.[6] And it all took form right next to Procter & Gamble.

The impact was galvanizing. William Procter and James Gamble may have been trained as traditional, small-scale artisans, but they sensed more radical opportunities before them. They had planted their business at a central nexus of trade, right at a defining point of economic inflection, and the partners busily began taking advantage.

The Flow of Business in the Commodity Era

Over the first several decades of operation, Procter & Gamble built up a thriving business, shipping candles and soap downriver on steamboats to New Orleans for transshipment on oceangoing ships up and down the Atlantic seaboard. The Ohio/Mississippi River system formed the company's central artery of distribution. Everything was geared to shipments downriver, on steamboats like the *Yorktown,* the *Persia,* the *Duke,* the *Winfield Scott,* and the *Tecumseh*.[7] Still, the firm was in no position to crank up a regular, steady, high-volume flow of production and distribution. The market was highly seasonal. Farmers tended to buy store goods only after harvest, and the rivers froze in the winter. "If you want another lot of Candles and could receive them before the close of navigation," the firm wrote to a wholesaler upriver (or "up-canal") in Detroit in November 1848, "we would sell at nine cents per pound."[8] Those kinds of letters and terms went out all the time: The fluctuations in business, and in prices, were entirely typical in this preindustrial era.[9]

A surviving cash book recording debits and credits from 1849 to 1852 captures the rhythms of business and the mechanisms of exchange in this early period. Procter & Gamble's accounts reveal a constant stream of outlays—for wages and for tallow and grease from Cincinnati's meat packers, principally, with additional charges for expenses such as insurance, boxes, freight, drayage (i.e., transporting boxes and crates to the levee), and so on. A second, parallel stream flowed in the opposite direction, as retailers paid for shipments. On both sides of the ledger, cash sometimes changed hands, but other forms of payment figured heavily as well. A sophisticated barter exchange helped lubricate transactions. The firm paid employees in cash on occasion, but also in goods such as starch, tea, flour, shoulders (of meat), ham, and sundries (miscellaneous goods), as well as, of course, boxes of soap and candles. Customers also paid in kind: Storekeepers paid for soap and candle shipments with cash, boxes, groceries, and the like. Between April and July 1845, for example, "Spencer, Blacksmith" paid for a series of soap and candle shipments with a buggy worth $150.[10]

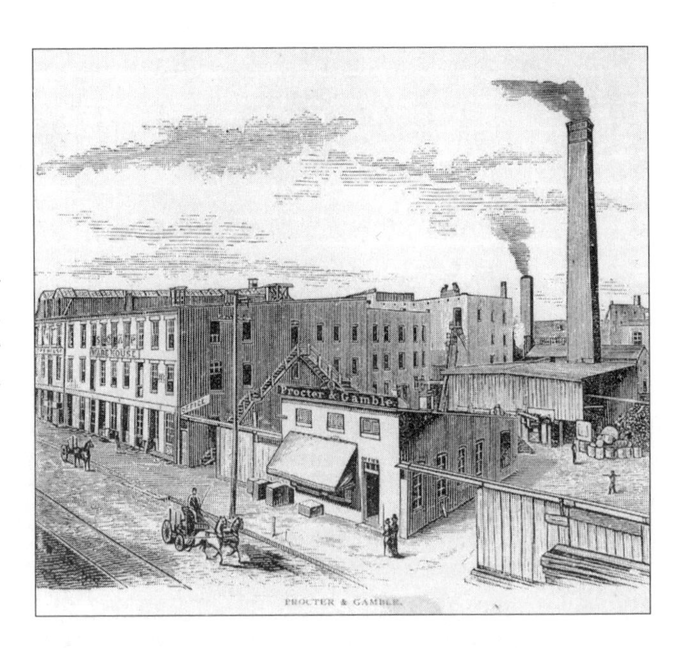

Procter & Gamble originally set up its manufacturing operations on Central Avenue in downtown Cincinnati.

The biggest accounts on the debit side of the ledger were the packers. Christian Pinger seems to have been a typical supplier. Between March 1844 and May 1845, he provided ten shipments of tallow, worth roughly $1,400. This accumulating balance was kept on the books as an open credit. Pinger drew on the account from time to time, for payments of between $25 and $100. Periodically, the company settled the balance; when the packer supplied another shipment of material, he started a new credit.[11]

For capital financing, the partners relied on local Cincinnati sources. "It always seemed possible to get all the accommodation at the banks [the firm] needed," an employee from this period recalled. A soap "factory" required a relatively small capital investment, holding little in the way of plant machinery. In any event, the partners had no access to anything like equity financing. It would be decades before a financial market for industrial stocks would take shape in the United States. By necessity, Procter & Gamble's partners funded their venture with modest financing on short terms. Essentially, the business was built on earnings.[12]

Marketing, in this environment, mainly consisted of establishing contact with wholesalers and storekeepers and earning their trust. Procter & Gamble did not really brand its soaps and candles over this period, though it did name them descriptively and insure that they measured up in terms of quality and full weight. Advertising expenditures were minimal. Products went to market with generic names like Rosin Soap (manufactured from rosin) and Mottled German Soap (a hard laundry soap of the so-called German type, made from oleic acid that mottled into red veins during the manufacturing process).

Creating Strategic Advantage

The commodity nature of the business and its minimal, generic marketing efforts did not mean that Procter & Gamble lacked strategic initiative, however. The firm did grow and adapt resourcefully, particularly as a second generation of Procters and Gambles entered the business in the mid-1800s. (See appendix 4 for a discussion of the founding families and the leadership of Procter & Gamble.) On the marketing front, the firm's network of trade dealers steadily expanded behind the impetus of George Procter, son of William Procter, and as it did, the scale of production grew. "Up to the time that Mr. George Procter made his first successful business visit to New York, Baltimore, Philadelphia and Chicago," one employee related, "the firm was making 100 to 120 boxes of soap a day, and from 50 to 75 boxes of candles. . . . Orders soon began to come in for large quantities of soap, and Mr. Gamble at once arranged for the increased work by securing larger kettles and employing more help and the output was increased to 500, 1000, 1500 and 2000 boxes a day."[13]

The spread of the railroads accelerated the firm's expansion. With the chartering of the Little Miami Railroad in 1836, Cincinnati started to build rail connections to Springfield, Ohio. The push soon connected Procter & Gamble (via other rail lines) to Lake Erie; a second Great Lakes railroad, the Cincinnati, Hamilton and Dayton line (incorporated in 1846), further opened markets in the northeastern United States.[14] Again, the infrastructure was fundamentally important. Unlike rivers and canals, railroads did not freeze over; rail traffic flowed year-round, in channels that were faster, more regular, and less expensive than steamboat freight. Forward-thinking manufacturers quickly adapted. Distribution and marketing possibilities grew considerably more flexible and diffuse. A Procter & Gamble ledger from 1864 indicates that by the end of the Civil War, the firm was managing a well-developed hinterland network that stretched across the midwestern United States. The ledger charts business with customers in scores of towns and small cities within a two-hundred-mile radius of Cincinnati. The network included locations in Ohio (Akron, Cairo, Cleveland, Columbus, Dayton, Marietta, and Toledo); Illinois (Chicago, Peoria, Springfield, and Urbana); and Indiana (Bloomington, Fort Wayne, Indianapolis, Lafayette, and Terre Haute); and several cities in other nearby states: Detroit, Kansas City, Louisville, Pittsburgh, Syracuse, and West Bend, Wisconsin.[15]

Perhaps even more significant than aggressive market expansion, though, was the firm's drive to master the technology of its products. Like most production in the pre- and early-industrial eras, the soap- and candle-making process learned and practiced by founders William Procter and James Gamble was more of an art than a science. The products they sold in the 1830s and 1840s—products such as No. 1 Palm Soap, No. 2 Rosin Soap, and Toilet and Shaving Soap—were made in kettles on the basis of craft knowledge. The makers followed uncodified recipes worked out through trial and error with only the vaguest understanding of the chemistry at work. Starting in the late 1850s, however, under the leadership of James Norris Gamble (son of founder James A. Gamble), the company began delving systematically and scientifically into the art.

As a young man preparing to enter the family business, Gamble had enrolled in college chemistry courses. Soon after graduating and joining the firm, he wrote to Campbell Morfit, a professor at the University of Maryland and a leading expert on soap and candle chemistry, for technical information. The contact deepened when Gamble visited Morfit's laboratory in New York the following year, in 1858, to conduct a series of chemical analyses of

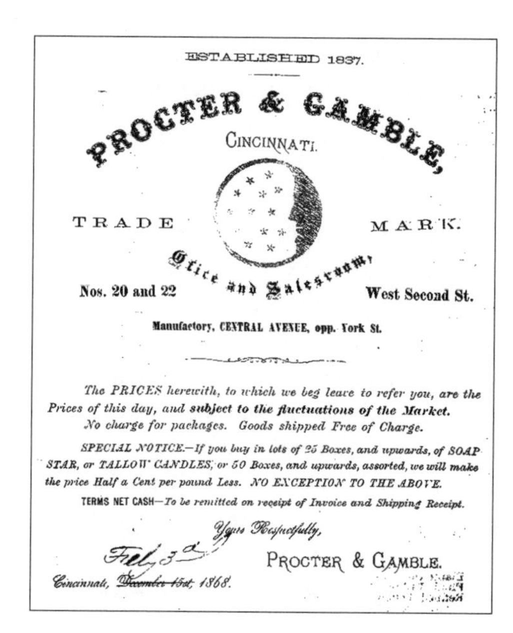
ESTABLISHED 1837.

PROCTER & GAMBLE,

CINCINNATI.

TRADE MARK.

Office and Salesroom,

Nos. 20 and 22 West Second St.

Manufactory, CENTRAL AVENUE, opp. York St.

The PRICES herewith, to which we beg leave to refer you, are the Prices of this day, and ***subject to the fluctuations of the Market.***
No charge for packages. Goods shipped Free of Charge.

SPECIAL NOTICE.—If you buy in lots of 25 Boxes, and upwards, of SOAP STAR, or TALLOW CANDLES, or 50 Boxes, and upwards, assorted, we will make the price Half a Cent per pound Less. NO EXCEPTION TO THE ABOVE.

TERMS NET CASH—*To be remitted on receipt of Invoice and Shipping Receipt.*

Yours Respectfully,

PROCTER & GAMBLE.

Feb 3d

Cincinnati, ~~December 15th~~, 1868.

Through most of the nineteenth century, Procter & Gamble sold unbranded soap and candles at prices that fluctuated according to market conditions.

soaps made by Procter & Gamble and rival companies. In addition to describing appearance, smell, specific gravity, and other physical properties, Gamble calculated each soap's water content, the amount of insoluble matter, and the levels of soda, fat, and salines, meticulously recording the results, soap by soap, in his lab notebook. In effect, he was reverse engineering competitive products and measuring them against Procter & Gamble's. Moreover, he was conducting his analyses from the consumer's point of view, using product he purchased from stores, "still fresh when used for analysis" (as he noted in his record of experiments with "Colgate & Co's Family Soap, obtained from Messrs. Colgate & Co Dutch St New York April 6 1858"*).[16]

Gamble continued periodic experimentation through the 1870s, carrying on his investigations even in periods when the firm was straining at breakneck speed to fill orders. He tried out different ingredients and formulas. Most significantly, he carefully recorded which specific processes produced what kinds and qualities of soaps. He was experimenting with floating soaps, for example, as early as the 1860s, and searching for inexpensive ways to manufacture high-end soaps. Eventually, these efforts would uncover a blockbuster product. On a more basic level, they trained Gamble and others

*This firm is the ancestor of today's Colgate-Palmolive Company, which has operated under several different legal names during its long history. For the sake of convenience, we reference it throughout the book simply as "Colgate."

working with him to approach manufacturing as a systematic, rigidly controlled process, designed to produce consistent, planned results.

A Turning Point

Over the years leading up to the U.S. Civil War, Procter & Gamble thus assembled the capacity for substantial production and wide distribution. Business still fluctuated, depending on prices, supplies, and seasonal markets, but the pieces were in place for enterprise on a massive scale, given market opportunities. The war provided those opportunities. Between 1861 and 1865, Procter & Gamble obtained large contracts from the national government to supply soap and candles to the Union army. These enormous procurements strained the firm's productive capacity to the breaking limits. Factories ran night and day, filling orders that ran in the hundreds and thousands of boxes per shipment. When martial law was declared for a time in Cincinnati (right across the river from Kentucky, a border state and slave state), Procter & Gamble was deemed vital to the war effort and permitted to stay open.

Getting business was easy. The dominant strategic preoccupation was obtaining enough raw materials to produce soap and candles in bulk. Shrewd maneuvering at the outbreak of the conflict proved critical later on. According to company lore, James Norris Gamble and William Alexander Procter (son of William Procter) were in New Orleans when news of the outbreak of hostilities broke. Quickly assessing the situation, they realized that hostilities would close off the Southern ports and send prices for raw materials soaring. The two bought all the rosin they could find, loaded it on a steamboat, and freighted it upriver to Cincinnati, where every available wagon was impressed to unload and haul the cargo to local warehouses. This timely stroke secured a cache of raw material that put Procter & Gamble in a position that its competitors could not match for months, as rosin prices did indeed spike dramatically.[17]

Though it strained in subsequent months to obtain enough raw material to fill its orders, Procter & Gamble came out on the other side of the war a substantially larger, more capable enterprise—indeed, a company doing business on a fundamentally enlarged scale of operation. The sharp eyes of the leading U.S. credit firm, Dun and Bradstreet, recognized the change in status. Through the 1850s, Dun and Bradstreet's local agents consistently rated the company as a strong, stable, prosperous business, with sales (they estimated) ranging in the tens of thousands of dollars, perhaps as much as $150,000 to $200,000 in flush years. When the credit firm visited Procter & Gamble in the years immediately after the war, it found what it estimated to be a million-dollar enterprise.[18]

Strategic Pressures and Opportunities

The Civil War created the opportunity for business on an unprecedented scale. Even as Procter & Gamble scrambled to capitalize, however, the ground beneath the company was shifting. Growth in its historical core business—candle manufacturing—stagnated starting in the 1860s. The 1859 discovery of oil in western Pennsylvania uncovered rich supplies of kerosene. Oil lamps began replacing candles in households, particularly as the oil-refining industry consolidated under John D. Rockefeller's Standard Oil in the 1860s and 1870s. The impact on Procter & Gamble's candle markets was pronounced: In 1867, the company's candle production peaked at 319,235 boxes (compared with 98,805 boxes of soap) and then began to slide. By 1876, when candle production sank below soap production for the first time in the company's history, there was no escaping the serious strategic crisis that the firm faced.[19] In order to continue expanding, the company needed to find new sources of growth on the soap side of the business.

All kinds of transformations, in fact, were destabilizing the company's traditional business patterns. On the supply side, Cincinnati's meat packers were coming under stiff competition from rival firms in Chicago, where superior rail connections were creating new opportunities for unprecedented consolidation and industrialization.[20] Sizable packing operations remained in Cincinnati, and resourceful experimentation by James Norris Gamble in the 1870s enabled the company to formulate new kinds of soap based on new raw ingredients such as vegetable oils. Nevertheless, the emergence of Chicago as a dynamic new hub of commerce and manufacturing (with soap makers of its own) signaled that the strategic landscape surrounding the company was shifting. The forces that had combined to create Procter & Gamble's initial opportunities were dissipating; the partners would have to find ways to create new kinds of opportunities based on new strategies.

Everywhere, railroads were overturning business patterns and opening vast new market possibilities. Procter & Gamble had originally expanded its markets along river transportation channels, shipping the bulk of its product on flatboats and steamboats down the Ohio River to New Orleans. With the onset of the Civil War, these channels were temporarily severed. Then the spread of the railroads more fundamentally redrew the map. The process had actually begun before the war, as early trunk lines hooked the Midwest more tightly and directly to New England and Middle Atlantic markets. In the years after the war, renewed railroad building penetrated the southern and western regions of the country, spinning a powerful new web of infrastructure across the continent, knitting previously isolated regions into an increasingly unified transportation network. Approximately 80,000 miles of railroad track were in operation in the United States by 1877; over the next dozen years, the figure would more than double, to 164,000.[21]

Nourished by the railroads, the pace of industrialization was quickening noticeably. Between 1870 and 1900, manufacturing surged past agriculture to become the dominant sector of the U.S. economy. The rate of urbanization was also accelerating. Although most Americans still lived in rural communities in 1878, urban centers were growing rapidly. Chicago's population was just reaching 500,000; smaller cities like Buffalo (155,000) and Minneapolis (47,000) were massing substantially, and a series of southern and western cities were poised for growth. Eleven U.S. cities held populations of at least 50,000 in 1870; by 1900, the number of such cities would be forty. Moreover, amid industrialization and urbanization, incomes were starting to climb—a critical point, from a consumer-goods point of view. U.S. per capita income grew at an annual rate of 2.1 percent from 1870 to 1910 (compared with 1.45 percent between 1840 and 1860). Between 1870 and 1915, the average American's spending power nearly tripled.[22]

Of course, Procter & Gamble's partners did not have these figures before them as they surveyed their business possibilities in the 1870s. But they did sense in a less quantifiable way that U.S. society was entering an era of sea change. Customers and potential customers were migrating out of rural areas and localized exchange (meaning cashless) economies into a national economic system. Fertile new markets were opening for entrepreneurs alert to the opportunity. And entrepreneurs were responding, creating bigger and more ambitious business enterprises than the world had ever known before. Andrew Carnegie was building massive new steel plants and staking a central position in the emerging U.S. steel industry. John D. Rockefeller was consolidating control over the petroleum industry. Chicago meat packers like Gustavus Swift and Philip Armour were assembling fleets of refrigerated boxcars and beginning to ship processed meats across the nation.[23]

Closer to home, as far as Procter & Gamble was concerned, came bold new ventures in packaged consumer goods, including brands and companies that would grow into multibillion-dollar businesses. Joseph Campbell was canning vegetables and condiments for broad retail distribution; soon he would add soups to his product line and so lay the foundations for the Campbell Soup Company. Henry J. Heinz, based up the Ohio River at Pittsburgh, was selling bottled condiments such as horseradish and ketchup, laying the foundation for what would become another multibillion-dollar corporation. The Anheuser-Busch brewery in St. Louis was launching Budweiser, "the King of Beers"; John and William Kellogg in Battle Creek, Michigan, were marketing the first boxed breakfast cereal that U.S. consumers had ever seen;

and Charles Hires was selling an extract of herbs, roots, and berries to make a new concoction called root beer. In the 1870s, the decade leading up to Ivory soap, a series of innovative product launches (to borrow an anachronistic term from a later business era) laid the groundwork for what would eventually become major packaged goods industries—soup, condiments, beer, breakfast cereal, and soda.[24] The U.S. economy was on the cusp of a massive market revolution.

In 1876, it would have taken a prophet to foresee all these changes. Still, Procter & Gamble's partners could hardly have ignored the new business energy and activity. Opportunity was quickening; entrepreneurial horizons were opening all around them. Heinz, for instance, had mounted an exhibit of his bottled preserves at the Cincinnati Exposition in 1875—one of numerous events the tireless promoter created in an effort to spread public awareness of his offerings. It must have looked like an intriguing venture, from Procter & Gamble's point of view.

In any event, it was becoming increasingly clear that business as usual would not be sustainable. By 1876, Procter & Gamble's traditional markets were breaking apart, while the outlines of wider new market opportunities were beginning to emerge. The company was approaching a crossroads.

The Period in Perspective, 1837–1890

Key milestones punctuated Procter & Gamble's first four decades of business. The establishment of the original partnership in 1837 marked the first, planting the seed from which the company grew. William Procter and James Gamble located their enterprise at the center of a vital cluster of industrial energy—the meatpacking industry of Porkopolis. This dynamic locale provided not only ample raw material for soap and candle manufacture, but also more basically exposure to what were then state-of-the-art production systems. The founding partners exploited these advantages skillfully, achieving superior operational excellence and outgrowing their local rivals. They also established a legacy of adaptive innovation, successfully executing a series of shifts in distribution and supply as the era of the railroads transformed U.S. business.

The unleashing of the U.S. Civil War marked a second milestone for Procter & Gamble, creating the opportunity for major expansion. The company did not merely endure this pressure; it met and managed it, demonstrating a capability for production and distribution on a national scale of operation.

Even as it ramped up to big-business proportions, however, the firm faced a troubling decline of its core candle business. By the mid-1870s, Procter & Gamble was searching urgently for new ways to sustain growth.

CHAPTER TWO

From Commodities to Consumer Goods

IVORY AND THE BIRTH OF THE BRAND

THE RESULT of Procter & Gamble's response to the strategic growth crisis of the 1870s was Ivory soap. This product represented the company's first sustained effort at mass-marketing its products by means of continuous advertising to consumers. In a case holding basic, formative lessons, Ivory began Procter & Gamble's long effort to learn and to master the art of brand building.

The development of Ivory soap came at a critical point of inflection in Procter & Gamble's history—a time when fundamental technological, social, and economic changes were undoing the strategic underpinnings of what had been forty years of profitable growth. Ivory represented the company's effort to adapt to those changes and seize the new opportunities they created. It was a highly creative response, one that vaulted Procter & Gamble into a leading position in a newly emerging national marketplace. It was also a high-stakes gambit, a venture into unexplored territory, a process filled with trial and error. The challenge of marketing the floating soap drew on many of the company's traditional skills and strengths, but it also forced Procter & Gamble to unlearn habits and assumptions that were rapidly becoming obsolete. No one yet knew how to sell in markets that were national in scale. Ivory taught Procter & Gamble how to do business in a new economy.

In adapting to the challenge, core values stood the company in good stead. Honest dealing and, in particular, the integrity of product quality remained critical selling points. But those features had to be translated into new, mass-market forms, framed for a much broader audience of distributors and consumers. Gradually the effort coalesced around the concept of the brand. In the period from 1880 to 1900, Procter & Gamble focused unprecedented strategic energy on Ivory, pouring more resources into marketing the soap than it had ever before lavished on a single product. In the process, Procter & Gamble became one of the largest advertisers in the United States, pioneering new media links to its consumers. In short, the company started building brands.

Putting that all together—making brands work and then fashioning new products and processes around them—changed the way Procter & Gamble did business in fundamental and far-reaching ways. The transformation did not happen all at once. But it gradually gathered momentum, for the company was closely and critically analyzing the experiment as it unfolded. One of the key outcomes of the Ivory experience was that Procter & Gamble began to cultivate a distinct, recognizable style of business. The company monitored, studied, and assessed the market continuously over the 1880s and 1890s. It ran small-scale experiments in test markets, measured the results, mapped out bigger moves. Ivory represented a bold venture of unprecedented resources, but also a highly disciplined one. The company was trying to figure out what levers, what mechanisms, would control this new mass market. And it found them. Ivory taught Procter & Gamble not just how to sell, but how to learn.

Developing Ivory

Company lore attributes the discovery of Ivory to an accident. The story has a distracted workman leaving a batch of white soap unattended in an automatic crutcher (mixer), which forced extra air into the mixture and, it was later discovered, accidentally produced a soap that floated. It makes an appealing tale, cloaking the product in an aura of fortuitous destiny. The account cannot be traced back to credible testimony, however, and does not ring true. To begin with, by 1878, the company had been experimenting for at least a dozen years with floating soaps. As early as 1863, James Norris Gamble was conferring with Samuel Lowry (then a partner of the company): "He spoke well of the floating soap I had given him," Norris recorded in a "Soapmaking Journal" he had begun keeping. "We will I think make all our soap stock in that way."

Years later, Gamble left a tantalizingly laconic account of Ivory's genesis: "We thought it might be well to make a soap similar to the castile soap, & I

James Norris Gamble played a leading role in developing Ivory and, more generally, converting the firm to scientific soap-making methods.

came in contact with a young man who was interested with others in making a soap of the same kind of ingredients, namely, vegetable oils . . . and he thought it would be well, as he was not doing very much in the business, to sell out their rights." The company bought the formula and then went to work modifying it. Ivory emerged from this process: "At first we made a soap which we mottled by partly coloring it partly red, so it would be similar to castile. But [we] concluded it would be better not to proceed with that, as we found that a soap made from vegetable oils and crutched would float. I do not think that the soap made by the parties from whom we obtained the prescription did float but our method of crutching produced the results."[1]

The account is revealing. It leaves open the possibility that the floating soap was discovered by accident, though Gamble strongly implies otherwise. In any event, he makes it clear that focused strategic thinking lay behind the project that became Ivory. The company was methodically developing a very specific kind of product, something outside Procter & Gamble's traditional line. Gamble and his partners were working on a soap made not of the company's traditional Porkopolis tallow, grease, or lard, but of vegetable oils. They were crafting a product comparable in quality to the castile soaps that commanded premium prices in the marketplace, but one inexpensive enough to be manufactured and sold in large quantities. This goal meant that these entrepreneurs needed to find a base oil cheaper than olive oil, the basis of castile soap. In short, they wanted a soap that would be something more than a commodity, sent in slabs to grocers to be sawed into nondescript chunks for the customers, yet something the company could make and sell in a mass market. To obtain such a product, the company was willing to move via either acquisition or internal development (Norris indicated that both strategies played a role). Clearly, Ivory represented something more than an accident on Procter & Gamble's part. The company was energetically looking for something new to make and sell.

In fact, the firm was scrambling. By 1878, active management of Procter & Gamble had passed to a second generation of two Procters and one Gamble. James Norris Gamble superintended the company's factories, William Alexander Procter was managing the lard oil business, and his brother Harley was assuming control of the company's sales and marketing efforts. They faced new challenges and sensed new opportunities in the shifting strategic landscape beneath them. The company's core business—candle manufacturing—was sliding into a long-term decline. The business environment that surrounded Procter & Gamble was one of both jarring displacement (decline in candles and lard oil) and intriguing entrepreneurial energy (the emergence of mass-market possibilities for consumer goods). An undertone of strategic urgency permeated the project that became Ivory, but at the same time, a stirring sense of strategic opportunity was propelling it forward.

Selling in a Mass Marketplace

By 1878, the team headed by James Norris Gamble had perfected the new soap and was preparing to take it to market. Made of a blend of palm and coconut oils—both substantially less expensive than olive oil—the new soap could be produced at costs that would permit large, nine-ounce (about 270 grams) cakes to be sold retail for ten cents. The product was priced, in other words, for an upscale mass market. The soap was distinctively colored—white—after an early mottled-red version was rejected. It lathered easily but remained solid and lasted longer than frothier, fancier "toilet soaps." And, of course, it floated. In sum, the company had a product distinctive enough to stand out in the fiercely competitive soap market, a product that offered clear quality advantages over lower-end soaps and equally clear price and performance advantages over the fancy, imported luxury soaps of the period.

Procter & Gamble initially marketed the product simply as "Procter & Gamble's White Soap," but that expedient was only a holding measure. Part of the strategy for selling the new soap entailed labeling it with a name that would mark it distinctively in grocery stores. As James Norris Gamble later recalled, "When we began to make the Ivory soap it was of course a white soap and that would not be an exclusive name so we had several meetings to discuss the matter as to what the name should be." It was Harley Procter who hit upon the solution, a divine inspiration that struck at church as Procter read aloud with the congregation. The next day, he convened the partners to read them the illuminating passage, from Psalms 45:8: "All thy garments smell of myrrh, and aloes, and cassia, out of the ivory palaces whereby they have made thee glad." "When he read it," Gamble later remembered, "he said, 'There, that is the name.' He proposed it to us and we agreed with him."[2] The company trademarked the term *Ivory* on July 18, 1879 (taking advantage of new federal trademark provisions established in 1870).[3] Harley Procter then sketched out a design for the product's packaging, creating a wrapping that was as distinctive as the new name: a checkerboard pattern in black and white, framing the legend "IVORY" in large letters.[4] It was an eye-catching container, tailored specifically for the grocer's shelf, to attract the attention of consumers who were just beginning to get accustomed to buying goods like soap in these kinds of forms.

By 1879, then, Ivory had acquired its labels, both figurative and literal. But, as the company gradually discovered, the branding of Ivory—the elaborate work of creating a cluster of associations and images around the product—was only beginning. Beyond naming and packaging the product, the company had to find ways of actually selling it, across a market that was expanding in scope by the year.

That effort began in tried and traditional ways. Harley Procter dispatched an assistant sales manager with samples to wholesale houses in New England and New York and took a trunkful himself to Chicago and other Midwestern outlets. These kinds of trips were already familiar and absolutely vital to the success of the product. Without the commitment of middlemen—the jobbers who bought products like Ivory from the manufacturers and sold them to the grocers and other retailers downstream—Ivory had little hope of making its way in substantial volume into grocery stores, where customers could buy it. It was an aspect of marketing that worked the company's traditional network of contacts, trading on Procter & Gamble's solid name and reputation for honest dealing.

At the same time, the company began to spread awareness of the new product among the storekeepers, who occupied the point of contact with the consumers themselves. The earliest Ivory advertising addressed the grocers directly. In 1879, the company took out a notice in the *Grocers' Criterion,* a trade journal, announcing "The IVORY" as "the only Laundry Soap that successfully answers for Toilet Use."[5] Few if any consumers would have seen such a notice. That same year, however, in what may well have been Ivory's first consumer-oriented commercial notice, Chicago's *Bon Ton Directory* ran an advertisement describing Ivory's unique qualities. An accompanying line drawing depicted two hands slicing a bar of the soap with string.

At this point, the marketing push behind Ivory was not particularly innovative and certainly did not amount to a concerted campaign. But Harley Procter, the youngest member of the second generation of family managers, was urging more energetic efforts and pressing his fellow partners to allocate a substantial advertising budget for Ivory. In 1881, he became a partner in the firm. The following year, in the midst of strong sales and healthy profits, he received eleven thousand dollars—an amount that doubled the level of the company's advertising spending—and immediately poured half of it into the new product.[6] What Harley had in mind for Ivory was going to take much greater amounts than what the company had traditionally spent. The new partner wanted to take Ivory into magazines.

Over the next decade or so, print advertising, and in particular magazine advertising, became the most prominent and most expensive aspect of Ivory's marketing. Millions of customers over the late nineteenth and early twentieth centuries came to know Ivory principally through the elegant, full-page advertisements Procter & Gamble ran in virtually all the major magazines in circulation by the 1890s. The company entered this new field tentatively, however. Building a marketing strategy around the magazines was not a clear-cut decision.

To begin with, magazine promotion was an expensive investment. Moreover, a good deal of the magazine advertising in circulation at the time was distinctly dubious in character. The "respectable," genteel magazines of the period—*Harper's, Scribner's,* and the like—carried very limited advertising in the 1870s. The most prominent advertisers of day were the patent medicine houses, pitching murky concoctions that claimed to cure everything from consumption to cancer, rickets to rheumatism. These kinds of products made up the single most important source of clients in 1877–1878 for N. W. Ayer and Son, probably the largest advertising agency of the late nineteenth century.[7]

The medium was in flux, though. Magazines were broadening their readerships and changing their contents, including their advertising content, by the early 1880s. By 1885, four general monthly magazines had reached circulations of more than one hundred thousand, for a combined readership of six hundred thousand. In addition, a spate of new periodicals was appearing. By 1880, highbrow periodicals like *Harper's* and *Scribner's* were also opening their pages to advertisers and even offering proportionally lower rates to those who bought entire pages.[8] The emergence of subscription-based magazines, most prominently *Ladies' Home Journal,* was another important development transforming the medium. Launched in 1883 by Cyrus H. K. Curtis (publisher of the *Saturday Evening Post*) at a subscription rate of fifty cents per year, one-sixth of what the leading women's periodical of the day charged, *Ladies' Home Journal* made up the lost subscription revenues by running twice as much advertising as its competitors. By the 1900s, Curtis was claiming more than a million subscribers.[9] Magazines, in short, were creating a new mass medium—one nearly as transformative as latter mass media such as radio, television, and the Internet would be. And in the process, magazines were opening new mass-marketing possibilities. By the early 1880s, other products were joining the patent medicines on the front and back ends of periodicals (where the ads were segregated): thread, sewing machines, silverware, and corsets. A few packaged goods companies were also hazarding the experiment—pioneers such as Sapolio (a household cleanser) and Royal Baking Powder (a brand powerhouse that survives today).

Procter & Gamble ventured into the arena in December 1882, running a half-column advertisement in the *Independent,* a religious weekly. The company had occasionally placed ads in these kinds of periodicals, as well as in local papers, in the past.[10] But in February 1883, the company forged into unmistakably new marketing territory when it placed an expanded version of the ad in *The Century Magazine,* the best-selling general monthly magazine of the day. Both of these ads employed the same line drawing illustration that had originally appeared in the Chicago directory several years before, accompanied by much of the same copy. These new ads also contained new elements, however, including the assurance that Ivory was "99 44-100 per cent. pure" and, in bold, that "the Ivory Soap will 'float.'"

Even with these catchphrases, the ad's appeal was straightforward and formal, even stately. No blandishment and no assumption of intimacy. Just a dignified and straightforward account of the product, its qualities, and its use, concluding with the pronouncement: "The price, compared to the quality and the size of the cakes, makes it the cheapest Soap for everybody, for every want."[11]

If the introduction seemed a little stilted, it may have been betraying just a bit of awkwardness on the company's part. The product was called *the* Ivory and bracketed in quotation marks: It was "the 'Ivory' soap." The claim for purity, which would remain a central focus of Ivory's marketing, was aimed principally at Ivory's competitors, of course. But one senses that the claim spoke, too, in a more indirect way, to lingering popular suspicions in the marketplace about packaged goods generally, and perhaps particularly to the stigma that patent medicine purveyors had cast on the idea of advertising proprietary, labeled articles. By the time the company was adapting the message for publication in *Century,* Harley Procter had gathered testimonials

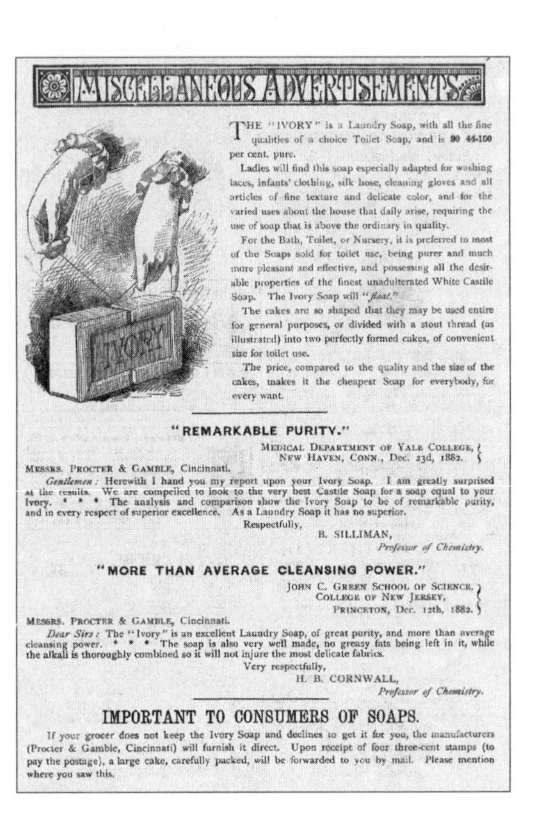

This ad, which appeared in The Century Magazine *in February 1883, introduced Ivory to the general public and launched Procter & Gamble into mass-market advertising.*

from several leading scientists, and he included these in the expanded ad. Benjamin Silliman, chemistry professor from the Yale Medical School, reported the soap to be "of remarkable purity" and equal to "the very best Castile Soap" in quality. His Princeton colleague H. B. Cornwall concurred: "The 'Ivory' is an excellent Laundry Soap, of great purity, and more than average cleansing power."

In addition to emphasizing the product's purity, the ad strove to convey a distinct sense of Ivory's market position. The soap was less expensive than castile soap and certainly economical (a message reinforced by the image of the soap being divided), but it was nevertheless of high quality. The company wanted to promote as wide a usage as possible, claiming that Ivory was suitable for all kinds of washing needs: face and hands, clothing, and delicate articles such as "laces, infants' clothing, silk hose, cleaning gloves and all articles of fine texture and delicate color." The ad's closing pitch—"the cheapest Soap for everybody, for every want"—underscored the product's versatility. To later generations of Procter & Gamble brand managers, the claims might sound dangerously ambitious, the market positioning crude and unfocused.

But it made sense at the time. Ivory's original developers and marketers were working in a highly fluid market environment. They were speaking to a consumer base that extended from affluent to middle-class to poorer families, and from urban to rural environments, along a rapidly evolving spectrum of development. Many middle-class households did not yet have hot running water; some had no running water at all. Households across the nation were just getting hooked up to plumbing networks (around the same time they started subscribing to periodicals like *Century*). The market was not yet segmented, not yet equipped for fine gradations of product definition.[12]

The company would take as much of the new ground as it could lay hold of, and it would do it by selling the brand. Accordingly, the other notable aspect of Ivory's original advertising was its focus on the product, not the company. The name Procter & Gamble appeared nowhere in the main body of the ad. It did make its way into the framing material: Both testimonials addressed themselves to "Messrs. Procter & Gamble," and a closing note "To Consumers of Soaps" advised people unable to obtain Ivory through their local grocers to write directly to the company in Cincinnati for a free cake. But the ad was selling Ivory, not Procter & Gamble. The company was forging the new relationship specifically between consumers and the particular product. The brand became the vehicle by which the company pushed its way into the mass market.[13]

Beyond these basic concepts, though, the company was still experimenting. For example, while the first national advertising already contained an early form of the two modern slogans that indelibly mark Ivory today ("99 44/100% Pure" and "It Floats"), these slogans were buried in five paragraphs' worth of copy. Under Harley Procter's direction, Procter & Gamble immediately began crafting and placing new ads, new artwork, and new copy. Ivory advertisements for the next several decades took constantly changing forms, revolving on a monthly basis: chemists and doctors pronouncing the product's chemical purity; swarms of brownies and elves boiling exotic oils in the woods; customers buying soaps in grocery stores; socialites blowing bubbles at bubble parties; cartoon frogs washing each other in the moonlight; charitable couples dropping cases off at orphanages; sewing circles admiring newspaper ads; and many, many mothers and children. Ivory never stayed tethered long to a single concept in those first years of experimental advertising. New images appeared every month, creating a diffuse range of associations. The company was apparently still looking for the right pitch, the right tone. It was, after all, trying to reach a consumer that was herself undergoing sharp social changes as she adapted to new surroundings, new markets, and a new material culture.[14]

Rescaling Production for Competitive Advantage

Procter & Gamble was undergoing internal changes of its own. A conversion to mass production accompanied the shift to mass marketing. As the advertising drive pushed up demand for Ivory, the company converted an increasing amount of its plant to making the new soap. Within a few years, though, Procter & Gamble began to bump up against the limits of incremental expansion. Branding and advertising may have differentiated the product to a degree, but they did not alter the fundamental dynamics of the industry. Making soap, including "the 'Ivory' soap," remained a fiercely competitive, low-margin business. "Soap is in excellent demand," Harley Procter reported in 1886, "but prices are low and profits small."[15] To fully exploit the Ivory campaign, the company had to capitalize on the opportunities it created for new operating efficiencies. Increased sales had to be translated into increased economies of scale. The need to float the soap in the marketplace had begun to transform the company's marketing strategies; keeping the brand afloat would require further transformations in manufacturing operations.

It was disaster that provided the opportunity for overhaul. On January 7, 1884, a fire broke out in the lard oil factory and quickly spread through the cluster of Central Avenue buildings that housed the company's manufacturing operations. The blaze consumed the candle works, lard oil facilities, warehouses, and a sizable portion of the soap operations. Only the north soap factory was left standing, along with a smaller satellite factory the company had recently acquired. These surviving facilities would bridge the company over the crisis, enabling some production to continue while Procter & Gamble rebuilt. Meanwhile, as the partners quickly grasped, the disaster had given them a chance to thoroughly redesign their plant and production techniques—to conduct, in other words, what a century later would be termed reengineering. Ivorydale, the new manufacturing complex that resulted, systematically expanded, restructured, and streamlined Procter & Gamble's manufacturing processes.

The geography was revealing. The old plant had been located on Central Avenue in downtown Cincinnati, a site oriented toward the Ohio River, the company's transportation lifeline. The new plant relocated production to the outskirts of the city, where Procter & Gamble could build on a massive new scale. A complex of thirty large buildings went up, giving Procter & Gamble a plant capable of making, packaging, and shipping two million boxes of soap per year (about 120 million pounds, or 55 million kilograms).[16] Although access to the river was no longer important, access to the railroads had become essential; Ivorydale, accordingly, transplanted operations to the confluence of several railroad lines. Feeder lines built and maintained by the

Built on the outskirts of Cincinnati in the mid-1880s, Ivorydale equipped Procter & Gamble for mass production on an industrial scale.

company ran right up alongside the plant's huge shipping warehouse, to a platform from which twenty cars could be loaded simultaneously. Procter & Gamble acquired a 65,000-pound locomotive engine to handle incoming and outgoing railroad cars; by the early twentieth century Ivorydale was running three locomotives and hundreds of cars, plying over ten miles (six kilometers) of track within the plant.[17]

Also telling was the new plant's name. *Ivorydale* signified commitment to the company's flagship brand, of course. But in a more general sense, the name marked the conversion from batch manufacturing, in which facilities adapted continuously to fluctuations in the price and availability of various potential raw materials, to dedicated plant, which regularly made fixed products in vast amounts. In 1876, the company's seven soap kettles made between thirty-eight and forty frames of soap at a time. Ivorydale went into operation with twelve kettles (and another dozen already under construction), each of them holding 150,000 pounds of soap, giving the company capacity to churn out between 200 and 360 frames at a time.[18]

As it was expanded, production was also smoothed, streamlined, and meshed into intricate coordination. A system of carts and trucks wheeled the soap from station to station, from boiling to framing to slabbing* to stamping, and a conveyor belt carried the formed cakes to wrapping and boxing stations. The new plant reconfigured soap production as a synchronized, continuous process, a steadily moving flow of operations—what the

---

**Slabbing* refers to the process of pouring the hot, liquefied soap into molds, where it is cooled and solidified into large slabs; the soap is then cut into individual bars.

company called "a vast, orderly exact machine, moving smoothly and accurately in the production of an output of uniform excellence."[19] The reengineering of the slabbing and packaging processes—the pivotal point in production whereby bulk blocks of soap became bars of Ivory—typified the larger transformation. At Central Avenue, old factory hands later recalled that "slabbing [had been] done by hand by means of a wire which had a wooden handle on either end. A notched stick showed where to run the wire."[20] A man known as the stamper then stamped each cake, one by one, with a pedal-activated die box.[21] Ivorydale mechanized and systematized the finishing processes. The company implemented automated slabbing machinery that cut frames into precisely uniform cakes, an entire frame at a time. From slabbing, the soap traveled to an apparatus that pressed the product into a pair of molds, stamping the name *Ivory* on each cake and spitting it onto a conveyor belt. Inspectors examined the cakes as the soap traveled down the line to women who wrapped them in their checkerboard packages.[22]

Product moved through this continuum in enormous volumes at steady rates, from raw material through a sequence of manufacturing stages to packaging and into warehouses, where it was stored for eventual rail shipment to distant markets. Ivorydale itself became an intricate, complex mechanism, geared for steady throughput. As a result, production became far more efficient and predictable than it had been at Central Avenue. It also became much more capital and resource intensive. As the company cranked the new machinery up to speed, maintaining the flow—which meant preventing any kind of interruption that might shut down production and idle workers—became a driving imperative. Consequently, alongside Ivorydale's railroad feeder lines, the company built an enormous bank of oil storage tanks, with a combined holding capacity of more than two million pounds, enabling plant managers to stockpile a vast reservoir of raw material in reserve to insure that the factory could be kept running steadily.

Reforging the Terms of Employment

Inevitably, ramping up to an industrial scale of production meant making an industrial community of the company's workforce, a transition that was not always smooth. By 1886, Procter & Gamble was employing hundreds of workers at Ivorydale and looking for ways to deepen their commitment to the enterprise. That year, fourteen separate walkouts and work stoppages erupted at the plant, each time disrupting the flow of production that was becoming so strategically vital. The Knights of Labor, a national labor organization, was trying to get a foothold in the new factory. And employee churn was approaching 50 percent: Nearly half the workers at Ivorydale were leaving over the course of a year.[23] In the midst of growth, Procter & Gamble needed to redefine the terms of participation in the enterprise. It could not afford to leave its workers behind.

A young William Cooper Procter, son of William Alexander Procter, just coming into the firm from college and starting on the factory floor, became the key figure in the company's search for a solution. In 1885, Procter convinced the partners to give workers Saturday afternoons off. The policy represented a liberal concession, coming at a time when most factory workers labored six days a week (and typically between ten and twelve hours a day). Still, it was no more than a gesture, Procter felt. Something more fundamental was needed. Over the next several years, he formulated and persuaded the partners to try a profit-sharing plan.

The company introduced the concept to the workers in April 1887. Under the terms of Procter's plan, Procter & Gamble committed to dividing profits between the employees and the company, in proportion to the expense of labor versus the firm's total cost of production. It was a formula, Proctor was convinced, that would result in improved productivity. More fundamentally, the plan represented a bold effort on the part of Procter & Gamble to expand the sense of ownership in the enterprise. Workers reportedly greeted the plan somewhat skeptically, but were certainly gratified when the company followed through later in the year. In October 1887, the company celebrated its first Dividend Day. James Norris Gamble addressed a meeting of workers gathered in one of Ivorydale's drying rooms, and company officers distributed 193 checks ranging from $14 to $280, a disbursement that totaled $9,026.66.[24]

In the coming years, the company would make repeated improvements to the profit-sharing plan to ensure that workers did not see the measure as simply a wage supplement—a monetary benefit, in other words—rather than a symbolic, substantial declaration of mutual faith and purpose. Nevertheless, the implementation of profit sharing represented a significant innovation on Procter & Gamble's part. William Cooper Procter had no term for it, but he was learning to manage the firm's human resources. If from the outside Ivorydale resembled other manufacturing plants mushrooming across the industrial landscape, on the inside Procter & Gamble was experimenting with radical new ways of redefining itself as a business and a community.

Selling Ivory, 1886–1900: The Marketing Message Coalesces

Procter & Gamble more than tripled its advertising spending during the construction of Ivorydale, from $45,000 in 1884 to $146,000 in 1886.[25] The company was building for growth and preparing its markets for growth. When a newspaper reporter asked Harley Procter in 1886 how widely the market for Cincinnati's soaps extended, he made it clear the company was thinking in broadly expansive terms. "From Maine to California and Canada to the Gulf of Mexico is the principal market," he replied grandly, "but some of her goods go to Mexico and South America, and even to Europe."[26] Initially spread among various products, the surge in marketing energy shifted to Ivory after 1886, as Ivorydale came on-line. By 1889, the company was spending $223,000 on advertising, with the lion's share, $158,000 (71 percent), backing Ivory specifically.[27]

Meanwhile, the company was also experimenting with promotional marketing initiatives. In April 1885, in the midst of building Ivorydale, Procter & Gamble sent out a mass mailing enclosing samples of Ivory along with a booklet compiling the brand's early print advertisements. "We mailed several of the books to other ladies in your state," a follow-up letter explained later in the year, "to get them as well as yourself to buy the Ivory Soap regularly of your grocer for we know that if one or two good housekeepers in a locality show their approval of an article by purchasing it regularly, the effect on the rest of the community is to create a general demand for it." In short, as the letter declared with disarming frankness, the company was trying to make "a patroness of you for the Ivory Soap." The letter reminded recipients of Ivory's purity, warned against "counterfeits," enclosed testimonials from "the most eminent men in their professions in the country," and urged would-be "patronesses" to demand Ivory specifically when shopping for soap and to reject any substitutes offered by their grocers.[28]

Like the brand's magazine advertising, these early Ivory mailings were groundbreaking steps for Procter & Gamble. Together with the ads, the promotions reveal how strategically vital steady sell-through was becoming for the company. Procter & Gamble was beginning to cast its energies downstream, looking for ways to exert more control over a sequence of transactions that took place beyond its traditional reach. The company's conventional marketing tactics had confined themselves for the most part to the wholesale houses, on which Procter & Gamble relied to push its products through to retailers. In turn, the soap maker hoped, retailers then extended the marketing momentum in selling to consumers at the far end of the chain. This structure had worked well enough up to this point, nourishing business of a certain scale, extending over a limited scope of operation. But it would not support what Procter & Gamble's senior managers envisioned for Ivory. They were opening up a direct, new channel of communication—magazine advertising—that in effect bypassed intervening jobbers and grocers to appeal directly to Procter & Gamble's ultimate customers downstream. Moves like the mass mailing sounded and deepened those channels, for the company now needed to generate and sustain a dependable, integrated flow of production and distribution. As it came to grips with that new imperative, Procter & Gamble began exploring ways of creating pull—consumer demand—to augment the push it traditionally exerted.

The imperative exposed troubling limitations with the system of distribution around which the company had built its traditional businesses. That system depended on a close alignment of interest between the manufacturer and the jobbers and grocers downstream. And it left Procter & Gamble distinctly vulnerable at what the company was coming to see as vitally strategic ground: the point of sale. Because the stores of the period were not self-service—instead, consumers requested products at counters—storekeepers could fairly easily persuade their customers to accept substitutes, as they would naturally try to do if they could sell competing soaps at higher profit margins. Procter & Gamble could, and did, bring pressure to bear on the storekeepers. But the critical relationship that was emerging here was with the consumer. "If your regular grocer refuses to get [Ivory] for you," Procter & Gamble pointedly suggested to the "patronesses" it solicited in November 1885, "there are undoubtedly others who recognize the fact that the increased volume of business done by reason of keeping the best customers more than compensates for the smaller profit and will take pleasure in getting it for you."[29]

To sustain Ivory's marketing momentum, then, Procter & Gamble needed to overcome possible resistance at multiple points in the distribution chain. Above all, the company had to innovate marketing tactics that would forge new bonds with its ultimate customer, the consumer. More mailings went out. One in 1889, for example, distributed another "little pamphlet which tells a few of the many good things about Ivory Soap," assuring "Madam" that the brand was eminently suited for washing "fine linen, fine embroideries, infants clothing or summer dresses and silk hose of delicate or brilliant color &c&c."[30] For children, the company offered a coloring book of Ivory ads, in exchange for Ivory wrappers.

The main marketing thrust behind Ivory, though, remained the magazine advertisements themselves. By the mid-1890s, the commitment to advertising had deepened into what amounted to a saturation campaign. The company maintained regular full-page spreads in every major magazine in the United States, an effort costing some hundred thousand dollars a year through the early 1890s and several times that figure by the late 1890s (as magazine circulations expanded and advertising rates rose).[31] "Ivory Soap advertisements appear in the principal magazines, in most of the farm journals, in the best of the religious periodicals, in practically all the women's publications and in scores of daily papers," the company informed wholesalers and retailers of the day. "Advertising is a permanent part of the policy of The Procter & Gamble Co. It is not a 'flash in the pan' proposition, intended to impress the dealer and get him to 'load up.' We have advertised regularly, systematically, persistently for nearly a quarter of a century."[32]

The ads themselves, meanwhile, were cohering increasingly tightly around core marketing messages. Claims for the soap's purity boiled down to the statistical formula, "99 44/100% Pure," which ads repeated so often that the statistic became fused in the popular imagination with the product. A second element began to acquire similar reflexive powers in 1891, when the company ran a full-page ad in *Century* with copy that read simply, "Ivory Soap. It Floats."[33]

By this point, Procter & Gamble had clearly found the pitch for Ivory. The ads were taking on a distinct look. They gave most of the page over to a single image, well-crafted and high-minded, even artistic, cultivating an impression of gentility and aesthetic taste. Images continued to rotate constantly, but they revolved increasingly around underlying themes. They tended to show women, households, families, children, and babies. These were and they remain, of course, touchstone concepts. But they played a distinct role in Victorian America. Ivory was tapping into complex iconography, identifying itself with concepts—purity, femininity, domesticity—that were acquiring a peculiar resonance in an age of rapid industrialization and urbanization, among a population of consumers adjusting themselves, sometimes uneasily, to participation in mass markets. To embed Ivory in the marketplace, the company had to embed it as a trusted staple in households and families. This the advertising did again and again, gradually creating a context of familiarity soothed and smoothed by comforting assurances of purity.

Assessing the Strategic Impact

The effort to establish Ivory in the marketplace pushed Procter & Gamble in new directions. In addition to its magazine and newspaper advertising, the company was deploying a battery of marketing initiatives, including mass distributions of samples, premiums, inserts, and other promotional materials; periodic rounds of exhibits and staged introductions; and a barrage of miscellaneous advertising mechanisms including wall signs, streetcar ads, streamers, and posters.[34] Meanwhile, the company was hammering the message home to wholesalers and retailers, tirelessly reciting the brand's benefits and urging committed selling. The brand had become a central strategic focus, consuming enormous resources, refashioning the company's marketing tactics, and, more broadly, reforging Procter & Gamble's collective sense of itself and its business.

These vigorous efforts certainly paid off in the marketplace. The company was not yet tracking market-share data per se, but it was moving a lot of product. Ivory shipments climbed up to just under a quarter-million boxes in 1892, slumped as the United States slid into a steep depression, then rebounded as conditions improved, reaching three hundred thousand boxes by 1900 and climbing steadily over the next decade.[35]

Procter & Gamble was creating a powerful new set of instruments for making markets, but it was still learning how to use those instruments, how to manipulate them, how to apply them for maximum effect. So, for example, when the 1893 depression hit, the company initially reduced Ivory's advertising spending, then reversed itself and resumed spending in an effort to shore up sales. As growth recovered, the company redoubled its efforts, hiking Ivory advertising up to nearly $400,000. Accordingly, when company strategists lined up shipment figures against Ivory advertising allocations over the 1890s, they found that Procter & Gamble had spent as little as thirty-four cents per case in 1892 and as much as $1.52 per case in 1899. Accordingly, advertising spending was reduced a little. (Sales continued to grow.)

By this point, Harley Procter was withdrawing from management responsibilities, but he had trained able pupils to sustain and sharpen the company's marketing efforts. Hastings French took over as sales manager, while Harry Brown assumed supervision of the advertising department. Under these managers, the company sifted through increasingly granular data, measuring the impact of specific marketing initiatives. They discovered, for example, that an exhibit promoting Ivory in Buffalo in 1896 (the exhibit distributed samples and cost the company more than $3,700) had not boosted sales as expected. In fact, average monthly sales of Ivory in the region had actually fallen off over the ensuing year. Similar calculations fill company notebooks from this period.[36]

Indeed, these kinds of calculations were becoming Procter & Gamble's hallmark. Point by point, the data was teaching sales and advertising people how to sell Ivory efficiently and effectively. On a more basic level, the numbers were teaching the company as a whole formative lessons about branding. As the scale of Procter & Gamble's commitment to mass marketing grew, it continuously sifted and resifted the data that the commitment was generating, searching for patterns, for causes and effects, for the levers that would work this intricate and still mysterious mechanism the company was constructing.

It was a style that contrasted sharply with the approach taken by many of the period's equally aggressive, but much less analytical, pioneers in mass marketing. Entrepreneurs like William Wrigley, for example, advertised just as vigorously and often as imaginatively as Harley Procter, Hastings French, and Harry Brown. (Wrigley sold soap, then baking powder, and eventually chewing gum—always offering flashy premiums to goose sales along.) But entrepreneurs like Wrigley worked by intuition for the most part, trusting their instincts. As another of the era's most flamboyant advertisers, Philadelphia department store magnate John Wanamaker, once famously quipped, he knew that half of the money he spent on advertising was wasted—he just did not know which half. Procter & Gamble, for its part, bent itself to figuring out just which half did work, and precisely how well.

Procter & Gamble made Ivory not just a bold risk, in other words, but an experiment for methodical, continuous study—one, moreover, that the company handled largely internally. Other manufacturing companies that began branding and advertising in mass markets in the late 1800s fairly quickly turned this aspect of the business over to the fledgling advertising agencies—J. Walter Thompson, Ayers, and others—which hurried in to make a profession out of the function.[37] James Buchanan Duke, for example, whose promotional efforts on behalf of Duke & Sons and later American Tobacco made the cigarette an item of mass consumption, left advertising to the agencies. For its part, Procter & Gamble kept close control over Ivory's public appearances. Although the company did eventually hire Cincinnati-based Procter & Collier Co. in 1900 to place its four-color magazine ads, Procter & Gamble continued to write and design its own advertising. Marketing had become too strategic a function to be outsourced.

That was a definitive decision on Procter & Gamble's part, for it implied unmistakably that the company was transforming itself into something more complicated than a soap manufacturer. Through the experience of developing, marketing, and distributing Ivory, the firm acquired a new set of skills, a new array of strategic competencies, and with them a new field of opportunity. As it involved itself more and more deeply in the lives and imaginations of its consumers, Procter & Gamble transformed itself into a builder of brands. In the coming century, these implicit understandings would point Procter & Gamble toward newer, bolder ventures.

The Birth of Ivory and Brand in Perspective

As the company's first sustained effort at branding its products, Ivory began the process of transforming Procter & Gamble in fundamental and far-reaching ways. Facing what was either (depending on one's point of view) a stark crisis or an unprecedented market opportunity, Procter & Gamble undertook a radically new series of marketing initiatives. In so doing, the firm triggered decisive changes in production, personnel, and strategic outlook. By 1890, Procter & Gamble was doing business on an unprecedented scale and beginning to internalize an entirely new set of business fundamentals.

This transformation was neither a planned program nor a single, fixed event. It was more like a chain reaction, as one round of change set off another somewhere else within the enterprise. Strategic crisis drove new product development, creating new marketing experiments (consumer packaging, branding, mass advertising), which in turn created new production imperatives (reinventing processes so that the brand could be used to build volume), which then required new mechanisms of human resource management (profit sharing). Staying the course meant being willing to follow through.

From an external point of view, though, the most dramatic impact came in the marketing of the product. Harley Procter and Ivory's other "brand managers" (to apply a term Procter & Gamble itself would not invent for another fifty years) were venturing into unexplored territory. They had no prior experience, either within Procter & Gamble or elsewhere in the business world, to guide them. The marketplace in which they were trying to do business was still taking shape. Only after a period of experimentation and analysis did the first, elemental understandings emerge about how brands were going to work.

Chief among these early lessons was the basic idea that to sell brands, Procter & Gamble had to connect with consumers. Before Ivory, the people whose purchasing decisions ultimately decided the fate of Procter & Gamble's products—the actors controlling the moments of truth—lay somewhere downstream, disconnected from the company. Ivory opened a dialog with them. Through advertising, the company reached out and addressed its consumers directly. Harley Procter had no tools of scientific market research to survey his consumers, but he tried resourcefully and continuously to respond to the signals they sent. The consumer may not yet have become "boss" by 1890, but Procter & Gamble was beginning to learn how to listen to her and certainly coming to understand that if it listened better than its competitors did, its brands would win in the marketplace.

The other key element in Ivory's marketing was the promise of keeping faith. Harley Procter and his partners searched around for a few years, but eventually settled on a brand equity (again, the term had not yet been invented, though the concept was beginning to crystallize) that resonated deeply and powerfully with consumers. The touchstones of this brand became purity ("99 44/100% Pure"), value, and domesticity. Images of mothers, children, families, and home imbued Ivory with an aura of familiarity and trustworthiness. The brand acquired the force of an article of faith between Procter & Gamble and its consumers.

CHAPTER THREE

Assembling the Elements of the Enterprise, 1890–1945

THE SUCCESS OF IVORY opened expansive strategic opportunities for Procter & Gamble. A new kind of marketplace was taking form, and Procter & Gamble was playing a leading role in staking out ground in it. But to hold that ground, the firm would have to restructure itself in fundamental and far-reaching ways. Having undertaken a boldly innovative marketing initiative, Procter & Gamble now faced the challenge of making that kind of initiative repeatable on a robust and regular basis. The company had made Ivory a groundbreaking brand by 1890, but had only started the deeper process of transforming itself into a builder of brands.

As it worked through this transformation between 1890 and 1945, Procter & Gamble underwent intensive, often wrenching changes. The firm became a public company. It built up a corporate R&D capacity. It reengineered its distribution infrastructure. It extended its advertising into a radical and unproven new medium—radio. It implemented and learned how to incorporate scientific market research. Finally, in a culminating step, Procter & Gamble reorganized its internal functions around the concept of brand management.

These moves did not unfold in a simple, straightforward sequence. Procter & Gamble adapted and evolved in the midst of pressing business, as it continued to make and market soap, rode out sharp economic fluctuations, and maneuvered for advantage in the midst of dramatic industry consolidation. The period from 1890 to 1930 was one of continuous experimentation. Procter & Gamble launched dozens of new brands. Some achieved breakout success, others proved modestly profitable, others failed. Critically, however, each experience taught the company more about how brands worked. Ventures such as developing Crisco and marketing Camay had impacts that went well beyond those specific products.

Working empirically, then, in piecemeal fashion, learning as it went along, but evolving steadily in strategic outlook, Procter & Gamble learned how to do business in a modern, brand-driven marketplace. By 1930, when William Cooper Procter turned the reins over to Richard R. "Red" Deupree, the first president of the company who was not a family member, a distinctly new Procter & Gamble had taken form: a company that was learning how to integrate product development, production, and marketing in a unique synthesis of corporate organization—a company, in other words, built around brand making.

Subsequent developments proved the resilience and resourcefulness of the enterprise. Between 1930 and 1945, Procter & Gamble weathered the worst depression in U.S. history, then adapted to the sharp dislocation of World War II. By the time the company emerged from war in 1945, it was poised for another round of expansion.

Incorporation: Procter & Gamble Goes Public

Procter & Gamble's partners laid the groundwork for basic transformation when they elected to take the company public, incorporating Procter & Gamble in the State of New Jersey in 1890.[1] The partners received $3 million in the transaction, $2.5 million of it in stock. The following year, the New York Stock Exchange began listing the stock.

Nobody was cashing out. The company remained closely held by the Procter and Gamble families and a few other investors. Indeed, as they took Procter & Gamble (P&G) public, the former partners agreed to hold $1 million of the shares they received for at least five years and to forgo dividends on those shares until the company paid a 12 percent dividend on the rest of the common stock. The second-generation patriarchs who had led the firm through the 1870s and 1880s took up senior management positions in the new corporation. William Alexander Procter became president, and James Norris Gamble became vice president. The former partners also figured heavily in the new company's board of directors: The initial slate of eleven board members included all the former partners except James A. Gamble (who was then eighty-seven years old). They were joined by a Cincinnati banker (Briggs S. Cunningham) and representatives of the underwriting interests (Henry B. Morehead from Morehead, Irwin & Co. and William M. Kidder from Kidder, Peabody & Co.).

Incorporation represented an effort to position P&G, already the largest soap manufacturer in the United States, for expansion and consolidation. The U.S. market for industrial equity was coming of age, and as it did so, in industry after industry, companies were merging to form combined enterprises capable of producing, marketing, and distributing in a mass market that was assuming national proportions.[2] Ivory had been P&G's first major foray into this opening territory. Incorporation represented the company's bid to stake a permanent place in the new arena.

At the same time, the move to take P&G public marked the coming of age of a new generation of family management. While the older partners remained heavily invested (literally and figuratively) in the enterprise, one new figure in particular was rising rapidly within the family ranks. William Cooper Procter, the son of William Alexander Procter and grandson of founder William Procter, had joined P&G as a factory worker in 1883. He became manager of Ivorydale as the plant went on-line a few years later, and joined the partnership as a junior member in 1887. In discussion among the partners, he advocated strongly for going public, and by the time Procter & Gamble incorporated, he was taking a position at the forefront of the company. In 1890, he became general manager. In 1907, he assumed the office of president, a position he held until retiring in 1930, at the age of sixty-eight, to become chairman of the board (the company's first chairman).

Previous generations of Procters and Gambles had made formative contributions to the company. The founders had joined forces and established the firm, of course. Their sons had both expanded and overhauled the enterprise they inherited, James Norris Gamble in product development and early R&D; Harley Procter in marketing. But arguably it was William Cooper Procter who would leave the biggest and most enduring mark on P&G.

Through a period of far-reaching change, he became the soul of the company. Arriving just as the Ivory venture was ramping up to scale, he assumed day-to-day senior management when everybody within the company—including the former partners—was adjusting to the demands of business on a corporate level of operation. He led P&G as it expanded its place within the new consumer marketplace and as it equipped itself to build successful brands.

Most important, Procter managed in the midst of these adaptations to sustain a vital, collective sense of the enterprise. As P&G grew to industrial proportions and then expanded to a national and ultimately international sphere of operation, the company naturally and necessarily grew massive in size. Nevertheless, under William Cooper Procter, the company nurtured a unique sense of belonging. His perspective was most likely shaped in fundamental ways by his early experiences working on the factory floor. In any event, Procter took progressive, highly imaginative steps to fuse a sense of common identity across company ranks. As discussed in chapter 2, in 1887 he persuaded the partners to offer profit sharing to workers.

"Colonel" Procter, as he was often called (because of his service in the Ohio National Guard), was not a naturally warm person. A tall and humorless man, he admitted that he was an uncomfortable public speaker. He was not sentimental, at least in public. "Any worthwhile change in the conduct of a business," he maintained, "must first and last have the element of lessening the cost." But he understood this issue in its broadest dimensions and felt a keen sense of responsibility to the company and its people. A man of firm conviction, he believed strongly that P&G had to avoid the cycle of exploitation, alienation, and unionization that was coming to characterize labor relations in most other large, industrial U.S. corporations. To avoid this, he believed, P&G would have to go beyond bland, paternalistic efforts to show workers that the company "cared about them."

Procter's goal in implementing profit sharing was to create a feeling of "perfect loyalty to the Company and mutual respect and confidence" between workers and management. The idea was slow to take hold. At first, workers looked upon the payments, or dividends, simply as bonuses. Procter made improvements to the plan. In 1892 he initiated an employee stock purchase program to encourage workers to become owners in the business by investing their profit-sharing dividend in company stock. In 1896 the company guaranteed employees at the lower end of the payscale against losses on investments in company stock up to one thousand dollars.

Then in 1899 labor unrest again erupted at the plant. Procter was shaken. "The fact that it was possible for a strike to be developed at Ivorydale," he wrote in a letter to the head of the employee committee, "was as disagreeable a disappointment as I could possibly have been given, showing as it does so plainly, how far short our profit sharing and other plans, for your welfare, have been from being appreciated, and how little benefit the Company has received from the money thus expended."

Despite the setback, Procter continued working on the plan. In 1903 profit sharing was restructured by tying payments to the purchase of Procter & Gamble stock. Still more changes followed in later years, as the company refined its efforts to foster a collective sense of ownership among its workers and managers.

The extension of profit sharing put P&G in the vanguard of what business historians have characterized as welfare capitalism. Taking form over the first several decades of the twentieth century, largely in response to the increasingly antagonistic confrontations between big business and labor unions, welfare capitalism represented an attempt to improve working conditions and thereby convince workers that they shared common interests with their employers. Most of these grand plans collapsed in the 1930s, under the economic pressures of the Great Depression.[3] Procter & Gamble, for its part, held fast to its commitment to the concept, demonstrating that both its work force and its management had deeply internalized the understanding that they were joined in a mutual enterprise.

Expansion: Building Capacity

Fortified by an influx of new capital and leadership, P&G expanded substantially in both scale and scope over the early 1900s. In 1903, the company began building a new plant in Kansas City, Kansas, its first major facility outside Cincinnati. Three years later, after floating more stock, P&G began work on a third plant, on Staten Island in New York Harbor. This third plant, Port Ivory, went on-line in 1907, establishing a major production capacity close to the dense markets of the eastern U.S. seaboard and to New York's shipping. In 1915, the company opened yet another plant, this one in Hamilton, Ontario, its first international plant.

Procter & Gamble also undertook a large-scale project in vertical integration, forming in 1901 a subsidiary, Buckeye Cotton Oil Co., to acquire and build cottonseed mills. Beginning in the 1870s, cottonseed oil had become an important raw material in soap formulation. Competition for supply subsequently rose, however, as major meat packers such as Swift and Armour started using cottonseed oil extract to manufacture lard compounds. Anxious to nail down supply, P&G formed Buckeye, which by 1905 was operating eight mills at various locations in the U.S. South. Eventually, this venture would lead P&G into a new product category (Crisco, discussed later in this chapter). Nevertheless, the company's principal concern originally was (in the words of a resolution passed in a special 1902 shareholder meeting to increase capital stock) to procure "better means and facilities for economically obtaining raw materials needed."[4]

P&G also expanded horizontally. In 1903, the company absorbed Schultz & Company of Zanesville, Ohio, principally to enter the laundry powder field through Schultz's Star brand (which P&G reformulated with naphtha, a petroleum derivative, and renamed Star Naphtha).[5] The Schultz acquisition initiated a series of mergers over the next several decades as P&G added capacity, expanded into new cleaning product markets, and more generally kept pace with industry consolidation. Between 1890 and 1929, the number of soap manufacturers in the United States dropped by more than 50 percent, from 578 to 282, while the size of the market expanded more than sixfold (from $46.6 million to $310.2 million).[6] Over this same period, P&G

acquired thirteen competitors, capping its leadership in the industry in 1930 with the acquisition of James S. Kirk & Co., Chicago's largest soap manufacturer. In that same year, moreover, P&G set up full-scale operations in England when it acquired Thomas Hedley & Co., Ltd.[7]

Integrating the Whole

Of course, building capacity was one thing; building *capability* was another. Many U.S. enterprises bulked up to massive dimensions in the late 1800s and early 1900s, but most eventually fell apart again or found themselves swamped by more capable competitors. Procter & Gamble outgrew its rivals in the first several decades of the twentieth century only by searching continuously for leverage and advantage. The effort to sustain growth, in other words, ultimately depended on P&G's ability to learn how to use the resources it was amassing better than rival soapers did.

More specifically, obtaining competitive leverage meant learning, and eventually mastering, the art of brand making. "To make money out of a universal commodity like soap you have to sell it in heroic amounts," *Fortune* observed in 1939. "The cost per unit is figured in pennies, and the profit per unit in mills, and unless you keep your tonnages flowing, you find that your penny costs multiply and your mills divide. . . . Practically all of your profits are tied up in your branded items, and these you must sell by the millions of cases if you are to survive."[8] These had become the essential facts of doing business in the modern marketplace, and while P&G grasped the basics readily, crafting a corporate organization capable of engineering success on these terms on a consistent, profitable basis took time, trial, and error. The company had to learn how to research and develop new technologies that could become new brands, how to merchandise and market them, and how to draw consumer insights into the process. Then, once these individual components of the larger process were functional, P&G had to learn how to organize the entire structure so that its various parts informed each other and worked in concert to create and sustain successful brands.

Research and Development

One vital component of brand building, as Ivory demonstrated, was the ability to develop new products and new technologies. The experimental work of James Norris Gamble in the mid-1800s had left craft knowledge behind and taken the firm out onto the leading edge of soap technology. The partners made an extended commitment to staying there in 1887, when they brought in Harley James Morrison (a nephew of the Procter brothers) to join Gamble in the lab. A chemistry student with a degree from Yale, Morrison came in looking both to expand P&G's technical expertise and deepen Gamble's probes into the basic underlying scientific processes at work in soap. Under his direction in 1890, the same year that P&G went public, the company established an analytical lab at Ivorydale to house Morrison's growing operation. The timing was not coincidental. Like incorporation, the establishment of a professional R&D arm represented an effort to harness technology as a corporate capability. Though small by modern standards, Morrison's operation was a bold innovation, one of the first corporate labs in the field of consumer goods.[9]

It took some time for the fledgling R&D operation to situate itself within the company. The establishment of a central lab was certainly useful in focusing R&D work, for example. Within a few years of carving out their own space within Ivorydale, however, the technical staff learned that they were going to have to spread themselves more widely through the everyday life of the company in order to have an impact. By the late 1800s, according to one chemist, "we were urging the Superintendent at Ivorydale and others to take some of the chemical men from the laboratory and put them in the plant," where they would be available to handle the problems that emerged in "departments like glycerine and fatty acid." At this stage, the R&D effort concentrated heavily on issues like quality and cost of raw materials as well as production issues, though Morrison and his staff did manage to carve out the time and resources for more basic research. Over the early 1900s, company researchers came into their own, working on projects such as developing a white naphtha laundry soap and perfecting the hydrogenation of edible oil.[10]

More fundamentally, Morrison and his team fostered a broad sense of the role of R&D within the company. "Most of the inventions of the nineteenth century were made by practical men, plant superintendents or factory managers, who could try out their new ideas right away," observed a researcher from a later period. "No research teams were involved and no bench-scale trials intervened. There were no pilot plants or process development operations. The entire development was by empiricism." Morrison's first challenge was to replace this reactive, trial-and-error mentality with a more sustained scientific outlook.[11]

Over time, as they integrated themselves within the factories and became a familiar presence in the managerial ranks, Morrison's staff wove R&D into the company's other processes. Pilot plants became part of factory architecture—and part of everyday assumptions throughout P&G about how the company developed, refined, and reformulated products. By the mid-1920s, the company's R&D effort had coalesced into a multitiered Chemical Division employing a staff of several hundred young men and women, with

Research, Process, and Products departments. The Research Department was charged with work on basic science, passing its findings onto the Process Department, which translated them into manufacturing processes. The Products Department, meanwhile, stationed itself downstream, working closely with salespeople and other marketing staff to refine product formulations.

Refining Brand Marketing

Technological shifts in one of P&G's key core markets—laundry soap—demonstrated the growing importance of maintaining a strong R&D operation. Between 1890 and 1930, consumers migrated from bar soap to flakes and chips, and then from flakes and chips to granules. Each shift required intensive R&D adjustments on P&G's part, in both process (designing and optimizing manufacturing equipment) and formulation. Each shift entailed massive conversions of plant. And each shift also taught the company important lessons about brand marketing. Indeed, much of P&G's formative understanding of how brands worked grew out of the company's experience in fighting to stay on top of the churning laundry soap market through the early 1900s.

At the turn of the twentieth century, P&G's most important brand, after Ivory, was Lenox, a yellow, rosin-based laundry bar that the company sold in enormous volume. Lenox itself had signaled the company's commitment to technological change: Taking the brand to market had meant cannibalizing P&G's Mottled German and Oleine soaps, a move the company nevertheless undertook without hesitation.[12] When a competitive brand incorporating naphtha began eating into Lenox's share, P&G undertook major R&D work on naphtha-based products, eventually acquiring and reformulating an external brand (Star Naphtha), as well as developing one internally (P&G White Naphtha). As customers then gravitated toward soap in ready-to-use forms (rather than bars, which consumers had to shave to add to wash water), P&G again moved aggressively to lead the transition by putting new brands with the new technologies on the market. The company launched Ivory Flakes in 1918, followed two years later by Chipso, a brand formulated especially for the new washing machines.

These changes were costly, calling for a continual commitment of resources. "The response from consumers [to the introduction of soap flakes] was so enthusiastic that for a ten year period the factories were kept busy buying and installing new flake dryers," recalled one scientist. "Meanwhile thousands of the steel frames used in the production of bar soap were scrapped because they were no longer needed." But even as flake sales increased rapidly, "development work was under way that resulted in making the flake dryers obsolete." Granules were more convenient for consumers and cheaper to manufacture. So between 1926 and 1946, "spray drying towers were built to produce granules." By 1945, some 60 percent of P&G's retail soap production was granular, and Oxydol had become the company's leading brand.[13]

At each stage in the evolution from bar soap to flakes to chips to granules, P&G was forced to adapt not just its technologies and plants, but more basically its array of brand positions. Each stage represented a very real risk for the company, threatening the brand equity it had built up to that point. Each stage called for new brand ventures. "When soap flakes became available," a P&G researcher recalled, "customers began switching from bar soaps and it was like a game of musical chairs to see which manufacturer would end up the winner."[14] The game never stopped. If P&G managed to come out a little further ahead each time the music stopped, the company learned that, to keep doing so, it had to rise and start moving as soon as the music started up again.

As it learned the rules of this game, the company's collective approach to marketing underwent a transition akin to the one that had shifted its understanding of R&D: Procter & Gamble gradually abandoned a hit-or-miss empirical approach—sticking with what experience showed worked, tinkering if things did not seem to be working—in search of more rigorous, proactive methods of analysis and application. The turning point in this transformation was the launch of Crisco in 1911.

Crisco: P&G Marketing Tactics Mature

In 1907, an independent scientist, E. C. Kayser, approached P&G with a technology he had developed, hydrogenation, that converted liquid oils into solid fats. Sensing market applications, the company set up a lab in Ivorydale for Kayser to continue development. Kayser left after a few months, but a research team led by Morrison and M. B. "Doc" Graff picked up the project, working in secret, behind frosted-glass windows. By 1910, they had a patentable product: an edible shortening composed of cottonseed oil mixed with cottonseed stearin. They called the substance Krispo.

The stuff was unlike anything P&G had tried to sell before. It was neither a soap nor a candle, of course, and so it represented a new product category for the company.[15] From the consumers' point of view, it was an entirely new kind of product altogether. To sell Krispo, the company would have to sell homemakers on the idea of replacing the lard, which they were accustomed to using for cooking. This challenge produced a marketing campaign bigger than anything P&G—or any other company—had ever tried before.[16] In

April 1911, the executive committee approved the brand name *Crisco* (after abandoning *Krispo,* because a Chicago cracker manufacturer had trademarked the name) and hired the J. Walter Thompson agency to handle the account. Stanley Resor, who had come to the agency from Procter and Collier, took charge of Crisco and brought in Helen Lansdowne as his copywriter.

This team, working closely with P&G at the senior-most level of management (both Resor and Lansdowne were invited to board of directors meetings, despite the rare presence of women in board rooms at that time), laid careful, intricate groundwork for the launch. The company sent samples of Crisco to university-based food researchers, nutritionists, and home economists. Local Cincinnati hotels, railroad dining cars, and restaurants were also provided with early supplies and solicited for endorsements and recipes. A general analysis of the shortening market was conducted. Meanwhile, Resor and Lansdowne tested alternative sales-promotion plans for Crisco in a series of test markets, running an all-newspaper advertising campaign in one city, an all-streetcar advertising campaign in another, and different mixes of store demonstrations and house-to-house samplings in others. The team tested eight alternative plans in all, tallying up results and measuring the varying impacts against each other.[17] This pilot marketing work then fed into a massive national launch in January 1912 (after every grocer in the United States had been sent a small case of the product). The launch was backed by saturation advertising and a precision battery of promotional events. It was the most ambitious product launch any company had ever undertaken, in all likelihood—and what was even more important, the most carefully and scientifically planned.

The Crisco campaign marked the maturing of P&G's branding powers. For decades after the launch of Ivory, the company had been gathering experience and knowledge. With Crisco, the company committed to applying that knowledge systematically, testing different approaches in advance and then mapping out larger campaigns on the basis of what the testing taught.

Selling Direct

As the company rebuilt its strategic orientation around brand marketing on a scale benchmarked by the Crisco campaign, P&G's traditional distribution structure began to show signs of stress. From its inception in 1837 through the early 1900s, the company had relied on wholesalers to reach the trade. Procter & Gamble sold to wholesalers (jobbers), who in turn sold to retailers, who in turn sold to consumers. As long as the company's product consisted mainly of commodities, channeling distribution through wholesalers worked admirably. The system also proved capable of moving large batches of a few branded goods in a more or less continuous flow. As P&G put more and more brands on the market, however, the system became increasingly cumbersome to operate. By 1910, it was becoming clear that P&G needed more intricate, responsive mechanisms of distribution. The result, after several years of experimentation, was a wrenching overhaul and a bold shift to a radically different infrastructure: Procter & Gamble began selling directly to retailers.

Background: Wholesaler Distribution

Structural weak points in P&G's wholesaler distribution system were already becoming apparent by the early 1900s. The company found, for example, that wholesalers waited for the manufacturer's prices to drop (in response to fluctuations in the cost of raw materials) and then purchased in large amounts they stockpiled in warehouses. The wholesalers could then draw down on these reserves once P&G's prices rose again. This sequence created a cyclical pattern of alternating slack and heavy demand, despite the ultimately steady consumption of the company's products downstream. Procter & Gamble, in other words, was missing out on an opportunity to smooth out production. The company was compelled to bring plants periodically on- and off-line, and was consequently unable to maintain a steady workforce.

Pricing disputes also arose. In 1909, a U.S. Supreme Court ruling made it illegal for manufacturers to enforce resale prices on goods they had sold through wholesalers. When this ruling was upheld on appeal in 1912, P&G was forced to relinquish long-standing efforts to hold the line on the resale prices that wholesalers offered retailers. The wholesalers consequently began discounting their prices and pressing P&G for greater discounts upstream. When P&G balked at increasing its traditional 10 percent discount rate (which amounted to the wholesalers' margin), wholesalers resisted and, in some regions, refused for a time to handle P&G products.[18]

The deeper problem with wholesale distribution, however, was that it was unwieldy. The system required that P&G bring an enormous, continuous effort to bear on third-party transactions that occurred beyond its control. The strain of that effort betrayed itself repeatedly in the stream of circular letters the company dispatched to wholesalers, urging them to sell P&G products energetically to retailers. "There is money in it for your firm, yourself and your customers," the company had to remind the jobbers repeatedly.[19] At its best, the system created a powerful partnership, smooth and seamless. Procter & Gamble offered the wholesalers "an opportunity to secure *lucrative, staple,* and *growing business* which should systematically attract your efforts to The Procter & Gamble Soaps."[20] At its worst, though, the system left P&G hostage to third-party agents. It was a filtered process—one that multiplied what a later generation of P&G strategists would call the moments of truth that determined success in the marketplace.

As P&G's marketing grew more sophisticated, meanwhile, the company required increasingly intricate machinery of execution. "Our samplers are now at work in your city," the company informed retailers in 1903–1904. "They will leave a pound package of Star Naphtha Washing Powder in every house in your city as well as a leaflet and a letter addressed to the lady of the house. 'Eight-sheet' posters advertising the brand will go on the boards right away. Street car advertising will begin as soon as the goods are generally distributed and will run for a period of six months after the work of sampling is completed. . . . The work we are doing will create an immediate demand for Star Naphtha Washing Powder. We want you to be in a position to satisfy this demand. Please, therefore, give your jobber an order for at least one case."[21] The launch of Crisco a handful of years later demanded even more rigorous planning. Brand marketing became a series of carefully sequenced campaigns, in which activities like advertising, sampling, and premiums unfolded in precisely coordinated stages.

Meanwhile, the number of brands P&G was putting on the marketplace was multiplying, even as the marketplace itself was becoming a contending multitude of brands from numerous competitors. In 1890, P&G was still putting most of its marketing energy behind a single brand: Ivory. By 1905, the company had broadened the effort considerably: "While the demand for Ivory is of great volume and continues to increase each year," one circular reminded the jobbers, "it is absolutely essential that Lenox, Clean Quick, Polo, Star, Tar Tar and other P&G brands should be *sold* and *pushed*."[22] Internally, P&G expanded its sales force from 30 to 175 over the first two decades of the 1900s in an effort to keep pace. "Instead of selling Ivory Soap and Lenox Soap . . . we have a number of brands," explained Richard Deupree in 1921. "We have Star Naphtha Powder, P&G White Naphtha Soap, Star Soap, and Crisco. . . . The new brands that were added could not be introduced to the public by selling the wholesale grocer. It was necessary to do very much more."[23]

"Very much more," inevitably, meant taking control of distribution. Typically, though, the company moved carefully, testing alternative methods. In 1913, P&G experimented with direct distribution in New York City, offering retailers the same discounts the company offered wholesalers (and pegging discount rates to quantities purchased). The results of this experiment were encouraging, indicating distribution costs comparable to those the company incurred distributing via wholesalers in the southwestern United States. In fact, when the wholesalers' discounts were factored in, P&G's costs were substantially lower.[24]

Of course, New York City presented highly atypical conditions; whether direct distribution would be feasible in a more dispersed retail environment remained unclear. Accordingly, the company expanded the experiment in 1919 to encompass the New England region. Again, the results looked encouraging, indicating that direct distribution looked both workable and economically feasible. On the other hand, the company's moves stirred opposition among wholesalers. Realizing that direct distribution would encounter resistance, P&G executives accelerated their plans in an effort to get a system up and running before opponents could fully mobilize. Behind the scenes, hasty preparations took place. A year later, on June 28, 1920, the company announced that it was going direct nationwide as of July 1, offering products to retailers on the same terms that it gave wholesalers.

Growing Pains: Implementing Direct Distribution

The transition to direct sales required a massive commitment of resources. According to Deupree: "To sell direct meant that we must be in position to deliver 5 boxes of soap to any retail grocer in the country. It meant store-door delivery to all dealers located in cities. It meant that all dealers have to be called upon regularly. Warehouses and trucking arrangements had to be established to give service."[25] From a sales operation that had been handling 20,000 accounts, the company expanded to an organization handling between 350,000 and 400,000 accounts. Warehouses, 150 of them initially, had to be secured, and more than 1,000 "cartage arrangements" were set up to handle transportation.[26] Ideally, the company would have rolled out the new system region by region. In fact, many P&G people still doubted they would be able to set up functional infrastructure in some sections of the United States—the Rocky Mountains, for example, and the Oklahoma/Texas region. Nevertheless, under the circumstances, the company did not feel it could afford to move incrementally. In Deupree's words: "We could not take the country piecemeal, we had to prepare to take it in one bite."[27]

Inevitably, glitches erupted. "We made a lot of mistakes, and these mistakes were costly," Deupree admitted. He added discreetly, "We found in building up one system for handling a territory that it did not fit that territory. There were changes, and a lot of changes."[28] The company discovered, for example, that it overbuilt initially, and had to substantially scale back its infrastructure. Between 1921 and 1926, P&G cut its sales force by half and its sales support staff by three-quarters, while at the same time slashing the

An editorial cartoon that appeared in the Interstate Grocer *in 1920, suggested what a bold and dangerous move Procter & Gamble was undertaking when it decided to sell its products directly to retailers.*

number of warehouses and "trucking arrangements" it had set up to operate the system.[29]

The company's most serious miscalculation, however, was the extent of resistance from the wholesalers. Procter & Gamble was the first major consumer goods producer to bypass the jobbers and set up direct sales to retailers. The jobbers were fighting for their life, and they threw themselves against the plan.[30] Wholesaler boycotts of P&G goods broke out, even as P&G struggled urgently to work the kinks and bugs out of its new system. "We had unlimited trouble in handling orders through our offices, we had considerable trouble in making deliveries; in giving service to the customer, and in handling customers' correspondence, and a lot of other things I can't think of at the moment," Deupree later conceded with a shudder. "The result was that within 15 days after we started direct, the wholesale grocer started out on the most intense campaign he ever indulged in to poison the mind of every retail grocer in the United States against our plan of marketing. For a while he succeeded admirably."[31]

The only way to proceed was to drive forward, learning and applying best practices as rapidly as they could be extracted from the confusion. On the one hand, P&G strained to preserve the support of the trade, assuring retailers (in Deupree's words), "We are not trying to browbeat a little dealer; we are not trying to build up a big dealer; we are simply trying to distribute goods to you at a more reasonable cost than we had been able to do before."[32] Meanwhile, the company scrambled frantically up its learning curve. It was in November or December 1920, by Deupree's account, that "one of our offices sort of stuck its head up from the rest with better sales and lower handling costs and less trouble." Seizing this basic blueprint, the company quickly restructured its other regional offices along the same lines. Slowly but perceptibly, the system began to achieve what Deupree called "at least a fair degree of efficiency."[33]

The rocky transition to direct sales, which happened to coincide with a slump in the U.S. economy, cost the company dearly. Procter & Gamble downplayed the extent of the disruption—the annual report for fiscal year (FY) 1920–1921 described the year as one "of readjustment and reconstruction"—but inevitably business suffered. Sales slipped from $188.8 million in FY 1919–1920 to $120 million the following year, and $105.7 million the next; not until FY 1925–1926 did they recover their previous levels. In 1922, William Cooper Procter reported (privately, to his niece) that "the business has been turned from going down hill and is starting up hill. . . . Our bad spots are pretty well cleaned up." Still, in January 1923, the Colonel conceded that P&G might not be able to pay a dividend (though it did, as things turned out) and fretted over the impact the news would have on the share price. Nevertheless, he maintained that "the present plan, with the now necessary change, has worked, and will work for the advantage of the average stockholder."[34]

Indeed, after a painful period of learning and adaptation, the company came out on the other side with a significantly more flexible distribution system, which strengthened P&G's marketing capability. That capability was further reinforced, moreover, by a pioneering effort to unlock the secrets of the consumer marketplace with new, scientific tools of understanding.

Learning Market Research

In 1924, shortly after setting up an Economic Research Department to analyze fluctuations in raw material prices, P&G hired D. Paul "Doc" Smelser, a Ph.D. economist from Johns Hopkins University. Smelser dutifully took on the assignment of price forecasting but quickly had carved out a significantly broader role for himself. He had a habit of posing basic questions that no one within the company had posed before or, at any rate, had figured out how to answer: How many consumers used Ivory for dish-washing, for example, and how many for washing their faces and hands? By his own account, Smelser was "a curious economist . . . who asked so many darn questions about our products that I was given the job of getting the answers."[35] A reporter probably came closer to the mark in describing him as "a short, round-faced gentleman who fully deserves his reputation of possessing one of the keenest commercial research intelligences in the world."[36]

Smelser issued his first report in October 1924, on salad oil. Several weeks later, he delivered a second, much more ambitious analysis, breaking out Ivory consumers by income and background and dissecting his findings in meticulous statistical detail. "Doc" would later advise market researchers to avoid using "technical terms, especially statistical terms" in their reports: "If you use correlation in determining a fact in a report, just refer to it as 'relationship.'"[37] Nevertheless, the data opened impressive insights into Ivory's market. Recognizing the value of this kind of information, the company pulled Smelser out of the Economic Research Department in 1925 and set him up in a new unit called the Market Research Department.

Smelser was working without the benefit of prior experience or established methodology—either within P&G or elsewhere in business. No company had undertaken market research before in a sustained, rigorous, applied way. Smelser had to improvise, making mistakes, learning as he went along. For example, to test perfumes for Camay, a perfumed toilet soap launched in 1926, he sent a researcher with bottles of the perfume to survey female employees working on another floor. "Of course," Smelser recounted, "all the perfume smelled like alcohol and thus we came to the great discovery that for a soap perfume to be really tested, it should be incorporated in soap." Not to mention, as the fledgling department continued to acquire experience, that the soap should not merely be sniffed, but actually used.[38]

By encountering and working through these kinds of issues, Smelser and his staff gradually developed a set of basic market research tools. Everything that would become second nature had to be learned, or as Smelser later put it, "practically every technique which the Company uses today in Market Research was developed by trial. . . . To make one touchdown we usually carried the ball several times the length of the field." Researchers found, for example, that there was "a definite art to the business of asking questions. . . . One needs to know to use words that are in our everyday language and string them together so they will communicate a very precise thought and yet, at the same time, do it in an objective way so that the person is not conditioned or prejudiced or misled in any way."[39]

The first brand to incorporate market research in its design was Camay. "Procedure was perfectly terrible by today's standards," Smelser later admitted, "with the only test worthwhile being made on the shape of the bar. Housewives were asked to choose one out of half a dozen possible bar shapes. This was confusing. However, we were *learning*." Thus, in a second round of market research to replace the brand's original packaging, the Market Research Department set up a much more elaborate series of tests. Sixty-three designs, arrayed in twelve groups, with six designs in each group, were submitted to 19,760 women. When this process had narrowed the field to two finalists, the competing designs were set up in paired display stands in grocery stores for a final runoff.[40]

As this work proved its worth, P&G built up the Market Research Department to substantial proportions. The first women investigators joined the staff in 1929, many of them transferring from Crisco's field crews (which were being disbanded as a result of the Depression). In 1931, Smelser decided the department would make a major commitment to field research, hiring female college graduates and sending them door-to-door to survey homemakers about all kinds of household products and habits. Within a few years, the department's staff grew to thirty-four, including dozens of field researchers. Between 1930 and 1942, despite the pressures of the Depression and mobilization for World War II, the Market Research Department's budget rose from $45,000 to $189,908.[41]

The emergence of scientific market research profoundly deepened P&G's understanding of its consumers and its brands. In the era of Ivory and Harley Procter, the company's branding, while resourceful and effective, had been top-down, issuing from the company outward to consumers, and had as a result been shaped almost entirely by managerial instinct. Even when the company sifted the data generated by its various marketing initiatives—

Beginning in the 1930s, P&G's market-research effort went door to door, sending young women into the field to interview homemakers about household products.

and P&G sifted especially carefully—it was still branding by fiat, still marketing empirically. Smelser's work opened vital feedback channels, drawing consumers into the process of branding. Procter & Gamble was learning to listen to its consumers.

Putting It All Together: Brand Management

The cultivation of cutting-edge R&D, the increasing sophistication of marketing campaigns such as that for Crisco, the rechanneling of distribution infrastructure, and the creation of state-of-the-art market research all represented important facets of brand making. As individual capabilities, they created powerful potential. What remained essential, however, was the ability to integrate them into a single, organic brand-building process. Research and development and market research had to communicate continuously with each other. Marketing initiatives had to be closely coordinated with distribution, and the entire process of developing, producing, merchandising, marketing, and distributing brands had to be structured so that its individual components worked in harness. In short, P&G ultimately had to craft an organizational structure capable of meshing the whole together.

The solution, brand management, emerged gradually and organically over the 1910s and 1920s. A new generation of managers rising to senior status during this period—people such as Deupree, Ralph Rogan, and Stockton Buzby—laid the groundwork for brand management as they decentralized responsibility for brand promotions. Launching Crisco was a formative experience in this regard.[42] The most influential figure in defining brand management, however, was Neil McElroy, and the pivotal brand was Camay.

As a perfumed beauty bar, Camay naturally challenged "99 44/100% Pure" Ivory, in message as well as market: The very positioning of Camay demanded independence. In any event, the experience of fighting for resources against P&G's entrenched, big-budget brands convinced McElroy, then a young advertising manager, that the company needed to formalize assignments of its marketers in brand-specific teams and to give these teams a large degree of autonomy in running specific marketing campaigns. From this background and with this impetus, brand management was already coalescing as a de facto policy by the mid-1920s. McElroy took a major step toward formalizing it as an organizational structure in a May 1931 memo, outlining what he referred to as "the duties and responsibilities of the brand men."[43]

Specifically, McElroy's memo charged brand managers with studying shipments of their brands by units and territories, analyzing where sales were heavy and where they were light, and extracting from that data conclusions about which tactics were working. "Where brand development is heavy and where it is progressing," McElroy directed, brand managers were to "examine carefully the combination of effort that seems to be clicking and try to apply this same treatment to other territories that are comparable." In addition, the memo charged brand managers with studying "the past advertising and promotional history of the brand," as well as dealers and consumers within various territories "at first hand." On the basis of this knowledge, the managers would work out "sales helps and all other necessary material" to pass along to sales personnel in the various districts for implementation. In addition, by spelling out responsibilities for "assistant brand men," McElroy's memo laid the preliminary groundwork for the formation of brand teams—although McElroy added that his plan "does not represent the situation as it is but as we will have it when we have sufficient man power."[44]

Reorganization around the principle of brand management culminated a gradual yet thoroughgoing reformulation of strategic outlook within P&G. From a geographically oriented sales perspective, the company shifted alignment internally to rearrange its people around its brands. That restructuring, which took place at the very heart of the company, where marketing initiatives were mapped out and critical resources allocated, focused managerial energy in fundamental and far-reaching ways. Procter & Gamble brand managers ultimately assumed responsibility for much more than marketing. They were, in fact, responsible for the coordination of all activities involving their brand including product development and field sales. As a result of this broad training, from McElroy on, every one of the company's chief executives would pass through the offices of assistant brand manager and brand manager on the way to executive ranks. Brand management became a crucible in which the company formed its sense of itself and its landscape.

This defining aspect marked P&G as a unique kind of company. A series of large industrial corporations were restructured over the 1920s, as they learned to do business on a massive scale. Much like P&G, they took themselves apart and reassembled themselves as multidivisional structures—or M-forms. Few, however, committed themselves as completely to the concept of brand management as P&G did. Companies such as Sears & Roebuck and Standard Oil built themselves around geographic regions, while at DuPont and General Motors, restructuring took place along product lines.[45] Procter & Gamble, for its part, defined the brand as the building block of the enterprise. After World War II, as P&G diversified into new product categories, the company would overlay a product line divisional structure onto the brand organization. By the time it did so, however, brand management had already solidified as a bedrock organizing principle.

Into Storms, 1930–1945

In 1930, William Cooper Procter retired as president of P&G, passing the torch to Richard Deupree. As mentioned, Deupree's ascension marked the first time that neither a Procter nor a Gamble was running the company on a day-to-day basis. (Colonel Procter did take up a new position as chairman of the board, holding the chair until he died, in 1934.) The company Deupree inherited proved durable and flexible, however, weathering two violent, external shocks in rapid succession over the next decade and a half. The Depression was already deepening as Procter stepped down, and beyond lay another world war.

P&G Faces a Depression

Procter & Gamble had by this point established a leading position within the soap industry. It was roughly twice the size of Colgate in terms of sales when the Depression struck, according to Wall Street estimates. What's more, the company was digesting several large acquisitions: William Waltke Co. of St. Louis (acquired in 1927 and giving the company the Lava soap and Oxydol detergent brands); James S. Kirk & Co. of Chicago (picked up in 1930); and Thomas Hedley & Co. in England (also 1930).[46] The Depression, however, hit business hard. By 1930, grocers were buying "hand-to-mouth" (in the phrase of P&G historian Alfred Lief), and inventory was piling up at Ivorydale some $6 million above normal levels.[47] Conditions continued to worsen, reaching their bleakest point in 1934. Nevertheless, the internal capabilities P&G had built up over the preceding decades withstood the economic storm. Procter & Gamble processes and structures proved durable and resilient. The company continued to pay out dividends. Perhaps most significantly, P&G managed to keep employment levels largely intact, even as surrounding companies were forced to make massive cutbacks.[48]

P&G Faces a New Medium

Another sign of internal soundness was the company's ability to manage the shift to radio advertising. Procter & Gamble was the largest magazine advertiser in the industry on the eve of radio broadcasting, outspending Colgate $3.3 million to $2.3 million. It was deeply staked, in other words, in the leading media of its day. But the advertising environment was about to undergo a seismic shift. A new media emerged in the late 1920s, one that would demand new types of advertising.[49]

Procter & Gamble sponsored The Puddle Family, *a popular radio soap opera in 1932. A forerunner of* Ma Perkins, *P&G's most successful and enduring soap opera, it helped usher in a new mass medium and, for the company, a new era in advertising.*

Radio took some time to define itself as a medium: The basic broadcast format (commercial broadcasting on national networks, sponsored by corporate advertising) took form slowly, in bits and pieces over the 1920s and early 1930s, as radio stations, studios, and commercial sponsors experimented with different ways of putting together programming. Procter & Gamble played a leading role in this process of definition, launching a series of creative (and expensive) initiatives. In 1933, with the national debut of *Ma Perkins,* the company found the formula. "Soap operas" became a fixture of radio and the centerpiece of P&G's marketing campaigns. By the time the Depression began to ease in the late 1930s, P&G had established itself as one of the biggest advertisers on the airwaves. Just as the company had four decades earlier in magazines (and would again several decades later in television), P&G had moved into the new medium while it was still experimental and found creative, resonant ways to embed its brands there.

The strategic landscape, meanwhile, stabilized during these years. Through the 1930s, P&G continued to do nearly all its business in two major sectors: soap (including laundry) and food products (shortening, accounting for roughly a third of sales). These markets, particularly the soap markets, were fragmented. According to *Fortune* magazine, in 1939 Procter & Gamble was marketing some 200 brands, including 140 soap brands. Nevertheless, 6 brands had achieved major sales and share positions: P&G White Naphtha (the biggest brand by volume, though it earned low margins), Oxydol (the biggest earner, with a healthier margin), Ivory (including soap, Ivory Flakes, and Ivory Snow), Chipso, Crisco, and Camay (which also enjoyed a relatively healthy margin).[50]

The company was certainly successful. Its position was not exactly comfortable, however. In the core laundry category in particular, P&G was still searching for decisive advantage. As R. A. Duncan, a researcher at P&G, characterized the situation, "the margin of P&G's lead over the other front runners was always narrow, which meant that the prizes for winning must be shared."[51]

P&G Faces a War

As the 1930s ended, greater forces broke in on the company and its business. Late in 1940, U.S. Army personnel approached P&G about building and running an ordnance plant, to load propellant charges into shells. The company responded, setting up a plant in Tennessee, then another in Mississippi. The war that had broken out in Europe was reaching the United States.

The U.S. government's choice of P&G, a consumer goods company, to take responsibility for ordnance production testified to the company's reputation as an efficient and reliable supplier. Nevertheless, World War II put immense pressure on P&G. The company strained to fill U.S. military procurement contracts on a vast scale, at the same time that it struggled to cope with shortages in raw materials. Meanwhile, a pressing worker shortage made labor supply a critical challenge. The crisis tested the ingenuity of managers and researchers alike, as the company scrambled to reformulate, retool factories, scrounge up supplies, and keep enough workers in the factory to continue making soap and shortening. Some brands were discontinued for the duration. Chipso, for example, disappeared from store shelves, never to reappear.

Although no one realized it yet, the entire laundry market, and indeed P&G itself, was about to enter another period of intense strategic flux. While the war consumed nearly everybody within the company, a few researchers in the lab were achieving new breakthroughs in formulating synthetic detergents capable of heavy cleaning. Things were never going to be the same again.

The Period in Perspective, 1890–1945

Over the period from 1890 to 1945, Procter & Gamble gradually acquired the capabilities it needed to build brands on a consistent basis. If Ivory had been merely an isolated event, the company's momentum would almost certainly have slowed down eventually—at least until another team had stumbled on another winning brand formula—for markets are always in flux. But P&G did not stumble forward. The company worked energetically and resourcefully to figure out what had been successful in developing and marketing Ivory. Building successive rounds of brands through the early 1900s, most of them now largely forgotten, helped the company to hone specific tactics and strategies. Procter & Gamble cut its teeth on Ivory, but refined its skills on brands such as Lenox, P&G White Naphtha, Oxydol, and Chipso. A major turning point in the learning curve came in 1911, with the launch of Crisco.

Gradually, over the course of these experiences, a larger vision took hold enterprisewide as P&G learned to apply and internalize brand building as a corporate pattern. It took time—decades, in fact—to restructure the company along these lines. A series of milestones marked continual, hard-won progress. The incorporation of the company in 1890 put P&G on a new institutional footing, preparing it for the time (still years ahead) when it would be carried on by senior managers named neither Procter nor Gamble. The implementation of a capacity for ongoing corporate R&D in 1890, including basic research and regular product and process application, represented another turning point. Equally critical was the establishment of a market research department in 1926, as well as the coalescence of brand management as a central organizing principle over the 1920s.

Each of these developments created new outlooks, deepening the collective sense of what happened when the company ventured out into the marketplace. In each case, however, implementing respective structural elements only began the more basic process of working through and integrating the new insights and outlooks that P&G was acquiring. Ultimately, P&G assembled a truly distinctive corporate capacity for brand building because it meshed together R&D, product development, market research, brand management, and a host of other functions in ways its competitors could not match.

CHAPTER FOUR

Science in the Washing Machine

THE STORY OF TIDE

OVER THE FIRST HALF of the twentieth century, P&G scraped and clawed its way to industry leadership. Its increasingly sophisticated capacity for brand building gave it a narrow competitive advantage over its rivals, enabling it to hold market leadership in its core soap categories. The company remained hard-pressed, however, and unable to achieve anything like breakout success against Colgate or Lever Brothers. Business was profitable, but by no means comfortable, through 1945.

Then, in a case rich with lessons in innovation and brand building, P&G decisively altered this ambiguous competitive position. By injecting a radical, new, disruptive technology and then masterfully exploiting the strategic opening thus created, the company built a brand bigger than anything it had created before. Tide was not just a new product, but a new *kind* of product, based on synthetic compounds rather than soap chemicals. Neil McElroy was scarcely exaggerating when he called synthetic detergents "the first big change in soapmaking in 2,000 years."[1] Indeed, it proved bigger than what P&G had initially planned: Tide quickly spilled over the boundaries that company strategists had drawn for the product and ripped through P&G's core markets. Within a handful of years, Tide displaced P&G's most profitable brands and its best-selling ones and sharply repositioned the company against its competitors.

That change worked just as powerfully internally, on P&G as it did on the marketplace. The experience of developing and marketing synthetic detergents rapidly dissolved and reconstituted the company's understanding of itself, its resources, and its opportunities. To an extent few people realized in 1946, when Tide went into test markets, P&G was undertaking a venture that would transform the company from the inside out. As one researcher described the shift in strategic outlook, P&G "would no longer be a soap company" in the wake of Tide, "it would become an industrial corporation with its future based on technology. We had done some things up until then . . . but we were still a soap company with these things as extras. With Tide, we were no longer a soap company."[2] For P&G, leveraging the technology of synthetic detergents ultimately meant managing a profound transition, from soap company to technology firm.

Procter & Gamble's success in managing that transition would position the company for decades of growth and expansion. But the transition did not come easily for a company that had, after all, been in the soap business for more than a hundred years, by 1946. Developing Tide meant pushing P&G in directions the company at times seemed collectively ambivalent about taking. Indeed, "Product X" (as the project was known before it was branded) very nearly died in the lab. And bringing it to market stretched the company as it had never been stretched before. From the outside, P&G appeared to ride Tide masterfully and smoothly to a commanding market position. But behind the scenes, piecing this technology together and readying it for market took courage and resourcefulness, a willingness to work against the rules and outside the confines of normal P&G processes. The experience drew deeply on the company's vaunted expertise, but also demanded improvisation and risk taking. Tide's original marketers would debut the product with declarations of a "Washday Revolution." The full implications of that revolution would take a little while to dawn on the company that was driving it. Procter & Gamble had invited a storm of creative destruction into its core business. Still, critically, the company recognized the opportunity it was creating and proved adept at modifying its resources and processes to exploit the opening.

Research and Development

Developing Tide was not a linear process. The company assembled the key technologies in fits and starts, by way of fortuitous accidents, vexing dead ends, and slow, laborious work. Actually, P&G almost missed the opportunity. The breakthrough grew out of a seemingly dead project—a line of research nearly everybody had given up on. Procter & Gamble did not march so much as lurch and crawl its way toward the breakthrough.

The Synthetic Breakthrough

The initial glimpse into the basic technology came unexpectedly, through a back door. In April 1931, Robert A. Duncan, one of P&G's process engineers, traveled to Europe on "a scouting expedition," as he later described it, "to see if I could learn anything concerning processes or products of interest to P&G." One of these stops brought Duncan to the I. G. Farben Research Laboratories in Ludwigshaften. Nothing he saw on his official tour looked particularly impressive, but afterward, things got interesting. "When I left it was approaching their quitting time," Duncan later recalled, "and one of their men asked to ride with me as far as his home. In the conversation en route I asked whether there were any other developments which might be of interest to P&G. After thinking a moment, he said, 'Yes, there is one development which I believe you will find interesting from an academic point of view, but I am sure it will be of no commercial interest to P&G.'" During World War I, when soap had been in desperately short supply, German chemists had discovered that a local textile mill was using bile from slaughtered cattle as a wetting agent for its dyeing operations. I. G. Farben had isolated the active ingredient within the bile, synthesized it, and marketed it to the textile trade as Igepon. The substance made a good wetting agent. It was, however, "hard to make, expensive, and with physical characteristics that would make it unsuitable for detergent use in the home," according to Duncan's source. "Just then we came to his village and he left."[3]

The casual information piqued Duncan's interest, though he was unsure about how to approach the lab for more information: "It did not seem tactful to go back to I. G. and ask them about something they had not officially told me about but I had learned through the back door." Instead Duncan called on another colleague at Deutsche Hydrierwerke in Berlin. That company knew about Igepon and was in fact in the process of launching a competitive product. Duncan promptly arranged a visit to the factory.

There it was, half-buried but, as Duncan recognized, a nevertheless tantalizing possibility. The properties that made this surface-active agent, or surfactant, an effective wetting agent—namely, its ability to bond with oil on one end of the molecule chain and water on the other (thus distributing the dye evenly through fabrics)—should theoretically also make it effective as a detergent. Moreover, a detergent with these properties would be able to wash clothes and dishes even in hard-water regions, where traditional soaps deposited a residue of scum, or *curds*. Deutsche Hydrierwerke "had no notion as to what value, if any, it had as a detergent for home use," Duncan recalled. He bought one hundred kilograms of the material, which he express-shipped home for further investigation.[4]

Procter & Gamble's R&D staff went to work on the new line of research in mid-1931. "Most of the people in the Chemical Division had some part in this testing," Duncan later recalled, "and perhaps one quarter to one third devoted full time to some phase of the evaluation work." Results were encouraging, and in 1932, P&G negotiated a license agreement to develop and market alkyl sulfates as synthetic detergents in the household and laundry fields. Thus, as the Depression deepened, P&G prepared to put its first synthetic detergents on the market. Deciding to lead with a granulated laundry soap and a liquid shampoo, the company launched Dreft (which entered test markets in 1933) and Drene (the shampoo, launched in 1934).

Dreft was an innovative but limited laundry detergent. It did clean clothes in hard water without leaving curds, an important benefit for consumers residing in hard-water regions (an area that stretched, broadly speaking, across the Midwest and into the western states to the Rocky Mountains). But the product was not strong enough to clean heavily soiled clothes. Procter & Gamble's chemical engineers managed to boost the formula's detergency to a limited degree by building the surfactant. That is, they added chemical compounds that enhanced the surfactant's ability to get to embedded soil. This solution created new problems, however: The chemical builders reacted with the hardness in the water, forming insoluble, granular deposits that adhered to clothes, leaving them harsh and stiff as they came out of the wash. Consequently, Dreft remained a light cleaner—a useful product, to be sure, but one with narrow market potential.

Slow Building

At this stage, progress on synthetic detergents stalled. Procter & Gamble's chemical engineers worked diligently on the surfactant-builder problem over much of the 1930s, trying to fashion an alkyl-sulfate-based detergent capable of heavy cleaning and clean rinsing. They tried building the surfactant with numerous compounds. They mixed soaps with synthetic detergents. They heated, cooled, extruded, pulverized, and flaked any number of formulas, none of which performed satisfactorily. By 1939, the research was looking like a dead end and management was shifting the company's R&D efforts to other, more promising projects.[5]

At this point, the key figure in the story became David "Dick" Byerly, a researcher in the Product Research Department. "I was very fond of Dick," one of his supervisors later recalled, "but you've got to understand the man to understand what he did. He was moody at times, and obstinate as all get

David "Dick" Byerly, the maverick researcher who developed Tide's synthetic formula, fought to keep "Product X" alive.

out. [His supervisors] had horrible times with Dick on occasion. Just tenacious as all hell." Not the kind of man, in other words, to give up on a project just because he was told to do so. Byerly kept picking away at the problem, experimenting with different ways of building the surfactant, even as company support for the work waned. "We had a system at P&G that every week you wrote a weekly report," one of Byerly's colleagues related years later. "Byerly had long since given up on putting this in his weekly report regularly since he had comments to the effect, 'What in the hell is he working on that for?'"[6]

In 1939, Tom Halberstadt assumed oversight of product development research for the company's soap brands. Among his other responsibilities, he inherited Byerly. According to Halberstadt's later account, Byerly regarded his new boss somewhat warily at first, gauging him for a month or two before revealing his covert work on the synthetic detergent problem. As Halberstadt told it, "He came to me one day and said, 'Now that you're here, I want to know, am I going to be allowed to work on what I think I should work on?' I didn't know what he was talking about. So he took me down to the lab, and we spent two days looking through all the records that he had for the last 4 to 5 years."[7]

It was a critical juncture in what would soon become known as Product X. Byerly was working alone, making uneven progress. Without support from somewhere in the administration, he would not be able to continue indefinitely. Halberstadt, for his part, was wary, but intrigued. Byerly's data indicated some interesting results with building the surfactant with sodium pyrophosphate, a compound that had recently become commercially available.

As Halberstadt put it, "I saw that the product was no good, but it had done something. He was able to get good cleaning. Maybe he could get rid of the fabric roughness. I didn't know how, but after all, everybody else said you couldn't even get cleaning before he got it." Halberstadt decided to take the case to his superior, Herb Coith (associate director of the Chemical Division, in charge of Product Research). Coith was surprised to learn that Byerly was still pursuing the work. Halberstadt argued they should let Byerly carry it on: "I knew we were short; we had trouble getting people, but Dick's the kind of guy that somehow or other he'll find a way. . . . Dick was that kind of guy. He would get it done." Whether swayed by the appeal, or impressed by the data, or perhaps just disinclined to lock horns with Byerly, Coith agreed. "Okay," he told Halberstadt, "but just don't get into any big deal about it. Don't go rushing in to Bruce Strain [who managed process development for detergents] and say you need samples made in their pilot plant."

So Byerly was permitted to continue his dogged progress. The onset of World War II put immense pressure on P&G, as people scrambled first to cope with raw-material shortages, then to convert to military supply and reformulate the company's soap products in response to wartime rationing. With so many process problems pressing, the strain on the company's chemical engineers grew intense. When Harvey Knowles (vice president of manufacturing) caught wind of Byerly's ongoing experimentation, he called Wesley Blair (chemical director) on the carpet. "How in the hell can your fellows fiddle around with a product we haven't even thought of making when we've got more unanswered problems out here in the factories?" Knowles demanded (according to Halberstadt's later recollection, as relayed through Coith). "You're just not giving us the right kind of service." Stung, Coith told Halberstadt to put the project on hold. After a few months, though, Halberstadt began pestering Coith for permission to "start up just doing a little of this." Eventually, Coith relented. Byerly could continue as long as the project did not interfere with anything else he was doing, though Coith did suggest that, again, Byerly keep his detergent work out of his weekly reports. By now, Product X had become an officially unofficial skunk works project. "There was a great deal of work done that was never reported," Halberstadt later confided. "We knew we couldn't. That was that."

Inevitably, though, the circle of involvement widened over 1943 and 1944. Coith had warned Byerly not to go to the pilot plants with requests for product samples, but research using material that was hand-mixed could only go so far. At some point, progress depended on working with product that had actually been granulated (or *blown*). Halberstadt felt compelled to wheedle support from Bruce Strain (who ran the pilot plants for process development) and his boss, Victor "Vic" Mills. "I would go to Bruce and say can't you put this in your pilot plant and blow some granules for us," Halberstadt related. "'Oh, we've got so damn much to do,' he would say. Maybe one time out of the three asked, we got a batch made." Still, they did get some batches made. Amid staggering pressures, pilot plant managers carved out time for Product X, keeping it alive. Blair, meanwhile, came around to cautious support as the wartime pressures on the plants eased a bit and Halberstadt revealed some of Byerly's data.[8]

Indeed, Byerly's results were getting better. The turning point came in a counterintuitive breakthrough, when the researcher tried inverting his builder-surfactant ratios. All prior experience with soaps had shown that reducing the amount of builder in a formula made it milder on clothing. Like everyone else, therefore, Byerly had assumed he wanted to keep the proportion of surfactant—the actual cleaning agent—as high as possible. He thought he needed to minimize the amount of builder (which, after all, was what was reacting with water hardness to create the stiffness and graying that plagued early formulations). When Byerly tried boosting the builder levels well above the surfactant levels, though, a surprising thing happened: The detergent continued to clean effectively, while the calcified residue (the gray deposit that stiffened washed clothes and left them harsh) diminished substantially. Why it worked, no one could yet say, but it worked.

By mid-1945, with Byerly and Halberstadt closing in on a formula and process, Coith decided that Product X was ready to be unveiled to senior management. First, he arranged a demonstration for Blair and R. K. Brodie (who had recently moved into headquarters as vice president of manufacturing and technical research). "Brodie was not the kind of man to get excited about anything," Halberstadt later recalled. "That was the most excited I had ever seen him. I can't remember his words, but he said it was different." Coith and Halberstadt hastily prepared a streamlined version of their exhibit to take downtown to what Halberstadt referred to as "the city office."

Strategizing: Planning for Rollout

Procter & Gamble's senior managers received their first detailed briefing on Product X sometime between late summer and early fall 1945, at a meeting that would turn out to be one of the most important executive sessions the company ever convened. Along with Brodie, President Richard Deupree, Ralph Rogan (vice president for advertising), and Neil McElroy (then an advertising manager) gathered to evaluate the demonstration staged by Coith and Halberstadt.[9] The executives heard out the researchers, agreed they had something big on their hands, and began mapping out strategies. How long, Deupree asked Rogan, would it take his people "to merchandise" a synthetic detergent based on the formulation the researchers had worked up? Several months to get samples, Rogan replied. Then P&G could set up blind tests in two or three cities and analyze the results. Allow five, maybe six months for that. Then, of course, further time would be needed to incorporate the modifications suggested by the blind testing. It would be a year or so, probably, before the company could gear up for shipping tests, try out advertising strategies, poll consumers, and hone the product and the marketing. In sum, Product X could be ready for test marketing in two years, with a national launch maybe a year or so after that.

That, at least, was the timetable dictated by normal procedures. Going by the book, Product X would take two or three years to roll out on a national basis—and P&G was a company famous for going by the book: studying thoroughly, preparing painstakingly, and moving forward slowly and methodically. Rogan was invoking deep and abiding business wisdom for P&G—wisdom, moreover, that seemed particularly applicable in this case. For in the case of Product X, P&G was dealing not with a new soap, which would have been relatively familiar, but with a new synthetic formula unlike anything it had taken to market before. Deupree took in Rogan's assessment, Halberstadt remembered, then turned to Brodie: "Kirk, do you fit into that schedule?"[10]

"We could," Brodie responded, "but I wonder if that's the best way to go." Brodie, having mulled over the situation since seeing the data back at the lab, was becoming convinced the situation called for bolder action. Sticking to the normal timetable would let Lever and Colgate get samples of the product soon after P&G started blind testing, allowing the competitors to put something comparable on the market shortly after. "Surely their product will not be as good as ours, but they will crowd the market with similar advertising and they will have a competitive product. We will not be alone," Brodie warned. Under the circumstances, he felt the company should seize and consolidate as much of the market opportunity as it could, which meant moving as quickly as possible. "We should bypass both the usual blind tests and the shipping and advertising tests," he urged. "This would give us almost two years start over Lever and Colgate." Rogan demurred, reminding people that this would mean a major and an essentially blind commitment of resources—at least $15 million, perhaps as much as $25 million, serious sums for a company doing less than $500 million in sales. Procter & Gamble had never moved without running blind tests or shipping tests, Rogan added. ("Kirk, you know we've never done that!" Halberstadt remembered Rogan protesting.) Brodie replied, "I know, but this product has so many advantages. It is in a different class from any other new product we have ever introduced. Certainly there are risks, but the potential is so great, I think we should take those risks."

It was a bold assessment—bolder, perhaps, than is easy to appreciate today. Procter & Gamble in 1946 had just weathered a long depression and a wrenching world war. Now it faced another reconversion to peacetime status, and uncertain economic prospects. Was it really the best time to make a major bet? In any event, long experience in the fiercely competitive soap business had keenly sharpened company tactics. The meticulous, methodical market and product research Rogan was proposing for Product X was what gave P&G its edge over Colgate and Lever. Brodie's proposal cut deeply against the grain of the company.

Still, there was the data; there were the results. And the men who stood over them knew enough about their business to share Brodie's sense of the opportunity at hand. Product X truly did look to be extraordinary. Perhaps it did call for extraordinary handling. According to Halberstadt's account, Deupree "looked from one to another and then said, 'I don't know, it's a real tough one.' Then, turning to Mr. McElroy he said, 'Mac, what do you think?' Mr. McElroy said, 'It sure is a tough one, but from what I have seen and heard today, I think it's the best prospect I have ever seen in P&G. For my money, I would take the chance and blast ahead as Mr. Brodie suggests. If the product turns out to be a winner as it appears to be, a two year lead would be like a license to steal.'" Deupree nodded. By now Rogan was getting caught up in the excitement, too. "It's a risk," he reiterated. "But since we all understand that[,] I would go along." "Okay, Kirk," Deupree declared, "crank her up. Full speed ahead!"

Branding

Product X had taken form on the periphery of the company, outside its main channels. Now, as the company shifted from product formulation to process engineering and merchandising, development accelerated rapidly. In short order, P&G's designers and marketers chose the name *Tide* and began assembling a brand identity to crystallize the product's qualities in the popular imagination.[11] Fittingly (and in typically cantankerous fashion), Byerly provided a key marketing element for the new brand when Tide's advertisers, Benton & Bowles, interviewed the product development team in search of marketing ideas. According to the recollection of another researcher who sat in on the meeting, "Each time [Byerly] would try to explain a feature of Tide, one of the agency people would ask about Tide's sudsing. After several interruptions of this type, [Byerly], a little exasperated, said, 'Oh, Tide makes oceans of suds.'" That slogan became a centerpiece of Tide's early marketing.

Arguably, though, it was the box itself that most dynamically conveyed the new product's extraordinary power. Tide appeared on supermarket shelves in a box radiating concentric rings of vivid orange and yellow, superimposed by the name Tide in blue. Crafted largely by P&G art director, Charlie Gerhart, in collaboration with input from the Compton agency, the layout registered a strong visceral impact. The bull's-eye motif, which the company had already featured in designs for the laundry soaps Dash and Oxydol, created a familiar context for the new product, while the coloring scheme conveyed an aggressive impression of the "rugged strength" of this detergent's cleaning power.[12]

The initial marketing strategy centered on the concept of the "Washday Miracle." Announcing that P&G had developed a revolutionary new technology, Tide advertising promised consumers to wash "cleaner than soap," with "oceans of suds." It all might have sounded hyperbolic or breathless—except, of course, that the technology *was* revolutionary and the performance truly superior. For millions of households in hard-water regions, the product truly did transform the experience of laundering clothes.

Tide's marketing played up the brand's compatibility with automatic top-loading washing machines, the new appliances that rapidly penetrated U.S. households after World War II.

Tide's early marketers also capitalized on a happy coincidence: the simultaneous spread of automatic washing machines in the United States. In the flush of postwar economic growth and consumer affluence, many households bought new appliances, including innovative, new top-loading agitator washers. With Tide coming onto the market at precisely the same time, P&G managed to fuse the two innovations in the popular imagination. Tide's advertisements picked up on the theme, prominently featuring the new machines. Exclusive agreements with washing machine manufacturers, in which boxes of Tide were packed in with new machines, reinforced the association. Eventually the U.S. Federal Trade Commission disallowed such exclusive agreements, but by the time it did, Tide had become embedded as the definitive product for use in the new appliances.[13]

Engineering Production

Given a two-year head start, Brodie and McElroy had argued, P&G could consolidate a commanding first-mover advantage over its competitors. The conviction created a driving, new imperative: Speed to market now became absolutely vital. Procter & Gamble was not necessarily geared for speed, but the opportunity at hand was energizing and Product X began hurtling to market. McElroy and his team drew up an improvised, streamlined rollout process with compressed test marketing and concurrent blind testing. Even while branding was still in the planning stage, the company laid plans to build four new towers to granulate, or *blow,* the new product. The expansion represented a major capital commitment, particularly in the context of the postwar environment, when steel and equipment suppliers were still recovering from the war effort. (The company's standing soap towers could not be converted to Tide production, since synthetic formulation required a fundamentally different granulation process.) Meanwhile, the company's process engineers began working out the manufacturing processes for granulating the new detergent.[14] At this stage, Bruce Strain played a key role in developing new patented processes and formula modifications.

Everyone had their job cut out for them. "There were no experimental towers as they have these days," recalled James Ewell, plant manager at St. Bernard, Ohio. "The first experiments were run over on the Dreft tower at Ivorydale, and they were failures. I know because all the product that was made, which was unusable, got shipped over to St. Bernard, and we had to incorporate it into soap just to sell it."[15] According to Dean Fite, cost chief at the St. Bernard Plant in 1946, "the first Tide produced came out in the shape and size of a baseball and was hard as marble."[16]

"Blowing a granule sounds like an easy thing, but it isn't," explained Ewell. "You can't get the right density, all sorts of strange things happen inside synthetic towers. And they didn't know enough about the operation of towers in those days, especially with a heavily built product like Tide. It had a lot of phosphate in it. Dreft didn't have any builders, so it was a completely different operation. Takes different spraying equipment, different swirl in the tower, all sorts of things must be changed."[17] Including the detergent itself, as it turned out. The initial formulation did not blow well, building up in the tower and the feeder valves, forcing frequent shutdowns to clean the equipment. Reformulation, and specifically the addition of a small dose of silicate, made for crisper granules that were more blowable and less mastic. "It took a lot of cutting and trying to get that just right. In the meantime, we made a lot of mastic material that wasn't suitable for putting into cartons," related Charles "Chuck" Fullgraf, who took over as plant manager from James Ewell in 1946 and thus was the first man to granulate Tide.[18]

Fullgraf was working under intense pressure. Everybody at St. Bernard felt it. "Any time the tower went down we had to call the plant manager—Chuck Fullgraf—immediately so he in turn could alert the Division Manager—Forrester Reid," remembered Robert Lake, one of the three foremen working in shifts on the start-up. "One time Mr. Reid called Chuck and asked why the tower was down. Chuck was in the process of saying that he did not think it was down when there was a loud bang over the phone and then it was dead. Only later did Chuck find out from the secretary that Mr. Reid had fallen out of his chair in Ivorydale straining to look out his window for the plume from the tower."[19]

Rollout proceeded in a flurry of activity. St. Bernard went on-line in early August 1946, followed shortly by new towers in Port Ivory, Chicago, and Dallas; by October 1, all four were on-line and Tide was going into its first pair of test markets. Within the first three weeks in October, Tide had entered six test markets: Springfield, Massachusetts; Albany, New York; Evansville, Indiana; Lima, Ohio; Wichita, Kansas; and Sioux Falls, South Dakota. Even as the company ran the detergent through blind testing in several other locations, it plunged in deeper on the capital end, commissioning an additional four towers. "There were four towers on the first wave, and then even before they got going, another four were authorized, which was absolutely amazing for a company the size of Procter at that time," marveled Ewell. "The investment that this required, the organizational strain that it imposed [in] getting people to handle it, was tremendous. But, we just had to move. McElroy said, 'we've got to get out there and get ahead of the other people.'"[20]

Tidal Wave: The Market Response

Tide took the market by storm. George Myers, a P&G salesman stationed in an Indiana territory, vividly remembered the excitement that radiated from the test market neighboring his district: "My main problem and concern was telling the grocers they couldn't have all they wanted (they knew how well it was selling in Fort Wayne)."[21] Bruce W. Price, Sr., a salesman covering Charlotte, North Carolina, endured similar clamor a year later, as Tide expanded toward his territory: "There were rumors, from people who had moved into my area from parts of the country where Tide was being sold[,] of a washday miracle. Then P&G lowered the boom on me by introducing Tide in Georgia, just 20 miles from my section headquarters. My retail stores, chains and wholesalers were all of a sudden interrupting my sales presentations with, 'When can you ship me some Tide?' Their customers were driving the short distance to Georgia, buying Tide and of course other groceries, also."[22] Max B. Schmidt, who later joined P&G but who was managing a Kroger grocery store in Wichita, Kansas, when Tide hit the market in 1947, tells the same story from the point of view of the trade. Having stocked what he assumed was a bountiful supply of the new detergent—enough, he assumed, to last several years—he arrived on the day Tide launched to find "customers . . . lined up for a block and more were coming. . . . The many years' stock of laundry soap was gone in a matter of four hours and no more available until the next week. I had never seen anything like this before and to my knowledge I have not seen anything like it since."[23]

Tide was selling as quickly as the company could make it. A lot depended on just how quickly the company could make it. Given the company's drive to consolidate as early and as commanding a first-mover advantage as possible, the pressure to build up production rapidly, before Colgate or Lever had a chance to marshal a response, grew enormous. Procter & Gamble's production engineers were scaling and scrambling their way up a steep learning curve. Particularly between 1947 and 1948, as Tide's markets expanded while the company waited for the second wave of towers to come on-line, process experts threw themselves into the problem of increasing production rates at the existing towers. Contributions by people like George Broadfoot, an engineer who had been studying the thermodynamics of granulation within soap towers for years, became critical. From an original production rate of six thousand pounds per hour per tower, the company managed to increase to twenty-one thousand pounds per hour by the end of 1949.[24]

Assessing the Strategic Impact

People across P&G had given the company the two-year head start that McElroy had called for. Colgate did not manage to put a synthetic detergent on the market until April 1948, when it launched Fab. Lever weighed in with Surf in July. Neither product performed as well as Tide, according to analysis within P&G and, independently, by *Consumer Reports*.[25] By 1950, with production ramped up to high volume, Tide was surging to new heights in the market (table 4-1).

The numbers were dramatic on several counts. They showed Tide claiming an unprecedented market share—more than twice what any earlier brand had been holding. They also indicated that Tide significantly boosted P&G's total share of the laundry market. Finally, P&G chartered a significant consolidation of brand focus: At the same time as P&G was increasing its total share, it was reducing the number of brands it was supporting in the category.

These statistics worked just as inexorably on the company itself as they did on its competitors. At the same time that the new detergent was eroding Colgate's and Lever's market positions, Tide was also eating into P&G's established laundry brands. Oxydol, for example, which had been P&G's top earner in the prewar years, slipped from a 12.8 percent share in 1948 to 8.5 percent by 1950, and 5.1 percent two years later. The company's market leader, Duz, fell nearly as far and just as fast, from a 12.9 percent share in 1948 to 6 percent in 1952. "Tide was introduced with the claim 'Tide gets clothes cleaner than any soap,'" related Edgar H. Lotspeich, copy brand manager for Tide during the launch. "How's that for a belief in the brand system? Here your business is soap. The soaps had to defend themselves. Tide didn't say 'we're better than Oxydol.' That's bad business. But it said 'Tide gets clothes cleaner than any soap.'"[26]

Procter & Gamble's soap brands countered as best they could. "Those new detergents may be all right for dishes, but your hands aren't made of china," warned ads for Ivory in the soap opera *The Road of Life*. "Duz does a wash like no detergent can—it's the soap in Duz that does it!" proclaimed ads during *The Guiding Light*.[27] To little effect. Tide swept relentlessly over the United States, displacing soap brands not just in hard-water regions (where the company had expected and planned for the shift), but in soft-water regions as well. In 1949, P&G reached a major historical watershed when, for the first time, the company's synthetic granule production surpassed its soap granule production.[28] Apart from a brief experiment in converting Oxydol to a synthetic formula, P&G's traditional laundry brands never recovered.[29]

TABLE 4-1

Tide Market Share in the United States, 1946–2002

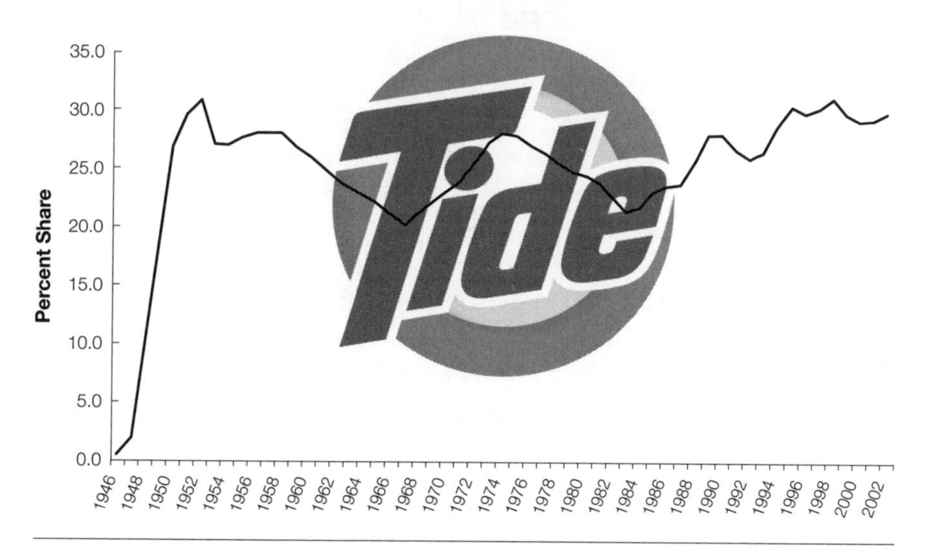

This development was unexpected. The runaway success of Tide seemed to catch even P&G by surprise, particularly as the phenomenon spread to soft-water districts. In October 1947, with the Tide rollout approaching national distribution, company president Deupree had assured shareholders: "In our judgment, there is small chance of synthetic detergents replacing soap products to any marked extent. They . . . will supplement rather than supplant soap products in most homes."[30] Even as late as 1950, Deupree noted "the change in the character of cleansing products being produced" and conceded that the development "very naturally affects soap brands." Nevertheless, he was still insisting, "We feel that the situation has clarified and more or less stabilized. We believe that, along with synthetics, the sales of regular soap products will show progress as a result of the increased population and increased consumption per family."

Of course, Deupree was wrong: As the market share data clearly showed, Tide would continue to erode P&G's soap brands over the next several years. Significantly, though, senior management's ambivalence did not slow Tide's spread. Aggressive plant expansion had signaled that P&G was committed to driving Tide as deeply into the market as it would go. Even as it became increasingly clear that this commitment would mean cannibalizing the company's soap brands, the company carried through unflinchingly.

The discipline that underlay that decision should not be underrated. Tide was rendering obsolete massive investments in manufacturing and was destroying decades' worth of hard-earned brand equity. A different company facing the same situation, with so much staked in soap, might easily have been overwhelmed, resisted the trend, or at least been too disoriented to adapt rapidly and ruthlessly. At P&G, though, the principle of brand management—the idea that brands had to live or die in the marketplace, in the heat of as much competition as P&G itself could bring to bear—provided the company with a powerful mechanism of stabilization and orientation. Deupree may have been flat wrong in asserting in 1947 that synthetic detergents would not replace soap products "to any marked extent," but the more important pronouncement was the one that he added immediately afterward. "The important fact to remember," he informed the shareholders, "is that no matter how active the trend to this type of product becomes, the Company is ready and able to market the popular leaders among synthetic detergents along with its standard soap brands." It was the company's commitment to brand management, in the end, that enabled P&G to ride out the shift in market currents while keeping its strategic bearings. And in that sense, it was particularly fitting that Neil McElroy, the original proponent of brand management, would oversee the process of creative destruction. As he assumed an increasingly prominent leadership role within P&G's executive team during the late 1940s, McElroy made himself Tide's champion. In other words, as things played out, the very architect of brand management was the manager called on to see the logic through to its conclusion.

The result of this commitment was a brand that became a megabrand: Once Tide had established a leading market share, P&G worked continuously to keep it atop the category. Tide's share of the laundry market briefly topped 30 percent then dropped into the high twenties as rivals finally mustered competitive synthetic brands of their own in the 1950s. Subsequently, the share slipped by degrees. Redoubled efforts on P&G's part, however, recovered the initiative. Over the years since Tide's launch the company has repeatedly refreshed the brand's cleansing technology, making sure Tide offers state-of-the-art laundry performance. The brand, as a result, has never relinquished its hold on market leadership. Having gained a decisive brand advantage in its core category, P&G held on tenaciously.

P&G in the Wake of Tide

As Tide surged to a leading share, it carried the company on to new strategic ground. This was not just an impressive brand; this was a decisive shakeout in the company's biggest and most important market. Between 1951 and 1956, P&G earned nearly a quarter of a billion dollars in profits in laundry, while both Lever and Colgate lost money in the category. The impact on the companies' various bottom lines was massive. Over the ten years following Tide's launch, P&G's net earnings nearly tripled, rising to $59 million in 1956 on sales of just over $1 billion. Colgate's U.S. earnings, meanwhile, fell sharply, from $16 million to $5 million. Lever fared even worse, barely breaking even over the early 1950s and earning only $3 million in 1956 (on sales of $282 million), about a third of prewar earnings.[31]

The implications reverberated widely. Tide put P&G in command of its core market just as the United States entered a period of sustained economic and demographic growth. Buoyed largely by Tide earnings, P&G found itself in a position to handle long-term, capital-intensive investments in a series of new ventures, including expansion into new countries (e.g., Mexico) and new product categories (e.g., paper products). Ventures such as Charmin toilet tissue, perhaps the most prominent example, took nearly a decade of investment to yield results. Critically, that decade coincided with Tide's ascendance to market leadership. Synthetic detergent revenues absorbed heavy development costs elsewhere in the company, sustained patience among the company's shareholders, and bolstered the company's confidence in its ability to win in other categories and other international markets.

The Development of Tide in Perspective

Tide represented a distinct turning point in the evolution of P&G's brand-building capability. Company researchers recognized the hidden potential within an obscure technology across the ocean and brought it back to Cincinnati to adapt as a synthetic detergent—a product chemically unlike anything P&G had made or marketed before. Ultimately, that technology became the basis of the biggest brand in P&G's history. More generally, the success of Tide conclusively demonstrated the power of creative R&D to transform even the most seemingly low-tech of categories. Tide demonstrated that P&G was and must remain a technology company.

The road to that result was not easy or straightforward, however. The technology originally imported by Duncan proved difficult to decode and adapt. The development of the formula that became Tide was nurtured by a maverick, Byerly, stubbornly sticking to a skunk works project his colleagues and supervisors had written off. Tide's development Product X grew out of an R&D structure that allowed room for individual initiative, experimentation, and serendipity.

Another striking aspect of Tide's development was the speed and resourcefulness P&G demonstrated in capitalizing on the opening created by the new technology. Product X may have nearly died in development, but as its full potential became clear, senior managers grasped the opportunity. Recognizing that getting to market faster than usual would create decisive first-mover advantage, they reengineered traditional test marketing processes and risked a massive commitment of resources. They knew enough about their business to recognize what they had on their hands, and they were flexible enough to improvise a new set of procedures that would equip them to take full advantage. Justly famous for its methodical, careful, rigorously disciplined approach to business, P&G proved equally capable of decisive action.

Moreover, the company did not flinch when it became clear, to nearly everybody's surprise, that Tide would cannibalize P&G's existing laundry brands. Though few realized it at first, the advent of synthetic detergents made P&G's soap-based brands obsolete virtually overnight. Within a handful of years, Tide had engulfed what had been P&G's biggest and most profitable brands. In a supreme test of brand management and of the principle that the consumer was boss, the company let the process happen, sacrificing massive plant investments and incalculable brand equity. That kind of dislocation might destabilize if not destroy most companies, yet P&G managed to ride out the transition and gain share as it did so.

The transition may have been jarring—it must have been. But the yield was enormous. For it was Tide, more than any other brand, that taught P&G how powerfully and disproportionately a big share rearranged the market. In the decades leading up to Tide, P&G held category leadership with a series of successful laundry brands and made respectable profits doing so. Tide, however, did not just take leadership in the category—it demolished the field. The company's competitors took decades to recover, while P&G gained a vastly more profitable business. This development was decisive, generating earnings and a sense of confidence that would carry P&G into a series of new categories, countries, and markets over the 1950s and 1960s.

PART II

The Science and Selling of Everyday Products 1945–1980

CHAPTER FIVE

An Explosion in Consumer Products

THE PERIOD FROM 1945 to the end of the 1960s saw P&G expand aggressively into new products and geographies. The phenomenal success of Tide gave the company both the confidence and the financial strength to explore new products and businesses, where P&G applied the branding expertise it had developed during the previous seventy-five years. From being a soap and shortening company, P&G became a diversified maker of household goods, entering the consumer paper products business and adding new items to its stable of food and toilet goods products. Drawing on its tradition of research and careful testing, the company achieved technological breakthroughs in shampoos (Head & Shoulders), tissues and towels (Charmin and Bounty), toothpaste (Crest), disposable diapers (Pampers and Luvs), and snack foods (Pringles) and began to acquire strong capabilities in pharmaceuticals. As John Smale, chief executive from 1981 to 1990, put it, "neither before, nor since that period, has there been such dramatic growth and change in the nature of what constitutes Procter & Gamble."[1]

The company's bold move into the most important new medium of the postwar era—television—assisted its new product introductions. The soap opera format that P&G pioneered for radio during the 1930s was quickly adapted to TV, which evolved into an effective and low-cost means of communicating with consumers. Filmed entertainment became an important P&G "product" that allowed the company to continue honing its skills in marketing. Another new marketing initiative, the Professional Services group, gave the company increased leverage among health professionals. Originally established in 1957 to educate dentists about Crest toothpaste,

Professional Services was eventually deployed to market Head & Shoulders dandruff shampoo, Pampers disposable diapers, and Scope mouthwash.

Pushing beyond its existing borders, P&G entered new markets around the world, becoming a true multinational rather than a U.S. company with a few overseas adjuncts. Europe became the most important locus of expansion, but significant operations were also established in Latin America and Asia, most prominently in Mexico, Venezuela, and Japan. By 1979, international sales totaled $2.8 billion, or nearly 31 percent of total revenues.

Yet, opportunities that seem obvious in hindsight often appeared ambiguous at the time. Many of the blockbusters developed during the "golden age" of the 1950s and 1960s first endured a period of uncertainty, frustration, and failure. The costs of entering the paper products business spiraled upward, pushing top executives to contemplate exiting after only a few years. The dental establishment cast a skeptical eye on Crest and initially resisted its anticavity claims. Pampers failed in its first three test markets. Regulatory obstacles to expansion included the U.S. government's antitrust policies, which in the 1960s resulted in consent decrees that severely limited the kinds of acquisitions that P&G could make. Throughout the 1970s, the company made no major acquisitions, focusing instead on digesting those of the previous two decades, and continued to invest heavily in the manufacturing lines for paper products and Pringles. Public concern about the environment was another obstacle, resulting in state laws that blocked the sale of phosphate detergents in some markets. Attempts to develop nonphosphate alternatives were expensive and diverted attention from other company priorities. A sharp rise in energy prices beginning in 1973 hurt both the top and the bottom lines, as consumers switched to lower-priced, private-label brands while manufacturing costs surged.

Through it all, growth remained the constant imperative. Procter & Gamble remained committed to its unofficial goal of doubling its business every ten years or so, in the belief that if growth and market share were achieved, profits would soon follow. Another continuity was the company's disciplined approach, which became legendary among U.S. companies. According to a 1974 article in *Fortune* magazine, P&G "manages every element of its business with a painstaking precision that most organizations fail to approach." In the 1970s, some Wall Street analysts began questioning whether such thoroughness slowed the introduction of new products. Procter & Gamble itself, however, rarely swerved from its philosophy that thorough research and testing minimized the risks associated with expansion. This philosophy also helped maintain the positioning of major brands, some of which were several decades old—no mean feat in an environment where, according to one study, the vast majority of new brands lose market share after only three years.[2]

The Postwar Era

Along with most other U.S. corporations, P&G benefited hugely from the postwar boom. The economic uncertainty that surfaced immediately after the war ended soon gave way to rapid growth, as the manufacturing infrastructure that had produced the victorious Allies' "arsenal of democracy" was quickly reconverted to civilian use. From 1940 to 1973, the real per capita gross national product (GNP) in the United States grew at a compound annual rate of 3 percent, more than doubling the rate of previous decades. Until the 1960s, output per hour worked remained more than twice that of most other industrialized nations.[3]

Despite two recessions, GNP increased by 50 percent during the 1950s, while inflation remained a manageable 1 to 2 percent a year. Household incomes rose while work hours declined. Americans began spending more on leisure pursuits, a circumstance made possible in part by the explosion in consumer credit. New materials such as plastics and aluminum expanded the range of affordable goods, which in turn created an even larger mass market. Ever-greater numbers of new appliances, such as automatic washing machines and dishwashers, heralded the arrival of the convenience society. With its cake mixes, laundry detergents, and, later, paper tissues, towels, and disposable diapers, P&G was well positioned to serve consumers eager to reduce the time they spent on cooking and cleaning. By 1956, ninety-five out of every one hundred U.S. homes used at least one P&G product, "a penetration unequaled by any other manufacturer of anything," according to *Fortune* magazine.[4]

Demographic shifts further fueled the economic expansion. The most significant was the baby boom. Between 1940 and 1960, the U.S. population swelled by some 48 million people, or 37 percent, a substantial gain for an advanced industrialized nation. As the largest U.S. corporations found a ready market for their goods and services, their average annual sales ballooned to $500 million, or about ten times the volume of the 1920s. Among these, P&G ranked among the very top. With revenues of just under $1 billion in 1955, it joined an elite group of only twenty-eight other American companies.

Inflation picked up during the 1960s, and social issues moved to the forefront of public consciousness. Yet through it all, the economy continued to expand, fueled partly by generous government spending on the Great Society social programs and the Vietnam War. Median family income nearly doubled, as the economy added ten million new jobs and more women entered the workforce. The proportion of Americans living below the poverty line—although still high at 11 percent—fell by nearly half.

Procter & Gamble's management ranks during the postwar period included many returning World War II veterans, such as Edward G. "Ed"

By the mid-1950s, P&G was a diversified producer of consumer goods ranging from soap to peanut butter and supported its strategy with a multidivisional structure.

Harness, who would later lead the company, and Dean Fite, who became vice president and comptroller in 1961. They were joined by new men such as Owen B. "Brad" Butler, chairman of the board from 1981 to 1986, and William Gurganus, president of P&G International from 1974 to 1980. In 1948, Richard "Red" Deupree stepped down as president and was replaced by forty-four-year-old Neil McElroy, the architect of P&G's famous brand management system. McElroy was more focused than Deupree on growth, and he laid the foundations for P&G's entry into new businesses and pushed harder for expansion into Europe. When President Eisenhower tapped McElroy to be U.S. secretary of defense in 1957, forty-six-year-old Howard Morgens assumed the presidency of P&G. (McElroy returned to P&G in 1959 as chairman of the board.)

Morgens continued his predecessors' strong focus on expansion. During his seventeen-year tenure, sales more than tripled and profits quadrupled.

But all of that growth was in the future when, as executive vice president, Morgens spearheaded a major reorganization that he hoped would facilitate P&G's entry into new consumer goods businesses.

The Creation of Divisions

In the decade following World War II, competitors Lever Brothers and Colgate grew at only a modest rate. In contrast, P&G's sales and operating income tripled, led by Tide and the company's other laundry products. Problems loomed, however, for although demand for these products remained strong, P&G was already the leading presence in many of its markets. According to *Fortune* magazine, in 1956 the company accounted for more than half of both packaged household soaps and detergents, and vegetable shortenings.[5]

The extent of the problem was not lost on Morgens, who was named executive vice president in charge of the U.S. business in 1954. A graduate of Washington University in St. Louis and Harvard Business School, Morgens joined P&G in 1933 as a retail soap salesman. Like McElroy before him, he soon transferred to the company's Advertising Department, becoming its manager in 1946. Morgens was elected vice president in charge of advertising in 1948, and two years later was named a director of the company. Simultaneously, he was given responsibility for the small drug products business, established in 1943.[6]

Before assuming his duties as executive vice president, Morgens took a three-week vacation in Europe, where the question of how to find additional revenue growth preoccupied him. On the return voyage, Morgens worked out a six-year plan. Looking at P&G's existing businesses, he was forced to conclude that the company "just couldn't add anything to soap," which "already had too many brands."[7] Morgens worried that P&G would not be able to double its business in the next ten years without getting into new businesses, and he also believed that food products would have to be separated from soaps and detergents before the foods business could expand.

Out of these insights came the idea that P&G should be reorganized into three divisions, each based around a different business. Morgens acted quickly, aware that there would be resistance from the powerful heads of departments such as Sales and Manufacturing who would suddenly find themselves "demoted" to staff positions. In 1955, Soaps and Detergents as well as Foods became separate divisions; Drug Products was renamed Toilet Goods. (When Morgens headed Drug Products in its carly days, he had succeeded in creating a minidivision of sorts, with its own separate managers.

He had this model in mind when he reorganized the company.) Each division was given its own general management, responsible for operations. Staff functions were created for the coordination of the separate divisions' activities, including basic research, engineering, advertising agency relations, media relations, and the supervision of sampling and couponing activities.[8]

In the ensuing years, the multidivisional structure eased P&G's expansion of existing businesses and entry into new ones and enhanced the company's ability to stay close to consumers.[9] The creation of divisions turned out to be the most significant organizational change since McElroy implemented brand management back in the 1930s. The new structure continued the basic idea behind brand management: to maximize independence and creativity while simultaneously enhancing the discipline within each unit and the coordination among them. Like many large U.S. manufacturers that expanded into new products and markets after the war, P&G began systematically to grapple with the problem of balancing discipline (centralization) and autonomy (decentralization).[10] Naturally, the challenge of maintaining that optimum balance became greater as the company expanded its product and brand offerings and became more international.

Expanding Old Businesses and Entering New Ones, 1950s and 1960s

The post–World War II period witnessed the appearance of some of P&G's most recognizable brands. Spic and Span was acquired in 1945. Joy dish-washing detergent debuted in 1949 and Blue Cheer laundry detergent in 1952. Dash (a low-sudsing detergent) entered the market in 1954 followed by Zest bar soap, and Cascade automatic dish-washing detergent in 1955. Comet, a household cleanser with chlorine bleach, appeared a year later. Procter & Gamble launched Ivory Liquid detergent in 1957, Mr. Clean household cleaner in 1958, Downy fabric softener in 1960, Safeguard deodorant soap in 1963, and Bold laundry detergent in 1965.

Internal Innovation

The small Toilet Goods Division began contributing more significantly to the overall P&G business, primarily in the areas of dentifrices and shampoos. Encouraged by the initial success of Drene shampoo, P&G had begun experimenting in 1936 with ways to use alkyl sulfate in a dentifrice product. The result was a liquid dentifrice called Teel, introduced in 1938. Teel achieved a modest, but short-lived success. Unwilling to exit the dentifrice category, P&G decided to invest in research that would identify some area of signifi-

Introduced in 1958, Mr. Clean added to a burgeoning line of household cleaners that included Spic and Span and Comet.

cant interest to consumers. In 1946, chemical director Wes Blair asked the Product Research group, headed by Verling Votaw, to make a recommendation. The one that eventually carried the day was antidecay, and the Product Research group immediately began searching for a chemical entity that would accomplish that goal.[11]

Procter & Gamble began a partnership with Indiana University in the late 1940s to look into the possibilities of stannous fluoride. The partnership produced Crest, launched nationally in 1955. Meanwhile, the company also developed a nonfluoride toothpaste, Gleem, expanded nationally in 1954 and backed by a substantial ad budget that surpassed even the promotion of Tide nearly a decade earlier.[12] Gleem was an immediate hit with consumers, largely because it tasted better than competitors' brands. It was Crest, however, that became the dentifrice category's star product, earning the first-ever acceptance by the American Dental Association in 1960 and overtaking Colgate for the number one spot. Along with Head & Shoulders and Scope, both introduced in the 1960s, Crest gave P&G competencies in therapeutic research that later helped lead the company into the health care and pharmaceutical business.

Shampoos were the other area of growth within the Toilet Goods Division. In the middle to late 1940s, Drug Products came up with new shampoo entries to add to Drene. Prell, a synthetic product packaged in a tube, was test marketed in 1946 and launched nationally the following year. Shasta

Cream Shampoo, with a combined soap and synthetic formulation, debuted in 1948. The shampoo research gave P&G deep knowledge of hair structure, and beginning in 1949, the company introduced a number of hair-waving products, including Lilt, Pace, and Pin It.[13] In mid-decade, the company tested another round of shampoos, including Velvet Blend and an Ivory-branded shampoo.[14]

In the late 1950s, researchers came up with an innovative product to control dandruff. They screened antifungal compounds developed by the Olin Chemical Company and isolated zinc pyrithione (ZPT). After tests were conducted by Vanderbilt University, the company test marketed Head & Shoulders in 1961. The shampoo "looked like green wall paint and smelled worse," one researcher admitted, but it performed well and proved popular with consumers.[15] By the late 1960s, P&G had consolidated a dominant position in the U.S. shampoo market, anchored by Head & Shoulders with a 25 percent share, and Prell with 22 percent.[16]

Entering New Businesses

The expansion of soap, laundry, dentifrice, and shampoo products was proceeding well, yet top executives pushed hard to get into new consumer goods businesses. In 1954, the company established a small Exploratory Development Division, headed by Victor Mills, to seek opportunities in new technology areas. (Mills called his division the "explorers' club."[17]) Externally, P&G's strategy was to acquire small companies that adhered to three general rules. First, the companies had to be in areas that had some technological connection to existing businesses. Second, the acquisition candidates should make products that could significantly be improved by applying P&G's technologies and know-how. Third, the companies should make low-cost, high-volume units that were bought from retail outlets, such as drug and grocery stores, with which P&G was familiar *(see the "Alternative Paths" box for two examples of billion-dollar brands launched during this era).*

Proceeding cautiously, P&G identified several small companies in the paper products and foods industries as pilot projects. In 1955, it purchased W. T. Young Foods of Lexington, Kentucky, maker of Big Top peanut butter. The following year, P&G bought some assets of Nebraska Consolidated Mills, including the Duncan Hines baking mixes, Hines-Park Foods, and the Duncan Hines Institute of Ithaca, New York. With the shortening and oils businesses, the properties in peanut butter and baking mixes constituted the foundation of the new Food Division. After the Duncan Hines acquisition, the Food Division accounted for more than a quarter of P&G's sales, a figure that would later prove to be the high-water mark for food products as a share of the company's total revenues.[18]

Researchers also launched a project to develop an engineered potato snack, eventually called Pringle's Newfangled Potato Chips. The snack was yet another project based on the company's expertise in oils and fats and in cooking. Although the initial research was begun in the 1950s, the project did not gather momentum until 1965. Procter & Gamble bet heavily on the product, which absorbed more than $70 million in the three-and-one-half years that elapsed from the restart of the program to test marketing. The product proved an overnight sensation, forcing competitors Frito-Lay, General Mills, and Nabisco to scramble to respond.

In 1963, P&G expanded into coffee by acquiring Folgers, a company established in 1850 during the California gold rush. Folgers attracted P&G's attention when research established that coffee was the nation's largest food import, drunk by 70 percent of the adult population. The coffee business in the United States was gargantuan, as big as the one for soaps and detergents.[19]

Bleach was another household product with obvious connections to P&G's existing businesses. In April 1957, an agreement was reached with Clorox Chemical Company of Oakland, California, for the acquisition of the properties and business of that company in exchange for P&G common stock. Almost immediately, the Federal Trade Commission (FTC) filed a proceeding against P&G, charging that its size and market dominance would stifle competition in the bleach industry.

Most significant for its future growth, P&G's expertise in cellulose led to a strong interest in consumer paper products, especially tissues and towels. Since 1920 the company had been involved in the processing of cotton linters into cellulose pulp, a by-product of cottonseed crushing, through a division of its Buckeye Cotton Oil subsidiary. Buckeye was started in 1901 when P&G discovered that speculators periodically cornered the market for cottonseed oil, an important ingredient in both shortening and soap. The only way to ensure access to affordable oil was for P&G to own its own supply so in the next few years, the company bought or built several cottonseed mills in the South. In the early 1950s P&G expanded into the processing of wood pulp by purchasing 25,000 acres of pine timberland in northern Florida and building a $25 million plant in Foley, Florida.[20] In 1957 P&G entered the consumer side of the paper business when it acquired Charmin Paper Mills, a relatively small regional manufacturer of tissues and towels based in Green Bay, Wisconsin.

Procter & Gamble had no interest in treating its acquisitions simply as arms-length financial investments. Instead, its managers and technical personnel sought to learn the new businesses thoroughly. In the process, they "Procterized" the acquired companies' systems and processes, upgrading and transforming them to comply with P&G standards.

ALTERNATIVE PATHS TO SUCCESS: DOWNY AND FOLGERS

In the post–World War II era, paper products and a close relative, disposable diapers, proved the biggest of P&G's new businesses, while Crest became the basis of a fast-growing oral care, and eventually health care, business. Two other brands introduced in this period also evolved into billion-dollar brands, although they resulted from different strategies. Downy fabric softener emerged from P&G's labs as an internal development. Folgers coffee, like Charmin, arrived via acquisition.

Downy addressed the small downside of the post–World War II laundry revolution. Washing with synthetic detergents results in cleaner, brighter clothes, but fabrics thus treated can have a stiff and harsh feel, especially in certain water conditions. The problem is compounded when the garments are moved to automatic dryers, where wrinkling tends to worsen and static cling may also result. In the 1950s, P&G researchers set about to remedy these problems, drawing on their extensive knowledge of surface chemistry and wash water. They discovered a material that would bond naturally to the surface of fabrics, leaving them feeling softer.

This discovery lay behind Downy liquid fabric softener, which P&G introduced in test markets in 1960. Added to the rinse cycle, Downy not only softened fabrics but also delivered pleasing scents and other benefits such as protection from rinse-water impurities that could cause fading or discoloration. Although it was not the first liquid conditioner on the market, Downy was the first to be rolled out nationally and backed by heavy advertising. The brand thrived, and P&G reinforced it through effective advertising and steady improvements and line extensions, including concentrated forms, dosing balls, a range of scents, and special antiwrinkle formulations.

Applying liquid softeners at the right time and in the right amount to the wash cycle, however, remained a problem for some consumers, especially if they did not want to have to monitor their washing machine. Although P&G introduced delivery systems such as dosing balls and worked with appliance manufacturers to introduce automatic dispensers sequenced with the rinse cycle, researchers also worked on alternative approaches. They found a way to deliver the same active ingredients in Downy to fabrics in dryers by embedding the substances in a sheet of nonwoven material. As the sheets and clothing tumble together in a hot dryer, the softening compounds are transferred from the softening sheet to the garments, with similar effects plus static control. This concept lay ➢

behind P&G's introduction of Bounce in 1972, another highly successful brand, as well as Downy sheets in 1987. (The same principles apply to the conditioning of hair, which is why some fashion models rub their hair with Bounce before a photo shoot.) Together, Downy and Bounce are the anchors of P&G's huge business in laundry aids and fabric treatments.

If Downy illustrates P&G's ability to build brands from scratch, Folgers illustrates the complementary ability to build brands that were purchased. Folgers turned out to be one of P&G's biggest (for the time) and best (for all time) acquisitions. Acquired in 1963 for considerations valued at $130 million—about 8 percent of P&G's revenues that year—Folgers was already the second-largest coffee company in the United States. At the time, however, its operations and markets were concentrated west of the Mississippi River. The coffee business was structurally attractive to P&G and complementary to its growing portfolio in foods. Coffee was a semi-perishable good sold through familiar channels, and in its striking red cans, Folgers was a popular brand in its territory. Folgers also offered potential for rapid growth based on P&G's technology in flavors and textures and its prowess in purchasing, manufacturing, and marketing.

Folgers prospered as part of P&G. During the 1970s, the company took the brand nationwide, helped by ubiquitous TV ads featuring the kindly Mrs. Olson, whose Swedish-accented commentary emphasized the social and communal benefits of drinking coffee. Procter & Gamble ➢

also supported the coffee unit's efforts to offer improved formulas and tastes, both in ground and instant, caffeinated and decaffeinated varieties. Although engaged in fierce competition with the Maxwell House brand of General Foods and later threatened by the rise of fresh roasted and specialty coffees, Folgers remained an enduring American staple.

In the mid-1980s, consumer research highlighted the significance of aroma to coffee drinkers. This insight changed P&G's fundamental understanding of how to market coffee, and the company repositioned Folgers under the famous slogan, "The best part of waking up is Folgers in your cup." The repositioning helped create a sustaining relationship with consumers and made the brand a trusted part of their lives and rituals. Folgers became a billion-dollar brand in 1994.

Over the years, Folgers spawned line extensions and sister brands and even helped tempt P&G to pursue other beverages such as orange juice, fruit juices, and soft drinks. Most of these ventures failed, although in 1995, P&G acquired Millstone Coffee, a premium, fresh-roasted brand with a modest presence in the northwestern United States. By the early 2000s, Millstone had become the leading specialty brand sold in grocery stores, drugstores, mass merchandisers, and club stores throughout the country. Together with Folgers, Millstone provides P&G with leadership across all major market segments.

Leading the Way in Television Advertising

As it expanded into new products and businesses, P&G moved quickly to exploit the new marketing potential of television. With some 20 percent of airtime devoted to commercials, television became an important medium for communicating with consumers. In a 1979 interview, chief executive Ed Harness explained why the company placed such a premium on radio and TV advertising: "There's a high frequency of purchase with [P&G's] products. That's why we use frequency of advertising, why we use daytime serials, where we talk to the audience every day. If we don't have [the consumer's] attention, somebody else will get it."[21]

When television began to appear in U.S. homes during the late 1940s, P&G immediately realized that the new medium was very different from radio. TV was much more expensive because it involved more elaborate casting and set design. In the early days, each show had to be done locally because there was no coast-to-coast transmission. Company executives debated about how much to invest in the new medium, while salespeople in rural areas resisted domestic shifts in advertising spending because few homes in their sales territories had TVs. But along with other large advertisers, P&G soon grasped the potential of TV commercials. In the seven years from 1949 to 1956, total dollars spent on TV ads in the United States rose from about one-tenth of the amount spent on radio ads to nearly two and one-half times as much. The cost of network airtime to advertisers nearly tripled, but the size of the audience increased so fast that the cost per household fell by more than half. By the early 1970s, P&G was spending some $200 million a year on television advertising. All by itself, the company accounted for a full *one-tenth* of the networks' total revenues. But even so, P&G estimated that it spent only one-quarter of one cent for each commercial that reached a U.S. household—far less than the cost of a postage stamp.[22]

On July 23, 1948 P&G aired its first regular TV broadcast, *Fashions on Parade,* jointly sponsored by Prell and Ivory Snow. Howard Morgens, who was then vice president of advertising, was a strong advocate of TV programming. In 1949 he formed P&G Productions to produce shows for company sponsorship. *Fireside Theatre,* the first P&G production, went on the air that same year. Within a few years, the company became one of the world's largest producers of live and filmed entertainment. Having learned the power of radio as a mass medium, P&G moved quickly to occupy the most desirable programming times in U.S. television. (The company would later do the same in Europe and South America.[23]) Of course, the popularity of the new TV shows could not have occurred without the rapid spread of TV and TV stations. The 1950s can properly be called the decade of television. Coast-to-coast transmission became available in 1951, and by the late 1960s, TV had become nearly universal, with 95 percent of U.S. homes having at least one set.[24]

At first, all the P&G shows were nighttime productions, but brand managers began urging the making of daytime shows. Debates arose about the effectiveness of such a move. Would women drop what they were doing and watch? What about men, most of whom would be out working? Such worries proved groundless. The company's first attempt at daytime television was a serial called *The First Hundred Years*. While that show lasted only two years, P&G's second effort became a hit. The radio program *The Guiding Light* moved to TV in 1952 and became the longest-running show in the history of electronic media. In 1956, P&G became the first company to produce half-hour serials, with the debut of *Another World* and *The Edge of Night*. At one point during the mid-1950s, P&G had thirteen different serials on TV, making it the world's biggest buyer of television time. Until the advent of cable television in the 1980s, the company was able to reach up to 90 percent of all U.S. households by sponsoring popular programs and placing ads in national magazines.[25]

Advertising Agencies

Procter & Gamble's advertising agencies were partners in these transitions. The company had used a full-service agency since 1922, when it assigned Ivory and Crisco to Blackman & Co., which later became Compton. In the 1930s, the brand management system was extended to advertising, when P&G retained a new agency, Pedler & Ryan, to take over the advertising for Camay. Pedler & Ryan was given full license to compete directly with Blackman and Ivory. Other agencies who became long-term suppliers and partners included Blackett Sample Hummert (later Dancer Fitzgerald Sample), first hired in 1933; Benton & Bowles (1941); Leo Burnett (1951); and Grey Advertising (1956). Mergers and acquisitions among the agencies resulted in numerous name changes over the years, but for most, the relationship with P&G remained a constant. The company earned a reputation in the advertising world as a demanding but loyal client who "moves an account only as a last resort," according to a 1963 article in *Advertising Age*. In part, the loyalty stemmed from the desire to maintain a consistent brand image. It also came from P&G's realization that switching agencies resulted in lost time, usually a year or more, before the replacement was up to speed.[26]

Some advertising executives complained about P&G's heavy-handedness and arrogance, others about its bureaucratic structure and resistance to change.[27] But as one of the world's largest advertisers, P&G inevitably commanded respect. Warren Albright of advertising agency N. W. Ayer explained the bond that developed between P&G and many of its agencies: "A lot of other clients don't respect their agencies; they treat their agencies like suppliers." In contrast, P&G worked "with their agencies in a partnership. . . . I think that's one of the things that make the bonds exist so well between P&G people and their agency people. It's what keeps people loyal to the P&G business."[28]

International Expansion

Prior to World War II, P&G's international businesses were located primarily in England and Canada, with smaller operations in the Philippines, Cuba, and Indonesia. (Procter & Gamble sold the Cuba business in 1959 and P&G closed the Indonesian operations in 1964 as a result of political instability.) Most U.S. corporations showed a similar pattern of having foreign subdivisions that were small, dependent outposts rather than full-fledged operations in their own right. After the war, however, large U.S. corporations began expanding abroad at a quickening pace, and their previously small outposts assumed much more independence and responsibility.

Neil McElroy, who after the war was clearly destined to be P&G's next president, believed that the company was facing "a marvelous opportunity" to expand abroad.[29] He persuaded Deupree to appoint an executive to manage all the existing operations and, more importantly, to expand into additional countries. Deupree went along with this plan, but, concerned about the potential instability in continental Europe, decreed that P&G would have no fixed investments there.[30] He may also have been reluctant to tackle head-on the strong, entrenched competitors such as Unilever and Henkel & Cie. GmbH, the latter a party to a technical exchange agreement with P&G. If so, he would have followed the example of many U.S. manufacturing companies, which had tacit agreements with European competitors in the 1920s and 1930s to leave each other's home markets alone.[31]

In late 1945 or early 1946, Walter "Jake" Lingle, a senior executive who had reported to McElroy in the Advertising Department, assumed the new responsibility as manager of foreign business. During the next few years, he spent most of his time attending to the war-ravaged operations in the Philippines and at Thomas Hedley & Co. in the United Kingdom. When McElroy took over as president in 1948, Deupree became chairman of the board and Lingle was elevated to vice president of a new International Division. Significantly, this was not always deemed a sufficiently large job. In 1954, Lingle was elected an executive vice president and assumed responsibility for

P&G's cellulose operations and oil mills. A few years later, he took on added duties overseeing the Toilet Goods and Paper divisions.[32]

Latin America

Given Deupree's reservations about Europe, Lingle was "very clearly directed" to focus first on Latin America, where the company already had achieved some success in Cuba. Geographical proximity and recent political events pointed to Mexico, which in 1948 became the first major foreign country P&G entered after the war. In 1946 Miguel Aleman had assumed the presidency of Mexico, ending decades of revolutionary instability and inaugurating a probusiness agenda, including courting foreign investment.[33] Procter & Gamble arrived with numerous other U.S. multinationals in what looked to be a rapidly growing market.

At first, Lingle looked for a soap company to buy. Finding nothing suitable, he arranged to acquire a small producer of edible fats. That venture soon soured, and P&G sold the business after several years. By then, however, Tide and other synthetic detergents had opened new possibilities for the company. In the late 1940s and early 1950s, P&G built or acquired operations for manufacturing detergents in Mexico, Venezuela, and Cuba.

Europe

At the same time that it was establishing itself in Latin America, P&G built a detergent plant in the United Kingdom to serve domestic demand and to supply exports to Belgium. Success in the venture enabled the company to overtake Unilever, which came late to the detergent revolution, as the category leader in the United Kingdom. Lingle harbored notions of expanding further into continental Europe, and in 1954, a serendipitous contact with the head of the Paris branch of J. P. Morgan allowed him to establish P&G's first foothold. From his Morgan contact, Lingle learned that Unilever, which had recently built a detergent plant in France, lacked the capacity to meet demand. He also learned that a failing soap company in Marseilles, Fournier-Ferrier, had started to build a new detergent plant but ran out of money before it was completed. Lingle knew that Deupree would never authorize an outright purchase of the plant. But with the backing of McElroy, Lingle was able to persuade Deupree to approve an arrangement whereby P&G would lease the Fournier-Ferrier plant for five years, with an option to buy. In the meantime, P&G would produce and market Tide in France.[34] The French venture got off to a fast start, with Tide garnering a 15 percent market share in its first year. Procter & Gamble's Bonux, a new, low-sudsing detergent better suited to French washing machines, was an even bigger hit. As sales accumulated, P&G built a second detergent plant near Paris and began to export to Italy.[35] The success of the company's exports into Western Europe prompted decisions to build detergent plants in Belgium (1955) and Italy (1958).

West Germany, which by the late 1950s had established itself as "the miracle economy in Europe" and a driving force behind the formation of the European Economic Community (EEC), was the next logical step. The country, however, already contained a strong local competitor, Henkel A.G. Before the war, the two companies had cooperated in the development of synthetic detergents, with P&G licensing Henkel's patents. After the war, the businesses resumed their technical-exchange agreement, with somewhat different motives. Henkel was eager to keep P&G out of Germany, whereas P&G respected Henkel's R&D capabilities and wanted a right of first refusal on any new technologies Henkel should develop. By the late 1950s, however, a multidivisional P&G had more than soaps, fats, and detergents to sell, and the prospect of serving 40 million affluent German consumers was too tempting to pass up. The company also anticipated the eventual integration of the region under the EEC. To establish itself as a viable competitor in Europe, P&G could hardly afford to bypass West Germany.

In 1960, P&G ended its technical exchanges with Henkel and negotiated with Rei-Werke A.G., a producer of soaps and light-duty detergents, to be its local sales agent. The deal was announced under terms that gave P&G an option to buy Rei-Werke within five years, an option duly exercised in 1965. Rei-Werke initially sold Camay and Spic and Span, with Lenor fabric softener in test marketing, as well as its own products. Soon after it partnered with Rei-Werke, P&G announced plans to erect a new, heavy-duty detergent (Dash) plant. Making the rare decision to build a factory before the demand for the product materialized, was a sure sign of P&G's commitment to the West German market.[36]

By the early 1960s, P&G was a growing presence throughout Western Europe, using the region as the launching pad for further expansion. In 1956, the company closed Hedley's export office in London and opened a new office in Geneva to coordinate exports to smaller markets throughout Europe, North Africa, and the Middle East. As volume grew, P&G sometimes established local sales offices and set up contract manufacturing agreements with local partners. When business moved beyond this stage, the company preferred a full ownership position of foreign assets but occasionally entered into joint venture agreements. It sought majority interests but sometimes agreed to fifty-fifty partnerships. The first such joint venture involved Iraq in 1959, closely followed by similar deals in Lebanon and Saudi Arabia.[37]

In 1962, like his friend and boss McElroy before him, Lingle took a leave of absence to work in Washington, first with the Agency for International Development and then with the National Aeronautics and Space Administration (NASA). When he returned in 1964, he found Morgens less eager to extend P&G's international reach; instead, Morgens preferred to increase control of P&G's now far-flung operations. "I was strong for pacing ourselves and taking one step at a time," Morgens later explained.[38] While Lingle was away, Morgens had divided the International Division into four separate operating divisions: Asia and Latin America; Britain, Canada, and Scandinavia; the Common Market; and Export and Special Operations. Each reported to a group vice president with full-time responsibility. Procter & Gamble focused on improving operations in these areas and developing local management talent, while taking a more deliberate approach to opening new markets.

Staffing the international offices was a constant problem. Because Morgens was so focused on growing and diversifying the domestic business, Lingle "had to really scramble to get the good people," recalled Chuck Fullgraf. William Gurganus, who succeeded Lingle in 1969, reported facing similar problems. By the mid-1970s, however, local talent had deepened considerably in Europe. Durk Jager, who would become chief executive in 1999, was an associate manager in the Netherlands. Talented advertising managers included Harald Einsmann in Germany, Jorge Montoya in Spain, and Michael Allen, who later became a group vice president in England.[39]

Japan

Looking beyond continental Europe and Latin America, Lingle became interested in the vast lands across the Pacific, especially Australia, India, and Japan. In P&G's parlance, these areas constituted the "white space," or markets wherein the company had as yet no presence. Lingle visited these countries with Business International, a U.S. organization, and met with top governmental officials. The inquiry left him cautious. The Australian market seemed too small to support entry, while India seemed too poor.

Japan, however, was another matter. Like West Germany, it had staged a miraculous economic comeback after the war and was a large, fast-growing, and affluent economy. But Lingle recognized in Japan some unique conditions that gave him pause. First were government restrictions that limited foreign ownership of Japanese companies to minority positions. This meant that P&G could not follow its now preferred mode of entry by acquiring or taking control of an existing company. Second was the presence of two strong, entrenched competitors, Kao and Lion. Both were old, established companies with strong brands, tight relationships with distributors, formidable technical capabilities (especially at Kao), and no inclination to form an alliance with P&G or any other foreign partner. What's more, Kao and Lion had already fended off challenges in dentifrices and soap from Colgate and Unilever, which had labored to make headway in Japan during the 1960s. Other U.S. consumer products companies such as General Mills and General Foods had also been forced to retreat from initial sallies in Japan.[40]

In the late 1960s, the prospect that the Japanese government would soon ease restrictions on foreign capital prompted P&G to reconsider entering Japan, by then the second-largest market in the non-Communist world. In 1968, shortly before Gurganus succeeded the retiring Lingle, P&G undertook a two-month study of the Japanese detergent market. This time, the analysis proved encouraging. In the early 1970s, P&G entered negotiations to form a joint venture for the manufacture and marketing of soaps, detergents, and household cleaning products in Japan.

The Middle East and Elsewhere

By the early 1970s, P&G had become a true multinational rather than a U.S. company with a few foreign subsidiaries and operations. The bulk of the company's overall growth in earnings occurred in its international operations, which in 1972 accounted for 27 percent of total earnings.[41] Within a few years, Ariel, marketed in Europe, Latin America, and the Middle East, would surpass Tide as the company's largest single detergent brand. From 1955 to 1979, P&G's foreign sales multiplied from $238 million to more than $1.3 billion, earnings increased eightfold, and overseas assets quadrupled from $81 million to $320 million. One-third of employee growth occurred outside the United States.[42] The company increasingly began to view itself as an international entity, becoming more vulnerable to the destabilizing events occurring in Asia, the Middle East, and Latin America.

As with its domestic acquisitions, P&G was determined to mold the international operations in the image of the parent firm. Lingle recognized the need to strike a balance between serving local interests and preserving the benefits of corporate experience, capabilities, and control. However, he also declared that "the best way to succeed in other countries is to build in each one an exact replica of the U.S Procter & Gamble."[43] By this assertion, he meant that each country would have a strong general manager with a full range of business functions. Procter & Gamble ensured that its new operations adhered to the company's principles of conducting thorough market research and providing superior products, as well as its primary values of honesty and integrity in business conduct. To that end, Lingle arranged for a number of international managers to spend time in Cincinnati. According to

Gurganus, transmitting the company's culture became easier when the status of the international operations began to rise within the company. As "some of the younger people from International developed the ability to carry heavy responsibility in the Company," they helped "to speed up this homogenization of the Procter & Gamble organizations worldwide."[44]

Obstacles to Expansion: Antitrust and the End of Acquisitions

In all likelihood, P&G would have continued acquiring companies as a way to enter new consumer goods businesses. The U.S. government's antitrust policies, however, altered that strategy. After World War II, the federal government resumed its strong enforcement of antitrust laws, continuing the trend begun during the Great Depression. In 1950, Congress enacted the Celler-Kefauver Act, making it difficult for companies to acquire or merge with others in related lines of business. The new law discounted intent; only size mattered. If a firm gained a large share of a market as a result of a merger or an acquisition, the courts could forbid the transaction even if no restraints of trade were involved. Inevitably, large corporations such as P&G, IBM, Alcoa, DuPont, and the United Shoe Machinery Company attracted the regulators' attention.

Problems had begun in 1952, when P&G and several other soap makers were named in a suit filed by the Justice Department charging restraint of competition and monopoly. The case was dismissed in 1961. A more serious charge was filed just one week after Morgens took over as P&G's new president in 1957. The FTC charged that the recent purchase of Clorox was in violation of the Clayton Act because it could result in market dominance in the household bleach industry. At the time, P&G was in the process of buying Charmin, and Morgens feared that the paper products company might prove to be P&G's last shot at entering a new business.[45]

Procter & Gamble publicly fought the Justice Department's charge. Deupree was especially bitter about what he and many other managers in corporate America regarded as the government's perverse logic, which punished companies just for having become large and successful. The case took ten years to wind its way to the Supreme Court, which in 1967 ruled against P&G, stating that the company's advertising and promotional resources represented a decisive threat to Clorox competitors. Clorox had to be divested.

Meanwhile, on June 26, 1966, the FTC served notice that it would seek divestiture of Folgers, which P&G had acquired three years earlier. Folgers was the second-largest coffee company in the United States. But coffee was a highly fragmented industry, and the Folgers business, concentrated primarily in the western states, accounted for only 11 percent of the national total. Disappointed by the FTC's notice, P&G nevertheless acted quickly to negotiate a consent decree, signed on February 9, 1967. Under the agreement, P&G was allowed to retain Folgers, but at significant cost. For seven years, P&G could not acquire, without prior consent of the FTC, any business in the United States that made household consumer products sold primarily in grocery stores. The company was further required to sell its Folgers coffee plant in Houston within the next five years to a purchaser approved by the FTC and was prohibited from acquiring any coffee business within the next ten years.[46]

The Clorox and Folgers episodes were serious blows, highlighting a persistent problem in U.S. antitrust cases: How should a market be defined? John Smale later pointed out that prior to the acquisitions P&G had not even been in the bleach or coffee businesses. But at the time, mere bigness was considered a punishable offense. The government believed that because P&G was such a force in grocery stores, it should not be allowed to enter new businesses by acquiring leading brands such as Clorox and Folgers. The Folgers decision was especially disheartening because, although it was a big brand west of the Mississippi, Folgers was not the leading brand nationally.[47]

Procter & Gamble insiders later confirmed that the rulings had a chilling effect on management's attitude about acquisitions. The company made no major purchases during the 1970s. It also declined to follow the lead of many other consumer goods companies, which, prevented by antitrust laws from acquiring firms in the same business, did not hesitate to venture into wholly unrelated lines. Conglomeration, as this strategy was called, was driven in part by the Justice Department's tendency not to challenge the mergers of firms in entirely different lines of business. The wisdom of conglomeration was also affirmed by the prevailing management philosophy, which stated that diversification would improve a firm's overall profit performance because operating in different industries would help spread risk and offset the negative effects of the business cycle. Wall Street took a favorable view of the conglomerate movement and rewarded these companies with higher valuations.[48]

Procter & Gamble, however, concentrated its energies on developing new products in-house, never swerving from its self-imposed rule of staying within existing and closely related product areas. It held to this policy even when the economy slowed in the 1970s, and the $130-billion-plus health care industry began to interest the company as one of the few that was outpacing the general economy. Fullgraf, who coordinated the exploration of the pharmaceuticals area as a potential new business during this time, reported that P&G "came up with no less than ten or twelve candidates for acquisition, any of which would have been a tremendous start for us . . . but management just couldn't see it being viable from an antitrust standpoint."[49] The company entered the health care industry only in 1982 with the acquisition of Norwich Eaton.

Procter & Gamble's reluctance to make acquisitions during the late 1960s and 1970s turned out to have at least one significant benefit. Many of the conglomerates failed to live up to investors' high hopes. Beginning in the late 1970s, corporate raiders such as T. Boone Pickens, Carl Icahn, and Michael Milken targeted a number of these firms, arguing that the conglomerates were mismanaged and therefore undervalued. Breaking them up, these raiders believed, would release the true value of the individual companies. They borrowed heavily to buy the firms, often relying on an instrument called the high-yield ("junk") bond.[50] Procter & Gamble's decision to grow internally and stick to related businesses spared it from the hostile takeover craze that continued into the late 1980s and early 1990s.

Environmental Issues

New public attitudes about the environment also acted as a brake on expansion. Concern about this area had been triggered by the 1962 publication of Rachel Carson's *Silent Spring,* which warned of the dangers posed by DDT and other pesticides. As a maker of detergents, P&G became a target of environmentalists concerned about the impact of chemicals in wash water discharged into public water supplies. Alkyl benzene sulfonate (ABS), the improved surfactant in Tide, occasionally caused foaming on the banks of rivers and streams. Public perception grew that detergent makers were to blame for significant water pollution. This issue was followed by concerns over enzymes, a new stain-removing ingredient being used in detergents. In Europe, enzyme-based detergents, such as Ariel, became widespread and generated little outcry. But in the United States, public fears arose about possible harmful effects (a misimpression created by ads depicting enzymes devouring dirt). Procter & Gamble was the first to introduce enzyme products in 1967, but soon felt pressured to abandon them. By 1971 the company, along with other detergent manufacturers, removed all enzymes from its U.S. laundry brands.

In the 1960s another detergent ingredient, phosphates, became a controversial issue. Phosphates are compounds containing the natural element phosphorus. (They are used in a wide range of industrial products and were added to laundry detergents to soften water and suspend the soil removed from clothes.) Phosphates were linked to accelerated eutrophication (a condition in which rich mineral and organic nutrients promote the proliferation of algae) in places like Lake Erie. Procter & Gamble maintained that phosphates from untreated sewage and fertilizer runoff were a far bigger problem than phosphate from detergents. But the public remained unconvinced by the company's claims.[51]

Several cities banned detergents with phosphates, and the FTC threatened to require detergents to be labeled "pollutants." In response to local laws, P&G stopped selling laundry detergents in the Miami, Buffalo, and Chicago areas in 1972. "We were faced with a dilemma," explained Tom Laco. "We couldn't make the products required by these laws in a responsible manner with the technology which was then available. It seemed wrong to replace phosphates with inert ingredients which would debase product performance without providing any environmental benefit. It seemed equally wrong to replace phosphates with unsafe alkaline materials. Under the circumstances, we felt the most responsible action we could take was to withdraw our laundry brands from these markets."[52]

Unlike the situation with enzymes, P&G held its ground during the phosphates controversy believing that its side of the story would eventually win out. The company also hoped that once consumers noticed the inferior performance of nonphosphate detergents, they would agitate to repeal the laws. But consumers saw little difference, and a grassroots campaign to allow the selling of phosphate detergents never materialized.[53] Eventually, company scientists developed alternative ingredients for phosphates that P&G felt provided acceptable performance and were safe. The company marketed these substitute formulas in areas where phosphates had been banned.

Like the antitrust cases brought against the company during the 1950s and 1960s, the phosphates controversy proved to be "a massive distraction," according to Ed Harness. Procter & Gamble spent more than $130 million searching for a phosphate replacement, which "had an effect of diminishing the productivity of our R&D work in [cleaning products] for a decade," Smale said. It wasn't "until the [19]80s that we really started to come up with some very significant product development . . . in the broad cleaning products area."[54]

Procter & Gamble had considered the media frenzy "emotional, political, and, at times, quite irrational." Harness, however, placed the issue in perspective. "Sure we paid a price, but it is the kind of price we will probably pay over and over in the future as the well-meaning world struggles through its search for a better life. Being Procter & Gamble we are willing to pay these prices in the long-term interest of the consumers of our products. Reason? If we take care of our consumer, the consumer will take care of us."[55] It was a sentiment that would soon be severely tested, when P&G confronted the Rely tampon crisis in 1980.

The 1970s: A More Difficult Business Climate

The long postwar period of economic expansion ended abruptly in the early 1970s, when the United States and most other Western industrialized nations entered a period of inflation combined with stagnation ("stagflation"). The decade began with the Nixon administration's imposition of wage and price controls. With each passing year, it became clear that economic growth could no longer be taken for granted. Worker productivity declined. Government deficits swelled as a result of increased military spending in Vietnam, expanded welfare programs, and environmental cleanup costs. International political developments imposed a series of economic shocks when, in 1973 and again in 1979, the Organization of Petroleum Exporting Countries (OPEC) raised its crude oil prices. Surging oil, chemical, and raw-material prices not only increased manufacturing costs for P&G; they also drove away consumers, who traded in the company's premium-priced brands for cheaper, generic versions.

In 1974, Harness succeeded Morgens, who stepped down as chief executive after a successful seventeen-year tenure. Like McElroy and Morgens, Harness rose through the ranks by way of the Advertising Department. He joined the company in 1940, spent four years in the military during World War II and then returned to P&G, becoming a brand promotion manager in 1954 and manager of the Soap Division's Advertising Department in 1960. In 1962 Harness was named manager of the Toilet Goods Division. He was then tapped by Morgens to head the struggling Paper Division a year later. In 1966, Harness was elected vice president–group executive, presiding over the Paper Division, the Cellulose and Specialties Division, and the Toilet Goods Division. He moved on to executive vice president in 1970, responsible for all the company's consumer products divisions in the United States, before assuming the presidency in 1971. As president, Harness was responsible for all the U.S. operating divisions, and in 1973, he was given the additional responsibilities for all the international operations.[56]

Procter & Gamble entered the 1970s at the top position in all its major businesses: laundry detergent (Tide), shampoo (Head & Shoulders), dentifrice (Crest), shortening (Crisco), disposable diapers (Pampers), and toilet tissue (Charmin). Despite the more difficult business climate, the company invested ever-higher amounts to expand its research facilities at Sharon Woods and Winton Hill, Ohio, and its manufacturing lines, especially those for paper products and Pringles. Overall, most of the investments made during the 1970s were warranted, but some, such as the manufacturing capacity for Pringles, did not pay off initially. The immense investments of both capital and personnel in the Paper Division also slowed progress in other areas of the company.[57]

Blocked by the Justice Department from making acquisitions in related lines of business, P&G concentrated on digesting those of the previous two decades and on expanding its brands into new territories, both in the United States and abroad. New product introductions continued, including Bounce fabric softener and Dawn dish-washing liquid (both immediately popular with consumers), Era heavy-duty detergent, Coast deodorant soap, Sure antiperspirant, and Puritan cooking oil. Motiv, a new dish-washing liquid detergent, was expanded nationally in both Germany and France. In 1973, researchers came up with an improved shaped and elasticized diaper, test marketed in 1976 as a separate brand, Luvs. The company also had great hopes for a new superabsorbent tampon, as well as a proprietary fat substitute that had been in development for more than a decade. Industrial products such as cellulose pulp and industrial foods (the latter sold primarily to restaurants) also grew, expanding eventually into some two hundred items. In the early 1970s, these divisions were grouped together under group vice president, Bill Snow.[58]

The record for the new consumer products was mixed. Pringles, Luvs, and Rely initially did well, but each later ran into severe problems. The Toilet Goods Division, too, lost its way as consumer habits changed and a flood of new shampoo brands entered the market. Development of the fat substitute olestra dragged on into the 1980s and 1990s.

Hopes ran high for Pringles, whose development began in the 1950s and accelerated during the following decade. It was, according to Fullgraf, "our breakthrough kind of hope, a mini Pampers if you will."[59] But by the mid-1970s, Pringles had hit a wall, and nothing P&G did to fix the brand seemed to work. In 1979, President Smale announced that unless Pringles could resume profitable growth within five years, it would be discontinued.

In shampoos, a series of shifts in the market during the early 1970s caught P&G off guard. Hairstyles changed, the use of blow dryers became prevalent, and consumers turned to shampoos and other hair care products promising fullness and more manageable hair. By 1974, Johnson & Johnson's Baby Shampoo had claimed market leadership, displacing Head & Shoulders and leaving P&G scrambling to regain its lead. Then Clairol (at the time a separate company) roiled the market again with Herbal Essences, an emerald-green shampoo with high fragrance content that filled bathrooms with a rich, sweet aroma. The brand rose within a few years to become the number-three-selling shampoo in the United States, ahead of Prell.[60] Procter & Gamble assigned its researchers the task of developing shampoos that improved hair's fullness, and high-perfume ones that could be pitted against Herbal Essences. These efforts produced Rejoice, which combined soap and synthetic ingredients, and Pert. But with new fads erupting and shaking up the market, consumers displayed little brand loyalty.[61]

The emergence of the blow dryer fundamentally altered hair care habits, reducing the time it took to wash and set hair from several hours to thirty minutes or less. As a result, consumers began washing their hair more often. Director of R&D, Cecilia Kuzma, conceded that P&G "spent an awful lot of time on how to develop superior cleaning—how to keep hair cleaner longer—when . . . 'cleaner longer' was no longer a need."[62] The company was still trying to adapt to the new environment as Pert moved out of test market in 1979.

Procter & Gamble also failed to react to market shifts in disposable diapers, a market it had pioneered with Pampers. After allocating its best technology to its new premium brand, Luvs, the company made Pampers vulnerable to Huggies, a strong competitor that hit the market in 1978. Pampers rapidly lost market share.

The problems with Rely tampons were of a different kind but were no less devastating *(see "The Rely Crisis" box)*. Launched on a regional basis beginning in 1978, Rely looked set to become P&G's next blockbuster. But a mysterious illness dubbed toxic shock syndrome and linked by the federal government to Rely, abruptly put an end to the brand. After the crisis struck in 1980, P&G withdrew Rely from the market amid a media frenzy that threatened to undermine severely the trust that consumers had in the company.

One bright spot was the company's increasing competence in health care and pharmaceuticals. Although it did not use the terminology at the time, the company first entered the health care business in the late 1950s and early 1960s, when it successfully introduced Crest as a therapeutic product. Head & Shoulders dandruff shampoo continued the process, as did Scope mouthwash, which fought against the bacteria that caused bad breath, among other oral care benefits. In combination with research on detergents, P&G's research on fluoride dentifrices provided knowledge of calcium, since tooth enamel is primarily made up of a calcium compound. Later, P&G researchers determined that common periodontal disease was a result of the buildup on the teeth of another primarily calcium compound called tartar. The researchers developed an agent that would remove this material without damaging the tooth enamel, a discovery that lay the foundation for development of Crest Tartar Control, introduced in 1985. From there, the research migrated to the next logical area. In the late 1970s, researchers began to extend the understanding and application of calcium-control technology from teeth to bones. The result was Didronel, a drug for the treatment of the bone disorder known as Paget's disease. Didronel represented P&G's first major entry into the pharmaceutical business; soon after, research was initiated on treatments for arthritis and osteoporosis.

As the end of the 1970s approached, "it became clear that we needed to generate more volume," explained Smale, who had succeeded Harness as

THE RELY CRISIS

In a 1972 management meeting, Ed Harness stated: "There are certain lasting things about the nature of this company which to me add up to its character. Some of these things can rightly be called policies. Some are basic principles which guide us. Others are really just continuing practices which we follow—ways of doing things which have become second nature with us."[63] Near the end of his tenure as chief executive, P&G's principles were put to a dramatic test in the most serious product liability case in the company's history.

In September 1980, the Center for Disease Control and Prevention (CDC), a federal research agency, notified P&G of a possible link between a mysterious and sometimes deadly new illness called toxic shock syndrome (TSS) and use of P&G's new Rely tampon. Introduced nationally in 1979 as the first superabsorbent tampon, Rely marked P&G's entry into the promising market for feminine care products and it looked like a possible blockbuster based on rapid market share gains during its first year. The CDC argued that TSS seemed more common among menstruating women who used tampons and suspected that the bacterium associated with TSS was more likely to flourish in superabsorbent models like Rely. The evidence was frustratingly inconclusive, but the situation posed a clear dilemma for P&G: Should it fight to defend the brand, as it had recently defended its detergents in the phosphates controversy, or should it withdraw Rely pending further research to clarify its causal connection to TSS?

Harness recognized that P&G would have to act quickly to resolve this dilemma. He placed the burden of proof squarely on P&G, asking whether the company could state unequivocally that its product was not culpable. The answer to this question would determine P&G's course of action.

TSS had been first identified in 1977—a year before P&G put Rely into test market—by Dr. James K. Todd, who found the puzzling condition in a small sample of children in Denver.[64] The symptoms were frightening: TSS began with a sudden high fever accompanied by diarrhea, vomiting, and sunburn-like rash. A dangerous drop in blood pressure was quickly followed by shock and, in the worst cases, death.

The disease caught the attention of the CDC, who tracked occurrences and initiated research studies. In May 1980 the agency published a report, based on fifty-two cases reported by the state departments of health, linking TSS with menstruation. Although the correlation between TSS and women of menstruating age was small—about three out of every one-hundred thousand individuals—the CDC began to investigate tampon ➢

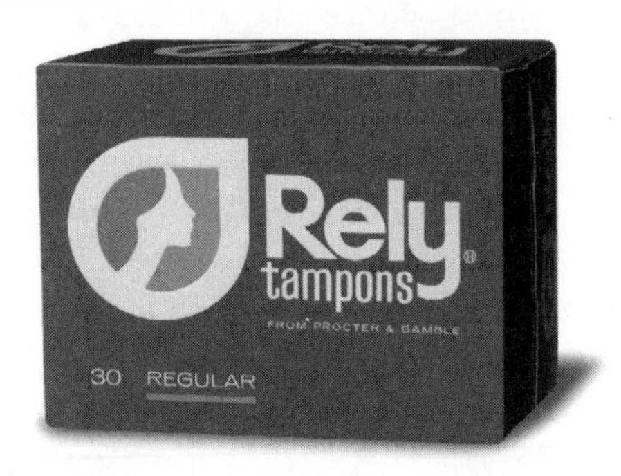

usage in TSS cases, obtaining the cooperation of P&G and other manufacturers. Several studies were inconclusive, but in early September, the CDC believed it had found a disturbing connection. After questioning 42 TSS victims and a control group of 150 healthy women, it reported that 71 percent of the afflicted group had used Rely compared with only 26 percent of the control group. To the CDC, this amounted to a "statistical association" between Rely and TSS, although it did not posit a causal link between tampon usage and the disease.[65]

Although P&G had concerns about the quality of this research and emerging conclusions, the company decided to seek impartial advice. On September 9 it established a panel of eminent physicians, microbiologists, and epidemiologists "to review the data and our assessment of it to help guide us toward a responsible course of action."[66] A week later, when the CDC formally notified P&G of the statistical association between Rely and TSS, Harness named Tom Laco, head of U.S. operations, to lead a crisis management team including senior executives and advisors. Procter & Gamble immediately suspended the production of Rely. Several days later, the CDC announced its findings publicly and in the ensuing media frenzy, some retailers took Rely off their shelves.

On Sunday, September 21, P&G convened its scientific advisory panel at Chicago's O'Hare airport, with Ed Harness and other top executives in attendance. Although the panel had been in existence less than two weeks, Harness wanted members' best answer to the key question: Could P&G claim, beyond any doubt, that Rely was not responsible for any of the TSS cases? Nearly all experts, even within the CDC itself, had acknowledged that the studies so far were inconclusive, but Harness did not want to delay a decision. When the panel could not categorically rule out Rely as a causal factor in TSS, Harness recalled: "that was the turning point . . . I knew what we had to do."[67] ➢

The next day, Harness announced that P&G would voluntarily withdraw Rely from the market. He added that the company had made the decision "despite the fact that we know of no defect in the Rely tampon and despite evidence that the withdrawal of Rely will not eliminate the occurrence of TSS, even if Rely's use is completely discontinued."

On Friday, September 26, P&G signed a consent agreement with the U.S. government. Procter & Gamble denied any violation of federal law or any product defect, a source of great concern given the number of potential lawsuits. The company agreed to buy back all unused products, including those that had been mailed free to women during the introductory campaign. Procter & Gamble also promised to cooperate with the CDC in researching the disease and to pay for and direct an extensive program educating consumers about TSS. Its three thousand-member sales force removed Rely from retailers' shelves within two weeks of the withdrawal announcement.[68]

Procter & Gamble subsequently announced the establishment of a $75 million reserve to cover product refunds as well as losses on inventory and fixed assets, and to provide some provisions against claims from lawsuits. Harness acknowledged that the "financial cost to the company of Rely's voluntary suspension will be high, but we believe we have done what is right and that our action is consistent with the long-held Procter & Gamble view that the company and the company alone is responsible for the safety of our products. To sacrifice this principle could over the years ahead be a far greater cost than the monetary losses we face on the Rely brand."[69]

Withdrawing Rely, he later said, was one of the easiest management decisions he ever had to make. It was the right thing to do not only for public health but also to protect P&G's reputation and maintain consumers' trust in its brands. Meanwhile, P&G did not abandon the feminine protection business. During the 1980 shareholders' meeting, Harness indicated that the termination of Rely "doesn't mean we have given up on the tampon or, alternatively, the sanitary napkin business. . . . Developments in coming months and years will be closely studied for opportunities to put us back in the [feminine hygiene] business, where we believe we have much to offer in superior technology."[70] In 1983, P&G introduced a new sanitary napkin, sold under the Always and Whisper brands. These became hot-selling global brands in the 1980s and beyond. It took longer for P&G to reenter the market for tampons, but it did so in a big way in 1997, when the company closed the $1.85 billion acquisition of Tambrands.

president in 1974. "We needed more brands. . . . We needed more avenues of growth."[71] After more than a decade of shying away from acquisitions, Smale was convinced that P&G needed to resume making deals to enter a new era of growth and diversification. The 1980s would see the company moving more firmly into health care and pharmaceuticals as well as new food products.

The Period in Perspective, 1945–1980

Over the thirty-five years following World War II, P&G rapidly assumed the proportions of a disciplined, diversified consumer goods colossus, doing business in an expanded range of product categories, with operations around the world. Having mastered the art of brand building in the years leading up to the war, the company applied these tactics across a steadily widening scope of enterprises between 1945 and 1980. Mainstay brands, including Crest, Charmin, Bounty, Pampers, Pringles, Folgers, Downy, and Bounce, all grew out of this period. Procter & Gamble as a whole consequently experienced enormous growth: The company's net sales increased more than thirty-fold, from $342.5 million in 1945 to $10.8 billion in 1980.

Numerous milestones marked this expansion. Restructuring into divisions in 1955 enabled P&G to extend its focus in new directions while at the same time adhering to disciplined, brand-oriented strategies. Even as it ventured into new markets, the company continued to operate in the familiar, proven patterns it had learned in its traditional core markets. Ventures in oral care, paper products, and foods took significant investments and patient nurturing before they bore fruit.

An intensified push into foreign markets also generated a string of milestones. With the establishment of the International Division in 1946, P&G gave a strong impetus to international expansion, creating momentum that carried it into Latin America (notably Mexico and Venezuela), continental Europe (starting with Belgium and France), and eventually markets farther afield (North Africa, the Middle East, and, with penetration into Japan in 1973, Asia). By 1980, the company had operations in twenty-two countries. Despite this expansion, P&G was not yet global in outlook. For example, it still broke down its businesses country by country, with few mechanisms to coordinate or leverage brand strategies across national boundaries. Even so, by the mid-1970s, P&G was planted in every continent and was cultivating a new generation of globally minded managers.

Finally, P&G continued to hone its expertise in brand building, which equipped the company to ride out profound shifts in its operating environment. Procter & Gamble managed the transition to television advertising almost seamlessly, adapting its radio advertising strategies and preserving its leadership role in broadcast media. It also adapted relatively smoothly to a major shift in retail distribution patterns, as a new network of large-scale distributors emerged in supermarkets and shopping centers, a trend that became even more pronounced during the 1980s and 1990s.

On the other hand, as this span of years drew to a close, the company encountered increasingly vexing social and political conditions. Antitrust policies checked various strategies for growth beginning in the 1960s. The rise of environmentalism and consumer activism in the 1960s and 1970s also presented major challenges. More fundamentally, the company's traditional markets steadily matured. By the late 1970s, it became clear that continued growth would require venturing into yet another ring of outlying markets.

Procter & Gamble Reinvents the Paper Products Business

SYNTHETIC DETERGENTS led P&G's growth during the 1950s and 1960s. Throughout the late 1960s and 1970s, however, it was the Paper Division that drove much of the company's expansion. The division's beginnings were modest: In 1957, P&G acquired an unexceptional Wisconsin-based tissue maker called Charmin as an entry point into the consumer paper products business, specifically tissues and towels. Eventually, the acquisition became the platform for launching several of P&G's best-known brands—but only after a decade of learning, experimentation, innovation, and unprecedented capital expenditures.

Developing Charmin and White Cloud toilet tissues, Bounty paper towels, Puffs facial tissue, and Pampers and Luvs disposable diapers involved many of the company's most talented technical personnel. These included Victor Mills, Bob Duncan, Harry Tecklenburg, Fred Wells, Jim Edwards, Jim Sisson, and Larry Sanford, all of whom came up with the innovations that established P&G as a leading force in the paper products business. Among the most important of these was CPF (Confidential Process F), a new process for improving the absorbency and softness of paper tissues and towels.* The technical team also improved the disposable diaper and then figured out how to bring down the manufacturing costs so that millions of parents could afford it.

*Process innovations at P&G were labeled with letters, beginning with A. CPF stood for Confidential Process F.

Entering the paper products business turned out to be the biggest financial risk P&G took during this period. Years later, veterans of the division described the huge capital expenditures on the manufacturing lines as being unanticipated and frightening. They agreed, however, that top management remained committed to the new business. In 1963, Howard Morgens appointed Ed Harness, then manager of the much larger Toilet Goods Division, to be head of the Paper Division. To ensure that the struggling division would succeed, Morgens gave Harness access to the company's most valuable technical and marketing personnel. Top management again showed its commitment during the lengthy development of Pampers, the world's first mass-produced disposable diaper. Although it failed in its first three test markets, Pampers eventually became the company's largest single brand and one of the most revolutionary consumer products of the postwar period.

Stretching a "Cellulose Connection"

Consumer paper products seemed a highly promising new business for P&G in the 1950s. As with a number of other consumer goods markets, demand for paper products had exploded after World War II. Morgens later confirmed that his interest had also been sparked by concern that disposable tissues and towels would eat into P&G's soap and detergent business. Why would consumers bother to clean a dishcloth or a rag if they could simply throw it away? Far better, he reasoned, for P&G to make a preemptive move and become part of an industry that might seriously undermine the company's own soap and detergent business.[1]

Some of Morgens's colleagues proved less sanguine, arguing that entry into the paper products industry would be too expensive. Skeptics pointed out that the level of investment needed to compete would dwarf anything in P&G's previous experience. Even so, in 1956 the company made the decision to enter paper products on a trial basis, and the following year, it completed the acquisition of Charmin Paper Mills, a manufacturer of paper towels and tissues based in Green Bay, Wisconsin.[2]

Morgens, Red Deupree, and Neil McElroy publicly supported the Charmin deal by citing the healthy growth rates in consumer paper goods.[3] They also stressed to shareholders and the media the logic of the acquisition. Making connections between different products had characterized the company's growth strategy in the past, when it had deftly used its existing businesses as bridges into successful, new ones.

Paper goods had two connections to the existing businesses. The first was technical. For thirty-five years, P&G had been involved in the R&D of cellulose fibers through its Buckeye Cotton Oil Co. subsidiary. The second connection involved P&G's long history of marketing and distributing low-cost consumer goods, especially cleaning products. Like soap and toilet goods, paper tissues and towels were sold through grocery stores, department stores, and drug outlets and therefore played to traditional P&G strengths.

In the ensuing years, P&G continued to emphasize the division's "cellulose connection" with Buckeye. But in reality, paper tissues and towels had few similarities with the cellulose business. Buckeye did not make paper products; instead, it manufactured intermediate materials that it supplied to other companies, which used them to make products such as rayon fiber and photographic film. And even with Buckeye's competencies, pulp making provided P&G with only a tiny wedge into the paper goods industry. Harness, who took charge of the Paper Division in 1963, came to believe that success required building an organization that was competent in every aspect of a vertically integrated process, stretching from the procurement of raw materials, to pulp making, papermaking, and converting, and finally to distribution.[4] Years later, P&G abandoned the idea of vertical integration; it sold the Buckeye business in the early 1990s.

Far from being a logical and inevitable move, the Charmin acquisition actually launched P&G into a largely unfamiliar business. To succeed, the company had to master new skills in product development, manufacturing, marketing, and distribution. It also had to fend off two large competitors, Scott Paper and Kimberly-Clark. Industry leader Scott Paper was a formidable rival—a vertically integrated, pure-play company with one of the highest profit margins in the business. A powerful marketer, Scott had virtually created the paper towel category, beginning in the 1930s.[5] Kimberly-Clark, the world's largest producer of cellulose wadding, had a two-decade head start in making and marketing consumer paper goods such as Kotex sanitary napkins, which accounted for 60 percent of the U.S. market, and facial tissues, which accounted for 50 percent of U.S. sales.[6] (Kimberly-Clark acquired Scott in 1995.) It seemed audacious for a soap and shortening company to take on such experienced and well-entrenched competitors.

Fixing Charmin

When P&G acquired Charmin Paper Mills in 1957, the smaller company had annual sales of $20 million, volume of a little over two million cases, and a workforce of twelve hundred people. Although in existence for sixty-six years, Charmin was primarily a regional competitor, with 80 to 90 percent of sales confined to the area that stretched from just west of Pittsburgh to just east of Denver, and south to the Kentucky-Tennessee border. The company manufactured toilet tissues under the Charmin and Lady Charmin brands in addition to paper towels, napkins, and private-label goods. It also sold products to industrial and institutional customers under the trade name Evergreen.[7] None of the products was a market leader; the strongest, Charmin toilet tissue, held only a 14 percent market share. In blind tests that P&G conducted in 1957, all of Charmin's products performed dismally against those of Scott Paper and Kimberly-Clark.

Privately, P&G executives described Charmin as a struggling company. The "paper machines were fifty years old," said Edwards. "They had one fairly modern machine, but even that [was only] about half the capacity of what it should have been."[8] Even so, Charmin provided P&G with a pilot project, a way to learn about the business and test new products in a limited geographic market. Procter & Gamble quickly decided that Charmin's coverage of its territory was too thin, and P&G actually retreated from some markets to improve distribution in key areas.[9] Not until 1962 did P&G attempt to expand outside Charmin's original territory.

Procter & Gamble executives moved slowly, allowing Charmin's management to continue running the company. A team of P&G advisers led by vice president of the paper products division, Schuyler Cole, flew to Green Bay every Monday to lend a hand. For the first three years, Cole's team focused on studying the business and designing new products and mill facilities rather than on expansion. Victor Mills and his staff at the Corporate Exploratory Development group were put in charge of updating Charmin's processes. Charmin benefited almost immediately from P&G's more sophisticated financial and marketing techniques, but the transfer of technical knowledge proved troublesome. At the time, papermaking was considered an art, in the same way soap making had been earlier in the century. Charmin "had no clearly established product or process standards," Mills recalled.[10]

Six to eight of P&G's chemical engineers were assigned to Green Bay for several months to learn Charmin's processes and determine what degree of control might be possible. They were regarded with suspicion by the Charmin people, an attitude that took some two years to overcome. The Paper Product Development Department changed Charmin's pulping methods, resulting in better quality control of the pulp and a 50 percent increase in production. Procter & Gamble also applied much higher safety standards. "When I first went to Green Bay," recalled engineer Larry Sanford, "old paper makers had lost fingers and thumbs. The statement to the neophyte was, 'Until you lose a finger or two, you're never going to be a paper maker!' "[11]

Progress in the tissue and towel products was strikingly less rapid than in the Food Division's new acquisition, Duncan Hines, partly because of "the lack of good *technical* background," said Mills. "In the case of prepared cake mixes, we started with six years of research and development background, whereas in the paper product field, we started with none."[12] Nevertheless, only one year after the acquisition, P&G test marketed its first new paper product, White Cloud, a two-ply toilet tissue that would replace Lady Charmin four years later. The plan was to build the paper business on the strength of White Cloud and a new facial tissue, Puffs, which went into test market in 1960 as a replacement for Charmin Facial.

Expanding into new markets was key to the division's success. But P&G found it extremely difficult to move beyond Charmin's original territory, which included only 57 percent of U.S. households. The "perimeter" included adjacent markets such as Syracuse and Utica, Oklahoma City and Denver, and Dallas and Fort Worth. Rivals carefully monitored P&G's expansion attempts and responded by improving their own offerings and incentives. The division's sales force struggled to introduce Charmin, White Cloud, and Puffs into markets that were being aggressively defended by Scott and Kimberly-Clark.[13]

Although aware of the division's problems, Morgens was at first reluctant to commit top management talent before the fundamental competencies were in place. In his opinion, it "would have been a real waste of those people" during a time when the company had its hands full developing its food business. The company's infiltration of the consumer tissues and towels business was so slow and low-key that it attracted little attention. In 1963, *Forbes* magazine described the impending battle between Scott and P&G as "one of the roughest competitive struggles of 20th-century American business." Yet, the article said, "many businessmen are unaware of the fact."[14]

After six years of mediocre results, Morgens decided to act. In 1963, he pulled Harness from his post as manager of the Toilet Goods Division and put him in charge of the Paper Division, replacing Cole. Morgens's brief was simple: Fix the problems, or the business would be sold. Harness's appointment was a clear sign of management's commitment; it greatly improved morale in the division. Harness himself, however, was ambivalent, wondering whether the appointment signaled the end of his chance at becoming president of the company. Whatever his reservations, it soon became clear that Morgens was prepared to back him with substantial resources, including P&G's best technical staff. Starting with Harry Tecklenburg (the future head of P&G's worldwide R&D), the "paper men" eventually included Fred Wells and Jim Edwards. "These guys were . . . the heart of the soap business in those days," said Ed Artzt, who was brought in during 1966 to help fix the division's problems in marketing and distribution. Nevertheless, Morgens willingly pulled them from the core Soap and Detergents Division to make the struggling paper business work.[15]

Geographical expansion meant enormous investments in plant and equipment, a requirement that became a constant source of anxiety for new division leader Harness. "How do we go before the Board of Directors," he asked in a 1964 memo, "and talk in terms of an undertaking which may mean in the next few years as much as $200 million in capital [investment] when we have not yet demonstrated ability to make a profit in present marketing areas?" (The division's estimated pretax losses for the following year were $4.7 million.) Harness later said that the experience amounted to "a liberal education for a guy who had grown up in the advertising side of the business. . . . I had never been confronted with major capital expenditures until I got involved in pulp and paper." Chuck Fullgraf, who succeeded Harness as head of the division in 1966 when Harness became a vice president and group executive, recalled that the sums involved proved to be "so off the scale from the company's normal experience" that many found it "shocking." Guidelines and targets for the older Soap and Toilet Goods divisions had little relevance for the Paper Division, and P&G found itself repeatedly underestimating the start-up costs for the new plants. Fullgraf later estimated that the cost to install an annual case of capacity for paper products was seven or eight times the cost for synthetic detergents, and even higher when compared to toilet goods.[16]

The massive costs appeared to confirm what top executives at Scott Paper had said when P&G first entered the business. Back in the late 1950s, they had estimated that P&G would have to spend nearly $1 billion—about the same amount as its annual revenues—to duplicate Scott's physical equipment. Scott's president, Harrison F. Dunning, implied that this staggering sum would force P&G to abandon its plans.[17]

Major expenditures involved the upgrading and expansion of Charmin's plants in Green Bay and Cheboygan, Michigan. By 1965, Green Bay had become the company's second biggest manufacturing complex after Ivorydale. In April of that year, P&G announced plans to spend even more by building a state-of-the-art plant in Mehoopany, near Scranton, Pennsylvania. Industry watchers saw the move as a direct challenge to Scott Paper, whose headquarters were located not far away in Philadelphia. Comprising 52 acres of working area, the new Mehoopany plant would be one of the largest of its kind in the world. The plant required hundreds of workers, for whom P&G built housing and contributed $100,000 for a hospital.[18] Throughout the 1960s and early 1970s, the company built or acquired additional paper plants in Cape Girardeau, Missouri; Modesto and Oxnard, California; Albany, Georgia; Euskirchen, West Germany; and Belleville, Ontario. In 1969, P&G significantly expanded its forest holdings by acquiring a crown lease on nearly 3.6 million acres in Grand Prairie, Alberta.

The Paper Division also required far more people than did Soap or Toilet Goods. Meeting its enormous staffing requirements meant pulling employees out of the other divisions and hiring and training thousands more. Finding enough support engineers was a constant problem. The Mehoopany start-up, Wells recalled, was a four-year process that was "terribly trying" because new paper machines were being installed about every six months. Wells credited Edwards with finding the talent to staff the new Mehoopany plant. Edwards "knew all the soap manufacturing networks" in P&G, and "he pulled in dozens and dozens—maybe hundreds [of] supervisors and managers from these soap plants and made paper and diaper-makers out of them."[19] For the first six months, qualified managers were so scarce that they had to be flown weekly into Mehoopany from the company's plants in Green Bay.

The CPF Breakthrough

Procter & Gamble remained bullish about the growth prospects for paper tissues and towels. Between 1960 and 1965, the industry grew by 7 percent a year, and by the end of that period, the volume of P&G's paper products surpassed that of many of its soaps and toilet goods. Consumers seemed willing to buy ever more disposable tissues and towels, even though the industry had achieved only small technological improvements in recent years. "There are few secrets to the manufacture of disposable paper products," *Forbes* noted in 1962, so that "almost anyone with sufficient capital can make them." (The magazine hastened to add, however, that making a profit from these products was much tougher.[20])

But the Paper Division was still having problems expanding out of Charmin's original marketing area. Harness was convinced that technological innovation was the key. From the beginning, Mills's engineering staff had worked to improve Charmin's unimpressive performance in blind tests. Puffs, introduced in 1960 to replace Charmin Facial, was the division's earliest and most pronounced success. As engineers began to understand tissue structure, the existing pulp was replaced with one that had a shorter fiber, resulting in a softer paper. Puffs was also the first perfumed tissue, an innovation that came out of engineer Dick Byerly's experience in the Soap Division.[21] Consumer preference for Puffs versus Scotties, the number two brand after Kleenex, shot up from 27 to 75 percent. Enhancements continued on all the products during the next few years, resulting in steady gains over competitors.

With the exception of Puffs, however, the gains were unsatisfying. According to Sanford, most of P&G's offerings were "still 'me-too' products." Incremental changes were inadequate; the existing processes could not simply be done faster or better than the competition. Instead, Harness and the technical staff believed that the division would have to come up with a higher level of improvements that consumers could readily perceive and that would translate into higher brand loyalty. The stakes in toilet tissue were particularly high. Procter & Gamble's paper towel brand, Bounty, was successful in its early markets, but it simply "wasn't big enough to really support" expansion, Artzt explained. To do that, a flagship toilet paper brand was needed, and Charmin "couldn't cut it."[22]

The groundbreaking innovation that changed the outlook for the paper products business was CPF, a process for manufacturing the softer and more absorbent tissue that consumers overwhelmingly preferred. Initially, the impetus for the new technology came not primarily out of a desire to make an improved product but out of the need to cut costs. The idea belonged to Tecklenburg, who believed that reducing the amount of fiber in the towels would result in significant savings.[23]

What began as a cost-saving exercise, however, became the innovation that put the Paper Division on a new and more promising track. Not only did CPF reduce costs, but more important, it resulted in a new fiber structure that produced softer and more absorbent paper. Traditional manufacturing processes were not conducive to these qualities. From the manufacturing point of view, strength was the most important consideration because the sheets had to go through the printers and winders without breaking. The problem was that the stronger the paper was made, the less soft it became. Furthermore, the traditional process limited the tissue's absorbency, because it resulted in too little void space between the individual wood fibers.

In 1962, engineers Larry Sanford and Jim Sisson were given a chance to develop a better sanitary paper tissue manufacturing process. A review of the literature revealed that researchers in Japan were working on forming paper on screens of monofilaments. Following this lead, Sanford and Sisson found that when the water in a wet paper web carried on such a screen was removed by a vacuum, the paper took on the shape of the weave. When dried against a drum dryer, the paper was bulkier, more absorbent, and softer—precisely the qualities that consumers repeatedly said they wanted. Producing this type of tissue at high speed, however, posed additional challenges. When the engineers added an air drying step between the vacuum treatment and the final drying stage, the CPF process became cost-effective.[24]

When he took over as division head the following year, Harness paid close attention to the CPF developments. Experimental runs on CPF paper were begun in October 1963 in Green Bay's East River plant, and a paper machine there was permanently converted to CPF in the summer of 1964. "[We] committed ourselves to Mehoopany and to the process largely on the basis of that pilot plant we had in Green Bay," said Edwards. "So we were up to our necks in CPF before we ever had a commercially feasible machine going. It was risk taking of the highest order." The question was: Could the new process become economically feasible? Each of the plastic webs "cost about ten thousand dollars apiece, and we were busting them after about 90 hours," said Edwards. "I can remember getting on the phone with Harness and saying, 'Well, we got 110 hours out of that one!' But then you'd be down for two days waiting" until the web could be replaced.[25]

The risks were formidable, but as a relative latecomer into the industry, P&G had an important advantage. High capital costs discouraged competitors from making process changes and encouraged them instead to concentrate on using their existing capacity more efficiently. Harness figured that Scott and Kimberly-Clark would find it difficult and expensive to catch up and would not have the will to scrap their older machines. Procter & Gamble's late entry also meant that engineers such as Sanford, who had come from the Soap Division, had to learn papermaking and converting from the ground up. In doing so, they stumbled on innovations, such as CPF, that had escaped P&G's more seasoned competitors.[26]

In early 1964, P&G completed market testing two versions of the new CPF one-ply toilet tissue. One version used the same amount of paper as the pre-CPF Charmin, resulting in an obviously superior product; the other used a lesser amount. Consumers overwhelmingly preferred both versions

These two-ton "parent rolls" waiting to be converted to finished products at P&G's Mehoopany, Pennsylvania facility, suggest the vast scale of the company's investment in manufacturing paper products.

to the old Charmin by a wide margin, seventy-three to twenty-seven. On the strength of these responses, most of P&G's mills were converted to CPF during the next five years, beginning with the East River plant in 1964, at a cost of between $640,000 to $1 million per machine. Delays occurred because the division's ambitious expansion required the mills to run almost at full capacity with little downtime. The bulkier paper also meant that rolls had to be resized and repackaged, another unforeseen delay.[27]

Charmin toilet tissue was the first to be converted to CPF. Procter & Gamble aimed to introduce the improved tissue quickly, aware that competitors would immediately try to duplicate it. Meanwhile, Bounty was improved by means of a process related to the CPF idea of using air to improve absorbency. To make the sheets more absorbent, each layer was embossed before being fitted together into a honeycomb pattern. The improved Bounty was test marketed in January 1965. (White Cloud was converted to CPF in 1967, Bounty in 1968. Puffs was the only brand that remained conventional; it was converted to CPN, a later technology, in 2000.[28])

Marketing and Distribution

By the mid-1960s, all the brands had been significantly improved. Unfortunately, however, every one of the seven perimeter test markets still showed lackluster results. The obstacle remained marketing and distribution. Lacking strong relationships with the trade, the division's salespeople continued to struggle with retailers who resisted stocking P&G's paper brands. The "trade had been given intensive presentations by our competitors on how unsuccessful we were in the early markets," said Artzt. "[Who] needs a brand that's been on the market for five or six years and is a weak number two or a weak number three in its category?" In addition, the trade "felt we were already too important in the household products business, in the personal care business, and they had a nice sort of friendly situation in paper with Scott dominating that market, and Kimberly and [American Can Company's] Northern [tissue brand] having a little piece of it, and there wasn't a lot of price cutting and competitive promotion."[29]

When Harness was promoted to group executive in 1966, he tapped Artzt to fix these problems. Artzt tried to transfer the paper brands to the other divisions' sales forces in the expansion areas, but he encountered resistance from them as well as from the Paper Division salespeople. The situation remained unresolved until the following year, when Owen B. "Brad" Butler, then P&G's head of sales, made the decision that the Toilet Goods Division would continue to sell Pampers, and that Bounty would go to Foods. Butler had Harness's strong support, but the effect was to depress the morale of the

Paper Division sales force even further. "Everybody wanted to leave Paper," Artzt recalled. "Plus, we had trouble recruiting. . . . The Paper business had huge growth potential," but it was "not considered one of the great career places to be."[30]

Meanwhile, an advertising campaign for CPF Charmin had to be developed. Since 1964, P&G had worked with ad agency Benton & Bowles to develop the "Please Don't Squeeze the Charmin!" campaign, featuring the fussy grocer, Mr. Whipple. Procter & Gamble decided to continue using the Whipple campaign for CPF Charmin, which was wrapped in a new, transparent packaging that replaced the older paper wraps. Thus newly formulated, packaged, and marketed, Charmin toilet tissue was launched in Columbus, Ohio, in the heart of the original Charmin marketing area. Artzt recalled that "the thing just took off like nothing had ever taken off before. We knew at that point that we had it."[31]

Success in Columbus finally gave P&G the needed boost to take its paper products into adjacent markets. According to Artzt, "all of the other [sales] people outside of the Charmin area that we were counting on to introduce Paper brands were now excited, whereas they took a look at Puffs and White Cloud prior to that and said, 'That's a headache we don't need.'" Within two years, Charmin was the top-selling bathroom tissue in its marketing area.[32] Meanwhile, P&G was able to communicate Bounty's superior absorbency to consumers. With the help of ad agency Dancer Fitzgerald Sample, Bounty memorably became the "Quicker Picker-Upper."

Expanding the tissue and towel products beyond Charmin's original marketing area took a full decade, during which the Paper Division perfected CPF and overcame serious obstacles to marketing and distribution. By the end of 1969, Harness was able to give an optimistic account of the division's achievements. He estimated that if the unit were combined with Pampers (then still being handled jointly with Toilet Goods) and Buckeye's Cellulose and Specialties Division to form a single entity, "it would be the fastest growing company in the pulp and paper industry. In total sales it would rank near the middle of *Fortune* Magazine's prestigious 'Top 500 List.'" During the 1960s, the division's case volume increased elevenfold, capital employed tenfold, and the number of management positions sevenfold (to seven hundred). Within a few years, the requisite manufacturing capacity would be fully in place to support national expansion of all the division's products.[33]

Pampers: Making Disposable Diapers a Mass-Market Product

Even as the Paper Division struggled to expand, it was also developing a revolutionary new product: an affordable disposable diaper. Until the late 1960s, the project was undertaken with the Toilet Goods Division, in part because disposable diapers initially were sold in drugstores, which had relationships with the Toilet Goods salespeople. Even before it entered the paper product business, P&G had recognized the potential market for disposable diapers. Demographic trends were compelling: More than three million babies were born in the United States every year, and all of them needed diapers for the first two to three years of their lives. Given the baby boom that began just after World War II ended, P&G knew that the number of childbearing-age women in the United States would continue to soar well into the future.[34]

Disposable diapers already had some history behind it. In wartime Japan, shortages of natural materials had led manufacturers to develop synthetics for use in diapers. Although not strictly disposable, the Japanese diaper pointed to the potential to improve on cloth. After the war, an inventor in Sweden developed a two-piece disposable diaper consisting of an absorbent insert and plastic pants. In the United States, Johnson & Johnson introduced a product in the early 1950s under the brand name Chux. By mid-decade, Johnson & Johnson's competitors included Kendall, a leading manufacturer of cloth diapers, and Parke-Davis.[35]

By the mid-1950s, disposable diapers were already found in more than 80 percent of U.S. households with infants, but they accounted for less than 1 percent of all diaper changes. Parents disliked the disposables because they leaked, didn't fit well, and had a tendency to crumble, leaving bits of paper on the baby's skin. Moreover, these so-called disposables were not so easily disposed of, leaving parents—not to mention hotels, motels, and gas stations—with the problem of getting rid of the used products.[36] On the other hand, traditional cloth diapers had serious deficiencies, too. They fit poorly, got soaked quickly, and necessitated the use of plastic pants, which often led to diaper rash and other discomforts. And cloth diapers had to be laundered frequently, an unpleasant task.

Even so, P&G doubted that disposables would ever fully replace cloth diapers. Instead, the company's initial plan was to position disposables as a convenience item, something that parents might use while traveling, for example. An analysis of the market suggested that a better disposable diaper could attract 6 or 7 percent of cloth-diaper users and generate significant revenues.[37] The challenge, then, was to develop a clearly superior product. Accomplishing this goal eventually involved a long partnership between several of the company's divisions. Mills's small Exploratory Division improved on the existing disposable-diaper designs, the Paper Division took responsibility for manufacturing and product development, the Engineering Development Division of Corporate R&D designed the manufacturing equipment, and the Toilet Goods sales force initially took responsibility for selling the new product.[38]

Early in 1956, Mills set up a part-time R&D group at the Miami Valley technical facility to investigate the potential in disposable diapers. Eighteen months later, work was far enough advanced that he could assign a top-flight engineer, Robert C. "Bob" Duncan (son of R. A. Duncan, the detergent pioneer), to lead the project on a full-time basis. (Duncan eventually transferred to Paper Products Development, where he continued to provide technical leadership to Pampers through the early 1970s.) The project turned out to be an extremely complex undertaking. A disposable diaper had to hold as much moisture as two cloth diapers because many parents resorted to wrapping their babies in two diapers for extra absorption. Studies revealed that the size of babies and individual output of urine varied considerably. Other technical problems such as flushability proved just as difficult to solve. To top it off, the product had to be affordable. At first, Mills and Duncan figured that to come out ahead, P&G could not sell the diapers for less than fifteen to seventeen cents each, far too costly to appeal to middle-class budgets.[39]

By early 1958, P&G had a disposable diaper ready for testing. The product consisted of a highly absorbent insert, folded into Z-pleats to form a bucket seat for better fit and absorption, and then encased in separate plastic pants. Procter & Gamble chose Dallas for the test. There the company quickly learned that the hot climate and lack of air-conditioning made parents reluctant to purchase the plastic pants. Sales were so low that some sales and marketing managers recommended abandoning the product altogether. Mills and Duncan dissented, convincing R&D director J. G. "Gib" Pleasants to let them try again.[40]

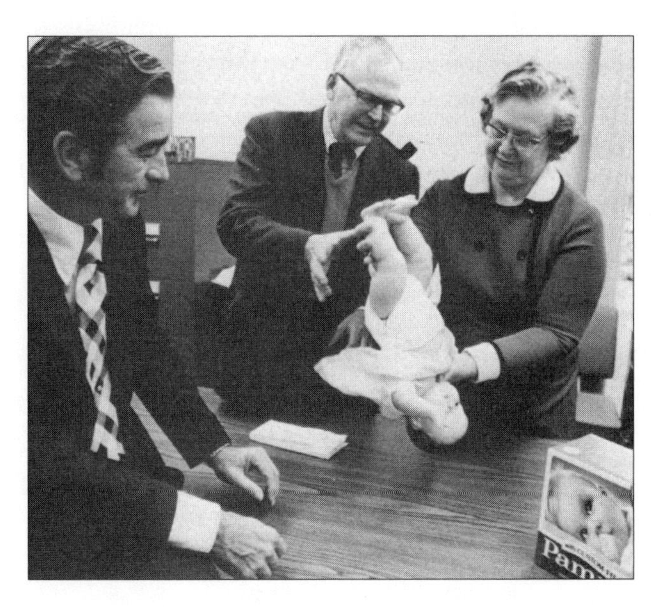

Pictured with patent attorney Richard Witte (left), *inventors Bob Duncan* (center) *and Norma Baker* (right) *demonstrate the use of Pampers on a doll used for the product's original design.*

The product designers went back to the drawing board. This time they focused on developing a one-piece, plastic-backed diaper that would eliminate the troublesome pants entirely. Six months later, an enhanced version was ready to be manufactured, and 37,000 of the new diapers were assembled largely by hand. When a further hundred cases were needed for another small test market, the Engineering Development Division was asked to build a pilot converting line to automate the process.

At first glance, manufacturing a rectangular disposable diaper appears simple: Take some absorbent wadding, fold it into Z-pleats, put the wadding between a stay-dry top sheet and a waterproof plastic back sheet, and then glue the whole thing together using hot-melt adhesives. In reality, the process was the most complex manufacturing challenge P&G had ever faced. The pilot converting line took a full year to be designed and built. The complex folding operation, in particular, determined how quickly the machines could run. To ensure quality, the purchasing departments had to work closely with raw-material suppliers to determine the best specifications for the Pampers materials. Thereafter, the company had to monitor the suppliers carefully to ensure consistency.[41]

Meanwhile, the brand group worked on a name for the diaper. *Pampers* was chosen over a number of others, including *Tads, Solos, Tenders, Dri-Dees, Winks, Zephyrs,* and *Larks*. The improved diaper made its debut in the first test market, Peoria, Illinois, in December 1961, and it contained a number of improvements that were eventually patented. One was a plastic back sheet that extended beyond the sides of the diaper to provide better containment. Another was a hydrophobic top sheet that Duncan designed to keep moisture in the middle layer. The top sheet not only kept the infant's skin drier, thereby reducing diaper rash, but also improved the middle layer's absorbency so that less wadding could be used.[42]

Even with these improvements, test results were mixed. Follow-up research revealed that mothers liked the product, but at ten cents each, the diapers were considered too expensive for regular use. The Peoria test revealed another problem: The company hadn't properly considered that consumers would buy diapers for a relatively short time, about two years per baby. Every month, therefore, a whole new group of first-time parents had to be introduced to Pampers and trained in their use. Research showed that mothers were much more likely to use Pampers if the product had been used on their newborns in the maternity ward. Procter & Gamble began to pay more attention to this channel, deploying its Professional Services group (originally established in 1957 to market Crest) to demonstrate to physicians and hospitals how Pampers could save on laundering costs. At the time, few hos-

By the 1970s, P&G was manufacturing Pampers on high-speed production lines at seven plants in the United States and two overseas.

pitals used plastic pants, so they had to wash not only a lot of cloth diapers but also considerable amounts of soiled bed linen.[43]

Distribution represented another problem. Since disposable diapers were traditionally sold only in drugstores, the Toilet Goods Division sales force saw an opportunity to introduce Pampers into grocery stores and supermarkets. But the salespeople considered Pampers a toiletry product to be displayed with other goods in the category. "That turned out not to be very smart," a marketing manager later admitted, "because when mothers went into the store looking for baby products, they didn't go to the toiletries section, they went to the baby food section." Relocating the product next to the baby food items in grocery stores proved no easy task, because these sections tended to be small and crowded, and diapers were a bulky product. Buyers in the trade initially were reluctant to replace baby food with a product whose sales potential was completely unknown.[44]

For Pampers to succeed, P&G needed to find solutions to all these problems. The first priority was to cut manufacturing costs. Tecklenburg recalled the process as being somewhat of a guessing game. "With a precision completely unjustified by the scantiness and spread of the data, we established the organizational goal at 6.2 cents per diaper," he wrote in an article for *Technology Management* in 1989. At first, P&G believed that it could achieve the lower price by shaving costs off the raw materials and the manufacturing process, but these measures turned out to be inadequate. Instead, something more radical was needed. Pampers would have to be repositioned as a mass-market product that would appeal to a much larger segment of the population. The company calculated that it would have to achieve more than a *five-fold* increase over the Peoria sales without incurring a proportional rise in costs. Manufacturing costs would eventually have to drop to 3 cents per diaper.[45]

Procter & Gamble engineers took on the immensely difficult problem of developing a continuous-process machine that could assemble diapers, one at a time, at high speeds. The new process enabled Pampers to be relaunched at 6 cents each in Sacramento in late 1962. The company had hoped to hit its target volume in seven months, but even at the lower price, it became clear by mid-1963 that the company would not reach its ambitious goal of 4.3 million cases. The price of Pampers was slashed again, to 5.5 cents per diaper, when P&G entered St. Louis in February 1964. Ad copy was changed to emphasize the benefits to the baby's skin. The target volume was achieved in seventeen months—better than Sacramento's twenty-three months, but still not good enough.[46]

The October 1964 launch in Indianapolis proved to be the turning point, reflecting all the lessons learned in Peoria, Sacramento, and St. Louis. The sales introduction went smoothly, and Indianapolis consumers began buying Pampers so fast that shipments were unable to keep up with demand.[47] The company began receiving letters and telephone calls from people asking where they could buy Pampers. Procter & Gamble achieved its target volume in Indianapolis in the hoped-for seven months.

One surprise was the kind of consumer the product appealed to. Originally, P&G had envisioned selling disposable diapers primarily to affluent parents, but when Pampers was launched in major urban areas, the company found that lower income consumers also desired the product. Procter & Gamble once received a phone call from a woman who lived in a New York tenement building. Without Pampers, the woman said, she was forced to take a pail of soiled diapers down four floors and then walk through an unsafe neighborhood to the coin laundry located two blocks away. The same pattern emerged when Pampers was launched worldwide. Consumers in countries where household washing machines and dryers were less common clamored for the product.[48]

Golden Times

Pampers began national rollout on the back of the Indianapolis success. By the time Pampers was introduced in the West Coast and Southeast in 1969, it had become P&G's second largest brand, after Tide. The following year, Pampers became available in the last two states, Hawaii and Alaska. At that point, marketing responsibility was finally transferred from the Toilet Goods to the Paper Division.[49] The pace of rollout was swift compared to P&G's tissue and towel products.

The amount of new manufacturing capacity needed to meet demand, and the complexity of the manufacturing process, resulted in delays. Procter & Gamble started with eight converting lines in the original Charmin company paper plant at Cheboygan, Michigan, in 1964. In all, an average of one line a month was added from 1966 through 1969 in Mehoopany and the other paper plants, eventually making Pampers the brand with the most production lines of any product in the company.[50] Continuous improvement of the diaper also slowed things down. In the late 1960s, for example, product developers substituted a fluff pulp for the original seven or eight layers of tissue, which the manufacturing organization had to learn to mass produce.

Developing the manufacturing lines was not only complicated; it was also expensive. According to a Harvard Business School case study of the diaper industry, in 1974, a basic disposable diaper machine required an investment of approximately $300,000. A complete line, including the building that housed it, cost between $2 million and $4 million. Three or four machines per plant were required in order to spread the costs of buildings, maintenance crews, and other overhead efficiently. Because of the high fixed costs, operating at optimal capacity was critical. The most efficient machines operated during 80 percent of the week and manufactured as many as four hundred diapers per minute. Outside suppliers provided the machines, but each diaper maker added its own proprietary and usually very expensive modifications to the design. Other considerations, such as maintenance and the extent of nonreusable rejects and scrap, also affected manufacturing costs. Learning to make diapers was so difficult that almost all firms experienced problems.[51]

Although often overlooked, P&G's manufacturing organization deserved a large share of the credit for the success of Pampers. In 1969, *Time* magazine characterized the effort that went into Pampers development as "worthy of the creation of a new line of automobiles." Tecklenburg himself compared it to Henry Ford's Model T: "In both cases, the knowledge of the price necessary to capture a mass market forced the innovation of a very efficient manufacturing system." Harness, too, pointed to manufacturing as critical to Pampers' success, commenting that while the "designing of Pampers was a brilliant job . . . the translating of that design into automated high-speed production is an equally outstanding achievement." He observed that in 1962 a competitor had tested a diaper similar to Pampers, but could not figure out how to produce it at high speeds. Consequently, the product flopped. In Harness's view, P&G's engineering personnel had provided the company with a running start of at least four years.[52]

By the early 1970s, P&G's diaper machines were manufacturing Pampers at a speed of 250 a minute, which was soon raised to as high as 400.[53] That pace would have astounded the engineers who had struggled to build the first Pampers manufacturing line some ten years earlier. (Curiously, the manufacturing organizations were later unable to imagine this kind of success for Luvs, the new-shaped diaper launched in 1976.) Instead, most projected a top speed of only 150 a minute. This mistake prevented the hourglass shape from being used on Pampers, P&G's flagship disposable diaper brand, until years after the competition had already done so.

With the success of Pampers, a number of competitors entered the market. In 1965, Borden began testing a two-piece disposable diaper called White Lamb. Baby Scott's went into test market in early 1966 in Denver, Dallas, and Minneapolis. Kimberly-Clark, which had experimented with disposable diapers even earlier than P&G, introduced Kimbies in 1968. Kimbies was priced at parity with Pampers, but benefited from a superior fluff pulp that Kimberly-Clark used in its sanitary napkins. It provided better absorbency and cost savings. Kimbies also featured adhesive tabs, which market research indicated consumers preferred to the pins used by competing products, including Pampers. Procter & Gamble switched to fluff pulp only in 1972 and to tapes in 1973; by 1974, all brands incorporated the tapes that Kimberly-Clark pioneered. Scott Paper, Borden, and International Paper all experimented with a two-piece disposable diaper that used snaps instead of pins.[54]

But the competition simply was unable to achieve P&G's manufacturing efficiencies, and they didn't have the same ability to communicate their products' advantages. In a 1969 speech, Harness expressed his belief that P&G was still several years ahead of the competition, which faced "the same capital investment and start-up problems [that] are largely behind us." By 1970, Pampers had a towering 92 percent of the market; it would soon become P&G's largest brand ever. The next few years saw an industry shakeout as Borden, Scott, International Paper, and Johnson & Johnson exited the business.[55]

Until the late 1970s, P&G's biggest worry was not competitors but adding capacity fast enough to meet demand. The company found itself having to delay expansion until sufficient production capacity could be developed. From late 1968 until 1970, Pampers was on allocation (limited availability) in over half the United States. Demand was so high that some customers bought Pampers at the sidewalk as the delivery trucks unloaded.[56]

With national rollout completed, P&G began expanding Pampers into Canada and Puerto Rico in late 1971 and early 1972. Europe was the next priority. If Pampers could establish an early presence there, the brand would likely become the market leader. At the time, European penetration of disposable diapers in Europe varied widely, with France at 98 percent, and southern Europe much lower. But overall, Pampers would have little strong competition, because although there were several country-specific players, there was no pan-European brand.[57]

Morgens and Harness thought it best to get Pampers into the first test market, Germany, even if this meant paying a high tariff, rather than waiting until P&G could build local manufacturing capacity. Diapers were initially sourced exclusively from the United States rather than produced locally, a strategy that was continued when P&G expanded into the Middle East, Japan, and other international markets. Local manufacturing capacity was built only when the viability of the market had been conclusively determined. Procter & Gamble opened a test market in Saar, Germany, in January 1973 and shipped its year 1 objective in only four months. Based on that success, the Euskirchen plant, near Bonn, was appropriated that summer, the Paper Division's first international plant outside of Canada.[58] Pampers became one of the first P&G products other than the company's traditional soaps and detergents to be heavily marketed outside the United States.

The European rollout took longer than the company anticipated, however. Later, there would be disagreement about why. William Gurganus, president of P&G International, and others believed that the company, struggling to meet demand in the United States, was reluctant to pour more resources into Europe at the expense of the domestic market. John Smale saw it somewhat differently: "[P&G] didn't delay the expansion offshore primarily because the market was growing so great in the U.S. Basically, it was delayed because we were not in that frame of mind." That is, the company was not trying to expand internationally as quickly as possible. Tecklenburg concurred: "[For] an American company, the joy is all here. . . . It's been a hard thing for the American mind to convert to a worldwide focus when two-thirds of the profits for a third of the effort are here."[59]

Artzt, who became group vice president for European operations in 1975, pointed to macroeconomic factors. The 1973–1974 oil shock caused a sudden and painful recession in most of the developed world just as P&G was considering entering Europe with Pampers. Oil prices quadrupled, resulting in huge increases in energy costs. People "were cutting their usage of detergent in half," as well as washing fewer loads, which hurt the detergents business. In 1974, profits in Europe dropped by a precipitous 65 percent, and the company's stock price fell. "We were in total disarray," said Artzt. "With our petrochemicals and the energy-intensive washing machines, we were hit a little harder than most people." Detergent consumption decreased by 7 or 8 percent, "which was just shocking, because we had never seen anything but growth." All the gains P&G had achieved in Europe since the end of World

War II suddenly appeared to be threatened. In that environment, the company was understandably very reluctant to undertake a costly expansion of its diaper business.[60]

Whether or not the European expansion can be characterized as delayed, P&G clearly had entered a new phase. Whereas the 1950s and 1960s were the decades of rolling out detergents internationally, by the late 1970s, attention had shifted to Pampers.[61]

The Paper Products Business in Perspective

The paper business stretched P&G radically. The category, markets, technologies, processes, and capital investment patterns of the business were all new, and P&G moved carefully into the unfamiliar field. For several years, executives focused on improving Charmin's existing products and processes and on learning the business thoroughly before hazarding major new initiatives. Because of competing demands in the Foods Division, Morgens waited six years before committing top P&G personnel. Finally, in 1963, he appointed Harness, one of the company's most promising rising executives, as head of the division and gave him the equivalent of a blank check to pull in several of the Soap Division's top manufacturing people.

Even then, the success of the venture remained very much in doubt, and Harness seriously considered recommending exit. Executives had come to realize that paper tissues and towels constituted a technologically unsophisticated (but capital-intensive) business, dominated by entrenched rivals that held long-established relationships with the trade. In the face of these conditions and with nothing to offer in the way of superior performance, Charmin remained an unprofitable brand contained within a limited marketing territory. "[We overestimated] how well we could do with conventional paper until we had already gotten far into this business and lost a lot of money," Artzt later acknowledged. Only by developing clearly superior products, communicating that message to consumers, and overcoming the reluctance of retailers to stock the new brands could P&G hope to compete against Scott and Kimberly-Clark and to expand into new territories.

But Harness elected not to exit. Instead, he argued that P&G should commit even more capital and people to the struggling business, based on the promise of CPF, a new technology that eventually gave P&G-branded paper products the performance edge they needed to distinguish themselves in the marketplace. Senior management trusted Harness's judgment and, more generally, maintained the long-term perspective the venture required to build winning brands and achieve profitability. Although it took more than a decade to begin paying out, the acquisition of Charmin became the basis of several billion-dollar brands and one of the company's leading growth producers.

The venture also served as the platform for the development of another mainstay brand that became one of P&G's most important contributions to modern material culture: Pampers and the mass-produced disposable diaper. Pampers failed in its first three test markets and looked like an unprofitable niche product. Yet P&G stayed the course, trusting its increasingly skilled product and process engineers to find ways to manufacture disposable diapers at prices that would sustain mass consumption. By the late 1960s, the improved Charmin, White Cloud, Bounty, Puffs, and (especially) Pampers had made the Paper Division one of P&G's most successful forays beyond its traditional core businesses.

CHAPTER SEVEN

Crest: A Therapeutic Breakthrough in Oral Care

LIKE TIDE, CREST toothpaste was a blockbuster brand that reshaped the way P&G viewed itself and its capabilities. Developing the brand's fluoride technology drew the company into the field of therapeutic research. (In medical terms, *therapeutic* refers to the treatment and cure of diseases.) Much as Tide had turned P&G from a soap maker into a technology powerhouse, Crest put the company on the path to health care and pharmaceuticals.

Navigating this new path was difficult, however. By the time it launched Crest in 1955, P&G had become one of the most savvy brand builders in the world, with a deep reservoir of experience in developing and marketing consumer products. But building a brand with credible claims to health benefits meant breaking old habits and learning new skills. Above all, Crest required an unprecedented commitment to strategic partnership. Its new stannous fluoride formula grew out of a closely nurtured relationship with researchers at Indiana University. Once the technology had been developed, the key became persuading the dental profession, specifically the American Dental Association (ADA), to recognize Crest's therapeutic benefits. Unfortunately, marketing strategies adopted for previous P&G dentifrice brands, as well as the ADA's commitment to community fluoridation of drinking water, complicated Crest's initial reception within the dental establishment. Nurturing dialogue with the ADA was critical to overcoming these obstacles, but the attempts tested P&G's diplomatic skills. For the first time, the company voluntarily submitted to an external, professional standard-setting body—a huge cultural shift for a company that had grown accustomed to micromanaging its brand marketing and dictating its own terms to advertising agencies.

Eventually, these efforts and adaptations paid off. From suspicion and outright hostility, the dental establishment eventually came to embrace fluoride dentifrices as a vital part of good oral hygiene. Others in the scientific establishment also came to recognize Crest's revolutionary benefits; in 1976, the American Chemical Society listed the brand's stannous fluoride as among the most notable developments of the previous one hundred years.[1] Crest became the cornerstone of P&G's Toilet Goods business. The product also earned a place in the history of U.S. public health by becoming part of an ambitious project undertaken by government, industry, and the dental profession to attack tooth decay, a serious public health problem until well into the latter half of the twentieth century.[2]

The Dentifrice Market and Fluoride Research

Before World War II, most toothpastes used soap as an emulsifying agent. Encouraged by the success of its Drene shampoo, P&G in 1936 began experimenting with ways to substitute alkyl sulfate for soap in a dentifrice product. The result was Teel liquid dentifrice, introduced in 1938. A liquid dentifrice was unusual for the time, but not entirely new. Liquids and tooth powders antedated toothpastes, and one of the most popular dentifrices during the late nineteenth century was a somewhat unpleasant-tasting red liquid called Sozodent, composed of 37 percent alcohol. Teel initially appealed to consumers partly because of its red color and pleasant cinnamon taste, and partly because of its convenience. Many people used it by taking a little in their mouth before starting to brush, or as a mouthwash.[3]

Dentifrices represented the largest of the new drug products categories and were therefore an important opportunity. But to make a significant impact, researchers knew they needed to identify an area that made a real difference to consumers. As mentioned in chapter 5, when Wes Blair asked the Product Research group to recommend such an area, the group recommended the development of an antidecay dentifrice, which Blair approved. Headed by Verling Votaw, the Product Research group immediately began searching for a chemical entity that would accomplish that goal.[4]

Today, it is difficult to imagine just how bad the problem of tooth decay was in the first half of the twentieth century. Most people were afflicted, and the most common treatment was the painful extraction of the affected teeth. Looking at rejection rate data for the U.S. military indicates the extent of the problem. During both world wars, failure to meet the minimum standard of having only six opposing teeth was the most common reason for rejection from military service. Healthy cleaning habits that might have prevented a lot of tooth decay were not well understood by the public. Studies conducted by P&G found that, in 1939, Americans brushed their teeth an average of less than once a week. Even in 1959, a year before the ADA acceptance of Crest, they were still brushing fewer than four times a week.[5]

When P&G entered the dentifrice business in the 1930s, it focused on three possible approaches to the problem of tooth decay. One was to search for an ingredient that would kill or retard the growth of bacteria that produced the enzymes responsible for decay-causing acids. Another was to try to eliminate the enzymes. The final option was to concentrate on making the tooth enamel more resistant to acid attack. Whichever approach was taken, top management knew that the outlays in time and money would be huge. Eventually, it was agreed that strengthening tooth enamel with fluoride constituted the most promising field of research. Procter & Gamble initiated a joint research program with Boston's Tufts University to investigate the use of sodium fluoride.[6]

Fluoride had been identified as a potentially effective treatment for tooth decay in the early 1930s, thanks largely to the earlier work of a dentist named Frederick S. McKay.[7] His findings might simply have been an interesting prelude to P&G's development of fluoride dentifrices, except that they led in 1931 to the establishment of the Dental Hygiene Unit at the National Institutes of Health (NIH). The unit was charged with continuing the research on mottled enamel, or *fluorosis,* the staining of teeth caused by a person's ingesting excessive amounts of fluoride. The NIH began conducting extensive testing that continued throughout the next three decades. What these scientists learned about fluoride confirmed Dr. McKay's earlier work: Too much fluoride could lead to stained ("mottled") tooth enamel, but in smaller amounts, fluoride was effective in preventing tooth decay. The findings led the NIH increasingly to support the fluoridation of community water sources.[8] These developments were critical to the story of Crest and of fluoride dentifrices generally. In rallying behind the community fluoridation efforts, the dental establishment became less predisposed to support the development of fluoride dentifrices, which they feared would distract the public from the importance of adding fluoride to drinking water.

By 1939, a small group of activists within the dental profession, along with some local officials, were pushing hard to add fluoride to community water supplies. Their persistence eventually carried the day. In 1950, the U.S. Public Health Service endorsed fluoridation; the ADA and the American Medical Association quickly followed. By the early 1950s, nearly the entire dental establishment was behind the fluoridation movement. (A small but very vocal minority of activists, however, resisted the trend. Although the number of communities opting for fluoridation grew quickly during the 1950s, opposition slowed the process in subsequent decades. As of 2000, some 100 million Americans, or about one-third of the population, still had no access to community water fluoridation.[9])

Meanwhile, beginning in 1936, P&G and Tufts University conducted tests of their own on the effectiveness of fluoride. Researchers concentrated on one kind, sodium fluoride, because a recent study of counties in Texas had found that the ingredient occurred naturally in the local water supply and substantially reduced tooth decay. The ingredient was added to Teel, and in 1942, researchers began testing this formula. Half of the test sample used Teel, half used a control dentifrice. The results were mixed, leading researchers to conclude that sodium fluoride's effectiveness, at least when added to dentifrice products, was seriously open to question.[10]

Teel was in trouble on a couple of other fronts. In 1943, the Federal Trade Commission (FTC), with the encouragement of the ADA, issued a complaint against P&G, charging the company with using false and misleading advertising. Procter & Gamble had developed an advertising campaign highlighting the lack of abrasives in Teel. According to the ads, competing tooth-

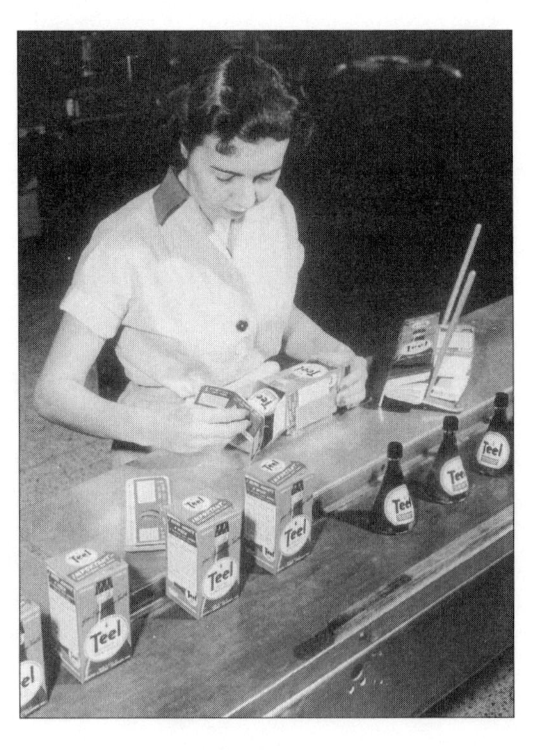

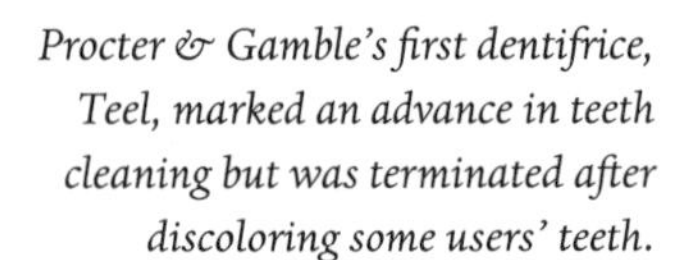
Procter & Gamble's first dentifrice, Teel, marked an advance in teeth cleaning but was terminated after discoloring some users' teeth.

pastes contained harsh abrasives that wore down teeth (actually, *dentin*, or the bone inside the tooth that becomes more and more exposed at the gum line as people age). The FTC took issue with this claim; it also objected to the ads' assertion that Teel's benefits were "revolutionary." Procter & Gamble resolved to fight the ADA's complaint. Votaw explained the reasoning: "If you give in then they're just on you again about something else and . . . you just become a patsy, and you're not running your own business!" The case dragged on until the commission dismissed it without prejudice, ten years after the complaint was filed. By that point, Teel had effectively been taken off the market, anyway.[11] The episode soured the relationship between the company and the ADA, making the association less willing to cooperate when P&G tried to present its clinical results for Crest.

While the FTC case was going on, some consumers began to complain that Teel left a dark stain on their teeth. The complaints perplexed P&G researchers, who were at first unable to identify the cause. Finally, they determined that the culprit was a film on the teeth, which they dubbed *pellicle*. Although transparent, pellicle could be affected by what a person ate, drank, or smoked. In about 20 percent of the population, the pellicle turned into a light- to dark-brown stain. Competing toothpastes contained abrasives, which removed the film. Adding an abrasive to Teel was the obvious solution; the problem, though, was that P&G had developed an advertising campaign touting Teel's lack of abrasives as its main benefit.

Procter & Gamble eventually concluded that a dentifrice without an abrasive could not possibly survive on a national basis, and they finally added one to Teel. But by then, Teel had lost a lot of credibility with the public and continued to be sold only because the wartime shortage of metal tubes (in which the main competitors were sold) severely limited the supply of competing toothpaste products. After the war, additional tests on sodium fluoride again showed mixed results, and researchers continued to debate the benefits of adding it to dentifrices.[12]

Building Alliances: Crest and University Research

By the late 1940s, the embattled Teel was clearly going out of business. The prospect of losing the company's only entry in the dentifrice market was not acceptable. Not only was the dentifrice market large, but there was also the competitive situation to consider. "Colgate was using profits from dentifrice to augment their . . . advertising and promotion of detergents," John Smale later explained. "[We felt] that if we can compete with these guys in dentifrice and in essence make them spend money against dentifrice rather than divert it to detergents, we're going to be better off."[13]

Procter & Gamble decided to initiate a two-pronged approach. The first used existing technology to develop the best possible dentifrice product as quickly as possible. Company researchers resolved to find something that removed the pellicle stain that had become such an issue with Teel, but one that did not damage the structure of teeth. The result was Gleem, a nonfluoride toothpaste. Gleem was not meant to be revolutionary; it made no claims to being therapeutic. Instead, its appeal lay in its superior flavor. Gleem was backed by a successful advertising campaign: "The toothpaste for people who cannot brush after every meal."[14]

The second project involved a contract with Indiana University to develop a dentifrice with stannous fluoride (rather than sodium fluoride) as the active ingredient. This was the project that produced Crest.

The partnership with Indiana University came about because P&G's earlier association with Tufts University had not produced the hoped-for results. Procter & Gamble decided to initiate partnerships with universities located closer to Cincinnati. Eventually, it established links with Ohio State, located in Columbus, and Indiana University at Bloomington. A partnership with a university made sense, according to Votaw: "We can't do clinical tests with any validity ourselves. You've got to have an unbiased professional [research institution] like Indiana University."[15]

Clinical research work was being done on stannous fluoride by a young Indiana University researcher named Joseph C. Muhler. Indiana University alumnus Votaw, who at the time was in charge of P&G's product work on dentifrices and shampoos, had been following Muhler's work closely and went to visit the young researcher in Bloomington. In 1949, P&G gave the university a $7,000 grant for fluoride research. Votaw and Bill Martin, who had responsibility for dentifrices within the Chemical Division, negotiated and signed the agreement in 1950. Procter & Gamble was not the only dentifrice manufacturer showing an interest in fluorides. The NIH's push for community fluoridation had ignited interest among several other toothpaste makers, including Colgate, Unilever, Bristol-Myers, Block Drug, and Warner-Lambert. None, however, focused on stannous fluoride.[16]

Muhler's work gave P&G a hopeful new direction. Even so, adding fluoride to toothpaste led to a serious technical problem that threatened to kill the project. Fluoride lacks stability because it is a chemically active substance that readily combines with other compounds, a characteristic that can render the fluoride itself inert and therefore useless. Company researchers had encountered the problem with Teel, when the sodium fluoride they had added reacted with the product's abrasive compound. Initially, sodium fluoride was to have been added to Gleem. But although its abrasive was differ-

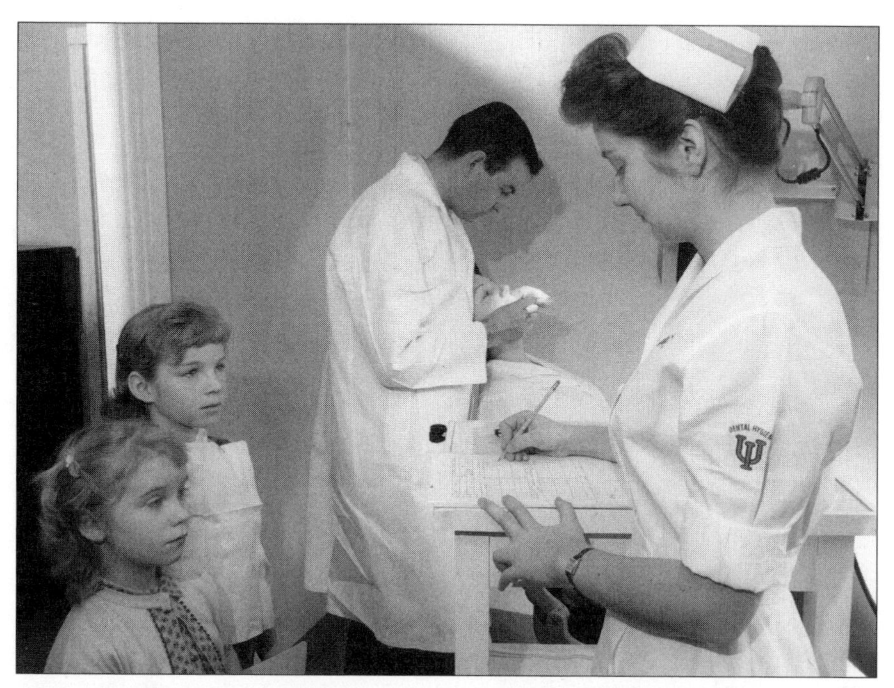

Starting in the late 1940s, P&G supported clinical research on tooth decay at Indiana University. Directed by Dr. Joseph Muhler (center), *the research prepared the way for Crest.*

ent from the one used in Teel, Gleem also had the problem of rendering fluoride inactive.[17]

The stability problem seemed unsolvable. In 1951, Muhler actually began a separate project on his own to search for other ways to deliver stannous fluoride to the population, perhaps by adding it to common foods such as bread, milk, and table salt. But a lucky break the following year put the toothpaste project back on track. Procter & Gamble had assigned the basic work on the abrasive to an Indiana University chemist, William H. Nebergall, in part because the company's process development people were too busy trying to get Gleem into production and could not devote time to developing the new abrasive until late 1951. One of the graduate students working for Nebergall used the laboratory oven to heat a sample of the toothpaste. This simple step converted the abrasive to calcium pyrophosphate, which was much more insoluble and therefore not prone to combine with the fluoride.[18]

What was equally important, the new formula could be patented, whereas simply using stannous fluoride as an antidecay agent could not. The Indiana University Foundation immediately filed a patent application in the United

States and sixteen other countries, under which P&G was granted exclusive license to the formulation in return for royalty payments. Other patents were also issued to company researchers. For legal protection, P&G gave the new formulation the trademark name Fluoristan. At the time, P&G was working closely with Monsanto on developing polyphosphates for use in laundry detergents, so the company had a ready partner to develop the new abrasive on a commercial basis.[19]

Convincing the ADA

The first human clinical test on Fluoristan was launched by Indiana University researchers in July 1952 in Bloomington. During the previous year, Votaw had initiated talks with the ADA in an attempt to interest its technical staff in the experiments. The association was far from welcoming. Chuck Fullgraf remembered that when he and Votaw went to the ADA in late 1951, the secretary of the ADA's Council on Dental Therapeutics, J. Roy Doty, was bitter, even hostile. The problem, it seemed, was that the association had built up substantial animosity toward P&G during the ten-year FTC investigation of Teel, which the ADA had backed. The association had long been frustrated by the inability of the FTC to curb advertising that the ADA regarded as misleading. The environment at the ADA was therefore "very, very hostile," Fullgraf reported, "about as intense as you can imagine." Even so, Doty agreed that P&G could informally show the ADA the results of clinical tests before they were published.[20]

Meanwhile, Gleem entered test market that year and was expanded nationally in 1954, backed by a substantial ad budget that surpassed even the promotion of Tide nearly a decade earlier. Gleem was an immediate hit with consumers, largely because it tasted better than competitors' brands. The toothpaste achieved a national share of 24 percent in 1955, making it a strong number two brand behind Colgate. Gleem's competitor countered by introducing a companion product to Colgate Dental Cream, called Colgate with Chlorophyll. The new product, however, ended up simply cannibalizing the original brand; when Colgate with Chlorophyll was discontinued, Colgate's total share dropped.[21]

By this time, Teel's sales volume was so low that it became impractical to keep the dentifrice in distribution. In 1955, P&G's Administrative Committee decided to suspend the manufacture and marketing of Teel.

Gleem was a success, but P&G forged on with the research on Crest with Fluoristan. Both the company and Muhler hoped that the new formulation would not compete with community efforts to fluoridate drinking water. Instead, they expected Crest to complement fluoridation, which was not yet available in many communities. Besides, unlike Crest's stannous fluoride, the widely used sodium fluoride appeared to have no effect on teeth once children reached a certain age. The researchers believed that there was room for all three approaches—community water fluoridation, sodium fluoride applied twice a year in dentists' offices, and Crest's stannous fluoride.[22]

In 1954, three clinical tests on Crest were conducted on some 3,600 Bloomington children and Indiana University students. The results were immensely positive, indicating a 35 percent reduction in new cavities. Because it planned to promote Crest as a therapeutic dentifrice, P&G had filed a new-drug application with the Food and Drug Administration (FDA) for Crest, the first P&G product ever to go through the process. The application was approved, clearing the way for test marketing to begin in February 1955. Votaw recalled that the process of obtaining the FDA approval was lengthy and that the regulators "were very hard to work with. [They] were anti-business and they had a lot of old chemists. . . . The anti-business didn't show very much—I mean, it didn't come out, but it was there in private conversations and so on. You picked it up all the time." Votaw attributed the FDA's uncooperative attitude to the understaffing of the agency after World War II. He vividly remembered how "one old fellow down there at a meeting got sort of irate, and he said, 'Do you know what we need? We need for you young guys not to invent anything for ten years in order that we can catch up.' Well, that was the attitude!"[23]

Positive test results, and the informal relationship that P&G had cultivated with the ADA, did not at first change the association's skepticism about adding fluorides to toothpaste. (The association's journal, however, regularly reported the results of the clinical tests.) Sales of Crest began in December 1955, for shipment the following month. It was officially introduced on a national basis in January with the campaign theme "Triumph over Tooth Decay." The ADA clearly was uncomfortable with the campaign slogan, believing that the clinical test results did not support a claim that seemed to promise the elimination of tooth decay. Earlier, the association had objected to Gleem's ads, which stated that the toothpaste was "for people who can't brush after every meal." The ADA feared that such claims would discourage people from brushing as often as they should. Bob Broge, the head of technical work, pointed out, however, that "at the time, people were brushing on the average [only] about three times a week!"[24] If anything, the Gleem promotions probably introduced the then-novel idea that people *should* brush after every meal.

In 1955, the ADA's Doty issued a statement responding to inquiries from the trade about fluoride's therapeutic effects: "We know of no present adequate demonstration that any dentifrice presently on the market is significantly useful in preventing tooth decay except as it assists the toothbrush in the prompt removal of sugar residues from the mouth." Doty added that the Council on Dental Therapeutics "knows of no substitute for fluoridation of public water supplies." The following year, Crest suffered another blow when the ADA responded specifically to questions about Fluoristan. In a public statement, the ADA declared that it was "not aware of evidence adequate to demonstrate the claimed dental caries prophylactic value of Crest." The association went on to say that evidence "of the value of adding a fluoride in other dentifrices is even less convincing. Therefore, the Association believes that all fluoride dentifrices are being marketed prematurely." Concerned that the claims made for fluoridated dentifrices would lead the public to a false sense of security, the association continued to insist that community water fluoridation was by far the more effective option. For children, there was the additional danger that the toothpaste would be repeatedly swallowed. The ADA feared that ingestion of large amounts of the fluoridated toothpastes would lead to stained tooth enamel, especially in communities where the drinking water already contained large amounts of fluoride. (Stained tooth enamel was a common occurrence in places with very high amounts of naturally occurring fluoride in the drinking water.[25])

Clinical tests conducted by P&G and Indiana University, however, indicated that Crest had significant therapeutic effects. The challenge lay in communicating that finding to the public. Reduced tooth decay was a difficult benefit to communicate, because users of Crest could not see the results immediately. And although a *reduction* in tooth decay was definitely an improvement, it lacked the drama of complete *elimination* of tooth decay, which no product yet devised could guarantee. Crest's message was also being drowned out by competing claims from other toothpaste makers. Despite the ADA's reservations, the market for fluoride toothpastes was becoming crowded with brands such as Block Drug's Super Amm-i-dent and Colgate's Brisk competing for advertising space. (Neither toothpaste, though, contained stannous fluoride.) Not everyone jumped on the fluoride bandwagon. Ads for Warner-Lambert's Listerine Antizyme, for example, actually emphasized that it did not contain fluoride, thereby taking advantage of the ADA's concern that large doses of the ingredient could be harmful to young children. Even P&G and Colgate continued to promote their nonfluoride toothpastes. Gleem's ads featured the virtues of GL-70 for fighting decay, while Colgate Dental Cream ads highlighted an ingredient called Gardol.[26]

Several members of P&G's technical staff continued to believe that there was some basis for an ADA acceptance. They pinned their hopes on the Council on Dental Therapeutics. Established in 1930 by the ADA, the council's purpose was to appraise and recognize products such as drugs and medical devices. The council served as a guide to the dental profession and helped monitor advertising that made therapeutic claims. When the program began, the council awarded its acceptance to several brands of cod liver oil for their therapeutic effects. But the council also accepted nontherapeutic dentifrices, as long as their claims were limited strictly to their efficacy in cleaning. Colgate Ribbon Dental Cream was awarded an acceptance in 1931 on this basis. Its advertising was careful to state that the product does "what a dentifrice should be expected to do—and the only thing a dentifrice can do—*it cleans teeth*."[27]

Clearly, the potential existed to convince the council about Crest's therapeutic benefits—its proven ability to go beyond mere cleaning and actually prevent decay. Appealing to the council also seemed a natural step, because Muhler and P&G researchers had been informally communicating their findings to the ADA since 1951.[28]

Aware of the association's lingering resentment about the Teel episode, a P&G team initiated monthly visits with the ADA in Chicago. The team included Broge as well as John Smale, who was then a young associate advertising manager for Crest. Smale had begun as an assistant brand manager on Gleem in 1952 and became a brand manager in 1954. The team reached an understanding with the ADA that the technical staffs of both sides would work together to reach agreement on the scientific facts surrounding Crest. It was the first agreement of its kind within the industry. Procter & Gamble agreed that its advertisements would say nothing that the ADA felt was inconsistent with the scientific data.[29]

Marketing Crest to Dentists and Consumers

In 1957, meanwhile, Votaw established the Crest Professional Services group to educate dentists about the benefits of using a fluoride toothpaste. Two years earlier, P&G had mailed the first issue of its *Crest Bulletin to the Dental Profession*. The "dentists started off being very skeptical," said Ernie Lewis, manager of Professional Services. "Most of them had read clinical studies on fluoride toothpastes that showed they did not work [and] assumed that Crest was hype rather than science." From 1957 to 1960, the goal was simply "to get to neutral"; that is, to get dentists to stop expressing doubts about Crest. Face-to-face contact with dentists to present the clinical research, informational pamphlets, and free samples for patients was the key to turning the situation around. In 1960, Votaw began a small detailing operation in a few cities, made up primarily of salespeople from the Toilet Goods Division retail sales force. The "detailers" managed to convince 12 percent of dentists to recommend Crest at least some of the time. Lewis recalled that

"that was considered pretty good." Even so, the operation was strictly considered experimental and did not become permanent until late 1964.[30]

Educating health professionals in order to create a market was, according to Lewis, "highly revolutionary at the time." The Professional Services group experimented with techniques such as direct mail and visits to grade schools to inform teachers and their students about the importance of good oral care. "I think our innovations came about because we really had to do basic Marketing 101 and go back to the drawing board. If we'd had an agreed-upon way to do it, we probably would have never [used the innovative approach], because we would have done it the time-honored, traditional way." The school programs, in particular, were controversial; parents and administrators objected that they were too commercial.[31]

In 1958, P&G introduced a new advertising theme for Crest: "Look, Mom—No Cavities!" created by Benton & Bowles. The company knew it had a lot riding on the campaign. Crest still had not come close to meeting its market objective, and the brand was in a weak fifth place behind Colgate, Gleem, Pepsodent, and Ipana. Procter & Gamble commissioned Norman Rockwell to provide illustrations, which featured smiling youngsters proudly showing off their dental reports. "Look, Mom" was also used in television commercials and became a memorable advertising slogan. But the ADA again objected, calling the slogan a "gross exaggeration and a misleading distortion."[32]

In July of that year, Crest again suffered a setback when the association testified about toothpaste advertising before the House Subcommittee on Legal and Monetary Affairs. The ADA felt that claims made by toothpaste makers misled people into thinking that brushing with these products alone constituted adequate oral hygiene. Sholom Pearlman, assistant secretary of the Council on Dental Therapeutics, went down a list of toothpaste products, criticizing the claims of each one in turn. When he came to Crest, Pearlman admitted that there was some clinical proof behind Crest's claims. But this did not stop him from accusing P&G of sacrificing "scientific integrity for the sake of commercial expediency."[33]

Pearlman refused to make a distinction between Crest and the other toothpastes, in part because researchers had changed Crest's original formulation by adding another ingredient, stannous pyrophosphate, to improve the fluoride's stability. The secretary believed that the original tests conducted on the older formulation no longer counted. He was also pessimistic about the results of tests then being conducted by the Minnesota State Health Department on the new formula. (P&G had also just started two other field studies, one at a military academy in Howe, Indiana, and the other in Bloomington.) As it turned out, Pearlman's criticisms were misplaced. A year later, all three field studies showed positive results. The Howe tests were especially promising and showed that users of Crest had 57 percent less decay than did the control group.[34]

Annual advertising support for Crest had fallen steadily since its introduction in 1956, from $20 million to only $5 million. Yet, in 1959, in the face of growing competition and the seeming intransigence of the ADA, Crest began to show some signs of life, thanks to the "Look, Mom—No Cavities!" campaign. The Professional Services group had also helped convince some dentists. Crest regained fourth place in the market behind Colgate Dental Cream (32 percent market share), Gleem (20.3 percent), and Pepsodent (11.5 percent), none of which contained fluoride.[35]

Earning the ADA's Acceptance

Votaw, Broge, and Fullgraf continued to believe that endorsement by the ADA of Fluoristan's efficacy, a result confirmed by the company's own test data, was a critical factor that would turn Crest from an also-ran to the market leader. "We decided that what we really needed was ADA support," said Broge. "We knew that if we had dental support for that product, we could make a success out of it, because we had been doing some work among dentists who knew the story, and who recommended the product. We had a big share among them; among the rest, we had nothing."[36] Broge's R&D team continued to keep in touch with the ADA and informed the association of new developments.

Finally, in 1959, the ADA agreed to have its Council on Dental Therapeutics review the Crest test results. This time, the council was persuaded by the evidence. In August 1960, the ADA awarded Crest a "B" Provisional Acceptance, the first ever for a dentifrice. Crest, the ADA stated in a public announcement, was "an effective decay preventive agent." The association's press release explained that a "B" Acceptance was awarded to products offering "reasonable evidence of usefulness and safety. They usually are undergoing further clinical dental trials to clarify final status"—meaning that an "A" Acceptance could be granted pending further testing. Concerned that the acceptance of Crest would be taken as a blanket approval of all fluoride toothpastes, the ADA emphasized that the council's "action applied only to this specified product. . . . None of the dentifrices previously evaluated by the council has been supported by evidence which was considered adequate to demonstrate substantial effectiveness"—wording that further enhanced Crest's position. The association was also careful to add that using Crest alone could not substitute for a comprehensive program of good oral hygiene and the continued fluoridation of community water sources, which "remains by far the most effective means for obtaining the benefits of fluorides."[37]

The ADA's about-face was a victory for Crest's research and marketing teams, particularly Smale. He went on to become manager of the Toilet Goods Division in 1966 and then executive vice president in charge of most of the U.S. businesses in 1972. Even when he became chief executive of P&G in 1981, Smale was still known inside and outside the company as the individual who had helped secure the ADA's recognition for Crest. However, the approval was clearly not the result of one individual's persistence; rather, it came about through years of carefully demonstrating Crest's therapeutic advantages. Smale's distinctive contribution, said Lewis, was getting the ADA to focus on the clinical tests as the basis for its acceptance. Smale argued that if the association found the clinical tests convincing, it had an ethical obligation to support the product. Later, he fully supported the idea that influential third parties would be the key to maintaining Crest's commercial superiority. According to Lewis, "John correctly analyzed that the battle would be for the growth in third-party support, and that the [ADA] acceptance was a foundation, not the be-all and end-all." The "breakthrough thought" was that P&G needed to continue cultivating the influence of professional third parties, "which was not just associations, but [also] the dentists on the firing line." Smale became an unwavering champion of the Professional Services group as well as the later programs to introduce Crest to schoolchildren. Later, the Professional Services program grew much larger and involved a number of P&G's other personal care products, including Pampers, Safeguard, and Head & Shoulders. "There's no question," said Lewis, "there were times that if it had not been for John Smale, and in some instances, Howard Morgens and Ed Harness, who became a strong supporter, that the program would have been emasculated, if not eliminated."[38]

Smale himself gave much credit to Harold Hillenbrand, the ADA's executive director. According to Smale, the director "took the position that the ADA was obligated to recognize the efficacy of a product if it was proven efficacious, even though it was a consumer advertised product, because of the potential health benefit to the country—particularly young people. He guided this whole process through the Council on Dental Therapeutics." Muhler's role was also critical. Although some privately described the young Indiana University researcher as a prima donna and somewhat unpredictable, Muhler's persistence and dynamism no doubt lent credibility to the claims. He was "very, very important in terms of the ADA even listening to us in those early sessions," said Fullgraf. Ironically, even the ADA's Doty, who had initially been so hostile to P&G, proved a staunch ally in the end. Fullgraf, Broge, and others remembered how the combative Doty later willingly put his reputation on the line to support the ADA's acceptance of Crest.[39]

Nearly all the country's major newspapers carried the story of the ADA's acceptance during the first few weeks of August 1960. The day after the announcement, P&G's stock opened an hour and a half late on the New York Stock Exchange because so many buy orders were received. By the next day, the shares had gone up by more than 15 percent. Thanks to the "Look, Mom—No Cavities!" campaign, Crest's market share was already above 13 percent and looked set to continue growing.[40] But sales soared after the ADA acceptance. A graph of Crest's historical market share shows the line vaulting upward between 1960 and 1961, a trend that continued until the mid-1970s. By the end of 1960, Crest had replaced Gleem as the nation's second-largest dentifrice brand, and in October 1961 Crest's 28.1 percent share overtook market leader Colgate. Colgate struck back in December with the national introduction of Colgate Fluoride, which contained stannous rather than sodium fluoride. Unilever's Pepsodent introduced its own stannous fluoride toothpaste the following February. But because the large-scale clinical trials necessary to obtain ADA acceptance would take a minimum of two years to conduct, Crest had the clear lead.[41]

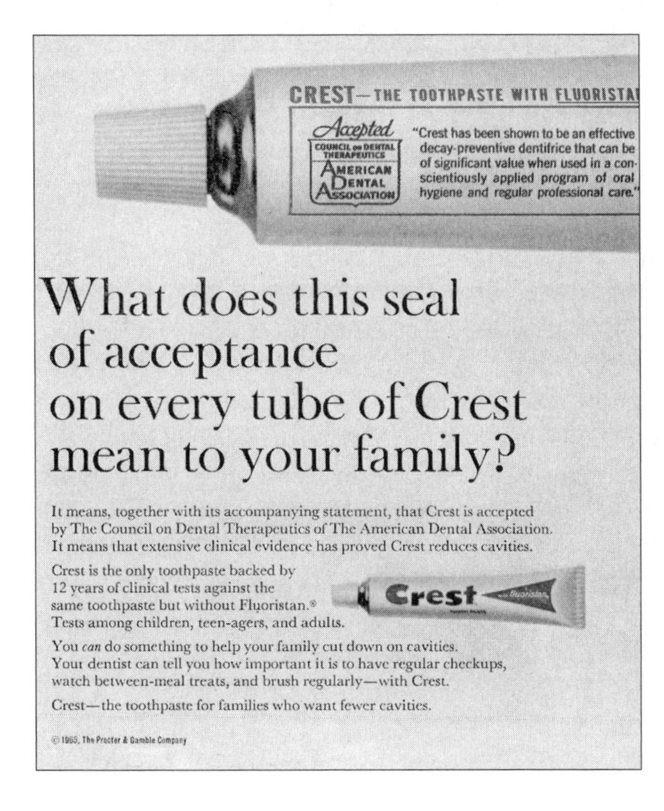

Soon after gaining the American Dental Association's acceptance in 1960, sales of Crest skyrocketed.

Surveys soon showed that dentist awareness of the ADA acceptance of Crest approached 100 percent, and that about 40 percent of them were actually recommending the brand. Demand increased so much that Crest was soon out of stock of some sizes in many geographic areas, and P&G had to run ads apologizing for the shortages. In 1964, the ADA raised Crest's rating to an "A" Acceptance, meaning that it had joined an elite group of products listed in the ADA's annual *Accepted Dental Remedies*.[42] Crest remained the only "A" classified toothpaste until Colgate's MFP was granted the classification in 1969.

The ADA's acceptance was a tremendous coup, but it had important implications for the way P&G advertised Crest. Concerned about how the acceptance would be perceived by its own members as well as by P&G's competitors, the ADA grew even more critical of Crest's ads. Prior to considering Crest for acceptance, the ADA had insisted on its right to review P&G's advertising of the toothpaste, an unprecedented concession that was opposed by some within the company, including chief executive Morgens. "Howard was not at all sure that giving a bunch of dentists control over our advertising was right for Crest," said Lewis. Morgens also feared that it would set a dangerous precedent that might affect other brands. According to Lewis, it was Smale who persuaded Morgens to accept the new restrictions.[43]

One of the first casualties was the "Look, Mom—No Cavities!" campaign, which the ADA thought gave the impression that Crest eliminated cavities altogether. Procter & Gamble was forced to discontinue the immensely successful campaign in 1961 after only three years. Instead, Crest ads began to focus on the successful clinical test results done in Bloomington (Minnesota), Bloomington (Indiana), and the Howe Military Academy. Later, the ads featured celebrity spokespeople such as Bing Crosby's wife, Kathy, and their children, and Nancy Reagan and her children. Smale described how closely the ADA began monitoring Crest's print and television ads: "When we would film commercials on Crest, [the ADA] had a representative there who would also be watching what was going on. Again, particularly when you are filming somebody like Kathy Crosby, the lines can get changed on the spot, and we needed to be sure that the association was comfortable with the change."[44]

The ADA's concerns about how some of its membership would react proved well founded. A number of dentists immediately objected to what they perceived to be the association's inappropriate endorsement of a consumer brand. According to Smale, the backlash was partly due to lack of information. The objectors "didn't really know or understand that ADA procedures provided for" the acceptance. "They assumed that the recognition program was really just for professional products." He added, "The people who were against the recognition did not question the efficacy of Crest. They were concerned about the act of endorsing a consumer product." Within the ADA, P&G found support from Paul Jeserich, the association's president. In a 1960 speech to the ADA Jeserich argued that "the Association would have no more right to withhold news of this scientific development than to withhold evidence of the efficacy of fluoridation of public water supplies. No profession, worthy of the name, has the right to withhold information with such a direct bearing on health merely because it runs counter to present opinion or dismisses some of our present prejudices."[45]

The Crest acceptance was hotly debated in the profession's annual convention in Los Angeles, held just a few weeks after the announcement was made. The issue became even more controversial the following year in Philadelphia, when 52 ADA delegates (out of a total of 416 voting delegates) signed an open letter charging that the endorsement had "become a tool for exploitation by commercial interests." Four North Carolina dentists offered a resolution that called on the association to rescind its acceptance of Crest. A sixty-four-page booklet with essentially the same message was distributed to the Philadelphia newspapers. According to *Newsweek*, however, "the grassroots movement that seemed to center in North Carolina had plainly been seeded in New York—specifically in the offices of P&G's top competitor—Colgate-Palmolive Co."[46] The ADA's house of delegates voted down the anti-Crest resolution, 292 to 72. Proposals were made again the following year, in Miami, but these were easily defeated. After that, the issue simply died away.

Crest had succeeded in delivering the first effective fluoride dentifrice to the nation's population. It paved the way for others, including the products of competitors that had tried to overturn the ADA acceptance. In addition, under the leadership of Paul Flory, who was brought in from P&G's Sales organization, the Professional Services programs convinced dentists that focusing on prevention would not put them out of business. At the time, a significant portion of dentists' revenues came from restorative work and extracting teeth. They had to be convinced that preventative dentistry could be as lucrative, if not more so. Lewis acknowledged that it was not "an easy sale, but that really set the stage for an amazing transformation in dentistry. We convinced the dental schools to start teaching prevention [rather than just treatment]. . . . [It's] safe to say that while one of the things that Crest did was to solve millions of instances of tooth decay, we also by our various actions actually oriented an entire profession from a restorative focus to a preventive focus and did that within five or six years."[47]

As vice president of research, Gib Pleasants and others would later put it, Crest was "one of the most exciting things we have ever done from the standpoint of providing something better for the public."[48]

Oral Care and Crest in Perspective

Crest was not the first P&G brand to grow out of what a later generation within the company would call "connect and develop." Of the company's three most important brands up to 1955—Ivory, Crisco, and Tide—none had been entirely developed in-house. In each case, initial formulas or technologies, or both, had been imported from external sources before being internally adapted and further developed.

With Crest, however, the experience of collaboration played a unique role. Accepting external ideas and cooperating with outside authorities became the driving force behind the development of stannous fluoride, then a central aspect of the brand's subsequent marketing campaign. Crest's success hinged on P&G's ability to negotiate and learn to work with outside partners.

These skills did not come naturally or easily, but ultimately they established Crest as the leading toothpaste in the U.S. market and, in the process, redefined the category. Crest required innovative approaches to marketing because conventional advertising techniques could not effectively demonstrate the brand's therapeutic, anticavity benefits to consumers. Both the dental establishment and the public viewed toothpastes and mouthwashes as cleaning products rather than preventative treatments for tooth decay. Faced with an increasingly crowded shelf of toothpaste brands, consumers had grown wary, and dentists had grown deeply distrustful, about inflated claims for dentifrice products. Procter & Gamble itself had contributed to this environment in its advertising for Teel and Gleem, paving a particularly difficult path for Crest. The efficacy of Crest's stannous fluoride was backed by ten years' worth of rigorous testing, but the company had to earn the trust of both the dental establishment and the public to get a new hearing.

Howard Morgens was initially skeptical about whether P&G would be able to secure the ADA's acceptance and if it would even be worth the effort. But others, including Verling Votaw, Chuck Fullgraf, Bob Broge, and, later, John Smale, realized that third-party endorsement of Crest by dental professionals and other experts would succeed where traditional marketing had failed. The result was a product that not only changed the dentifrice category, but also contributed significantly to the betterment of dental health within the United States.

CHAPTER EIGHT

Learning from Augusta, Lima, and Albany

ONE OF THE GREATEST LEGACIES bequeathed by the founding families to Procter & Gamble involved human relations, a philosophy and set of policies that sought to align and bind together the interests of the company and its employees. The philosophy was well expressed in an oft-quoted saying of Red Deupree: "If you leave us our buildings and our brands but take away our people the Company will fail. But if you take our money, our buildings and our brands, but leave us our people, we can rebuild the whole thing in a decade."[1] The policies included a range of measures, starting with profit sharing in 1887 and an employee stock purchase plan in 1892, continuing through steady employment (a guarantee of at least forty-eight weeks of work per year for eligible employees) in the 1920s, and a variety of medical and insurance benefits negotiated with independent unions in the 1940s and 1950s.

Procter & Gamble's philosophy and policies reflected a deeply held view that meeting employees' needs is good for business. The company's leaders believed that when employees have real ownership and share meaningfully in the fortunes of the business, they work more efficiently and productively. That behavior, in turn, supported the company's ability to keep its operating costs low—an essential part of building and sustaining brands.

But P&G did not always experience the best of relationships with its employees. After World War II, a time of trouble coincided with intensifying competitive rivalry and prepared the way for another significant milestone in employee relations: the introduction of the technician system, an early experiment in high-performance work systems. Innovations began in the early 1960s with a new work system design for a new detergent plant in Augusta,

Georgia. From there, they spread to other new facilities, including a Lima, Ohio, laundry products plant that achieved extraordinary business results, as well as to traditional operations. In the 1970s, P&G added another dimension to its employment policies by embracing race and gender diversity and making it a key design element at a new paper products plant in Albany, Georgia. Lessons learned at Augusta, Lima, and Albany remain at the heart of the company's twenty-first century integrated work system and its commitment to cultivating a diverse workforce.

The Technician System at Augusta

In the early post–World War II years, P&G experienced numerous minor labor disputes in its operations. The disputes concerned job rights and jurisdictions, performance evaluation, discipline, time bonus incentives, overtime distribution, and the contracting-out of work. Earlier agreements with P&G's independent unions had set the stage by giving the independent unions a strong voice in these matters. The unions had also become more vigorous in policing the contracts inside the plants. Management's attempts to bargain for more flexibility made little headway, because the unions were not interested in changing the status quo. Meanwhile, operating matters that management once handled routinely were now subject to continuing—frequently contentious—discussion and negotiation.[2]

From management's perspective, the imperative to address this problem arose soon after the opening of a brand-new detergent facility in Sacramento in 1953. Built to keep up with the soaring demand for Tide, the plant boasted the latest and best technology and was started up and staffed by experienced employees from other P&G facilities. The company's high hopes for Sacramento soon crashed, however. Employees brought with them the same contractual restrictions and adversarial attitudes that had developed in the older plants. Meanwhile, transfer of many employees added costs and triggered some personal and personnel problems among people dislocated from their families and friends. All these troubles showed up in the plant's disappointing results in cost, volume, and productivity.[3]

As the company looked ahead to the opening of additional new plants in laundry products and its newer businesses in food and paper products, it clearly needed to find a better way. In the late 1950s, P&G began looking for better ways by forming a small organization development group under Philip Willard in the corporate engineering organization. Responsible for designing new facilities, the group also began investigating fresh approaches to industrial relations and job design being developed at the Massachusetts Institute of Technology (MIT), Harvard Business School, University of Michigan, University of California–Los Angeles, and other institutions. Plans to open yet another new detergent plant in Augusta, Georgia, in 1963 offered an opportunity to put the new thinking to the test.

David Swanson, a young member of the Augusta design team, recommended that P&G retain one of his MIT professors, Douglas McGregor, as a consultant. Author of the influential book *The Human Side of Enterprise* (1960), McGregor believed that most industrial companies, which were organized as top-down, control-oriented hierarchies, failed to tap the full potential of their employees. This way of organizing and managing, he pointed out, rested on several unstated assumptions about human nature: (1) People have an inherent dislike of work and will avoid it if possible; (2) people need to be directed, want to avoid responsibility, have relatively little ambition, and want security above all; and (3) people need to be coerced, controlled, directed, and threatened with punishment to put forward adequate effort.[4]

McGregor characterized these assumptions as Theory X and rejected it in favor of what he called Theory Y, whose elements include the following: (1) Putting forth physical and mental effort in work is as natural among humans as play or rest; (2) the capacity for learning, ingenuity, creativity, and imagination is widely distributed in the population; (3) most people do not dislike work, although they may be placed in jobs that make them unhappy; (4) external control and threat of discipline are not the only or even the best motivational tools; and (5) commitment to objectives is directly related to rewards attached to achieving those objectives, including satisfaction of ego needs. The organizational implications of Theory Y were profound and extensive, calling for new administrative structures and ways of working.

The work design at the Augusta plant clearly reflected McGregor's influence. It was a nonunion facility. Employees were called technicians and were paid salaries. Top management in the plant committed to frequent, regular communications with the technicians about the state of the business, sharing information about safety, quality, productivity, and financial performance. Previously, the company had traditionally guarded this information closely. The idea, an observer later wrote, was "to build the technicians' knowledge of the business right up to that of the managers."[5]

The new building featured several conference rooms so that managers and technicians could meet in places other than the cafeteria or parking lot. The conference rooms also hosted regular meetings of the technicians. An adjustment to the production schedule called for thirty minutes of overlap at each change of shift. Technicians on the outgoing shift could thus share information with those succeeding them. Each shift was organized into work groups of about a dozen people. These groups were largely self-managed. For example, they scheduled production, hired peers, evaluated peers and managers, and interviewed prospective recruits. Role descriptions were defined broadly, and technicians performed a variety of operating and some maintenance tasks. Their pay could rise with mastery of certain skills. Finally, management invested heavily in establishing a positive work culture through formal and informal communications.[6]

Procter & Gamble's original objectives at Augusta were "quite modest," Swanson later recalled. "All we were trying to do, basically, was [to] eliminate the operating inflexibilities and reduce the level of conflict between managers and non-managers that had crept into our traditional plant operations over the years." He explained how the company would accomplish this: "We were trying to take away the rule book and substitute principle for mandate. The hypothesis here was that we wanted people to reach for responsibility."[7]

In fact, the achievements and innovations at Augusta proved quite dramatic, as Swanson again recounted, listing seven in particular:

1. Eliminate barriers between people—especially between managers and workers

2. Establish common objectives among all employees

3. Encourage genuine employee participation in the business by sharing important information

4. Substantially improve two-way communications by means of regular team meetings

5. Design a progression system that was based on skills acquisition and teamwork as opposed to seniority

6. Encourage change and high productivity in the absence of a monetary incentive

7. Establish and maintain a work environment in which employees would conclude that it was in their own best interest to operate without a union[8]

The Augusta plant proved extremely successful, with productivity levels by the mid-1960s about 30 percent above those of conventional detergent plants. Manufacturing managers, moreover, appreciated the technicians' flexibility and willingness to accommodate change. These results attracted the attention of top corporate executives, who encouraged the spread of the technician system to other plants on the drawing board as the company sought to meet soaring demand for its products in an expansive era. The Augusta plant was the first of ten new facilities P&G built or occupied in the United States between 1963 and 1975 as the laundry, paper, diapers, and food

Procter & Gamble's New U.S. Plants, 1963–1975

1963	Augusta, GA (laundry detergent)
1966	Mehoopany, PA (paper products)
1968	Lima, OH (laundry and cleaning products)
1969	Alexandria, LA (laundry detergent)
	Cape Girardeau, MO (paper products)
1971	Jackson, TN (food products)
	Modesto, CA (paper products)
1972	Albany, GA (paper products)
1973	Oxnard, CA (paper products)
1975	Greenville, NC (food products)

businesses boomed.[9] All these new facilities would feature the technician system, and all were successful in remaining nonunion.

Lima Concepts

After Augusta, the next new laundry plant to come on stream was in Lima, Ohio, a small city about one hundred miles north of Cincinnati. The plant was designed to make Downy fabric softener and Biz, a presoak (later described as a detergent booster and eventually reformulated as a color-safe bleach before being sold in 2000). The plant featured the latest and best systems in computers and factory automation, but its true distinguishing feature was the human systems around the technology. Although it drew on learning at Augusta and at Mehoopany, a paper products plant opened in 1966, Lima represented another major step forward in the empowerment of the workforce.[10]

Procter & Gamble chose the Lima site after carrying out the usual analyses of plant locations, looking at transportation networks, energy sources, workforce demographics, local incentives, and other factors.[11] In this instance, the company also valued a location near, but not too near, Cincinnati. Lima was close enough to enable corporate and division managers to keep a watchful eye on the plant but far enough away to remain isolated from the company's traditional ways of operating. James Ewell, corporate vice president of manufacturing, insisted that the new plant would avoid the inefficiencies of the traditional plants, and he protected it from the imposition of existing P&G policies, procedures, or staffing models that might have threatened a new way of operating.

Planning for Lima's work system began in 1966 under Bob Seitz and Charlie Krone. A manufacturing division manager and a former plant manager at several older facilities, Seitz was acutely aware of the problems and rigidities

Autonomous teams are a source of constant innovation and high efficiency at the Lima, Ohio, plant, which produces liquid detergents.

in the traditional plants. Krone hailed from a recently established corporate organizational development group formed to assist with implementation of the technician system in the new plants and the change initiatives elsewhere. He was a proponent of "open systems," the notion that organizations are living, organic entities that grow through constant interaction with and adaptation to their environments. As an observer later put it, an open-system organization "would never be 'finished'; it would never stop learning and evolving during its lifetime." The Lima plant came to embody these concepts.[12]

Like Augusta and other new plants, Lima was nonunion, with salaried technicians assigned to relatively autonomous work teams as the fundamental unit of organization. The only nonoperating (off-line) positions were the plant manager, the manager's administrative assistant, the personnel manager, and the accounting manager.

The plant was divided into separate businesses for Downy and Biz, with work teams of technicians and managers running each. Roles within teams were based on mastery of skills. These skills were divided into three levels: operation of the equipment, maintenance of the equipment, and improving the business and providing leadership to the teams. The technicians received no operating or maintenance overtime and no incentive pay. There were no first-level supervisors or general department supervisors—just managers acting as resources to the teams. Nor were there any barriers to cooperation inside the business or outside with suppliers, customers, or other parts of P&G.

Any technician could perform any job consistent with safe operation. The teams chose new members, decided who would do what work, what training might be required and how it would be obtained (even on the outside), and which projects to pursue. They even interviewed prospective managers. Rotation included both on- and off-line assignments. A technician could perform not more than two nonoperating jobs before returning to an operating position. Team leadership roles changed as required. The teams handled their own disciplinary matters, a responsibility they took very seriously and with standards stricter than those in traditional plants.[13]

Dave Guffey, the first plant manager at Lima, led the on-site management team that did the initial technician hiring. Lima sought individuals with entrepreneurial instinct, mechanical aptitude, and the ability to work as a team member—an unusual combination. As the final step in the hiring process, Guffey talked with each applicant before an offer of employment was made.

Lima began production in 1968 and quickly established itself as by far the most productive and efficient plant in P&G's system. The plant also recorded outstanding results in quality, safety, and control of absenteeism. Stories of breakthrough performance became legion and legendary inside the company. Some were amusing, such as the time when a team of technical people from a supplier came to install some equipment. They were met at the gate by a technician. One of the supplier group indicated that they were supposed to meet with an electrician, a machinist, and a pipe fitter from the plant to help them. "You're looking at her," said the technician.[14]

On another occasion in the early 1970s, Downy had become a major success and was on allocation throughout the United States. Retailers complained about short shipments and prompted top division managers to look for ways to expand capacity quickly. Some believed that the Lima workforce simply lacked the skills, especially in electrical and mechanical work, and could not be trained fast enough to get them. The division managers began making plans to hire extra technicians and skilled tradespeople in the community to help ramp up production. Seitz would have none of this, however. He made the two-hour drive to Lima and called a meeting of the Downy technicians to explain the situation and describe the necessary actions. Then he arranged for production to shut down for a week while the technicians made plans to run the lines faster and acquired the training to do the work themselves. After a week, the plant came back on stream and ran flat out to meet the orders for Downy.[15]

On still another occasion, a determined technician developed a revolutionary new process that changed the liquid fill industry. According to Seitz, the technician had watched the inefficient way that bottles of Downy were filled. Bottles came in from the supplier in cases, from which they were removed, filled, capped, and then put back in the case for shipping. The technician believed he could fashion equipment to enable the bottles to be filled and capped in the case, thus saving several time-consuming steps. The technician made his proposal to the Downy team and in turn to P&G. The project was funded, and the technician oversaw the installation and operation of the new equipment. The process worked as designed, resulting in significant savings for P&G along the way.[16]

Such performance garnered widespread attention inside P&G. As a result, many other P&G operations sent visitors to observe and appropriate as many techniques and lessons as they could.

The Diversity Dimension at Albany

By late 1971, when P&G was laying out plans to build a new paper products facility in Albany, Georgia, the company had already learned much about the benefits of the technician system, not only from Augusta and Lima, but also from Mehoopany; Cape Girardeau, Missouri; and Modesto, California, in paper products and Jackson, Mississippi, in food products. The company had accumulated ample evidence that the system could be scaled up from plants with a few hundred technicians to those with a thousand or more.

Race Relations

The principal difference between Albany and other technician plants stemmed from the company's commitment to making the plant work in a community with sharp racial divisions. Improved race relations and equal-opportunity performance was much on the minds of senior managers, and both Howard Morgens and Ed Harness addressed the topic at the company's end-of-year management meetings in 1971. "We must and we will continue to offer equal opportunity to blacks and to all other minority races," declared Morgens. "Furthermore, we must hire and train them up to the point where equal opportunity is meaningful. We must do this first of all because it is right to do and, secondly, because if we don't—this country will suffer greatly and we will all suffer along with it."[17]

In selecting Albany, Georgia, for the new plant, P&G chose a volatile site to put its principles to the test. Albany had a long history of segregation where the white power structure was extremely reluctant to desegregate. Albany witnessed a wave of civil rights demonstrations, and Martin Luther King, Jr., was jailed there on three separate occasions during 1961 and 1962. Massive protests continued, but four black churches were dynamited or burned during the disturbances. After one incident, twelve thousand U.S. National Guard troops were called in to restore peace.[18] In the end, the old guard grudgingly gave way and schools and other public facilities were integrated. Racial tensions subsided, but undercurrents remained. In the early 1970s, this history was fresh in everyone's minds, following a decade in the United States that had witnessed the major achievements of the civil rights movement but also a bitter aftermath—the urban riots in predominantly black neighborhoods of many Northern cities and the assassination of Dr. King.

At the outset, senior management in the Paper Products Division, including Jim Edwards, Charlie Carstarphen, and Dave Swanson, intended that the workforce at Albany would reflect the demographics of the local labor market: 60 percent white and 40 percent black, and an eighty-to-twenty ratio of males to females. Swanson recalled that P&G made this decision easily, knowing it was the right thing to do. But the company also recognized that it would need more than the usual amount of investment in design and training to make the plant a success.[19]

As at the other technician plants, the work systems design team included division and plant managers as well as an internal organization development

The paper products plant in Albany, Georgia, taught P&G valuable lessons about managing a diverse workforce and has also ranked as one of the company's top performers year after year.

consultant. Herb Stokes, who had participated in the design of the Modesto and Jackson plants, became the internal consultant at Albany. And like the other new plants, Albany would be designed using an "open socio-technical systems design" approach.[20]

Planning proceeded in phases. First came the setup of teams, which would be headed by the first Albany- and Cincinnati-based managers assigned to the plant. John Feldmann was the first plant manager. The next step occurred in March 1972, when about sixty people now engaged in planning the start-up met for two weeks in sessions that Stokes and his colleagues facilitated. The group included five African Americans: three managers assigned to Albany, one in Cincinnati, and a facilitator. The purpose of the sessions was to develop the preliminary design of the work systems before the start of hiring in the summer. The group broke up into subgroups to address issues ranging from identifying the major problems and constituencies in the plant's environment, especially in local government and the community; to the operating systems, support systems, and administrative systems in the plant; to the sequencing of the start-up; to long-term plans and other issues for the plant.

The work went smoothly until the second day of the session, when the company's hiring goals began to generate controversy. According to Stokes's record of the session, some in the group (whites, presumably) wondered "whether or not the Blacks would be able to do the work required, whether they would need preferential treatment (double standards). . . . This generated quite a bit of discussion. There was a lot of exchange between the black and white participants in the group." The group came to no consensus, but decided to form a racially mixed task group to explore the matter further.

After several more days of grappling with the issue of race relations, the task group "had what they called a 'tremendous experience,'" Stokes reported. "More or less spontaneously, they decided to explore their own feelings about the issues and proceeded to do so by sharing myths or stereotyped notions that whites had about blacks and vice versa." They debated the validity of these stereotypes and then talked about how their personal feelings and perceptions had changed as a result of their discussions during the session. The outcome of the session was a decision to put the race relations issue front and center in team building and training among the entire workforce of the plant.[21]

Procter & Gamble also reached outside for help with the race issue, retaining Price Cobbs and Ron Brown, two African American consultants. A psychiatrist, Cobbs had gained some notoriety in 1969 as the coauthor of *Black Rage,* a provocative book that probed the psychological effects of the informal, latent discrimination against blacks that persisted despite the civil rights legislation. Cobbs believed that much of this discrimination was rooted in unspoken and unexamined assumptions that both whites and blacks held about each other. He contended that true progress in race relations would ensue only after these assumptions were exposed. Racism, in short, was a pathology that could be treated with therapy, like other psychological disorders. Cobbs and Brown called their approach "ethnotherapy" and sought to force the members of work groups to face up to their unstated beliefs and assumptions about race.[22]

The first of a series of racial awareness workshops occurred in August 1972. The initial group consisted of thirteen managers, including eight whites and five blacks, drawn from the division and plant. They met over two days at a hotel near the Atlanta airport. The consultants ran a series of exercises and discussions to help surface hidden assumptions and preconceptions and to raise awareness of racial issues. After the session, Cobbs and Brown reported on their findings: "There was the predicted stereotyping of blacks with regard to their dispositions and capabilities but for this group anyway many of these attitudes were examined. A corollary of this phenomenon was the stereotyping of whites as to who was racist, liberal, or committed. If this is not strongly worked with there are, among other things, two disastrous outcomes. Blacks will feel that they must constantly prove their abilities and certain whites will feel that they must constantly prove their attitudes."[23]

The meeting produced several important outcomes. Managers of each race became more sensitized to the outlooks and perceptions of the other. "This was an intense and painful session," recalled Swanson, one of the senior whites in attendance. "It was difficult to have our views examined so thoroughly and unrelentingly in front of others. But it was eye-opening and it indicated that we had a lot of work to do on the race issue, not just in Albany but across P&G." At the same time, the meetings surfaced some black issues and concerns that the whites had not fully appreciated. For example, the local housing market was still segregated; black managers were unable to buy homes in certain areas of the community. As a result, P&G put together a housing task force led by plant manager Feldmann and used its influence with real estate agents, banks, and local government officials to break down racial barriers. Other significant outcomes included revamping the hiring process to expose and eliminate racial biases in job interviews; setting concrete goals to ensure that both races would be represented in approximate proportions on all teams, projects, and areas of the plant; and adding race relations workshops to the training that new managers and technicians would receive. The plant also hired a full-time racial interface manager, Jarrow Merenivitch, an organization development specialist and African

American who had been part of P&G's internal consulting group and who had participated in the design meetings in Cincinnati.[24]

As hiring for the plant began in the summer of 1972, P&G took care to ensure that its diversity goals were met. The company also recruited many of its black managers and supervisors from elsewhere in the division and company to ensure that management ranks at Albany were appropriately balanced in racial composition. As the plant geared up for production, all managers attended racial awareness workshops, as did, eventually, all technicians. Based on postworkshop surveys and interviews, Cobbs claimed that "the workshops have been able to facilitate beginning changes in racial attitudes" and pointed out that "discussions of racial factors have been legitimatized in the plant." As a result, he noted "a tremendous shift in the Plant climate resulting in a decrease of apprehension regarding the ability of blacks and whites to work together." Meanwhile, Merenivitch developed a so-called Racial Attitudes Sensing System to help catch potential incidents at an early stage before they flared up into major problems. This system consisted of a Race Relations Task Force with representatives drawn from each shift and area of the plant and equal numbers of blacks and whites. The task force met monthly and used surveys, interviews, and feedback sessions to ascertain emerging issues.[25]

Another key step was the formation of a Black Managers Task Force in January 1973. Initially, it served as a support group for black managers dealing with common problems in the community, such as the need to find suitable housing. It soon evolved into a more general support and advocacy group within the plant. For example, it pushed for modifications to recruiting and training and development policies to provide more opportunities for blacks in technical assignments and higher management ranks. The task force also succeeded in gaining sponsorship for a Black Manager Development Seminar and for changes in performance evaluation systems to overcome racial biases.

Gender Relations

Procter & Gamble was more visibly concerned with managing relationships between the races than with managing gender issues in the work place in the early years of the plant. The larger numbers of black employees (some of whom were female) and the potentially volatile context of local history made race relations a higher priority. Nonetheless, P&G also invested in making Albany a safe and productive working environment for female managers and technicians. There were some surprising discoveries, recalled Merenivitch, whose responsibilities included managing not only race relations but also gender relations. It was unusual for white women in the community to work in factories, for example, and initially, some women were embarrassed to be seen as blue-collar workers. They "would dress up as if they were going to the office, and come to work and change clothes and work. Their neighbors never knew they worked in the factory."[26]

The March 1972 design meetings had defined successful integration of women in the workforce "in terms of [their] being able to influence the organization, to learn and use new skills, not be discriminated against because of sex with regard to pay and advancement possibilities, and not lose individual identity." In working toward achieving that definition of success, P&G used methods similar to those used in dealing with race relations: high-visibility policy statements from senior corporate and plant executives, identification and removal of biases in interviewing and hiring, and training programs and workshops in gender awareness issues.[27]

In 1973, the company retained an outside, Dallas-based consultant, Nina Rosoff, a recent Ph.D. in organizational behavior, to lead the workshops and train Albany personnel to take over in the future. Rosoff employed an approach similar to ethnotherapy in the workshops, examining stereotypes and unstated assumptions in gender relations and leading the participants in developing new objectives and guidelines to govern their conduct at work. The workshop participants credited the sessions with stimulating significant changes in their beliefs and behaviors. One male participant, who had been reluctant to ask women to carry out what he perceived as physically demanding jobs, emerged more likely to assign women to almost any mechanical or operating task. For their part, many of the women recognized how their own behaviors fed the stereotypes. They vowed "to tackle previously 'frightening' jobs and be more aggressive in seeking out opportunities to learn and develop new skills." Finally, the workshops cumulatively developed an agenda on gender relationships for the attention of plant management, calling for more women to occupy managerial and technical roles and more training while recommending the formation of a plantwide task force to address gender issues on an ongoing basis.[28]

Early Returns

The actual work systems design at Albany resembled that at other technician plants, although it was not as self-governing as Lima. The plant was divided into modules based on stages of production, and within each module semiautonomous work teams constituted the basic organizational unit. The work teams were multicultural, balanced by race and gender. Other proven features of the technician system were present: a minimum number of job classifications, job rotation and skill-based progression and pay, boundary-spanning teams, frequent communication on goals and performance between management and each team and within each team.

The care that went into planning and operating Albany paid handsome dividends. At the outset, management had aspired to exceed the start-up at Mehoopany, which had taken more than three years from conception to operation at peak capacity. Albany achieved peak capacity in less than two years. Almost immediately, the plant ranked as the top performer in the division in virtually every important category: safety, productivity, quality, and cost.

Some of Albany's success was due to state-of-the-art equipment and the incorporation of lessons learned at other new plants in the division—the newest plants are often the most productive—but the designers credited the unique work culture at Albany stemming from the decision to have a diverse workforce. In the mid-1970s, research by Harvard Business School professor Richard Walton, an expert on high-commitment work systems, corroborated this view. As Merenivitch reported, Walton found that "the focus on people dealing effectively with conflict essentially helped the teams be more effective in working out their technical issues, because they were trained to not just sweep under the carpet issues of race—which were very tough to deal with. The spin-off effect was that [Albany] was a more effective technical organization as a result of what [we] had to go through in the early days."[29]

Albany justified the hopes of its designers in becoming a model for how to manage race relations specifically and diversity more generally. Looking back on the experience, Merenivitch was struck by how much progress occurred so quickly. "What I saw happen was that technicians who had never even looked at each other seriously on a human level started going fishing, started having beers after work, relating."[30] These attitudes and relationships gradually spilled over into the community, which became not only legally but also practically desegregated, with blacks and whites living together in the most desirable neighborhoods in the area. The plant, meanwhile, became a training ground for many black managers in P&G, including some who rose to senior ranks in manufacturing and in the company generally. Procter & Gamble's first black plant manager, Bob White, started as a supervisor in Albany and became plant manager there in 1984. By the twenty-fifth anniversary of the start-up, four African Americans with management experience at Albany had become corporate vice presidents. The company's current vice president of global diversity, Al Collins, served as human resources director at Albany in the mid-1970s. The company's first female plant manager, Mary Anne Gale, also served a stint in the Human Resources Department at Albany. (Gale is presently corporate vice president, global supply-chain operations.)[31]

This is not to claim that P&G succeeded in creating a small utopia at Albany. Indeed, the Black Managers Task Force and subsequent task forces for female managers and technicians continued to push the company and plant managers hard to make more progress toward diversity goals at a faster rate. But in Albany, the company developed an excellent training ground for dealing with and learning from the workforce management issues of the late twentieth and early twenty-first centuries.

Outcomes and Influence

During the 1960s, 1970s, and 1980s, the work systems at Augusta, Lima, Albany, and other technician plants proved themselves again and again. Augusta remains a model of manufacturing excellence forty years after its inception. Lima is one of the company's most productive plants and succeeded in becoming a sole-source operation for popular liquid detergents in the mid-1980s. Albany's results are nearly as impressive: It has been one of the Paper Products Division's top performers for many years.

Although work systems in the various technician plants differed from one plant to the next, P&G identified their common characteristics. These shared attributes became the basis for designing and planning more new plants, not only in the United States but around the world. In the 1980s, the company began using a new terminology to describe these high-performance organizations, or high-performance work systems. At the annual management meeting in Cincinnati in December 1980, two of P&G's internal consultants, M. J. Gowin and R. H. Beacham, reported on "new plant characteristics," drawing on experiences in twenty-one plants in six countries. About 40 percent of the company's employees worked in these facilities. Gowin and Beacham found nine characteristics that all these facilities had in common (see box, "New Plant Characteristics").[32]

In a major corporate initiative during the 1980s, P&G also sought to transfer as much of its learning from the new plants as possible to its traditional unionized plants. The results were positive although less spectacular than in the new plants. In the United States and Europe, national labor movements were on the defensive as rising global competitive rivalry upended the patterns in collective bargaining established in the post–World War II era. The 1980s witnessed concession bargaining and the migration of many manufacturing jobs from advanced economies to those with lower labor costs in Latin America, Asia, and southern Europe.

In these circumstances, P&G sought to restructure its work systems in the traditional plants in keeping with the principles of the technician plants. It proved a slow, arduous task, as managers and workers used to traditional

New Plant Characteristics

M. J. Gowin and R. H. Beacham
December 9, 1980

1. Respect for the capabilities of *all* employees
2. Common objectives
3. Management by principle
4. Results orientation
5. Goal setting/problem solving
6. Team orientation
7. Skill/contribution-based rewards
8. Multi-skill requirements
9. Communications, information, and training

ways of operating came to terms with the imperative to do things differently. All of the older plants made clear progress. The biggest breakthrough, oddly, came at one of the oldest, in Cheboygan, Michigan. Operating costs at the plant were significantly higher than in the technician plants, and in the late 1970s, a new plant manager, Homer Bullard, began making the case for change by sharing confidential business information with the local union. He also took union officers and other hourly workers to visit technician plants and other high-performance organizations in the United States. Then Bullard learned that P&G was considering adding capacity to make Attends, the adult incontinence brief. He persuaded the union that Cheboygan could get the business, but only if it adopted many of the features of the technician system, including fewer job classifications and skill-based pay and promotion. The union agreed, and although Attends was not a successful brand, the union learned that nontraditional ways of working need not be threatening.[33]

Once a few traditional plants changed, the rest were bound to follow. It sometimes took a crisis—the threat of loss of employment or even of a plant closing—to accelerate the rate of change. Always it took a significant investment in communications and training for the company to succeed. Finally, P&G learned that its own managers could constitute a major obstacle to change. Unions were not the only constituencies threatened by change. Supervisors and managers had to come to terms with a different role, from directing to coaching.[34]

The Lessons of Augusta, Lima, and Albany in Perspective

A key component of brand building is the ability to offer premium performance at attractive prices. That means constant effort to differentiate products through features that consumers value, the advertising of those products, and the reduction in total delivered cost. The Augusta, Lima, and Albany stories illustrate new and powerful approaches to achieving high performance in manufacturing. The stories also reveal important lessons about delivering outstanding results by unleashing the potential of all employees, whatever their backgrounds and outlooks.

The new facilities built in the 1960s and 1970s and the innovative work practices that later spread to older operations dramatically reaffirmed P&G's long-standing belief that mutuality of interest between employer and employee is the foundation of significant progress. This was not just a moral issue; it was also a strategic imperative and a source of competitive advantage. Savings from higher productivity and lower costs could be plowed back into the business to preserve existing brands and develop new ones. Similarly, P&G's embrace of a more diverse workforce at Albany paid off not just in terms of social justice, but also on the bottom line, in measurable productivity gains and an enviable reputation as a desirable place to work. Succeeding with a racially mixed workforce in Albany paid manifold dividends to P&G as it later applied its learning to managing a diverse global workforce.

Cultivating these innovations in human relations required strong leadership, careful staging, and committed follow-through. It took vision and courage. It built on a foundation of shared principles to guide decision making. And it took time. The transformation was not accomplished in one stroke, companywide. The new systems were nurtured in protected environments, then transplanted. The company set up experiments in greenfield locations, studied them, and then applied the learning to traditional plants. Repeated, explicit endorsement by senior management was necessary to maintain momentum.

PART III

Going Global

1980–1990

CHAPTER NINE

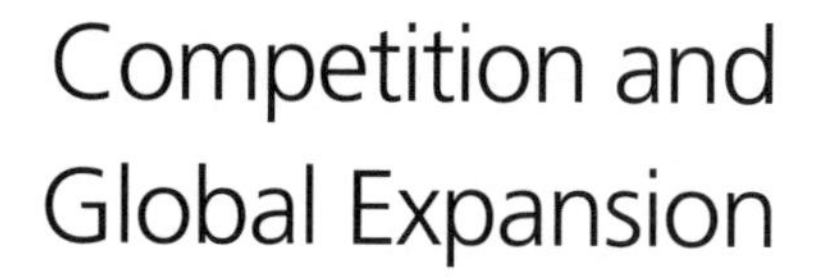

Competition and Global Expansion

AS PROCTER & GAMBLE entered the new decade of the 1980s, president and soon-to-be chief executive John Smale believed the company's primary challenge would be one of growth.[1] Although the company crossed the $10 billion revenue threshold during the 1979–1980 fiscal year, maintaining the historical pace of doubling the business every decade would require extraordinary means. The challenge was both one of sheer size—for virtually all big companies, growth rates tend to slacken once some multibillion-dollar revenue threshold is reached—and of structural changes in the markets in which P&G competed.

As for most U.S. manufacturing companies, the decade opened for P&G in struggle. A double-dip recession in 1981–1982 generated, at its low point, the worst economic conditions in the United States in fifty years, with interest rates approaching 20 percent and an unemployment rate of more than 10 percent. The aftereffects of the energy crises of the 1970s, including high inflation and high raw-materials costs, lingered while competitive rivalry, especially from Japanese manufacturers, escalated sharply. In a host of high-profile manufacturing industries—consumer electronics, machine tools, steel, and autos—global leadership passed from the United States to Japan. Although P&G's own industry, consumer products, seemed at first immune to the new competition, the company recognized that it had plenty to learn from Japanese manufacturers. It kept a wary eye on emerging Japanese rivals such as Kao, Lion, and Uni-Charm while redoubling its own efforts to penetrate the Japanese market.

In the United States, still by far P&G's biggest market, the company confronted ominous signs. The Rely crisis was a fresh and painful memory and a reminder of the difficulties inherent in developing new categories and brands. Pampers, the company's last megahit, had been introduced nearly twenty years earlier. Downy fabric softener, which made its debut in 1968, posted encouraging results, as did Bounce dryer sheets and Dawn dish detergent, but Pringles, after a promising start in the mid-1970s, had declined and struggled, leaving its long-term prospects much in doubt. Meanwhile, the company's core businesses encountered disturbing trends. Competitors were hacking away at P&G's once-dominant product lines in detergents, dentifrices, and disposable diapers.

In contending with these problems, P&G was no longer able to count on some of its most compelling traditional advantages. The growing popularity of cable and satellite TV networks fragmented the national TV advertising market in the United States and, along with the rise of two-career marriages, raised questions about the future value of the company's sponsorship of daytime soap operas. The retail sector was also in upheaval. In tough economic times, consumers were switching from premium brands to private-label and generic brands. Downward pressure on prices was intensifying. Meanwhile, P&G's leverage with the trade was beginning to lessen, as the bar codes and scanning gave retailers superior information about consumer purchasing patterns and meant that they no longer had to rely on manufacturers for such data.

Finally, distribution channels that P&G had commanded for decades were breaking down and giving way to alternatives that threatened to weaken the company's leverage with the trade. Young, aggressive mass merchandisers such as Kmart and Wal-Mart were gaining strides by offering brand-name goods at "everyday low prices." In the short run, this was good news for P&G, because the mass merchandisers needed top national brands to lure customers and therefore featured these brands prominently in more locations. In the long run, however, the rise of the new retailers portended still more pressure on prices, as well as the possibility that P&G could one day find itself dealing with customers bigger than itself. The gains of the mass merchandisers, moreover, occurred at the expense of P&G's traditional grocery supermarket accounts, which sought frantically to mount a counterattack. In the meantime, many of them underwent restructurings or were gobbled up in mergers and takeovers. Such developments also foreshadowed the tipping of the balance of power away from manufacturers and toward retailers.

For P&G, the 1980s would be a period of unusually complex and difficult challenges. The company would have to make significant changes in the products it sold, the markets it served, and the manner in which it conducted business.

Preparing for Change, 1980–1985

Procter & Gamble rose to meet the challenges of the 1980s under a new leadership team. In January 1981, the fifty-three-year-old Smale succeeded Ed Harness as the company's chief executive, and fifty-seven-year-old Brad Butler became chairman of the board. The Canadian-born Smale had joined P&G in 1952 after brief stints at two other companies, including Vick Chemical (which would eventually be renamed Richardson-Vicks and then, on chief executive Smale's watch, be absorbed into P&G). He began climbing the well-worn path for promising managers, starting as an assistant brand manager. His first brand was Gleem toothpaste; subsequently, he moved up to brand manager and then became associate advertising manager for Crest. This position proved a pivotal assignment that ultimately made his career when he helped to persuade the American Dental Association to give the brand its seal of acceptance. As Crest rocketed to market leadership, Smale rode along with it, rising swiftly through the organization: general manager of the Toilet Goods Division in 1966; vice president of Bar Soap and Household Cleaning Products, 1968; vice president of Packaged Soap and Detergents, 1969; group executive vice president, 1970; executive vice president, 1973; and president in 1974, a position in which he worked closely with Harness.[2]

Smale bore the usual attributes of P&G's top leaders: industriousness and a competitive streak, devotion to the company and its values, keen intelligence, and the manners of a gentleman. He was notably direct in communication, impatient with ideas and proposals not fully developed, and intolerant of lackluster results. Outwardly he epitomized P&G's conservative management style, often wearing a dark blue suit, a white shirt, and a tie featuring P&G's moon and stars logo. Quietly, however, he harbored radical ideas. As chief executive, he broke ranks with his predecessors in his willingness to deal with the financial community and media. During his first year, he caught the Cincinnati Society of Financial Analysts off guard by agreeing to speak to a gathering—the first P&G chief executive in twenty years to accept the annual invitation. Analysts and business reporters from across the United States flocked to Smale's coming-out party, as it was called, where they warmed up for the speech by touring the company's R&D facilities. Smale proved similarly open with P&G's trade customers, beginning to thaw frosty relationships that had emerged between a manufacturer perceived as haughty and dictatorial and retailers perceived as unwilling or unable to merchandise brands properly.[3]

A new management team joined Smale in the top ranks. Tom Laco and Ed Artzt became executive vice presidents with responsibility for U.S. and international business, respectively. Another key appointment was Wahib Zaki as senior vice president with responsibility for R&D.

The new team confronted a major problem in declining growth rates among several core U.S. categories, including detergents, paper products, and dentifrices. Some of the trouble was macroeconomic, but Smale and his colleagues believed that tough times in the short term masked adverse trends in the long term, a new and more challenging competitive environment. Most worrisome was the narrowing performance gap between P&G's brands and those of its major competitors.

Across a range of categories, the evidence of more effective competition was accumulating in P&G's falling market shares. New management teams arrived at Unilever, Colgate, and Kimberly-Clark and transformed their companies into notably tougher competitors. During the late 1970s and early 1980s in the United States, P&G lost five share points in detergents to low-cost competitors and heavy-duty liquid Wisk from Unilever. At the same time, Colgate and Beecham introduced dentifrices in gel forms and with new flavors that cost Crest and Gleem seven share points, and in diapers, Kimberly-Clark's Huggies, a fitted diaper with a superior fastening technology, took eight share points from Pampers and Luvs. "Ten or fifteen years ago," observed George Domolky, an industry specialist at Fidelity in 1983, "Procter & Gamble really had a commanding lead in management style, talent and structure. Procter & Gamble is still an excellent and sterling company, but due to the proliferation of their management style and staff defections from the company, the rest of the group learned a lot from P&G in defining their objectives and maximizing their potential. This makes the group relatively balanced. You can't make money based on the mistakes of the other guys, so that makes the going even tougher in a mature industry."[4]

Surveying these market and competitive trends, Smale and his colleagues moved quickly to reposition P&G in the new environment. Their new strategy had three principal components: an assault on costs, a drive to accelerate innovation, and a resumption of acquisitions to broaden the company's portfolio and hasten growth.

Attacking Costs

Smale declared that P&G would relentlessly pursue the goal of becoming the low-cost manufacturer in consumer products, and he handed the challenge first to Laco in U.S. operations. Laco understood that making P&G more cost efficient went far beyond the need to cut costs—although that was surely necessary. Rather, he saw his challenge as systemic and involving virtually every activity of the business, from purchasing, to R&D and engineering, to manufacturing, to sales and distribution.[5]

In the short term, P&G acted swiftly to improve its cost position, implementing hundreds of suggestions across the company. Some were straightforward and modest: using less ink on a box of Tide realized annual savings of about $2 million. Other suggestions were more consequential, such as using plastic instead of glass bottles for Crisco Oil and molding labels for Downy into the plastic bottles so that containers could be shipped without being unpacked. Procter & Gamble backed up these initiatives with significant changes in management policies and systems. For example, it altered its criteria for evaluating brand managers, adding cost control measures to the traditional gains in volume and market share. It also redirected spending toward automation and cost savings. By 1983, about a quarter of the company's capital expenditures were targeted at cost reduction, more than twice the level in the late 1970s. Finally, the company also thinned its managerial and technical ranks. Some reductions resulted from automation and attrition, but others reflected more demanding performance criteria. By some estimates, more than 10 percent of the salaried workforce was trimmed during the early 1980s.[6]

Beyond these measures, Smale and Laco also sought to change the way the company worked by breaking down functional and departmental barriers and encouraging more teamwork. Over the years, P&G's vaunted brand management system had produced some unhappy side effects, blocking internal information flows and inhibiting P&G's ability to leverage its capabilities across the company. Smale and Laco sought to redirect internal competition among brand managers outward, toward external competitors.

The initial vehicle of change was teamwork, which P&G used in a variety of contexts in the early 1980s. David Swanson, senior vice president of engineering, became a disciple of teamwork as a result of his investigations of the incipient total quality movement. Using cross-functional teams, he began running projects and experiments to achieve significant cost savings, improve product quality, and shorten the product development cycle. When sales of Pringles fell off after its promising introduction and management struggled for years to regain a growth trajectory, Smale appointed a cross-functional team to turn the business around. Procter & Gamble even began experimenting with teams involving customers. It formed a team with Kroger to develop a continuous-replenishment system that would take costs out of the supply chain, with the resulting savings to be shared between the partners and with the customers in the form of lower prices.[7]

Opening the Pipeline

One of the most fruitful applications of teamwork proved to be new-product introductions, which P&G accelerated dramatically during the early 1980s. Product introductions and upgrades to existing brands constituted the second component of P&G's strategy for growth. As the new head of R&D, Zaki's assignment was to reinvigorate the company's technical organization, institute a faster pace of innovation, and achieve better integration of technical work across departmental and geographical borders—goals he had already achieved in his previous position as director of P&G's European Technical Center in Brussels.[8]

Behind Zaki's charge lay disappointment with the major new product initiatives of the middle and late 1970s: Pringles and Rely. Although Pringles would eventually recover to become a leading global brand and P&G's withdrawal of Rely was not the result of a market failure, both projects had been expensive and highly publicized *(see the "Pringles and Perserverance" box)*. The company obviously had to do better. It also had to hasten the rate of new-product introductions, even if this meant taking more risks and moving from test markets to rollout at a faster clip.

During the early 1980s, P&G accelerated the rate of new-product introductions and upgrades. By early 1983, it had twenty-two new products in test markets—a record total—including some that departed from tradition by lacking distinctive performance advantages. Banner and Summit, for example, were two new, low-cost bathroom tissue brands designed to compete with generics on price. There was nothing remarkable about either new brand except that they were thinner and thus used less paper than Charmin. Other new brands in these years included another new bathroom tissue, Certain, which was impregnated with lotion; Pace, the first new dentifrice brand since Crest; Brigade, a toilet bowl cleaner; Encaprin, a coated aspirin for heavy users such as arthritics; Ivory shampoo; Attends adult incontinence briefs; Vibrant bleach; and Solo and Vizir liquid laundry detergents. Meanwhile, P&G unleashed a torrent of product upgrades and flankers (brand extensions), such as Spic and Span Pine Liquid, Liquid Lava, butter-flavored Crisco, Duncan Hines frosting, and Comet Liquid. Most of these new brands, upgrades, and flankers fizzled, but the faster tempo indicated important changes in the way P&G operated.[9]

The company placed its biggest bets on two major new products, Duncan Hines soft cookies and Always sanitary pads (known as Whisper in Japan and other parts of Asia). The first proved another disappointment, but the second became a huge success and P&G's first truly global brand.

The Cookie Wars

Procter & Gamble held out high hopes for its new cookies. By the early 1980s, Duncan Hines was by far the biggest producer of cookie mixes in the United States, but this market was tiny in comparison with that for packaged, ready-to-eat cookies, which Nabisco dominated with its Oreo, Chips Ahoy, and Nilla brands. Although these brands had passionate adherents, P&G scientists believed in the late 1970s that they had found an opening. By using two types of dough and "special manipulation of the sugar crystals in different parts of the product," P&G successfully created a ready-to-eat, soft cookie comparable to one baked at home.[10]

Procter & Gamble applied for patents on the soft cookie formulation and the process for making it in 1979, but the product was not ready for market testing until nearly four years and $30 million in development costs later. In January 1983, P&G began testing six varieties of soft cookies in Kansas City, where Frito-Lay was also testing a similar product. By the summer, P&G's cookies had surged to a 30 percent share in the segment, a result that made it one of the most successful test markets in the company's history. Convinced that it had a runaway hit on its hands, P&G decided to go national with Duncan Hines soft cookies as quickly as possible. This was a major investment decision, involving several hundred million dollars for the construction of manufacturing facilities in Jackson, Tennessee, and Brockville, Ontario, and for national TV advertising.[11]

Within months, however, Nabisco and Keebler had similar soft cookies on the market. Protesting that these rivals had illegally copied the Duncan Hines formula and process, P&G filed patent infringement suits against them. Undeterred, the competitors pressed ahead, and a full-scale cookie war was on. From the beginning, P&G was disadvantaged. The competitors all had developed distribution systems for delivering reasonably fresh baked and fried goods (cookies, crackers, and snack foods)—systems that P&G could not match without still more big investments. Another serious problem was the public's slowing appetite for soft cookies of all types. Repeat sales trended down after about a half dozen purchases. "People just didn't like the cookies," concluded Lawrence D. "Mike" Milligan, general manager of the Food Products Division. They "tasted like raw dough," said an industry analyst.[12]

Sales of soft cookies peaked at $450 million in 1985 and plunged by a third the following year. Procter & Gamble held out until 1987, but with annual losses of $100 million (according to some estimates) piling up, it all but closed down the business. Meanwhile, the company zealously pursued its

PRINGLES AND PERSEVERANCE: THE IMPROBABLE MAKING OF A GLOBAL BRAND

In the mid-1950s, P&G launched an intriguing effort to develop an engineered potato chip. Decades later, Pringles Crisps became one of P&G's biggest brands, with special appeal to youth all over the world. The path between these endpoints was hardly smooth, however. Rather, difficulties and disappointments marked Pringles' first quarter century and the brand was nearly terminated before P&G's perseverance was rewarded. Pringles is one of the rare instances in consumer marketing of a dying brand returning to health.

The Pringles story began when Vic Mills, head of process development at the Miami Valley Laboratory, and his colleague Ken Hawley brainstormed a way for P&G to enter the potato chip industry—a tremendous market—well known to the company as a leading supplier of fats and oils. Given that P&G's distribution system was geared to nonperishable items, however, Mills and Hawley recognized that the company would have to reinvent the potato chip and its packaging. The product "had to be packed in nitrogen if it was going to keep . . . [yet] you can't have a big bulky package. That would be too expensive. So you had to shape it so that it would stack. . . ."[13]

During the next several years, P&G researcher Fred Baur took charge of the potato chip project, looking at alternative sources of raw materials and different processes for manufacturing and packaging. An interesting question involved how best to form the chips so that they would survive frying and be both strong and stackable. Baur experimented with flat discs or rectangles, but a serendipitous discussion with an astronomer prompted investigation of a curved saddle shape, which increased the bulk density of the chips when stacked. Not long after, P&G applied for a patent on "packaging of chip-type snack food products."[14]

In 1965, after an eight-year hiatus while P&G attended to other priorities, researchers developed the basic Pringles formula of dehydrated potato flakes combined with starch and water that was beaten into dough. The dough was then rolled into a flat sheet, molded into individual pieces, and fried. The next challenge was to ramp up the process, a complex and expensive undertaking. Mills, who was simultaneously leading the development of P&G's new paper machines, thought big, imagining that one or two huge factories could supply the potato chip needs of the ➢

entire country. As a result, P&G's engineers developed "a totally integrated, continuous stream manufacturing operation which goes from dry ingredients to packed finished product without interruption in a matter of minutes." In all, Pringles' development absorbed more than $70 million between 1965 and 1968, when test marketing began.[15]

Marketing Pringles also proved a difficult challenge, although the initial signs were encouraging. Buoyed by heavy national TV advertising, Pringles got off to a fast start, surging to a 25 percent share in some metropolitan areas, despite premium prices. Revenues surpassed $105 million in 1973, speeding toward a target of $250 million in sales within five years. "The arrival of Pringles on the scene in a big way," declared the trade magazine *Monthly Chipper,* "would seem to present the potato-chip industry with the most serious challenge in its history."[16]

In fact, Pringles was reaching a high-water mark. Shipments crested at about 15 percent of the market in 1975 before tumbling to a 4.3 percent share at the end of the decade. The brand was clearly ailing. Consumers complained about Pringles' flavor and texture, while makers of traditional chips counterattacked by lampooning the synthetic nature of Pringles to a public increasingly drawn to natural foods. In 1975, P&G suffered a major setback when the FDA required disclosure in bold type on Pringles' packages that the crisps were made from dehydrated potatoes. In 1979, P&G discontinued Pringles' national TV advertising and incoming chief executive John Smale drew a line in the sand. He announced that unless Pringles could resume profitable growth within five years it would be discontinued.[17]

Pringles rebounded in stages. First, a cross-functional business team—an unprecedented approach for P&G—halted the decline in sales by instituting dramatic changes. Revamping the production process enabled Pringles to be priced at parity with traditional chips. Scientists and engineers developed a patented technique to spray the chips with oil, which imparted a more pleasing taste and texture. Procter & Gamble also introduced more flavor varieties, starting with the popular Pringles Cheez'Ums. Meanwhile, the company resumed its spending on advertising, modifying its message to emphasize the taste and variety benefits of the Pringles line. In combination, the measures taken by the Pringles management team proved effective. Three years into the turnaround the brand became profitable for the first time in its history. And it began again to grow, with shipments up more than 50 percent, by 1983–1984. ➢

Mass producing Pringles proved a difficult and costly challenge but the payoff was enormous when demand finally caught up with capacity.

The second, breakthrough stage of the brand's revival followed later in the decade, when Smale asked Bob Gill, category manager for salty snacks, to transform Pringles into a much bigger and more profitable business.[18] Gill and his colleagues, including Randy Potts in R&D, Dan Millisor in product supply, Paul Beck in sales, and Jeff Ansell in marketing, formed a cohesive team focused on building Pringles as a significant corporate brand.

The new team rethought Pringles from the ground up, starting with the demand side. Certain steps seemed relatively clear. The new supply-chain partnerships between P&G and its trade customers opened up new distribution channels at mass merchandisers, the dollar stores, and discount drug chains. Procter & Gamble also began an export initiative, working with Fouad Kraytem and Henrik Svennas at P&G's Export and Special Operations group in Geneva to promote the product in Europe, the Middle East, and Africa.[19] ➢

The Pringles team's coup—reconceiving the product and changing it from a "potato chip" to a "potato crisp"—was a modest change in the eyes of consumers but one that freed P&G from having to disclose the source of its raw materials in bold type. At the same time, P&G gained the ability to modify the dough formula to achieve better flavor and, due to greater ease in handling and processing, achieve significant cost reductions. It also became easier to introduce new flavors; P&G brought out an average of nearly two new flavor varieties per year during the 1990s.

By far the biggest change in Pringles' positioning followed after the team and agency reps collaborated on a fresh study of the potato snack market. "We found we were No. 10 in the market, ranked from an image standpoint with adults," said Gill, "but amongst kids, we were No. 1." That finding prompted further study of the tastes and consuming habits of children and teenagers as well as a key strategic decision to focus on the youth market. A wholly new advertising campaign featured young actors, loud music, the sound of crunching chips, and little or no text, all produced in the hip, quick-cutting style of music videos. The ads poked fun at the shortcomings of traditional chips—greasiness, bags full of air, and the crumbs at the bottom—while simultaneously emphasizing the fun of playing with Pringles and the sheer enjoyment of eating them. The sound of the can opening prompted a new slogan—"Once you pop, you can't stop!"—that became the basis of an extremely effective, award-winning ad campaign.

The new advertising campaign proved not only powerful in the United States, but around the world. Procter & Gamble discovered that the purchasing patterns and tastes of the world's teenagers and youth were similar. Thus the company advertised Pringles in London, Tokyo, and Rio de Janeiro with the same message and essentially the same TV ads as those that ran in the United States, with astonishing effect. In the mid-1990s, a Japanese teen magazine asked Japanese girls to name the one food they would take with them if stranded on a desert island. The answer: Sour Cream & Onion Pringles.[20]

By the late-1990s, after decades of perseverance, Pringles had established itself as one of P&G's most powerful global brands, with more than $1 billion in annual sales and particular strength in the developed economies. The volume split evenly between North America and the rest of the world.

patent suits and finally won in September 1989, with a settlement in which three rivals were to pay a total of $125 million in royalties and damages. The outcome eased some of the hurt in a painful experience, but by then, the soft cookie wars were over.[21]

Always Success

The company had much better luck with another big bet: Always/Whisper sanitary pads. At the annual meeting of management in October 1981, Harness declared that, the Rely experience notwithstanding, P&G had no intention of giving up on the feminine hygiene market. The reasons that the company had invested in Rely still held true: The population of potential customers remained large and growing, with especially bright prospects overseas; P&G's proprietary technology could deliver distinctive product benefits; and the business complemented and extended P&G's line of personal care products.[22]

Although competitors were focusing on the use of superabsorbent materials in the core of pads to make them smaller, P&G's market research revealed that one of the biggest complaints was the feeling of stickiness that many users experienced. This problem was similar to one that P&G had solved years earlier in disposable diapers, and researchers saw an opportunity to use that knowledge in pads. The company had an ideal material, a perforated polyethylene polymer film called CPT, for use in the top sheet. For the interior of the pads, P&G chose wood pulp fibers.[23]

Procter & Gamble introduced Always in the spring of 1983 as "a complete system of feminine protection products" consisting of maxipads, minipads, and panty liners into test markets in Minneapolis/St. Paul and the Dakotas. Promotional materials and advertisements emphasized the benefits of the Dri-Weave top sheet and "the clean, dry feeling of protection" that it made possible. Ads also highlighted how the lining's "microtextured pattern" simulated the feel of cloth. The packaging, too, was innovative. A full 70 percent smaller than competing brands, the packages gave retailers a much better return on shelf space.[24]

The decision to introduce a single brand as an umbrella for the entire line of feminine care products contrasted not only with P&G's traditional practice in detergents, dentifrices, and diapers, but also with the competition: Johnson & Johnson, for example, marketed its panty liners under two brand names, Assure and Stay Free. By managing the products as a single brand, moreover, P&G was able to focus its marketing campaign while also saving on ad spending.[25]

After the Rely disappointment, P&G continued to target the feminine care products market. In the 1980s Always feminine pads (Whisper in Asia) became one of P&G's first global brands.

Another key decision was to roll out the product nationally after just a year in the original test market—a marked contrast to P&G's traditional pattern of testing in multiple markets and tweaking the product and advertising over years to get them just right. Introduced in May 1984, Always entered a crowded market, but it became an immediate hit. Procter & Gamble knew that the original feature advantages of the product would not sustain its long-term success, and it began adding new features. Market research found that about two-thirds of women thought that the existing pads left their undergarments unprotected, suggesting a need for more coverage rather than greater absorbency. In 1986, the company introduced patented undergarment protectors in the United States as Always Plus. Women in consumer tests dubbed the protectors "wings," because the material extended on both sides from the center of the pad and folded around the underwear edge to fasten on the bottom side.[26]

Meanwhile, at the insistence of Ed Artzt, P&G moved aggressively to launch Always overseas. The company had taken seven years to expand Pampers into sixty countries, but Artzt was determined to accomplish the same goal for Always in less than half the time. "We knew we would have a better chance of success if we could get established before competition could react to our U.S. product in their overseas markets," he said. Shortly after the original U.S. test in February 1983, Always moved into test or country expansion in Canada, Saudi Arabia, Singapore (as Whisper), France, and Puerto Rico—all lead markets in their respective regions. The elapsed time between the start of the U.S. test and the foreign introductions was just eighteen months.[27]

Building New Businesses Through Acquisitions

Before Smale became chief executive in January 1981, he recognized that for P&G to remain on its historical growth trajectory of doubling revenues every decade, even accelerated internal development would not be enough. Rather, the company would need to resume making acquisitions. Fortunately for P&G, this means of growth became possible again, as the Reagan administration in Washington, D.C., relaxed antitrust enforcement. At the same time, the 1980s became a decade of restructuring and financial engineering, and many companies and divisions came on the market.

Procter & Gamble was not interested in making acquisitions merely for the sake of growth, however. The deals had to fit with P&G values, technology, and capabilities. Shortly before Smale became chief executive, he commissioned a group led by Margaret Wyant to analyze every product category sold in supermarkets and drugstores in a search for products compatible with P&G's. The group looked at branded consumer goods, nonperishable, and any other product category that provided opportunities to differentiate based on the company's capabilities in technology, manufacturing, and marketing. At the same time, the categories had to offer stronger growth potential than those in which the company already competed.[28] In the course of Wyant's work, some attractive candidates emerged: bottled soft drinks, in which P&G could offer flavor technology; orange juice, a category that no national brands yet dominated; and over-the-counter drugs for self-medication, a category in which the company's marketing clout might make a difference. In the early 1980s, P&G entered all these businesses via acquisition.

In July 1980, P&G completed its first significant acquisition in seventeen years (since Folgers). It spent $53 million to purchase the soft-drink operations outside Canada from Toronto-based Crush International Limited. (Procter & Gamble acquired the Canadian business four years later.) Procter & Gamble thus became the sixth-biggest soft-drink maker in the United States, with a 4 percent market share and brands including Orange Crush soda, Hires root beer, and Sun-Drop lemon-lime soda. Although Coca-Cola and

PepsiCo dominated the category and dwarfed P&G, the company nonetheless contended that it could jump over rivals such as Dr. Pepper and 7-Up to gain the number three position.[29]

The next significant deal, in the fall of 1981, brought the citrus processing business of Frostproof, from Florida-based Ben Hill Griffin. The business had annual revenues of approximately $175 million and about seven hundred employees. The juices were sold under regional or private label brands in the southeastern United States, but P&G harbored big plans to develop a national brand to compete with the market leaders, Minute Maid (Coca-Cola) and Tropicana (Beatrice Foods). Several companies were experimenting with freeze-dried orange juice that consumers could later reconstitute by adding water. Such juice would be much cheaper than chilled fresh juice, which sold at high prices to offset high freight costs, and simpler and more convenient for consumers than dealing with frozen concentrate. Procter & Gamble followed this path and believed that it could also deliver a superior juice by enhancing its flavor, aroma, and texture through proprietary technology.[30]

The initial returns in P&G's new beverage businesses were encouraging. Consumer research revealed that consumers of root beer valued a foamy, creamy beverage, so P&G adjusted the formula of Hires accordingly. It also modified Orange Crush to deliver a flavor "more orangey" than that of its principal direct competitor, Sunkist orange soda. In orange juice, when researchers failed to make the freeze-dried technology work, the company decided instead to launch a new brand, Citrus Hill, made from frozen concentrate and featuring proprietary flavor technology. Test markets indicated that consumers preferred Citrus Hill's "natural taste, sweetness and texture to that of other leading brands." Rolled out nationally in 1983, Citrus Hill hit 12 to 14 percent of the market for refrigerated orange juice and 7 percent for frozen concentrate within two years.[31]

Procter & Gamble placed another big bet on over-the-counter (OTC) remedies and prescription drugs. In the early 1980s, the company already had several prescription products on the market and some promising OTC drugs in development, including a new mouthwash and a new "delivery system" for aspirin. Procter & Gamble was making steady progress on these efforts when it learned of a significant acquisition opportunity. Early in 1982, Goldman Sachs notified the company that Morton-Norwich, a diversified corporation that needed cash to buy back 20 percent of its equity from an erstwhile venture partner, was putting up for bid its subsidiary, Norwich Eaton Pharmaceuticals. In March, P&G won the auction, agreeing to pay $371 million for the unit. During the previous year, Norwich Eaton had reported a net income of $15 million on annual sales of $235 million. It employed about three thousand people, a third of whom were based in Norwich, New York, home of the administrative headquarters and R&D laboratory. The unit also maintained production facilities in the United States, the United Kingdom, Canada, Mexico, and Colombia and sales offices in many other countries. Norwich Eaton also held a 50 percent stake in Röhm Pharma, a joint venture with Röhm GmbH in West Germany.[32]

Norwich Eaton managed two principal lines of business: OTC health care products (44 percent of sales; 66 percent of profit) and ethical (prescription) drugs (56 percent of sales; 34 percent of profit). Procter & Gamble was principally interested in Norwich Eaton's leading OTC brands, Pepto-Bismol (the number two remedy for upset stomach and diarrhea) and Chloraseptic (since its 1976 introduction the leading product in the relatively small market for oral antiseptics/anesthetics for sore throats).[33]

Norwich Eaton's prescription drugs included Macrodantin and Furadantin (treatments for urinary tract infections), Dantrium (a skeletal muscle relaxant), Vivonex (elemental diets and feeding devices), Entex L.A. (for relief of respiratory congestion), and some other products. At the time of P&G's acquisition, the prescription business was growing rapidly in the United States and accounted for all but a tiny fraction of Norwich Eaton's overseas revenues.[34]

In presenting the Norwich Eaton deal to P&G's board of directors, an enthusiastic Smale claimed that the OTC lines would "telescope our entry" into the field "by several years," especially considering the amount of time necessary to develop leading brands comparable to Pepto-Bismol and Chloraseptic. At the same time, Smale believed that P&G could provide Norwich Eaton with manufacturing and marketing capabilities that would significantly improve the drug company's cost position and market coverage. He also believed that the deal would "accelerate the development of a pharmaceutical business into a break-even proposition for [P&G], four or five years earlier than we might otherwise."[35]

Three years later, P&G dramatically strengthened its OTC business by closing two more deals, the second one a blockbuster. The first purchase, for $312 million, brought in the OTC lines of Monsanto's pharmaceutical subsidiary, G. D. Searle & Co., including Metamucil, the leading laxative in the United States.[36] The second and much bigger acquisition occurred suddenly and nearly simultaneously in October 1985, when P&G launched a friendly bid to acquire Richardson-Vicks Inc. (RVI), which was looking to stave off a hostile takeover bid by Unilever. In the previous fiscal year, RVI had earned $72.2 million on sales of $1.2 billion, with nearly half of these revenues originating in sales outside the United States, and employed eleven thousand people. Like Norwich Eaton, RVI was an old company, harking back to 1905, when Lunsford Richardson, a druggist in Greensboro, North Carolina, had formulated an ointment as a cold remedy for children—the precursor of Vicks VapoRub. From there, Richardson and his successors had developed a family of related products, including cough syrup (Vicks Formula 44), nasal decongestants (Sinex), and cough and cold remedies (DayCare [later DayQuil] and NyQuil). RVI had subsequently diversified primarily through acquisitions into personal care products—Oil of Olay (skin care), Clearasil (acne care), Pantene and Vidal Sassoon (hair care), and Fixodent and Fasteeth (denture adhesives)—and other miscellaneous lines ranging from wood refinishing products to nutritional snacks to medical and chemical instruments.[37]

The contest for control of RVI proved spirited. Procter & Gamble had to carry out its due diligence under intense time pressure while also debating internally the scope and structure of an appropriate bid. Unilever was offering more than $1.1 billion, a price that some senior P&G executives believed was already too high. Smale nonetheless pushed hard for the deal, and P&G proposed an all-stock transaction that topped Unilever's bid by one dollar per share. The RVI board accepted P&G's offer, which came to $1.2 billion.[38] By far the biggest acquisition in P&G's history at the time, the arrival of RVI carried profound implications not only for P&G's burgeoning OTC health care business but also for its hair care and skin care lines. The RVI deal also added significant operations in Europe and especially in southeast Asia, where it greatly boosted P&G's initiatives in the region.

Reorganization and Rebound, 1985–1989

In June 1985, P&G occupied the new twin tower office building adjacent to the old limestone headquarters opened in 1956. The top executives remained on the eleventh floor of the old building, which was integrated into the new complex by a bridge, walkways, and landscaping.[39] The marriage of old and new P&G constituted a metaphor for the company itself as it sought in the mid-1980s to preserve the best of its traditions while continuing to adjust to new business imperatives.

The timing of the new building's dedication proved somewhat awkward, as it coincided with the conclusion of P&G's fiscal year and the company's first annual earnings decline (28 percent) since 1952. Management attributed the problem to high expenses associated with new product and business development, but the major problem was fierce competition in the company's core brands, especially diapers. The once overwhelming market share of Pampers had fallen below 50 percent, while Kimberly-Clark now had a third of the market. To defend its lead, P&G had made huge capital investments to retool the diaper lines to make fitted, and later ultrathin, Pampers.

Unfortunately for the company, the returns on this investment lay some years into the future. Another problem was dentifrices, in which P&G's share dropped from 42 to 28 percent between 1979 and 1985, while Colgate's climbed from 18 to 25 percent. Colgate's rise was partly based on the strength of pump dispensers, an innovation to which P&G had responded slowly.[40]

On the supply side, the initiatives in productivity, quality, and trade relations were gathering momentum under the leadership of Laco, who became vice chairman in 1984, and his successor as head of U.S. operations, forty-five-year-old John Pepper. Procter & Gamble was at last beginning to push back the competitive onslaught in the United States. Liquid Tide, introduced in 1984, halted the inroads made by Unilever's Wisk and positioned P&G to assume leadership of the fast-growing liquid-detergent category. Procter & Gamble built on its lead with a steady stream of improvements to both its powder and liquid versions, starting with Tide with Bleach (1988). The new Pampers models became huge successes in North America and Europe. In dentifrices, P&G began to reverse its slide with the introduction of Tartar Control Crest, the most significant innovation in the category since fluoridation.[41]

Procter & Gamble introduced Liquid Tide in 1984 and immediately gained the offensive in the liquid-detergent category.

These efforts to generate faster growth, however, produced decidedly mixed results. Always/Whisper and the health care lines, bolstered by the RVI and Searle acquisitions, continued to grow rapidly. Unfortunately, P&G's plans to develop new categories in orange juice and carbonated beverages ran awry. Despite several reformulations, including the addition of a proprietary calcium ingredient, Citrus Hill's market share remained tiny as brand managers at Minute Maid and Tropicana aggressively defended their turf. In carbonated beverages, P&G encountered a similar problem, as Coca-Cola and PepsiCo fought back with new brands and heavy spending on advertising and promotion.

As the company's 150th year in business wound down in June 1987, earnings from operations had recovered from the dip two years earlier. Nonetheless, management elected to take an $800 million charge to restructure its business. Most of the money was used to pay for scaling back in soft cookies, but some covered the costs of closing three powdered-detergent plants as markets in North America and Europe moved toward liquids. Other payments went toward expenses associated with consolidating facilities and operations after the RVI and Searle acquisitions.[42]

Fully conscious that it was deviating from its steady-employment practice instituted in the 1920s (to ensure an annual forty-eight weeks of work to every employee with two years of continuous employment), P&G undertook the plant closings and other moves to streamline its operations. Although the policy was never ironclad, most experienced production workers at P&G believed they had a job for life. By the mid-1980s, however, competitive pressures and the cumulative impact of investments in new work systems and automation that had made operations much more efficient rendered the guarantee of employment no longer sustainable. According to David Swanson, a senior manufacturing executive, top management abandoned the policy reluctantly while the company took "extraordinary measures . . . to treat people with care, dignity, and very generous separation benefits." The impact was manifested initially in the company's older plants but eventually reached newer operations, including some of the high-performance facilities and overseas locations. "The trauma . . . felt in the organization was significant," Swanson recalled. "There were special problems for both those who were separated and those who were administering the separations."[43]

Reorganization

At the same time that P&G was facing these plant and personnel reductions, changes in organization accompanied changes in longtime policy.

Smale and Pepper, who had become president of the company in 1986, took a hard look at P&G's portfolio of brands and the organization structure and management systems that supported them. Several problems were evident. In some categories, such as laundry and cleaning products, the company simply had too many brands that competed against each other for R&D support, plant capacity, marketing dollars, and management attention. Not enough thought was being given to how they might fit together and complement each other. Second, internal competition among brand managers had many virtues, as Neil McElroy had anticipated in 1931, but there were also disadvantages that became increasingly evident in the face of tough external competition in the 1980s. Procter & Gamble was not realizing the benefits of its vast scale and scope, as brand managers competed with each other and cooperated only on special projects. As a result, the company was missing opportunities to collaborate and share information and learning. Third, P&G lacked a coordinated strategy in each of its major categories, because it was no one's business to identify segments and opportunities that might be served with line extensions or even new brands. And fourth, the success of brand teams on Always/Whisper and some other brands had demonstrated that greater cross-functional collaboration could hasten new products to market not only in the United States but around the world.

To address these problems and opportunities, in October, Smale and Pepper announced a major reorganization of U.S. operations—"the most significant reorganization of the Company in 30 years." Category business units (CBUs) were established in the space between the product divisions and brand managers. A CBU aggregated "all brands and products in a particular business category, such as disposable diapers or oral care products, . . . organizationally in the same unit." The general managers of these CBUs had reporting to them not only the brand managers in their portfolio but also representatives from sales, finance, and product development. The new structure included thirty-nine CBUs in the United States, led by twenty-six CBU managers, some of whom were responsible for more than one category. This change affected not only the brand managers, but also the division general managers, who became, in effect, group vice presidents. Publicity around the change emphasized that P&G was not adding a new layer of management, but rather pushing some decision making down in the organization, closer to the operating level and the trade customers and consumers. At the same time, a new Profit Improvement Program (PIP) triggered significant changes as managers shifted their focus from selling more cases to generating bigger profits.[44]

In another related change, the once separate functions of manufacturing, engineering, purchasing, and distribution were gathered in a new organization called Product Supply, under Swanson. This unit became a single point of contact for coordinating the movement of materials and goods across the entire supply chain, from purchasing through delivery to the trade. Approximately twenty Product Supply units supported the new CBUs. Smale and Swanson believed that the new organization would extend the productivity and quality initiatives of the early 1980s and have a major continuing impact on the corporate bottom line. "I have the growing conviction," said Smale, "that the product supply concept is perhaps the single most important thing that can influence our profit performance over the next several years." He predicted—rightly, as it turned out—that the change would result in more than $1 billion in cost savings by 1990.[45]

Two other important events accompanied the category management and product supply reorganizations. To simplify top-level decision making, the company abandoned the Administrative Committee, the forty-person group of senior operating and staff executives who had met every Tuesday morning for decades to review operations and approve expenditures. The committee was replaced with a twenty-member executive committee, which concerned itself primarily with the most pressing strategic and operating issues. At the same time, greater authority over routine expenditures was handed to the division and category management levels.

The final important change was the development of a formal statement of P&G's purpose, values, and principles. The statement was necessary, Smale and Pepper believed, because as a huge, fast-changing company operating on a global scale with an increasingly diverse workforce, P&G needed to codify its deepest beliefs and values to ensure their continuing role as guides to decision making and operating. The statement also served both to inspire individual employees and to give them a common language—a glue to bind the company together. The essence of P&G began with the statement of purpose: "We will provide products of superior quality and value that improve the lives of the world's consumers. As a result, consumers will reward us with leadership sales and profit growth, allowing our people, our shareholders, and the communities in which we live and work to prosper." From there flowed crisp statements of the core values by which the company and its employees sought to live and the principles and supporting behaviors that followed from the statements of purpose and values.[46]

It is hard to overestimate the magnitude of the 1987 reorganizations and events. Procter & Gamble was making itself over from a top-down hierarchical, command-and-control mode of operating into a leaner, flatter, and more responsive organization. At the same time, it was thinking hard about the essence of the company, distinguishing its fundamental qualities that should be preserved from those aspects of the business and organization that had to change along with changing times.

Rebound

In the late 1980s, the efforts of P&G to make itself over during the early and middle years of the decade paid off handsomely as the company enjoyed rapid growth and high profitability. Return on sales climbed back steadily from a low of 4.7 percent in 1985 to 5.6 percent four years later, an encouraging trend. Liquid Tide, Ultra Pampers, and Tartar Control Crest preserved the company's leadership in its biggest categories, although competition remained fierce and there was no time to relax. Meanwhile, P&G's development and introduction of two-in-one shampoos that combined cleaning and conditioning stirred a sensation in the hair care market. Pert Plus (Rejoy or Rejoice in Asia) became a major success, followed by an even bigger hit when two-in-one technology was transferred to the upscale Pantene brand acquired with RVI.

In food products and paper products, the news was similarly good. In foods, a new management team at Pringles was in the process of reformulating the product and rejuvenating the brand in North America and readying it for introduction around the world. In 1989, P&G added to its foundation in salty snacks by acquiring Fisher Nuts from RJR Nabisco.

In tissue/towel, under the leadership of general manager Gary Martin, P&G followed a three-pronged strategy to raise the profitability of the business and prepare to take it global. The first component involved reducing the cost per case by more than two dollars primarily through process reliability and maximizing the running time of the paper machines. The second component entailed a steady stream of upgrades to Charmin and Bounty, such as new packaging, new colored designs, and other features that consumers valued. The third component was development of the next-generation process technology for making structured paper to succeed CPF (Confidential Process F), which was nearing the end of its life under patent protection.[47]

The OTC health care brands acquired from Norwich Eaton and RVI thrived under P&G's ownership, with Pepto-Bismol, Metamucil, and the Vicks brands making particularly good use of corporate capabilities in product supply, marketing, and advertising. In 1988, P&G signed a joint venture agreement with Syntex Corporation, a California-based pharmaceutical company, to bring its Naprosyn prescription analgesic, a rival to ibuprofen, to the OTC drug market. The OTC version, called Aleve, held potential to become a billion-dollar brand in the 1990s. Procter & Gamble also had high hopes for several prescription drugs in development, including risedronate, a third-generation treatment for osteoporosis, and Asacol, a drug for ulcerative colitis.

The other new business acquired in the early 1980s, cold beverages, continued to struggle, leading the company to restructure its portfolio of brands. In August 1989, the company finally exited carbonated beverages by selling its Crush International business to Britain's Cadbury Schweppes PLC for $220 million. Although P&G had managed to triple sales of Crush between 1980 and 1989, industry leaders Coca-Cola and PepsiCo grew their brands still faster.[48]

Procter & Gamble was also reconsidering its fresh-juice business. Food and Beverage Division general manager Jurgen Hintz worked on a new strategy, convinced that the company could deliver benefits in taste, nutritional needs, and value sought by consumers in the category. In 1989, he sought to bolster P&G's position by negotiating the acquisition of Sundor Company, producer of Sunny Delight (a blend of orange juice and other ingredients into an orange punch) and several regional brands of grapefruit, apple, and cranberry juices.[49]

While P&G reassessed its beverage business, it also began building another new business, beauty care, via acquisition. Oil of Olay skin care cream, an RVI brand, had become a major global success in part by drawing on P&G's capabilities in distribution and advertising. In 1989, the company decided to extend its foundation in beauty care by acquiring for $1.34 billion the Noxell Company, maker of Noxzema skin creams, Cover Girl cosmetics, and other brands. The deal, the biggest in P&G's history at the time, signaled a major growth thrust in beauty care in the 1990s.

Among many internal initiatives, P&G held out high hopes for an unusual product. In 1968, researchers Fred Mattson and Bob Volpenhein had serendipitously discovered some interesting properties in a compound called sucrose polyester (SPE). These properties made it potentially attractive as a replacement for fat in foods and cooking oils. Known replacements had significant drawbacks: They broke down at cooking temperatures and thus could not be used in preparing foods; they failed to match the effects of natural fats in cooking and flavoring, imparting an unappetizing "mouthfeel" in flavor and texture; or they reduced fat but not calories. But SPE possessed none of these disadvantages, and P&G soon applied for patents on its production and use.[50]

The company initiated discussions with the FDA about SPE in May 1971 and followed up with an exhaustive series of clinical studies and trials that consumed much of the next decade and a half. The company also explored various ways to use SPE and investigated food products in which to introduce it. All this work yielded generally encouraging results. In some clinical studies, SPE cut cholesterol levels by as much as 20 percent—another desirable property to go along with stability at high temperatures, low calorie content, and resistance to absorption by the body.[51]

By the mid-1980s, many at P&G and some outside observers were convinced that SPE held blockbuster potential, a product that could easily swell into a billion-dollar business within a few years of its introduction. Vast amounts of research on low-fat, low-calorie diets fueled a fast-growing industry in dietary foods and supplements. The medical establishment touted the benefits of a healthy (low-fat, low-calorie) diet, advice widely endorsed and echoed in the fashion and entertainment industries and in popular culture generally. Nutrasweet, a division of Monsanto, introduced its noncaloric artificial sweetener aspartame in 1981 and watched it mushroom into a huge financial success as a key ingredient of diet sodas. It did not seem fanciful to imagine that P&G's SPE formulation, called olestra (branded as Olean), could generate similar dazzling returns.[52]

In May 1987, P&G applied for FDA approval of olestra as a calorie-free replacement for fat in shortening and cooking oil. Although P&G recognized that it might be several more years before approval—the FDA had taken seven years to give aspartame the nod—the company nonetheless sought to be ready. In 1989, it set up a division of about eighty people to develop a marketing campaign and oversee the commercialization of the product. Critical choices loomed about the point of entry—health foods versus snacks and fried foods—and the scale of investment.[53]

Going Global

While press coverage of P&G in the late 1980s focused on the company's competitive wars, acquisitions, and new products such as olestra, its thriving business overseas was a major development behind the scenes. During the 1980s, P&G's foreign sales grew by nearly 150 percent, from $3.5 billion to $8.5 billion, and the share of total revenues from 32 percent to 40 percent. Growth in earnings was even more impressive, from $149 million to $417 million, and from 23 percent to 35 percent of the corporate total.[54]

Several factors accounted for this strong performance. To begin with, P&G was maturing as an international organization. Having entered most markets in the developed world during the previous two decades, it now possessed the key ingredients of success: proven leadership and policies, a cadre of experienced international managers, and a growing number of local managers with significant responsibilities. These local people brought to the company pipelines into leading universities and other sources of local managerial and technical talent, and a deep, accumulating knowledge of local customers and consumption patterns.

Procter & Gamble fared especially well in Western Europe, which in some years accounted for as much as 40 percent of the company's overall profits *(see "Leading and Learning in Western Europe" box).* This performance resulted from the company's transnational character and vigorous leadership. In the late 1970s, under Artzt and with support from Zaki, Pepper, Harald Einsmann, and many other executives, the company had pursued a strategy to anticipate and then capitalize on the growing economic and political integration of the region. To leverage capabilities and scale across the region, coordinate new product and marketing initiatives, and avoid costly duplication of effort, P&G established a series of organizational mechanisms that linked its various national subsidiaries. Euro Brand Teams, for example, formed to promote particular brands, with the team leader chosen from a national subsidiary with an especially strong competence in the relevant area. In the early 1980s, a Euro Brand Team led by product developers at P&G in Germany introduced Vizir liquid detergent, which became a hit and validated the transnational approach.[55]

By the mid-1980s, P&G in Western Europe had evolved a matrix structure that featured senior executives doubling as national subsidiary heads and as category managers for the region. The beauty of the system, as Einsmann put it, was that these executives came to understand the importance and value of each perspective. "Rather than getting the response, 'It is different in France,' which we used to get often from the local general managers, there was a spirit of very positive cooperation." The matrix, Einsmann added, created "a healthy tension . . . and excellent strategic thinking, as well as very good execution."[56]

By the late 1980s, P&G held leading positions in most major categories in the major markets of Western Europe and was expanding into smaller territory in the Iberian Peninsula, Scandinavia, and the Balkans. Acquisitions further strengthened the company's fortunes in the region. Several of the RVI brands were strong in the United Kingdom. In the fall of 1987, P&G strengthened its business in Germany by acquiring the Blendax Group, a leading maker of health (especially oral) and beauty care products. Based in Mainz, Blendax accounted for roughly a quarter of the domestic market in oral hygiene, with Blend-a-Med dentifrice a particularly popular brand. The deal boosted West Germany past the United Kingdom to become P&G's second-largest national market after the United States. It also provided P&G a base from which to expand in Central and Eastern Europe, where Blendax had established export operations.[57]

At the same time, P&G marched ahead aggressively in other regions of the world. In Latin America, P&G poured more investments and categories into the region. At the outset of the decade, P&G had operations in only five

LEADING AND LEARNING IN WESTERN EUROPE

Western Europe has been a major source of both business and learning for P&G since the acquisition of Thomas Hedley in the United Kingdom in 1930 and its initial ventures on the European continent in the 1950s. In building leading positions in its major categories, the company learned significant lessons about striking a balance between serving the particular needs of local consumers while enjoying the advantages of regional scale. For P&G, success in Western Europe proved a critical step on the path to becoming a global force in consumer products.

Procter & Gamble met and overcame a host of challenges in Western Europe in its early years on the continent. One of the biggest was making headway in laundry products, where rivals Unilever and Henkel were well entrenched. In the mid-1960s, P&G found an approach that worked, listening closely to local consumers and designing products specifically for them. Given that most European washing machines were front-loading, had relatively small capacity, and operated at high temperatures, Tide had limited prospects in the region. Accordingly, at the European Technical Center in Brussels, P&G researchers developed a low-suds detergent called Dash. Introduced in West Germany, Dash proved popular not only locally but also across the continent. Procter & Gamble replicated this success with Lenor fabric softener and then followed with a much bigger hit: Ariel, P&G's first enzyme detergent. Also introduced in West Germany, in 1967, Ariel grew into a megabrand not only in Europe but also in Latin America and Asia. Since the 1970s, Ariel has vied with Tide for leadership among P&G's laundry brands.

Procter & Gamble's ability to manage across borders blossomed as it built on successes like Ariel and addressed other challenges in the region. One such challenge was a mixed record in rolling out some of its North American brands across Europe. Mr. Proper (or Mr. Propre)—Mr. Clean in the United States—for example, fared well in Northern Europe but not in the south. Pampers was a success in West Germany (where the Paper Products Division built its first plant outside the United States in 1974) and Belgium but faltered initially in Italy and other countries. Meanwhile, some locally developed products, such as Monsavon bar soap in France, also struggled when P&G attempted to sell them in other European markets.

Procter & Gamble traced these frustrations largely to a fragmented organization in which operations in each nation were managed as autonomous units. Each country's organization initially included responsibility for product development, manufacturing, advertising, and marketing and ➢

In the 1980s, P&G bolstered its position in Western Europe with popular liquid detergents and such packaging innovations as dosing balls.

maintained its own finance and accounting departments. In addition to causing numerous problems in brand building across the region, these arrangements raised administrative costs in overhead, duplicated services, incompatible systems, and other areas. Following the oil crisis of 1973 and 1974, which raised raw materials costs dramatically, P&G decided to act, implementing a regionalization strategy under Ed Artzt. The new strategy began with more coordinated R&D and gradually encompassed purchasing, manufacturing, and marketing. The new strategy also anticipated the growing economic and political integration of Western Europe.

In the mid-1980s, P&G took the next step by placing responsibility for Pampers in Western Europe under a single manager who reported to Harald Einsmann as the top executive for the region. Procter & Gamble also recognized that trans-border television offered great opportunities in advertising common brands and logos across Europe. Within five years of the new "Europeanization" program, Pampers' share of the Western European market doubled to more than 50 percent. Procter & Gamble achieved similarly impressive results with the rapid, regionwide introduction of Always.

During the late 1980s, P&G Europe became one of the company's strongest and most profitable units. It was a training ground for top U.S. executives, such as Ed Artzt, John Pepper, and Bruce Byrnes, while supplying the company with such talented European executives as Einsmann, Durk Jager, Wolfgang Berndt, Paul Polman, and Dimitri Panayotopoulos. Meanwhile, the success of regional category managers and the Europeanization program helped pave the way for P&G's global reorganization a decade later under the Organization 2005 initiative.

of twenty-four countries in Latin America, with significant strength only in Venezuela and Mexico. Detergent and laundry products accounted for more than two-thirds of revenues and profits. Although it had to contend with high inflation and other macroeconomic problems in many countries, most governments abandoned restrictive policies and welcomed foreign investment. Taking advantage of this trend, P&G had entered seven additional countries in Latin America by 1990. Meanwhile, the company diversified its business, finding growing markets for diapers, feminine protection products, personal and beauty care products, and even Pringles. By 1990, for example, P&G was present in sixteen categories in Mexico, with two-thirds of profits coming from products outside laundry. Overall sales in Latin America that year surged past $1 billion.[58]

Under Samih Sherif and Fouad Kraytem, P&G's Export and Special Operations organization in Geneva also negotiated entry into a score of countries during the decade. The company fanned out in several directions from its base around the Mediterranean and in the Middle East, north into the Balkans, and south into sub-Saharan Africa. Following a proven strategy, P&G typically started joint ventures with local partners. Procter & Gamble sometimes began with minority positions but always exerted managerial control and usually had provisions that enabled it, over time, to acquire large majority stakes if not full ownership.[59]

In Asia, P&G transformed its struggling operations in Japan into a huge, profitable success that by the end of the decade contended with West Germany to become the company's number-two national market. After losing money for more than a decade after its 1972 entry into Japan, P&G executed a turnaround under the creative leadership of Durk Jager. In 1985, Jager and his management team developed a new strategy, the "Great Flying Leap," which had several key components, including better understanding of the unique and exacting requirements of Japanese customers, products tailored to these customers, and culturally sensitive advertising. Following these principles, P&G introduced a new, very thin and superabsorbent version of Pampers that vaulted the company to market leadership ahead of Uni-Charm, a tough, local competitor that had pioneered the new designs. Procter & Gamble gleaned technology and learning from the Japanese front of the diaper wars to develop Ultra Pampers for sale in North America and Europe and won back market share ceded to Kimberly-Clark. Whisper sanitary pads (Always in the United States) became another raging success in Japan, with features developed locally to meet the needs of demanding Japanese consumers. The knowledge that the company gained from understanding the Japanese purchaser also transferred to P&G's benefit around the world. Once the company figured out how to compete in Japan—how to innovate, distribute, and win over consumers—most of its products and categories began to flourish.

Artzt also prompted P&G to look beyond Japan and its long-standing operations in the Philippines to penetrate other parts of Asia. The company established a joint venture in Taiwan in 1984, making it the launching pad for an enormous business in shampoos that would erupt in the region and, like Ultra Pampers and Whisper in Japan, spread rapidly around the globe. Procter & Gamble was also pursuing plans to enter Hong Kong and southern Asia when the 1985 RVI acquisition brought thriving operations in Hong Kong, Indonesia, Thailand, and other countries in the region, as well as in the United Kingdom in Europe. Three years later, P&G added to its operations in northern Asia by forming a joint venture in Korea. At the same time, the company kept a watchful eye on the main prize in the region: the People's Republic of China. During the late 1970s and early 1980s, the government of Deng Xiaoping pursued liberal economic policies and encouraged Western companies to invest there. More than a billion prospective customers beckoned, and in 1988, P&G formed a joint venture with Hutchison (China) Trade Holdings Ltd., a unit of a Hong Kong–based trading company, to acquire an interest in a soap factory in Guangzhou. This was the start of a burgeoning investment in China that would pay significant dividends in the next decade and beyond.

Procter & Gamble also responded swiftly to economic liberalization in Central and Eastern Europe. As the Soviet bloc disintegrated and dissolved in the middle and late 1980s, many Western companies, including P&G, recognized another vast opportunity. Led by Wolfgang Berndt, vice president for Canada, Latin America, and the Philippines, P&G carried out an intensive study of markets in Central and Eastern Europe. The outcome was a decision to forgo P&G's traditional country-by-country strategy of entry in favor of a tightly coordinated and sequenced regional strategy to occupy the biggest markets in major categories as quickly as possible. In the spring of 1989—six months before the fall of the Berlin Wall—P&G took its first formal step, charging management at Blendax to seek investment opportunities in East Germany. At the same time, the company drafted plans to enter Poland, Hungary, and the Czech Republic in close succession before 1990, with entry in the Soviet Union to follow soon thereafter. By 1991, P&G expected to produce and sell dentifrices, detergents, diapers, feminine protection products, shampoos, and soaps and cleaners, as well as other products throughout the region.

The speed and scale of P&G's global buildup were unprecedented in the company and caught many of its rivals by surprise. Although Colgate and Unilever remained well entrenched in Latin America and Unilever maintained its traditional stronghold in Southeast Asia, P&G raced ahead to market leadership in most of its categories in the new "white spaces" of Central and Eastern Europe and China. There, and in both the developed and developing economies, the basis of competition in household and consumer products was shifting from national to global scale. In the process, several of P&G's flagship products, including Tide and Ariel, Pampers, Always/Whisper, Pantene, Pert/Rejoy/Rejoice, and even Pringles, became global brands.

The Period in Perspective, 1980–1990

The 1980s proved a significant and decisive decade of change for P&G. The company vigorously pursued growth, accelerating the rate of innovation, entering new businesses via acquisition, and expanding aggressively into new geographies. While outward changes were highly visible and dramatic, changes inside the company were also profound. The most important internal changes involved the category management reorganization of 1987 and the accompanying reforms in compensation (from that based on volume and share growth to that based on profitability), management philosophy (the formal statement of the company's purpose, values, and principles), and product supply, which together thoroughly revamped the way the company operated internally.

The outcome of all this activity was generally positive. Procter & Gamble hit its historical targets for growth: Revenues doubled between 1980 and 1989, from $10.8 to $21.4 billion, with a similar surge in net earnings, from $643 million to $1.2 billion. At the same time, employment climbed to 92,500, an increase of 50 percent. The company successfully defended and renewed its biggest brands, with the introductions of Liquid Tide, Tartar Control Crest, and Ultra Pampers. Always/Whisper proved a major global hit, an especially gratifying outcome given the disappointment of Rely, its first venture into feminine care products, and the company laid the groundwork for shampoos and Pringles to become big global success stories in the following decade. The acquisitions of Norwich Eaton, the Searle OTC business, and RVI provided P&G with a strong foundation in OTC health care products and a promising toehold in prescription drugs. At the same time, RVI contributed major brands in hair and skin care—brands that in later years would constitute the basis of a burgeoning beauty care business.

Procter & Gamble also made important strides in its international ventures. In 1980, sales outside the United States accounted for just under one-third of corporate revenues. Nine years later, foreign revenues had climbed to 40 percent of the total—an impressive result, given the fast growth of the company as a whole. Procter & Gamble maintained operations in forty-five countries in 1989, up from twenty-two countries in 1980. As the volume and complexity of its international activities grew, the company was also learning new ways to manage and coordinate them and was transforming several of its biggest brands into global powerhouses.

Yet the company also coped with some significant disappointments during the 1980s. Many of the smaller brand initiatives begun early in the decade—in bathroom tissue (Banner, Summit, and Certain), laundry (Vibrant), and toilet-bowl cleaners (Brigade) failed to pan out. Some—the low-cost bathroom tissue brands—did not offer significantly better benefits than did generics and store brands. Vibrant was poorly positioned, whereas Brigade suffered from insufficient testing and failed to find a broad market. Meanwhile, the defeat in the soft cookie wars was costly. Not only did it result in a hefty restructuring charge, but when combined with struggles in the acquired soft drink and orange juice businesses, the cookie defeat also caused the company to ponder afresh its entire position in foods and beverages. Moreover, these results heightened P&G's appreciation of the risks of acquisitions, with happy stories (Norwich Eaton, RVI) tempered by cautionary tales (Crush International, Ben Hill Griffin).

The aggressive pursuit of growth in the 1980s generated several important lessons. First, the failure of the smaller brand initiatives indicated that it was risky to speed new products to market without thoroughly understanding consumer needs and doing the detailed prework for which P&G had become justly famous.

Second—and related—an underappreciated risk of the focus on growth and accelerated innovation was the diversion of management attention away from the company's core brands. In an era of heightened competition, P&G could ill afford to pause in upgrading and refreshing Tide and Ariel, Pampers, and Crest. Unfortunately, P&G would relearn both of these lessons in the 1990s.

Third, P&G could only match the accelerating pace of change on the outside by accelerating the rate of change on the inside. Guided by Smale, P&G thus undertook a major reorganization, installed new incentives for managers, and developed new ways of managing through teamwork and collaboration.

Finally, P&G maintained its historical growth trajectory during the 1980s through a combination of sound strategy and effective implementation. It succeeded in finding and cultivating new businesses, such as feminine protection, health care, and beauty care—businesses that would grow faster than the core businesses—and in accelerating overseas expansion. The impact of these moves was particularly strong in the second half of the decade. At the end of the 1980s, however, P&G's prospects for sustaining historical growth rates into the coming decade in a more intensely competitive environment seemed unclear. Despite the uncertainty, the opening of vast new territory in Central and Eastern Europe, the Soviet Union, and China, where two billion potential consumers beckoned, offered ample cause for optimism.

As indicated throughout this chapter, P&G learned some important lessons during the period of heightened competition and globalization in the 1980s. In the following chapters, we recount some of these important learning episodes.

CHAPTER TEN

Learning to Compete in Japan

IN 1972, Procter & Gamble entered Japan, the last major country in the developed world that the company penetrated during the expansive era following World War II. By then, the company had set up operations in more than two dozen nations in Europe, Latin America, North Africa, and the Middle East and was following a well-worn path. The company started by studying the market for detergents to learn about consumers and the channels through which to reach them. It then formed a partnership with a local manufacturer to gain assets and access to distributors, retailers, and customers. And then it pushed to transfer products, people, and technologies proven elsewhere into Japan. Although P&G expected to lose money for several years, it believed that before too long, it would succeed, just as it had elsewhere.

It was a proven formula, except this time, it didn't work.

Procter & Gamble learned from this experience and eventually established a large, vital business in Japan. The company succeeded by rejecting its original approach to market entry and returning to fundamentals: a focus on the particular needs of Japanese consumers, a drive to meet those needs with demonstrably superior products, a commitment to constant innovation, a determination to build and sustain a strong organization. In the early twenty-first century, P&G's operations in Japan face bright prospects for growth and provide a foundation on which P&G is establishing a major presence in northeast Asia. At the same time, the exacting requirements of consumers and a fiercely competitive environment in Japan have pushed and stretched P&G to reach new levels of performance. Japan is a hotbed of innovation that benefits P&G not only locally and regionally, but also globally.

When P&G first thought about entering Japan, however, it had much more modest expectations. As it turned out, even these would be dashed before the company discovered how to succeed in Japan and become a truly global competitor.

Entry into Japan

In the late 1960s, the prospect that the Japanese government would soon ease restrictions on foreign capital prompted P&G to consider entering Japan. In 1968, P&G undertook a two-month study of the Japanese detergent market. The analysis proved encouraging. To begin with, the market was large and growing at 15 percent per year. Powerful cultural and religious factors helped propel this growth. Women managed Japanese households and made most purchasing decisions for consumer products. Japanese women had high standards for personal cleanliness and order—standards necessitated and reinforced by the relatively small living space occupied by typical households. They bathed frequently and typically washed laundry twice per day. They consumed (on a per capita basis) twice the volume of soaps, detergents, cleansers, and personal care products that their counterparts in North America and Europe used. Japanese women also had extraordinarily high expectations for the products they purchased and were finely attuned to product features and quality. This concern for cleanliness and order had roots in the dominant religions in Japan, Buddhism and Shintoism. In both religions, evil is associated with dirtiness and good with cleanliness. For many Japanese, then, a business reporter pointed out, "cleanliness is not next to godliness, it is godliness."[1]

While bullish about the Japanese market, P&G remained concerned about the competition. It was well aware that two domestic competitors, Kao and Lion, would prove tough, resourceful rivals. At the same time, however, P&G believed that neither company could match its experience, technical prowess, marketing savvy, and financial clout and that ultimately P&G would prevail.

A bigger concern was the complex and highly fragmented nature of distribution in Japan. In the 1970s, packaged goods typically were sold through small retail outlets or convenience stores, although there was an incipient trend toward self-service supermarket chains. There were nearly 1.7 million retail stores in Japan, one for every 375 people and about four times the store density in the United States. Approximately 17,000 Japanese wholesalers supplied these stores, with responsibilities including selling, physical movement of goods, collection of money, and returns. At least two, and sometimes three, wholesalers typically handled packaged goods between manufacturers' warehouses and retail outlets. Procter & Gamble had no prospect of arranging exclusive agreements with any of these wholesalers, most of whom already had strong relationships with Kao and Lion. Learning to navigate through this thicket of wholesalers and distributors, P&G recognized, would constitute a major challenge.[2]

The outcome of P&G's 1968 study was a decision to enter Japan, although the means remained as yet undecided. News of the company's activity nonetheless sent tremors through the Japanese soap and detergent industry, alarming competitors, who fretted about P&G's "vast resources—its revenues amounted to nine times the combined revenues of Kao and Lion—and ability to spend heavily on advertising."[3]

In September 1970, the Japanese government implemented new regulations that permitted foreign owners to acquire up to a 50 percent interest in Japanese companies. Within a month, William Gurganus, head of P&G International, and Ed Shutt, manager of the Asia and Latin America Division, were in Japan for talks with prospective partners. Neither Kao nor Lion was interested, so P&G turned its attention first to Nihon Yushi (Nippon Oils and Fats), the number four soap maker in Japan. Initial discussions seemed to go well, and an imminent deal was reported in the Japanese business press.[4] The talks broke off, however, and P&G eventually shifted its focus to Nippon Sunhome, the industry's third-largest competitor.

A joint venture between three chemical companies—Daiichi Kogyo Seiyaka (DKS), Asahi Denka Kogyo (ADK), and Mitsuwa—Nippon Sunhome had formed in 1969 in Osaka under the supervision of the Japanese Ministry of International Trade and Industry (MITI). None of the constituent companies had recently fared well in soaps and detergents, and MITI hoped that pooling their resources would produce a stronger competitor. That hope proved ill founded, however. By 1972, P&G learned through both Morgan Bank and C. Itoh, a Japanese trading company, that Nippon Sunhome was failing and that its owners might be willing to listen to offers. Shutt quickly followed up the lead and hammered out the terms for a deal: Procter & Gamble would acquire 50 percent of Nippon Sunhome, with 45 percent owned by DKS and ADK, and 5 percent by C. Itoh. Mitsuwa dropped out of the venture altogether. The new company would be called P&G Sunhome, with a capitalization of two billion yen, and P&G would possess management control.[5]

Procter & Gamble's senior executives disagreed sharply about using Sunhome as a vehicle for entry into Japan. Shutt pushed hard for the deal, while his boss believed that Sunhome was too weak as a partner. Gurganus predicted that it might take ten to fifteen years for P&G to reach breakeven. He argued further that a wiser course would be to wait for a better opportunity—either a stronger partner or a more distinctive product than detergents. Neil

McElroy, still a member of the executive committee of the board, concurred. Chief executive Howard Morgens agreed with Shutt, however. In making the case for the deal to P&G's board, Morgens argued that "unless we know how to compete with Japan, *in Japan,* we're going to have to compete with them all over the world, and we'd better learn" (emphasis in original).[6] This view prevailed, and it would become a recurring theme in the company, as well as a periodic reminder of the strategic significance of the Japanese market.

A Rocky Start

Complicated decision-making arrangements encumbered the early years of P&G Sunhome. When Gurganus declined to take responsibility for the venture, citing priorities in Europe, Brad Butler, a senior sales executive who would shortly become vice chairman of the board, assumed top-level oversight. Shutt remained the top executive for the region and kept a close watch on the new general manager, Jack Nedell, a veteran international executive—so close, in fact, that Nedell was known as "Mr. Telex" because he had to clear even minor decisions with his boss. Since Nedell did not speak Japanese, he relied heavily on managers from the joint venture partners to understand local conditions. He also valued the advice of several other expatriate managers. With heavy input from Cincinnati, Nedell and his colleagues crafted a strategy to weed out all but two of Sunhome's traditional brands and introduce three P&G brands: Cheer laundry detergent powder, Bonus liquid laundry detergent (Era in the United States), and Camay.

Procter & Gamble placed the biggest bet on Cheer, then thriving in the United States under its positioning as an all-temperature detergent. Although Japanese consumers typically washed their clothes in cold tap water—or sometimes by recycling tepid bathtub water—P&G reasoned that the all-temperature attribute of Cheer would help differentiate the product and call to mind its high-tech, U.S. origins. This attribute was emphasized in ad campaigns carried out by Leo Burnett Kyodo, the Tokyo branch of a U.S. agency staffed by American expatriates. In an all-out drive to gain market share, P&G Sunhome advertised aggressively and offered low introductory prices. The company also worked directly with large retailers to feature Cheer—a common practice in the United States but unheard of in Japan and cause for unhappiness among distributors and smaller retailers who had to pay more for the product than consumers at some outlets.

P&G Sunhome's strategy and tactics delivered promising early results. Between 1973 and 1978, gross revenues more than doubled (reaching ¥42.1 billion). The company still lost money, however, because of heavy investments in advertising, in promotion, and in upgrading and expanding produc-

Procter & Gamble entered Japan with high hopes for Cheer. The company eventually became a factor in detergents, but its long-term fortunes in Japan depended on expanding its categories.

tion facilities. These actions strained the resources of P&G's Japanese partners. As the government eased restrictions on foreign ownership, P&G gradually increased its stake, acquiring P&G Sunhome outright in 1978. By then, the company's total capitalization had reached ¥24 billion. The company had also realigned its decision-making process following Shutt's retirement. For a time, Nedell reported directly to Butler before a new general manager, Fred Kruse, arrived on the scene.[7]

As these events and changes played out at P&G Sunhome, P&G mounted a complementary effort to launch other product lines in Japan. The idea was to generate more volume to gain leverage in the fragmented distribution channels. Aware that its partners in P&G Sunhome were ill equipped to support such a strategy, in 1976 P&G incorporated a wholly owned subsidiary, P&G Japan K.K. In the next several years, P&G Japan K.K. test marketed numerous brands in Japan, but only one—Pampers disposable diapers—seemed promising. Imported from the United States, Pampers fared well initially despite little effort to customize the product for the Japanese market. Designs and sizes, for example, were identical to those in the United States. Procter & Gamble also sold the product at a hefty premium. By one calculation, the exclusive use of Pampers cost an average household about twelve thousand yen per month—approximately the same as the home's utility bill. The company backed the national rollout with a blitz of TV advertising, retail trade presentations, and donations of samples to maternity clinics and households with babies. The company even hired vans equipped with loudspeakers to drive through neighborhoods, announcing "if you need a diaper, please hang one on your balcony." Such actions helped increase the penetration of disposable diapers from 2 percent to 10 percent of all diaper changes by 1979. In that year, P&G began construction of a new Pampers plant in Akashi.[8]

At first glance, P&G's steady gains in volume in detergents and disposable diapers appeared to signal that it was on track. Serious problems, however, lurked below the surface. The company's aggressive pricing in detergents had touched off a trade war with Kao and Lion, a circumstance in which no one benefited. The big jump in raw-materials prices triggered by the energy crisis of 1973 to 1974 worsened the situation, putting a tight squeeze on margins. In 1977, moreover, Kao introduced a new detergent, Wonderful, that quickly ate into Cheer's share. Two years later, Lion announced its own entry, Top, which featured the superior cleaning power of enzymes. Within eighteen months, Top surpassed Cheer as the leading product in the detergent category. Meanwhile, to stem share losses, P&G cut prices on Cheer just in time for a second energy crisis in 1979. In that year, the company's operating losses were greater than during the introductory period of 1973 to 1974.

Nor was the situation better in Pampers. Although P&G had successfully created the market for disposable diapers, it soon found itself on the defensive. One problem was the extraordinarily high standard for quality in Japan. The imported Pampers met U.S. standards for quality, which in Japan were considered wholly unsatisfactory. Product failures rarely occurred, but when they did, consumers were furious and some stores threatened to discontinue the brand.[9] While P&G rushed to improve product quality, a strong domestic competitor suddenly appeared on the scene. In 1981, the Japanese company Uni-Charm introduced its Moony disposable diaper at a 40 percent premium to Pampers and quickly cornered a 23 percent share in its first year. In contrast to Pampers, Moony was a slimmer, fitted product similar to P&G's Luvs brand sold in the United States. Japanese mothers changed diapers more frequently than did their American counterparts, a practice that meant each diaper would carry less load and could be less bulky. In retrospect, Butler believed that P&G erred by not introducing Luvs into Japan. Meanwhile, P&G was saddled with a new Akashi plant that would take a year and many millions of dollars to be retooled for a new Pampers design.[10]

Other problems were also manifest. The company had inherited from its joint venture partners a sales force of 150 people, who in turn were expected to call on approximately three thousand wholesalers each week. Butler noted that the sales reps "made very few calls," and because few of them lived in their sales territories, "their travel expenses were terrible, their effectiveness in calls per day was terrible." None of the wholesalers had exclusive rights to P&G brands, which accounted for a tiny fraction (on average, less than 2 percent) of their business, and they had limited interest in pushing P&G's products. Some wholesalers also distributed for Kao, Lion, or Uni-Charm, invariably older and bigger accounts that naturally commanded their loyalty. Finally, some geographical territories overlapped, causing internal competition among the wholesalers.[11]

Internally, P&G Sunhome faced tensions between some expatriate and Japanese managers. Expatriates occupied the most powerful positions in the company, while some Japanese managers continued to identify with their original employers before the formation of the joint venture. By the early 1980s, this latter group had aged into an old guard that moved slowly, resisted change, and impeded efforts to recruit younger managers. And recruiting was already a difficult challenge because most bright and ambitious Japanese students preferred to work for established Japanese companies. Procter & Gamble made some progress with a program that promised to send the best of its recruits after one year for a one-year assignment at corporate headquarters, including an English immersion program at the University of Cincinnati. Still, it would take ten to fifteen years to see how these young recruits would pan out.[12]

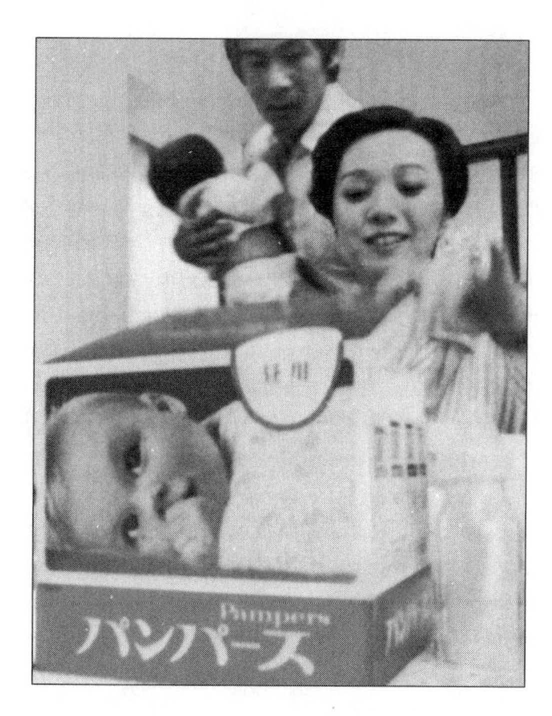

Pampers eventually proved a big hit in Japan—after P&G learned how to meet the needs of extremely demanding consumers through fast-cycle innovations and upgrades.

By 1983, after its first decade, P&G Japan was clearly in trouble. Cheer had slipped well behind Wonderful and Top, even as new and improved, phosphate-free formulations of those products came on the market. Thus, P&G had fallen at least two technology generations behind its competitors and could only anticipate that things would get worse during the twelve to eighteen months typically needed to reformulate a detergent. At the same time, Moony had become the leading disposable diaper in its second full year in the market, with Pampers losing one to two points of market share per month. Worse, Kao was test marketing a shaped and fitted diaper similar to Moony called Merries, which consumers also preferred to Pampers. Not only did P&G management face big investments to retool the Akashi plant, but repositioning Pampers, regarded as an inferior product, to compete at price parity with Moony and Merries was a daunting prospect. Meanwhile, no other P&G brands had made much headway in Japan; the company overall had lost $300 million, with the prospect of payback nowhere in sight. And together, P&G Sunhome and P&G Japan K.K. had already accumulated a combined debt of $250 million. Retailers and wholesalers were unhappy. Internally, morale had reached a low ebb. Some observers wondered how much longer P&G could sustain such performance, while rumors swirled to the effect that the top ranks of corporate management were divided, with some senior executives and board members urging P&G to withdraw from Japan altogether for the time being.

The Great Flying Leap

The dawning awareness of P&G's predicament in Japan coincided with the ascendancy of new management in Cincinnati. In 1980, Ed Artzt succeeded Gurganus as head of P&G International; a year later, John Smale succeeded Ed Harness as chief executive of the corporation. Artzt arrived fresh off a highly successful stint as head of P&G operations in Europe, and neither he nor Smale was about to concede defeat in Japan. Like Morgens before him, Artzt believed that P&G simply had to succeed in Japan to remain a viable global competitor in consumer products. "Compete with them in their own backyard," he said, "for you will eventually compete with them at home. . . . We need to be in business in Japan, and we cannot afford to be anything but successful there."[13]

With Smale's backing, Artzt reorganized P&G's international operations to remove the layer of regional division management, so that the presidents of operations in major markets, including Japan, reported directly to him. He also saw a need for a strong, new management team in Japan. In the summer of 1982, he placed Russell Marsden and Durk Jager, two young, high-potential executives from Europe, in charge. Marsden, the new general manager, had been responsible for P&G's operations in Southern Europe, where Jager, country manager for Austria, had reported to him. Jager became head of the advertising department in Japan.

Reviewing the first decade of P&G's experience in Japan, Marsden and Jager saw numerous mistakes, most of them rooted in the natural but counterproductive arrogance of a highly successful American multinational. As Artzt later summarized it, the company "stormed into the Japanese market with American products, American managers, American advertising, American sales methods and American promotion strategy. . . . It was a near disaster." Turning the operation around called for a radically new approach.[14]

Assured of Artzt's strong support, early in 1983, Marsden and Jager recommended a set of initiatives collected under the general rubric "A Fresh Start." The initiatives began with structural, financial, and organizational changes. Procter & Gamble created a new, wholly owned subsidiary, P&G Far East, which in turn acquired P&G Sunhome and P&G Japan K.K., in the process removing all debt from the balance sheet. The new operating company in Japan thus began its work debt-free. At the same time, the officers of both P&G Sunhome and P&G Japan K.K. resigned, allowing P&G Far East to form a new executive team and a leaner organization. Most of the new executives were rehired from P&G Sunhome or P&G Japan K.K., although a few came from elsewhere within P&G. Japanese nationals held key positions in manufacturing and personnel.[15]

Marsden and Jager also acted swiftly and decisively to address challenges in detergents and disposable diapers. They compressed the timetable for reformulating Cheer from the normal twelve- to eighteen-month period to six months, introducing a higher-performance Cheer in new packaging in the summer of 1983. The new Cheer was sold at higher prices, enabling distributors and retailers to reap higher margins. Procter & Gamble also believed that Kao and Lion were selling below cost in order to keep P&G in a loss position and force its eventual withdrawal. The company petitioned MITI to investigate and later enlisted the support of the U.S. government to urge the Japanese government to pursue the matter. Although P&G's leaders held little hope that these efforts would prove effectual, they felt obliged nonetheless to pursue them.[16]

In the meantime, P&G collaborated with wholesalers and retailers to revise terms of trade so that the entire process of distribution could be streamlined—a development the Japanese business press hailed as "an epoch-making change."[17] Marsden and Jager also sought to reposition Pampers with new designs calling for a slimmer, fitted product. The old production lines were written off and new ones ordered to begin a national rollout by the end of 1984—in time to cut into the growth of Kao's Merries, if not Uni-Charm's Moony.

In February 1985, before the new strategies were fully tested, Marsden suffered a debilitating stroke that led eventually to his premature retirement from P&G. Artzt installed Jager as general manager. Jager saw clearly the dimensions of the task, which he conveyed to his management team: "Pull together or we're out of business."[18]

Jager made a few key changes in top management, installing Kerry Clark as advertising manager and promoting Ryozo Shin-i as personnel manager and a direct report. These managers, along with Fred Caswell (sales), Minoru Shimada (manufacturing), Tatsuhisa Miyanoiri (distribution), and I. Imai (corporate relations) worked as a team to develop a new three-year plan to reach breakeven. Called *Ichidai Hiyaku* ("The Great Flying Leap"), the plan called for dramatic gains in growth while stemming operating losses. *Ichidai Hiyaku* included five key points:

1. UNDERSTAND JAPANESE CONSUMERS. The all-temperature quality of Cheer, for example, meant little in Japan, since the Japanese customarily washed their clothes in cold water. Henceforth, P&G products sold in Japan would be pitched to the needs of Japanese consumers. Detergents, for example, would emphasize their cleaning power in cold-water conditions.

2. TAILOR PRODUCTS TO JAPAN. Pampers, for example, would be again completely redesigned for reduced bulk, increased absorbency, and better fit—all qualities prized by Japanese consumers.

3. MARKET WITH SENSITIVITY TO CULTURE. New advertising would reflect subtleties and nuances in Japanese culture and would be made with more input from Japanese ad agency professionals. For example, a Camay ad from the 1970s depicted a man meeting a woman for the first time and immediately comparing her skin to that of a fine porcelain doll. The ad flopped, said a Japanese ad agency executive: "For a Japanese man to say something like that to a Japanese woman means he's either unsophisticated or rude." Procter & Gamble's agency reps warned that Japanese women would find the ad offensive, but the company "just wouldn't listen."[19] After this episode, P&G would listen attentively.

4. SELL THE COMPANY'S IMAGE. The P&G name would be attached to the brand name in packaging and advertising to emphasize the company behind the brand—a common practice in Japan.

5. PENETRATE THE JAPANESE DISTRIBUTION SYSTEM. The company would redouble its efforts to gain leverage with wholesalers and ensure that its products were available and prominently displayed in stores.

Adhering to these principles, P&G began a series of major product initiatives in the mid- to late 1980s. The company made the Japanese market a focal point of R&D on diapers worldwide. Drawing heavily on corporate R&D and investment, P&G retooled the Akashi plant and upgraded Pampers four times in three years. Improvements focused especially on removing bulk, enabling tighter fits, and simplifying fastening. At the same time, manufacturing process and management changes in Akashi enabled the plant to run at significantly lower cost. The result was a technical breakthrough—the world's thinnest and most absorbent diaper—and a business hit. By 1990, Pampers had regained the number one position in Japan, while usage had nearly tripled, from about 10 percent to 27 percent in nine years. The turnaround demonstrated, said Jager, "that with relentless pursuit of design and production quality it is possible to recapture business from sophisticated Japanese competition."[20]

The detergent business remained a struggle for P&G. Earlier changes to Cheer had halted the downward spiral, but had not enabled a rebound. In 1987, Kao introduced a new compact detergent called Attack, which vaulted well past Cheer to the number two market position within six months. By then, it was clear to P&G management that no amount of effort would enable Cheer to catch up. Rather, the company introduced its own new compact detergent, called Ariel, in 1988. Like the redesigned Pampers, Ariel incorporated P&G's best technology worldwide, including a low-temperature bleach activator and new surfactants. Ariel surged quickly to the number three position behind both Lion's leading brand, Top, and Kao's Attack, but progress from there would be slow.

Encouraging signs from Pampers and Ariel notwithstanding, Jager recognized that P&G needed a broader line of offerings to increase leverage with distributors and bolster its position in the marketplace. At the same time, Artzt believed that the company had to put more pressure on Kao's major product contributors that were subsidizing its losses in detergents. Between 1985 and 1988, P&G launched more than a dozen new or upgraded brands, including Monogen Uni liquid laundry detergent (for fine fabrics), Attento (Attends in the United States) adult incontinent briefs, Whisper feminine protection pads (Always in the United States), Rejoy two-in-one shampoo (Pert Plus in the United States), Bounce liquid fabric softener, Shasta moisturizing lotion, and Sinex nasal decongestant (a product obtained through P&G's 1985 acquisition of Richardson-Vicks Inc.).[21]

Among these newcomers, Whisper proved by far the most successful and a major contributor to P&G's strong rebound. The company introduced the brand in 1986, tailoring it in size to fit Japanese women. Procter & Gamble backed Whisper with heavy expenditures in promotion and advertising. Free samples were distributed outside subway stations. For the first time in Japan, a feminine protection product was advertised on television. Advertisements developed with the Japanese agency Dentsu emphasized the unobtrusive nature and cleanliness of the product, targeting young women in their late teens and early twenties. Brand manager Hiroko Wada explained Dentsu's approach:

> *To appeal to these women in our television advertising, we chose a minor celebrity who is the perfect role model for our target audience. She is a well-known photographer and epitomizes the emergence of professional working women in Japan.*
>
> *The dialogue of the commercial reflects the open and frank way the Japanese women talk to one another about sanitary products and is represented by the selling line that using Whisper feels like wearing just-washed underwear.*[22]

Introduced at a 24 percent price premium, Whisper became a runaway market leader behind superior consumer satisfaction and value ratings.

Behind the scenes, P&G made significant progress in simplifying the distribution of its products. Assisted by the consulting firm Booz Allen Hamilton, the company concentrated its business in the hands of about 40 core wholesalers and 1,000 secondary wholesalers—down from 500 and 3,000, respectively. The core wholesalers were given exclusive distribution rights to P&G products by geography or trade channel, and, according to distribution manager Miyanoiri, they "began aggressively supporting [P&G] brands following their selection." At the same time, P&G set up electronic links with its core wholesalers and instituted twenty-four-hour delivery service. Procter & Gamble also established a national accounts division to penetrate and develop the top fifty retail chains in Japan. In the first year after the change, the company's volume with these customers surged by 40 percent.[23]

Internally, P&G revamped its entire system of human resource management. It supplemented the informal hierarchy based on Japanese titles with English titles. It also abandoned the traditional Japanese practice of basing promotion and compensation on age and seniority in favor of merit-based criteria. The company instituted an early-retirement program that induced several dozen managers to leave. In recruiting, personnel manager Shin-i targeted students in the top eight schools in Japan. He attempted to lure them by emphasizing that P&G would give young people significant responsibility, advance them on the basis of their performance, and tolerate no sex dis-

In the late 1980s, Whisper became a huge success in Japan, symbolizing the turnaround of P&G's fortunes.

crimination. Such policies attracted strong applicants, particularly among young Japanese women, whose career prospects in traditional Japanese organizations were more limited. Although P&G conducted much of its internal business in English, it did not require facility in English as a condition of employment. Promising recruits who did not speak English were sent to language immersion programs at company expense. In 1986, Jager reported that the most recent recruiting cycle had netted "35 top-rate people versus a maximum of 10 in the past."[24]

A new corporate public relations initiative simultaneously aided P&G's business and recruiting. Jager made himself freely available to reporters and held periodic press conferences. The company sponsored receptions for the press and business community when launching new products or making major announcements. It instituted the first toll-free telephone number for consumers in Japan. The company also promoted its institutional identity. In 1986, it registered its stock on the Tokyo Stock Exchange. The P&G logo was featured on all packaging, advertising, and printed matter, including business cards and stationery, and a video signature was added at the close of all TV advertisements. The company also started two new publications: *P&G Tsushin* ("Communicating P&G") provided monthly updates on company activities to the press and public, and *P&G Tradebeams* covered topics of interest to the company's wholesalers and retailers.[25]

In combination, the policies, events, and activities of the Great Flying Leap produced outstanding performance for P&G in Japan. Between 1985 and 1988, P&G's sales in Japan surged from $132 million to $566 million. The company moved past breakeven in 1987, earning its first annual profit after nearly fifteen years in Japan. These results impressed even the competition. "P&G has learned how to make products the Japanese consumer likes," observed Kazaburo Sagawa, chairman of Kao. "We're very impressed with their ability to get products right for Japan now."[26]

In reflecting on these events and outcomes a decade later, Jager declared that *Ichidai Hiyaku* was more than a slogan:

> *We moved away from sugar-coated, paternalistic company-employee relations. We were candid on our results and with each other (i.e., the reward system). We met with 20–25 senior managers every quarter to discuss our results, where we've done well, and particularly, where we failed. We reviewed the programs for the next 3, 6, or 12 months by business or discipline. These plans became corporate commitments and every one of these meetings was concluded with a sushi/sashimi/beer/sake party.*
>
> *. . . what I recall the best is that we were having real fun. We were very close to defeat, had nothing to lose, and thus had to stretch, had to innovate, and had to be fast on our feet.*[27]

Relearning How to Compete in Japan

After Jager left Japan in 1989 for other assignments, momentum established under *Ichidai Hiyaku* carried on for several more years. In 1990, P&G's sales in Japan climbed past $1 billion, and the company committed $215 million to build a combined headquarters and technical center on Rokko Island in Osaka Bay. The R&D unit was a visible symbol of the company's view of the Japanese market as a powerful laboratory for learning. The facility was designed not only to support initiatives in Japan but also those elsewhere in Asia, as the company continued an aggressive drive in the region.[28]

In the early 1990s, however, the rapid growth of the Japanese economy tapered off noticeably. To sustain volume, P&G cut its prices an average of 3 percent per year between 1991 and 1995, but the competition matched the cuts, resulting in declining volume and profitability. The company fell prey to a vicious cycle: Lower prices meant pressure to cut production costs, which resulted in reduced performance, which prompted still lower prices. In detergents, price competition proved especially fierce. At one point, the cost of the water to do a load of laundry exceeded the cost of the detergent. Procter & Gamble compounded its troubles by deciding to remove the low-temperature-activated bleach from Ariel as a cost-saving measure. This action robbed the product of one of its distinctive features and made it vulnerable to criticism that it was no longer a high-performance detergent.[29]

By 1996, at a management meeting in Cincinnati to review the performance of the company's brands in each category worldwide, P&G executives came to an unhappy realization. Bob McDonald, general manager of laundry and hair care products in P&G Asia (successor to P&G Far East), recalled the discussion about the merits of each brand: "We kept hearing that ours was the best—except in Japan." He heard this from A. G. Lafley, the senior executive responsible for P&G's business in Asia. Lafley had noticed that "except in Japan" was becoming a litany. In fact, as he reported to the board, only two of P&G's fourteen brands—lipstick and Bonus liquid laundry detergent—clearly outperformed the competition. Even Whisper had fallen behind a Japanese rival whose products delivered "extra protection." The troubles showed up in declining growth rates and falling market share throughout P&G Japan. For a time, appreciation of the yen (from 126 to the dollar, to 85 to the dollar between 1992 and 1995) masked the serious nature of the problem. By 1996, however, nothing could hide the need for immediate, strong actions.[30]

Procter & Gamble again installed new management, calling on McDonald. Supported by Jager and Lafley, McDonald quickly assembled a team and acted decisively to improve the company's cost position. The company wrote off $71 million of waste, closed two plants and a number of offices and warehouses, and retired or separated more than eleven hundred employees—more than a quarter of the workforce. At the same time, the new team, again assisted by Jager and Lafley, articulated a new vision of growth and the strategies to achieve it. The new strategies recalled the lessons of the Great Flying Leap and placed renewed emphasis on innovation, changing the rules of the game, and strengthening the organization.[31]

Innovation began with key improvements to existing product lines. Brand managers for Ariel, for example, worked closely with expert panels of consumers and determined that users wanted their washed garments sanitized as well as cleaned and brightened. Drawing on corporate R&D, P&G reformulated Ariel to deliver superior sanitization—a higher-order benefit called *seiketsu*—and the brand began to make significant headway against Attack. Similar interventions helped put Whisper back on track.[32]

In the mid- to late 1990s, P&G followed with a blitzkrieg of new product introductions and product line extensions, averaging ten per year. The goal was to market "products that are clearly different, often unique, and always better."[33] New items, all of which were priced at premiums, included "new-to-the world" products such as Pampers Pants and newly positioned brands such as the SK-II skin care line, which proved a big winner. Meanwhile, P&G Japan also introduced Pringles through an arrangement with a local broker. The product also fared well, and P&G subsequently formed its own field sales force in a steady drive to record performance, year after year.[34]

Again, P&G sought to change the competitive rules of the game through innovative products and marketing. In 1995, the company had introduced in Japan a concentrated dish-washing liquid called Joy, which became for the late 1990s what Whisper had been a decade earlier: a blockbuster hit. Joy featured state-of-the-art grease-cutting technology, as well as compact and convenient packaging. Within two years, the brand soared to a 20 percent market share against entrenched competitors Kao and Lion, while selling at a 20 percent premium and leading the market toward concentrated dish-washing detergents.[35]

Procter & Gamble also brought Efficient Consumer Response (ECR) practices to Japan. The result included simplified supply chains, the elimination of temporary price reductions and deep discounting, and the adoption of global standard systems like electronic data interchange. At the same time, P&G itself became much more streamlined, operating with half the number of plants and 10 percent of the warehouses it had used previously.[36]

By early in the twenty-first century, P&G Japan had rebounded again to become one of P&G's strongest international units. Under Werner Geissler's leadership, it posted revenues of $1.7 billion and was growing profitably and at a significantly faster clip than any of its competitors, despite a troubled economy. Procter & Gamble Japan also served as a test bed for new products and concepts for the corporation as a whole. As McDonald put it, "Japan is an R&D developer's dream."[37]

The Japanese Experience in Perspective

Procter & Gamble's long struggle and ultimate success in Japan validated the conviction of its top officers—from John Smale and Ed Artzt to Durk Jager and A. G. Lafley—that winning in Japan would be a foundation for winning around the world. By meeting the expectations of the world's most demanding consumers for quality and innovation, P&G gained significant advantage. In detergents, disposable diapers, feminine care, and other products and categories, the technology and marketing behind P&G's success in Japan facilitated gains in many other markets.

Reaching this result, however, proved fraught with difficulty and required persisting through major setbacks. Although success came only after years of struggle, P&G benefited from the timing of its entry. In the early 1970s, neither Kao nor Lion was as yet a global competitor. By attacking them on their home turf, P&G weakened its rivals, delayed their international expansion, and gained deep insight into the local marketplace.

Procter & Gamble began to make progress, however, only after it dispatched some of its best young management talent to Japan while also engaging focused attention from Artzt, the company's top international officer. The magnitude of the crisis in the early 1980s required an unusually creative response, and the long-term, competitive stakes meant that the company could ill afford subsequent mistakes. Procter & Gamble started winning once it changed the game by tailoring its products and marketing messages to the exacting requirements of Japanese consumers and taking the lead in revamping the country's complex system of distribution. Along the way, P&G Japan became a proving ground for three future P&G chief executives—Artzt, Jager, and Lafley—as well as other prominent technical and managerial personnel.

CHAPTER ELEVEN

The Diaper Wars

THROUGHOUT the late 1960s and early 1970s, P&G rode high with Pampers, the blockbuster brand that almost single-handedly created the mass market for disposable diapers in the United States. Despite its resounding success, the company continued to search for ways to improve the product. Market research studies begun in the mid-1960s revealed that disposable diapers tended to leak because they lost their fit, especially around the legs. After identifying this problem, researchers at the Miami Valley and Winton Hill technical facilities in Ohio began working on a solution. In 1973, they perfected an hourglass-shaped pad with flexible, elastic gathers. Three years later, P&G made the fateful decision to test market the new design not on Pampers but on a separate premium brand called Luvs.[1]

The decision to restrict the premium technology to the smaller, more expensive Luvs brand exposed Pampers to attack. In 1978, Kimberly-Clark struck hard, introducing its brand, Huggies, as a technologically superior diaper for the masses. The success of Huggies came at the expense of both Pampers and Luvs, and Kimberly-Clark followed through with a series of timely and significant improvements. As a result, although P&G remained the worldwide market leader in disposable diapers, it lost its commanding lead in the United States. As of the early 2000s P&G was locked in fierce competition with Kimberly-Clark in North America, with Kimberly-Clark and several European competitors, and with Uni-Charm and other tough rivals in Japan and Asia.

Procter & Gamble's reversal of fortune in disposable diapers became a cautionary tale inside the company, a great might-have-been that has been taught and studied by managers and technical personnel ever since. The Pampers/Luvs case was an early lesson about brand equity, a contentious issue that later reemerged with Crest. Even more fundamentally, the experience typified the way a market leader in a newly competitive industry received its comeuppance from a nimbler and more savvy rival. Incredibly, the company that prided itself on knowing more about consumers than almost any other company, badly misjudged what its own consumers wanted.

Luvs: A Lesson in Brand Equity

In hindsight, the decision to put all the premium features on a separate, higher-priced brand proved disastrous. But at the time, the strategy struck nearly everyone as eminently sensible. In 1980, the company's own in-house newsletter, *Moonbeams,* asked, "Why has P&G introduced a second disposable diaper called Luvs?" The article went on to quote Chuck Lieppe, advertising manager for the Paper Division: "While Pampers has been improved many times, we simply couldn't add the premium performance features some parents wanted in a diaper and keep Pampers' relative cost down." Articulating the decisions made by top management, Lieppe went on to say that marketers had "identified specific consumer needs for both products." Researchers had "found that many parents choose both Pampers and Luvs for their babies and use them at different times."[2]

As Lieppe indicated, the differential in cost strongly argued for the separate-brand strategy. The company's engineering and manufacturing experts, including Chuck Fullgraf, Jim Edwards, and Harry Tecklenburg, agreed that the premium features on Luvs could not be transferred to a high-volume product like Pampers. The hourglass design of the Luvs diaper used a new manufacturing process to mold the diaper's inner core, which added 30 percent to costs. Top line speed reached only 130 per minute, compared with around 400 for Pampers. Attaching the elastic on the leg openings was also tricky, because the gathers sometimes caused the diaper to bunch up on the production line, making the diaper difficult to fold. These problems had been so difficult to fix that they necessitated two entirely new processes that eventually were patented.[3]

Procter & Gamble priced Luvs about 30 percent higher than Pampers to reflect the higher manufacturing costs and to prevent direct competition between the two brands. Initial consumer research indicated that only a minority of mothers was willing to pay significantly more for improved performance. Consumers, P&G believed, would always be divided between those who wanted a medium-priced product, and a much smaller segment who was willing to pay for premium features. Historical data on P&G's other products appeared to support the conclusion. "When we looked at our

In 1976 P&G fatefully decided to offer its best technology on Luvs, a new premium diaper brand. An unintended consequence was to expose Pampers to competitive attack.

other categories," a company spokesman later explained, "we saw that very few brands with such a level of premium pricing had ever gained a major share of their category."[4]

Decades of experience reinforced the decision. Anyone who doubted the wisdom of the multibrand strategy needed only to look at the company's detergents. Tide was sold as the premium product, Cheer cleaned colors safely, Gain had fresh scent, and Oxydol contained bleach. By separately supporting several closely related products, P&G found that it could satisfy a wider spectrum of consumers. Howard Morgens summed up the philosophy in a 1994 interview: "We had better be the first to find [the better product] and to bring it out rather than let a competitor do it. If Cheer could take business away from Tide, somebody else could do it. That was the principle, only what we did then was say we want a different brand name on it."[5]

This way of thinking about brand equity was so firmly entrenched that the idea of putting the best technology on Pampers, rather than creating a separate brand, "was not even a remote possibility," said Mark Ketchum, who became the global manager for diapers in 1996. Introducing a new benefit to Pampers was seen as "an inappropriate distillation of the existing brand equity." Consequently, "there was no discussion, really no serious discussion, about making this a Pampers product. . . . [W]e didn't have any model in the company for line extending into something, for instance like Pampers Ultra." The division was clear: Luvs diapers' appeal was superior comfort, fit, and absorbency; Pampers concentrated on its heritage of dryness.[6]

In retrospect, such an approach failed to take account of the competition and limited the company's ability to respond quickly. In 1978, just as P&G began the international rollout of Pampers and Luvs, Kimberly-Clark introduced Huggies at a slight premium to Pampers. Huggies represented a significant improvement not only over Kimberly-Clark's original Kimbies brand, but also over Pampers. It had an hourglass shape that fit better, offered better absorbency, and featured an improved tape fastening system—all for pennies more than Pampers.[7]

Huggies proved immensely popular with consumers, and it steadily gained share, going from 7 percent of the U.S. market in 1980 to a remarkable 32 percent by 1989. (Procter & Gamble's 70 percent U.S. share, meanwhile, dropped to 48 percent.) The diapers became Kimberly-Clark's largest single product, contributing $1.4 billion to 1989 sales and an estimated 37 percent in net income.[8] Johnson & Johnson, which in 1978 had a 20 percent share of the market, also fell behind Kimberly-Clark. In 1981, Johnson & Johnson admitted defeat and exited the branded disposable-diaper business, although it continued to produce for private-label customers.

The huge investments P&G had made in the older diaper machines hampered its ability to respond quickly. The situation represented an ironic reversal of P&G's Paper Division strategy a decade earlier, when the company's late arrival in the industry had allowed engineers to reconceive the papermaking process and leapfrog the competition. This time, P&G had been the first mover, with the sunk costs.[9]

But the company made the problem worse by focusing on maintaining differentiation between Pampers and Luvs. By the 1980s, the products were no longer competing primarily against cloth diapers but with other disposables, including low-cost private-label brands. Increasing numbers of women with very young children were working outside the home, and two-income households could afford to pay higher prices for better performance. Consumers polarized into those who wanted premium diapers and those who just wanted cheap ones. Positioned in the increasingly unsustainable middle segment, Pampers began to lose sales. When P&G began getting reports of softening sales at retail, it was unsure whether the numbers represented an unusual occurrence or a more permanent trend. As it turned out, the dip in sales "was a fundamental change in the market," a spokesman later admitted, "but one that was difficult to recognize." (Kimberly-Clark faced the same problem with its older Kimbies brand, which it withdrew in 1986.[10])

Despite the greater competition, Pampers remained P&G's biggest brand worldwide in the early 1980s. Pampers and Luvs combined had nearly half of the worldwide disposable-diaper volume and more than twice the share of

Huggies. Had it been a separate company, P&G's disposable-diaper business would have ranked in the top half of the *Fortune* 500 list. And significant potential remained; in the United States, for example, cloth continued to represent about 35 percent of all diaper changes.[11]

Even so, the situation deteriorated rapidly, as new-shaped diapers appeared not just in the United States but all over the world. In addition to Huggies, Pampers competed against Born in Germany, Tendress in France, and a growing list of others. The situation was even more dire in Japan, where in the space of three years, Pampers relinquished its first-place position to become a distant third behind Moony and Merries. Similar stories were reported in Italy, the United Kingdom, France, Canada, and Hong Kong. According to Ketchum, "what we ended up with was a large global Pampers brand and a small North American and European Luvs brand. So this Luvs brand had the top-end technology. . . . Yet, our big global brand in terms of its presence and scope and so on was Pampers."[12]

The loss of market share proved devastating to P&G, because of the high fixed costs of diaper production plants. As the market reached saturation point, manufacturers found that they could no longer rely on total market growth as a hedge against idle plant capacity. Even small dips in market share represented substantial profit losses.

Repositioning Pampers

Slowly, P&G began repositioning Pampers as a premium brand. In February 1982, Pampers with Stay-Dry Gathers, an elasticized version similar to Luvs but without the hourglass-shaped core, was introduced in Fort Wayne, Indiana, and Berlin, West Germany. Within twelve months, the new Pampers was available in eighty countries. Although the changes were incremental rather than truly radical, modifications to the production line were still immensely complicated. More than forty suppliers were required to provide P&G-designed modifications for some one hundred components for each of the lines. According to one manager, the company had "never attempted a technological change of this magnitude under this kind of timing in the past . . . [W]e were starting up a new production line every few days for almost a year."[13]

By the end of 1984, however, it became clear that incremental improvements to the old, rectangular Pampers design were inadequate and that something more radical had to be done.[14] Product development and marketing managers from the United States, Canada, Europe, and Japan gathered in Cincinnati to confront the problem. Two distinctly different strategies were debated at length and, at times, rancorously. The first, Blue Ribbon Pampers, would keep the rectangular shape but introduce a thicker cellulose pad; double elastic leg gathers; a blue, leak-proof waist shield; and "breathable" leg cuffs. The price tag to implement this change was about $150 million in capital and another $100 million for marketing expenses.

The second option was to accept that a rectangular diaper could never match the containment performance of an hourglass-shaped diaper. The proposed design would have the hourglass shape of Luvs; a waist shield; and an absorbent pad of a new, thin, superabsorbent material. To achieve this, the Pampers converting lines would have to be almost totally rebuilt, at a capital cost of about $500 million plus the attendant marketing expenses. Ultra Pampers, as the second option came to be called, risked raising the price of Pampers at a time when lower-cost, private-label diapers were fast becoming a major competitive factor.

Deciding which course to pursue was difficult. Two important points emerged. First, breathable cuffs had been tested in the Buffalo market, and the consumer had hardly noticed. Second, almost everyone agreed that the hourglass design was markedly superior in containing waste, a feature of critical importance to consumers. According to Jim Edwards, "Smale finally had to make the decision—and he did. 'Go with the shaped-diaper design, and make it work!'"[15] At last, P&G committed to the shaped design, years after Kimberly-Clark had done so. Both Blue Ribbon and Ultra Pampers would be introduced as shaped diapers.

Procter & Gamble ended up investing $500 million to upgrade its production system and an additional $225 million for advertising and promotion. The figures were unprecedented for a P&G diaper product and contributed to P&G's profit decline in fiscal 1985, the first full-year drop in profits from operations since 1952. Moving to shaped diapers became the largest single construction and start-up project in the company's history, involving more than one hundred Pampers converting lines around the world. Procter & Gamble set itself an ambitious target of designing and building new lines, retraining its line operators, and developing a new packaging and marketing program within two years' time.[16]

In 1985, R&D executive Dick Andre emphasized the project's scale and complexity:

To support this massive effort, we actually talked to every qualified machine tool company in the United States and in many countries around the world. We had 200 of our best engineering people and more than 3,000 designers, fabricators, and assemblers who went to work on an around-the-clock, seven-day basis, in more than 100 separate locations around the world. We moved teams of plant technicians and manufacturing managers from Cape Girardeau to

Cleveland, from Germany to Nashville, and from Akashi to Cape Girardeau. We even expedited the delivery of our first international converters to their destinations in Germany and Japan by chartering eight Boeing 747 jets. This mammoth effort resulted in starting up two new machines every week for the past year.[17]

It was a massive undertaking and, according to some within the company, one that occurred too late. In an interview he gave at the time, Tecklenburg said that the changes were "not things which couldn't have been done five or six or seven years ago. It probably would have been a little tougher to do, but they could have been done."[18]

Blue Ribbon Pampers was rolled out beginning in 1984, and superabsorbent Ultra Pampers was introduced in 1986. The latter was made with polyacrylate granules, a new material that swelled and formed a gel when it came in contact with fluid, which prevented the moisture from being squeezed back out. The granules were an improvement over cellulose alone, which soaked water like a sponge and was therefore unable to guard against the squeezing motions of a baby's twisting and turning. Interspersed in the diaper's cellulose, the granules were so absorbent that P&G was able to reduce the cellulose content from fifty to only thirty grams. Although the superabsorbent diapers had higher manufacturing costs, the company could sell them for about the same price, because the smaller product cost less to package, ship, and store. Japan had developed the new technology, and because P&G was in that market and had access to the technology, the company was able to introduce the improved product nine months earlier than Kimberly-Clark introduced its version. The diapers were positioned as a premium product, reaffirming that both P&G and Kimberly-Clark had largely abandoned the middle segment of the market. Neither company, however, made much headway in low-cost diapers, because retailers preferred to stock their own higher-margin, private-label products.[19]

Although a markedly superior product, Ultra Pampers posed a new set of problems. First, consumers had to be convinced that thinner pads could hold more moisture than their thicker predecessors. Even within the company, some questioned the need for such a product, especially when Blue Ribbon Pampers achieved market leadership in late 1985. Reports from Japan indicated that the key was simply to get consumers to try the product. Consequently, in addition to sampling, P&G organized a series of novel events, called the Baby Olympics, to attract consumer interest. Getting enough of the raw materials was another obstacle. The total world supply of absorbent gelling materials amounted to only 1 percent of what would be needed within a year of the launch of Ultra Pampers. In a very short space of time,

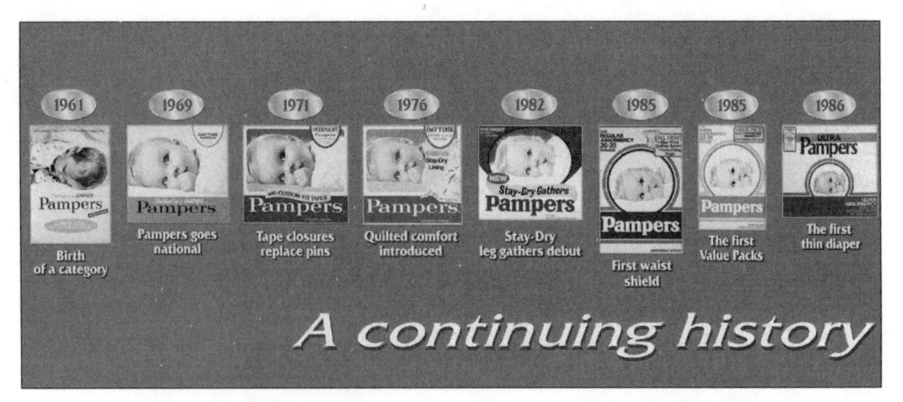

Since the mid-1970s, P&G's primary weapon in the fierce, worldwide rivalry in disposable diapers has been constant innovation. There is

P&G had to create a $200 million industry in what was then a new technology to guarantee its own supply base. A major concern was that the company would contract for too much raw material, thereby inadvertently providing a source of supply for the competition. Projected needs had to be calculated extremely carefully, so that neither too much nor too little was produced by contractors.[20]

Within eleven months of its introduction, Ultra Pampers was available nationally, a record for the company. The product quickly went on allocation, as P&G again faced the problem of keeping retailers adequately supplied. The company had to develop a drop-shipment approach, which bypassed the retailers' central warehouses so that the individual stores received the diapers directly. Drop shipment placed increased complexity on the delivery process because it obliged P&G to take on the added responsibility of ensuring that every store received the diapers it had ordered. Out-of-stocks were another problem; diaper boxes were bulky and had to be continually replenished. Retailers needed to pay better attention to this issue: The company demonstrated that 34 percent of diaper consumers who could not find their brand of diaper went to another store. Shelf graphics software helped retailers make the best use of their space, and P&G trained a group of specialists to work with retailers in using the technology.[21]

With Pampers so vastly improved, its price could at last be raised. But by then, Luvs and Pampers had become "virtually indistinguishable in terms of their performance," said Ketchum. "[Procter & Gamble] struggled for another ten years [but was] unable to differentiate these two." Finally, in the late 1990s, P&G transformed Luvs into a mid-tier product, dropping its price and some of its performance enhancements.[22]

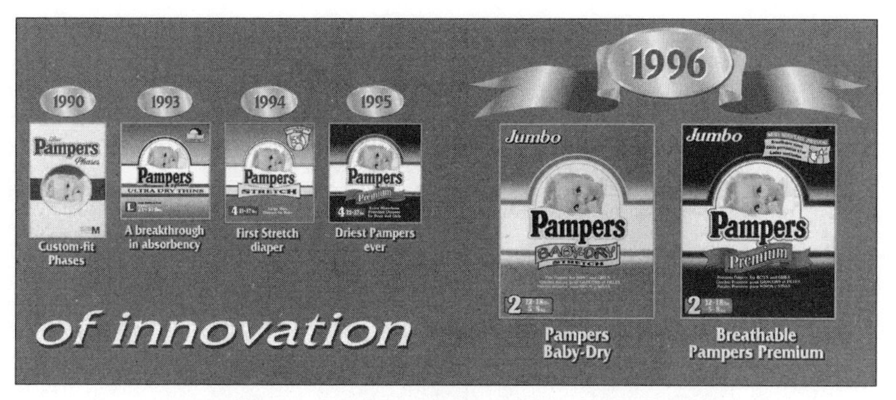

no standing pat, as indicated by this graphic, produced in 1996, on the thirty-fifth anniversary of Pamper's introduction.

Although Luvs remained a factor in the North American marketplace and some foreign brands continued to thrive, the main event on the global stage became a fierce struggle between Pampers and Huggies. Many economists and business analysts viewed the diaper wars as a duopoly similar to the cola wars between Coke and Pepsi. Procter & Gamble and Kimberly-Clark split the North American market, with P&G having the upper hand in other regions. Competition became an unending sequence of rapid moves and countermoves, as one company quickly matched improvements the other made. Kimberly-Clark had "to spend a ton of money. As they spend a ton of money, we defend. . . . To defend, we have to spend a ton of money too," Ketchum explained.[23] Consumers turned out to be the true winners, as diapers became thinner, better fitting, easier to fasten, decorated, color coordinated, more comfortable, and more hygienic.

Meanwhile, the rivals expanded the competition in related products such as pull-ups (an important niche that P&G was late in entering), training pants, swimmers, and wipes. Beginning in the 1990s, the focus shifted more heavily to these line extensions targeted to small market niches, which managed to attract a 2 or 3 percent share of the total market. But "it is not hard for the first entrant to get an 80 or 100 percent share of that small segment," said Ketchum. In a business where gains could only be incremental, both P&G and Kimberly-Clark went after these with a vengeance.[24]

The Diaper Wars in Perspective

Procter & Gamble's fate in the diaper wars offers a classic illustration of the dilemmas faced by first movers in a new technology or market. The company's early dominance gave it a huge scale advantage in producing rectangular diapers. But this very success later became an obstacle. "[Procter & Gamble] had very little flexibility for quick or low-cost change," said group vice president, Sandy Weiner. "This gave the competition the opportunity to leapfrog our technology, which they did."[25] Ironically, Harness had been keenly aware of this dynamic when he pushed to expand the Paper Division's manufacturing capacity during the mid-1960s and 1970s. Back then, P&G had been the latecomer trailing first-movers Scott Paper and Kimberly-Clark. Procter & Gamble's new process technology enabled it to leap ahead of its more established rivals. In disposable diapers, Kimberly-Clark turned the tables. It was not until 1984, six years after the introduction of Huggies, that P&G made the commitment to convert all its manufacturing lines to produce shaped diapers. There was general agreement later that the company should have made the decision sooner. The high costs, moreover, pointed to the importance of investing in more flexible and adaptable manufacturing equipment, which became a priority in the 1990s.[26]

In a class he taught at P&G College in the early 1990s, Artzt examined the Pampers/Luvs decision and its aftermath and drew from them five strategic lessons. Perhaps the most important is the first: Never give your consumer a product reason to switch to a competitor's brand. Such a scenario could have been avoided had managers understood Artzt's third and fourth lessons: that a feature considered premium when first introduced can quickly become generic. This was the case with the Luvs hourglass design, which was swiftly matched first by Huggies and then by other rivals. For too long, P&G continued to treat the shaped design as a premium feature, restricting it to the much smaller Luvs brand. Research, along with previous experience on its other products, convinced the company that only a few consumers would ever be willing to pay for such features. In tissues and towels, for example, consumers ignored clear technological superiority if the price was even slightly higher than competitors'.[27]

Ironically, the lesson that a premium feature can quickly become generic had already been suggested some fifteen years earlier, when Crest was recognized by the American Dental Association. At the time, Gleem was the second-largest U.S. brand, with more than a 20 percent share. But P&G "didn't want to risk losing this important non-fluoride brand franchise," said John Smale, so it "did not put fluoride in Gleem until much later. When we finally added fluoride to Gleem to try and resurrect the brand—it was too late."[28]

The other, related mistake was the assumption that the company would not be able to reduce the costs of manufacturing a shaped diaper. Artzt later observed that although P&G made Herculean efforts to reduce the selling price of Pampers during the early 1960s, the process was not repeated in the

Musica

Sep 15 - Oct 3, 2010

BEEHIVE THE 1960'S GIRL GROUP MUSICAL

Remember when hair was hard and life was easy? This major musical will have you dancing in your seat as we witness the journey of women through the girl groups that spoke for a generation. The Shirelles, Brenda Lee, The Chiffons, Lesley Gore, The Supremes, Connie Francis, Petula Clark, Lulu, Dusty Springfield, The Shangri-Las, Tina Turner, "Mama" Cass Elliot...and more!

Five Strategic Lessons from the Diaper Wars

Ed Artzt

1. Never give your consumer a product-based reason to switch away from your brand.
2. Think of every brand that we have, and treat every brand that we have, as though it were our only brand.
3. Always determine whether a product innovation is brand-specific or generic.
4. Competition will always follow your technology, not your brand.
5. After you have defined your options, always test your worst-case scenario in the market. If you don't, and if you have made the wrong move, the market *will be* the worst-case scenario.

1970s and early 1980s. There "were only two questions they needed to ask at that time," Artzt argued. "One is, what would happen to the economics of Pampers if we could produce shaped diapers at 400 pads a minute instead of 130? And the answer is we'd have a parity-price diaper." As it turned out, the manufacturing organization succeeded in dramatically improving the production rate on shaped Pampers.[29] The second question was how consumers would react to the new benefit on Pampers. "Had we gone into the market in the early days with . . . shaped Pampers as a flanker alongside of Pampers in both the Luvs test market and a non-Luvs test market, we would have found out immediately [that] the Pampers users wanted it."[30]

Artzt also stressed his fifth and final lesson: Always consider the worst-case scenario. Procter & Gamble accepted that Luvs would take some share from Pampers, but failed to take into account the possibility that a competitor could match its technology. The result was a costly mistake that the company took years to rectify.

CHAPTER TWELVE

En Rio Revuelto

FINDING THE FORMULA IN MEXICO AND LATIN AMERICA

THE LOGIC that drew P&G into Mexico in 1948 was straightforward and compelling. Mexico was the last untapped territory in North America, offering the prospect of extending the company's sphere of operation across the continent. Procter & Gamble was in an expansive frame of mind, having set up an Overseas Division in 1946. And the company was confident. In the United States, it was rolling out a blockbuster new technology—synthetic detergents—and rapidly consolidating a dominant position in its core laundry and dish-washing markets. Some of that momentum, surely, could be carried over into Mexico, where the company would presumably enjoy the halo effect of a massive market presence just north of the border. Although P&G knew little about Mexican markets specifically, it did know how to put together a world-class consumer goods operation. All in all, P&G's prospects in Mexico looked promising.

What lay ahead, though, would defy the company's expectations and test its ingenuity. For all its marketing experience, its technological leadership, its imposing resources, P&G struggled to get a solid footing in Mexico. The country was right next door, from the point of view of U.S. headquarters, but at the same time it was a world away. The economic environment and market conditions were sharply different. So too were the habits and standards of Mexican consumers—different in ways P&G did not anticipate and only slowly came to understand. Colgate, meanwhile, was already entrenched in the region and much more knowledgeable about Mexican market conditions and consumers. Only after repeated missteps and nearly two decades of perseverance did P&G finally begin building effective brands in Mexico.

Even after establishing a solid position in the marketplace, P&G Mexico struggled to achieve steady profitability. Successive economic crises rocked the business in the 1980s and again in the 1990s. Moreover, the subsidiary weathered a period of strained relations with the Mexican government. As a developing economy with (initially) a deeply foreign (to P&G) culture, Mexico presented daunting challenges to brand building. Though the venture grew into a substantial enterprise in its own right, it took deft maneuvering and imaginative crisis management to keep the business viable. More than once P&G came close to exiting Mexico.

Nevertheless, Mexico grew increasingly important as the company's larger global strategy took form. By the early 1990s, P&G was doing a billion dollars in sales annually in the country, making it not only P&G's biggest market outside of the United States and Western Europe, but also the linchpin of the Latin American region. Ultimately, the company had to figure out how to make Mexico both a market stronghold and a platform for Latin American expansion and global business structures.

Entry and Early Going

Procter & Gamble entered Mexico in March 1948, acquiring a vegetable oil mill and shortening plant on the outskirts of Mexico City. Entry via acquisition was already a time-tested strategy, having created openings for the company in England, Cuba, and the Philippines during the 1930s. But the effort to build from a ready-made platform in Mexico ran into early complications. Jake Lingle, the head of the Overseas Division, had hoped to find a soap company, settling for an edible-oils factory only after failing to uncover anything more suitable. Theoretically, P&G knew the business, at least in a U.S. context, having gained considerable experience through its work on Crisco. In Mexico, however, unfamiliar business conditions prevailed. The local industry hinged on returnable glass bottling. By refusing to return bottles to the manufacturer, retailers exerted considerable leverage and used that leverage to demand high return prices and substantially improved terms of sale. Accustomed to selling product and packaging together, P&G struggled to cope with the alien situation and maneuvered clumsily.[1] Moreover, the plant that the company had acquired proved to be run-down and obsolete. The edible-oil business struggled from the start. Within a few years, P&G was looking to exit.

The market possibilities for detergent, meanwhile, initially looked limited. Given the underdeveloped nature of the Mexican economy and the low per capita income of its consumers, potential demand for a high-end product like synthetic detergent appeared insignificant. "I had no concept of the opportunity for detergents in those countries," Lingle would later admit. "We all tended to think detergents were too high-priced. People won't pay for them and we've got to sell something they can pay for. We did not understand their willingness or ability to pay for packaged products." (Underestimating the willingness of Latin American consumers to pay for performance and value in cleaning products was a mistake P&G would make repeatedly in the years ahead.) Then, an entrepreneur in Venezuela began importing Tide and uncovered a surprisingly robust market. Venezuela was "awash in money, black gold" from its oil business, an old P&G hand related, and consumers lined up to buy cases of the American detergent. Intrigued, the company bought out the business and expanded sales of imported Tide to Cuba and Mexico. "We suddenly saw that there was a real detergent opportunity in Latin America," said Lingle.[2] When word reached headquarters that Colgate was building a detergent plant in Mexico, P&G quickly put together plans to build a detergent plant of its own, in Nuevo Vallejo, Mexico.[3]

The rival plants went into operation within months of each other, pitting P&G against what turned out to be formidable competition. Procter & Gamble went to market with Ace, a brand based loosely on the U.S. Tide formulation, but modified for Mexican washing conditions with a somewhat higher active level and more sudsing. Colgate countered with Fab, in a formulation offering a significantly higher active level and heavier perfume content than either its U.S. namesake or Ace. Those were critical differences. Mexican consumers measured performance closely, on the basis of their experience as they washed, and they expected value. The vast majority of them laundered their clothes by hand, in cold water, in streams or metal tubs. Under these conditions, Fab significantly outperformed Ace.[4] Within a few years, as a result, Colgate's brand had grown so embedded in the market that Mexican consumers buying detergents at store counters (in Mexico at the time, there were virtually no self-service stores) asked for "Fab" generically. Ace (which was packaged in a red box) they requested by asking for "red Fab."[5]

In the face of such market dominance, P&G struggled to broaden its beachhead in Mexico. The subsidiary had to battle, for example, to get its ads on the radio (which was then the dominant mass medium in Mexico), as Colgate blanketed prime programming slots and pressured station owners to keep P&G ads off the Mexican airwaves. Only when Neil McElroy requested a personal interview with Mexican radio baron Emilio Azcarraga and obtained his commitment to grant fairer treatment was Colgate's stranglehold loosened. Still, radio access remained limited. "There was never any question about getting as equal a voice as Colgate had," recalled Claude Salomon (who worked as a brand manager in Mexico during this period). "We had a very small share of total voice in Mexico."[6]

Claude Salomon joined P&G Mexico as a young assistant brand manager in the early, difficult years of the venture. Following a string of assignments in other countries, he would return as the subsidiary's general manager in the 1970s.

Unable to marshal the mass media, P&G Mexico jury-rigged alternatives. In an effort to literally drive its message across the countryside, the company equipped small trucks with loudspeakers and dispatched them through the hinterland, advertising P&G's brands and projecting cartoons and movies in open-air screenings to assembled inhabitants.[7] The brunt of the campaign came at the sales level, though, at the point of contact with the trade, where P&G Mexico scrapped tenaciously for territory. Decades later, veteran senior managers would credit the young sales force with making key inroads during these years. Because marketing resources were so limited, development occurred regionally, concentrating in pockets and skirting Colgate strongholds. "Where the business was strong and we were making headway against Colgate we increased our marketing investment," explained Salomon. "We were prepared to under-spend in relative terms in the areas where we were struggling because of the dominance of Colgate."[8]

In addition to the Sales Department, the subsidiary organized a Market Research Department. In basic respects, this arm of P&G Mexico duplicated its U.S. counterpart, hiring young women, training them in scientific market research methods, and dispatching them across the landscape to gather Mexican homemakers' reactions to the company's products, packaging, and advertising. The department was small, however, and faced daunting conditions trying to canvas a population that was still largely rural and widely dispersed across a countryside unevenly connected by poor infrastructure. The "research girls" (in the language of the day) embarked in automobile caravans to the north and south of Mexico City in trips that often took several days. When they reached their destination, the women would use portable record players to test radio commercials.[9]

Market research, under these conditions, was a tedious, painstaking process. Only slowly did market insights filter in from the countryside. In any event, with only rudimentary product development resources, the Mexican operation remained almost entirely dependent on the Overseas Division for technical support. The Overseas Division, however, was understaffed, particularly in technical support. The responsibility for detergent formulation therefore fell to the head of manufacturing back in Cincinnati, where the thinking ran, "We'll give the Mexicans the best product we know how to make: U.S. Tide." Unfortunately, as one former advertising manager observed, U.S. Tide "might have been one of the best products north of the border, but was one of the worst selections south of the border."[10]

Staying Afloat

Hampered by lack of resources and kept in check by a fiercely competitive and well-entrenched Colgate operation, P&G lost the first detergent round decisively in Mexico. Still, over the 1950s, the company did manage at least to get itself off the ground and to begin building capability, accumulating experience, and extending its market presence. By the mid-1950s, the operation was passing out of its uneven infancy. It was about to face a grueling rite of passage.

In 1955, Lingle visited Mexico with a stern message. The operation was bleeding money and the parent company was running out of patience. Headquarters had decided to cut off further infusions of operating capital. "Consider yourselves a Mexican company," Lingle in effect told local managers. "You don't have any Uncle Sam in Cincinnati to supply funds to bail you out. You're on your own. . . . And the first thing I suggest you do is cut all your advertising."[11]

The news was jarring. Kingston Fletcher, who had just arrived in Mexico several weeks before and who promptly found himself thrust into the position of the company's advertising manager (his first posting out of training), remembers being shaken. Nevertheless, the dictum "proved to be a very good decision," in his opinion, forcing the company "to think long and hard about any activity that it undertook."[12] The subsidiary suspended all advertising for several months to cut losses and stabilize its fiscal position. It planned its next venture very carefully, pooling resources and mapping out new promotional tactics. In 1956, the company launched Star, a detergent better formulated for cold-water washing and supported with an innovative yet disciplined marketing campaign built around premiums: Boxes of Star came packed with small plastic gifts, toys, utensils, movie tickets, and the like.

Star scarcely dented Fab's leading share, but it did at least pay out for P&G. Encouraged by the modest success, the company expanded the premiums to its other detergent brands. "We had all sorts of laundry detergents with premium exchange deals—bring me a box top from this detergent and pay one peso and you get a fork, knife, or spoon," Salomon recalled. Fab held stubbornly to its market lead. Nevertheless, P&G's premiums "kept the brands alive."[13] Gradually the company's finances improved, enabling P&G Mexico to carry its own overhead and begin generating modest earnings. Morale and confidence within the company started to rise. "We weren't making a penny, we were following the Lingle idea of breaking even, but every cent we had we put back into the business—in advertising, promotion, personnel," Fletcher recounted.[14]

Turnaround: Rapido

In 1958, P&G marked its tenth year in Mexico. After several false starts, the company was marketing competitive products, though it still trailed Colgate in the market and was barely profitable. On the other hand, the operation was battle-hardened by this point, its staff growing seasoned and market-savvy. And the detergent market was starting to shift. In the mid-1950s, several local producers brought detergent plants of their own on-line in Mexico, making nonbranded product that was considerably degraded compared to Ace or Fab, but much cheaper, too. These detergents, produced by Mexican companies like La Corona and 1-2-3, were sold in bulk, in large barrels or sacks, to be doled out by storekeepers to consumers in makeshift cones of newspaper. It was a different value proposition, one that brought synthetic detergent within reach of a much broader cross-section of Mexican consumers, in amounts retailing for prices as low as a peso or two. The business was marginally profitable, though in volume, it did generate earnings, particularly if a company happened already to be running a detergent plant. Both P&G and Colgate joined the new competition, selling nonbranded product in bulk.

The bulk business damaged Colgate badly, however, for it eroded the brand equity that the company had built up in Fab. Consumers buying bulk product continued to ask for "Fab," retailers sold it as such, and, fairly rapidly, the associations attached to the brand shifted. "Fab" came to signify a degraded product that significantly underperformed the boxed detergent itself. What had been a decisive advantage rebounded disastrously. Colgate recognized what was happening and fought desperately to protect the brand name, but the effort proved futile.[15]

Procter & Gamble sensed that it was facing a market opportunity. In 1958, the company responded with Rapido. Blue-colored, formulated for cold-water washing and Mexican consumer preferences, with boosted levels of perfume and higher sudsing performance than its bulk competitors, Rapido for the first time reflected P&G's hard-won market understanding. The detergent was also packaged in polyethylene bags, an innovation that created a water-tight container (unlike the newspaper cones in which bulk detergents were wrapped) that was significantly less expensive to produce than cardboard boxes. Moreover, the shift to poly-bagging enabled P&G to market Rapido in small 250- and 100-gram packages that retailed for as little as a peso (the equivalent of eight cents). Procter & Gamble positioned the new brand on the basis of a bluing/bleaching/whitening strategy.[16]

With Rapido, P&G Mexico found a new sweet spot in the market. The product offered better performance than bulk detergent, yet better economy than boxed detergents, retailing at levels 25 to 40 percent below other packaged brands. Propelled by effective advertising crafted by Young & Rubicam-Noble, Rapido grew robustly between 1958 and 1963. Colgate responded with Magico in 1962, but now found itself on the defensive: Procter & Gamble

Rapido detergent, launched in 1958, marked the beginning of the turnaround for P&G in Mexico.

had already seized the concept and effectively held on to it through the 1960s as Rapido worked its way to a share in the mid-teens. By 1970, the brand had achieved market leadership with a 15.8 percent share.[17]

Breakaway: Ariel

Although Rapido marked P&G's coming of age in Mexico, the company was not yet winning comfortably in the laundry category. As the relatively modest share numbers indicate, Colgate remained a force, and local Mexican companies continued to offer capable competition, with La Corona emerging as a particularly strong rival. In fact, Mexico remained a fiercely competitive laundry market through the 1970s: Rapido held brand leadership only briefly before another low-priced brand, La Corona's Roma, slipped ahead.[18] Nevertheless, Rapido represented the company's first unequivocally successful brand in Mexico, anchoring a diversifying portfolio of cleaning brands. Over the 1950s and 1960s, P&G Mexico added soap (Camay, launched in 1953), toothpaste (Gleem, 1957), cleaners (Spic and Span, 1958; Maestro Limpio [in the United States, Mr. Clean], 1959), and deodorant soap (Escudo, 1966). Detergent continued to generate the lion's share of the company's earnings, though, with Rapido driving the category.

Though few sensed it, P&G Mexico had positioned itself for breakaway. In 1967, the company decided to launch a new detergent based on enzyme technology that P&G had developed in Europe. Because it was expensive, Ariel did not look likely to contend for major market share in Mexico. But enzymes cleaned stains impervious to ordinary detergents, and the technology was particularly well suited to Mexican laundry patterns, since it delivered superior performance across a wide range of washing conditions, including hand washing in cold water with high levels of water hardness. The company ran Ariel in test markets in January 1968 (in Chihuahua, Sinaloa, and Sonara), and rolled out nationally in May. Based on Ariel's premium pricing, P&G Mexico projected that the new brand would attract less than a 5 percent share.[19]

Once again, however, Mexican consumers demonstrated that they recognized superior performance and were willing to pay for it. The numbers for Ariel quickly climbed past the company's original targets, indicating that consumers judged the brand as a genuine value proposition, even at a price point nearly 150 percent higher than that of Rapido.[20] Taken by surprise, but recognizing nevertheless that it faced a golden opportunity, P&G adapted its marketing strategy, putting more media weight behind the new brand. Thus, one of P&G Mexico's most effective advertising campaigns took form.

Based on enzyme formulations originally developed in Europe, Ariel became P&G's first blockbuster brand in Mexico, anchoring an increasingly strong market presence in the region.

"The creative challenge [in marketing Ariel in Mexico] was to develop a copy campaign . . . that would sell a very sophisticated product . . . for use in a very unsophisticated washing method—by hand, in a bucket," said Mexico supervisor W. O. Coleman. The solution, devised by Young & Rubicam-Noble, was masterful. Ariel's advertising introduced a continuing character, Señor Jimeno, who circulated among women at *lavaderos* (public washing areas with running water), talking up the new brand. Specifically, to demonstrate the cleaning power of Ariel, Jimeno poured the product into a bucket of laundry, which he then began agitating like an automatic washer. It was Ariel's unique enzyme formulation, Jimeno explained, that enabled the bucket to clean like a washing machine, giving washes a *chaca, chaca* (duplicating the sound of a washing machine). In a market just beginning to adopt washing machines and yet still dominated by hand washing, the image struck a powerful chord, communicating the invisible process of enzyme cleaning in a way consumers readily grasped and responded to. Ariel amassed increasing share over the 1970s, reaching number one in 1977.[21]

This time, share leadership represented a market win with decisive implications: Ariel catapulted P&G from competitiveness to command in Mexico. Unlike Rapido, Ariel was technologically advanced and demonstrably superior in performance. And by the late 1970s, it had established itself in the marketplace as a superior value, despite its premium pricing. In short, P&G Mexico had the makings of a megabrand on its hands. By the time Martha Miller de Lombera came on board as an assistant brand manager in 1976, strategic thinking was coalescing around the concept. "Ariel continued to do better and better as we gave it product technology, upgrades, more advertising and support," Lombera related. "Eventually the shift was really quite dramatic, with Rapido becoming a small brand and Ariel becoming the horsepower brand of the company."[22]

As the company's strategic focus shifted, Ariel became P&G Mexico's top technological priority. Thus, in 1979, two years after Ariel achieved brand leadership, the company upgraded the formula by adding an optical (i.e., light-activated) bleach, Ariel BH. The new formulation, which P&G debuted in Mexico, proved ideally suited to the country, where line drying remained widely prevalent. Procter & Gamble supported the upgrade with heavy marketing: Señor Jimeno saturated the airwaves to explain how the optical bleach worked. In the consumer imagination as well as internally within the company, the optical-bleach technology bolstered Ariel's position not only as the market leader but also as the brand platform for state-of-the-art laundry technology. And Ariel BH was just the beginning: In subsequent years, Ariel underwent repeated reformulation, reflecting its status as P&G Mexico's cornerstone brand. By the mid-1980s, Ariel had become, according to P&G Mexico general manager Jaime Davila, "a symbol of absolute quality for the consumer."[23]

The strategy delivered impressive results. Even as economic conditions deteriorated and government controls tightened around the company, P&G continued to refresh Ariel's technology, continued to back it with megabrand-level marketing resources, continued to build share and volume. By FY 1988–1989, at the tail end of a very difficult period for Mexico, Ariel was anchoring the company's 54.1 percent share in the laundry category, the central component of P&G's $341 million business in the country.[24] A new advertising campaign animated and accelerated the brand's momentum. Building on "a Latin insight that the housewife wants to be the heroine with her family" (according to Salomon), P&G fashioned a new marketing campaign based on the concept of family recognition that the homemaker or mother can successfully overcome even the greatest challenges: *Tu siempre puedes* ("You always can"). By 1993, Ariel was holding a 50-percent-plus share.[25]

The implications of Ariel's emergence as a megabrand rippled out across Latin America. Over the late 1970s and early 1980s, as P&G reorganized its international business around global divisions and expanded into a new round of Latin American markets, P&G Mexico became a platform for launching wider regional strategic initiatives, with Ariel as the spearhead brand. In 1980, synthetic detergents made up 80 percent of the Latin American Division's volume, with Ariel alone accounting for 60 percent.[26] The "*Tu siempre puedes*" campaign, which the company exported from Mexico to other Latin countries in the 1980s as the brand's core marketing message, consolidated Ariel's megabrand status: By 1990 Ariel was making up 65 percent of P&G's total synthetic detergent volume in Latin America.[27]

Mounting Government Pressures

In 1974–1975, even as Ariel closed in on brand leadership, the Mexican government imposed price controls on a wide range of consumer goods, including soaps and detergents. For P &G, the impact was immediate, triggering what Salomon described as "a near disastrous slide in our profitability."[28] Just as P&G had begun to break away from the pack in Mexico, the country became a much more complicated environment in which to do business.

The implementation of price controls marked the beginning of a new stage in the relationship between the Mexican government and P&G. Starting in the 1970s and running through the 1980s, the government asserted broad powers of economic control, dictating which product categories companies like P&G could and could not enter. Efforts to obtain relief from price controls encountered stiff bureaucratic resistance, even as raw-material prices surged. "We had a whole group of people working on justifying pricing," recalled Lombera. "In the finance group there were probably thirty or forty people, in [what was] a fairly small organization, doing nothing but figuring out how to validate the requests [for price increases] that we were making."[29] More often than not, the requests were denied. The Mexican administrations of the 1970s and 1980s were suspicious of foreign-owned corporations like P&G, challenging everything from fine-grained data to basic working assumptions.

For example, Mexican authorities scrutinized the company's advertising, looking for anything that might be deceptive or misleading. Ads in the United States were similarly reviewed by the U.S. Federal Trade Commission, of course, but in Mexico the scrutiny was rigorous and literal-minded. Did Ariel really cause washing buckets to agitate like automatic washing machines? Of course not; the image was metaphorical. Ariel's ads were ruled unacceptable. Procter & Gamble and Young & Rubicam-Noble returned with ads in which the foam sloshed around inside stationary buckets. These were permitted for a time. Then the government decided that they, too, might confuse consumers. So, new ads were worked up, this time simply showing people looking into buckets and exclaiming "Ah!" leaving it to viewers to infer the *chaca, chaca* at work within. "We spent a lot of time and effort," Lombera concluded, "justifying the imagery that we were trying to convey in what is a creative medium to people who . . . thought that the consumer was really stupid. Whereas the consumer is very, very smart."

Inevitably in this climate, profitability suffered, especially when Mexico's economic conditions began to deteriorate. As inflation climbed and earnings fell, concern grew in Cincinnati. In Mexico, though, the company fought fiercely not just to preserve the ground it had won, but to use the opportunity to consolidate and expand its position. "We were unwilling to forgo our volume growth track record," Salomon reported in a presentation at headquarters in 1981, "since this would be the basis for major profit opportunities as Mexico's government saw the light on the deleterious effects of price controls." So P&G Mexico turned inward to undertake a rigorous cost-tightening and productivity drive, wringing out efficiencies, streamlining personnel, driving volume up 62 percent from 1977 to 1981 while over the same period raising its cases-per-employee index by 45 percent.[30]

Figuring results in terms of cases per employee was not typical P&G thinking in 1981, when the company worldwide was more attuned to metrics such as market share, volume, and brand support case rates. But the pressurized atmosphere in Mexico was forcing all kinds of tough choices. Negotiating for position under price controls, for example, fostered a distinct, disciplined approach to marketing. Mexican officials regarded expenses like promotional spending suspiciously. "They'd say, 'Why are you spending that much when supposedly you're not making money?'" Lombera related. "So . . . the majority of our marketing support was spent on advertising. Almost none was spent on promotion. . . . How could we justify to the government if we're under such a price squeeze and we're pushing for cents on pricing that now we're going to go and give it back to the consumer?"[31]

Well before the concept of value pricing gained currency in the United States, then, managers in Mexico were learning to adjust to it and to use it to fortify their brands. The curtailment of promotional activity raised questions in Cincinnati. "Why aren't you doing trial-generating events?" Lombera remembered hearing from headquarters. "Why aren't you doing in-store activities?" But in Mexico, these were costly luxuries, to be spent in tiny, concentrated amounts calculated for maximum effect. The company reserved nearly all its limited marketing resources for more basic brand investments. "When we would have a new launch, we would sample very, very carefully, because that [was] a huge cost for us," Lombera recounted. "The bulk [went] into advertising, to building awareness and to making sure . . . that awareness was built around a really relevant story." The approach ran counter to the standard P&G thinking of the time, but it paid off: "We weren't prostituting the market with all these high-low offers and things that are really irrelevant and at some stage teach your consumers very bad habits, . . . teaches them to wait, not to be product loyal. We were doing all of the basics as well as we could with a great deal of discipline."[32]

So P&G Mexico adapted to a challenging regulatory environment in Mexico. Productivity became a driving imperative, a way back to profitability and, more basically, a matter of survival. Earnings were low but the company was building volume. Scarce marketing resources were concentrating around basic advertising, consolidating long-term brand equity. A new mentality, a new frame of mind, was taking hold within the company. Lombera offered a Mexican proverb by way of illustration: *"En rio revuelto, ganacia de pescadores"*—"A river in turmoil benefits the fisherman."

Economic Collapse

The waters were about to get much choppier. By mid-1982, Mexico's external national debt exceeded $80 billion—a level, it became increasingly obvious, that the country would be unable to repay as oil prices fell on the world market. In August, the peso collapsed, sending the Mexican economy into a severe depression that would last for the rest of the decade.

The collapse tipped P&G Mexico into crisis. Virtually all the company's volume—98.5 percent, by an internal calculation—was locked in products falling under price controls, forcing the company to pay world prices for imported raw materials to make product it was able to sell "at half world levels" (according to Davila, who inherited the unfortunate situation from Salomon in 1983). By 1984, raw-material costs had swollen to 70 percent of total sales realization. The Mexican government, responding to pressure from the International Monetary Fund, cut import permits drastically, exacerbating material shortages. Meanwhile, the company's financing costs escalated alarmingly. A dollar of debt representing 25 pesos at the end of FY 1981–1982 had climbed to 150 pesos by the end of FY 1982–1983. And in the midst of these tightening financial pressures, the company's markets contracted sharply, detergents shrinking by 8 percent in 1983–1984, and toilet bars by 6 percent, after shrinking 9.5 percent the year before.[33]

The company scrambled to contain the spreading damage. The Purchasing and Distribution Department waded into turbulent markets, fighting to stabilize the company's cost position. Sales tightened the company's trade terms significantly, shortening payment schedules in an effort to get on top of the country's hyperinflation. Products Development redoubled efforts to replace imported raw materials with local substitutes that would not degrade product quality. The Marketing Department rationed out reduced brand support; the Manufacturing Department scoured the plants for inefficiencies.[34]

Conditions became so bad that executives felt compelled to at least consider exiting. On July 11, 1986, the finance manager of P&G Mexico, J. S. Lafferty, submitted a report to P&G Latin America head Jorge Montoya "dimensionaliz[ing] the P & (L) impact of permanently shutting down our business in Mexico." Montoya passed the report on to Artzt with the comment "For your information. Since this issue has been raised a few times we are now prepared." Artzt appended a handwritten note: "Pretty awful prospect. We are hopeful of solving the problem." To which Smale added, "We'd better!"[35]

On the ground in Mexico, meanwhile, another state of mind took hold. Now staffed largely by local managers who had spent decades building the business, P&G Mexico resolved in the depths of the crisis not just to stanch the red ink, not just to retrench, but to use conditions to bolster their strategic position. "If I could summarize in a phrase the central concept of our approach to managing in the worst of times in Mexico," Davila proclaimed in 1984, "it is that we are in the business for the long term."[36] So, for example, while competitors tried to sustain sales volumes and offset category shrinkage by returning to the use of trade allowance activity and heavy trade loading against price increases, P&G resisted the trend. The company registered short-term volume losses, but sweated it out for a while before volume stabilized, then began to recover, even as the overall market contracted.[37]

First and foremost, the company protected its brands' claim to value and quality. Needing, as Davila put it, to manufacture product "with raw materials that many times were apparently non-existent," the company reformulated using local substitutes. Executives decreed, though, that reformulation must not degrade product, and while tensions sometimes emerged as local managers and company executives searched for workable solutions, quality standards were upheld. In fact, many of the locally procured substitutes improvised in the midst of the crisis proved superior in performance and thus survived once import restrictions loosened.[38]

On the marketing front, the company had already learned to conserve and apply brand support resources "where experience had taught us they would do the most good," Davila reported. The crisis further concentrated spending: In 1983 to 1984, the company devoted fully 84 percent of its marketing resources to media spending and another 6 percent to TV and radio commercials. Davila did the math: "Net, 90 percent of our brand support was committed to making our copy work for us, was committed to the long term health of our business. And the bulk of the balance . . . went into long term trial programs such as washing machine sampling and new mothers sampling."[39]

Similar adherence to company principles shaped the company's response to the crisis on another front, in human resources. Conditions looked "almost frighteningly bad," Davila admitted. The company was undergoing a "hair raising" episode, Salomon agreed. Signifying the extent of the crisis, the company curtailed profit-sharing distribution in 1983. Inevitably, as conditions worsened and inflation outpaced wages and salaries, anxieties mounted in the company's offices and plants. The situation called for what Davila characterized as "extraordinary attention to the needs of the people in the organization. This was a top priority, everyday activity." Though it was scraping for every peso, the company put "unusual and visible emphasis on training," Davila reported, both to boost morale and to demonstrate a corporate commitment to employees' personal growth. In the same spirit, the company strained to pay its people as well as difficult circumstances would permit, and actually stepped up its campus recruiting. "Hold on to the organization as a first priority," Davila declared. "Take care of the people, and they will take care of the brands."[40]

An Injection of Zest

In the depths of the crisis, one of the few bright spots for P&G Mexico was Zest. The staff at P&G Mexico had first detected a potential market for the brand in the early 1970s, when they noticed that consumers in the Baja region bordering the United States (where liberal import rules prevailed) were buying large quantities of the synthetic cleaning bar. "It must have had a 60 or 65 share. Nobody could really understand," remembered Salomon. "Partly [it was] the water conditions." The Baja region was hard water, making Zest's synthetic cleaning system much more effective than traditional soap. Sensing a broader opportunity, P&G Mexico's staff petitioned headquarters for permission to build a plant in Mexico and market Zest countrywide. Because the product was expensive to manufacture, executives in Cincinnati hesitated to undertake the capital cost. Eventually, however, they signed off on the project.[41]

Early returns were gratifying. Zest found a fertile market in Mexico, particularly as the company conducted and exploited local market research, which revealed that consumers were using Zest for shampooing. Hair care thus became a point of entry for Zest (in Salomon's term): "Once [consumers] used it for shampooing, they used it in even greater quantities for everything else."[42]

The imposition of price controls cut deeply into Zest's margins, however—wiped them out, in fact, since the product was initially classified as a conventional soap bar and priced accordingly, though it was much more expensive to produce. Yet in this case, at least, the company found a way to reverse the situation. After engineering a significant product upgrade, P&G

petitioned the government to reclassify Zest in a new category: The product was not really a soap, the company argued, but rather a *dermo-limpiador*—a skin cleanser, made up of synthetic, nonsoap ingredients. A study from the National University of Mexico buttressed the claim, and eventually, the government was persuaded to reclassify Zest.

It was a modest victory in the midst of a dismal stretch, but for a company starving for earnings, the brand now began generating desperately needed cash flow. Already Mexico's leading toilet bar, Zest was soon yielding a price premium index of 53 percent compared with other complexion bars on the market. In Mexico as in the United States, the marketing revolved around the concept of revivification: "*Vuelve a la vida con* Zest!" For P&G Mexico, it was a slogan with uncanny internal resonance.[43]

Recovery: From Stranglehold to Stronghold

Small victories like Zest fed the starving business. Gradually, incrementally, meanwhile, general conditions improved in Mexico. Successive presidential administrations began loosening price controls and other economic restrictions. The economy slowly picked up. Toughened by the crisis, P&G Mexico fortified its market position.

In fact, the company emerged from the crisis of the 1980s a highly disciplined and stronger business. Forced to operate under stringent price controls, operations grew extraordinarily efficient. By the late 1980s, P&G's manufacturing costs for laundry detergent and bar soap were lower in Mexico, and its productivity higher, than in any other part of the world.[44] The commitment to preserving long-term strategic viability by fortifying brand equity, meanwhile, resulted in substantial growth in volume and share in those core categories. It was during these years that Ariel and Zest solidified their brand leadership positions. Procter & Gamble's category share in laundry reached 58.7 percent by FY 1988–1989; in toilet soaps, the share was 52.1 percent.[45]

These accomplishments made Mexico an increasingly important point on the map, strategically speaking, particularly as P&G pushed into new Latin American markets over the late 1980s. For all its troubles, P&G Mexico was generating $341 million in net sales by FY 1987–1988, making it the largest earner outside of the United States, Canada, and Europe, and more than twice as large as any other Latin American operation. (Venezuela was second, with $170 million.[46]) By the late 1980s, the company was laying plans to compete for market leadership in all sixteen categories in which P&G (then) did business.[47] Corporate executives were coming to think of Mexico as holding a "unique role as the learning center and gateway for expansion throughout Latin America."[48]

This understanding of Mexico's role in the larger picture reflected a fundamental reorganization of the company's Latin American operations. The model for structural change came from Europe, where reorganization around regional divisions, with Europe-wide brand teams, had created powerful mechanisms for strategic flexibility, included coordinated product improvements and rapidly sequenced brand introductions, along with significant cost savings. A meeting of Latin American senior managers in Cincinnati in June 1984 began the process of reorganizing along similar lines. General managers running operations in specific countries raised concerns about being able to respond flexibly to varying competitive positions and market conditions. Profit and loss responsibility, it was agreed, should remain with line managers, along with final decision-making authority on brand initiatives. Nevertheless, brand teams were implemented for major brands (including Ariel, Ace, and Camay), in order to facilitate the sharing of experience and help leverage knowledge from one country to another.

In 1987, the process of regionalization deepened with the decision to relocate the headquarters for the Latin American division from Cincinnati to Caracas, Venezuela, and to set up two dedicated R&D centers in the region, in Caracas and Mexico City. The specific contours of the regional structure were revisited several times, in 1988 and again in 1993, as people wrestled with the challenge of bringing category and subsidiary management into balance. Category teams were reshaped, and their specific responsibilities delineated. Ultimately, it was decided that the two alignments had to be meshed together in a matrix structure: Neither a breakdown along pure sector lines nor a purely geographic structure would allow for an optimal balance of local responsiveness and regional efficiency. "There will be gray areas," Montoya admitted. Ultimately, people needed to let go of the idea that lines of authority should run exclusively in either sector or geographic alignments: "We need to change the paradigm that strategy only applies to certain aspects of the business. The subsidiary and category managers must both deal with strategy and execution in their respective roles."[49]

In essence, Montoya and his generation of country and brand managers were inheriting and working through the same kinds of issues that had defined P&G's experience in Mexico from the outset. The company had gone into Mexico with little local knowledge, counting on its technical expertise and marketing ability to carry the business—counting, in other words, on leveraging its learning (to borrow a phrase from a later era of business) to create a profitable market. What P&G learned, in fact, was that a company still needed local knowledge, local market understanding, rigorously and imaginatively applied, to compete. Until it learned how to listen and respond to Mexican consumers, P&G Mexico foundered. Eventually, after hard trials, the company achieved impressive success. Now came the challenge of exploiting the global possibilities that success created—while at the same time preserving the local responsiveness that had made it possible.

The Mexican Lessons in Perspective

The experience of establishing, and then defending, positions in Mexico's teeming and turbulent markets yielded invaluable insights about doing business in developing economies, adapting to non-Anglo cultures, and ultimately adopting a global outlook on P&G's brands. The company did not encounter what it had expected to find when it entered Mexico in 1948, and a difficult and unprofitable period of adjustment followed. The first set of laundry brands P&G put on the market were not well formulated for local conditions and washing habits. Although the company had developed deep knowledge of U.S. consumers, their households, and their daily lives—indeed, had made that knowledge the basis of brand building—the company had nothing comparable to work with in Mexico. Moreover, P&G faced entrenched competition from Colgate, which had been doing business in Mexico for decades by the time P&G arrived. Inevitably, P&G's early efforts at building brands here suffered. Only through dogged determination did the company manage to establish and maintain a tenuous toehold in the country. Furthermore, only when P&G began putting products on the market that met local standards of quality, value, and performance did it begin building winning brands. Rapido (launched in 1958) marked the turning point; Ariel (1968) became the breakthrough.

In other words, P&G had to relearn a sharp lesson as it shifted from Ace to Rapido to Ariel. Mexican consumers may have had lower per capita incomes than their counterparts in the United States, but they were discerning, they demanded performance, and, to an extent that headquarters initially underestimated, they proved willing to pay for value. "You have to be respectful," concluded Lombera. "Sometimes we think that because consumers have a lower income, we can sort of tell them what to do." Wrong. Procter & Gamble did not make headway in Mexico until it learned how to give local consumers what Lombera described as "a story that makes sense to them, and then a product that delivers on that story." In Mexico as anywhere else, the consumer was still the boss.

The company turned the corner, after decades of hard lessons and hard work. But even then, the road remained rocky. When the economy collapsed in the mid-1980s, P&G Mexico very nearly went under, having to confront conditions bleaker than anything P&G had experienced in the United States. What sustained the enterprise through this dark episode was the capability and sense of commitment P&G had built on the ground in Mexico. Passionate ownership on a local level proved vital to success. Meeting, and matching, a supreme test, P&G Mexico emerged from economic turmoil in the late 1980s with one of the leanest, most efficient, most capable local organizations the company had ever fielded.

Mexico thus became important not just for what it had to teach P&G about building brands, but also for what it had to teach the company about building organizations. In order to operate globally, P&G had to be able to conduct business in the midst of crisis. Economic collapses like the one that struck Mexico in the early 1980s are endemic in developing markets. The price of doing business is being able to weather those setbacks. Montoya described a major turning point in the company's outlook in the mid-1980s: "We decided that rather than wait for crisis to be over, we assumed that crisis of some kind would always exist in our region."[50] Ultimately, winning in this environment was not a matter of crisis containment, but of capitalizing on opportunity.

CHAPTER THIRTEEN

Pantene

BUILDING A GLOBAL BEAUTY BRAND

PROCTER & GAMBLE built its first billion-dollar beauty brand from what would have seemed, a decade and a half before, to be the most unlikely of sources. When it acquired Pantene in the Richardson-Vicks Inc. (RVI) deal in 1985, the shampoo and conditioner brand had been a minor prestige label distributed through the narrowest of distribution channels. The marketing strategy that subsequently restaged the brand, moreover, had come together in a distant corner of the globe, in Taiwan, where P&G's small subsidiary was still consolidating ground. Nevertheless, from this niche and this nook, Pantene surged over the 1990s to a central place in the company's beauty care strategy.

As a case in brand building, Pantene has stretched the company in new and unfamiliar ways. It is a technology story, incorporating both innovative research and creative application through a series of branding decisions. It is also a branding and positioning story, in which P&G had to learn to market not only on the basis of performance, but also on less tangible, less measurable qualities. Finally, the Pantene experience is a story about building brands globally, offering a compelling example of the possibilities of leveraging knowledge and ideas from everywhere within the company—not just from in the United States—and coordinating rapid deployment around the world.

Background: Procter & Gamble in the Hair Care Category

Though the company had been successful in hair care since the 1930s, P&G went into the 1980s facing a crisis. What had been a leading position in the category, anchored by brand mainstays Head & Shoulders (25 percent share in the late 1960s) and Prell (22 percent share), had been dislodged by a series of jarring market shifts.[1] Hairstyles had changed, aggressive new competition had shaken up the industry, and the company was responding sluggishly.

Part of the challenge stemmed from fundamental industry dynamics. In categories like laundry detergent or paper, P&G was accustomed to competing against a small circle of heavyweight contenders, each backing one or two megabrands. Manufacturing costs were high and economies of scale decisive, creating imposing entry barriers. Shampoos, on the other hand, as *Advertising Age* observed, were relatively inexpensive to manufacture, with low entry barriers, numerous competitors, and a host of brands vying for attention. The company found itself competing without any proprietary technological advantages. Most products in hair care were "very similar, without much differentiation," a marketing consultant warned in 1983. "Marketers will have to be satisfied with smaller shares of the market for each brand and having many brands to add up to a total large share for the company."[2]

Given these conditions, the industry had become crowded and chaotic. "In this volatile, highly fragmented market, any number can play, and dozens do," *Advertising Age* reported in 1980. "One share point may mean $10,000,000; a brand with a 2 percent share can afford to advertise and several manage to thrive." Surveys indicated that 40 percent of consumers preferred specialty shampoos "purporting to combat dandruff, grease or split ends; add body or fragrance, or simply resuscitate lackluster locks." New fads kept erupting and shaking up the market. Consumers seemed to adopt and abandon brands nearly as quickly as they finished one bottle of shampoo and bought another.[3]

The company hoped to turn this trend around with the introduction of a new brand, Pert, in 1979. The original marketing concept behind Pert was "Coast for your hair," explained R&D director, Cecilia Kuzma. The product was positioned on refreshment and included a bubble-adorned label design that recalled the soap brand Coast (also positioned on refreshment) and a green, high-scent formulation. Even as the company prepared Pert for market, however, competitors were introducing a new product category that was called conditioners and was taking the market by storm. In response, Pert's brand team hastily reworked its positioning, adding conditioning ingredients and working up a marketing campaign positioning the brand with the promise of "Wash and Go." The amount of conditioning that could be added with existing technology was relatively minor, however, making Pert "claimably and perceptually better than a plain shampoo," Kuzma admitted, "but nowhere close to what a conditioner was providing—maybe 10 percent of what a conditioner did."[4]

Not surprisingly, Pert failed to catch on with consumers. By the early 1980s, some in the company were developing serious doubts about staying in the shampoo category. Head & Shoulders was still generating healthy earnings, but the company's other brands were losing money, dragging the beauty care unit as a whole below the profitability level. Market growth, fostered by the increase in shampoo frequency, had sustained sales levels yet masked deeper problems. Apart from Head & Shoulders, P&G's brands were steadily losing market share.

Concerned, division management created a task force, consisting of Kuzma from R&D, Marc Pritchard from Finance, and John Bess from Hair Care to study whether P&G should exit the category by shifting Head & Shoulders over to the company's health care unit and selling off all the other shampoo brands. The argument for exit was clear enough. Although P&G had proven capable of achieving notable technology breakthroughs in the past (including synthetic cleaning with Drene in the 1930s and effective dandruff control with Head & Shoulders in the early 1960s), the company had lost these technological edges and found itself unable to sustain market leadership. Particularly during the 1970s, hair care had grown more fluid and less governable than the company's traditional household product markets. Shampoos were becoming a commodity product driven by marketing on the basis of aesthetics. Fighting for middle-tier shares in a fragmented market was not a formula for success for a company like P&G.

On the other hand, several reasons argued for staying in the category—arguments that eventually swayed the task force. First, there was the resilience of Head & Shoulders. Procter & Gamble's leading shampoo brand continued to hold share, continued to justify premium pricing, and continued to sell profitably. The earnings were important but even more significant to the task force, was what Head & Shoulders suggested about consumers in the hair care market, according to Kuzma. "Head & Shoulders represented the success model that said P&G could compete in this business if we made performance our goal, as opposed to just aesthetics. . . . What Head & Shoulders represented, was a combination of performance and aesthetics. It was far and away the best liked dandruff shampoo, and the best performing dandruff shampoo. That seemed to be the recipe for success."[5]

Applying the formula to other shampoo brands depended on achieving a superior performance advantage, of course, and that in turn depended on applying new technologies. Procter & Gamble's technical people thought they had a major breakthrough on their hands. This technological promise was the other factor that persuaded the task force that the company should stay in shampoos. Kuzma's researchers were testing a new kind of shampoo in building panels, and employee panelists kept coming back for more samples. "[Procter & Gamble] R&D people are very demanding on their products," Kuzma later recounted, "and when you have people coming in asking you for more after they've been on a building panel for you, coming back week after week after week, you know you've got something because they're very particular and very demanding."

The test product was a shampoo that not only cleaned hair, but left it feeling remarkably smooth and silky. Coded BC-18 (beauty care product 18), the product was the result of decades of painstaking learning on the vexing problem of combining shampoo with real consumer-perceptible conditioning benefits in a single, two-in-one product.

The Technology Breakthrough: BC-18

The problem of conditioning had intermittently occupied P&G's hair care researchers since the late 1930s, as the implications of Drene's superior cleaning power and harsh side effects became apparent. Synthetic shampoos cleaned so well that they washed out natural hair oils and left hair difficult to comb. "Hair needs to have something left behind on it," explained P&G researcher Ray Bolich. "Up to this point, most shampoos were [nonsynthetic] soap shampoos, which left a small amount of soap scum on the hair that made it feel like it had been conditioned."[6] Mixing a little soap with synthetic detergents generated enough soap scum to create a conditioning effect. However, while making hair a little easier to comb, soap left hair feeling heavy, dirty, and coated.

The obvious technical solution was to distribute a small amount of fat back in the hair during the rinse stage, to replace the natural oils washed out by the shampoo. As researchers dug into the problem, however, they found it defied quick solutions. Shampoo surfactants removed fats, of course, and eggs, proteins, and other conditioning ingredients researchers tried adding to shampoo formulas washed out during rinsing. What was needed was to somehow deposit a very thin layer of conditioning molecules that would coat the surface of the hair, that would not be cleaned out by the shampoo, and that would survive rinsing. One possible approach was to put a positive charge on the molecules, so that they would spread and cling evenly to hair (which is negatively charged) during the rinse step. Unfortunately, almost all synthetic detergents are negatively charged, meaning that the detergent molecules would bond with the conditioner molecules in the bottle before either had a chance to get at the hair. The result, Bolich reported, is "an insoluble precipitate. It doesn't do anything. It doesn't lather any more, and it doesn't go down on the hair. It's a chunk of hard wax that doesn't do anything."

The development process that solved this problem got under way in 1980, when the company appointed a new research team to the quest for a two-in-one shampoo and conditioner formula. The team initially identified three novel approaches that seemed promising. The first, building off an observation that clay softened hair, tried formulating a conditioner that incorporated clay—a technology used in laundry detergents with built-in softener (e.g., Bold 3 in the United Kingdom). The second took a surfactant that did not lather, but that did stay on hair during rinsing, creating a conditioning effect. The third approach incorporated compounds called betaine surfactants, which are doubly charged. Investigation over the next year winnowed out the first two approaches. Clay did soften hair, but only when injected at unworkably high levels of formulation. ("We were turning Prell shampoo into bricks," Bolich remembered.) And efforts to get the conditioning surfactant to lather failed. The team's work with betaines did make headway, however.

Then, as the project approached market feasibility tests, serious problems emerged. Some test subjects reacted with severe eye irritation. BC-18 had run into what research supervisor Jim Monton would later characterize as a "dire need for [a] radical fix."[7] Fortunately for P&G, Bolich had discovered just such a fix while working on an unrelated project.

The Magic Ingredient

Bolich's team had been investigating rinse-off conditioners, trying to develop formulations that would counter their tendency to make hair get dirtier more rapidly. The fatty tails of many conditioner molecules, the team found, interacted with *sebum* (the hair's natural oils), causing a large, greasy complex that would not rinse off the hair. Bolich's efforts to isolate conditioning molecules with fatty tails that would not interact with sebum came up empty. Then the research team took a different tack. Bolich's hobby of refurbishing old automobiles had familiarized him with the lubricating properties of a range of oils, in particular silicone oil. Because it was uncharged and had no long fatty chains, volatile silicone oil, he found, evaporated off the hair within a few hours of washing, making it unlikely to complex with sebum or other conditioning ingredients. It did not deposit easily on hair, however, requiring formulations with high oil concentrations. The team tried mixing the silicone oil with other oils (that deposited more effectively). These efforts yielded a product that performed better, but still left hair rather oily.

Then came a breakthrough from out of the blue—or at any rate, out of what Bolich called "blue-sky thinking." While on a camping trip, he ran out of detergent and used shampoo to wash his frying pan. The cooking oil, he noticed, rinsed easily out of his pan, while the bacon fat remained, coating and sticking to the pan. Why? he wondered. The answer lay evidently in the difference in their viscosity. Cooking oil was thin and fluid, while bacon fat was of more intermediate viscosity—somewhere between oil and solid wax. Bolich's thinking turned to the conditioning problem he was working on back in the lab. What would happen if he could somehow thicken the silicone oil? If it were thick, he reasoned, "when it hits the hair it's not going to be mobile. If it hits the hair [and] sticks to it, it's probably not going to come off the hair during rinsing."[8]

Returning to the lab, Bolich began working with silicone. He and his team screened many compounds and polymers, experimenting with different ways to thicken the oil. One compound in particular, silicone gum, high in molecular weight and nonvolatile, proved soluble and effective. "We had all kinds of problems breaking that thick goo up into small particles," Bolich remembered. Eventually, he found a blend of gum and liquid silicone oil thin enough to disperse while still staying viscous enough to stay on the hair.

The formulation worked well on hair switches in the lab. And then, when testing moved to human subjects, something unexpected happened. Test subjects reported that the conditioner left their hair feeling soft and silky. That caught the researchers' attention. "We hadn't seen that in the labs. We weren't looking for it," Bolich recalled. "So, we increased the level and we tried it on some people that had some really unruly hair and hair problems. They said, 'Gee, this does something that no conditioner has ever done.'" It not only provided the combing and detangling benefits expected from conditioners, but also provided new dry-hair benefits such as smoothness, softness, and shine. And all without the dirty, oily feel that traditional conditioners created.

Bolich's combination of perseverance, nonlinear experimentation, and the good sense to recognize and pursue an unexpected opportunity had uncovered something totally new. "Silicone gum, it's like a magic ingredient. It ought to be useful somewhere,'" thought Bolich.

Indeed, Bolich's "magic ingredient" became the key to solving the decades-old puzzle of creating a two-in-one shampoo. The BC-18 two-in-one shampoo team had originally tried silicone and rejected it because it prevented shampoo from lathering. Or at least, silicone *oil* did. Bolich's magic blend of silicone oil and silicone gum, however, worked well with shampoos. "I put it into a simple surfactant system and I washed the switch. It worked. I played with it a little bit more, and it worked really well."

Critically, Bolich's supervisors gave him the latitude to pursue his hunch and the support to test his formulations. "My boss was saying, 'Hey, Ray—where's our new mousse?' I'd say, 'Well, I've got this idea. I've got to check it out.'" Once his tests began to yield results, moreover, other people in the hair care division were also supportive. "I took it to the lab in back of me, to Theresa Bakken [who was supervising the BC-18 formulation project]. Normally, what people do when you take them an idea is they say, 'Fine, we'll throw it in, and when we get time, we'll test it.' People are very protective. They only want to test their own ideas. She was very open. . . . She took this shampoo and championed it, gave it to product research persons and said, 'Try this.' They tried it and they loved it."

BC-18 was not yet fully realized. Various problems still had to be smoothed out. For example, the team had to figure out how to suspend the silicone mixture in the shampoo. Other P&G researchers made important contributions, too, including making the shampoo pearlescent, optimizing silicone gum-to-oil ratios, and reformulating to prevent a reaction between other elements in the shampoo. Eventually, multiple process teams worked out various aspects of the final formula.

As the elements of BC-18 cohered, excitement began to build up in the lab. "We had focus group response and HPT [home panel test] response like we'd never seen before," Kuzma related. "Consumers would come back, fill in their questionnaires, and refuse to bring their bottle of shampoo back. . . . Those of us in R&D knew we had something. BC-18 was engendering consumer responses like nothing we had ever seen before."

That awareness bolstered internal confidence that P&G would be able to bring winning new technologies to shampoos—a decisive factor in the company's determination not to pull out of the category in the mid-1980s. "Had we not had BC-18," Kuzma affirmed, "I'm not sure we would have said we could do performance." And delivering superior performance, the task force decided, was the key to winning in shampoos. Kuzma explained: "We came out of that task force with a strategy that said, 'We're not going to win by trying to play the commodity business. We're going to win by trying to play the superior performance business.'"[9]

Marketing the Technology: The First Branding Decision

Of course, the technology still had to be marketed. Once P&G had bottled BC-18, the question became what brand to put on the bottle. And that turned out to be a complicated question. Shampoos had promised consumers two-in-one benefits before and had not yet delivered. Procter & Gamble had a product on its hands that actually did deliver genuine, measurable, unique performance, but making BC-18 stand out, attracting skeptical consumers and persuading them to give it a chance, was going to be challenging. "The benefits had been advertised before, albeit without an effective product, and had not generated a strong response," said John Pepper, then head of U.S. operations. "We were not sure how well it would do. There was a lot of consumer skepticism."[10] The company itself had contributed to the skepticism with offerings such as Pert in the early 1980s, which despite its promise of "bounce and behavior" had provided little in the way of real conditioning.

Under the circumstances, many felt the company should launch BC-18, the new two-in-one technology, with a new brand. The marketing people began working up brand names and packaging design prototypes even as the development teams finalized the formula. "They were looking at names, and one of the names was China Silk. I remember seeing bottles and packages, and there were two or three other names, really exotic, hip, great names," Bolich recalled, watching the process from the labs. Examples of several proposals tested in market surveys survive in P&G Archives. *Silk Blossom,* for example, enticed consumers with a floral, art deco label design and copy that promised "a totally new beauty treatment for sensuously silky, radiant hair."[11]

Ultimately, though, the company decided to bring the new technology to market as Pert Plus. "We had vehicles already," Kuzma explained, "and with Pert having been introduced as a conditioning shampoo . . . it was the logical place, [given] the company's mindset of giving your newest technologies to your current brands first."[12]

Pert Plus

Whatever the mind-set, the choice was risky. Pert was a failing brand. Test marketed in 1979, it had originally been conceived as a green, pearly, high-perfume shampoo to counter Clairol's Herbal Essences, a popular emerald-green product with a high fragrance content, and to help expand the category of "refreshing" shampoos.[13] As previously noted, soap conditioners had been added late in the development stage, though in minor amounts that provided only minimal conditioning. After rapidly climbing to a share of near 6 percent, the brand had fallen off almost as quickly. By the time the company decided to apply BC-18, Pert was "a sick brand," in Kuzma's characterization, with a share that had sunk to 1.9 percent.[14] Some doubted whether BC-18 would be enough to revive it. "We went into test in Seattle wondering whether we would be able to save the brand or not," said Pep-

Pert Plus's original marketing stressed the convenience of effective two-in-one shampoo and conditioning—a positioning that created early market leadership but not a defensible brand equity.

per.[15] The results, however, were too encouraging to ignore: The brand doubled, then tripled in share.

Pert Plus expanded nationally in 1987. Procter & Gamble positioned the brand behind the promise of "great-looking hair with a minimum of fuss," backed by support elements proclaiming a "revolutionary cleaning and conditioning formula [that] works so well it eliminates the need for a separate conditioner." To drive the message home, Pert's first advertising campaign, called "Lockers" (because the ads were staged in locker rooms), began airing in January. As the brand team conceptualized the Pert Plus consumer, she was "independent, self-confident and enjoys an active lifestyle."[16] The company supported the brand with heavy sampling, distributing more than sixty million samples between 1987 and 1990.[17]

For several years, Pert Plus slowly, incrementally acquired share. Launched as a twelve-month payout proposition, the brand managed to break even over FY 1986–1987 and garner a 3.7-point share. The following year, Pert Plus picked up another point and began earning profits, which the company plowed back into the brand. Growth dipped when the brand reduced sampling, but picked up again when sampling resumed. By 1989, the company was projecting Pert Plus as a "leadership (5 percent plus case share) brand."[18] Then, in February 1989, *Consumer Reports* published the results of a shampoo survey that check-rated both Pert Plus Extra Body Fine Hair and Pert Plus Normal Hair for "lather[ing] more lushly than most shampoos" and leaving hair "very easy to comb when wet and exceptionally silky when dry."[19] BC-18 had been recognized. Momentum accelerated when the television program *Good Morning America* picked up on the story and echoed the *Consumer Reports* recommendation. On the strength of these independent testimonials, sales of Pert Plus surged, driving the share to 7 percent. By early 1990, the brand had become the number one dollar-volume shampoo in the United States.[20] Globally, rebranded as Vidal Sassoon Wash & Go (in some European markets) and Rejoice or Rejoy (in Asia), the brand scored further impressive gains.[21]

The Competitors Catch Up

Procter & Gamble's initial effort at marketing BC-18 looked like a triumph. Certainly, Pert Plus's growth through the 1980s vindicated the decision to stay in shampoos. Growth tailed off in the early 1990s, however, as the limitations of the brand's marketing strategy became apparent. The company had positioned Pert Plus on a convenience platform, identifying it as a brand offering "great-looking hair" with minimal "fuss." The brand had gone to market, in other words, on what U.S. hair care manager Martin Neuchtern later characterized as a "functional positioning," emphasizing what was "really a generic benefit."[22] Though it took competitors several years to catch up, by July 1991, no fewer than ten rival two-in-one brands were coming on-line, most of them (internal P&G analysis indicated) offering "adequate or comparable product formulation compared to ours." If all Pert Plus stood for in consumers' minds was convenience, the product was not going to be able to hold the ground it had won. "We need to create an ownable positioning which focuses on hair performance rather than convenience benefits and builds on our distinct character," the brand team warned as it prepared for the oncoming competition.[23]

The apprehension proved justified. The company tinkered with its "Lockers" ads, shifting the "executional emphasis . . . from convenience to great looking hair." Meanwhile, Pert Plus weathered what its brand team called a "year of reckoning." Its share inched up to 7.5 percent, over calendar year 1991, but volume growth plateaued and total shipments actually declined. The "high quality and overall image" of Pert Plus needed shoring up, the brand team concluded. The team needed to create "performance based copy . . . that will convince non-users to try Pert and will compel users to remain loyal."[24]

In retrospect, beauty care supervisor Rob Matteucci suggested, "We really didn't understand what the essence of the brand was." In Matteucci's terms, P&G had mastered the science, but not yet the art.[25]

Round Two: Restaging Pantene

Pert Plus, BC-18, and more basically P&G's rededication to selling hair care on the basis of performance had rescued a flagging business and recovered strategic initiative. To maintain momentum, though, the company needed to sell something beyond performance. It needed to tap into more mysterious forces, stir deeper consumer aspirations, capture and bring to market ineffable, intangible qualities. In a word, P&G needed to sell beauty. In BC-18, the company had developed a technology with significant beauty potential, Monton later observed, but the first effort to brand and market that technology had failed to create a beauty brand.

Meanwhile, in one of P&G's smallest and (from the perspective of headquarters in Cincinnati) most distant outposts, a fledgling operation was restaging one of the company's smaller prestige brands in a bold, new marketing package.

The Taiwan Twist

Procter & Gamble had entered Taiwan in 1985. The venture's first round of brands, including Pampers and a series of toilet soap brands, sold fairly well, but earned little profit.[26] After a few years of struggling to break even, local managers decided to redirect their strategy, launching feminine protection brands, pulling out of soaps, and concentrating instead on hair care. "We felt that the Taiwanese were willing to pay something for beauty and that they were more interested in getting an international brand," explained James Wei, a native Taiwanese who was then a young brand manager. "Also, beauty care was a category where we felt that we only needed a niche brand to be successful—unlike soap, laundry detergent, or diapers."[27] In 1986, the company introduced Head & Shoulders, followed in 1987 by Pert Plus.

Both brands did well, rapidly establishing themselves in the Taiwan market with respectable, if not dominant, shares. Still, the company's position was not exactly comfortable. In fact, it closely resembled the situation facing U.S. managers. Like the U.S. market, the Taiwan hair care market was fragmented, with only four brands holding shares larger than 5 percent in 1990. Pert, as the first two-in-one product on the market, had claimed an 11 percent share; Head & Shoulders was holding 7 percent. In total share terms, P&G trailed Kao, which had claimed 25 percent of the market. Procter & Gamble's brands held a total share of 18 points, and the company was bracing for a new round of competition. Kao Sifone (with "soft smooth hair" positioning) and Lux (positioned behind the promise of shiny hair) were both entering the two-in-one field, encroaching on P&G's position in what was clearly the growth segment of the market.[28]

Surveying the situation—in Taiwan specifically and Asia more generally—Durk Jager, the P&G executive overseeing business in the region, directed Taiwan's managers to work up a third hair care brand, suggesting they try Pantene. He chose the Taiwan group, Wei later surmised, because this group had "the longest experience in hair care in Asia," though that experience amounted to only a handful of years. Pantene seemed promising because it had a history as an international brand—although a tenuous one that had not extended to Asia.

In other respects, though, Pantene seemed an unlikely choice. When P&G inherited Pantene through the acquisition of RVI in 1985, the product looked like a minor, if profitable, property. Richardson-Vicks itself had acquired Pantene only a few years before being folded into P&G and had marketed the shampoo in the United States as a prestige brand distributed through department stores, professional salons, and selected drug outlets. As P&G moved in, RVI was preparing a mass-market campaign, which P&G carried through. Still, Pantene remained a limited, upscale marketing concept. As then formulated, "it was basic shampoo and conditioner technology," Kuzma reported. "It was an image brand all the way."[29]

A strong health and beauty heritage had nourished the brand since its introduction in 1945, however. The name derived from an ingredient, panthenol, discovered by a team of Swiss developers working in the 1940s. Panthenol penetrated the hair cuticle, strengthening the hair and making it more elastic. RVI's positioning had fortified the concept: Company literature described Pantene products as "upscale, treatment/health-oriented with an emphasis on the scientific approach to hair care." Elegant packaging in bottles with distinctive gold caps had underscored the beauty element.[30]

Restaging Pantene

In recommending Pantene for restaging and launch in Taiwan, Jager suggested that the product be perfume based, with variances based on fragrance, each in different colors. Taiwan's brand managers took a different approach, however. Their R&D people advised that basing variance on fragrance and color would be too expensive. In any event, the brand manager assigned to the project brought different instincts to the problem. Wei was, in his own words, "a young, enthusiastic marketing executive who had not known failure." He had worked on Head & Shoulders and Pert Plus in Taiwan, but he had also absorbed key lessons while training as a brand manager in the United States, where he had worked on laundry brands, not hair care. That experience proved formative. "We took the laundry approach of common technology and common perfume," Wei explained. Adopt the basic technology chassis, and adapt to meet specific brand equity needs. If BC-18 was the best shampoo and conditioner technology the company had to offer, in other words, then it should go into the new brand.[31]

On the other hand, Pantene's new custodians in Taiwan were determined to take advantage of the brand's science and health image and its beauty mystique. Having established itself in the Taiwan market with two functional brands, local managers had already decided "that the third brand should be something closer to beauty care," Wei related.[32] A Taiwan habits and practices study revealed key insights to exploit. "Shiny hair and healthy hair" emerged as "top hair-care attributes," remembered John Lee, then the marketing manager for hair care products in Taiwan. "Given that other key attributes—antidandruff and softeners/smoothness—were already addressed by Head & Shoulders and Pert, we concluded that a positioning using shiny and healthy attributes, combined with a 2-in-1 technology, could be a unique one."[33]

As they assembled the basic brand concept, Taiwan's marketing managers scavenged bits and pieces of marketing from other Pantene campaigns in other countries. The brand team was attracted, for example, to both the beauty-through-health positioning the brand had cultivated in the United States and a shine-outside/strength-inside positioning that brand managers had established in France. But the U.S. version seemed vague, while the French version sounded too complicated to be conveyed effectively. Combining the two ideas, the Taiwan concept became "shine through health," which tested well in market research.[34] At that point, continued Wei, "we had a concept that had something to do with health. Therefore, it made sense to connect health with vitamins. So R&D improved the formula by putting [original] Pantene's pro-vitamin [B-5] in the BC-18 formula to make this product work."[35]

It was a classic case of what Neuchtern termed "steal and improve" (and the company, less bluntly, has come to call "search and reapply"). Taiwan had appropriated elements from Pantene campaigns in other markets, tailored them to local market conditions, and in the process created a strong new platform for the brand. "Taiwan at the time was a very small market," Wei explained. "We tended to be on the receiving end." In other words, there was no room for not-invented-here thinking.

Procter & Gamble launched Pantene Pro-V (Pan-Ting Pro-V in Chinese) in Taiwan in April 1990. The line was originally limited to shampoos (no conditioners), which came in four versions: normal, oily, dry, and permed. The gold caps were scrapped, and the bottle redesigned as an oval cylinder. Following the "rainbow" U.S. coloring scheme, the bottles came in pearlescent pastel shades: ivory for the oily version, yellow for normal, pink for dry, and lavender for permed. Market testing also indicated that Taiwan consumers preferred a graphic design modeled on the U.S. pattern, rather than the latest Euro-Pantene design.[36]

The advertising campaign came together as the brand launched, with the local brand team and the agency continuing to employ search-and-apply tactics. The first round of ads adopted copy from U.S. Pantene commercials, in which fashion models urged, "Don't hate me because I'm beautiful." To stress the shampoo's effectiveness on difficult hair, the campaign used models with permed hair. The result was not great. "We couldn't catch any shine in the permed hair," Wei conceded. And Taiwan consumers responded uneasily to the tag line, which in retrospect was "too much for the Taiwanese culture," according to Wei. Recognizing that the campaign needed tweaking, the brand team worked up a second round of commercials with the modified tag line "Don't envy my healthy, shiny hair." The team also drew from Japan, which had decided to launch a Pantene restaging along similar lines, and (drawing on the resources of a bigger and more seasoned operation) had shot its own ads. The Japanese ads featured "a beautiful visual of someone with straight hair," Wei recalled. "We said, 'Wow! Some of those hair shots look pretty good.'"[37] After trying to get comparable visuals using models with permed hair, Taiwan's Pantene team switched to straight hair. With that shift, everything clicked. The stunning, shiny hair visual and the transformation approach became the centerpiece of the brand's marketing campaign.

The original marketing plan for Pantene in Taiwan had projected a 3 percent share in the brand's first year. It took Pantene Pro-V only six months to double that goal. A postlaunch usage and attitude study indicated brand awareness of 70 percent and advertising awareness of 60 percent.[38] Pantene took Taiwan by storm. By combining consumer desire for healthy, shiny hair with BC-18 technology that delivered superior shine, silkiness, and softness, P&G had made a beauty brand out of BC-18.

Globalizing Pantene

Pantene Pro-V spread rapidly beyond its original borders. Larry Dare played a key role in expanding the brand through Asia using the Taiwan model, appointing Taiwan General Manager Koos Groot to spearhead the expan-

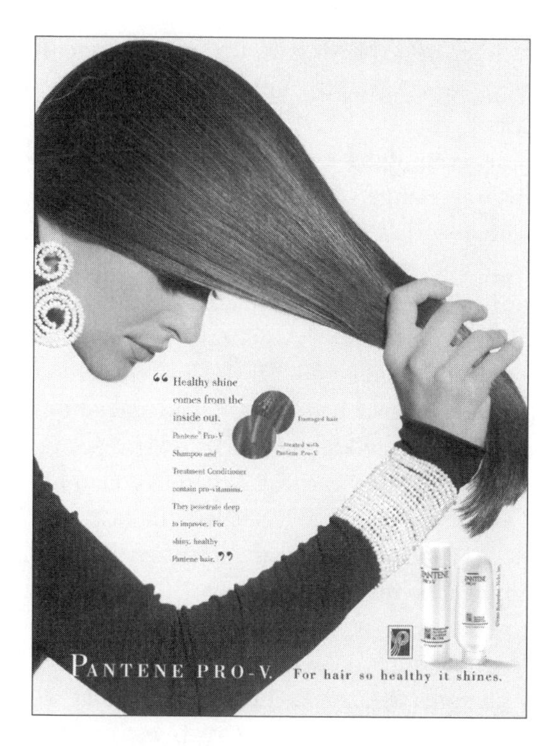

Instead of selling the shampoo on the basis of functional performance, Pantene Pro-V's ads imbued the brand with an intangible aura of beauty.

sion. Groot started in the Philippines, then moved to Thailand, and soon established the brand in markets across the region. Impressed, Bob Blanchard, then vice president in charge of international strategic planning, became a champion for broader expansion in Latin American and European markets. In the space of less than two years, with energetic support at the corporate level from chief executive Ed Artzt, who was drumming global thinking into heads everywhere, P&G had rolled Pantene out nearly across the globe.[39] The expansion of P&G's first round of BC-18 brands had unfolded in uncoordinated, haphazard fashion: What launched as Pert Plus in the United States became Vidal Sassoon Wash & Go in Europe, and Rejoice (or Rejoy) in Japan. As Matteucci put it, "we had this technology, and we put it on whatever happened to be there."[40] The second time around, with Pro-V, the company worked in tighter alignment, taking the basic elements that had proven themselves in Taiwan, making relatively minor adjustments for local markets, and launching in rapid sequence around the globe.

The real test, of course, waited in the United States. The stakes were higher there: "It's one thing to roll the dice in a small country like Taiwan," Monton pointed out. "You might lose $5 million. It's another thing to roll the dice in the United States, where you're talking $50 to $60 million."[41] More basically,

U.S. brand managers were accustomed to exporting, not importing, ideas. Even in the face of Pantene's impressive international market performance, there was hesitation in P&G's parent country. "For the first time in beauty care," Monton observed, "ideas start coming back to the U.S. from international. This was a very difficult cultural change."[42]

Nevertheless, circumstances were clearly calling for action. As Pert Plus positioning deteriorated, P&G was coming under mounting competitive pressure. Helene Curtis had become a particularly formidable threat, claiming the number one ranking in hair care products throughout the 1980s and early 1990s. Its flagship brand, Suave, held solid ground at the low end of the market, and two other brands, Salon Selectives and Finesse, had staked out strong positions at the high end. Most seriously, Helene Curtis was preparing a massive launch for Vibrance, a new high-end brand.[43] Procter & Gamble needed a strong contender in the same segment, and it needed one fast.

With some urgency, then, P&G's U.S. beauty care managers turned to the Taiwan model. The company tapped Neuchtern, then in Japan, to run the U.S. hair care business in the summer of 1991, with the specific mission of launching Pantene. He had to work quickly, without the usual battery of extensive market testing. "We changed the proposition so much and we didn't have time to test it," he recalled. "We knew Helene Curtis was coming out with a new prestige brand, so we just had to go." The company ran BASES testing (an early, pre-test–market round of testing) in September 1991 and launched nationally in February 1992. Even before national launch of Pantene Pro-V, Neuchtern was running the new "healthy, shiny hair" ad campaign in modified forms to advertise the old Pantene. He was determined not to let another company get to the North American market first with the concept P&G had pioneered in Taiwan.[44]

Expectations were fairly modest, as Pantene Pro-V launched in the United States. After a rocky first year and hasty modifications to what had been a rushed execution (tinkering with package sizes and so on), the brand began to grow, incrementally at first, then with gathering momentum. Neuchtern described the iterative process: "We had limited money in the beginning—I had a terrible profit at the end of my year one. But then we really kind of got into the rhythm, increasing media weight, building the business, testing, sampling, building the business, increasing media weight, building the business, more sampling, and then it began just chugging out." At each level, the company tested the impact of increasing media weight and discovered more growth potential. At each level, the brand paid out. Against expectations, Pantene grew to megabrand status. Procter & Gamble had fused the science (BC-18) and the art (healthy, shiny hair) and built a beauty brand.

The Pantene Story in Perspective

Establishing leadership in hair care over the 1980s and 1990s took repeated attempts on P&G's part. From Pert to BC-18, from BC-18 to Pert Plus, and from Pert Plus to Pantene Pro-V, the company redirected its hair care strategies several times. By the late 1990s, though, P&G was assembling not only the elements of a new billion-dollar brand, but more basically a new model of brand leadership.

As with many other episodes in P&G history, technology and superior performance played critical roles in the outcome. Formulating a two-in-one shampoo and conditioning chassis (BC-18) that delivered real benefits created the opportunity the company needed to build (or rebuild) brands with unique value propositions. Procter & Gamble's scientists and chemical engineers managed to regain the technological edge, giving the company the potential to put products on the market that clearly outperformed competitive brands. To this extent, the first part of this case—the story of BC-18 and Pert Plus—resembles stories like Ivory in the 1880s, Tide in the 1940s, and Crest in the 1960s.

But then the story takes a very different turn, for capitalizing on the opportunity created by BC-18 and creating sustainable brand leadership eventually took P&G beyond inherited assumptions about brand building. Competitive products offering comparable performance appeared on the market within a few years of the Pert Plus launch. Brand managers soon realized that branding hair care products on the basis of functionality and performance was not going to create defensible brand equity or sustainable market leadership. In other words, technology alone would not hold the field for long.

Accordingly, after a few years of growth, BC-18's first brand iteration stalled. Fortunately, P&G spread itself out as it searched for ways to keep momentum, discovering new attributes within the technology and applying BC-18 in new brand forms that capitalized on those attributes. "When you get a good piece of technology," Monton observed, referring to Pert Plus and Pantene, "you can use that technology in different ways. There isn't just one positioning."

Thus the technology that first served as the basis for the revitalization of Pert migrated to another brand, Pantene Pro-V. And this time, brand managers took a very different approach when positioning the brand. They described the product in terms and imagery that not only demonstrated tangible benefits such as performance and functionality, but also cloaked it with a glamorous, ineffable, mysterious aura. In short, they made Pantene a beauty brand. The evolution was not necessarily easy or natural for a company from P&G's background. Nevertheless, it created a compelling chemistry, becoming the basis for a new blockbuster. "You have to deliver both the art and the science," said Matteucci. "Then you can begin to build loyalty. And that's when you really start to get the big brands, . . . the ones that are sustainable."

Finally, the other striking aspect of the Pantene story is geographic. Unlike the usual route of other leading P&G products, the components of what rapidly grew into a global powerhouse were initially assembled far from Cincinnati. Within a small operation establishing itself on what was (from headquarters' point of view) the periphery of the company, a handful of managers and researchers were working with passionate initiative to build up a new business. Once Jager made the initial suggestion, Wei, in Taiwan, took ownership of the idea and crafted a winning campaign. The company's ability to inspire that sense of ownership to begin with, then recognize the strength of the work it created, and roll out an innovation on a rapidly sequenced global basis represented a milestone in the redefinition of P&G as a global enterprise.

First-generation immigrants William Procter (left) and James Gamble (pictured as a younger man, above) met in Cincinnati, where they married sisters Elizabeth Ann and Olivia Norris. In 1837, the brothers-in-law decided to go into business together selling soap and candles.

Harley T. Procter, a younger son of the co-founder, was the marketing genius behind the creation of P&G's—and one of the world's first—consumer brands in household products. Ivory paved the way for everything that followed.

I look and long to touch her lips,
Or steal one curl among the tresses
Through which the summer sunlight slips
And summer breezes blow caresses:

"What makes you always fair?" I cry,
But she says naught until I force her,
And then demurely makes reply:
"Why, just pure Ivory Soap, of course, Sir!"

Grandson of the co-founder, William Cooper Procter (left) served in senior management positions in the company between 1890 and his death in 1934. He is credited with diversifying P&G's business into food products, building the direct sales force, and articulating many of its enduring values, especially the fair treatment of employees.

Three leaders of the mid-twentieth century: the first head of the company from outside of the founding families, Richard R. "Red" Deupree (below, center) guided P&G through economic and military crises from 1930 to 1948, while successors Neil McElroy (below, right) and Howard Morgens (below, left) presided over the company's vast postwar expansion and diversification from 1948 to 1957 and 1957 to 1974, respectively.

OPPOSITE: *P&G ran its first color print ad in 1896 in a ladies' magazine. It was not immediately evident that Ivory soap was being advertised. Instead, the ad communicated something subtler and ultimately more powerful—a set of associations that P&G cultivated for the brand, including femininity, gentility, and cleanliness.*

The advertising campaign accompanying Tide's launch in 1946 heralded a "revolutionary" new product, and the claim was not just hype. The new synthetic detergent performed far better than traditional soaps, vaulting P&G to new heights in its core market. Along with automatic washing machines, Tide eased an ancient chore and changed consumer habits. It was the company's biggest brand for decades, and although later eclipsed by Pampers, Tide remains a major source of earnings nearly sixty years after its introduction.

Time Life Pictures / Getty Images.

Procter & Gamble's rapid growth and overseas expansion after World War II attracted widespread public interest and helped to make President Neil McElroy a star in American industry. Several years after appearing on the cover of Time, *McElroy moved on to Washington, D.C., as U.S. Secretary of Defense.*

P&G and its agency partners produced many memorable advertising campaigns, including this famous print ad for Crest using artwork by Norman Rockwell. The ad emphasized the wholesome therapeutic benefits of Crest, but the brand really took off several years later, following acceptance by the American Dental Association.

A pioneer in print and radio advertising and radio and TV soap operas, P&G also invested early and heavily in TV advertising. Pictured at left: Actor Ken Roberts pitches Ivory to daytime viewers.

P&G entered the papermaking arena by acquiring Charmin in 1957. The business proved successful, but not before the company had made a huge financial bet and mastered a wholly new technology.

In addition to new technology, P&G brought its formidable capabilities in marketing and advertising to its new paper brands, establishing popular television characters as spokespersons. Mr. Whipple (right), who couldn't resist squeezing the Charmin, emphasized the softness of the product, while Rosie (below) showed that Bounty was "the quicker picker upper," with unusual absorbency and wet strength.

One of P&G's most able executives, Ed Harness (above) moved from the company's core business in packaged soap and detergent products to become general manager of paper products in 1963. Under his leadership, the business turned around, with Pampers and Bounty becoming blockbuster brands. Harness also rocketed upward, becoming president in 1970 and chairman and chief executive upon Howard Morgens's retirement in 1974.

John Smale (above) succeeded Harness as chairman and chief executive in 1981 and served in the top job for nine years. Smale displayed outstanding abilities and future promise in the late 1950s and early 1960s as an advertising manager for Crest as it surged to market leadership. As chief executive, Smale led P&G into new businesses in health care and beauty care, accelerated its global expansion, and presided over a major reorganization.

Ed Artzt (pictured in front of the headquarters towers opened in 1985) distinguished himself in a range of P&G businesses before taking charge of operations in Europe in 1975. There he built an integrated regional operation that propelled P&G to market leadership in many areas. From there, Artzt championed rapid expansion in Latin America, Asia, and Central and Eastern Europe. In 1991, he succeeded John Smale as chairman and chief executive.

Not everything P&G touched turned to gold. 1980s ventures into soft drinks and orange juice (right) foundered as the company acquired and introduced brands but was unable to compete with much bigger, well-entrenched, and sophisticated rivals. P&G sold off most of its cold beverage brands by the early 1990s.

P&G's famous "moon-and-stars" logo evolved from uncertain origins. During its early decades, the company sold a popular type of "star" (short for stearic acid) candles, and lore has it that an image of a five-pointed star in a circle adorned the shipping crates. If so, by the late 1850s, the star in a circle had morphed into a more arresting image featuring 13 stars (in honor of the 13 original American states) and the man in the moon, a popular icon of the era. In 1882, the logo was registered as a trademark, and the image was modified occasionally in later years, assuming the familiar modern design (by sculptor Ernest Haswell) around 1930. In the early 1980s, the logo became controversial as unfounded rumors proclaimed it to be a symbol of Satanism—rumors that still resurface occasionally. In the 1990s, the company gradually weaned itself from the moon and stars, converting to a contemporary logo based on its abbreviated name, one of the most recognized in the global economy.

late 1850s

1882

1930

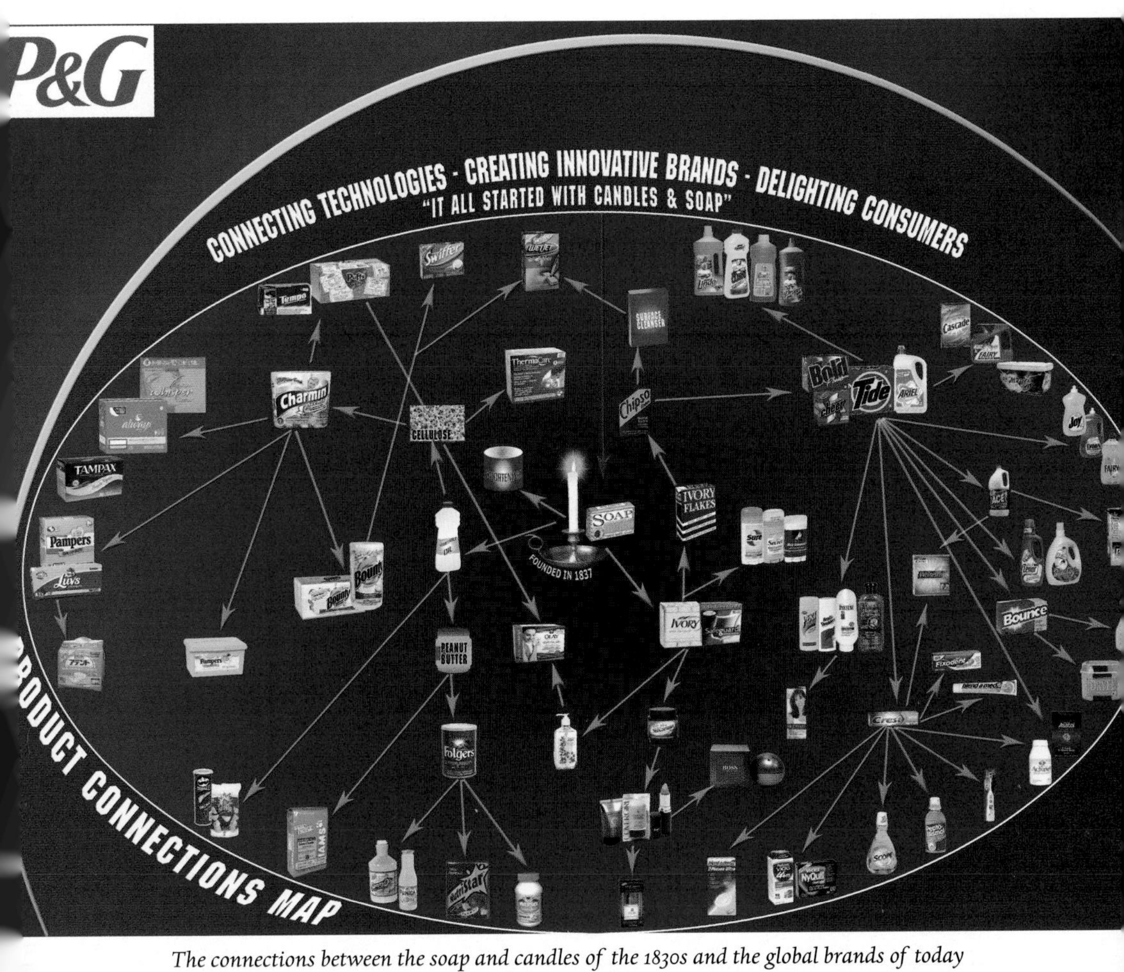

The connections between the soap and candles of the 1830s and the global brands of today are tangible and tight. Procter & Gamble has remained focused on household consumer products from the beginning. Its growth has been organic, as one product technology led to another or as acquisitions brought positions in related markets.

1991

2003

The European Technical Center in Brussels (above) opened in the early 1960s, a sign of the company's growing commitment to international business. The original facility is the H-shaped structure in the rear. Expanded several times and now also housing administrative offices, the complex is one of P&G's biggest in Europe, a resource not only for the region but also, as part of the company's network of technology centers, for operations around the world.

P&G has maintained operations in Latin America since the 1940s and built market-leading positions in Mexico, Central America, and Venezuela. These are supported from the Latin American Market Development Organization, based in Caracas (below).

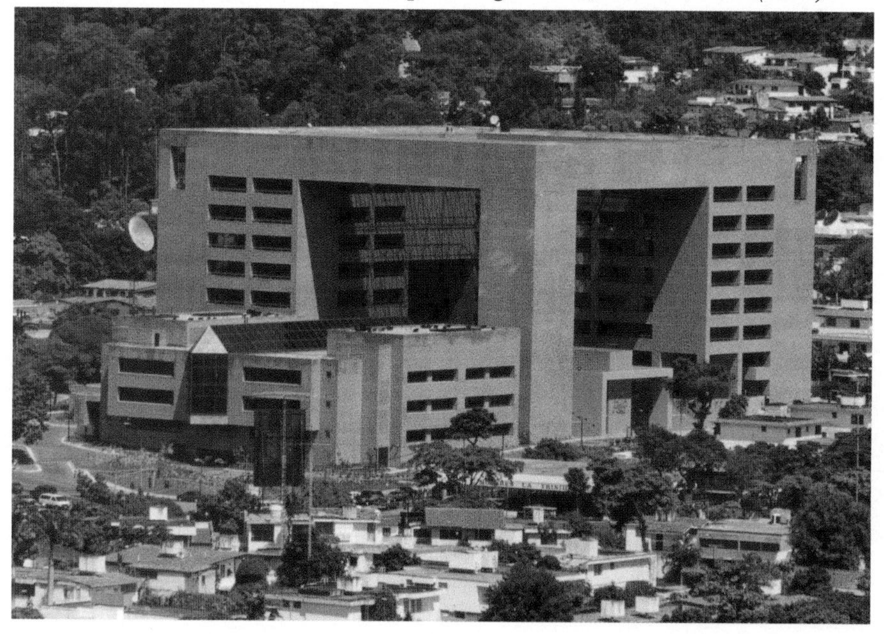

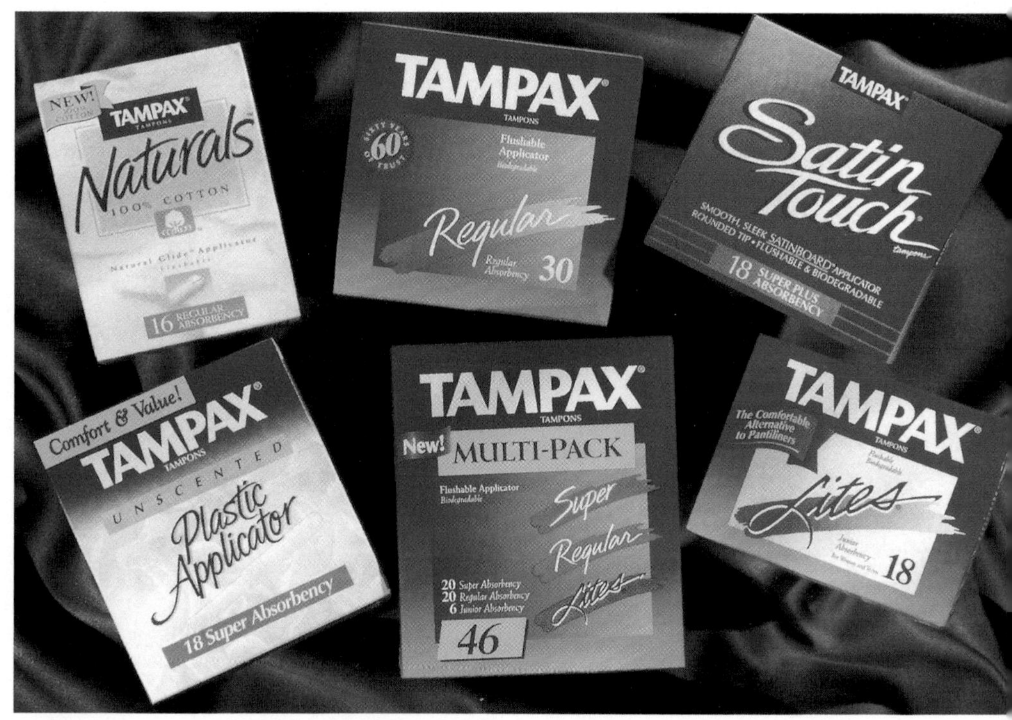

P&G's first entry into feminine products, Rely tampons, ended with a massive voluntary product recall and termination of the brand in 1980. Undeterred, the company offered Always sanitary pads (marketed as Whisper in Asia), which became one of its first global brands in the mid-1980s. P&G followed up by acquiring Tambrands in 1995. The deal cemented the company's position as the global market leader in feminine protection products.

John Pepper (left) served as chairman and chief executive between 1995 and 1998, years of rapid change in the company as it pushed aggressively into health care, accelerated the pace of new product introductions, integrated a major acquisition (Tambrands), and prepared for a massive worldwide reorganization. A prime mover in developing the company's formal statement of Purpose, Values, and Principles, Pepper tirelessly championed P&G's efforts to hold true to its core beliefs.

In the 1980s, Durk Jager (right) led P&G's impressive turnaround in Japan. In the early 1990s, he headed the North American business, guiding P&G through a necessary restructuring of its relationships with its trade customers. Jager's tenure as chief executive (1998–2000) ended prematurely but included the hugely successful acquisition of Iams, which became a billion-dollar brand in pet nutrition.

A. G. Lafley, chief executive since 2000 and chairman and chief executive since 2002, refocused P&G on its biggest brands, biggest markets, and biggest customers. Under his quiet, inspirational leadership, the company delivered strong results based on winning at the two moments of truth: when consumers choose P&G products in stores, and when they put those products to use in their homes.

In 1985, P&G bought Richardson-Vicks for its renowned over-the-counter cough-and-cold remedies. A minor part of the deal, but no mere fringe benefit, was the Pantene line of hair care products. In the 1990s, P&G built Pantene into a billion-dollar global beauty brand and a key component of its burgeoning portfolio of hair care and beauty care brands.

Like Pantene, SK-II was a hidden jewel in a business acquired for other reasons. After P&G bought Max Factor in 1991, it discovered SK-II, an upscale beauty brand with global potential.

24 DECEMBER 13, 1999 · ADVERTISING AGE

Best of the best: Brilliant leadership, brand building, compelling advertising and use of the media mix are what makes history; by vote of the editors, here are the top five

Marketers *of the* Century

Creating a brand management system was only the start of a legacy devoted to nurturing of brands by leaders who understood consumers

1 Procter & Gamble

In December 1999, Advertising Age, *the bible of the advertising industry, hailed P&G as the number one "marketer of the century." Long the world's biggest spender on advertising, the company was lauded not only for its commitment but also for its pioneering campaigns in print, electronic, and interactive media and its leadership in building and sustaining brands.*

PART IV

Competing in a Shrinking World: Procter & Gamble Since 1990

CHAPTER FOURTEEN

Reshaping Procter & Gamble

AFTER 1990, P&G continued to face dramatic and rapid changes in its major businesses and markets. The company entered the decade with $1.6 billion in net income on revenues of $24.1 billion (6.7 percent return on sales after tax) and employed approximately 89,000 people in 47 countries. Major business segments included laundry and cleaning, personal care, food and beverage, and pulp and chemicals. About 38 percent of sales and 47 percent of corporate assets fell outside the United States—indications of the company's increasingly global outlook and operations.

By the early twenty-first century, P&G was a markedly changed enterprise. In 2003, the company reported $5.1 billion in net income on revenues of $43.3 billion (11 percent return on sales after tax), and employed 98,000 people in more than 80 countries. The collapse of Communism in Central and Eastern Europe and liberal economic policies in China permitted P&G to gain access to approximately 2 billion new customers who were hungry for Western goods.

Outwardly, the company's portfolio of businesses looked markedly different. Procter & Gamble no longer reported a pulp and chemicals segment, whereas fast-rising young businesses in beauty care and health care (including oral care) complemented the steady growth of traditional, strong contributors in fabric and home care and paper products (including feminine protection). Major acquisitions of the period included Max Factor (1991), Tambrands (1997), Iams (1999), Clairol (2001), and Wella (2003). Departures included such longtime brands as Crisco, Spic and Span, Biz, Duncan Hines, and Jif, as well as some 1980s ventures in foods and beverages such as Citrus

Hill and Fisher Nuts. The continuing rise of megacustomers such as Wal-Mart, Target, Carrefour, and METRO, which themselves were globalizing rapidly, carried enormous implications for how P&G marketed and sold its products. The advent of the Internet brought more changes in supply-chain management and marketing and portended still more.

All these dramatic, even revolutionary, events in P&G's businesses and markets constituted the outward signs of equally dramatic, even revolutionary, events on the inside. On two occasions, the company restructured its operations and eliminated thousands of positions, all the while laboring diligently to deliver superior value to consumers, in part by lowering costs. It revamped its approach to new-product development in pursuit of new brands and categories. And in 1998–1999, under new chief executive Durk Jager, P&G launched the biggest reorganization in the company's history. Carried out under the rubric of Organization 2005 (O-2005), the reorganization changed nearly everything about how the company organized and managed itself. It shifted the basis of the company's operations from geographical profit centers to a global matrix featuring worldwide product groups and geographical marketing organizations. Under the watchwords "stretch, innovation, and speed," the company sought to accelerate both its rate of innovation and its global growth.

The transition to the new structure was rocky, however. The stretch proved a little too far, the speed a little too fast. Built for global growth, the company's cost structure became burdensome when that growth failed to materialize. The stock tumbled, resulting in a change in top management. A new chief executive, A. G. Lafley, led a comeback by reorienting P&G toward what it did best, focusing on sustaining the biggest brands, penetrating the biggest customers, and winning in the biggest geographical markets. At the same time, the company revamped its cost structure and developed a new approach to innovation based on partnership and rapid commercialization of new products.

By 2003, changes associated with O-2005 and its aftermath continued to ripple through P&G. Nonetheless, the most recent returns are encouraging, apparently fulfilling the intent of the O-2005 reorganization and subsequent changes: global leadership in major categories, global leadership brands, global leadership in innovation, global scale, and a return to consistent earnings growth.

In 1990, when Ed Artzt succeeded John Smale as chairman and chief executive, few observers (inside or outside P&G) would have predicted the magnitude of the coming changes. Nevertheless, everyone knew that changes were inevitable and suspected they would be unusually dramatic.

Throttle Forward, 1990–1995

The election of fifty-nine-year-old Artzt as chief executive caught some observers by surprise, although he was one of two obvious internal candidates. The other, John Pepper, age fifty, would later occupy the top job when Artzt reached mandatory retirement age in 1995.[1] During the fifteen years before taking over, Artzt had spearheaded P&G's rapid and extensive international expansion, starting as group vice president for European operations in 1975 and continuing with his elevations to executive vice president (international operations) in 1980 and vice chairman and president of P&G International four years later. He presided over the reorganization of P&G's business in Western Europe, grouping the autonomous, country-based subsidiaries into a more centralized and coordinated regional structure that cut direct and indirect costs throughout the value chain. He also provided vigorous leadership to P&G's thrusts into Japan, Taiwan, China, and Southeast Asia, as well as into Central and Eastern Europe with the collapse of the Soviet bloc. Before that, he had followed the traditional upward path, establishing himself as a hardworking, hard-driving brand manager and general manager across a range of businesses including laundry, paper, and food products. A former collegiate basketball player, Artzt was a highly competitive executive with a sharp intellect, a blunt manner, and a knack for getting results. Although stories of his quick temper circulated widely in the company, he also possessed great personal charm, which he deployed skillfully as a motivational tool.

The primary signal sent by Artzt's election was P&G's continuing resolve to become a more global company. At the same time, two new executive vice presidents, Durk Jager and Jurgen Hintz, both foreign-born with most of their careers spent outside the United States, joined the senior management team. Pepper, meanwhile, succeeded Artzt as president of P&G International. This was a team with broad and deep international experience and a decidedly global outlook.[2]

In the early 1990s, P&G faced some unexpected—and unexpectedly big—opportunities, especially in China and Central and Eastern Europe. At the same time, the company had to respond to familiar challenges: continuing assaults on core businesses by longtime rivals Unilever, Kimberly-Clark, Colgate, Henkel, and Kao; the disappointing performance of several beverage and food units; the ongoing need to find new growth opportunities via acquisition and internal development; operating costs that remained too high; and the ongoing trade revolution, led by Wal-Mart.

Although P&G was already hard at work on these matters, Artzt was impatient with the progress. As he sought to push the throttle forward, the early 1990s became a hectic time. Procter & Gamble mounted major initiatives to accelerate international growth, weed and sort the company's portfolio of businesses, restructure relations with the trade, reengineer the company's operations, launch a new approach to innovation, and revamp internal training and development to prepare P&G to prosper in a smaller, faster, more competitive world.[3]

Global Growth

The most obvious growth opportunities appeared in the "white spaces" of China and Central and Eastern Europe—spaces that P&G rushed aggressively to fill. Departing from its usual practice of measured entry via joint venture, one country at a time, P&G pursued a regional strategy in Central and Eastern Europe that featured simultaneous entry in multiple markets with multiple categories. By the early 1990s, P&G had operations on the ground in Hungary, Poland, Czech Republic, and Russia and had surged ahead of its Western competitors in laundry products, disposable diapers, and dentifrices. Similarly in China, where P&G had entered via a joint venture in 1988, the company concluded agreements with the city of Guangzhou and Guangdong Province to build the biggest consumer products factory in the country. Opened in 1991, the Huangpu plant enabled P&G to surge to market leadership in hair care and personal care products like soaps and moisturizing creams and to lay a firm foundation for growth in oral care.

Meanwhile, P&G supplemented its invasion of the white space with other major foreign investments to bolster its global position. In 1991, the company broke ground on a new R&D center on Rokko Island (near Osaka), Japan, to incorporate learning from, and develop products tailored to, that nation's demanding customers. In Europe, P&G invested more than $1 billion to increase its technical and production capabilities, including a major expansion of the European Technical Center in Brussels, the acquisition of a paper products company in Germany, and a new Pringles factory in Belgium. In Latin America, in 1993, P&G broke ground in Caracas, Venezuela, for the headquarters building of a new Latin American Division, with responsibility for developing and overseeing a coordinated strategy for the region. The Middle East, Africa, and General Export organization in Geneva continued to cultivate new markets through exports and joint ventures in the countries for which it was responsible. All this activity helped reorient P&G from a U.S. to a global corporation: In 1993, for the first time in its history, P&G's revenues from overseas surpassed those from the United States.[4]

Remixing the Portfolio

While P&G accelerated its overseas thrusts, top management also reevaluated the company's portfolio of businesses, seeking to bolster the core and prune marginal operations. During the 1990s, patterns of competition that had emerged earlier in the core businesses continued to play out. In laundry and home care, for example, Tide and Ariel sustained leadership in global markets, while smaller detergent brands and the major dish care and fabric softener brands also fared well. Unilever remained a strong rival, especially in Europe, Latin America, and other developing countries and regions, while Henkel in Europe and Kao in Asia were also tough, resourceful competitors that also were globalizing. Although P&G held the leading position in North America in tissues and towels, Kimberly-Clark proved a formidable foe in disposable diapers, and its Huggies brand eclipsed Pampers for market leadership in the United States. Colgate, meanwhile, maintained its ferocious assault on Crest.

Artzt expected most of P&G's leading brands to become global leaders, at least in the developed world. This was no idle dream, given the international success of Tide/Ariel, Pampers, Always/Whisper, and Pringles, among other brands. As detailed earlier, in the early 1990s, Pantene Pro-V shampoo became P&G's next global superstar.

While seeking to promote its global brands (and revive Pampers and Crest), P&G invested heavily in its younger businesses, including cosmetics and fragrances and health care, to generate faster growth. The future seemed bright in both businesses, which P&G had built primarily through acquisitions.

In cosmetics and fragrances, the 1989 purchase of the Noxell Company had brought with it not only the Noxzema brand of skin care products, but also the Cover Girl (the U.S. market leader) and Clarion lines of cosmetics and skin treatment products and Navy perfume. The cosmetics and fragrances business possessed many structural characteristics appealing to P&G: It drew on familiar science and technology, its products were distributed through the same channels as P&G's core brands, and it depended heavily on advertising to build and sustain brands. Like many P&G ventures into new territory, the initial transaction was made to learn a new business and ascertain how P&G's capabilities in R&D, manufacturing, and marketing could add value and create competitive advantage. It took only a brief time to validate optimistic assessments. "I don't know of any place that's not a good beauty-care market," said Artzt.[5]

Soon thereafter, P&G acquired American Cyanamid's Shulton division, maker of Old Spice and Santa Fe men's toiletries and fragrances. In 1991, the company followed up with the purchase of the Max Factor and Betrix businesses from Revlon. These new properties included significant overseas business, and Max Factor's SK-II ultimately turned out to be a hidden jewel. Two years later, P&G added Giorgio cosmetics from Avon. By then, P&G had doubled the initial investment in Noxell, spending $2.7 billion on acquisitions to become a significant factor in the industry worldwide. When combined with P&G's fashionable brands in hair care (Pantene, Vidal Sassoon) and skin care (Oil of Olay), the company possessed the foundation of a promising global business in beauty care.[6]

Procter & Gamble continued to make big investments in health care, another industry with attractive structural characteristics and growth prospects. In 1991, the company committed more than $300 million to build a new Health Care Research Center near Cincinnati. Additionally, P&G negotiated a series of licensing deals, acquisitions, joint ventures, and cooperative marketing agreements pertaining to a range of new prescription drugs. The company's portfolio of prescription drugs included Asacol (a widely prescribed treatment for ulcerative colitis) and two potential blockbuster drugs with annual sales potential of $1 billion: Stedicor (a remedy for heart arrhythmia) and Actonel (a P&G discovery for treating osteoporosis). In the OTC marketplace, P&G brought its formidable capabilities in product supply, marketing, and advertising to bear on the major brands acquired in the 1980s, including Pepto-Bismol, Metamucil, and the Vicks cough and cold remedies. By the mid-1990s, P&G's health care segment, which included Crest and other oral care products, had achieved $2.5 billion in sales.

The flip side of the strategy to support core brands and fund new growth opportunities was a sober assessment of the long-term viability of underperforming brands and businesses. In 1992, P&G began to sell off its operations in cotton linters and wood pulp, including the P&G Cellulose (formerly Buckeye) subsidiary established in the early twentieth century. The business had been struggling for several years, with prices falling based on the growing popularity of cheaper, noncellulose pulps and excess capacity among traditional pulp manufacturers. Artzt concluded that P&G "would be better off working with raw materials suppliers rather than continuing to create much of [its] own raw material supply internally."[7]

Another business that drew a hard look was the Food and Beverage Division, which Artzt had once headed. Although Folgers remained a powerhouse brand in the United States, and Pringles, after years of fits and starts, was beginning its global breakout, other brands in the division were troubled. Changing consumer tastes that favored low-fat and low-calorie foods created problems for Crisco and Duncan Hines in the United States. Neither brand had any real hope of growing abroad, where consumer preferences and practices were different. Meanwhile, several food and beverage acquisitions from the 1980s failed to deliver acceptable results, and some investors and analysts believed that P&G would be better off getting out of foods and beverages altogether. In June 1991, rumors swirled that the company had the business on the block.[8]

In fact, P&G was very concerned about its Citrus Hill orange juice and Fisher Nuts units. After failing to find a potential buyer, the company finally decided in September 1992 to liquidate Citrus Hill (along with selling off some other minor juice brands) and absorb a write-off of $200 million. Similarly, P&G was unhappy with Fisher Nuts, acquired in 1989 to complement Pringles in the salty-snack category. Procter & Gamble soon discovered that it could bring nothing distinctive to the nut business. In 1995, after six years of accumulating modest losses, P&G sold the business to John B. San Filippo & Son for a fraction of the initial acquisition price.[9]

Extending the Supply-Chain Revolution

A third priority was to position P&G in the United States, and eventually in the rest of the world, to profit from the revolution in supply-chain management that new information technology made possible and Wal-Mart led. In 1988, P&G had formed a customer team with Wal-Mart, the first in a series of similar teams with major mass merchandisers. In 1992, under the leadership of Jager and Lawrence D. "Mike" Milligan, the company gathered and regrouped its sales force under a new organization called Customer Business Development (CBD). Structured around national (and eventually global) accounts, CBD forged close relationships with its customers to streamline the supply chain, with the resulting cost savings split among itself, its customers, and the consumers. Between 1991 and 1993, Jager directed P&G to convert all its business with the North American trade to *value pricing,* an everyday low price. The adoption of value pricing marked the end of the large, periodic cash discounts and other incentives P&G had traditionally provided its trade customers to influence the merchandising of its brands. Procter & Gamble's move sent shock waves through the trade, which had come to depend on these incentives. Many retailers began to reorganize their operations to maintain margins on lower prices. With up to 70 percent of its volume affected by lower prices, P&G itself undertook a probing review of its internal management systems and practices, especially in product supply. It also discontinued several minor brands.[10]

In 1993, P&G took a leading role in the establishment of Efficient Consumer Response (ECR), a cooperative initiative sponsored by the Food Marketing Institute and the Grocery Manufacturers of America, the two leading trade associations in the grocery industry. The ECR initiative modeled many of its practices on supply-chain innovations at Wal-Mart and other leading retailers. Procter & Gamble took a particularly active role in the establishment of standards and practices for the continuous replenishment of stocks. In the place of a time-consuming, labor-intensive process prone to human error came an automated system for managing inventories and just-in-time deliveries to trade distribution centers.

Becoming Leaner and Faster

Procter & Gamble concluded FY 1992–1993 in excellent shape—in its own words, "a healthy, growing business, [with] a strong balance sheet, positive cash flow, state-of-the-art products and a well-stocked technology pipeline with plenty of opportunities for growth."[11] Management forecast record earnings of more than $2 billion, a total representing double-digit growth. Nonetheless, the company was not content to rest. Indeed, Artzt fretted that the rate of change internally was not keeping pace with the rate of change in the external environment. A company release put the challenge into words: "We believe that we must slim down to stay competitive in a very competitive world. Internally, the dramatic growth of our business during the past decade—including more than 40 acquisitions, plus entry into 29 new countries and 20 new business categories—has created a more complex work environment. Externally, customers want better value, and our competitors are getting leaner and quicker. We are simply going to have to run faster to stay ahead, and we intend to do that."[12]

More specifically, P&G noted that since 1982, it had acquired seventy-nine new plant sites and closed only twenty-four, "leaving a significant number of opportunities to consolidate to lower product costs." At the same time, the "ongoing move to global brands and common formulas and packages on a regional basis, wherever possible, results in economies of scale and the need for fewer operations."[13]

To realize these efficiencies and accelerate the pace of internal change, P&G turned to business-process reengineering techniques that were sweeping the industrial landscape in the United States. In the early 1990s, a deep recession, advances in information technology, and increasing global competitive rivalry combined to prompt many big U.S. companies to reexamine and redesign their core business processes.[14] In December 1992, P&G caught the wave and launched a reengineering initiative called Strengthening Global

Effectiveness (SGE). Eleven cross-functional and multilevel teams tackled every important business process in the company, looking for ways to streamline and simplify operations, cut costs, and achieve breakthrough gains in productivity. The teams operated with four rules: (1) change the work, (2) do more with less, (3) eliminate rework, and (4) reduce costs that can't be recovered through pricing.[15]

The process of study and analysis consumed seven months and culminated in numerous proposals and recommendations. Many of these, however, proved hard to implement or incapable of generating lasting effects. The primary impact of SGE resulted from downsizing. Procter & Gamble closed 30 plants (of the total of 147), removed three layers of management, and eliminated thirteen thousand jobs—about 12 percent of P&G's total workforce.[16]

To pay for SGE, P&G set aside a restructuring reserve of $1.5 billion, which caused an accounting loss for the fiscal year. Nonetheless, the company expected to recoup the investment at a rate of more than $500 million per year, beginning in the 1995 fiscal year. The impact of SGE carried beyond its financial and economic effects to dampen morale. Although most employees accepted the logic of downsizing, for others, the experience proved disillusioning and lessened the loyalty they felt toward the company.[17]

More Innovation, Faster

The SGE initiative delivered an immediate impact on P&G's bottom line. Return on sales (as reported) jumped from an average of about 10 percent during the late 1980s and early 1990s to between 15 and 17 percent in 1994 and 1995. Unfortunately, noted an executive, "we had little top line growth. . . . Our earnings growth was largely fueled by cost reduction, and we realized that there was a limit to the costs you could take out of the system." Another executive pointed out that despite the huge number of introductions of new packaged goods in the United States since 1990, only a small number had achieved sales of $100 million or more. For P&G, that was sobering news. Incremental innovations, product line extensions, and flanker brands would not do the job. Something more was needed. In addition to pushing each business line for faster growth, P&G needed to accelerate the development of major new brands and new lines of business.[18]

In 1993, Artzt established an Innovation Leadership Team consisting of six top executives: Pepper, Jager, Wolfgang Berndt (executive vice president, North America), Gordon Brunner (senior vice president and chief technical officer), Gary Martin (senior vice president, information services and product supply), and Eric Nelson (senior vice president and chief financial officer). The team reviewed all new-product and new-venture initiatives in the company and looked for opportunities to develop new products that would draw on P&G capabilities but cut across organizational lines of responsibility. Such ideas typically languished because of lack of funding and internal sponsorship. To redress these problems, the team set up a Corporate Innovation Fund to provide "a small amount of seed money to explore new ideas." In 1994, the Innovation Leadership Team followed up by establishing a Corporate New Ventures (CNV) organization at headquarters and charged it to launch major new projects and develop "an efficient, reliable innovation process."

The CNV group declared its mission as "to have an important, direct role in the development of at least one major new business per year." The group drew on high-potential managerial and technical talent across the company and sought to foster a stimulating working environment at its quarters on the sixteenth floor of the headquarters towers. An open space with no private offices, the CNV quarters featured couches, white boards, a stock of refreshments. Some envious employees dubbed it "the penthouse."[19]

It would take time for CNV to do its work. Nonetheless, in its first months, it identified several projects to pursue, including a new electrostatic mop, a home dry-cleaning kit, a treatment for fabrics (including curtains and upholstery) to remove odors, and a thermal heat wrap to treat muscle pain.

Combat Training

Artzt's final major initiative was to emphasize aspects of P&G's values and culture that he deemed critical to the company's success in the new environment. When he had been a young manager, he and his peers could still interact with Neil McElroy, Howard Morgens, and other senior figures on an informal basis. By the 1990s, however, P&G's global growth and vast scale placed limits on personal contact with top leaders. To help transmit the company's traditions, values, and culture, late in 1991 Artzt founded P&G College. Modeled loosely on General Electric's renowned Management Development Institute at Crotonville, New York, the new institution was designed especially to reinforce P&G's passion to win and to equip the company with strategies and tactics to best the competition. The use of military terms was not accidental: Artzt dubbed the program "combat training," and he wanted it to deliver "a quantum leap in the quality and speed of our execution."[20]

P&G College offered programs for entry-level managers, who were required to attend three- or four-day sessions during their first year, as well as for higher-ups in need of indoctrination in P&G's new ways. In all, some four thousand employees rotated through the college each year.

Preparing for the Twenty-First Century, 1995–1998

In the spring of 1995, P&G's board of directors elected Pepper, at age fifty-six, to succeed Artzt as chairman and chief executive. Like his predecessors, Pepper rose to the top on a record of extraordinary achievement as a brand manager and general manager. His track record included an initial overseas stint in the mid-1970s as head of P&G in Italy and a tour as general manager of the Packaged Soap and Detergent Division. From there he held increasingly responsible group executive positions before being named in 1984 as head of all U.S. business. Two years later, he was elected president of the company, a position he held until he succeeded Artzt as president of P&G International.[21]

Pepper's management style reflected his warmth and interpersonal skills. He was a consensus builder who was more likely to motivate with the carrot than the stick. In 1986, he had taken a prime role in developing the company's statement of purpose, values, and principles. Many employees regarded him as the embodiment of that statement, especially noting his integrity, unflagging commitment to the company, attention to detail, and respect for people. In his extensive travels across the company, Pepper frequently delivered brief, inspirational messages about the essence of the company, in whose accomplishments he took great pride.[22]

Jager, who became the company's president and first-ever chief operating officer, joined Pepper at the top of P&G. The business press viewed the new team as something of an odd couple, a good cop/bad cop routine with obvious and distinct roles for the two leaders. Nonetheless, they saw eye to eye on the major opportunities and challenges facing the company. Both had been intimately involved in P&G's most significant decisions and initiatives since 1990, and they contemplated few changes in direction. "Much of what we've been doing," Pepper pointed out after about a year in the job, "is on a continuum."[23]

Pepper took particular interest in promoting continuing expansion overseas, especially in Russia and China, where revenues in each market were surging toward $1 billion. He also looked toward growth plans in beauty care, health care, and feminine protection and the creative efforts of the CNV organization to find new blockbuster categories and brands. In the cosmetics and fragrances part of beauty care, for example, P&G sought to reinvent the concept of cosmetics from "hope in a bottle" to something that added tangible skin care benefits. In 1996, the company introduced its Oil of Olay line of cosmetics in the United States and Europe, building on the popularity of the global skin care treatment and its recent extension into a successful body wash.

Internally, Pepper authorized many changes in the way P&G approached and managed all its activities. These ranged from small symbols, such as a new dress code of informal, business-appropriate attire to emphasize a more relaxed atmosphere at work, to major efforts in support of increasing diversity in management ranks. He proved a tireless champion of diversity, insisting on the promotion of women, minorities, and foreign-born employees, monitoring their progress and providing support. He promoted across the company the use of a simple technique, a one-page statement of objectives, goals, strategies, and measurements (OGSM), updated annually, as the basis of planning and evaluation at all levels of management. Finally, he encouraged the CNV initiative to change the way P&G developed major new products and brands. By the late 1990s, CNV's efforts were beginning to bear fruit with the test marketing of Swiffer, the electrostatic mop; Dryel, the home dry-cleaning kit; and ThermaCare, the pain-relieving, disposable heat pad.[24]

Jager, meanwhile, concentrated on three priorities: picking up the pace of innovation, finding new sources of growth, and pushing to reduce total delivered cost. In the last area, he encouraged the ongoing process of slashing costs from the supply chain and a major initiative in manufacturing to marry new techniques of reliability engineering and Total Productive Maintenance with the company's high-performance work systems. Jager also supported the continuing quest to simplify internal processes and eliminate errors through standardized formulas and packages, fewer trade promotions, and the end of consumer coupons. Marginal brands and flankers were subjected to close scrutiny. During 1995 and 1996, P&G sold or discontinued eleven brands, including Lestoil, Bain de Soleil, Prell, Ivory shampoo, and Lava soap. Jager turned a sharp eye to the company's marketing budgets, slowing the rate of spending increases and reexamining traditional practices. The company saved millions of dollars by consolidating most of its media buying in the United States at a single agency.[25]

While P&G relentlessly attacked costs and pushed continuous improvement of existing operations and practices, it also completed a major strategic acquisition to bolster its already commanding position in feminine protection products. By the mid-1990s, one of every four feminine protection pads and panty liners sold worldwide was made by P&G, and revenues surpassed $1.6 billion. In 1997, the company added to this foundation by acquiring Tambrands for considerations worth approximately $2 billion. Tambrands had pioneered the tampon in the 1930s, and its Tampax brand had been the market leader in the United States ever since.[26] In 1996, Tambrands reported operating income of $92 million on sales of $662 million. The company posted some sales overseas but lacked the scale and resources to develop its business abroad—hence P&G's interest. Recalling the unfortunate

Rely experience, the Tambrands acquisition gave some senior executives and board members pause. On the other hand, more than fifteen years of research had failed to establish a strong correlation between tampon usage and toxic shock syndrome. Meanwhile, Tambrands continued to thrive. Combined with Always/Whisper and Alldays panty liners, Tampax made P&G by far the world's leading producer of feminine protection products.[27]

Organization 2005

When he assumed P&G's helm in 1995, Pepper sought to maintain the company's historic growth rate, fixing a goal to double sales to $70 billion by 2005. Although new product initiatives and acquisitions would help, Pepper and Jager recognized that the company would have to make dramatic internal changes to match the accelerating pace of change in the outside world. The company was confronting new circumstances on an almost daily basis: a new geopolitical environment, the continuing rise and globalization of powerhouse trade customers, the arrival of large-scale computer networks, the emergence of global brands, the increasing globalization of competition.[28]

In such a world, Pepper and Jager believed that P&G's organization structure and many of its operating policies were increasingly inadequate. The organization structure, for example, now featured some anomalies. The category management approach, pioneered in Western Europe in the 1980s, had evolved into matrix structure as operations sprouted and spread around the planet. In 1989, P&G appointed its first global category executive, in health and beauty care, to coordinate strategy and operations, although profit and loss (P&L) responsibilities remained with regional and country managers. During the next six years, P&G followed up by appointing global category executives for all the company's core categories and gradually increasing their authority and responsibility, albeit without giving them responsibility for the bottom line. Marketing and brand managers in the field thus had two bosses: the category manager in Cincinnati and the president of their local country organization. In 1995, P&G coordinated its business around the world through four executive vice presidents, each responsible for a major region (North America; Europe, Middle East, and Africa; Asia; and Latin America).[29]

The trend toward global categories coincided with other significant organizational changes, including the formation of CBD. Although this innovation took root first in North America, it was spreading around the world as big customers like Wal-Mart and Carrefour set up foreign operations. By the mid-1990s, Pepper and Jager were concerned that "the evolution in structure" since the late 1980s had made P&G's "operation far too complex to meet the needs of the business."[30] With two clear goals in mind—"to better serve our consumers and customers" and "to grow our business faster," Pepper and Jager commissioned a major organization review.

Launched late in 1997, the review considered structures based on three alternative organizing principles. The "sector-is-king" approach would base the organization around three to five worldwide product sectors, each with P&L responsibility. A second alternative, called "small is beautiful" (later, "consumer is boss") would extend the existing category management organization around the world, with twenty or more global category units as the basic organizational unit with P&L responsibility. The third alternative, "large-region-large-sector," was a matrix structure in which P&L responsibilities would be divided around the world, sometimes on a global sector basis and sometimes on a geographical basis. Study teams led by high-level executives fleshed out these alternatives and their implications and reported back in April 1998.[31]

Pepper and Jager saw advantages and drawbacks to each approach. During the summer, another executive team worked on combining elements from all three into a new recommended structure. The result was a matrix in which along one axis P&G grouped its businesses into seven global business units (GBUs), and along the other axis into eight geographically based market development organizations (MDOs). The theory was that P&G would get the benefit of both axes of the matrix: The GBUs would develop and manage strong global brands, while the MDOs would plan and execute on winning in the marketplace. The structure thus would balance global advantages of scale with the particular demands of local circumstances.

In September, Pepper and Jager enthusiastically announced that P&G would follow the recommended reorganization under the aforementioned rubric, O-2005—P&G's management structure for the twenty-first century. Under O-2005, the GBUs became fully responsible for overall business strategy and planning, brand development, and brand management. Each GBU possessed "all of the capability required to do this work, including Research & Development, Product Supply, Marketing, Customer Business Development, Information Technology, Finance & Accounting, and Human Resources." Befitting its global orientation, P&G based two of the GBUs outside Cincinnati: the Fabric and Home Care GBU in Brussels, Belgium, and the Feminine Protection GBU in Kobe, Japan. The MDOs, meanwhile, had four principal capabilities: market strategy and planning, customer development, external relations, and organization development, including local recruiting. Procter & Gamble split P&L responsibility between the GBUs and the MDOs, depending on geographical location. In developed regions such as North America, Western Europe, Latin America, and northeast Asia

Organization 2005 Structure

SEPTEMBER 1998

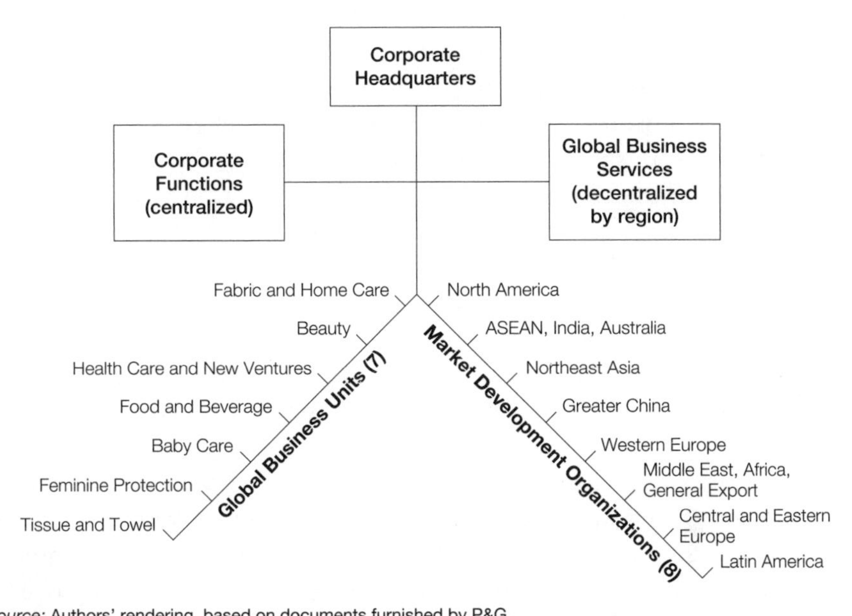

Source: Authors' rendering, based on documents furnished by P&G.

(Japan and Korea), the responsibility belonged to the GBU presidents, but elsewhere, it belonged to the MDO presidents.[32]

Procter & Gamble defined two additional organizations in O-2005. Global Business Services combined a number of corporate services, including accounting, employee benefits and payroll, order management, and information technology services, into a new worldwide organization that operated out of regional centers. Finally, Corporate Functions consisted of central responsibilities lodged at the corporate headquarters in Cincinnati: CBD, finance, human resources, IT, legal, marketing and market research, product supply, public affairs, and R&D.

The organization designers were careful to avoid overly detailing the new structure. Procter & Gamble wanted the various entities to find the most effective way to collaborate with others. As the company put it in press materials accompanying the announcement: "That may mean it makes sense for a Global Business Unit and Market Development Organization in a particular country to agree that some important business unit work will be done by Market Development teams—or vice versa. Corporate Function experts may be brought in to help with a product launch. Someone from

Global Business Services may be tapped to help a Function push toward a new capability or innovation. The principle is 'flow to the work.' We cannot overstate how important this is."

The organization designers also planned a deliberate transition to the new structure. Some changes, including a shift in managing and reporting, would become effective in July 1999, whereas others would take longer. Jager estimated that it would take about eighteen months before the first phase of the global matrix structure became operational and three to four years beyond that for the Global Business Services transition to be completed. In all, the designers envisioned that the entire transition would unfold over about six years. Inevitably, the changes involved some downsizing. The company expected to close ten plants and eliminate about fifteen thousand jobs, two-thirds of which would fall outside North America. Most job losses would result from consolidations and other administrative efficiencies under the new structure. To pay for it all, P&G set aside a restructuring charge of $2 billion.

The design also included a deliberate effort to change P&G's culture, which the architects deemed too slow, cautious, and risk-averse for a highly competitive environment. Rather, they sought "a culture that drives stretch, innovation and speed. A culture that rewards going for breakthrough goals, that supports stretching, taking risks—even if there is a chance of falling short . . . a culture that stimulates robust innovation—big ideas that change the game—and encourages visionary leadership. A culture that encourages collaboration and emphasizes learning and sharing new knowledge. A culture that values speed and fosters fast, streamlined decision-making." To stimulate the drift toward the new culture, P&G revamped its leadership assessment criteria, training programs, and policies for executive compensation and recognition.[33]

A change in management oversight accompanied the change in structure. The Executive Committee, which had consisted of the top thirty officers, was abolished and replaced by a smaller Global Leadership Council of about twelve, including the chief executive, chief operating officer, GBU heads, and corporate officers responsible for CBD, finance, R&D, and human resources. The council took as its mission to "provide overall corporate strategic direction and ensure the fulfillment of the Company's Purpose, Values and Principles."[34] The Operations Committee—the annual gathering of the top several hundred managers—was also disbanded, replaced by an annual meeting of the top forty to sixty senior managers.

The final component of the new organization was a change in leadership. In September 1998, Pepper announced his phased retirement, and the board of directors elected Jager to succeed him as chief executive in January 1999 and as chairman the following September. Pepper recommended these changes to the board of directors because of his "belief that this major organizational change should be led from the beginning by the team who will be leading it in the years ahead."[35]

Aftermath

During 1998 and 1999, P&G began the complex transition to the O-2005 organization under Jager's direction. A very bright, tough-minded, and hard-driving manager, he had attracted Artzt's attention in the 1970s as general manager of P&G in Austria during the extremely successful rollout of Pampers. In the early 1980s, Artzt recruited Jager to Japan as part of a new management team to rescue the company's flagging operations there. When a stroke felled the general manager of P&G in Japan, Jager took his place and presided over a dramatic turnaround. His next assignment was as group vice president for P&G's Far East and Asia Pacific Divisions, a position in which he served briefly and also joined the corporate board of directors. Although he had worked a short time in Cincinnati in the 1970s, his first sustained exposure to headquarters came in the early 1990s, when he ran P&G's business in North America. He strongly supported the transformation of the sales organization into CBD and led the transition to value pricing. As president and chief operating officer (and heir apparent) after 1995, he was intimately involved in the planning of O-2005.

Jager's priorities as chief executive were to accelerate growth, build new business, and bring out new brands through "stretch, innovation, and speed." As he stepped into his new job, a lot was already happening at P&G: the integration of the Tambrands acquisition; the press for faster growth; new categories, brands, and products beginning to spill out of the development pipeline; and a massive worldwide reorganization. Things were happening faster outside the company, too. To some observers, the explosive growth of the Internet and the rise of the so-called new economy of dot-coms heralded a brave new world.

Procter & Gamble viewed the Internet as a potentially significant channel for distributing its brands. Virtual grocery and drugstores were sprouting up in many cities and regions, especially in North America. The company ran collaborative experiments with some of these ventures, establishing systems, practices, and procedures to test the new channel. At the same time, P&G recognized the potential of the Internet to help build brands and form communities of interest around them. The new medium proved ideal for market research, enabling rapid surveys of large test samples. Brand managers experimented with Web page design and content, featuring information specific to products and their usage, reinforcing brand messages, and providing more general product-related information in attractive, easy-to-use formats. Pampers.com, for example, offered a wealth of advice on infant care to parents, with discussion areas and links to related resources. At A. G. Lafley's behest, P&G also invested directly in reflect.com. This Silicon Valley–based start-up provided personalized, interactive beauty care advice to women and enabled them to order customized packages of beauty care products.[36]

Jager recognized that P&G could not reach its growth targets simply by developing additional new categories and brands and by investing in new ventures such as reflect.com, important as such initiatives were. Procter & Gamble also needed acquisitions, and in August 1999, the company announced two new deals. First, it paid $265 million in cash to acquire Recovery Engineering, Inc., the maker of PUR household drinking water systems and filters. With the filtered-water market growing fast in the United States, Jager believed that, with P&G's help, the market could grow fast elsewhere, especially in countries with inadequate supplies of clean water.[37]

The second deal was much bigger. Procter & Gamble agreed to acquire The Iams Company, a global leader in premium pet nutrition, for considerations worth approximately $2.3 billion—a new record in P&G history. Based near Dayton, Ohio, Iams was challenging for leadership in the premium segment of the $25 billion pet food market, with annual sales of $800 million and twenty-one hundred employees worldwide. The CNV organization had targeted pet nutrition as an area of potential interest, and once P&G's gaze settled on the industry, Iams represented the most attractive point of entry. It possessed outstanding R&D capabilities and strong brands in Iams and Eukanuba. Privately held and growing fast, Iams recognized that joining with P&G would help them gain access to investment capital, new distribution channels, and marketing expertise to accelerate its global expansion. Indeed, the two companies seemed almost fated for each other, sharing similar values and aspirations, as well as geographical proximity and even some history. Founder Paul F. Iams had worked for P&G before World War II *(see "Anatomy of a Successful Acquisition" box).*[38]

During 1999, a bull market reacted favorably to P&G's many initiatives and activities. Although the company had encountered a devastating reversal of fortune in Russia as a result of a huge currency devaluation in the fall of 1998 and weathered softer markets in Asia and Latin America, its shares traded at record highs (above $110) late in 1999 and its prospects seemed exceptionally bright. The following year, however, was to tell another story.

ANATOMY OF A SUCCESSFUL ACQUISITON: THE COMING TOGETHER OF IAMS AND P&G

John Pepper considers P&G's purchase of The Iams Company as "the most successful acquisition through this point in its history that I have seen in my forty-year career."[39] The foundation of the deal was an excellent company in Iams. Founder Paul F. Iams introduced his first branded product, "Iams 999"—a 99.9 percent pure, "perfectly balanced" pet food in 1950. Nineteen years later he added a second premium brand, Eukanuba, named for an expression apparently used by jazz musician Hoagy Carmichael to mean something supreme or "the ultimate." Iams sold these brands to breeders, at cat and dog shows, and through veterinarians, relying heavily on word-of-mouth referrals.

In 1982, Clay Mathile, a top executive, acquired The Iams Company. Under his leadership the company pioneered numerous advances in pet nutrition that promoted healthy digestion and shiny coats. It also developed customized foods for dogs and cats at different stages of their life cycles. Many innovations originated at the Paul F. Iams Research Center in Lewisburg, Ohio, a facility opened in 1987.

By the late 1990s domestic growth had slowed, and Iams sought to expand distribution into grocery stores and mass merchandise channels and to penetrate markets overseas. Recognizing that the company needed outside help, Mathile put Iams up for sale and quickly found a buyer in P&G. Under P&G's umbrella, Iams accelerated its growth by adding capabilities in branding and distribution and expanding into areas such as dental health. The Iams brand has surged from the number-five pet-food brand in North America to number one while the Iams company climbed from number six to number two among North American manufacturers.

Jeff Ansell, a 23-year P&G veteran who became Iams' president in 1999, believes the acquisition story provides many lessons for P&G. He attributes the merger's success so far to several key actions and decisions. First, he worked closely with Mathile to introduce P&G to the Iams employees, visiting thirty locations together in thirty days. The world tour, said Ansell, provided "a chance for Clay to say farewell and explain why he sold the company, and a chance for me to introduce myself and P&G, and quickly put a face on what otherwise could have seemed a faceless company. Employees saw us unified, consistent in our messages, and clearly amicable. Employees soon learned P&G is an honest and fair company that treats people fairly and with respect, just as Iams always did."[40] ➢

Three generations: Paul Iams (right) *founded the company and developed its brands; Clay Mathile* (left) *presided over two decades of rapid growth; Jeff Ansell* (center) *helped make the company a model acquisition for P&G.*

Second, P&G and Iams carried the spirit of cooperation forward into the top management team, which balances P&G and Iams veterans. A set of "smart integration" principles determined the basis for choosing where and where not to integrate. "The team focused," says Ansell, on "integrating what's right to drive the Iams/Eukanuba business and develop the organization. We didn't integrate for integration's sake . . . but ultimately we did realize significant cost savings to help fuel innovation, brand building, and profit growth."

Third, the team set growth as the top priority, ahead of cost savings from administrative efficiencies. Six months after acquisition, the Iams brand was expanded into traditional P&G channels simultaneously in the United States and Canada in P&G's largest-ever single-day product expansion. The Iams brand embarked on an unbroken string of more than forty-eight consecutive months of share gains and surging to market leadership in North America. Globally, Iams/Eukanuba roughly doubled its volume in the first four years after the acquisition.

Fourth, Iams pursued superior innovation and superior branding relentlessly. Innovations included dental care formulas; an across-the-line upgrade with vitamin-rich fish oils for healthier skin and coat; new weight-control and large-breed diets; and other initiatives.

Finally, the new management routinely celebrates Iams employees and accomplishments so they feel valued and appreciated by P&G. "This is incredibly important to creating an inspired group of new P&G employees," Ansell points out. "It makes a group of newly acquired employees feel appreciated and valued when their business is highlighted as a success."

Crisis

The first indications of trouble occurred in January 2000, when rumors leaked that P&G was in serious talks with Warner-Lambert and American Home Products about a potential blockbuster merger. Had it been consummated, the deal would have transformed P&G into a major factor in the OTC health care industry. Investors greeted the rumors harshly, however, and the value of P&G's stock plunged about 15 percent. Although P&G quickly broke off the talks, its stock price did not rebound, hovering in the high $80 range.[41]

About six weeks later came another disturbing sign. The company revised its earnings forecast for the second half of the fiscal year from an increase of 7 to 9 percent over the prior year performance to a drop of 10 to 11 percent. Procter & Gamble attributed the disappointing news to several factors: First, higher-than-anticipated pulp costs dragged down results in the Tissue and Towel GBU. Second, delayed regulatory approval of Actonel in the United States caused the company to miss collecting a significant milestone payment from P&G's joint venture partner. Third, aggressive competitive pricing in Latin America eroded margins. And finally, the company cited "higher manufacturing, inventory, and logistical costs in Europe associated with a large number of new initiatives launched in the region at a time of unprecedented organizational change."[42] Although Jager and chief financial officer, Clayt Daley, sought to allay analysts' concerns, the stock market reacted swiftly and harshly. Within days of the earnings-revision announcement, the stock price plunged to the low-to-mid-$50 range.

The sharp decline in P&G's valuation placed top management under scrutiny, as this event coincided with the collapse of the new-economy stocks and a looming recession in North America and Europe. The pressure on Jager built not only from the outside, but also—because of P&G's broad base of employee owners and retirees—from the inside. Although the company took immediate actions to clamp down on costs and curtail nonessential projects and activities, the stock showed no signs of recovering. Finally, in June, Jager resigned. He was replaced as chairman of the board by a returning Pepper and as president and chief executive by fifty-three-year-old A. G. Lafley, previously head of the North American business and the Beauty Care GBU.

By then it was clear that some of P&G's troubles reflected several interrelated problems resulting from the O-2005 changes. First, the final design had included features that weren't working. The division of P&L responsibilities among the GBUs and MDOs created serious morale issues in Europe and North America. Before O-2005, the country managers in Europe had been sovereigns in their domains. As MDO heads without control over profits, however, some now felt disempowered and consigned to lesser jobs. Similarly, many executives in the North American MDO felt that they had become second-class citizens to their counterparts in the GBUs. Morale and status issues thus inhibited the collaboration that was supposed to occur between managers on the respective axes of the matrix structure.

Second, the company's management systems could not be reengineered quickly enough to support the new structure. Executives in the GBUs encountered frustrating difficulties and delays in getting basic information about operations. Kerry Clark, president of the Global Feminine Care GBU and the Northeast Asia MDO, pointed out that all the company's reporting systems for years had been geared to generating data by country: "Then, all of a sudden, we wanted global business data. . . . It just wasn't there. It was all being cobbled together. . . . Just trying to figure out what was going on in our worldwide business was a nightmare!" Getting answers to basic questions—shipments of a particular stock-keeping unit (SKU)—could entail a dozen phone calls, faxes, or e-mails and other costly time delays.[43]

A third significant problem was the high overhead costs for several smaller GBUs, which lacked the scale to support their management structures. The Feminine Care, Baby Care, and Tissue and Towel GBUs were particularly disadvantaged.

A series of lesser issues and transition costs compounded these major problems. Based in Kobe, Japan, Clark felt disconnected from other GBU heads, most of whom remained in Cincinnati. "It was a mistake to put the GBU in Asia," he recalled. "We were too far away from the resources we needed." Meanwhile, another controversial action in Europe was the decision to set up a new regional headquarters organization for GBUs and the Western Europe MDO in Geneva, Switzerland. This decision resulted in the concentration of about twenty-five hundred employees, including more than a thousand who moved from other European locations. The influx of personnel created nightmarish difficulties in finding affordable housing and suitable schools. Meanwhile, many executives found themselves reporting to new bosses, sometimes in distant time zones that impeded direct communications.[44]

Looking back on the experience, P&G's leaders attributed some problems to inevitable growing pains accompanying any major reorganization. They also believed they had set their goals too high and tried to accomplish too much, too fast. Ill effects then multiplied. The company lost control of cash flow and costs and suffered delays and frustrations in untangling ambiguous and overlapping responsibilities. To reach ambitious revenue targets, managers attempted to sustain high prices in the face of fierce competition and pushed new brands into the market before they were ready. Management lost focus on the company's biggest brands and markets. It also violated P&G custom by mounting an enormous change without first conducting tests and pilot-scale experiments to limit risk and to apply new learning as they moved ahead. Lafley compared P&G's experience of simultaneously trying to conduct business normally while undergoing a massive reorganization to living in a house while it was being rehabbed: "We took down the kitchen and bathrooms at the same time, when you're living there."[45]

Back on Track

The new chief executive, like his predecessors, was a career employee of P&G. Lafley had joined the company in 1977 after a five-year tour of duty in the U.S. Navy and fresh from the M.B.A. program at Harvard Business School. He started as a brand assistant on Joy and climbed rapidly through brand and advertising assignments in the Packaged Soaps and Detergents Division, including advertising manager during the highly successful launch of Liquid Tide. In 1988, he earned his first general management assignment as head of Laundry Products under the category management structure, and he rose to become president of Laundry and Cleaning Products in Procter & Gamble USA four years later. In 1994, he took his first international assignment—an essential prerequisite for top management—as president of P&G Far East, a nearly five-year stint. Upon his return, he served as president of P&G North America, a job he combined with his position as president of the Global Beauty Care GBU under O-2005. Given his impressive track record and increasing responsibilities, many observers predicted that one day Lafley would succeed Jager. The prediction came true all too abruptly.

Thrust into the top job during a crisis, Lafley calmly set about the task of restoring investor and employee confidence in P&G. Working closely with Chairman Pepper and CFO Daley, Lafley assured the financial community that the company would indeed meet its revised earnings forecast and had taken actions to prevent similar missteps in the future. For the longer term, the company proclaimed its intention to maintain total return to shareholders that placed it in the top third of a group of peer companies while posting annual growth rates of between 4 and 6 percent.[46] To help boost morale in Europe, Lafley (after just ten days in office) and Pepper traveled there to listen to complaints and address concerns. They also signaled their intention to address the shortcomings of the O-2005 structure while likewise moderating the pace of internal change. In many of these meetings and countless more during his first months, Lafley used a common framework to structure his remarks, drawing on his core beliefs about the fundamentals of the business, including some that P&G did well and others that would require change and improvement (see "Ten Things I Believe").

Having reached out to P&G's key constituencies, Lafley moved on to focus the company's strategy and fix new priorities. The company abandoned the slogan "stretch, innovation, and speed," but not the underlying imperative to strive for significantly better performance. Lafley set three new priorities. First, the company "had to come to grips with reality" and acknowledge the specific ways P&G was underperforming, with costs that were too high, lackluster results in some major categories and brands, and frayed relationships with important trade customers. The widespread adoption of total shareholder return as the principal performance measure, replacing traditional emphases on volume and profit, helped underscore the new reality. An integrative and holistic measure, total share return, Lafley believed, "would drive clear choices throughout the organization: it helps define business goals, it's a screener for strategic choices, it helps discriminate among plan options, [and] it's a criterion for compensation."[47]

Second, P&G set about making clear choices. These entailed resetting goals that were more realistic while focusing more intensely on the company's biggest brands and biggest customers and on succeeding in its biggest markets. It made little sense to push Febreze and Dryel if Tide and Ariel suffered relative neglect. Likewise, why promote Physique, a new family of beauty care products including shampoo, when Pantene had reached a plateau? Crest, recently eclipsed by Colgate as the leading dentifrice in the United States, required particular attention. Lafley urged P&G to focus on building and sustaining its core brands as global leaders. Similarly, he believed that P&G should take special care to strengthen its partnerships with its top ten customers worldwide while also focusing on its top ten geographical markets, where it possessed deep understanding.[48]

Other choices involved modifying the O-2005 organization structure. Procter & Gamble simplified matters and lowered costs by reducing the number of GBUs. Three units—Baby Care, Feminine Care, and Tissue and Towel—were merged into a new Baby Care and Family Care GBU, with headquarters in Cincinnati. At the same time, Lafley appointed Clark president of the MDOs, giving the MDO heads a top-level champion in Cincinnati with easy access to the chief executive.

These organization changes reflected Lafley's conviction that "the consumer is boss" and positioned P&G to win over the long term in what he called "the two moments of truth with consumers." The first occurred thirty million times a day in more than 160 countries, when consumers stood in front of a shelf or counter and chose to buy a P&G or competing product,

Ten Things I Believe

A. G. Lafley
June 2000

1. Lead Change
   - Change is inevitable and coming faster. It's far better to lead it than to ignore or resist it
   - Leading change requires that we know the major currents of change impacting consumers, customers, and the business, and we get in front of them
2. The Consumer Is Boss
   - We must understand consumer needs, wants, and dreams and desired consumer experiences to create loyal customers and passionate ambassadors
   - This understanding focuses technology, product, and brand choices so we're more effective and faster to market
   - We must understand *total* consumer experiences—shopping, usage, bonding—to enable us to build a relationship, be where he/she lives, and become a trusted partner in his/her life
3. Innovation Is Our Lifeblood
   - Leading innovation is the only way to become/stay market leader
   - Watch out: P&G has a tendency to become molecule myopic/product myopic
4. Power of Strategy
   - We must make clear choices about where to play and how to win
   - We must exploit core capabilities and P&G strengths
5. Power of Execution
   - This is what consumers, customers, and competitors see
   - Win in the two moments of truth: purchase decision and usage experience
6. Power of Brands
   - Global . . . "Glocal" . . .
   - Category leaders: #1, #2, unique niche . . . or divest/nurture for cash/profit
7. Power of Knowledge and Learning
   - Manifested when turned into superior strategies/business plans
8. Power of P&G People
   - Without us—P&G people—there are no strategies, no brands, no execution
   - At the center/the core of everything we are and everything we do, and everything we want to become
9. Direct, Simple, and Transparent
   - What you see is what you get
10. Take P&G's statement of Purpose, Values, Principles seriously
    - Values that are particularly important now: Leadership; Ownership, Integrity; Trust, Passion for Winning
    - P&G Principles—a few opportunities for improvement: Respect for Individuals; Valuing Differences; Strategically Focused; Externally Focused; Mutual Interdependence as a Way of Life

deciding on the basis of brand promise and store price. These myriad moments were the responsibilities of the MDOs. The second moment of truth occurred nearly two billion times each day, when a consumer put a P&G product to the test, checking whether it lived up to its promises. These innumerable moments were the responsibility of the GBUs. The moments of truth thus provided a compelling rationale for P&G's global matrix structure and clarified the respective roles of the GBU and MDO organizations.[49]

The hard choices continued with decisions affecting P&G's cost structure. "The hardest choice of all," said Lafley, "[was] to right-size the organization." In the mid- to late 1990s, P&G had staffed up to become a $50 billion business. The problem was that revenues were still hovering around $40 billion and the company's new projections for growth were much less bullish. Thus job cuts were necessary. In March 2001, P&G eliminated an additional ten thousand jobs. Meanwhile, the company slashed capital spending from nearly 8 percent to less than 4 percent of sales.

Procter & Gamble also shut down underperforming businesses and exited nonstrategic ones. It discontinued the struggling Olay line of cosmetics and wrote off a huge investment in olestra, the fat replacement that had failed to catch on. Jif, Crisco, and Comet were put on the block. Procter & Gamble entered serious talks with Coca-Cola to form a joint venture that would oversee P&G's Pringles and Sunny Delight brands along with several of Coke's juice brands. Although the deal ultimately collapsed, Lafley remained convinced that joint ventures could be useful vehicles to help the company realize greater value from some of its assets.[50]

The company's willingness to enter major alliances represented a sharp departure from its tradition of going it alone. This change was especially obvious in the company's new approach to innovation. Lafley believed the company was too wedded to a narrow understanding of the sources of innovation. Procter & Gamble need not itself invent and develop every new category and brand, he argued. Rather, it could accelerate the rate of commercialization of new brands and products by forming partnerships with others. He wanted this connect-and-develop approach to account for more than half of all the company's innovations—up from about 10 percent in 2000. The company formed partnerships to develop Crest SpinBrush, a new diabetes drug, and (with Clorox) Glad food bags and wraps. The new approach meant that P&G could also generate more innovations faster and with less expense. Accordingly, the company cut back the corporate innovation fund, terminating two-thirds of projects under way.

Lafley's third priority, and the enabler of the others, was the building of a new global leadership team. "In June 2000," he observed, "we weren't a team. We were all firefighting and trying to fix problems in our individual businesses." To address this problem, Lafley reconstituted the top executive ranks and introduced more collaborative ways of working. During his first two years, over half of the company's top thirty officers turned over, with replacements younger, more diverse, and more broadly experienced, especially in assignments outside the United States. Lafley jumped over dozens of general managers, for example, in promoting forty-two-year-old Deb Henretta to head the North American baby-care unit. He also instituted a program on inspirational leadership, which he helped teach to handpicked students in weeklong sessions.[51]

The top team met in person or electronically every Monday morning to touch base and work on common issues. Lafley also initiated regular quarterly meetings of the twenty-some presidents of the businesses. To further improve communications, P&G redesigned its headquarters in Cincinnati and Geneva to feature open offices and ample spaces for spontaneous meetings. This more informal and collaborative way of working even spilled over to meetings of the board of directors, where traditionally "speakers generally stood at a podium and read prepared presentations which were backed with elaborate, multi-media visual aids." In 2000, the board moved out of its formal boardroom into a conference room featuring a circular table, around which everyone, including presenters, spoke on an equal footing. According to one director, the change produced "an increasingly informal environment in which questions (and challenges) could be more readily raised—and give and take in conversation could enhance the transfer of information."[52]

During the early 2000s, P&G's revenues picked up despite a worldwide economic slowdown. Iams proved to be an especially valuable acquisition that meshed tightly with P&G's values and ways of operating while contributing strong growth and earnings. New initiatives in the major brands also paid off. A new formulation of Tide, Tide Clean Breeze, showed promise of becoming a big hit. Two extensions—Crest SpinBrush and Crest Whitestrips—helped build Crest into a billion-dollar brand. Late in 2001, P&G closed on another huge acquisition, the Clairol hair care business, purchased from Bristol-Myers Squibb for considerations valued at $4.95 billion. The transaction brought with it the Clairol brand of hair-coloring products, Herbal Essences shampoos and conditioners, and other brands. With annual sales of $1.6 billion, Clairol became a major component of P&G's burgeoning portfolio of beauty care brands. In 2003, P&G further bolstered the business by acquiring Wella AG, a leading German hair products company, for $7 billion, including assumption of net debt. In 2002, Wella reported revenues of 3.4 billion euros.[53]

Meanwhile P&G continued to watch its cost structure closely, balancing competitive imperatives with concern for the welfare of its employees. The company's focus on essential activities and its willingness to form partnerships elsewhere prompted two significant outsourcing deals during early 2003. In April, P&G concluded a deal with Trillium, a Canadian contractor, to undertake all the manufacturing of bar soap at Ivorydale. The following month, P&G signed a contract with Hewlett-Packard to take over P&G's IT operations. In negotiating these and other agreements—and others to come—P&G took care to protect the jobs and benefits of those affected.[54]

Procter & Gamble surged toward global leadership in hair care through the acquisitions of Clairol (including the popular Herbal Essences brand, pictured here) in 2002 and Wella in 2003.

In 2002, when he succeeded Pepper as chairman of the board, Lafley pointed to encouraging signs that P&G was back on track, "returning to the consistent, reliable earnings and cash growth that shareholders expect." Revenue growth had hit the target of 4 to 6 percent per year, a year ahead of schedule, and net earnings growth in all the company's segments ran into double digits. The company was faring well in all its major brand and market initiatives, and it was looking forward to new opportunities and challenges in the business of building brands in the twenty-first century.

The Period in Perspective, Since 1990

During the 1980s, P&G had pushed rapidly around the world, setting up shop in a score of countries and at the end of the decade rushed to fill the white spaces vacated by the collapse of Communist regimes. In the 1990s, with production facilities and offices all over the world and a growing portfolio of global brands, the company faced the challenge of organizing and operating as a global company—to reap the advantages of global scale without losing the benefits of responsiveness to local conditions. Procter & Gamble's adoption of the O-2005 global matrix structure was thus a pivotal move designed to balance global and local advantages and considerations. With modifications and adjustments, by 2002 the new structure and way of managing showed indications of achieving its designers' objectives.

The 1990s and early 2000s posed other formidable challenges to P&G: to find new and faster sources of growth, to generate new brands and categories, to build better relationships with its biggest customers, to win (and not simply participate) in the white spaces, to exploit new media to build brands, and to balance sales and earnings growth. These challenges came thick and fast after 1990, requiring quick thinking and timely action in response. Procter & Gamble made significant headway against each of these challenges, although not without difficulty and pain. The company fostered young businesses in health care and beauty care into significant components of the corporate portfolio. It introduced new brands in Swiffer, Febreze, ThermaCare, and Actonel. Taking advantage of new IT and ways of managing, P&G streamlined its supply chain, reduced its operating costs, and extended and deepened partnerships with its trade customers. In Central and Eastern Europe, Russia, and China, P&G vaulted to leadership in many of its core categories while coping with the political and economic uncertainties of operating in freshly (and, in China's case, incompletely) free markets. A flowering of Internet initiatives and ventures provided insight into the power of the technology to reach consumers and build brands. And, at the end of this period, the company restored the balance between sales and earnings growth by following its strategy to focus on the biggest brands, biggest customers, and biggest markets.

Making progress simultaneously on all these fronts required P&G to tap deep reservoirs of experience and capability. Advances, retreats, and new advances punctuated the years after 1990. In the end, progress resulted, as it had throughout most of the company's long corporate life, from focus on the fundamentals of brand building: differentiated products, distinctive advertising, disciplined management, constant focus on costs and value, and deep understanding of consumers and customers.

CHAPTER FIFTEEN

Rewriting the Rules

RECONFIGURING THE SUPPLY CHAIN

PERIODICALLY P&G has rewritten the rules of competition in its industry. Examples include:

- The successful campaign to brand Ivory, which differentiated an age-old commodity, a bar of soap
- The decision to sell direct in 1920, which enabled the company to synchronize supply and demand better and to stabilize employment
- The establishment of market research, which afforded unparalleled insights into consumer behavior and the use of P&G products
- The production of radio and TV soap operas, which helped the company establish a commanding position in electronic media advertising to homemakers
- A sequence of impressive technological breakthroughs in detergents, disposable diapers, feminine care products, shampoos, and other products

The list goes on. And in the 1980s and 1990s, P&G rewrote the rules again, this time using new management approaches and IT to streamline its operations and forge stronger links to its trade customers in a thoroughgoing restructuring of the supply chain in consumer products. The result was a company stronger, leaner, and more competitive than ever. But along the way, P&G underwent significant internal changes involving a major reorganization and the adoption of many new management practices.

A Decade of Challenge

In the 1980s, P&G began to face up to a problem that had been brewing for years. Grocery wholesalers and retailers in North America accounted for most of the company's sales, yet P&G's relationship with the trade was rocky. According to longtime sales executive Lou Pritchett, "most suppliers, including P&G, looked upon the [trade] customer as a necessary evil—a link in the distribution chain, a middleman whose only job was that of a conduit between the manufacturer and the end user." This attitude promoted "an adversarial win/lose relationship," a problem that P&G's sales practices and behaviors tended to magnify. "When you came out of a store," Pritchett said, "[the questions asked were] Did you win? Did you impose your will upon that store? . . . Did you get a price corrected? Did you get a display? Did you get volume?" Procter & Gamble's incentives, meanwhile, drove the month-end surge, in which inventories transferred from company warehouses to trade customers "to make the numbers look good," that is, to meet that month's estimated shipments.[1]

These problems with the wholesale and retail trade had worsened in the years after the first energy crisis of the 1970s. To keep goods moving in an era of soaring inflation, P&G and other manufacturers increased spending on promotions while also undertaking a wider assortment of such deals. The idea was to maintain a relatively high list price but offer frequent and various ways to bring in-store pricing down through short-term merchandising and featuring by customers. These tactics came with hidden costs, however. Frequent price cuts were eroding the everyday value of P&G's brands, while the amount of money available for promotions grew large in relation to sales (from 7 to 20 percent during the 1970s and 1980s) and the myriad of requirements for customers to earn this money became a bureaucratic nightmare. Trade deductions—the practice whereby customers deducted from their invoice payments the allowance they believed they had qualified for under a promotion, regardless of the formal merchandising agreement—ballooned from $20 million to $180 million per year. The resolution of disputes about these deductions became a costly and lengthy headache.[2]

A final serious problem was sheer duplication of effort. Procter & Gamble's sales force was organized by product divisions, and within each division in North America, in geographical regions. There were no national accounts to serve the fast-growing mass merchandisers and discount drug chains. Buyers in regional grocery chains might entertain a dozen P&G sales reps a month, with sometimes comical, sometimes embarrassing, sometimes nightmarish results. As Lawrence D. "Mike" Milligan, another veteran sales

In the 1980s bar code scanners and other new information technologies created opportunities for manufacturers and retailers to restructure their traditional relationship.

executive, put it, the P&G people "were all trying to cope with the same problems, predictably in different ways. No [P&G unit] had the same order entry, invoice, discount terms, promotion values or performance requirements." With only a modest effort to economize on distribution present within the company, products were often shipped on different trucks. Reward and recognition systems differed markedly. Customers played P&G against itself; "rancor and backbiting" within P&G and between P&G and its trade customers were "common fare."[3]

Rethinking Internal Systems and External Relationships

Procter & Gamble began to address these problems through a series of initiatives in the early 1980s. Chief executive John Smale made the reduction of operating costs a top priority and recognized that the effort would entail systemic change across the company, including how it distributed and marketed its products. Smale and Tom Laco, executive vice president, also encouraged the use of cross-functional teams to tackle business challenges ranging from reviving struggling brands such as Pringles to hastening the rate of innovation. Meanwhile, groups inside the company were independently investigating the total quality movement, seeking not only to improve product and process quality but also to make operations more efficient. David Swanson, senior vice president of engineering, became a convert to the teachings of W. Edwards Deming, a notable expert on quality management. A revered figure in Japan, where the nation's most prestigious industrial quality award is named for him, Deming was a prophet without honor in his homeland until the late 1970s, when a handful of U.S. manufacturers, including P&G, began to pay heed.

After attending Deming seminars, recalled Swanson, "a few courageous [P&G] engineers" followed up with numerous small-scale projects that nonetheless yielded "breakthroughs in product quality, plant reliability, labor productivity, and cost reduction."[4] These experiences "Deming-ized" Swanson, who in turn convinced Laco that a total quality initiative could provide "a means of substantially improving our ability to translate consumer needs and preferences into consistently superior products." Laco and Swanson arranged for their senior colleagues to visit companies like 3M and Motorola (where John Pepper served on the board) that had committed to total quality and for Deming to spend a week at P&G. These measures helped build momentum behind a total quality initiative, which the company launched under a corporate quality office headed by Marvin Womack, a vice president.[5]

Another sign of change was P&G's new willingness to listen to retailers. Long viewed (and derided) by the trade as arrogant, dictatorial, and domineering, P&G began to reassess long-standing practices and behaviors and to modify some of them. The company, for example, selectively gave the trade greater freedom to respond to local market conditions in the placement of advertising and the choice of brands to feature and promote.[6]

Meanwhile, trade customers and P&G were evaluating significant changes in their operations and organization. The availability of new information technologies, such as bar code scanners and personal computers, prompted P&G to set up small-scale experiments with a few retailers to build and share electronic databases. Following the Japanese practice of just-in-time delivery, P&G collaborated with some retailers to explore ways to reduce inventory and ensure timely replenishment of its products in retail stores. More changes flowed from more efficient practices in the trade and from the centralization of purchasing decisions among bigger and more sophisticated customers. Some reformers in P&G's sales organization began to question the continuing viability and high cost of the company's traditional practice of sending an army of sales reps to take orders from individual store managers. The reformers set up a test of an alternative model in Florida. One or two sales reps began to handle orders for a range of products across the divisions, and P&G gained a richer understanding of its customers' strategy and decision-making processes.

The Juggernaut

These initiatives and experiments were gathering momentum, when still more forces converged to persuade P&G to rethink the nature and structure of its dealings with trade customers. In the mid-1980s, P&G woke up to the new retailing phenomenon known as Wal-Mart. Founded by Sam Walton in 1962 as a discount department store in Rogers, Arkansas, Wal-Mart had become the fastest-growing retail chain in history. Walton's formula was simple: Offer quality goods at the lowest possible prices; provide large, clean, and well-lighted stores; and welcome customers with a friendly greeting and a smile. Wal-Mart also adopted a clever and careful approach to geographical expansion. Starting from its base in northwestern Arkansas, the company targeted small cities in nearby regions that other mass merchandisers had neglected. The company supported its geographical growth with an impressive logistical infrastructure and a relentless drive to reduce operating costs. At one point, Wal-Mart even leased its own communications satellite to hasten the flow of information through its network of warehouses and stores. The formula proved wildly successful. As it approached its twenty-fifth anniversary in 1987, the Wal-Mart empire totaled more than a thousand stores and boasted revenues of nearly $12 billion. It was growing at 40 percent per year. Wal-Mart was also experimenting with—and learning from—new retail formats, including supercenters, hypermarkets, and Sam's Club stores.[7]

In 1985, Lou Pritchett returned from a stint in the Philippines to become P&G's general sales manager in North America.[8] At his first meeting with his top reports, he pointed out that Wal-Mart, of which he had been only dimly aware during his last U.S. assignment, had now become P&G's third-largest domestic customer, with annual sales of several hundred million dollars. At the same time, P&G had become one of Wal-Mart's biggest suppliers. Nevertheless, the relationship between the two companies was hardly robust. None of P&G's division sales managers possessed extensive knowledge of Wal-Mart or had developed good relationships with its leaders. For his part, Walton was frustrated in his dealings with P&G. His colleagues claimed that among Wal-Mart's suppliers, "P&G was the hardest company to do business with" and that P&G had "an extremely overcomplicated and inflexible sales organization." In 1985, Walton sought to address this problem at the top. He called P&G headquarters to say that Wal-Mart wanted to honor P&G as its vendor of the year. The megastore founder had hoped that this recognition would open a new dialogue between the companies. When his call was not returned, however, Walton decided to recognize another supplier, and he shifted his attention from P&G to other matters.[9]

Learning of this story, Pritchett sought a fresh start. A mutual friend helped arrange an invitation for Pritchett to join Walton on a canoe trip. When the two men finally met in July 1987, they quickly established a tight bond; both were Southerners and Eagle Scouts, and they tended to view the world in similar ways. Although the occasion was ostensibly a getaway, Walton and Pritchett talked extensively about business and relations between the two companies. Pritchett later summarized the conversation: "Basically we discussed the opportunities available by working more closely together with the mutual objective of increasing both our companies' profits." Pritchett also relayed Walton's view "that the whole buyer/seller relationship which has served the industry so well in the past must be redesigned for the future. Electronic ordering will make the jobs obsolete, therefore, Sales people must serve a different and more strategic role." Finally, Walton added that "the days of automatically passing cost increases through to the customer are over, and only when customers/suppliers work on a partnership basis will excess costs be wrung out of the system."[10]

The outcome of the canoe trip was an agreement for P&G to work with Wal-Mart in three areas: knowledge transfer, total system efficiency, and total quality. Procter & Gamble sent a senior sales manager to Bentonville, Arkansas, for three months to observe how Wal-Mart ran its business. The companies began sharing their experiences with electronic ordering, custom-built displays, and new sources of cost reduction. Finally, Pritchett arranged for Walton and his management team to attend a two-day Deming seminar with P&G executives in Cincinnati.

The joint seminar soon took place, complete with a demonstration of Walton's legendary parsimony. When P&G arranged rooms for the Wal-Mart executives in a good, but not highest-quality hotel, the executives called to inquire if less expensive accommodations might be available. In the end, they doubled up in rooms at the Queen City Club for forty-five dollars a night.[11] The seminar itself proved extremely productive. After two days of talk and exercises illustrating how total quality management drives out systems costs between suppliers and customers and ultimately benefits consumers, Walton wrapped up the meeting by saying, "O.K., let's do it." Procter & Gamble was not used to moving at such a rapid clip, and an executive reportedly asked, "Do what?" Walton countered with "This thing we've been talking about for two days: change the way we do business together." Wal-Mart was ready to get started; the question was whether P&G was also ready, and if so, how this would be accomplished.[12]

An Experiment in Customer Relations

The top-level dialogue between P&G and Wal-Mart coincided almost exactly with P&G's reorganization in 1987 around category business units (CBUs) and the formation of the Product Supply organization, which centralized logistics and manufacturing under Swanson. In planning for the new structure, Laco, with Pritchett's support, had commissioned a team of promising middle managers drawn from a variety of divisions and functions for an intensive, six-month study of how P&G should go to market in 2000. Tom Muccio, formerly national sales manager in the Food Division, assumed a leading role on the team. It was clear to the team that Laco and his senior colleagues expected radical recommendations, including the collapse of the seven product divisions, which still existed above the thirty-nine CBUs, into a smaller number of units, as well as a restructuring of the North American sales operation. Such changes would not only continue and extend the CBU reorganization, but would also trigger a fundamental change in how P&G related to its customers.

In tackling the future marketplace assignment, the P&G team members traveled widely to examine interactions between suppliers and customers in a host of industries and settings. They met with consultants and business academics and conducted extensive interviews inside P&G. Throughout the process, they met periodically with a group of prominent category managers, including Tom Moore, Jeff Jones, Gary Martin, and A. G. Lafley, as well as with Pritchett and Bob Herbold, P&G's chief information officer. As the interviews and visits proceeded, and as data gathering moved into data analysis, the preliminary conclusions of the team seemed clear and strong:

- Customers were becoming much more sophisticated in their use of IT and in inventory management
- Purchasing decisions in customer organizations were shifting from traditional criteria such as prices and allowances to a more holistic set of criteria
- Multiple points of contact inside customer organizations required a coordinated, multifunctional approach from major suppliers
- Procter & Gamble could no longer afford to go to market with many decentralized, duplicative units and multiple policies and systems for billing and shipping orders

With these conclusions in mind, the team realized that the company risked alienating customers, losing its advantage of scale, and missing opportunities to leverage learning across its operations and customer base.[13]

The sector general managers and their respective sales forces greeted these conclusions coolly. The conclusions, however, dovetailed with the wrap-up of the P&G/Wal-Mart total quality seminar, and the study team gave Laco and Pritchett the ammunition they needed to launch a new experiment in customer relations. That experiment, in time, would grow into a fundamentally new way for P&G to approach its customers, from big, national—ultimately global—accounts like Wal-Mart to regional grocery and drugstore chains, to individual retailers. And what P&G and Wal-Mart accomplished together would rewrite the rules in the consumer products industry.

Moving to Arkansas

In June 1988, P&G and Wal-Mart launched their joint experiment in supply-chain management. A multifunctional team of managers headed by Muccio moved to Fayetteville, Arkansas, about twenty miles south of Wal-Mart's headquarters in Bentonville. The team included representatives of sales, marketing, operations, IT, product supply, and finance. The members went through a period of team building, training, and study of Wal-Mart's operations. At the same time, Wal-Mart formed a mirror team consisting of an executive coordinator and representatives of the same functions and followed its own process of training and development. And then the two teams began to meet to hammer out a common mission and objectives and outline ways to work together on particular projects.

In the beginning, recalled Muccio, the work was heavy going, because the parties had little experience in sharing and a legacy of mistrust. The two sides eventually agreed on a few general principles: that discussion would proceed in the spirit of solving problems rather than stating positions, that it would not matter who was right as long as the right thing was done, and that project expenses would be shared equally. The two parties also hammered out a mission statement to guide their interactions, with the following goal: "to achieve the long-term business objectives of both companies by building a total system partnership that leads our respective companies and industries to better serve our mutual customer—the consumer."[14] Muccio later summarized the basis for a new relationship in bullet points:

- We have the same consumer.
- This same consumer wants better value (not just better price).
- A manufacturer's job and profits are not in selling to retailers, and a retailer's job and profits are not in buying from suppliers.

- Together, our job and profits come from creating better consumer value across the total supply chain to exceed our mutual customers' expectations.[15]

Meeting as often as every few weeks through the fall and winter of 1988–1989, the mirror teams identified a series of projects and assigned action teams to address them. One major project focused on integrating the information systems of the respective companies, so that the two parties could share the data they gathered. In the era before the Internet, this entailed building a proprietary data-delivery highway between the computer systems of the respective companies—a complex information systems problem. Another project involved developing joint scorecards and measurements so that each side would have the same information on which to base decisions. Mike Graen, a P&G IT specialist, recalled that at the outset it was difficult to answer even basic questions about the business, because of misaligned objectives and incompatible systems. The two companies had different fiscal years and operating benchmarks. Wal-Mart tracked all its activities by dollar sales and dollar profits, whereas P&G followed statistical cases, an internal measurement designed to equate the value of the business from one product division to another. Wal-Mart measured P&G's profitability contribution to its own profitability by SKU and by brand. On the other hand, P&G was oblivious to customer profitability issues on its brands, believing that the value of the brands stemmed from their ability to draw consumers into retailers' stores. "The net of all this," said Muccio, "[was] that we didn't have systems, measurements, or scorecards that talked the same language on the same timeframe, and that made it extremely difficult to solve business problems."[16]

The development of the data-delivery highway consumed a year and a half. By the time it came on-line, however, the two companies had also developed tracking measures useful to both parties. The common assumption was the need to make the supply chain more efficient, hence driving down everyone's costs and enabling better value for consumers.

Other projects focused on faster replenishment of inventory based on data received from Wal-Mart's distribution centers. A process that once took nearly two weeks could now be performed in three or four days. By stationing a P&G employee in the Wal-Mart Accounts Payable Department to observe the handling of P&G invoices, P&G learned of dramatic discrepancies between purchase orders and invoices. These discrepancies were costing both companies millions of dollars each year in nonproductive time and interest charges. The problem was quickly fixed. The two companies developed a system combining P&G's insights about consumers with Wal-Mart's point-of-sale information and third-party market research data into a powerful tool for decision making about products to feature and promote.[17]

The benefits of this collaboration surfaced almost immediately. Between 1989 and 1990, P&G's sales to Wal-Mart leaped by more than $250 million, beginning an unbroken, annual string of rising sales and increasing market share for P&G and improved profitability on P&G brands for Wal-Mart. These results validated the partnership experiment and helped accelerate changes in retailing generally, as well as within P&G itself.[18]

The Widening Revolution

The collaboration between P&G and Wal-Mart proved extraordinarily robust, delivering impressive results, year after year. The P&G team in Arkansas took time to reflect on the experience and develop a general model of how to restructure relationships with other top customers.[19] A simple graphic explained the basic architectural principles. Procter & Gamble traditionally approached customers through a single point of contact, a sales representative backed up by a functional organization. This sales rep, in turn, met with a Wal-Mart counterpart who also sat atop a functional pyramid. Muccio expressed this interaction by drawing two triangles, with the apex of each corresponding to the P&G sales rep and the Wal-Mart buyer. Then he turned the triangles on their sides and pushed them together in the shape of a bow tie. The point of contact served as a filter through which information flowed. In the new relationship, however, matters were reversed, with the base of the respective triangles pushed together, forming a "reverse bow tie," or diamond shape. Suddenly, there were multiple points of contact, with functional specialists meeting directly with their counterparts, and a steady flow of benefits. *(See illustrations.)*

By the summer of 1989, teams were in place not only at Wal-Mart but also at Kmart, Target, Club/Convenience Stores, and other retailers.[20] Procter & Gamble's market shares at these customers surged almost immediately, while structural costs in the supply chain tumbled. At Kmart, for example, P&G's volume doubled while inventory was reduced by $40 million.[21]

Procter & Gamble took the unusual step of setting up these teams to report outside the traditional product division, geographical, and CBU structures. Muccio and his counterparts at other teams reported up through the worldwide functional head of sales, Milligan, who succeeded Pritchett in the job. This channel of reporting, noted Milligan, was established because Smale recognized that "the U.S. sectors and functions would stone to death these highly innovative but status-quo-threatening endeavors." The employ-

These "bow-tie" and "reverse bow-tie" charts depict the emergence of a new relationship between P&G and its customers in the 1990s.

ees who staffed the teams were handpicked for their "courage, skill, and willingness to risk." Milligan called them Pathfinders, after the Allied reconnaissance paratrooper teams who guided the troops landing in the 1944 D day invasion.[22]

The Pathfinders continued to form customer teams with invariably positive results, and by 1992, nearly a third of P&G's North American business was managed by teams. Meanwhile, other pressures on traditional ways of going to market continued to mount. Although the Florida experiment (in which only a few sales reps handled many divisions) was terminated, it had nonetheless validated a centralized approach to dealing even with smaller trade customers. The trends that had prompted the experiment—centralized purchasing and more efficient practices in the trade generally—remained vital.

Value Pricing

Just as centralized purchasing and more efficient trade practices drove down costs, so did the new approach to pricing. Procter & Gamble's deepening partnerships with leading mass merchandisers did not distract it from the need to address concerns about the soaring costs of promotions, the erosion of consumer loyalty, and conflicting signals about the value of its brands across the trade. Consumers had learned to shop for deals and no longer expected to pay premium prices for brand-name goods. These trends, said Durk Jager, newly appointed executive vice president in charge of P&G's business in North America, portended danger:

> *If you look at the market value of the company and subtract what our balance sheet says the company is worth, the difference is basically the future earning power of our brands at net present value. If you agree that brands are your source of value creation, then you have to ask, "What are we doing to create strong brands?" The stronger you make them, the more value they add to the company. You make strong brand franchises by creating strong customer loyalty. As a consumer, if I came into a grocery store and saw Tide at half the price I paid the week before, I'd be angry.*[23]

An internal P&G study in 1989–1990 revealed a connection between its concerns and those of its biggest customers. The study showed that merchandisers offering low and stable prices—everyday low pricing (EDLP)—were much more efficient than those relying on a combination of high list prices and frequent discounts—so-called Hi-Lo merchandisers. Indeed, EDLP merchandising was a powerful competitive advantage in the trade and was fueling the revolution in supply-chain management. Yet P&G's traditional go-to-market strategy, the new customer teams notwithstanding, was still based on serving Hi-Lo customers.[24]

In the winter of 1990–1991, Jager determined to act on these concerns and findings, to remove the clutter created by waves of promotions, and to make the company's offerings more transparent. Procter & Gamble sent ripples through the trade in North America by announcing that it would begin converting its trade terms to value pricing—a single list price, or EDLP—starting with dish-washing liquid and other soap and laundry brands in the Packaged Soap Division headed by Lafley. This pricing policy meant not only a substantial reduction in list price—from 12 to 14 percent—but also a reduction and redesign of its merchandising programs. Promotional funds were cut by more than half and were credited to future purchases, as opposed to being deducted from payment by retailers.[25]

During the next two years, P&G shifted virtually all its offerings to value pricing. A gutsy move, it stirred strong reactions. Some wholesalers discontinued or deemphasized P&G brands. SuperValu added a special surcharge to P&G products, and Certified Growers Midwest, a big distributor, removed forty P&G SKUs from its product list. Many retailers also objected to the move. Von's, a leading grocery chain in Southern California, stopped selling thirteen P&G items in its stores. Lew Schaeneman, chief executive of Stop & Shop, the biggest grocery chain in New England, proclaimed that "P&G is acting like a dictator, and like all dictators, they will fall. We will do everything in our power to undermine their plan."[26] Meanwhile, P&G's competitors stormed into the breach, offering substantial deals to promote their products. Less visibly, however, many retailers adapted quickly to the new terms and worked with P&G to manage the transition. Meanwhile, the rivals who jumped on the value pricing announcement understood the logic of P&G's position and quietly began preparations to follow suit.

For P&G, value pricing meant more than an effort to restore and preserve brand equity. It also reinforced efforts to streamline the supply chain. Over the years, the company's internal systems had adapted to the cycles of discounts and promotions and the trade practices that the Hi-Lo system had engendered. As a result, it proved difficult for P&G to forecast demand accurately. To accommodate the large fluctuations in demand that occurred periodically, the company stockpiled large inventories. The inefficiencies were not confined to distribution channels. They rippled backward to the factories, where inefficiencies complicated scheduling and raised manufacturing and logistics costs. The shift to value pricing enabled P&G's Product Supply organization to focus on eliminating such inefficiencies. At the same time, the company accelerated its work with a growing number of customers on redesigning order processes, continuous-replenishment programs, and other initiatives to improve supply-chain management.[27]

All these factors fed into a major overhaul of P&G's North American sales force in 1992. Jager directed that the entire organization be restructured around customer teams—an initiative subsequently known as Customer Business Development (CBD). Jager further charged each team and the North American organization as a whole "to simplify, standardize, and mechanize" all processes and activities that did not add value. This reorganization was a controversial and risky decision, because it pulled the sales force out of the stores and sent them to customer headquarters while also eliminating many sales jobs.[28]

Efficient Consumer Response

Meanwhile, the revolution in merchandising and retailing continued to spread, prompting still more changes in the trade. To remain competitive, traditional retailers accelerated their efforts to squeeze costs out of their own supply chains. In January 1993, the Food Marketing Institute and the Grocery Manufacturers of America, the leading trade associations, formed the Joint Industry Committee to restructure supply chains and improve customer service. The vision was simple, said Milligan: "a smooth continuous flow of product driven by what consumers purchase, supported by a timely, accurate flow of information which enables the supply chain to give customers what they want at a better value." At stake was an estimated $30 billion in savings—more than 5 percent of total industry costs.[29]

The joint committee included representatives from grocers, distributors, wholesalers, and manufacturers, and it launched thrusts in four areas under the rubric of Efficient Consumer Response (ECR). The thrusts were known as the four Es:

1. Efficient assortment, combining manufacturers' consumer research on brand and category-specific purchasing behavior with geo-demographic and product movement history to make better choices on the ways products and categories should be merchandised and promoted

2. Efficient product introductions, to combine available market research and geo-demographic information to make better decisions about new product introductions

3. Efficient promotion, aimed at making pricing more stable and predictable and discouraging special deals

4. Efficient (continuous) replenishment, with the goal to squeeze out inventory and use scanner data to drive the replenishment cycle

Procter & Gamble, which had already been working on these issues intensively for several years and on some for nearly a decade, quickly assumed a leading role on the Joint Industry Committee, with Jager serving as the first cochair. The company proved particularly influential on the thrust for efficient (continuous) replenishment, which according to some estimates accounted for nearly 40 percent of total savings from supply-chain reform. The company made available proprietary continuous-replacement software it had developed in the 1980s, and the software became the official standard for ECR.[30]

Summing Up a Decade of Revolutionary Change

By the late 1990s, numerous tributaries, both from the 1980s (total quality management, category management, product supply, experiments in customer relations, and customer teams) and from the early 1990s (value pricing, business process reengineering, CBD, and ECR) had converged to change the rules of engagement in the consumer products industry. Most of the innovations originated in North America, but they spread quickly around the world. Everywhere, manufacturers, distributors, and retailers were collaborating to lower systems costs throughout the supply chain, to gather better and more useful information as the basis for making decisions, and to deliver improved service and value to consumers.

For P&G, the dividends from these changes—many of which the company initiated and all of which it embraced—proved large and readily apparent. In 1995, Milligan ticked them off in a speech: SKUs, down 25 percent; rate of volume growth, up more than 100 percent; sales staffing (including additions), down 30 percent; combined CBD/ECR cost savings, more than $500 million after tax; unit costs, down 14 percent; days receivable, down 20 percent; inventory on hand, down 15 percent; improved customer value (through reduced list prices), $7 billion. At the same time, P&G's business in North America grew dramatically and savings from supply-chain innovations flowed directly to the bottom line.[31]

Reconfigured Supply Chains in Perspective

The revamping of supply chains in the consumer products industry—an initiative P&G joined at an early date and then helped lead—carried profound implications for consumers, the trade, and for the company itself. Once P&G and its trade partners understood and began to manage the supply chain as a total system with interrelated parts stretching from the purchase of raw materials; through manufacturing, logistics, advertising, and merchandising; to the point of sale, enormous savings in time and money became possible. Suppliers, customers, and consumers benefited alike from smoother, more efficient operations and the free flow of information. Procter & Gamble could produce goods faster and at lower cost, with tighter connections between demand for its products and the output of its factories. Merchandiser customers economized on inventory without having to worry about shortages of its best-selling and most profitable items. Consumers gained better-performing products, easier-to-understand product usage and benefits, better awareness and access to the categories and brands of their choice, and enhanced overall value.

For P&G, its customers became a source of powerful learning. By collaborating with customers in research on shoppers, both parties gained a richer understanding of how consumers make purchase decisions, with indications of how to influence these decisions to mutual benefit. Some customers also opened up new marketing venues. As Muccio noted, in the United States in 2002, it took 117 prime-time commercials to reach 80 percent of eighteen- to forty-nine-year-olds. By comparison, 50 percent of the U.S. population shopped at Wal-Mart each week, and 80 percent of households shopped there each month. By tailoring its message to such consumers, P&G has been able to drive its sales and profits up, year after year.[32]

Procter & Gamble's role in the vanguard of the supply-chain revolution enabled it to reap significant advantages and gain new sources of both learning and profits to help extend its market leadership. But the company's actions also came with costs. The corporation had to reexamine nearly everything it did and be willing to change some time-honored practices. This scrutiny took many acts of courage, from the intrepid engineers who championed the total quality principles; to the front-line members of the customer teams; to the top leaders of the company who approved the new approach to product supply, customer business development, and value pricing. In the end, the company reasoned rightly—as it had on many previous occasions—that it was far better to help lead an industry through transition than to follow.

Winning in the White Space

PROCTER & GAMBLE IN CENTRAL AND EASTERN EUROPE AND RUSSIA

DURING the mid- to late 1980s, P&G executives watched with great interest the growing popular agitation for liberal economic reform in the Communist countries of Central and Eastern Europe. Poland, Hungary, Czechoslovakia, and the Baltic republics—Latvia, Estonia, and Lithuania—were all cautiously exploring liberal economic policies, including private ownership and free-market enterprise. Even the Soviet Union was encouraging small-scale experiments in capitalism.

For many Western companies, the temptation to enter the region was powerful. The region as a whole included more than 400 million people, about equal to the population of Western Europe. Residents did not enjoy high personal incomes, but they were well educated and attracted to Western culture and products. Most could be reached by nationwide TV advertising. The local competition, meanwhile, posed minimal threat, offering markedly inferior products and lacking basic skills in marketing and advertising. Yet the risks of entry for Western companies were also glaringly apparent: Currencies were not convertible to dollars, the infrastructure for distributing and retailing consumer goods was virtually nonexistent, and the course of political liberalization could easily be disrupted and perhaps reversed.

For P&G in particular, the prospect of competing in Central and Eastern Europe raised numerous questions, most importantly, how to ensure not only that the company would succeed but also that it would win in the long term in a region undergoing rapid political and economic transformation.

An Atypical Entry Strategy

In the spring of 1990—after the fall of the Berlin Wall but before the collapse of the Soviet Union—P&G determined to enter the most promising markets of the region as aggressively as possible. In contrast to earlier international ventures, in which the company had proceeded deliberately and on a market-by-market basis, the company this time decided to move fast and simultaneously on several fronts.

Led by Wolfgang Berndt, P&G sorted the nations in the region into categories based on their commercial attractiveness: safety and stability, per capita incomes, TV penetration, and government commitment to free-market reforms. The most inviting A markets included Czechoslovakia, Hungary, Poland, and urban Russia (Moscow and St. Petersburg, as Leningrad was renamed in 1991). The Balkans, the Baltic republics, and other urban areas of the Soviet Union were designated B markets, and rural areas of the Soviet Union were classified as C markets. Procter & Gamble made entry into the A markets its top priority and would cultivate the B and C markets later on.[1]

The next decision was how to enter. Just as it had with countries in the region, P&G sorted its business into categories, with the A list consisting of those with the biggest volume and profit potential: laundry detergent, disposable diapers, hair care, feminine care, and dentifrices. The B categories featured personal cleaning, dish care, fabric softening, household cleaning, skin care, and cough and cold; the C list included tissues, deodorants, foods and beverages, cosmetics, fragrances, and pharmaceuticals. The company planned to penetrate each market on a scale big enough to justify and spread the costs of heavy investments in advertising, distribution, and administration. Moreover, simultaneous arrival in multiple categories would enable P&G to build a more efficient distribution system and claim a greater share of shelf space and consumer spending.

Uncharacteristically, P&G chose to pursue a regional, as opposed to country-based, entry strategy. "The idea," said Herbert Schmitz, an experienced international executive who led the charge, was "to do it fast, do it on the ground, and develop the business[es] in parallel to get critical mass early." Respective A countries took responsibility for production and marketing campaigns for particular A categories: Poland, for hair care and diapers; Hungary, for feminine protection and dentifrices; and Czechoslovakia, for fabric care. "These lead markets," Berndt pointed out, "developed introductory plans for their lead categories with a view to using the same product, packaging and marketing plans in the other markets as well—if successful in the first market. This approach of 'flying in formation' shared the workload and generated far superior speed."[2]

Procter & Gamble's major rivals, meanwhile, had chosen to enter Central and Eastern Europe in time-honored ways. They bought plants or formed joint ventures in each country, assuming that the region would develop like Latin America, with protectionist trade and investment policies impeding cross-border activity. Procter & Gamble, in contrast, believed that the pace and extent of liberalization across the region would spark enthusiasm for free trade. Trends in privatization and regional integration in North America and Western Europe reinforced the belief. Accordingly, P&G prepared white papers dealing with public policy issues in each market and the region as a whole as the basis of discussion with host governments and institutional stakeholders. Procter & Gamble argued against "investment-distorting" practices such as local content laws, tax holidays, trade quotas, and high tariffs. In the long term, the company believed, liberal trade policies would foster competition and promote regional development and integration. Berndt and Schmitz discovered that P&G's views "gained us very high credibility" with host country governments.[3]

Procter & Gamble also found that its beliefs and reputation proved to be important assets when it came to negotiating with local partners. In Czechoslovakia, for example, several Western companies competed keenly for the right to acquire Rakona, a leading local manufacturer of detergents, cleaners, and shampoos. In the end, P&G captured the prize, in part because of its values. When representatives from competitors toured the Czech facilities most of their questions concerned ways to maximize production and lower costs. The visitors from P&G, in contrast, inquired first about improving performance in quality, safety, hygiene, and protecting the environment. When employees at Rakona voted on the choice of a Western partner, P&G won handily.

Securing government approval of the purchase also proceeded smoothly, as Czech ministry officials welcomed P&G's plans to use Rakona as a base from which to supply products to the entire region. The deal—the first large acquisition in Czechoslovakia by a Western company—was concluded in principle in the spring of 1991. Production of Ariel began in August—nearly two years earlier than would have been possible had P&G built a green-field plant.[4]

Elsewhere in the region, P&G managed entry through joint ventures. In Poland, P&G and a British partner purchased a large complex of warehouses

Procter & Gamble acquired Rakona in the Czech Republic in 1991. The deal gave the company a head start and a base for exporting throughout Central and Eastern Europe.

near Warsaw to serve as a central distribution network. In 1993, the venture acquired a partially completed manufacturing plant, also near Warsaw, as a site from which to produce diapers, shampoo, and bleach. In Hungary, P&G formed several joint ventures. On the supply side, it found a local partner to invest in a plant to make feminine protection products; on the demand side, it formed joint ventures to market and distribute shampoos, soap, dentifrices, and skin care products.

Procter & Gamble trod more cautiously in entering the Soviet Union, allying with an unusual partner: the University of St. Petersburg. Enzo Ferraris, marketing manager for the country (and later the company's first general manager in Russia), identified the opportunity while taking Russian language classes at the university. A faculty member who had helped several Western businesspeople navigate through the government bureaucracy to obtain permits and authorization offered to help P&G, and an institutional relationship began to blossom.[5] Schmitz considered the St. Petersburg venture "a laboratory for Russia" that helped P&G learn the terrain. Partnership with the university, said Schmitz, also offered "prestige . . . , the absence of corruption, the absence of old-time thinking. And this partnership gave us a political base, a social entry base, and administrative entry to help."[6]

Meanwhile, P&G had structured itself for a strong, continuing push in the region. By the fall of 1991, it had formed country organizations in each of the A markets, with responsibility for selling, distribution, advertising, pricing, finance, human resources, public relations, and local market research and customer service. The company grouped the four country units under a new organization, P&G Central and Eastern Europe (C&EE), with Schmitz at its head. The new organization assumed responsibility for coordinating business development in the region, as well as for R&D, manufacturing and product supply (until the country organizations developed local capacity), product technology, packaging, and exports.[7]

The initial returns from P&G's activities in Central and Eastern Europe proved highly gratifying. In 1990–1991, the company reported sales of $29 million in the region; the following year, sales soared to $366 million and seemed likely to surpass $1 billion within another year or two. Better still, P&G surged ahead of its Western rivals in every category, with market share leads ranging from 10 to 50 percent.[8] The company seemed likely to sustain its leadership in the region as long as it attended to the challenges of managing rapid growth and kept a wary eye on the progress of economic and political reform. Procter & Gamble's experiences in Russia illustrated the benefits and pitfalls of conducting business in the region, as well as the value of perseverance and focusing on the fundamentals when adversity arrived.

Rapid Rise in Russia

During the early and mid-1990s, P&G continued to enjoy rapid growth throughout Central and Eastern Europe. Revenues reached $1.3 billion in 1996–1997, and Schmitz expected annual growth rates to continue at 20 to 30 percent per year into the near future. Procter & Gamble continued to outpace its Western competitors and held leading positions in its major categories. The business was profitable in every market and category, a performance that encouraged P&G to proceed with plans to launch operations in the B and C markets and introduce offerings from its B and C categories.[9]

The company was also increasingly optimistic about opportunities in the Russian Federation (the biggest constituent of what had been the Soviet Union before its disintegration at the end of 1991). The world's largest nation by geographic area, Russia spanned eleven time zones. Its economy was very shaky, however, with low per capita incomes, and with rates of development well below those in the strongest economies of Central Europe, and the ultimate direction and extent of political reforms in Russia were anything but certain.

Aware of these risks, P&G proceeded swiftly to build its business in Russia. Early in 1992, just weeks after the collapse of the Soviet Union, P&G opened an office in Moscow with intentions eventually to establish its national headquarters there. The company faced daunting challenges on many fronts. One of the biggest involved setting up distribution in a country woefully lacking in retail outlets and the infrastructure to support them. The government-controlled distribution system of the Soviet era had simply collapsed, forcing P&G to develop new channels from scratch. Retail coverage, such as it was, included department stores in urban areas and many thousands of small, neighborhood shops around the country. Another important outlet was rapidly taking shape: open-air markets, where vendors and incipient entrepreneurs began peddling goods from stalls, carts, and tables. During the early 1990s, P&G contracted with warehouse operations in St. Petersburg and Moscow and shipped products directly to "two hundred or three hundred" retail stores in St. Petersburg and Moscow.[10]

One legacy of the Soviet era, the national media, proved a boon. State control of information had been a top priority, with the result that TV sets (most of them color) adorned more than 95 percent of households. (In contrast, only about half of Russian households had telephones.) Procter & Gamble immediately became the nation's biggest advertiser by far, accounting for about 10 percent of all TV advertising expenditures in Russia. Maria Bjork, P&G's media manager in Moscow, pointed out that "the market is relatively cheap and uncluttered" and that "advertising remains [a] very good value in global terms, and the limited number of major advertisers means that continuity achievement is better than almost anywhere else in the world."[11]

Securing Local Supply

On the supply side, P&G imported most of its products from Western and Central Europe, including from the fledgling operations in Hungary, Poland, and Czechoslovakia. It was clear, however, that the company would soon need to develop its own extensive production capacity in Russia. Otto Hausknecht, the product supply manager reporting to Schmitz, toured Russia and nearby countries extensively, looking for potential partners. Most of the factories he saw, unfortunately, were "way below standard: too little productivity, poor safety and hygiene, sporadic production, poor air quality." Early in 1992, however, he found a suitable candidate: Novomoskovskbytkhim (Novo). Based in Novomoskovsk, a city about 200 kilometers southwest of Moscow, Novo operated by far the biggest detergent factory in Russia and had recently modernized its equipment. In addition to a popular but low-tech detergent called Myth, in which P&G saw possibilities, Novo also manufactured many other products, such as linoleum and varnish, in which P&G had no interest. At the same time, the factory suffered from the organizational pathologies of the Communist era: lax work practices, a workforce five or six times bigger than necessary, inattention to working conditions and the environment, and generally inefficient and unfocused operations.[12]

The decision to pursue Novo provoked sharp internal debates at P&G, including pointed and skeptical questioning from Ed Artzt. Nonetheless, Schmitz and Hausknecht were convinced that Novo constituted P&G's best alternative. They began negotiating with Novo's management in April 1992, starting with contracts to manufacture and market P&G products. This proved the start of a long and complex mating dance that unfolded over the next several years as P&G sought to gain control of Novo and restructure its operations. In August 1993, the parties signed a business cooperation agreement in which P&G would acquire 51 percent of Novo in return for a $50 million investment over five years. Procter & Gamble also acquired additional shares on the open market, finally obtaining outright control in 1997. By then, the plant was producing not only detergents but also Always and other P&G brands. It had also undergone a major restructuring, which included the installation of new equipment and processes, job redesigns, and significant reduction of the workforce.

Serving Soaring Demand

During P&G's first years in Russia, while the company conducted its experiments in St. Petersburg and Moscow, revenues crept up slowly, with shipments of 1.8 million cases and revenues of $40 million in 1993–1994. By then, new leadership had arrived on the scene. Ferraris's successor, Peter Smit, presided over a period of rapid expansion based on strong successes in dentifrices and shampoos.

As the first Western products in their categories to hit the market in Russia, Head & Shoulders shampoo and Blend-a-Med dentifrice surged ahead to market-leading positions.[13] In both instances, advertising played a major role in the early success. Head & Shoulders benefited from an amusing ad that showed people in an elevator noticing a man with an obvious dandruff problem. The message was that Head & Shoulders would not only cure the problem but also enhance the user's self-esteem and confidence in social settings. Ads for Blend-a-Med, meanwhile, echoed those of P&G dentifrices elsewhere, especially in North America and in Germany. The company quickly secured and then promoted heavily the endorsement of the Russian Dental Association, trumpeting the therapeutic, anticavity benefits of Blend-a-Med. Procter & Gamble also launched a research study with schools in Novomoskovsk, providing students with Blend-a-Med as part of an ongoing program in dental care. Other big winners for P&G included the laundry products manufactured at Novo, and Pampers imported from Poland. For some brands, managers in Russia worked with product supply personnel elsewhere in the region or in Western Europe to develop customized packaging, including small sizes that Russian consumers found affordable.

Buoyed by encouraging results, in 1995 P&G redoubled its efforts to cultivate the market, with management setting an ambitious goal of $1 billion in revenues by the middle of 2000. The company followed the exclusive regional distributor success model developed in Poland by Bob Fregolle. In May 1995, Kevin Edwards, who had worked with Fregolle in Poland, moved to Russia to push sales beyond St. Petersburg and Moscow to the rest of urban Russia—the more than 150 cities with populations greater than half a million inhabitants. Under the so-called McVan Program in Poland, P&G had identified promising distributors and provided them with vans, hand-held computer equipment, working capital, and intensive training in return for exclusive agreements to market P&G products in their territory. Edwards instituted a similar program in Russia. Teams from P&G offices worked with these distributors, offering training in inventory management, sales, credit policy, and accounting, and consulting support on a weekly basis. The distributors served the retail trade, while P&G reached the open-air vendors through independent wholesalers, who rushed in to fill the vacuum created by the demise of the Soviet-era distribution system.[14]

As the McVan Program and other changes took hold, P&G experienced phenomenal growth. In 1994–1995, after just three years and significant investments in Russia, the company turned its first annual profit. During the next three years, volume skyrocketed, from 3.8 million cases to 28.9 million, with sales soaring from $78 million to $629 million. Laurent Philippe, who succeeded Smit as country manager in July 1996, attributed P&G's success to several factors. He mentioned the ruble exchange rate, which was artificially high against the dollar and made Western goods relatively attractive to Russian consumers. But P&G's lead over its Western competitors, its ability to maintain high market shares in category after category, depended on more fundamental factors. Philippe credited the decision by Berndt and Schmitz, with backing from John Pepper, to pursue rapid growth. As a result, P&G achieved "the volume and the size to really spread our fixed cost and investments across a very large amount of business."[15]

Philippe also pointed out that P&G had developed a very strong organization and a very positive reputation in Russia. Although the company experienced inevitable turnover as other Western companies arrived and raided talent from the early pioneers, the management team at P&G Russia worked together with extraordinary cohesion that was born of sharing in a groundbreaking venture, as well as in a remarkable success. "We have slept in airports, on benches all night, in the cold," noted Philippe. "We've had flat tires in the winter on the freeways, whatever we call freeways in Russia. We were in military coups; we had great parties, big disappointments, frustrations, governments changing rules every week; we had threats [including] Mafia threats."[16]

Nevertheless, the difficulties, the dangers, and the effort proved rewarding, not only financially for P&G shareholders but also psychologically for

Pictured in front of St. Basil's cathedral in Moscow, this van was part of a P&G program to equip and train independent entrepreneurs as distributors of the company's brands.

employees. Some exulted from participating in historic events; others, particularly Russians, reveled in the experience of succeeding in a wholly new environment. Although experienced international managers in P&G occupied most senior positions in Russia, the company offered Russian employees an abundance of opportunities for personal growth and development. Such opportunities were unthinkable in the Soviet era. Recent college graduates became assistant brand managers with significant responsibilities for advertising and pricing or members of the financial staff to track sales and profits. Translators and drivers moved into management ranks to develop the product supply network or to help run the central and branch offices. Ludmila Biriukova, an employee in human resources, noted that in Soviet times, she had worked about two hours per day, spending the rest of her time drinking tea and chatting with colleagues. Procter & Gamble, in contrast, was all work and long hours. But she came to love it—it was "a hard lesson, but exciting." In product supply, Natasha Glazova, an administrative assistant, expressed delight at the prospect of coming to work each day and was constantly surprised by exciting opportunities to learn. Ruslan Giniyatov, a young finance manager, considered working at P&G "a dream come true."[17]

As P&G's business mushroomed, the company's values helped reinforce the cohesiveness of employees and guide them on the job. Many employees mentioned P&G's philosophy and clean reputation as important factors influencing their decisions to join the company. Employees also witnessed the values at work every day. They and their counterparts at other Western companies were frequently put to the test when commercial agents or bureaucratic officials sought bribes, gifts, and favors before agreeing to process petitions or expedite requests. Procter & Gamble's policy was not to comply, even if it meant protracted delays and loss of business.

Alexander Filatov, a young sales manager, believed that the policy offered hope for employees that some of the most cynical and characteristic administrative practices of the Soviet era would eventually disappear. Filatov himself offered a case in point. He was charged to set up a series of promotional lotteries in Moscow department stores. Customers who bought a P&G product would receive a coupon making them eligible for a drawing to win prizes such as TVs and other appliances. He targeted the top fifty stores and persuaded forty-seven of them to sign up. Managers in the three remaining stores—including one of the city's biggest retailers—offered to participate only if they received special incentives. Filatov refused. The promotion worked so well at the competitive outlets, however, that the three outliers eventually relented, seeing that they could attract more traffic and make more money by conducting business aboveboard.[18]

During 1997–1998, P&G continued its aggressive push for more business, venturing into new territory, selling more products, introducing new brands, and hiring new people. Employment climbed to 550 people. The company leased land about 60 miles (100 kilometers) east of Moscow to build a new Pampers plant. Many signs indicated a bright future for P&G. All told, it seemed likely that the company would cross the $1 billion sales threshold at least a year early.

Surprise and Crisis

Procter & Gamble's optimistic projections of future business in Russia were shattered on a single day in the summer of 1998. On August 17, 1998, Prime Minister Sergei Kiriyenko shocked the economy by announcing that the ruble, which had traded at about 6 to the dollar, would henceforth trade at 9.5 to the dollar—a 50 percent devaluation. During the next few weeks, with the props removed, the ruble slid to 12 to the dollar and threatened to dive deeper still. As millions of Russians saw their life savings wiped out, the hopes that many had voiced for a new Russia after the collapse of the Soviet Union were dashed.

For foreign companies operating in Russia, the August 17 announcement triggered a deep financial crisis. Procter & Gamble had just made the investments and was taking on employment to manage a $1 billion operation. Suddenly, it was looking at annual revenues of less than—maybe much less than—half that amount. Indeed, a major short-term problem was the difficulty in assessing the magnitude of the crisis. For a while, it appeared that the ruble might stabilize at about 14 to the dollar—a dismal but not disastrous prospect. But a pattern was soon evident. The ruble would rally when banks intervened or when investors decided to convert at what they considered favorable exchange rates. The value would then hold at equilibrium for a few days, sometimes longer, before sliding again. The uncertainty proved nerve-racking for businesses, which found it nearly impossible to stabilize prices, manage inventories, and plan production. While a downward trend was unmistakable, no one knew where the ruble would bottom out or how long it would take to get there.

One thing was certain, though: Procter & Gamble needed to make difficult choices, and fast. After meeting with his department heads, Philippe announced a freeze on hiring and discretionary spending. Work on the new Pampers plant was halted and eventually terminated. Temporary employees and contractors were advised to look elsewhere for jobs. The company also set new priorities among its categories and ceased promoting minor and struggling brands. Through it all, Philippe and his colleagues communicated frequently with employees to keep them abreast of emerging developments and their implications for the business.

The human cost of the crisis and the anxieties it generated were terribly demoralizing. Luba Pelikhova, a compensation specialist (and subsequently head of human resources), recalled that the bank that used to handle the payroll simply froze all assets and would not allow employees to access their accounts for an indefinite period, which turned out to be several months. The bank, one of the six biggest in the country, eventually failed, resulting in dreadful hardships for employees and other account holders. For the interim, P&G arranged to pay salaries in cash (in dollars), engaging a local security firm to bring money to the office and guard it while human-resources managers sorted the bills into envelopes.[19]

Realignment for a New Reality

Beyond the challenge of dealing with the immediate crisis loomed formidable, long-term strategic challenges. Only about 30 percent of P&G's offerings—chiefly detergents, some cleaning products, and Always—were manufactured locally; the other 70 percent were imported in exchange for dollars. The only way to sell the imported goods at a profit was to raise prices dramatically. That, in turn, meant accepting much lower volume. "We had to face the truth and the reality that there would be far fewer Russian consumers with a disposable income to buy our products," said Philippe. "We found that we needed to face the moment of truth, where we offered to consumers our product priced where it ought to be priced and see how many were still willing to reach for their money and buy."[20] The questions were how far, and how fast, demand would plunge.

The answers were not long in coming. By October, it was painfully clear that Russian consumers had become extremely conscious of prices. Procter & Gamble lost half its volume and seemed likely to lose still more. It was also apparent that two of P&G's most successful categories—shampoos and dentifrices—would be particularly hard hit. Russian consumers recognized the benefits of P&G's brands, but could no longer afford to pay for them, especially because much cheaper alternatives made locally were deemed good enough. Market shares began trending down and the company was draining cash at the rate of $10 million per month.

Having made the decision to preserve premium pricing, P&G made another important decision in the fall of 1998. It set an ambitious goal to return to a pretax profit, however modest, by the start of the next fiscal year, on July 1, 1999. The means to accomplish this goal were hammered out in plans presented to regional and top corporate management in December 1998.[21] The first step was to agree on realistic volume forecasts. Second, the company restructured its internal processes and workloads in light of the new forecast. Third, P&G reevaluated its supply chain, looking for ways to economize and simplify operations. Fourth, the company prepared severance packages for the employees it could no longer support. Finally, it accelerated plans to localize management and production.[22]

In facing its difficult choices, P&G adhered to several principles. First, it avoided doing anything that would undermine the competitive advantages it had worked so hard to create before the crisis. Thus, the company would not do anything to erode the value of its brands or eviscerate its distribution network. Procter & Gamble would continue to be Russia's leading TV advertiser, albeit paying significantly reduced rates and airing ads less often. While reductions in personnel seemed inevitable, they would be handled fairly and with an eye to preserving the strength of the organization as a whole.

In product supply, the challenge suddenly reversed from developing the systems and finding the warehouse space to move 35 million cases per year to finding ways, fast, to liquidate inventory and cut back on capacity. The company's recently signed contracts with warehouse operators and trucking companies all over Russia complicated matters. Not only were these deals freshly minted, but also P&G had not worked with its partners long enough to differentiate between the strong and the weak. Even with the strong, there was much yet to learn about how to work together effectively. On the other hand, recalled Angelike Gaedtke, a product supply manager, all parties recognized the situation. Because many Western companies were prepared to abandon Russia altogether, it was somewhat easier for companies like P&G, which chose to remain, to restructure terms and negotiate lower prices.[23]

During the fall, the product supply organization formed task forces to reduce inventory and optimize the logistics for much lower demand. Addressing these problems meant buying back inventory from distributors and reallocating it to markets with the greatest likelihood of sales. It also meant canceling contracts for warehouse space and renegotiating lease terms: Prices in the Moscow area dropped from twelve to three dollars per square meter. Another step was the restructuring of deals with carriers. In each instance, Gaedtke noted, P&G treated its vendors like partners: "Everything [was] very practical and cost-oriented. [It was] a give and take, in fact. During the time of volume growth [the partners] all made good money. Now we needed to get something back as Procter & Gamble to limit the impact and losses so that we could stay in this market." Procter & Gamble's statements of philosophy and values proved helpful in framing these discussions, she added. "[We got] very practical and positive outcomes of this."[24]

As painful as the exercise proved, Gaedtke believed that P&G emerged from it with a stronger, battle-tested organization, better relationships with its partners, and an inventory management system that was more tightly integrated across the nation. With P&G consigning rather than selling goods to the distributors, the company was better able to manage and replenish inventory in a timely way. It was also much more sensitive to costs in the system and worked continuously on lowering them.[25]

On the distribution side, P&G took a similar approach, renegotiating terms and consolidating its business in the hands of fewer distributors. When the crisis hit, P&G had thirty-three distributors across Russia. Within a year, the number had dropped to sixteen. Fewer distributors meant fewer vans (from 1,050 to 750) and less investment and training. Procter & Gamble also renegotiated terms that lowered margins throughout the supply chain; in return, the company permitted distributors to carry goods from other Western suppliers such as BIC and Energizer.[26]

By the fall of 1998, given the new and much lower demand forecasts, the need to reduce employment was paramount. An always difficult and unhappy task, it proved especially so in this instance, said Philippe, "on two grounds. It was painful because we had built a very strong local organization, so separating early from these people was an emotionally difficult thing to do." Second, "the Russian people coming out of the Soviet era had been very hopeful and optimistic about what an open society and a Western form of capitalism and business would bring them in terms of benefits. This currency crisis came up as a very sober reminder that the path forward to progress would not be . . . without pain and difficulties."[27]

Procter & Gamble's analysis determined that about sixty people above and beyond temporary employees and contractors would have to be let go. Department heads worked with human-resources managers to ensure that the best performers would be retained and that those leaving the company would be fairly compensated. Procter & Gamble prepared voluntary-separation packages more generous than those required by Russian law. The deal included two months' notice, during which the departing employees received outplacement assistance, four months' wages in a lump sum, and extended repayment terms for loans that some departing employees had taken to finance housing purchases. Marketing director Shannan Stevenson found the process of letting people go especially poignant when a number of employees, on hearing the news, thanked him for the opportunity to work at P&G and for exceeding expectations in handling the separations.[28]

The company also took a hard look at the number of international managers on its staff. When the crisis hit, expatriates accounted for nearly 10 percent of total employment. They had proved invaluable as the business ramped up during the early 1990s, but, given the massive devaluation of the ruble and their dollar-denominated salaries, these managers were now too costly to retain in such numbers. During the fall and winter of 1998–1999, P&G sought to transfer as many expatriates as possible to other countries and regions, replacing them with Russians, many of whom had only a few years of experience with the company, as well as with capitalism generally. Expatriates remained in the most senior positions, but all but disappeared from the ranks of middle management.[29]

Although P&G had made a gloomy forecast in November and December, results in the first quarter of 1999 proved even worse. By April, volume was so low that P&G was forced to cut another sixty-five jobs. At the same time, after conducting surveys of other Western employers in Russia, P&G "dedollarized" or "rublized" the salaries for those remaining. That is, the salaries were converted from dollars to rubles at the exchange rate of the previous November. In effect, this conversion constituted a pay cut of approximately 20 percent. The step caused obvious unhappiness, but it kept P&G in line with other Western employers in Russia.[30]

During 1998–1999, P&G saw its volume in Russia drop by more than 50 percent, and the company lost approximately $100 million. About half of the financial loss involved one-time charges, including the write-off of inventories and costs associated with separating employees and restructuring contracts with suppliers and distributors. But P&G Russia succeeded in meeting the short-term goal set in the aftermath of the crisis: By the summer of 1999, it was no longer losing money in Russia. With the business stabilized and the organization much streamlined, Philippe and his colleagues looked ahead to the challenge of reconstructing the business.

Coming Back

In the fall of 1998, Philippe had asked P&G's financial staff in Russia to calculate how long it would take the company to regain the business lost due to the crisis. The estimates that came back were sobering: Procter & Gamble would need at least three years to recover the production volume and as many as seven years to recoup the sales value. The delay in value recovery reflected the renewed competitiveness of local Russian industries. Western competitors had all but driven them out of business before 1998, but thereafter, they gained new life. With effective low-cost and low-price competitors, it would be a long time before P&G could again expect significant premiums for its products.[31]

The company continued to press for cost reductions and search for more efficient ways to conduct business, but the young, now largely Russian management team also determined to regain lost ground. A key part of the recovery plan was based on protecting and preserving the advantages the company had worked so hard to establish before the crisis. The fundamentals of the distribution system remained intact, although P&G worked with fewer distributors and less overall investment. Improvements and de-dollarization during 1998–1999 gave the company some flexibility to lower prices, with a corresponding rise in volume. Meanwhile, P&G modified its advertising messages to take account of the new environment. In the laundry and cleaning categories, for example, the company proclaimed that its products performed much better than the local competition's, justifying P&G's higher prices. Ads for P&G's Fairy dish-washing liquid emphasized that a few drops were enough to wash the evening dishes. For Ariel laundry detergent, P&G filmed a schoolteacher (representing an occupation widely known as poorly compensated) professing that P&G's products were safer for garments, enabling them to last longer, despite repeated washing.[32]

Challenges to rebuild the dentifrice and shampoo businesses proved more daunting—although young brand managers Anton Andreev and Vitalius Paulus approached the challenges as tremendous opportunities to prove themselves. In dentifrices, Russian and Bulgarian competitors mimicked P&G's

product claims, endorsements, and packaging. Combined with improved products, these tactics worked well, at the cost of Blend-a-Med's market share. The benefits of anticavity protection, moreover, were frustratingly difficult to demonstrate: The effects of ceasing to use Blend-a-Med would not show up for many months. In market research and consumer interviews, Andreev kept hearing deep skepticism about P&G's claims and hostility toward its high prices. Fortunately, P&G's clinical studies in the Novomoskovsk schools had been launched before the crisis and were now delivering results. The company filmed a series of ads featuring children talking about the differences that Blend-a-Med had made: significantly fewer cavities, significantly less gingivitis. These claims, backed by independent and authoritative research, helped turn the tide back in P&G's favor.[33]

In shampoos, P&G reformulated advertising copy to emphasize new benefits that extended, but remained consistent with, earlier benefits. Before the crisis, for example, copy for Head & Shoulders and Pantene had communicated social and emotional benefits: Use the product, and feel more at ease in social settings. After the crisis, the copy for both brands focused on creating stronger hair, a desirable characteristic in the Russian consumer's mind, perhaps because it suggested that the shampoos protected hair better between washings, which naturally occurred less often with higher-priced shampoos. Procter & Gamble also modified the packaging, offering smaller sizes and single-use sachets that were less expensive to purchase and could be used for special occasions and as gifts.[34]

The results of such efforts were positive. During 1999–2000, although production volume continued its decline, slipping to 9.6 million cases, about one-third the level of the precrisis peak, P&G eked out a small profit. In 2000–2001, results continued to improve, with volume up to 13.6 million cases and profits much healthier. Meanwhile, P&G stemmed its market share losses and began again to grow in key categories such as laundry, dentifrices, and hair care. Finally, with the return of prosperity, the company maintained its vigilant watch over costs. Head counts held steady at about 375 employees, while managers continued to find new savings in optimizing the supply chain and distribution network.

In 2000, in recognition of the turnaround, as well as the fundamental strength and significance of the company, key managers in P&G Russia took on additional duties for business development in the region. The company was designated the anchor of a new organizational unit, P&G Eastern Europe, with responsibilities for operations and marketing in Russia, Ukraine, and Belarus. And under the leadership of Daniela Riccardi, an international manager who succeeded Philippe in 2001, P&G Russia has sustained its momentum.

Expansion into Central and Eastern Europe and Russia in Perspective

Procter & Gamble surged to market leadership throughout white space of Central and Eastern Europe and Russia in the early 1990s because it saw that exploiting an unprecedented opportunity would require unconventional tactics. The company departed boldly from its own traditions—and the examples of other Western competitors—in hastening to create a strong, multimarket, multicategory presence in the region as quickly as possible. "If you ask me to single out three important reasons [for P&G's success]," offered Schmitz, "I would say speed, earliness on the ground, and scale. . . . We knew the window [of opportunity in the region] in terms of being first, [and] being able to operate when costs are still low would not be open forever. So, we said a little bit of imperfection is better than a lot of delay."[35]

By the mid-1990s, P&G had become the clear market leader in most of its major categories across the region. Along the way, P&G found that the same principles and practices of business that worked in its traditional markets also worked in these former Communist countries. Effective nationwide TV advertising, for example, proved as important to success in Prague as in Paris or Pittsburgh. Similarly, efficient product supply and good relationships with distributors and trade customers were as vital to success in Central and Eastern Europe as in Western Europe or North America. Meanwhile, P&G's reputation for ethical behavior did not present a disadvantage in places where black markets and corruption were accepted and where citizens tend to be cynical about large institutions. On the contrary, the company's determination to do the right thing made it attractive to promising recruits and partners and facilitated discussions with local and national governments.

The experience in Russia taught the company several key lessons about managing in crises. First was the importance of fixing aggressive but attainable goals to force the determination of priorities among possible actions. The decision to recover the full dollar cost of selling imported goods provided great clarity of purpose and made subsequent actions clear. High prices meant lower volume, which in turn meant restructuring and downsizing to operate at a cost level that would allow profitable operations. A related forcing decision was to strive to return to profitability within ten months of the onset of the economic crisis. Setting that goal created a sense of urgency and energized employees to move fast and work in a common direction. Achieving the goal validated the strategy and the teamwork that brought it off.

Second, P&G avoided taking any actions that could erode or threaten the advantages it had worked so hard to achieve. It continued nationwide advertising to communicate the benefits and value of its strong brands. It did not retreat from nationwide distribution and maintained its relationships with local partners. It retained and rewarded the company's best performers to ensure the strongest possible organization. "We were very, very conscious," said Stevenson, "that we [ought to be] in a position to ramp everything back up again whenever things picked up."[36]

Finally, the crisis in Russia proved an opportunity to test and develop P&G's cadre of young managers. Procter & Gamble reaped the benefit of excellent recruiting and training during its early years in Russia after the crisis forced the company to reduce the number of expatriates. The young Russians and Eastern Europeans thrust into responsibility proved quick on their feet and adept in responding to the crisis. When handed the new goals and objectives, these managers were given wide latitude to carry out their work. As a result, the crisis became empowering and P&G benefited from employee creativity and ingenuity. A longer-term benefit is that P&G Russia developed a young, battle-tested management team with an unusually strong can-do spirit.

CHAPTER SEVENTEEN

Ivory, Crest, and Olay

REDEFINING THE BOUNDARIES OF THE BRAND

OVER THE 1980S AND 1990S, competitive pressures bore in on many of P&G's core brands. Rivals such as Colgate, Kimberly-Clark, and Unilever put a host of new products on the market, crowding store shelves with line extensions, while at the same time a growing number of consumers turned to low-cost generic and private-label offerings. As a result, flagship brands such as Tide, Pampers, Crest, Bounty, and Charmin lost share.

Procter & Gamble's brands had slipped before, but by the mid-1990s, what had originally seemed like a cluster of individual setbacks was assuming the outlines of a broader trend. The company was getting outflanked in the marketplace. Brand managers, confronting innovative competitive offerings and rapidly evolving consumer expectations, were struggling to recover the initiative, and, as they did so, were finding it difficult to maneuver effectively within the boundaries that had been drawn around their brands.

Deep-rooted corporate wisdom warned against tampering with brands. Stretch them too far, past experience had demonstrated, and brands quickly lost meaning for consumers. Trying to make Crest, for example, stand for something more than cavity protection risked diluting its unique essence. Nevertheless, by the late 1990s, the need to revitalize Crest—and a number of other core brands—was growing inescapable. Consumers were indicating that they wanted new benefits and new value equations. Moreover, the relentless imperative of innovation was also demanding evolution. In response, the company prepared a series of moves taking some of its most closely and carefully guarded brands in directions never before attempted. As they launched new initiatives under such venerable, cherished names as

Crest, Pampers, and Olay, brand managers could not be entirely sure whether they were revitalizing the brands or extending them beyond recognition. But the managers sensed untapped potential hidden within the equities that those names signified. By the first years of the twenty-first century, P&G was coming to new outlooks on some of its oldest brands.

Ivory and the Paradox of Purity

The problem of where to draw brand boundaries had been with P&G from the very beginning. Ivory, the company's first brand, taught how powerful a tightly focused and carefully disciplined branding strategy could be—and over time, how constrictive, too. Within a few years of launch, Ivory's marketing message had cohered around several key points of reference. Central among these was the offer of new convenience and economy ("It Floats"), and the promise of purity: The soap, advertisements relentlessly repeated, was "99 44/100% Pure." That formula fixed Ivory in the public imagination as a trusted part of household kitchens and bathrooms. The brand became an article of faith between the company and consumers.

The impact of this strategy was enormous, both externally in the marketplace and also within P&G, which was then internalizing its initial, formative lessons in brand building. Ivory's claim to purity played an essential role in establishing Ivory as the leading soap brand in the United States well into the twentieth century. Meanwhile, P&G's solemn vow to preserve that purity deeply shaped the company's sense of how brands should be put together and sustained, warning against tampering with consumer expectations or experimenting casually with proven formulas.

But Ivory's core branding elements, the benefit of floating and the promise of purity, became increasingly problematic over time. Ivory soap's ability to float had translated, when clothes and bodies were washed in tubs, into both convenience and economy—yet that benefit grew less relevant as showers replaced baths and automatic washing machines replaced the hand washing of laundry. Worse, the idea of purity grew restrictive, implying, or seeming to imply, an assurance of immutability. The trademark "99 44/100% Pure" proved to be a formula for long decades of success, but also for eventual obsolescence, leaving precisely 0.56 percent room for innovation or adaptation.

The limits of this strategy only gradually became clear. In 1954, on the occasion of Ivory's seventy-fifth anniversary, P&G historian Alfred Lief could credibly claim that Ivory was "not only America's largest selling soap but also a kind of national institution."[1] Three years later, however, when

Unilever launched the synthetic cleaning bar Dove, Ivory was in no position to formulate an effective response. Over the following decades, a series of researchers and brand managers tried to refashion a relevant, new strategy for the brand. But repeatedly they met resistance from above. In the 1980s, for example, P&G researchers tested a series of ideas that scored well with consumers, including Ivory with Aloe, Ivory with Baby Powder, and the like. None made it to market, however, as again and again, senior management rejected proposals with the decision that "it was not Ivory." "The success [criterion] was always, 'change Ivory but in a way that consumers will never know,'" researcher Mary Carethers summarized. "It had to be 100 percent soap, it had to have the Ivopo [a proprietary perfume], it had to float."[2]

In retrospect, a later generation of P&G brand managers would come to see Ivory as a story of missed opportunity. The boundaries the company drew around the brand were too narrow, causing the people who inherited and worked with Ivory in the late twentieth century to misread its deeper equity. Gina Drosos, vice president of beauty care, for example, pointed out that when it first came on the market, Ivory was replacing lye soap. Compared to these strong soaps, Ivory was the best on the market and the mildest on skin. "In a sense," Drosos concluded, "it was the company's first beauty product. . . . It was about purity, naturalness, and caring for your skin." When Dove came onto the market in the 1950s, it displaced this position. Dove's synthetic formulation was in fact more "pure" than Ivory, because it was milder on skin. Yet P&G had decided long ago that Ivory meant "99 44/100% Pure." The company defined the brand in terms of narrow, formula-specific aspects and thus chained Ivory to what eventually became old-fashioned technology. Ivory remained pure in formula, but forfeited its claim to a deeper, more consumer-relevant sense of the brand equity that "purity" signified.[3]

Crest: Revitalizing the Brand

Similar reservations and restrictions hobbled Crest. During the process of establishing the brand as a therapeutic toothpaste beginning in the late 1950s, P&G had focused tightly on the benefits of fluoride formulation and cavity prevention. An enormous and extremely resourceful campaign had backed the brand, with marketing that remained relentlessly on-message, for P&G was not just introducing a new product, it was redefining the category around an entirely new set of product benefits. As with Ivory, the company created a very strong brand in the process—but not a particularly flexible or resilient one.

Moving Beyond Therapeutic

Problems began to emerge in the U.S. market in the 1980s, when after nearly two decades at the top spot in the dentifrice category, Crest lost marketplace initiative. Ironically, the brand's very success had laid the groundwork for this development, by making fluoride-based cavity protection a generic benefit shared by rival toothpastes. By 1980, virtually every household in the United States used some kind of fluoride toothpaste, leaving Crest little room for differentiation. Having staked so much of its business on decay prevention, P&G confronted a mature market in which no brand could demonstrate overwhelming superiority.[4] The only route to growth was to come up with value-added features and then charge a premium for them.

Not surprisingly, given the company's ingrained instinct to protect Crest's claim to state-of-the-art oral health, P&G directed its efforts toward therapeutic benefits. Between 1979 and 1985, while Crest's share plunged from 42 to 28 percent, researchers prepared what they were convinced would be the next evolution in the dentifrice category, effective treatment of tartar. This tactic temporarily recovered initiative. Crest Tartar Control, launched in 1985, gave Crest a huge lift, restoring the brand's share to the 40 percent mark. Within P&G, that success was taken as a vindication of traditional wisdom. In the words of Michael Kehoe, who took over as vice president of Global Oral Care in 1998, the success signaled that "we were on the right track" in trying to find the next big therapeutic innovation.[5]

Procter & Gamble's rivals, meanwhile, were pushing their dentifrice brands in other directions, including nontherapeutic, cosmetic areas of research, and consumers were following. Baking soda first caught the public imagination in 1988, when Church & Dwight Co. placed its Arm & Hammer brand name on a toothpaste product. For many Americans, Arm & Hammer *was* baking soda, and when some dentists recommended brushing with the old-fashioned ingredient, the new toothpaste grabbed 10 percent of the market.[6] Procter & Gamble noted the phenomenon, but was reluctant to counter with its own version. In fact, the American Dental Association was stating that baking soda had no effect on gum disease and, as an abrasive, had no advantage in cleaning teeth.[7] Similarly, the company also resisted another new trend: the use of peroxide as a regulated whitening ingredient.[8]

Dental research may have been on the company's side, but the market was shifting. As P&G stubbornly continued to hold out for a big therapeutic breakthrough, it again found itself losing ground to competitors. In 1990, a relatively small company called Den-Mat became the first to position its whitener, Rembrandt, as a replacement to everyday toothpaste.[9] Dental offices began distributing whitening kits around this time, intensifying consumer interest in products such as Rembrandt. In 1993–1994, Unilever raised the stakes with the launch of Mentadent. Positioned as a baking soda and peroxide combination, the new toothpaste was delivered in a pump format that cleverly showcased the two benefits, with the baking soda in one side and the peroxide in the other. Mentadent quickly established a large foothold. Colgate and Aquafresh reacted swiftly. For its part, said Kehoe, P&G seemed reluctant to admit that the playing field had shifted: "We've now got a new game being played, and it's not our game."[10]

Another attempt at a therapeutic breakthrough, Crest Gum Care, was launched in 1995. Crest Gum Care was the first dentifrice in the United States specifically designed to combat gingivitis (gum disease). The product had two big problems, however: It tasted terrible, and—like the ill-fated Teel liquid dentifrice of the 1940s and 1950s—it stained teeth. (Staining was due to the active ingredient used to prevent gingivitis.) At any rate, it turned out that consumers were not attracted to a toothpaste whose sole claim was that it fought gum disease. After turning in lackluster results, Crest Gum Care was withdrawn.

Not until 1996 did P&G finally respond to the consumer demand for baking soda. Crest's share was down 10 points by this time, and the business press was highlighting the brand's decline. In 1997, the *New York Times* labeled Crest's stumble as "one of P&G's biggest missteps in recent years and certainly among its most embarrassing."[11]

The final blow occurred in 1997–1998, with Colgate's U.S. introduction of Total, an all-in-one formula that combined all the available therapeutic and cosmetic benefits. Total had been sold abroad since 1992, but had been bogged down in the FDA approval process in the United States. When Total finally launched in 1997, Colgate pulled out all the stops, spending a record $100 million, the biggest marketing campaign in the company's history. In less than six months, Total overtook Crest to become the best-selling toothpaste in the United States and the only one with an FDA-approved claim that it helped prevent gum disease. Total's distinguishing claim, in addition to the combination of benefits, was that it contained triclosan, an antibacterial ingredient found in no other toothpaste in the United States. Procter & Gamble sold triclosan-based Crest Ultra in Canada, but its own clinical trials suggested that triclosan was a relatively weak active ingredient. Colgate's clinical trials and savvy marketing created a compelling case that triclosan worked, however, making Total the most significant U.S. dentifrice launch in a decade. In its first year, Colgate gained 5.6 percentage points of market share, pushing its overall share to 29 percent, versus P&G's 26 percent. Pundits characterized Colgate's victory over Crest as the equivalent of Pepsi beating Coke, Burger King trouncing McDonald's, or Avis overtaking Hertz. The perennial number two brand had knocked out the U.S. champion.[12]

Procter & Gamble had been well aware of Total's success abroad, but drew the wrong lesson about its significance. The impending threat focused P&G even more tightly on searching for an elusive therapeutic breakthrough. Ironically, P&G itself had developed an all-in-one platform, Multi-Care, and had actually launched it several months before Total. But Multi-Care was not backed by the deep clinical research and all-out marketing blitz that characterized Total—or, for that matter, the original Crest. Instead, Multi-Care was primarily a defensive move. "Total had a far bigger set of claims that it could make relative to Multi-Care," Kehoe acknowledged, referring to the fifteen to twenty years of clinical experience behind Total's U.S. launch. Colgate "bet the company on it" and "consolidated itself in the eyes of Wall Street as a winning company. . . . [It] was a calculated bet and, frankly, a very good one."[13]

Internationally, Colgate also raced ahead. Both it and Unilever had pushed into overseas markets significantly before P&G, so they enjoyed first-mover advantages as the market became global. Colgate, for example, standardized the formula and packaging of its toothpaste in the early 1980s. Although P&G had pioneered tartar control, in 1986 it was Colgate that launched tartar-control products around the world, using the same advertising in twenty countries. Meanwhile, Crest continued to hold only a minuscule share in the United Kingdom. The P&G entrant in Germany, Blend-a-Med (part of the 1987 Blendax acquisition), and the one in Italy, AZ (part of the 1985 Richardson-Vicks acquisition), had higher but not dominant shares.[14] In 2001, John Smale, who had been instrumental in Crest's early U.S. success, acknowledged that in "hindsight, it was a major failure" not to have taken Crest international after the 1960 acceptance by the American Dental Association. He cited the lack of interest among the international managers, who "had their hands full in trying to get their way into leadership positions in laundry products in Europe."[15] Afterward, Pampers, hair care, and then Always were given higher priority over the oral care products.

Moving Brand Equity into New Categories: SpinBrush and Whitestrips

Whitening toothpastes was the one subcategory in oral care that proved able to withstand the Total juggernaut.[16] Retailers looked to whiteners as the most promising way to regain consumer interest in the dentifrice category as well as an excellent way to increase gross margins. In the early 1980s, toothpaste prices were based largely on tube size, with the average being about

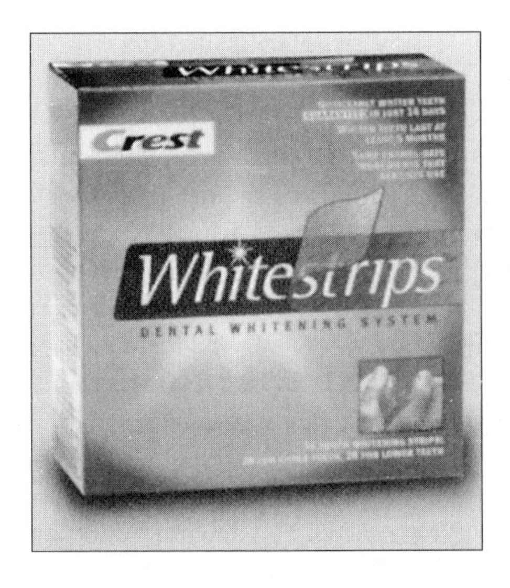

With the introduction of Crest Whitestrips in 2000, P&G significantly expanded the brand franchise, acknowledging that Crest had to stand for more than its therapeutic benefits.

$1.99; seven or eight years later, a six-ounce tube of one whitening paste sold for $7.00.[17] Procter & Gamble itself belatedly entered the growing segment, with Crest Extra Whitening toothpaste, at the end of 1997. With an innovative abrasive, the product pushed Crest's share appreciably higher. But in reality, the brand was still playing catch-up rather than truly innovating.

Finally, in the late 1990s, P&G achieved a breakthrough in the laboratory: a whitening product that paralleled the expensive bleaching techniques used by dentists. Crest Whitestrips, as the product came to be called, signaled that P&G had finally embraced the idea that consumers wanted cosmetic, or what the company labeled social, benefits.

As with many of its most significant innovations, the breakthrough happened almost serendipitously. The story began with a partnership that developed between thirty-year company veteran Bob Dirksing and a young chemical engineer named Paul Sagel.[18] Dirksing was a fellow of the prestigious Victor Mills Society, a singular R&D honor within P&G. A recognized innovator, he taught creativity classes to company employees around the world. In January 1997, Sagel made his first trip to Winton Hill Technical Center to meet Dirksing. The two immediately hit it off and spent several hours talking about bleaching. At the time, tooth bleaching had begun to attract greater consumer interest, a natural outgrowth of the recent popularity of whitening toothpastes. But it was done almost exclusively by dentists, who charged anywhere from three hundred to eight hundred dollars for the procedure. Still a small business, bleaching was nevertheless growing rapidly and attracted much excited attention from the media. Prospects for growing this market were clearly good, but existing home-bleaching systems performed poorly compared to what dentists achieved. Concerns about safety, reinforced by dentists' desire for bleaching to be supervised, inhibited the development of home bleaching products.

This was the state of affairs when Dirksing, Sagel, and the rest of the tooth-bleaching team began kicking ideas around. Typical of a P&G development project, this one began by their first asking a basic question: Does tooth bleaching work at all? According to Sagel, Crest technicians tended to think "that you could not change tooth color—it was impossible." The team conducted clinical trials, which confirmed that tooth color could indeed be changed. With that finding established, Dirksing and Sagel went on to the next problem: How can the gel be applied to teeth and remain there long enough to do its work? The initial approach we were taking," Sagel explained, "was 'let's go make a better mousetrap.'" They worked on an improved version of the device used by dentists. The two spent a couple of weeks prototyping trays that consumers could use at home.

Sagel soon noticed that the amount of bleaching gel needed to accomplish the job was actually very small: "The only thing that really matters is surface concentration of peroxide on the tooth, which would drive it in there to get the bleaching effect." Sagel and Dirksing concluded that what was needed was some way to keep a very thin layer of gel on the teeth. They first attempted to mold a thin wax sheet into trays. But, Sagel recalled, "as I thought about it, I said, 'Bob, if we could just find a *film* that was even thinner—I still think the tray is too thick—we'd be in good shape.'" In February 1997, Sagel went to see Dirksing at Winton Hill. "It just so happened that he had the Impress food wrap [an experimental plastic film that eventually became part of a joint venture with Clorox and Glad Wrap] sitting there, and we looked at it, and I said, 'This is it. This is what we need.'" The two smeared gel on the Impress film and cut it into small strips. "I put it on my teeth, stuck it on, and said, 'That's it!' We knew we had it instantly."

The secret to the effectiveness of Whitestrips was not the bleaching; using peroxide to whiten teeth had been around since at least the nineteenth century. Rather, the revolution lay in the delivery system, the thin film that could be put on the teeth in a matter of seconds. Whitestrips was sent out for product tests by the end of the summer of 1997. Patent protection was of particular concern, and Dirksing and Sagel spent between early and mid-1997 writing the patents themselves. "We didn't patent polyethylene strips because then you could use rubber. We patented the drapability . . . the thinness and the ability to conform to teeth," said Sagel.

Debate ensued about whether putting the Crest name on the whitening strips was appropriate. Those who disagreed feared the repercussions should the new product later prove unsuccessful or, worse, harmful. But supporters of putting the Crest brand name on the new product carried the day.

Crest Whitestrips was launched in mid-2000, in dentists' offices. Concerns about a backlash among this group were high because the product was an inexpensive alternative to a practice that some dentists found lucrative. But P&G had invested in building a strong clinical database to support the safety and efficacy of Whitestrips, precisely because it anticipated that professionals and consumers needed such reassurance. Members of the profession soon began confirming that the product was effective. According to one clinical professor at the University of Michigan School of Dentistry, "We used the Whitestrips when they first came out, and they work." He added, "It's not something we like to tell everybody."[19]

As in the original Crest launch, a team of professionals visited dental practitioners to answer questions. Face-to-face consultation helped communicate the benefits and ease of use. Some dentists even began arguing that Whitestrips could inspire people to take more interest in their teeth. Research showed that more than 50 percent of consumers wanted whiter teeth, but fewer than 5 percent actually had them professionally bleached. Whitestrips was positioned as an entry point to the more complete whitening that was done in dentists' offices. Procter & Gamble also offered dentists a professional kit containing strips with a higher gel concentration, a toothbrush, and toothpaste, which the dentists could offer for sale to their patients.[20]

In September 2000, Crest Whitestrips was made available for sale to the public through the Internet. A few months later, it was also offered through a TV home-shopping channel purveyor. Begun nine to twelve months in advance of the full retail launch, these seeding efforts were targeted at adventuresome consumers who were interested in trying new products and were undeterred by price. The retail price of the product was a concern; initially, Whitestrips sold for $44 a unit, well above most oral care products. But the buzz surrounding Whitestrips built quickly, allowing P&G to generate a large public relations campaign while concurrently conducting demonstrations for retailers. More than half a million units were sold through the Internet during these early months.[21]

Crest Whitestrips was launched in retail stores in May 2001. Almost single-handedly, it boosted sales in the fledgling over-the-counter whitening kit category by fivefold. Thirteen months after the full retail launch, more than five million people had tried Whitestrips, with some 90 percent indicating that they would recommend the product to an average of five people. In its first year, retail sales of Whitestrips totaled $225 million, making it one of the most successful consumer product launches of the previous five years.[22]

Meanwhile, another initiative was under way in the oral care unit, this one in power toothbrushes. Procter & Gamble had earlier recognized that the category represented a growing trend, but believed that the company's core competencies were not suited to producing an electrical product. In 2000, a fast-selling, battery-operated toothbrush called SpinBrush caught the eye of the oral care team. The SpinBrush had been developed two years earlier by a small start-up called Dr. John's, specifically with the idea of selling it to P&G. SpinBrush was already outselling by a wide margin all other power toothbrushes, including Colgate's recently launched Actibrush. Dr. John's got an appointment to see P&G in July 2000. Six months later, P&G acquired the company for $475 million, agreeing to retain three of the original founders for a year and half to help expand SpinBrush's market. *BusinessWeek* commented that the move was "unheard of at the insular company." Procter & Gamble "adopted a very external focus," confirmed Shekhar Mitra, global manager for oral care R&D. "This was a first for the Crest brand in a long, long time."[23]

Crest SpinBrush offered a benefit similar to Whitestrips in that it dramatically reduced the price of something that had previously been perceived as too expensive. Most consumers had shied away from power toothbrushes because it meant trading in their $3 manual toothbrushes for ones costing between $30 to well over $100. SpinBrush bridged the gap by delivering a power toothbrush that could be sold for $5 to $6.

Unlike other Crest products, the SpinBrush arrived externally via acquisition.

In addition to its substantially lower cost, SpinBrush featured two patented innovations. One was using a rotating head in combination with a fixed head, which gave the user a feeling that was similar to a manual toothbrush. "It was bigger," Kehoe explained. "There was more brush up against the teeth than just the standard little rotary heads that you see in many of the electric brushes today." The other important invention was the "try me" button on the package, which consumers could press in the store. The feature came from the toy industry and was an important element in persuading people to try the product.[24]

With SpinBrush, P&G envisaged leading manual toothbrush users to power ones, in much the same way that Pampers had led parents from cloth to disposable diapers. Because the aim was to change a practice that people already engaged in, rather than to create a wholly new and unfamiliar one, the potential market was huge: Nine out of every ten brushes bought in the United States were manual brushes. Company research showed that significant health benefits could be gained by switching to a power toothbrush. "The classic dilemma in the United States is that dentists say you should brush for one and a half to two minutes," said Bruce Byrnes, president of global health care. But the "average American brushes for 47 seconds." Brushing for much longer with a conventional toothbrush was simply a chore for most people, and children, in particular, tended not to do it thoroughly. Switching to a power toothbrush mitigated many of the problems. "We've got clinical studies showing much better plaque removal, much better brushing habits [with SpinBrush]," said Kehoe. "One of the great things is that both the kids and adults brush about 30 to 40 percent longer." Crest SpinBrush sales quadrupled during the first year of ownership, as P&G took it to more than twenty countries, one of the company's quickest-ever global rollouts. In the United States, SpinBrush soon outsold all other toothbrushes, manual or power.[25]

Whitestrips and SpinBrush revitalized the Crest brand in the United States and established P&G as an innovator in new oral care categories. Unlike the situation during the 1980s and 1990s, said Kehoe, the company was now "anticipating the trend before it happened and driving it." Crest toothpaste recovered from its low point, which occurred some four or five months after Total hit the market in 1998. Both Crest and Colgate grew at the expense of others, as consumers increasingly turned to the most trusted toothpaste brands for benefits such as whitening, tartar control, and breath freshening. Although Colgate sold more toothpaste, SpinBrush and Whitestrips vaulted Crest back in the lead in the overall oral care business as measured by dollar share. In 2001–2002, Crest became P&G's twelfth billion-dollar brand. Industry observers pointed to the brand's success in new categories as a model for how P&G could grow in the future.[26]

The International Market

Internationally, the story of the previous two decades also began to change. The 1990s saw the oral care business helping lead the charge into Central and Eastern Europe as well as China. Learning from past mistakes, P&G was quicker to take advantage of international opportunities, including the breakup of the former Soviet Union, and the Chinese government's attempts to open the country gradually to outside market forces. In both cases, P&G entered on a more equal footing with Colgate and Unilever than was the case in Western Europe and Latin America. However, both companies preceded P&G into the new regions by several years and represented serious competitive threats.

At the start of the twenty-first century, P&G's oral care business had largely regained its lost leadership in the United States and was growing rapidly in a number of foreign markets. Previously, said Paul Cootes, associate director of R&D in the Beijing Technical Center, the unspoken questions had been "Is Oral Care part of our future? What do we do with this Crest brand?" With Whitestrips and SpinBrush, and with the business growing substantially in Eastern Europe and in China, oral care "is again back in the center of things."[27]

Olay: From "Oil of Old Lady" to Billion-Dollar Brand

The effort to broaden Crest's brand equity is a story of recovery. The expansion of the brand started reactively, as a response to competitors' moves, then subsequently acquired coherent, strategic, internal direction and momentum. The case of Olay offers a parallel story—of broadening the equity and stretching the brand—in a different strategic context. Over the 1990s, P&G took what had been a strong but static brand in a niche category, Oil of Olay, and refashioned it as the basis for a series of initiatives in a suddenly fast-growing category. By 2003, Olay had joined the roster of billion-dollar P&G brands. If Crest illustrates the possibilities brand equity holds for revitalization, Olay illustrates the opportunities the concept opens for proactive innovation and growth.

Procter & Gamble inherited Olay when it acquired Richardson-Vicks Inc., in 1985. The brand had not weighed heavily in the decision to make the acquisition (which had drawn P&G's interest mainly because of RVI's over-the-counter drug brands and global scope of operations). Oil of Olay (as the brand was then known) was solidly entrenched in its market niche, holding leading shares in the United States, United Kingdom, Canada, Australia, and the Philippines; smaller though substantial shares in major Western European markets; and a strong number two position in Hong Kong.[28] That niche was closely bounded, however. In the consumer imagination, Oil of Olay represented a pink moisturizing beauty lotion used mainly by older women. It was a healthy brand but a relatively minor one, with an aging customer base and narrow prospects—"a solid performer, but not a star," in the characterization of Susan Arnold, head of P&G's beauty and feminine protection unit. Within the industry, the brand was known as "Oil of Old Lady."[29]

On the other hand, the skin care market was entering a period of rapid growth and evolution. Through the late 1980s and into the 1990s, the face creams and lotions category grew at an average annual rate of 10 percent in the United States, with internal company research indicating the market would reach one billion dollars by 1995 and continue to grow in following years, making it "a true 'core' category for the mass retail outlets."[30] Aging populations in the United States and Europe, coupled with increasing consumer awareness of the effects of sun on skin and the emergence of a multitude of new skin care products, all contributed to the trend.

Procter & Gamble saw the opportunity opening, but vacillated over how to respond. As Gina Drosos (who would later acquire oversight of Olay) pointed out, the company was still relatively inexperienced in marketing beauty brands, unfamiliar with the skin care market specifically, and dealing moreover with brands it had inherited rather than grown internally. Over the late 1980s, the company acquired a cluster of skin care brands, including Oil of Olay (1985), Clearasil (also acquired via RVI, 1985), Bain de Soleil (1987), Noxzema (1989), and SK-II (1991, via Max Factor), each offering distinct benefits, each focused on different market segments. It took some time to sort through this somewhat scattered portfolio and craft a cohesive strategy.[31]

Oil of Olay, meanwhile, remained relatively static. Procter & Gamble put some basic innovation into the brand in the years immediately following acquisition, including a Cleansing line in 1990, Daily UV Protectant in 1991, an Olay beauty bar in 1993, and Body Wash in 1994. Momentum behind the brand then slowed, however, as Oil of Olay entered what Drosos conceded was "a pretty blank period of innovation for a few years." Significantly, strategic indecision coincided with dramatic shifts in the marketplace. By the mid-1990s, competitors were launching products incorporating impressive new skin care technologies. For example, Unilever's successful global relaunch of Ponds, which incorporated an alpha hydroxy formulation, offered consumers state-of-the-art, new antiaging benefits. "We've been out-ideaed this past year," admitted beauty care head Robert Blanchard in 1996. In the face of these developments, Olay's share slipped significantly.[32]

The turning point was coming, however. The eye-opening success of the alpha-hydroxy-based new skin care brands sent a powerful wake-up call. If

P&G wanted to stay in the category, its beauty care strategists realized, they would have to innovate. At the same time, consensus was settling on Oil of Olay as the brand vehicle for innovation. Research indicated the brand had established a unique relationship with consumers. "Women trusted it," Drosos explained. "They did not always use it—'That's my grandmother's brand,' we'd hear—but they trusted it."[33] It was also a brand with particularly promising global prospects, a formerly obscure aspect of Olay that grew more prominent as the company reorganized its brands within globalized matrix structures over the late 1990s. Belatedly, then, but with growing strategic commitment, P&G identified Olay as a brand with substantial untapped possibilities.

To realize this potential, the brand needed to recover its innovation edge and reestablish its relevance to women's lives and aspirations. Accordingly, P&G undertook an intensive research program interviewing thousands of consumers worldwide, probing deeply and widely into their perceptions and experiences of aging, appearance, skin care, and a host of related issues. Key insights emerged. Women, researchers discovered, worried about much more than lines and wrinkles. When they thought about their skin, they also thought about tone, texture, dryness, age spots, and other symptoms of creeping age. Besides wanting to preserve their skin's appearance, they also worried about their skin's health. Refining a mass of data, the company identified what it called the Seven Signs of Aging. It then assigned an R&D team in its skin care labs in the Sharon Woods Technical Center in Cincinnati, Ohio, to develop a line of products that would treat all seven in a comprehensive, holistically therapeutic way.

The result of this initiative was Olay Total Effects, a line of products that incorporated breakthrough skin care innovations. Based on a patented formulation the company labeled Vitaniacin, which blended vitamin E, provitamin B5 (panthenol), and niacinamide (vitamin B3), Total Effects brought a unique offering to market.[34] "Anti-aging products tend to be singly-focused," explained P&G marketing director Michael Kuremsky. "Total Effects delivers against both vectors—skin's beauty and skin's health."[35] To mark the occasion, P&G formally dropped "Oil of" and rechristened the brand simply "Olay." "Love the Skin You're In" became the clever marketing catchphrase.

Rechanneling the Brand: Crafting Olay's First Moment of Truth

In working its way toward Total Effects, P&G had begun to significantly broaden Olay's brand equity. The goal was not simply to refresh the brand, but to fundamentally reposition it on a substantially bigger platform. Procter

& Gamble had moved boldly, but not unilaterally. Hard-earned, carefully sifted consumer understanding shaped the initiative. The Seven Signs of Aging had come directly out of this process. So too had an even more ambitious effort to rechannel Olay's positioning and distribution. What P&G heard when it talked to consumers about skin care was that women believed that the best skin care products were sold in department stores, at significantly higher prices than the brands available in mass outlets. In short, women felt they got what they paid for. Accordingly, Olay's strategists mapped out a highly distinctive, even revolutionary strategy for distributing the brand. They were determined to position Olay at the high end of the market, dramatically recentering its underlying equity. At the same time, they recognized that limiting distribution to so-called prestige outlets, meaning beauty counters in department stores, would consign Olay to a small corner of a market that research indicated could be much wider. Oil of Olay had retailed (in the United States) at around $6, as compared to an average price for a mass-distributed facial moisturizer of $8. Total Effects went to market with a price point of $19.99. Yet it went to the mass market, including outlets like Wal-Mart.

It was this aspect of Total Effects that stirred up the most internal debate as P&G weighed whether to commit to launch. To this point, Olay's story represented classic P&G tactics, time-honored and market-tested: Recognizing the need to reconnect to consumers, the company undertook a massive round of market research and product development. On the other hand, the decision to reposition the brand in such a sharply different segment of the market at a premium of more than 250 percent of the brand's former price

The preparation and testing for the launch of Olay Total Effects focused as much on the brand's retail presentation as it did on the product and packaging.

point represented a dramatic departure. For what Total Effects proposed, essentially, was to carve out an entirely new market segment, straddling the prestige market in department stores and the mass market in supermarket and drugstore outlets. "It was a really big jump for Olay," Drosos acknowledged. Yet it was not a blind one. Procter & Gamble was planning on the basis of rigorous market research, a hallmark approach that bolstered confidence in the new strategy. "The thing that made us feel comfortable . . . was getting close to the consumer and understanding what she wanted . . . knowing that we had a really powerful technology that worked better than even what she thought the best brands could do. And being bold enough to make that comparison."[36]

Major retail partners were skeptical about the new line, at first. After all, twenty-dollar bottles of skin lotion were not standard items in inventories like Wal-Mart's. Consequently, P&G, working in a new spirit of partnership and collaboration with its customers, took care to invite retailers in early in the planning process, sharing research, soliciting input and ideas, and specifically asking retailers what aspects of the brand's marketing they wanted tested. The test market, which ran in Peoria for seven months, covered supermarkets, drug outlets, and other mass merchandisers, combing the stores for different presentation techniques. At the same time, the Total Effects team benchmarked department store merchandising techniques, including the in-store theater techniques (e.g., stationing live "testers" by display counters) that gave department store brands their aura of prestige. Consumers, too, were consulted. The marketing team asked them what they liked and did not like about buying products like skin care lotion in outlets like department stores. In other words, Olay's marketing was envisioned in broad, comprehensive terms, paying close attention to what A. G. Lafley (who would shortly be assuming leadership as P&G's chief executive) called the "first moment of truth"—the in-store purchasing experience. These efforts cemented customers' commitment to the campaign and fine-tuned a marketing package that performed excellently in Peoria's test market, leading to national launch seven months later.

The results were impressive. Total Effects, in combination with a new line of lathering cleansing cloths called Daily Facials, quickly acquired marketplace momentum. By 2003, the Olay brand was passing the threshold to join P&G's elite category of billion-dollar brands.

The Boundaries of Brand Equity

Reconfiguring brands in terms of brand equity does not make them endlessly elastic. They remain every bit as prone to overextension and irrelevance as ever. Olay itself illustrates the limits of ill-conceived application. In 1999, even as it was preparing Total Effects for launch, the company launched a major initiative in color cosmetics under the Olay brand. Beginning in Europe, the program marshaled a massive marketing support plan costing several hundred million dollars . . . and failed to catch on with consumers.

In retrospect, Olay's brand team found flaws in the color cosmetics initiative. The venture did not, for example, build off Olay's core associations. Rather than offer state-of-the-art skin care products as consumers would expect from Olay, it went to market with me-too technology. In fact, the foundations did not even contain UV protection or antiaging ingredients. Efforts to reposition the campaign took the brand even further astray, generating very color-oriented, Revlon-like copy and imagery. The result was not disastrous, in marketplace terms. But the costly initiative fell short of performance goals and was pulled from shelves.

The lesson, in hindsight, is clear: Brand equity needs to be nurtured and extended organically, staying true to consumers' perceptions and understanding of a given brand. Extensions and initiatives still need to be tested rigorously and planned carefully. Discipline remains absolutely essential. Which means, as global marketing officer Jim Stengel has pointed out, that the concept of brand equity is in fact classic P&G: a tool for analysis and understanding, rather than a license for haphazard expansion.

At the same time, the concept has significantly reoriented thinking within the company about its brands and their potentials. "We've always thought about what's different about our brands. That's been part of our heritage for decades and decades," Stengel observed. "I think, as our brands become larger and more multidimensional, we started thinking about their essence and what they mean to the consumer in a deeper way."[37]

As with other stages in P&G's evolution of brand building, learning the rules of brand equity has been an intensive process, with considerable experimentation and a number of missteps. Indeed, Stengel conceded, the company probably had more negative experiences than positive ones in its early days of learning the concept: "We missed many opportunities by not thinking broadly and aspirationally about our brands." Nevertheless, P&G has been learning steadily, he maintained, and in the process developing a powerful new set of tools for building and rebuilding its brands.

Redefining Brands in Perspective

Procter & Gamble's efforts over the late 1990s to revitalize brands and redefine the nature of their underlying equity were as varied as the brands themselves. Nevertheless, common themes were emerging by the first years of the twenty-first century. In general terms, P&G was significantly deepening its sense of brand equity. Traditional wisdom held that different benefits required the creation of different brands. Trying to make Crest stand for something more than cavity protection, this line of thinking ran, risked confusing the consumer and diluting the brand. After all, it was the single-message focus of Crest's original marketing campaigns that had indelibly established Crest in the marketplace as the dentifrice that controlled cavities—a positioning that had redefined the category and upheld market leadership for decades. Not surprisingly, it was hard to let go of that understanding of the brand.

Ultimately, however, P&G had to do just that—in the case of Crest and a series of other P&G brands. What P&G learned, over this period of experimentation, was that brands had big shoulders. Managed skillfully and sensitively, continuing to honor core promises, they could be deepened and broadened beyond original performance benefits. Brands were not limitlessly elastic, however. The company could not dictate the terms of brand equity. It still had to listen to consumer feedback and adhere to what it heard—more closely than ever, in fact. In short, the consumer remained boss. But once understood in its fullest dimensions, brand equity could become a platform for creative expansion and significant growth. So, for example, Crest could stand not just for cavity protection, but for "healthy, beautiful smiles." Olay could be applied not just to a high-end skin lotion, but to a range of skin care products tied to core technologies and marketing elements.

Other opportunities beckoned in other brands. The Pampers brand team, for example, redefined its brand equity as signifying not just disposable diapers or drier bottoms, but loving baby care. In Iams, brand managers took the core product of pet food as a basis for crafting a deeper equity in health-oriented pet care. Bounty became "mother's indispensable helper." In each of these cases and in a range of other P&G products, a broadening of the company's understanding of what the brand signified injected new energy and innovation and became the basis of revitalization over the 1990s and beyond.

The implications ran deep. Thinking in terms of brand equity still warned against tampering with the essential elements or understandings at the core of a brand. Specifically, the concept preserved the fundamental imperative that a brand stands for something inviolable. Reconceptualizing Crest as a brand equity gave the company license, in effect, to apply the brand to closely related products such as teeth whiteners and electric toothbrushes—as long as they clustered within the equity concept and delivered real, brand-relevant performance. Crest could not be applied, though, to beverages or lipstick.

On the other hand, using brand equity as a basis for revitalizing brands also helped prevent complacency or rigid, static adherence to inherited brand definitions. Indeed, the brand-equity concept underscored the need for continuous innovation and constant responsiveness to consumer signals. Crest's historical association with therapeutic benefits had limited the company's acceptance of cosmetic benefits for too long. After more than a decade of denial, said Kehoe, P&G finally acknowledged that "the consumer wants a combination of social and health" benefits. "They don't want a trade-off. So if the consumer is telling you that, you'd better be there."[38]

Finally, in the most basic sense, the story of revitalizing flagship brands and the concept of brand equities reminded people throughout P&G that even after more than a hundred years of experience, the company could still learn new things about its brands. Much as Crest could not afford to remain a rigid formula or a static set of products, P&G could not and cannot let itself imagine that it has ever fully mastered or definitively blueprinted the art of brand building. There is always more to learn, relearn, and unlearn.

CHAPTER EIGHTEEN

Prescription for Growth in Health Care

AT THE DAWN of the twenty-first century, P&G's leaders regard health care as one of the company's brightest business prospects. The health care business unit is smaller than those in fabric and home care, and baby and family care, but it is growing faster and is ultimately a much larger opportunity. And the business is changing P&G in the process, pushing in new directions, driving toward higher technology, stretching its vaunted skills in advertising and marketing, requiring more alliances, and demanding patience while awaiting the returns. Indeed, looking at the differences between slow-developing health care products and the fast-moving consumer goods for which P&G is justly famous, some outside analysts question whether the company's various interests are compatible. The health care industry is structurally quite different from the consumer products industry, with dissimilar economics, customers, and competitors. Procter & Gamble, it seems to such observers, does not belong in health care and is a long shot to succeed against entrenched giants such as Johnson & Johnson, Merck, Pfizer, GlaxoSmithKline, Novartis, Aventis, Bristol-Myers Squibb, and Wyeth.

Procter & Gamble, of course, looks at it differently.

While acutely aware of the contrasts between consumer and medical products, P&G also recognizes and values the similarities. For a company pursuing a purpose "to improve the lives of consumers," what better products to make than those that enhance consumers' health? A major segment of the health care industry, over-the-counter (OTC) drugs, moreover, plays to P&G's historical strengths in manufacturing, packaging, distribution, advertising, and branding. Even on the prescription-drug side, P&G developed its first pharmaceuticals through internal research, drawing on its deep knowledge of skin and oral care and its mastery of industrial chemistry. Before all these factors could contribute to P&G's success in health care, however, the company had to make acquisitions and be willing to form partnerships.

Procter & Gamble's experience in health care illustrates several important topics and themes in the company's history. First, it provides yet one more illustration of the theme of technological connections, that is, how R&D and other capabilities of the business could combine to create new opportunities. Second, it shows how the company has built a major growth business via a combination of internal development, acquisitions, and alliances. And third, the case story demonstrates the continuing evolution of the business portfolio as P&G proceeds on its long journey from making soap and candles in nineteenth-century Cincinnati to operating today as a diversified, high-technology, and global consumer products and life sciences company.

Entry

In 1981, Harry Tecklenburg, senior vice president for R&D, reflected on the origins of P&G's fledgling business in health care. Brands such as Crest and Head & Shoulders helped prepare the way by delivering important medical benefits. However, the company's real interest in health care, noted Tecklenburg, arose "directly from leads developed in our consumer product research activities in the 1960s and early 1970s. Specifically, our long-standing and continuing research programs in nutrition, dentistry, lipids, and skin have led to specific pharmaceutical products leads. In a very real sense, we have done nothing more than follow our noses."[1]

The trail that P&G's researchers sniffed out began in the late 1960s with the discovery of the unlikely connection between wash water and gum disease. In studying the chemistry of wash water, research scientist Willy Lange had learned from Henkel about a diphosphonate (more familiarly called a bisphosphonate) compound, ethane-l-hydroxy-l,l-diphosphonate (EHDP). This compound acted as a chelating agent to suspend minerals such as calcium and magnesium and prevent them from depositing on garments. To Lange and others at P&G, EHDP held promise of solving a nagging problem with synthetic detergents: the tendency of minerals in the wash water to tinge garments with a grayish hue. Eventually, EHDP was formulated into Tide, where it succeeded in banishing "tattletale gray."[2]

While research on EHDP as an ingredient of detergents was under way, another P&G research team grew interested in the compound. At Miami Valley Laboratories, M. David Francis, a biochemist who had worked on the fluoridation of Crest, had turned his attention to another common oral malady: the buildup of calculus (tartar) on teeth, which, unchecked over time,

Chemist David Francis's research on tartar-control dentifrices opened up P&G's path into pharmaceuticals.

caused serious periodontal problems. News of EHDP intrigued Francis. He reasoned that a chelating agent that suspended calcium in wash water might also keep the mineral, a main constituent of tartar, from building up on teeth. When he first experimented with EHDP, Francis was amazed: "I couldn't believe my eyes because it was such a strong chelator." Although he feared that the compound would destroy the surface of teeth, Francis's research showed just the opposite: "It did not do *any* damage to the enamel."[3]

Further investigations into EHDP revealed that the compound inhibited the formation and growth of calcium crystals and thus had high potential to protect teeth against tartar buildup. This work was the genesis of Tartar Control Crest, but Francis and his colleague John Gray did not stop there. They saw still more potential for bisphosphonates in treating other medical conditions, especially bone diseases. With another colleague, Bill King, Francis undertook "a really extensive biological study of the systemic effect of EHDP" on bones. In this study, the researchers found that the compound could both inhibit bone growth and block the dissolution of bone material. In other words, as Francis later put it, bisphosphonates could provide a chemical mechanism "to place calcium where it's needed, and keep it from forming where it shouldn't be."[4]

During the late 1960s and early 1970s, Francis and his colleagues continued to work on EHDP, focusing on a compound called etidronate, which offered potential to treat some bone conditions such as heterotopic ossification (the calcification of the soft tissue surrounding bones and joints), Paget's disease (the abnormal remodeling of bone, causing pain and usually weakness and the tendency to fracture), and osteoporosis (thinning of bone, a common problem in elderly people, especially women). Another application of etidronate was in combination with another compound as a bone-scanning agent. In 1973, P&G secured regulatory approval for the scanning agent and introduced its first trademarked pharmaceutical product, Osteoscan.[5]

Meanwhile, Francis and his colleagues worked on the expensive, time-consuming, and laborious process of obtaining approval from regulatory agencies in the United States and other nations for use of etidronate as a drug to treat metabolic bone conditions such as Paget's disease and osteoporosis. In the United States, the FDA approval process entailed repeated, rigorous testing and evaluation and clinical trials. Although the process typically consumed eight and one-half years, it often took longer—sometimes nearly twice as long.[6] In 1978, P&G finally obtained its first FDA approval of a prescription drug, Didronel (etidronate), as a treatment for Paget's disease. Approval for treatment of various forms of heterotopic ossification followed several years later. The company also began the long, arduous process of gaining approval for Didronel in the United States and abroad as a treatment for osteoporosis, a much more common malady that afflicted many millions of elderly people.

During the 1970s, P&G also developed another prescription drug product, Topicycline, a topical treatment for acne, which also received FDA approval in 1978. The product, which delivers the antibiotic tetracycline quickly to infected areas by penetrating the skin, had tapped the company's knowledge about skin, surface chemistry, and oils and creams. Procter & Gamble researchers were also investigating other medical products, including those that could be sold OTC, as well as those requiring a doctor's prescription. With an eye on the huge OTC market for analgesics (pain remedies), for example, a team of researchers was investigating a new aspirin-delivery mechanism featuring coated particles in a capsule. Another project was closely related to the company's expertise in oral care and involved a new treatment for gingivitis.[7]

Procter & Gamble marketed its medical products through the Special Products Group, which included a handful of "detail" representatives who called on dental and medical specialists and also oversaw the company's institutional accounts with hospitals and schools. At the dawn of the 1980s, the medical business was very small—approximately five million dollars in revenues, as compared with total corporate sales of ten billion. As it invested to establish the new business of medical products, the company was also accepting losses significantly larger than revenues.[8]

While it was losing money, P&G was also gaining insight into how to succeed in health care. Tecklenburg pointed out that the success of Didronel "reduced some . . . uncertainty" and enabled him to claim in 1981 that P&G's "confidence and sophistication are increasing."[9]

Procter & Gamble's early experiences in medical products also taught the value of focus. Given the magnitude of investments necessary to succeed, Tecklenburg pointed out that the company could ill afford to pursue "a very diverse and unconnected program" that spread its research and marketing resources "broadly and thinly across a number of categories rather than in depth in several categories. Concentration is necessary to achieve sufficient learning necessary for success." In 1981, he proposed that P&G should emphasize two fundamental areas: bone metabolism and hyperglycemia. A shrewd, efficient program of investment, he believed, would enable the company to break even within five years. The company might reach that goal faster by acquiring "a freestanding and viable pharmaceutical operation."[10]

The First Big Bets

The health care industry in the early 1980s held many temptations for P&G. To begin with, it was vast, global, and growing rapidly. The sheer scale was staggering: The market was more than ten times the size of fabric care, paper, or other big industries in which P&G had made its mark. Demographic trends in the developed economies were also highly encouraging. The population in many nations had bulged after World War II, and by the 1980s, the average age was inching up into the upper thirties and low forties. These trends would drive rising demand for medical products for decades. Another big attraction was the fragmented structure of the industry. While the field was populated with large companies, none possessed even a 10 percent share. No company dominated more than a few segments or had a commanding global position.

In the early 1980s, the pharmaceutical industry was undergoing profound changes and generating opportunities for new entrants. Before World War II, the industry had been small, rather sleepy, and not especially profitable. The leading competitors included dozens of old-line companies, many of which were nearly as old as P&G. Some of these companies manufactured or supplied intermediate chemicals for home remedies—what later became the OTC market, as distinct from the newer, prescription-drug market. In the 1940s and 1950s, a series of technological breakthroughs (including government-supported research on antibiotics during the war) combined with an explosion of investment in heath care, much of it funded by health insurance, to stimulate the market for prescription drugs. Whereas prescription drugs had accounted for only 32 percent of all consumer expenditures on medicines in 1929, they accounted for 83 percent by 1969.[11]

The 1970s and 1980s witnessed still more technological changes, as scientists gained better understanding of microbial biology and enzymology and developed new techniques for drug discovery and genetic engineering. The industry became more research-intensive, requiring much higher investments, but also producing bigger rewards for significant breakthroughs. During the 1980s, a number of companies developed blockbuster drugs with annual sales surpassing $500 million and generating huge profits. Among these were Glaxo's Zantac and SmithKline Beecham's Tagamet (treatments for gastric ulcers), Squibb's Capoten and Merck's Vasotec (treatments for hypertension and congestive heart failure), Syntex Corporation's Naprosyn (anti-inflammatory analgesic), and Eli Lilly's Prozac (antidepressant). The R&D expenditures in the industry began to average 10 percent or more of sales, while the leading competitors enjoyed returns on capital of 20 percent or more. The heavy investments and big risks exacted a toll on the industry, however, and the 1980s witnessed the beginnings of consolidation. There were mergers between SmithKline and Beecham, Bristol-Myers and Squibb, and Rorer and Rhône-Poulenc; a wave of acquisitions that saw the sales of A. H. Robins and Sterling Drug; and numerous joint ventures, including Merck's separate deals with DuPont and Johnson & Johnson.[12]

In sum, the health care industry in the 1980s seemed highly promising to P&G—if the company could find the right path and overcome the entry barriers. The company was first and primarily interested in the OTC segment, where its core strengths, senior managers believed, would enable it to succeed rapidly. But P&G also continued to pursue development of prescription drugs. As John Smale later put it, "an underlying factor" in the company's decision to proceed "was the confidence the management had built up over time in P&G's inherent product innovation abilities."[13]

As discussed earlier in the book, P&G boosted its fortunes in both the OTC and the prescription segments by several key acquisitions in the mid-1980s. Norwich Eaton, acquired in 1982 for $371 million, provided P&G with popular OTC brands such as Pepto-Bismol, a remedy for a variety of stomach ailments, and Chloraseptic, a sore-throat remedy, as well as several prescription drugs. Besides these products, the acquisition included an R&D organization in Norwich, New York, and a joint venture in West Germany.

The next several years constituted a crash course for P&G in learning a new business. Although many Norwich Eaton managers remained in place, a team of P&G executives led by Charlie Carroll took charge of the OTC product lines. They focused primarily on Pepto-Bismol and Chloraseptic, and P&G's advertising capabilities and greater market coverage provided an immediate boost to both brands. Sales of both medications surged nearly 30 percent in the year after the acquisition. At the same time, P&G launched programs to refresh and reposition Pepto-Bismol and Chloraseptic. Although the basic product formulas were monographic—that is, the FDA specified them—P&G could and did modify packaging, delivery regimens, and brand messages. Meanwhile, P&G weeded and pruned other brands from Norwich Eaton's OTC portfolio, divesting minor brands and products, including Unguentine antiseptic, saccharin tablets, and an athlete's foot remedy.[14]

In the fall of 1985, P&G dramatically strengthened its OTC business by closing two more deals. The first, at a cost of $312 million, involved the OTC lines of Monsanto's pharmaceutical subsidiary, G. D. Searle & Co. These products included Metamucil, the leading laxative in the United States; Dramamine, the leading anti-motion-sickness remedy; and Icy Hot, a topical pain reliever for sore muscles and other minor ailments. Procter & Gamble was especially interested in Metamucil as a complement to Pepto-Bismol in stomach remedies. Immediately after the deal, P&G began to work some of the same magic on Metamucil that it had on Pepto-Bismol and Chloraseptic.[15]

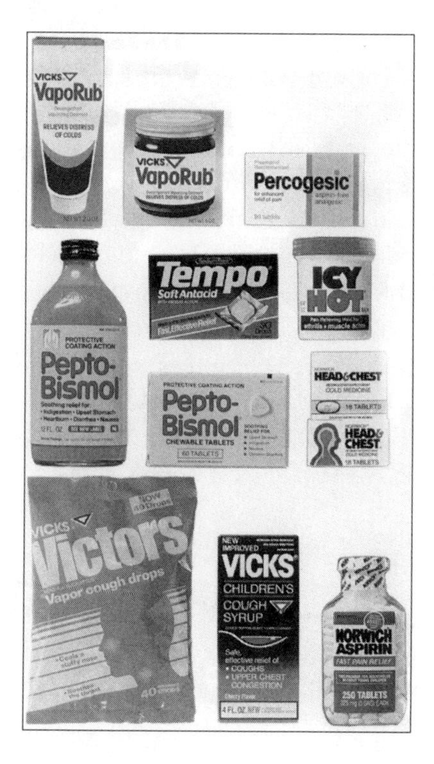

Brands acquired from Norwich Eaton (1982), Searle (1985), and Richardson-Vicks (1985) boosted P&G's presence in over-the-counter medicines (not all shown here).

The second and much bigger acquisition in 1985 was Richardson-Vicks Inc. (RVI). A company that resembled P&G in important ways, RVI was a diversified maker of consumer products with a substantial portfolio of OTC brands. These included cough syrup (Vicks Formula 44), nasal decongestants (Vicks VapoRub and Sinex), and cough and cold remedies (NyQuil and DayCare).[16]

The Searle and RVI acquisitions, added to the Norwich Eaton deal, meant that P&G had invested approximately one billion dollars between 1982 and 1985 to become a major factor in health care. The company's dominance was especially apparent on the OTC side, with a product portfolio accounting for about 10 percent of the total U.S. market.[17] Nor was P&G through with acquisitions, although it resumed a discriminating approach to making deals, looking for brands and businesses like those of Searle, which would complement those already in-house, as opposed to opportunities that would take the company into wholly new areas. At the same time, P&G sought to grow via joint venture, especially in collaborating with pharmaceutical companies in switching their prescription drugs to OTC markets. During the 1980s, so-called OTC switches became increasingly popular, as drug companies entered or prepared for a new phase of competition after the expiration of patents on their leading drugs. Several blockbuster drugs, including the anti-peptic ulcer drugs SmithKline Beecham's Tagamet and Glaxo's Zantac, were among the candidates to be switched in the 1990s.[18]

In 1988, P&G formed a fifty-fifty joint venture with Palo Alto, California–based Syntex Corporation, producer of the blockbuster analgesic Naprosyn, to market an OTC version of the drug, as well as other products in both companies' pipelines. The partners planned to introduce a reformulated version of Naprosyn under the trade name Aleve. Procter & Gamble brought to the Syntex joint venture essentially the same qualities that it had contributed to Norwich Eaton, Searle, and RVI: its finely honed capabilities in product supply, marketing, and advertising, as well as its greater clout in the marketplace.[19]

By the late 1980s, P&G had succeeded in building a prominent OTC products business. On a related front, it was also making significant progress in prescription drugs.

Expanding the Foundation in Prescription Drugs

After the 1982 acquisition of Norwich Eaton, P&G operated that company's pharmaceutical business as an independent subsidiary, Norwich Eaton Pharmaceuticals, Inc. (NEPI). The idea was to use NEPI as a learning vehicle, much as P&G had used previous small acquisitions to learn more about food and paper. As Smale put it, the Norwich Eaton deal did not represent "a commitment that Procter [was] hell bound to get into the pharmaceutical business one way or another. It was a decision strategically that the company was going to pursue an experience in the pharmaceutical business. . . . Had we concluded that there were systemic reasons why we could not succeed . . . we would have turned away from it."[20]

With approximately two hundred research scientists on staff, NEPI significantly bolstered P&G's R&D capabilities in pharmaceuticals, including the capacity to conduct clinical studies and trials and manage the process of regulatory approval. At the same time, NEPI maintained a technical sales force of 330 people and far extended the reach of the handful of professional reps in P&G's Special Products Group.[21]

During the balance of the decade, P&G focused on sorting through its prescription-drug product lines and formulating a strategy for competing in the industry. The issues ranged from short-term developments such as bringing to market products already in the pipeline (e.g., P&G's Peridex antigingivitis mouthwash and NEPI's Macrobid for treatment of urinary tract infections), to medium-term challenges such as qualifying Didronel as a treatment for osteoporosis, to longer-term decisions about potential drugs at the beginning of the development cycle. At the same time, P&G had to think through basic strategic issues: In what segments of the industry would the company compete? How would it balance growth through internal development versus growth via licensing and acquisitions? And how would the company's efforts in OTC and prescription drugs relate?

In 1983, senior technical personnel at P&G proclaimed an "overall goal . . . to become a major factor in the healthcare industry, worldwide, in the 1990's." The company expected to succeed "via an intensive internal Research and Product Development effort in combination with an aggressive program to acquire externally developed products, technology, and scientific understanding." The company now identified five health care focus areas in which it would concentrate: (1) bone and tooth disorders, (2) gastrointestinal disorders, (3) pain, (4) infections, and (5) nutritional disorders. In selecting these focus areas, the company considered four factors: market size, needs unmet in the market, P&G's "technical right to succeed," and interactions between the focus areas that could produce synergistic benefits.[22]

Procter & Gamble was already positioned in each focus area through its own R&D and operations (on bone and tooth disorders) or that of NEPI. In some cases (pain relief and nutritional disorders), both entities had relevant experience and expertise. In nutritional disorders, for example, P&G had been working for decades on sucrose polyester (SPE), the progenitor of olestra, as a potential medical remedy for obesity; the company also had in development calcium compounds as potential additives to foods and beverages. Meanwhile, NEPI was already in the marketplace with Vivonex, its prescription nutritional supplement.

During the next several years, P&G carried out experiments, investigated new drugs, and explored acquisition and alliance opportunities in these focus areas. Learning from these efforts and initiatives fed back into decision making about whether to proceed in each area. Although Tecklenburg and other leaders recognized that they would eventually have to narrow P&G's focus further, they were reluctant to narrow their options too soon, "given the quality of leads in each area."[23]

In 1985, P&G scientists synthesized risedronate, the third-generation bisphosphonate. Risedronate held potential to become a far more powerful treatment for osteoporosis and osteoarthritis than either Didronel or the second-generation drug alendronate, which Merck would market under license as Fosamax. In 1988, P&G researchers achieved another breakthrough by identifying azilimide, a potassium channel blocker, for treatment of heart arrhythmia.[24]

Procter & Gamble also enhanced its position in prescription drugs through licensing and acquisitions. In 1985, for example, it obtained from Tillots-Pharma, a Swiss company, the rights to market Asacol, a drug for ulcerative colitis, in the Western Hemisphere. (Asacol was immediately cleared for use in Canada and approved in the United States in 1992.) In 1986, NEPI acquired Nativelle, a French specialist in cardiovascular drugs, and two years later, P&G bought Blendax, the German oral care products company. These deals bolstered P&G's presence in Europe, although the company still had to contend with the time-consuming process of securing regulatory approval in each national market. Meanwhile, the RVI acquisition further enhanced P&G's ability to market its health care products overseas.[25]

By the late 1980s, prescription pharmaceuticals remained a relatively small business for P&G (approximately $250 million in revenues), and because the company was investing heavily in R&D ahead of product introductions, the business was not profitable. Nonetheless, the company was making enough headway in prescription drugs that it began to rethink its strategy for competing in both OTC and prescription products. It was time for the next stage.

Commitment

Late in 1988, a study team took a fresh look at the strategy and structure of P&G's health care businesses. The team recommended the formation of a new organizational sector that would take responsibility for oral care, OTC, and prescription products. The recommendations took as given that the health care industry, broadly defined, "should be the Corporation's primary focus area for growth and profit in the years ahead." The group believed that by 2000, P&G could achieve $1 billion in prescription drug revenues, with an average after-tax margin of 20 percent. Combined with an OTC business (including oral care) projected at $2.7 billion and an after-tax margin of 12.5 percent, the total P&G health care business would reach $3.7 billion and $540 million of after-tax earnings. The proposed health care unit would include separate marketing organizations for OTC and prescription products, but common organizations for R&D and licensing and acquisitions.[26]

In 1990, P&G began acting on the study team's recommendations by forming a health care unit, with Mal Jozoff as the initial general manager. The unit included a Personal Health Care Division, under Tom Moore, with responsibility for OTC products in the United States, and NEPI, which was renamed P&G Pharmaceuticals in 1992 under Gil Cloyd. Procter & Gamble set its ambitions high. It sought to be a top ten health care company in the United States by 2000 and, by 2015, to be "the leading health care company worldwide."[27]

In 1991, P&G announced plans to consolidate its OTC and prescription drug operations at a massive new technical center in Mason, Ohio, some fifteen miles north of Cincinnati. Dedicated in July 1995, the new Health Care Research Center (HCRC) represented an investment of more than $300 million and housed up to twenty-five hundred people, including personnel drawn together from the Miami Valley Laboratory; Norwich, New York; and Shelton, Connecticut. At the dedication of HCRC, chief executive John Pepper pointed out that "we've made this tremendous investment in this complex . . . because health care is a foundation for the future growth of our Company. Our goals for growth in health care are aggressive and it is vital that we meet them. We intend to do that becoming the worldwide leader in over the counter health care products and we also intend to be the leader in pharmaceutical products in several major therapeutic areas where we are convinced that we can bring superior benefits to consumers."[28]

Although HCRC constituted a big bet on the future, it was only one of a number of significant initiatives and investments in health care that P&G made in the early 1990s. In 1991, azilimide (branded as Stedicor) entered phase 1 trials. Two years later, the company formally entered the cardiovascular market by forming a collaborative marketing agreement with Lederle Laboratories for Ziac and Zebeta, two agents for the treatment of hypertension. Procter & Gamble formed a joint venture with Mountain View, California–based Alza Corp. to commercialize drugs for the treatment of periodontal disease. Procter & Gamble also formed R&D partnerships in biotechnology with Houghten Pharmaceuticals and Genta, two San Diego–based firms, and with the University of Cincinnati Medical Center, for research in the areas of respiratory and pulmonary medicine. Another promising deal in 1992 was an agreement in principle with Pfizer to pursue the joint development of risedronate, later branded as Actonel. Moore estimated that the deal would save P&G about $200 million in R&D costs, hasten time to market, and permit P&G to share in the rights to several Pfizer drugs, including the promising antibiotic Zithromax.[29]

Procter & Gamble also expanded its activities overseas. In 1992, the company acquired complete ownership of Röhm Pharma, the fifty-fifty joint venture that had come with the Norwich Eaton acquisition. The new purchase gave P&G the rights to approximately two dozen pharmaceuticals, diagnostics, and vaccines and bolstered its presence in Europe's biggest national market. And after another two years, P&G closed a comparable deal, obtaining the assets and business of SmithKline Beecham's Italian subsidiary, which included the rights to manufacture and market five prescription drugs.[30]

Despite these significant investments, P&G struggled to attain its growth objectives. For one thing, growth across the industry was slowing down. By the early 1990s, an era of unparalleled prosperity for drug makers in the developed economies seemed to be ended, in part due to the spread of managed care in the United States and stricter price controls elsewhere. In the United States, for example, prescriptions for generic drugs (as opposed to brand-name drugs) rose from about 30 percent of prescriptions written in 1988 to about 50 percent in 1995.[31]

Meanwhile, P&G seriously underestimated the time and expense necessary to obtain approval of new drugs both in the United States and abroad. As drugs neared final approval, the resource commitments and risks for manufacturers climbed sharply. It was imperative to ensure that final clinical studies and trials went well.[32] Procter & Gamble learned this lesson bitterly in the case of Didronel. Although the company gained authorization to market the drug as a treatment for osteoporosis in Canada, the United Kingdom, and more than a dozen other countries, the drug failed to win FDA approval in the United States, where regulators were concerned that Didronel could increase risk of bone fractures after three years. This U.S. rejection was a devastating blow, since it denied P&G access to millions of potential customers and an annual business opportunity estimated at more than $500 million. It also enabled Merck's Fosamax to become by far the most common treatment for osteoporosis in the United States.[33]

Meanwhile, the joint venture with Pfizer to market Actonel collapsed in the early going, leaving P&G solely responsible for heavy development expenditures while searching for another partner. For a time, P&G considered developing and commercializing Actonel on its own, but eventually concluded that it was important to join forces with another big pharmaceutical company for the coming rivalry with Merck's Fosamax. On its own, P&G pushed Actonel into phase 3 trials in 1993. The development was one of the most comprehensive in the industry, involving more than 330 clinical investigators and sixteen thousand patients in eighteen countries. The payoff was potentially enormous, given estimates that 200 million people around the world would be at risk of osteoporosis within the following ten years.[34]

On the OTC side, P&G's results were mixed in the mid-1990s. On the one hand, many of its strongest brands—Pepto-Bismol, Metamucil, NyQuil, DayQuil (as DayCare was known after its repositioning), and Vicks Formula 44 fared well, buoyed by strong advertising and marketing. Even amid the OTC switches in gastrointestinal products—Tagamet, Zantac, Pepcid—Pepto-Bismol remained a popular remedy. The reason, said Tom Blinn, a manager who worked on the brand, is excellent marketing. "Technically, we did not do all that much to [the brand]. What makes Pepto-Bismol truly unique is its multisymptom positioning. It treats five symptoms: upset stomach, nausea, indigestion, diarrhea, and heartburn." Competitive products, he noted, focused on only one or two of these indications. Thus P&G could position Pepto-Bismol as "first aid for your stomach," securing its leading place in the consumer's eyes.[35]

Procter & Gamble had bad luck in its efforts to work with other pharmaceutical companies on OTC switches, however, although the company's joint venture with Syntex started out promising. Introduced in 1992 and backed by heavy advertising, Procter-Syntex's Aleve achieved more than $100 million in sales in its first year. The partners also collaborated on the introduction of Femstat 3, a promising new treatment for vaginal yeast infections. In 1994, however, P&G saw its hopes for the venture dashed when Roche Pharmaceuticals acquired Syntex. Suddenly, P&G found itself in a relationship in which the parties had different aims and priorities. In 1996, the partners agreed to go their separate ways. Although P&G realized a significant profit on the sale of its interest to Roche, it proved a disappointing end to a venture in which the company had placed high hopes.

As a result of this series of adverse trends, P&G revised its financial objectives for health care downward in 1994 and again in 1996. Soon after 1996, however, the company saw signs of a pickup. Perhaps P&G would come close to realizing its hopes for achieving a multibillion-dollar business, profitable in all segments, by the early twenty-first century.

Payoff

The biggest decision Pepper faced in his first eighteen months as chief executive involved P&G's future in pharmaceuticals: whether to continue or exit.

He asked the leaders of P&G's health care businesses, Bruce Byrnes and Gil Cloyd, to carry out a thorough review of the business to present to the board of directors. In March 1996, they came back with a powerful case to stay the course. According to Byrnes, "top management and the board of directors reaffirmed their belief that Pharmaceuticals represents important growth potential for P&G, and that we should continue making our investment. This was done with full understanding that net losses would be significant for the next six years."[36]

The confidence of senior management and the board was based on a new short-term objective: "establish the Pharmaceuticals Business as a sustainable and financially viable unit of P&G, making significant contribution to consumer health and to P&G shareholder value." During the late 1990s, the company had ample reason to be optimistic. Didronel remained a popular prescription remedy for osteoporosis in Europe and elsewhere, accounting for more than $100 million in revenues each year. Macrobid achieved strong sales in the United States and Canada. Among the licensed drugs, Asacol proved a big winner. In delayed-release tablet form, the drug escalated into the leading treatment for ulcerative colitis, a condition that afflicted more than one million people in the United States and other countries in which P&G owned the marketing rights to the drug. Another licensed drug, Ziac, a treatment for cardiovascular conditions, also sold well.

Procter & Gamble researchers steadily pushed Actonel and Stedicor through the process of regulatory approval. In May 1997, the company alleviated some financial pressure by reaching agreement with Hoechst Marion Roussel (now Aventis) to form a global alliance to commercialize Actonel. The deal included provision for Hoechst Marion Roussel to make milestone payments to P&G to help offset the huge investments already made in the therapy.[37] In 1998, U.S. regulators approved Actonel for treatment of Paget's disease. Although Fosamax was by then a well-established blockbuster, P&G had high hopes that Actonel, which generated fewer adverse side effects, would quickly gain ground once it received expected FDA approval in 2000. Meanwhile, Stedicor entered phase 3 clinical trials in 1995. During the next several years, P&G readied new drug applications and marketing authorization applications for the drug in the United States and other countries, with initial expectations of a U.S. launch in 2000. In 1998, P&G formed an agreement with Tanabe in Japan to market Stedicor in certain Asian markets.[38]

Procter & Gamble also explored new areas and launched new products with new partners. In April 1995, the company formed an alliance with TheraTech, Inc., a small pharmaceutical company based in Utah and now part of Watson Pharmaceuticals, to codevelop hormone replacement products for women. The drug would be delivered transdermally, via patches. Intrinsa,

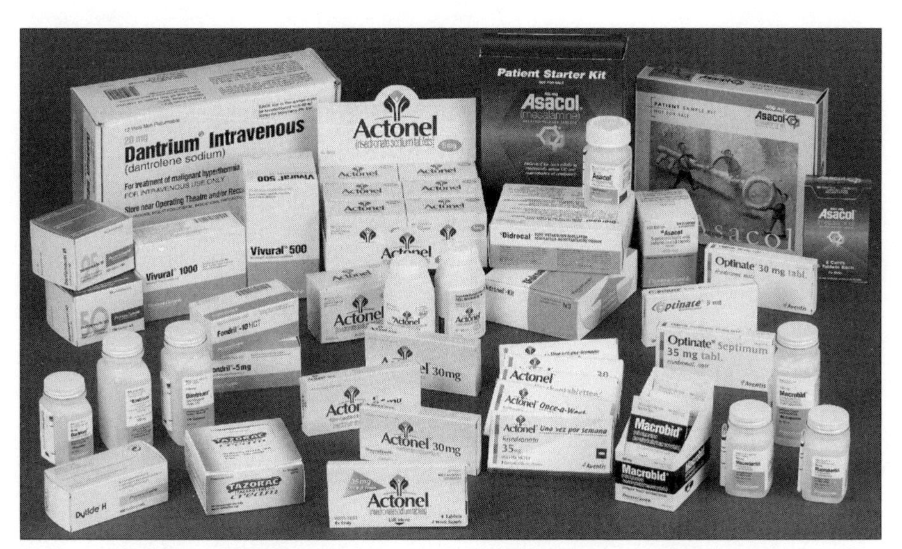

By the early 2000s, P&G manufactured and marketed a variety of prescription drugs.

which delivers testosterone via a transdermal patch to counteract loss of sexual desire and other conditions associated with low levels of the hormone in women, was in phase 3 development in 2001.[39]

In the late 1990s, P&G formed partnerships with several pharmaceutical companies. In 1997, it joined forces with Regeneron Pharmaceuticals, a small biopharmaceutical research company with expertise in various areas, including cancer, rheumatoid arthritis, muscle atrophy, and obesity. The same year, Gene Logic, a leader in genomics research, and P&G formed a partnership to discover new targets for the development of drugs to treat congestive heart failure and osteoporosis. Finally, Procter & Gamble and Alexion Pharmaceuticals entered a joint agreement in 1999 to develop pexelizumab, a compound to reduce complications resulting from cardiopulmonary bypass surgery and certain heart conditions.[40]

The pharmaceutical ventures were beginning to pay off. In FY 2001–2002, P&G's pharmaceutical sales surpassed $1 billion. In terms of profit contribution, Asacol ranked as one of the company's top dozen brands.

On the OTC side, business leaders were also bullish at the dawn of the new century. The optimism partly reflected excellent and consistent management of Pepto-Bismol, Metamucil, and the Vicks brands during the decade. The optimism also stemmed from several major coups that P&G scored in the late 1990s. First, in 1998, it negotiated a deal with AstraZeneca (now Astra-Merck) to collaborate on switching Prilosec from the prescription to the OTC marketplace. The leading treatment for acid reflux disease, including heartburn and certain types of ulcers, Prilosec was then the best-selling drug in the world, with $6 billion in annual revenues. It was expected to stimulate significant sales in OTC versions after FDA approval in 2003.[41]

Second, in the late 1990s and early 2000s, P&G transformed DayQuil, once "just another multisymptom product for daytime relief" into a powerful brand in the cough and cold remedy category. According to Blinn, head of the Personal Health Care Division, "really good consumer insight work" that P&G commissioned "determined that the strongest possible positioning for DayQuil was as NyQuil's daytime partner." The result was a new brand message: "The power of NyQuil for the day." The effect of the new positioning was pronounced: DayQuil became the fastest-growing brand in the cough and cold remedy category, a place it held for several years running.[42]

Finally, P&G developed an intriguing new pain relief product, ThermaCare, a chemically activated heat wrap for treatment of muscular/skeletal pain. The product originated in the mid-1990s under the Corporate New Ventures initiative, which sought (among other goals) to generate new business opportunities through greater collaboration across the company's diverse operating units. ThermaCare provided an early demonstration of the concept, involving participation not only from health care but also from the paper, diapers, and feminine protection business units. The initial product—designed to provide relief to sufferers from lower back pain—was also rooted in P&G fundamentals, Blinn pointed out. "We started with the consumer first," then identified "a major need" that conventional remedies failed to meet. In the case of lower back pain, there was "immense consumer dissatisfaction with what's out there," chiefly a steady diet of ibuprofen or other systemic painkillers.[43]

ThermaCare consisted of heat chemistry in individual cells embedded in a wide belt made from P&G paper similar to the materials used in Pampers. The product began working when the user opened the package and oxygen triggered a chemical reaction in the heat cell. After about thirty minutes, the cell heated to forty degrees Celsius, a level "therapeutically warm but safe." The user then strapped the belt around his or her waist, where it would maintain a constant temperature for at least eight hours. "What it does," explained Blinn, "is promote blood flow through tightened muscles, and that . . . provides the pain relief and increased mobility." The result, market tests revealed, is pain relief "superior to either ibuprofen or acetaminophen for back pain and mobility."[44]

The advent of ThermaCare brought P&G back into the huge global market for pain relief for the first time since the sale of its interest in Procter-Syntex in 1996. Procter & Gamble thus competed in the three biggest OTC segments (cough, cold, and allergies; gastrointestinal; and pain relief), which together amounted to a $36 billion market worldwide. Although P&G held global leadership positions in the first two segments (number one in the cough, cold, and allergies segment, and number four in gastrointestinal) and had high hopes for ThermaCare, its revenues in OTC products were relatively modest by P&G standards, amounting to approximately $1 billion globally in 2001–2002. To Blinn, that meant P&G had ample room to grow, especially in view of trends showing that consumers were assuming a greater voice in their own health care. For example, about 15 percent of all Internet traffic in the United States in 2001 flowed to health care sites.[45] The fragmented structure of the industry also fueled Blinn's optimism. Major growth spurts could result from acquisitions and OTC switches. Should attractive opportunities crop up in major OTC segments such as respiratory, gastrointestinal, weight management, or cholesterol reduction, P&G would be very interested. The company also kept a vigilant eye on opportunities to blend health care technology into traditional consumer products, creating, for example, "nutriceuticals" from fruit drinks, or "cosmoceuticals" from beauty care products.[46]

Among the Giants

During the late 1990s, the global pharmaceutical industry continued on the path toward consolidation begun in the previous decade. Megamergers, including some that crossed national and geographical borders, became common fare with a general slowdown of economic growth around the world and the spread of managed care and other public and private efforts to curtail rising health care costs. Roche acquired Syntex and Genentech; American Home Products bought American Cyanamid (which had earlier bought Lederle Laboratories) and Genetics Institute; Glaxo acquired Wellcome and then merged with SmithKline Beecham; Ciba-Geigy merged with Sandoz to form Novartis; Astra joined with Zeneca and then formed an alliance with Merck; Pharmacia acquired Upjohn and Monsanto's pharmaceutical businesses; Hoechst Marion Roussel (a mid-1990s consolidation) merged with Rhône-Poulenc Rorer (another recent consolidation), to form Aventis.[47]

The rising scale and concentration of the global pharmaceutical industry raised questions about whether P&G could survive, much less succeed, in the long run. And in fact, P&G briefly considered joining in the consolidation spree, entertaining a possible three-way merger with American Home Products and Warner-Lambert that, had it been consummated, would have created a behemoth with a market value exceeding $200 billion. Talks quickly broke down after investors reacted to the proposed deal with profound skepticism. Perhaps they wondered what business a renowned consumer products company like P&G had in attempting to stake out a major position in the research-intensive, fast-changing, high-tech world of pharmaceuticals.

In view of P&G's long history in health care, however, the megamerger was not so far-fetched. The company had built, at times painstakingly, a promising health care business and appeared to be positioned to benefit from trends shaping the industry. On its own or in partnership, the company had cultivated capabilities in developing and marketing both OTC and prescription products. Although P&G continues to face significant challenges in both pharmaceuticals and its OTC business, leaders of these units believe that one day the company may be as well known for its capabilities in life sciences as for its prowess in making and selling branded consumer products.[48]

Whether that vision will materialize, of course, is presently unknowable. Nevertheless, the company clearly has painstakingly built a new growth business in health care by dint of hard work, internal development, acquisitions, and alliances. Along the way, these initiatives depended on and benefited from the patient, unwavering support of chief executives, from Ed Harness to A. G. Lafley. Today, leaders of the health care business (including vice chairman Bruce Byrnes) believe that P&G can continue to thrive in an industry dominated by giants by targeting opportunities carefully and being selective in making acquisitions and forming partnerships.

Procter & Gamble's Health Care Business in Perspective

In the late 1970s and early 1980s, P&G determined that it could succeed in health care, believing the industry compatible with the company's traditional beliefs, values, and strengths. For one thing, P&G held a commitment to bettering the lives of consumers. Then there was the company's underappreciated level of technology in its products, its proclivity for proceeding through tests and experiments, and its willingness and ability to acquire and ally with partners possessing complementary capabilities.

The path to success in health care, however, proved longer and marked by more obstacles than P&G originally foresaw. The business, especially the pharmaceutical segment, contrasted with P&G's traditional core businesses in ways beyond the differences between, say, detergents and disposable diapers. Developing prescription drugs requires bigger investments and longer lead times, while sales and marketing must focus on narrower channels and specialized customers. Success requires a high level of competence not only in the scientific and management disciplines but also in the design and conduct of clinical studies and in negotiating regulatory processes. Procter & Gamble had to learn these things, and at times—such as with the failure to win FDA clearance for Didronel as a treatment for osteoporosis in the United States—the lesson proved costly and painful.

Procter & Gamble's gains so far have reflected a cautious approach to the marketplace in prescription drugs as well as more aggressive moves in the OTC segment. On the prescription side, the company has possessed the discipline to maintain focus on its own areas of strength, such as bone conditions, in which it possesses deep knowledge and significant capability. The company has been very selective in entering other prescription drug areas. At the same time, P&G has repeatedly tested its strategies for reasonableness and competitive responses.

On the OTC side, the company has marshaled its capabilities in product supply, marketing, and branding effectively—as evidenced by the success of Pepto-Bismol, Metamucil, and the Vicks brands. Meanwhile, as patents on prescription drugs expire, these drugs will migrate into OTC channels, where again P&G's capabilities will come into play. At the same time, traditional markets for prescription drugs are becoming more competitive, with marketing and distribution becoming significant sources of advantage. As P&G becomes more capable in research, clinical testing, and regulatory compliance, its traditional strengths, the company's leaders believe, will continue to serve it well.

Finally, competing in health care has reaffirmed for P&G the value of forming alliances. Although it entered the business organically, first by adding therapeutic features to consumer products and then by developing prescription drugs from science and technology it was mastering, alliances have proved invaluable for P&G. Such arrangements have afforded access to new sources of innovation and talent, providing greater leverage for P&G capabilities and accelerating the timetable for success.

Challenges in China

MORE THAN A BILLION PEOPLE. A market teeming with potential consumers, well educated, with widespread access to television. Western rivals still waiting on the borders. Local competitors still scattered and unskilled in modern marketing. In the late 1980s, P&G launched one of the biggest, most consequential ventures the company had ever undertaken, in China.

The risks were substantial. The country still had a Communist government (unlike Russia or Eastern Europe, by the time P&G went in), and whether the ruling regime was truly committed to economic liberalization remained uncertain. Moreover, P&G was still establishing itself in the region: As of 1985, the company had managed to establish full-scale operations in only one other east Asian country, Japan. China, of course, was massively different. It was just plain massive, to begin with, with a large rural population that remained poor by Western standards and a labor force accustomed to the "iron rice-bowl" of state ownership. A host of unknowns surrounded the idea. History itself seemed to caution against the venture. For centuries, Western merchants and multinationals had been trying to penetrate this market, and most had found the going difficult. Few had managed to sustain long-term success.

On the other hand, staying out of China might ultimately prove even riskier. The size of the opportunity was breathtaking. If P&G held off while competitors moved in, it would be relinquishing potentially vital strategic ground. Once entrenched in the market, competitors would not be dislodged for decades and would meanwhile be in a position to dominate the region. Moreover, there was the threat—and the opportunity—of rising Chinese competitors. Executives like Ed Artzt, who strongly championed entry, argued from the basis of P&G's experience in Japan, where ferocious competition had taught P&G invaluable lessons about brand building and operational discipline. Ultimately, the logic for entry into China became inexorable.

Nothing was inevitable about what followed, however. Procter & Gamble's expansion into China turned out to be full of surprises.

The venture got off to a roaring start. Entering with hair care and skin care offerings, P&G triggered a surge of consumer demand in major urban markets and rapidly established leading brands. Within a few years of entry, the company was laying ambitious plans for expansion, both geographically (beyond the largest urban markets) and in category terms (adding paper, toilet soap, laundry, and oral care brands to its hair care and skin care entries).

As the scale of the venture expanded, however, the challenges facing P&G grew more difficult. In oral care, P&G encountered stiff competition from Colgate, which had entered the category earlier and staked out strong positions behind low-price, low-end products. In feminine care, local competitors proved skilled at copying Western products, making them cheaply and selling them at very low prices. And in the laundry category, the emergence of strong, local competition rapidly altered market conditions. By the late 1990s, it was becoming clear that winning decisively across all categories in China would require more than simply getting better at what P&G already knew how to do. It was going to take a thoroughgoing rethinking of the business fundamentals.

All of which does not so much overturn as vindicate the decision to enter China. If P&G were to win globally, it had to learn how to compete in China. The story of P&G in China is not one of straightforward, linear growth—nor of setback and retreat. Rather, it is one of learning and adaptation in the midst of intense economic flux, as the company acquired and still acquires experience in one of the most challenging, and certainly the biggest, markets it has ever encountered.

Advance Scouting and Strategizing

Procter & Gamble began paying serious attention to China in the early 1980s, as the government began to open local markets to foreign investment. In 1980, China established the first of what became a series of special economic zones (SEZs)—contained staging grounds for free enterprise. The most prominent SEZ took root near the village of Shenzhen, in Guangdong Province on the border of the New Territories adjacent to Hong Kong and Macao. Explosive industrial growth transformed the region as a result. In 1984, China expanded the number of SEZs to fourteen, further widening the scope of capitalist activity. Procter & Gamble watched these developments with growing interest.

The company ran its first market research probes in Beijing and Shanghai in 1985. Foreign commerce remained strictly contained at this point, channeled through "friendship stores," where consumers with access to hard (i.e., foreign) currency could buy a limited range of imported goods. In other words, there was no real Chinese consumer market yet. Nevertheless, P&G wanted to put a team on the ground to get a feel for what it would be like to operate in China. Export & Special Operations (E&SO) took up the project, sending in Berenike Ullmann, a young, Chinese-speaking market researcher, to break the ground. The experience was as unfamiliar to Chinese authorities as it was to the company. In Beijing, Ullmann recounted, local police "raided our TV Test Central Location—as we were suspected of engaging in industrial espionage—but were happy to watch TV and answer *our* questions instead!"[1]

The company was laying careful groundwork. Before putting products on the market or setting up local operations, P&G wanted to introduce itself as a corporate entity to political authorities and the Chinese public. Ullmann's specific goal was to test the effectiveness of several P&G corporate ads. "We went into the market two or three years before we actually started selling products, and started advertising to build up a reputation for the company," Artzt related. "It was very, very effective. Every commercial ended with the words P&G. . . . We must have said that a billion times."[2]

The Entry Strategy

The company's first impulse, as it weighed strategies for entering the market, was to go in with laundry brands. After all, P&G dominated the category in the United States with Tide and was in the process of making Ariel a billion-dollar brand globally, with strong positions in numerous European markets and a commanding lead in several Latin American countries as well. Accordingly, when P&G dispatched Ullmann back to China in 1986, it was to conduct a laundry research program. Ullmann, accompanied by agency staff from Hong Kong, recalled taking "cameras, fishhook scales, bottles containing samples of beef blood, spaghetti sauce and grass for staining laundry samples, . . . as well as two large cartons with 750 small plastic bottles."[3]

The results were not particularly encouraging. Procter & Gamble brands far outperformed local alternatives. But Ullmann's tests also revealed that Chinese consumers held relatively low standards for detergent performance. Marketing P&G brands on the basis of whiteness, brightness, or superior cleaning power did not look promising.

On the other hand, Ullmann's work did uncover more intriguing results in other areas. Near the end of the laundry testing, at the request of E&SO

supervisors back in Geneva, the team tacked on some hair care research. Here they found definite potential. Chinese consumers bought their shampoo in bulk, bringing containers into shops to collect a product that had the consistency of jelly. Against the distinctly low performance of these local brands, Ullmann's team tested Head & Shoulders and Pert Plus (then still in test market in the United States). Consumer response registered dramatically.

Procter & Gamble's entry planning thus shifted toward hair care, and several advantages emerged. The capital investment would be much cheaper. The acquisition of Richardson-Vicks Inc. during this period also reinforced thinking along these new lines, providing P&G with ready-made bases of operation in nearby Hong Kong and Singapore. Finally, the case of Taiwan, where the company had recently decided to focus on feminine protection and hair care, also influenced P&G's China strategists. The company thought of Taiwan as a kind of large-scale test market for China as well as a market in its own right, observed James Wei, a brand manager in Taiwan at the time.[4]

Efforts to identify potential laundry partners, meanwhile, had bogged down. Chinese regulations dictated that foreign businesses enter the country in partnership with local businesses—an approach P&G preferred as well. Chinese detergent manufacturers reacted coolly to P&G's overtures, however, and local government authorities seemed reluctant to cede to foreign investors control of factories with high numbers of employees.[5] When it became apparent that the company would be unable, for several years at least, to secure partnership agreements on acceptable terms with local

In China, P&G's traditional market research discipline provided key insights into a rapidly changing consumer population.

detergent manufacturers, P&G swung decisively to hair care as its lead entry category.

Other elements of the plan fell into place more easily. Confronting a huge country broken up into powerful provincial regulatory regimes and fractured markets, with patchy infrastructure, the company decided to concentrate its initial penetration in China's three largest urban markets. Guangzhou (formerly known to Westerners as Canton), on the Pearl River in South China, would provide the first point of entry. This move would plant the venture near Hong Kong, where expatriate P&G managers would actually live and base their operation for the first several years. It also positioned the company in one of China's most dynamic markets, the region near the Shenzhen SEZ, which was experiencing explosive growth. In addition, the company targeted Beijing (a natural choice, given both the scale of the local market and the importance of cultivating a partnering relationship with the national government), and Shanghai, China's largest city, also experiencing booming growth.

To facilitate entry, P&G joined with Hutchison Whampoa, Ltd., a huge trading company based in Hong Kong and increasingly active in China. With Hutchison's help, P&G identified the Guangzhou Soap Factory as a promising initial joint venture partner. In August 1988, P&G and Hutchison struck the deal. Procter & Gamble assumed management control over the new company, called P&G (Guangzhou) Ltd., drawing from P&G's Hong Kong office to provide most of the needed managerial talent. Peter Hempstead, a veteran of the E&SO organization, moved in as general manager of the venture, reporting to Winfried Kastner, who supervised Hong Kong and Taiwan in addition to China.

Getting Under Way

The new venture got off to a fast start. Incoming P&G managers established an effective working relationship with Ma Fuxiang, who had been general manager of the Guangzhou Soap Factory. Wedged into a small alley in a busy section of downtown Guangzhou, the multistory factory received raw materials carted by tricycles down a narrow alley. The factory then loaded manufactured product on the same trikes to be ferried out to trucks waiting in the street outside. The venture led with Head & Shoulders, producing its first batch in October 1988.

The introduction of Head & Shoulders unleashed a torrent of consumer demand. Guangzhou residents were just beginning to earn disposable income and getting their first exposure to Western brands. "In those early days," recalled Dimitri Panayotopoulos, general manager of P&G China from 1993 to 2001, "our brand launches used to be featured on the evening television news, and consumers used to queue in the department stores in the hope of buying them."[6] The appearance of a high-performing shampoo, moreover, proved particularly sensational. Chinese consumers had small disposable incomes by Western standards, but they placed high value on personal appearance, especially attractive skin and hair. Head & Shoulders sold (often in single-use sachets priced at half a reminbi [RMB] each, the equivalent of fourteen U.S. cents) as quickly as P&G could make it. Even in the outlying countryside, where incomes were much lower, consumers splurged to buy sachets for special occasions such as weddings and celebrations.[7]

During these heady early years, P&G's main challenge was ramping up production to keep pace with demand. Within twelve months of launch, Head & Shoulders had claimed a 15 percent share in urban Guangdong (the province containing Guangzhou), easily beating company targets. Buoyed by this success, the company began constructing a larger, green-field plant (100,000 square meters, or almost 25 acres, in area, to employ a workforce of one thousand) in Huangpu, outside of Guangzhou. The factory was to include facilities to produce surfactants and perfumes locally. Meanwhile, as P&G acquired operational experience on the ground in China, the company expanded its brand portfolio. In May 1989, the company entered the skin care category with Oil of Ulan (Oil of Olay). A second hair care brand, Rejoice (Pert Plus), followed several months later in October.

The results remained highly encouraging. Presenting to P&G's board of directors in June 1989, John Pepper reported that the company had invested $4.5 million to date in China, and that the "start-up has by far exceeded our own and our partners' expectations." Even with sales still concentrated almost entirely (85 percent) in Guangzhou and the surrounding region, China had already become the fifth-largest market for Head & Shoulders in the world.[8] The new Huangpu plant came on-line in January 1991, providing capacity to produce other brands and serve demand in Beijing and Shanghai. Whisper, a feminine care brand that the company had begun importing in small batches in late 1990, went into local production beginning in August 1991, entering test markets in Guangzhou. A few months later, in March 1992, the company launched Pantene Pro-V, its new global powerhouse brand, followed shortly by Safeguard bar soap. With each step, overall sales climbed, passing $50 million by late 1991, when the venture achieved profitability, and approaching $100 million by FY 1992–1993.[9]

Not that growth was easy or smooth. Operational issues like distribution posed significant challenges, particularly as P&G and its partners expanded beyond the big cities. "There was no distribution," recalled Panayotopoulos. "Because there were only local brands, there was no national distribution system for our type of goods. That had to be set up, too."[10] Kenneth Zhu, a native Chinese lawyer who studied in the United States and joined P&G shortly after returning to the region, explained that this aspect of business required painstaking efforts. Existing Chinese distribution networks were not only confined to regional spheres of operation, but were also transaction-oriented, rather than mutually supportive relationships. Zhu summarized the state of mind: "You buy my product, I don't care how you are going to make a profit or how you sell." Most Western multinationals entering the market were content to fit themselves into these channels. For its part, P&G China quickly decided that more collaborative, robust relationships would have to be nurtured. Local distributors were still learning how to build business and operate profitably in a free-enterprise, consumer-market-driven environment. "We had to initiate the consumer consumption," Zhu elaborated. "We had to direct the distribution company how to sell, how to use incentive programs, for example. These things were new, for China. Local companies just didn't understand how they could make a profit and build business."[11]

Teaching these skills, in turn, meant learning how to read distribution flows and correct bottlenecks. At one point early in the process, Panayotopoulos recalled, sell-through levels backed up as inventory gluts accumulated in distributors' warehouses. "We thought this business was going out all over China, . . . but we suddenly realized, no, actually, we were building inventory because [wholesalers] basically didn't know how to get" broader distribution. Accounts receivable problems also backed up, initially, before the company tightened terms and established patterns of punctual payment.[12]

Meanwhile, as it built out basic structures of production and distribution, the company learned more about Chinese consumers. Safeguard's ad campaign, for example, required significant modifications as local brand managers learned the market. Initially, the company imported the advertising from abroad, with minimal modifications. "We simply took the very successful Safeguard advertising from the Philippines, and re-shot it with Chinese talent," Panayotopoulos recalled. "There were several copies: one was a father coming home grimy, sweaty and smelly from his football game, one was a teenager worried about her pimples, and one was a little boy who grazed his knee, and his mother used Safeguard to prevent bacteria growth. These copies had built the business to a 46 percent share in the Philippines."[13] In China, however, the ads failed to connect with homemakers. "Chinese consumers take advertising very literally," Panayotopoulos explained. "So, women who watched the adapted Philippines copy thought Safeguard was designed to treat children's cuts and bruises, and to deodorize sweaty men. They told us, 'we don't get dirty and sweaty like the men—so we don't need Safeguard.'" Once P&G put in place new advertising that stressed usage by the entire family, the brand began to acquire stronger share.[14]

Similar adaptations characterized advertising for Rejoice. At first, the company adopted the "Locker Room" copy devised in the United States (for Pert Plus) and used effectively in numerous other global markets. Since Chinese consumers were unfamiliar with conditioners, however, positioning Rejoice on the basis of convenience as a two-in-one product was confusing and meaningless. Procter & Gamble struck a much more resonant note in a new campaign, called "Secret," in 1994. Depicting an airline stewardess, the copy evoked images of travel (particularly exotic to Chinese at the time, with travel restrictions just beginning to loosen). At the same time, the ad also played off a traditional Chinese proverb about telling secrets: Telling one person tells ten, who tell one hundred, who tell . . .[15] Rejoice, as a result, came to combine aspirational imagery (air travel) and traditional (proverbial) wisdom, an aura that established powerful brand equity.

Building the Organization

This kind of skillful adaptation to local culture revealed the presence of a rapidly cohering local organization behind P&G China's brands. Performance in the marketplace, category by category, would be crucial in establishing the company in China. Yet, in the long run, the creation of a sustainable presence in China depended on tapping into latent Chinese managerial talent, technology, and entrepreneurial initiative. This effort began virtually from the outset of the venture. Within months of setting up in Guangzhou, the company launched a recruiting program, visiting a round of Chinese universities in June 1988 to identify promising graduates and postgraduate students. "In '89 we recruited 12 people," recounted Raymond Co, director of human resources. "In the second batch, we went to 60, and the third batch, we went to 100. . . . After that, it's been averaging 100 to 120. We had our peak in 1995 when we recruited 200 people."[16]

An early, extended visit to China by P&G President Pepper in 1991 affirmed both the central role China was assuming in the company's long-range strategic thinking and the company's commitment to building a robust and well-rooted organization. Pepper spent two weeks touring operations and meeting with Chinese customers, consumers, and government officials, including Vice Premier Wu Xueqian and the mayors of Shanghai and Guangzhou. China represented "one of the significant strategic growth opportunities for the company over the next 10–20–30 years," Pepper reported to the board shortly after returning. Capitalizing on the opportunity was going to depend not only on the quality of the brands P&G put on the market, but also on the character and nature of the company's long-term investment in the country. Specifically, Pepper argued, success in China would depend on three factors. The first would be to introduce "very best [world-class] technology, well ahead of existing products." The second would be to cultivate "strong relationships, with the government, at the national and especially provincial and local levels," with the general aim of "making ourselves a company of China"—one that sourced raw material locally and assembled benchmark-quality local production operations. And the third would be to commit to developing the strongest possible local organization, "starting with the management group now including young Chinese coming on board."[17]

In short, P&G approached China not as a market to be invaded, but as an opportunity to build new partnerships and develop local capabilities—a challenge, in Pepper's phrase, to "make ourselves a company of China." Winfried Kastner underscored the point in his own presentation to the board several months later. As of November 1991, Kastner reported, P&G was "the only company that presents and recruits directly at the top universities across the country." Other multinational competitors, including Unilever, SC Johnson, Kao, and Colgate, had launched brands in China, but none had prioritized local organization building the way P&G had. In recognition of this commitment, the Chinese government granted the company unusual concessions, including permitting employees to travel across provincial boundaries and to obtain visas for overseas training.[18]

By the summer of 1993, when Panayotopoulos arrived in China to assume control of the health and beauty care business from Peter Hempstead, the foundational elements of the organization were coming together. Most expatriate managers were moving from Hong Kong into local headquarters facilities in Guangzhou, joining a growing number of increasingly savvy Chinese personnel.

Launching Laundry

With successful entries in hair care, skin care, feminine care, and personal cleansing, and with the basic elements of local organization falling into place, P&G restarted efforts to establish itself in laundry. Some aspects of market research remained unsettling, in particular the relatively low priority Chinese consumers placed on detergent performance. Testing showed that Chinese consumers categorized detergents as an "item on which to scrimp" rather than splurge. Homemakers doing laundry dosed with tiny amounts—as little as one-tenth what their counterparts in the West used.[19] On the other hand, ongoing talks with potential joint venture partners suggested a growing willingness on the Chinese side to work collaboratively, and the competitive landscape remained wide open. Local production was fragmented geographically, with each of the thirty provinces forming self-contained local markets. Most Chinese laundry manufacturers were large but unwieldy operations, state-owned and heavily overstaffed, by Western standards. There were no national brands, although some regional brands such as Gaofuli near Guangzhou, Panda near Beijing, and Shanghai White Cat along the eastern coast had strong local followings. Based on generic, low-performing formulas, the brands themselves remained undifferentiated. The industry, in short, was still in the early stages of development. As markets grew national in scale, there was going be a shakeout, and P&G intended to be a consolidator.

As a first step, in February 1993, P&G distributed 300,000 free sachets of Ariel in Guangzhou. The initial reception, bolstered by heavy local advertising, was encouraging. Consumers rated the brand highly, recognizing that it performed better than local alternatives. Procter & Gamble began selling Ariel as a premium brand in the spring, building up modest sales in its first year. The company did run into skepticism about its prices, however. Ullmann recalled a consumer in a focus group pointing out that it was cheaper to buy a new shirt than a bag of Ariel.[20]

Nevertheless, by the fall of 1993, P&G was sufficiently encouraged to commit investment and commence local manufacturing. As the Chinese government relaxed its restrictions on foreign control of the industry's large factories, P&G and Hutchison in quick succession acquired controlling interest in four local detergent companies.[21] Together, the investments gave P&G control of three of China's eight biggest detergent facilities and a substantial proportion of the country's total production capacity.[22] The deals also brought with them the rights to several promising local brands, including Panda, Gaofuli, and Lanxiang (in Chengdu).

These investments formed the core of a multipronged strategy to penetrate and cultivate the market. As Panayotopoulos outlined the strategy to corporate directors, P&G would position Ariel at the high end of the market (the top 5 percent, he estimated); Tide in the middle tier (15 percent); and local brands acquired through joint venture partners—Panda, Gaofuli, and Lanxiang—in the lower tier. "We are currently the only Company with this 3 tier laundry strategy," Panayotopoulos observed. "Each brand has its own distinctive positioning. Ariel stands for the best cleaning evidenced by superior stain removal. Tide stands for everyday cleaning evidenced by collars and cuffs, and good value. Our local joint-venture brands stand for basic cleaning at an everyday price."[23]

This strategy would create a strong total share and a solid brand portfolio, Panayotopoulos predicted, although he added that formidable competition was also developing. Not surprisingly, "given the size of the prize," Unilever, Henkel, and Kao were "already very active in China." Unilever, for example, had bought into a joint venture near Shanghai and was scaling up for national distribution. He also observed that local competitors were gaining strength. Chinese producers tended to have "low quality products and limited geographical presence," but they were "learning fast, improving product quality, upgrading packaging and expanding distribution." The emergence of local brands, Panayotopoulos anticipated, would soon require P&G to "develop the products and marketing plans to compete as effectively against them as we do against our international competitors."[24]

Critical Mass and the Onslaught of Local Competition

With new laundry revenues coming on-stream, brands in core categories such as hair and skin care continuing to perform impressively, and market penetration steadily widening, P&G's business grew by leaps and bounds in the mid-1990s. By March 1994, monthly sales shipments were already reaching four million cases, putting the operation well ahead of schedule and making China already one of the company's top ten subsidiaries in volume terms. Many Western companies started in the same top three cities in which P&G had begun, Panayotopoulos informed P&G directors in 1995, and the more ambitious firms were targeting a second ring of the fifty largest cities: "*We* are going for *all 570 cities* in China."[25]

Creating strong positions in the laundry category figured particularly important in the overall plan. Through the mid-1990s, P&G upgraded operations in the joint venture plants while building Tide, Ariel, and the local brands. Results in the marketplace, if not meteoric, were encouraging. Tide steadily gained share in laundry, climbing above 10 percent in 1998 and, for a few months, becoming the best-selling detergent in China.[26] To keep pace with demand, P&G arranged with two state-owned companies to manufacture detergent on contract. Meanwhile, after a series of sticky negotiations, P&G bought out its Chinese partners and assumed full ownership of the laundry ventures. All during this time, growth continued at a rapid pace. Sales surged to nearly $800 million in FY 1995–1996 and continued to climb over the next several years.

Then momentum shifted. In 1998, a financial crisis hit the Asia region, sending China's economy into a tailspin. Foreign investment dried up, unemployment spread, and consumer spending dropped sharply. "Chinese consumers are cutting down on categories that are seen as less essential," Panayotopoulos reported to headquarters in February 1999. "They were willing to splurge when times were good, but now that times are hard, they cut back or trade down. They find coping mechanisms for categories. . . . They still wash laundry, but they scrimp on the products, and find substitutes, such as [soap] bars."[27]

The impact on P&G, particularly on its laundry business, was sharp. The company had gone to market with high-quality brands at premium prices. Even its lower-tier brands had grown more expensive as the company upgraded factories, distribution, and marketing. This strategy had established strong brand equity and a reputation for quality, but it had left considerable room at the lower end of the market for competitors—both legitimate and illegitimate. In the latter category, the phenomenon of counterfeiting (which had plagued P&G from the early 1990s) became rampant. One manager estimated that, by 1999, more than half of all sales of Panda in greater Beijing were actually of counterfeit products.[28]

In the long term, however, the emergence of increasingly strong, legitimate competition was more serious. By the time economic recession hit China, the local competitors Panayotopoulos had seen on the horizon were reaching scale and learning how to market their brands. Seizing advantage of the opening P&G had created in lower-tier market segments, one company in particular, Zhejiang Nice Group, expanded astonishingly fast. Originally an undistinguished, state-owned operation in Lishui City, a small city in Zhejiang Province in eastern China, Nice came under new entrepreneurial management in the mid-1990s. The entrepreneurs took local brand Diaopai national with saturation TV advertising and, over the next few years, built it into China's leading laundry brand.

Nice was a competitor unlike any P&G had faced before. The company ran numerous small operations on shoestring budgets, contracting out for extra capacity when necessary. Although it used old equipment, the company offset this lack of automation with a vast supply of cheap labor. Nice worked relationships with suppliers to get raw materials at extremely low cost, and with distributors to get its product in shops across the nation, again at extremely low cost. Content to make a product that was good enough for most consumers, the company spent very little on R&D. It operated with razor-thin margins, pouring profits into attractive packaging and ubiquitous TV ads, building market share, and driving out less efficient rivals.[29] And under this strategy, it brought Diaopai into the market at a price point less than one-third of Tide's. Explained a Nice official: "We cover more markets and we offer low prices to let our consumers share the profits."[30]

The Diaopai TV ads revealed how swiftly Chinese competitors were acquiring Western marketing skills. One ad portrayed a family situation in which a young girl did the family's laundry while her unemployed mother walked the streets in search of work. "Very empathetic," conceded Austin Lally, the Glasgow-born marketing director who arrived in 1999 to take charge of P&G's laundry products in China. Diaopai's message spoke to the needs of the Chinese consumer: "She wanted cheap detergent. [Nice] gave [her] a great price . . . on detergent and a brand that she felt good about using because of the emotional values associated with it, at a time when western manufacturers, in the eyes of [many Chinese], were basically charging outrageous price premiums." They were ads, Lally concluded, that "P&G would have been proud to have aired."[31]

Thus it was Nice, not P&G or another global competitor, that became the great consolidator in the Chinese detergent industry in the late 1990s. Along with other global competitors, P&G absorbed heavy losses in the laundry category and was forced to respond with strong measures. The company slashed prices on Tide (bringing them closer to, but not as low as, Diaopai's price points) and sold off plants in Shaoguan and Guangzhou Lonkey, consolidating production in Chengdu and Beijing. It also sold off its money-losing local brands, repositioning Tide to regain the lost ground.[32]

These were only short-gap measures, however. Lally quickly became convinced that sustainable, long-term success in laundry products depended on figuring out how to radically reengineer P&G's processes in ways that brought the company's costs close to Nice's. "Anybody can reduce prices," he pointed out. "The problem is you can only reduce prices if the cost structure in your business allows you the flexibility to do so. People say to me, 'Well, Austin, in China you had a pricing problem.' I didn't have a pricing problem; I had a cost problem."[33]

Lally and other managers also faced intensifying logistics difficulties on the ground, where miscalculation in sales and distribution resources soon compounded macroeconomic market pressures in China. In the years prior to the downturn, global mass retailers such as Wal-Mart, METRO, and Carrefour had planted beachhead operations in China's largest cities. Procter & Gamble, which of course was forging close relationships with these partners in other countries, responded rapidly, swinging much of its sales force and focus to the entering retailers. "We wanted to be right there at the beginning," explained chief executive A. G. Lafley (who was supervising Asia operations at the time). But in the context of China, the move was premature, for it left local distribution partners underrepresented and alienated. Having built up a local distribution capacity that had conferred critical competitive advantage, the company now seemed to be walking away from it. Inevitably, sales suffered.

Investment in Organization: The Beijing Technical Center

The economic downturn, the setback in the laundry segment, and distribution problems put extraordinary pressure on P&G China. A decade into the venture, the challenge of competing had escalated dramatically. Managers began digging into the numbers, looking everywhere for ways to cut costs. One of the most obvious measures was to reduce the number of expatriates (whom the company supported at considerable expense) and place more of the business in the hands of locally recruited people. The crisis amounted to a baptism by fire, not just for P&G's brands, but for the local organization that the company had been assembling.

Critically, that organization was reaching maturity. Though only a decade old, P&G China had been building energetically from the outset, and by the late 1990s, those efforts were bearing fruit. The most visible sign that P&G China was coming of age was the establishment of the Beijing Technical Center (BJTC).

The impetus behind the BJTC had coalesced in the mid-1990s. P&G China did its early technical work in Guangzhou, undertaking modest projects such as product design and some product research. In 1995, with the business expanding aggressively, the parent company established expanded facilities in its Huangpu plant, which was equipped for state-of-the-art research. When a major earthquake temporarily shut down the Kobe Technical Center in Japan in January 1995, a number of researchers moved to Huangpu. Initially the transfer was considered a temporary expedient. It coincided, however, with a significant shift in thinking about P&G's technical work in the region. Executives such as Shekhar Mitra, global manager for oral care research, felt the company needed to deepen what he called "local consumer sensing" in China. Products designed exclusively for western consumers, Mitra argued, would not serve Chinese consumers. This market would require high quality products at better values. In order to achieve those values, the company needed to embed its R&D work on site, in China itself.[34]

The Huangpu location had its drawbacks, however. Its setting in south China made it an unappealing assignment for Chinese researchers and staff from the northern part of the country. "[It was] difficult to get the really good university graduates to go down there," conceded researcher Chris Buckley, "particularly in the sciences." More fundamentally, some people within the company sensed broader opportunities. Like other Western companies, P&G was discovering deep reservoirs of technical and scientific knowledge

Brands such as Oil of Ulan created a particularly strong market presence for P&G in China's major cities.

in China. In universities that were starkly poor and seemingly underequipped by Western standards, remarkable research was under way. Few in the West had realized the extent of the potential for technological partnership.

Inspired by the opportunity and prodded in particular by the persuasive advocacy of Nabil Sakkab, vice president of R&D, P&G Far East, P&G laid plans for a bold commitment. In April 1998, a decade after setting up its first joint venture, the company opened the BJTC in affiliation with Tsinghua University, the country's premiere science and technology institution. Like other aspects of the company's China business, the venture was structured as a partnership with local institutions: In this case, P&G leased on-campus space from the university, helped underwrite construction of a world-class laboratory complex, and set up a research fund of 10.7 million RMB to sponsor selected R&D projects by faculty and students. For its part, P&G transferred the bulk of its technical work from Huangpu to Beijing, designating BJTC as a major facility responsible for core technology work with global brand applications. Within two years, the facility had grown into the company's largest technical center working on R&D for developing regions (surpassing the center in Caracas, Venezuela), with a staff of more than 150. Deborah Caswell, manager of R&D at BJTC, described the center's mission as "developmental entrepreneurial": In addition to on-site R&D, the center screens patents, maintains liaisons with Chinese universities and other technical institutions, and more generally seeks to connect with, and develop opportunities for, technical collaboration.[35] "Connect and develop" has become the catchphrase, signifying a continuous, proactive outreach campaign.

Oral Care: Drawing on Local Capabilities

The benefits of deepening local capabilities proved themselves in oral care, a category also hit hard by the economic downturn, but one that recovered the initiative and made new headway as conditions improved. With high hopes, the company had established P&G Oral Care (Guangzhou) Ltd. in September 1995. Local dentifrices were markedly inferior. Using low-quality natural chalk as an abrasive, Chinese toothpastes were gritty, offered minimal cavity protection, and tended to scour teeth with scratches. Procter & Gamble positioned Crest at the high end of this market, as a quality brand signaling premium performance. Working with the National Committee on Oral Health and the China Medical Association, P&G managed to demonstrate Crest's cavity protection properties and earn official endorsement in June 1996. Subsequent programs in public education, notably the Oral Health Long March program in September 1997, effectively spread popular awareness of cavity protection as Crest hit the market and rapidly started establishing a strong equity. However, the product came in at premium pricing that only the more affluent consumers could afford. Still, this segment of the population amounted to a market fully as big as Crest's markets in middle-sized European countries.[36]

Other companies took different strategies. Unilever bought a leading local brand, Zhonghua, which gave the Western company a mass brand with solid share numbers in the lower segments of the market. Colgate, which had entered the market in the early 1990s, also aimed for the middle market and share leadership. It maintained its Colgate brand in several forms, including a less expensive formulation that preserved the aesthetics of the appearance yet relied on a cheaper abrasive and offered diminished fluoride bioavailability (relative to U.S. formulations). Branded (in translation) "Colgate Super Strong" and hitting the market just as Crest launched, the product retailed for a fraction of Crest's price—3.5 RMB per tube, versus between 9 and 10 RMB for Colgate premium and more than 10 RMB for Crest.[37]

Within P&G, debate went back and forth over whether to join Unilever and Colgate at the lower end of the market. On the one hand, putting the name *Crest* on a degraded product would erode brand equity and, more fundamentally, would violate P&G's corporate ethos. The idea of working up "a very quick and dirty, watered-down version of our premium product," did not appeal to Mitra.[38] In a vigorous effort to protect Crest's claim to safe and superior cavity protection, the company set up a Crest Research Institute, cultivating relationships with leading Chinese academics through a top-notch advisory board. Still, with Crest's premium pricing placing it well out of reach of a huge group of potential customers, strategists remained concerned, in Buckley's words, "that we were not going to get critical mass in the market."[39]

Persuaded that P&G had to find some way deeper into the market, the company turned to its local technical staff. Mitra laid down demanding guidelines: The reformulation must not compromise the brand's efficacy and safety, and of course must be built around premium Crest's proprietary Fluorostat system, yet must also be made affordable to Chinese consumers. A team led by Jiang Yue went to work. Experimentation began in Huangpu and moved to Beijing as the BJTC came on-line. By 2000, the work was yielding breakthrough results. A new formulation platform, which the team labeled "Snow," substituted other ingredients for glycerin (one of the most costly components of traditional toothpastes) in a stable fluoride formula that performed to Crest's traditional standards.

Concurrently, Mitra and his team dug more deeply into consumer understanding. By closely differentiating the needs of China's premium and mid-tier consumers, the team developed a segmentation model that enabled P&G to tailor product and package designs to specific slices of the market. Snow-formulated Crest launched in the market's mid-tier, while premium Crest received a new round of innovation and benefits. Procter & Gamble's toothpaste business in China more than tripled in three and a half years.

Those results attracted attention within the company's technical community. Many P&G researchers outside of China had been skeptical that an aesthetically appealing, high performing toothpaste could be made with lower cost ingredients. But the product won the skeptics over: a toothpaste that looked glossy, tasted good, stood up well, and yet cost substantially less to make.[40] By 2002, P&G was exploring the adaptation of the Snow formulation for use in other developing markets globally.[41]

Restructuring Laundry

Learning to make competitively priced laundry products will require the same kind of resourcefulness and innovative approach that transformed dentifrices. If it hopes to compete for the emerging heart of the market in China, P&G will have to examine every element of its cost structure and benchmark it against Chinese competitors, in laundry as in other categories. That effort is already well under way. Charles Yang, head of product R&D

for fabric and home care at the BJTC, reports that technical investigation was uncovering ways to substantially reduce laundry formula costs. Other changes had yielded more savings—for example, in distribution: "We significantly reduced the shipping cost from the plant to different distributors by improving the powder integrity so we can stack the product higher to make more efficient use of the warehouse."[42]

Incremental cost savings by traditional methods will probably not bring P&G's prices down to levels competitive with products like Diaopai, however. In all likelihood, P&G will have to undertake even more radical measures to contend for leadership in China's evolving laundry market. As Lally observed from the front lines: "The pricing benchmarks on the market here are established at much lower levels than P&G is used to. If you want to be competitive you have to learn how to make a case of laundry product significantly cheaper than you've done anywhere else in the world so far." In other words, winning in China will require the company to push itself beyond its current assumptions about how its business operates. Without losing its unique capabilities and competitive advantages, P&G will have to systematically take apart, examine, and reassemble its business fundamentals in new, more efficient forms.

China in Perspective

What sustains all these efforts, and what distinguishes P&G's investment in China from those made by many other global companies that set up operations there in the bonanza years of the late 1980s and early 1990s, is the company's steady eye on the long term. Procter & Gamble has scored notable successes in China, including continuing share leadership and healthy profitability in categories such as skin and hair care. Other categories have met more challenging competition, and in some cases encountered sharp setbacks. Yet the deeper, long-term project of dedicated organization building and organic partnership has equipped P&G China to respond robustly. China has always represented more to P&G than a market in which to sell or a setting in which to set up low-cost factories. That outlook is now sustaining the venture through some of the most challenging conditions the company has ever faced.

Brand by brand, then, P&G has scored major wins in China, including leadership in several core categories. Head & Shoulders, Rejoice, and Oil of Ulan disappeared from store shelves as fast as the company could make and distribute these products when they first launched, creating a massive new market for some of P&G's most important brands. Comparable successes in other categories have subsequently extended the business. On the other hand, the company has also met reverses and responded with perseverance and resourceful adaptation. Lessons are just beginning to emerge from the venture.

To begin with, the China case warns against underestimating the competition—or making quick assumptions about where it is going to come from. When P&G entered China, local competitors were very weak in most consumer categories. With surprising resourcefulness, however, they adapted to the arrival of the multinationals, rapidly acquiring Western marketing techniques while manufacturing and distributing at a fraction of the costs that companies like P&G had grown accustomed to carrying. Instead of contending with familiar rivals like Colgate, Unilever, Kao, and Henkel for China's laundry market, P&G found itself losing ground to Nice, a resourceful local producer that coupled effective advertising and masterful production and distribution structures with extraordinarily frugal manufacturing. Procter & Gamble's ability to win in China in this category will depend on adapting as rapidly and resourcefully as Nice is doing.

The imperative of adaptation and further innovation does not mean that competing in laundry in China was a mistake, though. Far from it. Just as competing in Japan taught P&G the need to achieve higher standards of quality and a faster pace of innovation, competing in China is teaching new models of competition, especially in manufacturing and distribution. If P&G succeeds in this category in China, the lessons learned there will help the company sustain its lead elsewhere.

In the meantime, the laundry experience in China (like other cases in other markets) strongly suggests that putting a portfolio of brands in key categories creates a stronger, more durable market presence. In environments like China and other developing economies, competing at the lower price tiers not only rounds out the company's brand offerings, but also forces efficiencies and keeps the company closely tied to consumers' value standards.

In the final analysis, however, long-term success or failure in China cannot be measured by the market shares of any given brand or set of brands. Ultimately, P&G will stand on the strength of the organization it builds there and the capacity of that organization to contribute to the enterprise as a global whole. The overriding lesson in China remains deeply familiar: Build for the long term. China is proving to be more than an enormous market and more than a series of low-cost factory sites. It is turning into a series of invaluable opportunities for new partnership, new technologies, and new entrepreneurial energy for P&G as it navigates through the next century.

Principles of Brand Building

THROUGHOUT ITS HISTORY, P&G has sought consciously to learn from its experiences, as well as from deep study of consumers, competitors, and markets. Before this book was written, the company twice authorized histories to be published.[1] In the early 1990s, Ed Artzt institutionalized the study of the company's experience by identifying historical management cases to be studied as part of the curriculum in P&G College, the internal forum for management training and development. Beyond these formal inquiries into P&G's past, the company is a font of stories and lore, about the key innovation in this brand, the terrible mistake made in that one, the contributions of this individual, the impact of and response to that unforeseen event. Some of these stories are posted on P&G's intranet, where they serve as illustrations and reminders of how the company works and makes progress.

Procter & Gamble recounts and propagates these stories and, from time to time, inquires systematically into its past because it recognizes that its experience is a unique source of learning and advantage. The trick in examining experience is to distill from it the important and enduring conclusions and to distinguish these from the insignificant and ephemeral.[2]

Procter & Gamble's business and long-term formula for success is building consumer brands: developing and offering products with features and associations that consumers value above their alternatives. Ideally, the features will enhance performance and make P&G's products superior to those of the competition. Similarly, the associations should create in the consumer feelings of safety, reliability, and trust. A strong brand promises a positive experience and creates an enduring relationship. The company thus strives to make the purchase of a P&G brand the best choice and the use of it a source of complete satisfaction. As A. G. Lafley put it, the company wins at the two moments of truth: when a consumer chooses to buy a P&G product instead of an alternative, and when the consumer puts that P&G product to use.[3]

Brand building in this sense is much more than a marketing activity. It involves developing products with performance features that consumers value, and it involves constantly upgrading them. It includes manufacturing and distributing these products at costs permitting prices consumers are willing to pay and guaranteeing margins acceptable to the company and its wholesalers and retailers. And, of course, brand building does include the marketing and advertising that communicates the brands' promise. All this has to be coordinated and done well. Brand building, in short, engages the entire organization in the ongoing quest to deliver superior value to consumers.

Tried and Tested Principles

During the course of its long life, P&G has identified principles of brand building. Taking these principles from its most vivid experiences, the company has then attempted to use them in introducing new brands, preserving old ones, entering new markets, and competing in old ones. Many of the principles originated in the company's earliest days, and a few surfaced in more recent times. Some principles are made explicit in the company's official publications; some are communicated informally on the job. Whenever and however they emerged, the principles act as guidelines to the company's operation. Here are ten that emerged from review and discussion inside P&G as it reflected on its first 165 years.

1. Do the Right Thing

The company separated itself from many of its competitors in the nineteenth century by insisting on unadulterated ingredients, quality products, and high ethical standards in business conduct. The founders were upright men, and they established a reputation for rectitude, integrity, and fairness that remain hallmarks of the company today.

In the 1980s, P&G articulated formal statements of purpose, values, and principles that are foundational to all its activities and operations. Virtually all companies, of course, proclaim ethical behavior and integrity as primary values. For a company to do the right thing every day, however, it must not only espouse the principle but also enact it. Procter & Gamble has sought to do both with constancy of purpose, disciplining transgressors, walking away from deals involving questionable payments, and terminating products and brands that could tarnish the company's reputation.

Another manifestation of the principle is P&G's commitment to the communities in which it operates and to public service generally. This commitment originated not in idealism but in pragmatism, to win and retain consumers, attract and inspire employees, improve the communities where the company operates, and bolster the company's image—its brand, if you will. Wherever significant concentrations of P&G personnel are found, significant contributions by P&G to community welfare will also be found. Most of these contributions—such as leadership in civic associations, support for local charities, and volunteer initiatives in education and health care—are so routine as to be scarcely noticeable. Other contributions, however, such as P&G's role in helping Albany, Georgia, overcome racial barriers and the company's humanitarian relief efforts after a devastating earthquake in Kobe, Japan, were quite dramatic.

2. Cultivate a Passion for Winning

The imperative to succeed, to best the competition, to win, is a longstanding principle in P&G's history. The company is intensely competitive, an attitude that goes back to its founders, when William Procter and James Gamble's company emerged as the leader of the pack among scores of soap and candle makers in nineteenth-century Cincinnati. Long before it became fashionable for corporate leaders to proclaim that their companies would become number one or number two in their businesses or they would exit, P&G was pursuing the same goal. Except that with core brands, number two is not acceptable. When Colgate passed Crest as the leading dentifrice in the United States in the late 1990s, the pain at P&G was palpable—just as was the determination to reclaim the lead at the earliest possible moment.

Procter & Gamble institutionalized its competitiveness in the 1920s and 1930s through the brand management system. Not only would the company strive to outdo rival makers of household products, but it would also strive to outdo itself, with brand managers of Camay trying to maximize volume and share, even if some share of the latter came from Ivory. Competitiveness remains *the* salient characteristic of brand managers and most other employees. The best people in the company are bright, articulate, committed, determined, hardworking, and creative—all of that. Most of all, though, they want to win. Winning is not exclusively defined as developing the next blockbuster category or brand, although that remains a constant objective. Rather, winning often consists of many incremental gains, a significant reduction of total delivered cost here, a share point taken from the competition there. These accumulate, and P&G has encouraged the attitudes and developed the supporting systems and policies to produce these small gains, time after time.

3. Sustaining Brands Is a Never-Ending Challenge

Another old discovery involves the power of branding—the ability to implant in a consumer's mind a set of positive associations around even a humdrum, everyday product like a bar of soap. Brands can command loyalty. Ivory was not just another soap—as everyone in the United States knows, it floats—but it had no secret ingredients, lower costs, or other features that made it wash and clean better than any other well-made bar of soap. What it did have were qualities that P&G fashioned into an image that consumers came to understand and value: quality, reliability, convenience, mildness, familiarity, and home-and-hearth values. Procter & Gamble carefully crafted and nurtured these associations over time. The creation of the Ivory brand is a hugely significant story. Not only did it accelerate P&G's progress, but it also set the example in the consumer products industry and in the larger history of the modern consumer economy. There is a tangible, quantifiable, and valuable difference between two similar products with different brand images. Procter & Gamble was one of the first, and remains one of the best, teachers of this lesson.

Unfortunately for P&G, Ivory also illustrates an important caveat: Once built, brands cannot be neglected, lest they languish. In the middle of the twentieth century, Ivory was allowed to wither and fade. The soap became old-fashioned, and lost its distinctive positioning. In this episode of brand erosion, P&G learned a lesson that it vowed never to repeat with its subsequent major brands. The huge efforts poured into keeping Tide an evergreen brand provide a positive example of the same point.

4. The Consumer Is Boss

Procter & Gamble's approach to building brands continues to evolve. The principal reason is another old lesson occasionally forgotten and painfully relearned: The consumer must be at the heart of everything the company does. That is why P&G invests so heavily in market research and test markets and why, in the vast majority of instances, consumers come to prize the company's brands. The brands are customized to their needs and preferences, even when, initially, consumers aren't fully aware of these. Sometimes, listening takes a long time, as happened with Pringles, a loser for decades before it became a big hit. And sometimes, for all the sensing the company does, it makes mistakes. Whoppers, even. The biggest and most damaging occurred in the 1970s and 1980s, when P&G underestimated its competition across a range of core categories in laundry products, oral care, and disposable diapers. Although it quickly recovered in laundry products and never lost its lead to Unilever, P&G did eventually fall behind Colgate in oral care and remains in a ferocious fight for leadership with Kimberly-Clark in disposable diapers. In these instances, P&G's competitors listened better to consumers and offered innovative features at prices people were prepared to pay. Wedded to formulas, features, and positionings that had worked in the past, P&G was slow to recognize changing consumer tastes.

5. Individuals Make a Difference

Still another old lesson lies in the recognition that the company consists of individuals whose contributions sum up to the performance of the whole.[4] No company grows fast and large on the abilities of its owners alone. Much earlier than most large companies, P&G recognized and acted on the notion that the interests of employer and its employees are inseparable, and individuals should be treated with dignity. This recognition lay behind the institution of profit sharing in 1887 and the subsequent spread of employee stock ownership, as well as the policy of promotion from within. Recognition of the individual remains at the heart of the integrated (high-performance) work systems in P&G's production facilities today.

Literal ownership is an important factor at P&G, but metaphorical ownership—taking responsibility and being held accountable, thinking and behaving like an owner—is equally important. The company encourages individual initiative and tolerates nonconformists and mavericks within certain bounds, recognizing that individuals make a difference. The most celebrated instance is the technology behind Tide, which proceeded in fits and starts—mainly the former—for more than a decade before determined scientists, engineers, and managers made it work. The result enabled the launch of two of the biggest brands in the company's history. This story is replicated in every successful P&G brand, market initiative, process, and program: An individual or a small team of people did something new or different and extraordinary. The individual or team took ownership and refused to be deflected off course. After more than 150 years, that's no accident: Procter & Gamble has figured out ways for (or allowed) it to happen, again and again.

6. Discipline Counts

Another important principle in P&G history involved the hard thinking and work channeled into getting something right. The company learned to gather a mass of data and analyze and reflect on it before developing a plan of action. It then staged trials, analyzed and reflected on these, and proceeded to develop better plans of action. This became a continuous process, the P&G way of learning, managing, and competing. Operational discipline is embedded in the company's daily procedures and activities as well as in its approach to new initiatives. There are no shortcuts, no substitutes for the intensive effort necessary to sustain success.

The roots of P&G's operational discipline reach back to Harley Procter and the branding of Ivory. Other important elements were grafted on during the twentieth century. The discipline has many manifestations. For example, there are the rigorous market research and bounded test markets that precede every product launch and major marketing campaign. Another example is the once famous one-page memos that are harder and more time-consuming to write than something longer and less well conceived. The company's discipline is also evident in the comprehensive quality-control systems and procedures characteristic of P&G plants. Finally, there are the strict and closely monitored financial controls the company applies to its programs and projects.

7. Innovate Constantly, Everywhere

Constant, meaningful product innovation has been a primary tool for P&G in building and sustaining brands, especially after the introduction of Tide in the late 1940s. The company's best brands are distinctive in ways that consumers recognize and value in both moments of truth: when they are shopping for a product and when they use it. Winning in these moments, in turn, requires significant investment in R&D. Procter & Gamble sells detergents confidently, because it believes they are better for the consumer than competitive products and alternatives, and it has stacks of research studies to back up its claims.

Procter & Gamble's ability to innovate in products and processes has been a key factor in its long-term success. The company spends between 4 and 5 percent of net revenues on R&D—it spent $1.7 billion in 2001–2002. The costly business of pharmaceutical research somewhat inflates the total, but P&G has been by far the biggest R&D spender in its industry since the 1930s. The company maintains a network of technical centers around the world, including seven in the United States (five near Cincinnati) and a dozen others scattered across Europe, Asia, and Latin America. It also funds research projects in more than one hundred universities in the United States and abroad. Procter & Gamble is one of only two consumer products companies—Johnson & Johnson is the other—to be awarded the National Medal of Technology in the United States.

At an early stage, P&G learned to think of and value innovation more broadly than as a responsibility of its technical organization, just as it does not consider brand building the sole responsibility of its marketing organization.

Innovations that reduce total delivered cost—in purchasing, manufacturing, logistics, and overhead—are potent competitive weapons. Similarly, innovations that enhance differentiation—in packaging, advertising, and promotion, as well as in R&D—are essential to building strong, enduring brands.

8. Lead Change

In business generally and in P&G's industry particularly, companies do not sustain success without anticipating and leading innovation and change. Throughout its history, P&G periodically triggered significant change in its markets and organization and sometimes reacted to or resisted it. It tended to fare better when championing change than when observing or opposing it. As the pioneer of direct selling, market research, brand management, radio and TV advertising, retailer partnerships, and a host of significant product, process, and management innovations, P&G reaped significant competitive advantages.

An important part of P&G's success is an attitude about change expressed in common sayings around the company that is determined periodically to "reinvent itself" and "change the game." It seeks to breed in employees not only "a restless dissatisfaction with the status quo," but also (reflecting P&G's competitiveness) "a relentless quest to be the best." Procter & Gamble has learned how to do that, through a willingness to change not only the outside world but also the inside. Hence came the institution of brand management in the 1930s, divisionalization in the 1950s, high-performance work systems in the 1960s and 1970s, category management in the 1980s, and integrated work systems and the global matrix organization in the 1990s and 2000s. All these initiatives propelled the company ahead.

9. Alliances Create Advantage

Procter & Gamble discovered the benefits of partnerships early on, when it developed enduring alliances with ad agencies to promote brands and negotiated technical agreements with third parties to introduce and improve products and processes. Technical agreements, for example, hastened the development of Crisco, synthetic detergents, dentifrices, and pharmaceuticals, where these agreements remain an especially important source of advantage today. The benefits of partnerships are apparent in the company's recent emphasis on "connect and develop" rather than always going it alone in new-product development.

Procter & Gamble embraced another form of alliance, the joint venture, as its customary mode of entry into many new geographic markets.

Partnerships are a mechanism for blurring the boundaries of the company, providing access to information and innovation, gaining speed, saving money, and generating better returns. In the early 2000s, alliances even allowed the company to outsource activities such as routine business services not directly contributing to P&G's competitive differentiation.

10. Partner with Customers

Since the 1980s, P&G has learned to extend the concept of alliance to its trade customers, which include distributors and retailers of all sizes and modes of operating all over the world. The company hardly ignored its trade customers before the 1980s, but viewed them more as parties in a transaction rather than as partners in a common purpose to serve their shopper, who also is P&G's consumer. Several factors prompted the change in P&G's thinking: the total quality movement's focus on the customer, advances in information technology that enabled real-time gathering and analysis of consumer decisions and behavior, and the rise of mass merchandisers such as Wal-Mart and Carrefour and their own store brands. At P&G, these factors led the company to establish a single organization to coordinate purchasing, manufacturing, and distribution activities; recast the sales function as "customer business development," a customer relationship management activity; and participate in and often lead industrywide cooperative programs to take costs out of the supply chain.

By the mid-1990s, these initiatives had all delivered tangible benefits to P&G and its partners. At the same time, P&G's efforts to collaborate with its trade customers had graduated from an intriguing set of experiments to a new principle by which the company would henceforth conduct its business.

The principles of brand building just enumerated are hardly unique. Many of them, with slight variations, might be found in other large consumer products companies. But the timing, context, and ways in which they were learned and how they cumulate and interact give them particular meaning and force within this company. How well and how consistently the company has executed them around the world have largely determined its fortunes. The principles thus helped gather and guide the rising tide that we take as a metaphor for P&G's evolution and expansion—the waves of change originating in Cincinnati in 1837 and still swelling and surging through time and across distance today.

APPENDIXES

Appendix 1

Graphical Timeline Prepared by P&G Corporate Archives

Appendix 2

Financial Results Summary 1929–2003

Appendix 3

Selected Brand Introduction Dates

Appendix 4

Procters, Gambles, and the Leaders of Procter & Gamble 1837–Present

Appendix 1

Graphical Timeline Prepared by P&G Corporate Archives

		1837	1860	1870	1880
Leaders		William Procter, James Gamble Founders			
Organizational Design	Structure	Family Partnership			
	Culture and Values				Half Day Off Saturday Profit Sharing
	Corporate Innovations				P&G Brand Advertising Begins
Business Environment			U.S. Civil War 1861–1865		
P&G Growth	P&G Technical Innovations		Scientific Analysis and Soapmaking Process		Ivory Bar "99-44/100% Pure" Analysis
	Categories	Candles and Soaps			
	Markets	Cincinnati		Regional U.S. Markets	U.S. National Market
	Potential Market Size	46,000			50,262,000
	Net Sales		$1 million		
		1837	1860	1870	1880

Partnership Years

	1890	1900	1910	1920	1930	1940
	William A. Procter 1890–1907		William Cooper Procter 1907–1930		R. R. Deupree 1930–1948	
	Company Incorporated				Brand Management	
			Eight-hour Workday	Steady Employment	Five-day Workweek	
	First Color Print Aid			First Radio Ad Direct Selling to Customers Market Research Department	Radio Soap Operas First TV Ad	
	Financial Panic Depression 1893–1897		World War I 1914–1918	Increased United States/ European Trade	Great Depression Government Regulation Collective Bargaining	World War II 1939–1945
	Corporate R&D Lab	Hydrogenization of Edible Oils		Standardization of Soapmaking Process	Synthetic Detergents and Shampoos	Continuous Bar Soapmaking Process
			Shortening and Oil	Machine Laundry Products	Hair Care Oral Care	Hard Surface Cleaners
			Canada		United Kingdom Philippines Cuba	
				115,249,000		159,629,000
					$192 million	$343 million

1890 1900 1910 1920 1930 1940

Innovation and Brand Building

Graphical Timeline *(continued)*

		1950	1960	1970
Leaders		Neil McElroy 1948–1957	Howard Morgens 1957–1974	Ed Harness 1974–1981
Organizational Design	Structure	Divisionalization; Country Management		
	Culture and Values		Minority Hiring; High-Performance Work Organizations	
	Corporate Innovations	P&G TV Programming		Consumer 1-800-Number
Business Environment		Post-War Era Huge Economic Growth United States/ Europe/Japan; Formation of the EEC	Asian and Latin American Economies Developing	Oil Crises 1973 and 1979
P&G Growth	P&G Technical Innovations	MVL Opens; First Fluoride Toothpaste	CPF Paper-making Process; European Technical Center; Disposable Diapers	Enzyme Laundry Detergent; Stacked Potato Chips; First Rx Products; Dryer-added Fabric Conditioner
	Categories	Dish Care; Deodorants/ Antiperspirants; Paper Products; Peanut Butter	Fabric Conditioner; Disposable Diapers; Coffee	Salted Snacks; Bone Health; Feminine Protection; Skin Care
	Markets	Puerto Rico; Venezuela; France; Mexico; Switzerland; Italy; Belgium; Peru; Saudi Arabia; Lebanon	Greece; Morocco; Germany; Netherlands; Austria	Singapore; Hong Kong; Indonesia; Spain; Sweden; Finland; Malaysia; Japan
	Potential Market Size		535,236,000	
	Net Sales	$1 billion		$2.9 billion
		1950	1960	1970

Diversification and International Expansion

1980 **1990** **2000**

John Smale 1981–1990 | Ed Artzt 1990–1995 | John Pepper 1995–1999 | Durk Jager 1999–2000 | A. G. Lafley 2000–

Teamwork | Category Management | Product Supply | Global Category Teams | Customer Business Development | Strengthening Global Effectiveness | Corporate New Ventures | Global R&D Network | Organization 2005

Rely Withdrawal | Purpose, Values, and Principles | Reliability Engineering | Corporate Sustainability | Integrated Work Systems | Consumer Is Boss

First P&G Cable TV Program | Vic Mills Society Created | Innovation Leadership Team | First Digital TV Ad | PG.com | Reflect.com | Technology Donations and Licensing

Great Merger Wave | ASEAN | China Opens for Trade | Cold War Ends | Collapse of Communism | European Union | NAFTA | Russian Economic Collapse | Asian Financial Crisis | European Monetary Union

High Protection Feminine Pads | Tartar Control Toothpaste | Super Absorbent Thin Diaper | 2-in-1 Shampoo | Laundry Detergents •Compact •Bleach | Structured Tissue/Towels | Kobe Technical Center | Beijing Technical Center | Olestra | Non-woven Materials | Fabric Odor Elimination | Tooth Whitening

Juice | Gastrointestinal | Hair Conditioner | Respiratory Care | Cosmetics | Fragrances | Baby Wipes | Pet Nutrition | Home Dry Cleaning | Hair Coloring | Water Purification

Colombia | Chile | Ireland | Taiwan | Australia | Guatemala | Honduras | India | Kenya | New Zealand | Nicaragua | Thailand | Caribbean | Egypt | Turkey | Brazil | China | El Salvador | Korea | Pakistan | Portugal | Argentina | Czech Republic | Hungary | Poland | Russia | Slovak Republic | Ukraine | Norway | Denmark | Nigeria | Bulgaria | Romania | South Africa | Vietnam | Bangladesh | Belarus | Costa Rica | Estonia | Croatia | Kazakhstan | Slovenia | Sri Lanka | Uzbekistan | Yugoslavia | Latvia | Uganda | Yemen | Azerbaijan | Boznia-Herzegovina | Ghana | Macedonia | Syria | Lithuania | Tanzania | Algeria | Israel | Panama | United Arab Emirates

3,653,110,000 | 4,984,000,000 | 5,255,000,000

$10.7 billion | $24 billion | $40 billion

1980 **1990** **2000**

Global Leadership

Appendix 2

Financial Results Summary, 1929–2003

Fiscal Year Ending	Net Sales (millions of dollars)	Net Earnings (millions of dollars)	Average Shareholder's Equity (millions of dollars)	After Tax Margin %	Return on Equity %	
2003	43,377	5,186	14,945.9	12.0%	34.7%	
2002	40,238	4,352	12,858.0	10.8%	33.8%	
2001	39,244	2,922	12,148.6	7.4%	24.1%	(A)
2000	39,951	3,542	12,172.5	8.9%	29.1%	(B)
1999	38,125	3,763	12,147.0	9.9%	31.0%	(C)
1998	37,154	3,780	12,141.1	10.2%	31.1%	
1997	35,764	3,415	11,884.0	9.5%	28.7%	
1996	35,284	3,046	11,155.5	8.6%	27.3%	
1995	33,482	2,645	9,710.5	7.9%	27.2%	
1994	30,385	2,211	8,136.5	7.3%	27.2%	
1993	30,433	–656	8,256.0	–2.2%	–7.9%	(D)
1992	29,362	1,872	8,403.5	6.4%	22.3%	
1991	27,026	1,773	7,627.0	6.6%	23.2%	
1990	24,081	1,602	6,866.5	6.7%	23.3%	
1989	21,398	1,206	6,276.0	5.6%	19.2%	
1988	19,336	1,020	6,164.0	5.3%	16.5%	
1987	17,000	327	5,972.0	1.9%	5.5%	(E)
1986	15,439	709	5,613.0	4.6%	12.6%	
1985	13,552	635	5,176.0	4.7%	12.3%	
1984	12,946	890	4,841.0	6.9%	18.4%	
1983	12,452	866	4,383.0	7.0%	19.8%	
1982	11,994	777	4,014.0	6.5%	19.4%	
1981	11,416	593	3,723.0	5.2%	15.9%	(F)
1980	10,772	640	3,397.0	5.9%	18.8%	
1979	9,329	575	3,056.0	6.2%	18.8%	
1978	8,100	510	2,756.0	6.3%	18.5%	
1977	7,284	460	2,479.0	6.3%	18.6%	

Fiscal Year Ending	Net Sales (millions of dollars)	Net Earnings (millions of dollars)	Average Shareholder's Equity (millions of dollars)	After Tax Margin %	Return on Equity %
1976	6,513	400	2,227.0	6.1%	18.0%
1975	6,082	332	2,017.0	5.5%	16.5%
1974	4,912	316	1,838.0	6.4%	17.2%
1973	3,907	302	1,662.0	7.7%	18.2%
1972	3,514	276	1,483.8	7.9%	18.6%
1971	3,178	238	1,336.6	7.5%	17.8%
1970	2,979	212	1,218.4	7.1%	17.4%
1969	2,708	187	1,135.5	6.9%	16.5%
1968	2,543	183	1,057.6	7.2%	17.3%
1967	2,439	174	978.4	7.1%	17.8%
1966	2,243	149	932.6	6.6%	16.0%
1965	2,059	133	904.5	6.5%	14.7%
1964	1,914	131	837.9	6.8%	15.6%
1963	1,654	116	757.3	7.0%	15.3%
1962	1,619	109	704.4	6.7%	15.5%
1961	1,542	107	648.7	6.9%	16.5%
1960	1,442	98	593.6	6.8%	16.5%
1959	1,369	82	547.1	6.0%	15.0%
1958	1,295	73	494.3	5.6%	14.8%
1957	1,156	68	435.7	5.9%	15.6%
1956	1,038	59	395.4	5.7%	14.9%
1955	966	57	368.3	5.9%	15.5%
1954	911	52	344.3	5.7%	15.1%
1953	850	42	325.1	4.9%	12.9%
1952	818	42	308.4	5.1%	13.6%
1951	861	51	288.9	5.9%	17.7%
1950	633	61	262.6	9.6%	23.2%
1949	697	29	246.2	4.2%	11.8%
1948	724	65	224.6	9.0%	28.9%
1947	534	47	183.5	8.8%	25.6%
1946	310	21	158.7	6.8%	13.2%
1945	343	20	157.1	5.8%	12.7%

(continued)

Appendix 2

Financial Results Summary, 1929–2003 *(continued)*

Fiscal Year Ending	Net Sales (millions of dollars)	Net Earnings (millions of dollars)	Average Shareholder's Equity (millions of dollars)	After Tax Margin %	Return on Equity %
1944	326	19	157.4	5.8%	12.1%
1943	302	21	149.4	7.0%	14.1%
1942	271	21	141.1	7.7%	14.9%
1941	220	28	134.5	12.7%	20.8%
1940	205	29	130.2	14.1%	22.3%
1939	211	25	129.0	11.8%	19.4%
1938	209	15	128.0	7.2%	11.7%
1937	219	27	124.3	12.3%	21.7%
1936	170	17	118.1	10.0%	14.4%
1935	148	19	112.3	12.8%	16.9%
1934	108	14	107.9	13.0%	13.0%
1933	94	11	107.3	11.7%	10.3%
1932	128	18	112.4	14.1%	16.0%
1931	176	23	111.8	13.1%	20.6%
1930	192	22	97.0	11.5%	22.7%
1929	193	19	82.9	9.8%	22.9%

(A) Includes charges of $131 million in net sales and $1.474 billion in after tax income related to the Organization 2005 program.
(B) Includes charges of $688 million in after tax income related to the Organization 2005 program.
(C) Includes charges of $385 million in after tax income related to the Organization 2005 program.
(D) Includes charges of $1.746 billion in after tax income related to the Strengthening Global Effectiveness program and charges of $925 million in after tax income related to an earlier accounting change.
(E) Includes charges of $459 million in after tax income related to the June 1987 restructuring program.
(F) Includes an extraordinary charge of $75 million after tax for the suspension of the sale of Rely tampons.

Appendix 3

Selected Brand Introduction Dates

This is a partial *list of selected P&G consumer brands, listing the date and country of introduction. The list provides only the initial use of the brand name and does not include product extensions or flanker brands (e.g., it includes Always feminine care pads but not Always Plus, Always Ultra, Always Pantiliners with Wings, etc.) or introduction in foreign markets. The list includes some brands acquired and some discontinued; it does not include brands that failed in test markets or within three years of introduction. More detailed information is available in the P&G Corporate Archives.*

NA indicates information not available

Brand	Company	Country of Introduction	Date
Ace (bleach)	P&G	Italy	1960s
Ace (laundry detergent)	P&G	Cuba	1948
Actonel (prescription drug)	P&G	United States	1998
Always (feminine care)	P&G	United States	1983
Ariel (laundry detergent)	P&G	Germany	1967
Asacol (prescription drug)	Tillots-Pharma	Switzerland	1992
Attends (adult incontinence)	P&G	United States	1978–1979
Baby Fresh (baby wipes) Babysan (diapers)	Acquired from Kimberly-Clark	United States	1996
Bain de Soleil (skin care)	Acquired, 1987	Europe	1937; sold, 1995
Big Top (peanut butter)	Acquired, 1955	United States	discontinued, 1960s
Biz (bleach)	P&G	United States	1967; sold, 2000
Biz (laundry detergent)	P&G	United States	1956, later discontinued
Blend-a-Med (dentifrice)	Blendax, acquired in 1987	Germany	1951
Blendax (dentifrice)	Blendax, acquired in 1987	Germany	1932
Bold (laundry detergent)	P&G	United States	1965
Bonus (laundry detergent)	P&G	United States	1965
Bonux (laundry detergent)	P&G	France	1958
Bounce (dryer sheets)	P&G	United States	1972
Bounty (paper towels)	P&G	United States	1965
Brothers Coffee	Acquired, 1999	United States	1984
Camay (bar soap)	P&G	United States	1926
Cascade (dish detergent)	P&G	United States	1955
Certain (bathroom tissue)	P&G	United States	1981; discontinued, 1987
Charmin (bathroom tissue)	Acquired, 1957	United States	1928
Cheer (laundry detergent)	P&G	United States	1950
Chloraseptic (OTC medicine)	Acquired with Norwich, 1982	United States	1957
Cinch (household cleaner)	P&G	United States	1966, later discontinued
Citrus Hill Orange Juice	Acquired 1982	United States	sold, 1993

(continued)

Brand	Company	Country of Introduction	Date
Clarion (beauty care)	Acquired with Noxell, 1989	United States	1986; discontinued, 1994
Clairol (hair care)	Acquired, 2001	United States	1931
Clearasil (acne remedy)	Acquired with Richardson-Vicks, 1985	United States	sold, 2000
Clorox (bleach)	Acquired, 1957	United States	divested, 1969
Coast (bar soap)	P&G	United States	1974; sold, 2000
Comet (abrasive cleaner)	P&G	United States	1956; sold, 2001
Cover Girl (beauty care)	Acquired with Noxell, 1989	United States	1958
Crest (dentifrice)	P&G	United States	1955
Crisco (shortening)	P&G	United States	1911; sold, 2001
Crush (beverages)	Acquired, 1981	United States	sold, 1989
Dantrium (prescription drug)	Acquired with Norwich, 1982	United States	1974
Dash (laundry detergent)	P&G	United States	1954
Dawn (dish detergent)	P&G	United States	1972
DayQuil (OTC medicine)	P&G	United States	1992
Daz (laundry detergent)	P&G	United Kingdom	1953
Denquel (dentifrice)	Acquired with Richardson-Vicks, 1985	United States	1981; discontinued, 1994
Didronel (prescription drug)	P&G	United States	1978
Downy (fabric softener)	P&G	United States	1960
Dramamine	Acquired from Searle, 1985	United States	sold, 1991
Dreft (laundry detergent)	P&G	United States	1933
Drene (shampoo)	P&G	United States	1934; sold, 2000
Duffy (disposable diaper)	Eguimad, S.A	Argentina	acquired, 1991
Duncan Hines (cake mix)	Acquired, 1956	United States	sold, 1997
Duz (laundry soap)	Acquired, 1929	United States	discontinued, 1978
Dryel (fabric care)	P&G	United States	1999
Ela (feminine care)	Pro-Higiene, acquired, 1993	Brazil	1970s
Ellen Betrix (beauty care)	Acquired from Revlon, 1991	Germany	1930s
Entex (prescription drug)	Acquired with Norwich, 1982	United States	sold, 1996
Era (laundry detergent)	P&G	United States	1972
Escudo (beauty care)	P&G	Mexico	1966
Eukanuba	Acquired with Iams, 1999	United States	1969
Evax (feminine care)	Agrolimen	Spain	acquired, 1989
Fairy (bar soap)	Hedley	United Kingdom	1898; acquired, 1930
Febreze (fabric treatment)	P&G	United States	1996
Fisher Nuts (snack)	Acquired, 1989	United States	sold, 1995
Fixodent (denture adhesive)	Acquired with Richardson-Vicks, 1985	United States	1936
Flash (hard surface cleanser)	P&G	United Kingdom	1958
Fluffo (shortening)	P&G	United States	1953; later sold
Folgers (coffee)	Acquired, 1963	United States	1850

Brand	Company	Country of Introduction	Date
Formula 44 (OTC medicine)	Acquired with Richardson-Vicks, 1985	United States	1972
Fresco (bar soaps)	NA	Mexico	1989
Furadantin	Acquired with Norwich, 1982	United States	1953
Gain (laundry detergent)	P&G	United States	1960
Gleem (dentifrice)	P&G	United States	1952
Giorgio of Beverly Hills (fragrance)	Acquired from Avon, 1994	United States	1981
Hawaiian Punch (beverage)	Acquired from Del Monte/ RJR Nabisco, 1990	United States	1930s; sold, 1999
Head & Chest (OTC medicine)	Acquired with Norwich, 1982	United States	1982; discontinued, 1987
Head & Shoulders (shampoo)	P&G	United States	1961
Hegor (shampoo)	Acquired	France	1929
Herbal Essences (hair care; originally Herbal Essence)	Acquired, 2002	United States	1972
Hidden Magic (hair spray)	P&G	United States	1959; relaunched, 1965, discontinued, 1971
High Point (decaffeinated coffee)	P&G	United States	1975; discontinued, 1993
Hires Root Beer (beverage)	Acquired, 1981	United States	sold, 1989
Hugo Boss (fragrance)	Acquired with Eurocos, 1991	NA	1985
Iams (pet nutrition)	Acquired, 1999	United States	1950
Inextra (laundry detergent)	Inextra	Colombia	1956
Ivory (bar soap)	P&G	United States	1879
Jar (dish detergent)	Rakona	Czech/Slovak Republics	relaunched, 1992
Jif (peanut butter)	P&G	United States	1956; sold, 2001
Joy (dish detergent)	P&G	United States	1949
Joy (fragrance)	Acquired from Jean Patou, 2001	France	1930
Kamill (skin care)	Acquired with Blendax	Germany	1983
Kirk's Castile (bar soap)	Acquired, 1930	United States	discontinued, 1996
Ladysan (feminine care)	Compania Manufac-turera dePapeles y Cartones (CMPC)	Argentina	acquired,1993
Laura Biagotti's Roma (fragrance)	Acquired with Eurocos, 1991	NA	1988
Lava (bar soap)	Acquired with William Waltke, 1927	United States	1893; sold, 1995
Le Jardin (fragrance)	Acquired with Max Factor, 1991	United States	1983; sold, 1996
Lenor (fabric softener)	P&G	Germany	1963
Lenox (bar soap)	P&G	United States	1884; discontinued, 1930s?
Lestoil	Acquired with Noxell, 1989	United States	1936; sold, 1996
Lilt (hair care)	P&G	United States	1949; sold, 1990

(continued)

Brand	Company	Country of Introduction	Date
Lincoln juices	Acquired with Sundor, 1989	United States	sold, 1993
Luvs (disposable diapers)	P&G	United States	1976
Macrobid (prescription drug)	P&G	United States	1994
Macrodantin (prescription drug)	Acquired with Norwich, 1982	United States	1968
Max Factor (beauty care)	Acquired from Revlon, 1991	United States	1909
Metamucil (nutritional supplement)	Acquired from Searle, 1985	United States	1934
Millstone Coffee	Acquired, 1995	United States	1978
Monogen Baby (laundry detergent)	P&G	Japan	1986
Monogen Uni (laundry detergent)	Acquired	Japan	1937
Monsavon (bar soap)	Acquired	France	1930
Muse (bar soap)	Acquired	Japan	1953
Mr. Clean (household cleaner)	P&G	United States	1958
Myth (laundry detergent)	Acquired, 1992	Soviet Union (Russia)	NA
Navy (fragrance)	Acquired, 1990	United States	sold, 1996
NE (bar soap)	P&G	Mexico	1993
Norwich Aspirin (OTC medicine)	Acquired with Norwich, 1982	United States	1927; sold, 1992
Noxzema (skin care)	Acquired with Noxell, 1989	United States	1914
NyQuil (OTC medicine)	Acquired with Richardson-Vicks, 1985	United States	1966
Oil of Olay	Acquired with Richardson-Vicks, 1985	South Africa	Early 1950s
Old Spice (deodorant)	Acquired with Shulton, 1990	United States	1937
Otros Dias (catamenials)	Acquired, 1991	Argentina	NA
Oxydol (laundry soap)	Acquired with William Waltke, 1928	United States	sold, 2000
P&G White Naptha (soap)	P&G	United States	1905; discontinued, 1963
Pampers (disposable diapers)	P&G	United States	1961
Pantene	Acquired with Richardson-Vicks, 1985	Europe	1947
Party Curl (hair care)	P&G	United States	1953; discontinued, 1965
Pepto-Bismol	Acquired with Norwich, 1982	United States	1901
Peridex (prescription oral rinse)	P&G	United States	1986; sold, 1997
Pert Plus (hair care; original Pert brand test marketed in 1979)	P&G	United States	1986
Petrole Hahn (shampoo)	Acquired	France	1885

Brand	Company	Country of Introduction	Date
Prell (shampoo)	P&G	United States	1946; sold, 1999
Prilosec OTC (medicine)	Cooperative agreement with AstraZeneca	United States	2003
Pringles (potato snack)	P&G	United States	1968
Puffs (facial tissue)	P&G	United States	1960
Punica (beverage)	Dittmeyer, acquired, 1989	Germany	1976
PUR (water treatment)	Acquired, 1999	United States	1986
Puritan (cooking oil)	P&G	United States	1976; sold, 2001
Radar (hair care)	P&G	United States	1962; discontinued, 1967
RainTree (skin care)	Acquired with Noxell, 1989	United States	discontinued, 1993
Rapido (laundry detergent)	P&G	Mexico	1959
Red (fragrance)	Acquired with Giorgio, 1994	United States	1988
Rejoice (shampoo)	P&G	Asia	early 1980s
Rejoy (shampoo)	P&G	Asia	early 1980s
Rei (laundry)	Rei-Werke	Germany	1969
Rely (feminine care)	P&G	United States	1974; discontinued, 1980
Roge Cavailles (beauty care)	Acquired	France	1924
Royale paper brands	Acquired, 1991	Canada	1929
Safeguard (bar soap)	P&G	United States	1963
Salvo (dish detergent)	P&G	Mexico	1977
Salvo (laundry detergent)	P&G	United States	1960; discontinued, 1978
Sapon (hard surface cleanser)	Rakona	Czech/Slovak Republics	relaunched, 1992
Scope (oral rinse)	P&G	United States	1965
Secret (deodorant; originally home permanent, 1955)	P&G	United States	1956
Shamtu (hair care)	Acquired with Blendax, 1987	Germany	1968
Shasta (shampoo)	P&G	United States	1948; discontinued, 1962
Sinex (OTC medicine)	Acquired with Richardson-Vicks, 1985	United States	1959
Siren (laundry detergent)	Inextra	Colombia	1985
SK-II (beauty care)	Acquired with Max Factor, 1991	Japan	1981
Solo (laundry detergent)	P&G	United States	1979
Spic and Span (household cleaner)	Acquired, 1945	United States	1926; sold, 2001
Summit (bathroom tissue)	P&G	United States	1981; discontinued, 1990s
Sunny Delight (beverage)	Acquired with Sundor, 1989	United States	1964
Supremo (laundry detergent)	Acquired with Inextra, 1987	Colombia	1972

(continued)

Brand	Company	Country of Introduction	Date
Sure (deodorant)	P&G	United States	1972
Swiffer (cleaning product)	P&G	United States	1999
Tampax (feminine care)	Acquired with Tambrands, 1997	United States	1931
Teel (dentifrice)	P&G	United States	1938; discontinued, 1953
Tempo (facial tissue)	Acquired with VP-Schickedanz AG, 1994	Germany	1929
Tender Leaf Tea	Acquired from Standard Brands, 1983	United States	discontinued but brand licensed outside
Texsun (beverage)	Acquired with Sundor, 1989	United States	sold, 1993
ThermaCare (OTC medicine)	P&G	United States	2001
Thrill (laundry detergent)	P&G	United States	1959; discontinued, 1978
Tide (laundry detergent)	P&G	United States	1946
Top Job (household cleaner)	P&G	United States	1963; discontinued, 1994
Tras (dish detergent)	Acquired with Inextra, 1987	Colombia	1981
Unijab (laundry detergent)	Acquired with Inextra, 1987	Colombia	1966
Valensina (beverage)	Acquired with Dittmeyer, 1984	Germany	1967
Viakal (limescale remover)	P&G	France	1991
Vibrant (bleach)	P&G	United States	1981; discontinued, 1986
Vicks (OTC medicine)	Acquired with Richardson-Vicks, 1985	United States	1890
Vidal Sassoon	Acquired with Richardson-Vicks, 1985	United States	1974
Vizir (laundry detergent)	P&G	Germany	1981
Wella (hair care)	Acquired controlling interest, 2003	Germany	1880
Whirl (shortening)	P&G	United States	1955; discontinued, 1964
Whisper	P&G	Singapore	1983–1984
White Cloud (bathroom tissue)	P&G	United States	1958; sold, 1993
Wings (fragrance)	Acquired with Giorgio, 1994	United States	1993
Wondra (skin care; originally shampoo, 1959)	P&G	United States	1977; discontinued, 1993
Ya (laundry detergent)	Acquired with Inextra, 1987	Colombia	1982
Yes (feminine care)	Acquired, 1991	Argentina	NA
Zest (bar soap)	P&G	United States	1955
Ziac (prescription medicine)	P&G	United States	1993

Appendix 4

Procters, Gambles, and the Leaders of Procter & Gamble, 1837–Present

Procter & Gamble operated as a partnership between 1837 and 1890, when it was legally incorporated in New Jersey.[1] During its first three decades, founders William Procter (1801–1884) and James Gamble (1803–1891) shared responsibility for the firm's leadership. After the Civil War, Procter brought his sons, William A., George H., and Harley T. Procter into the partnership, tapering off his own involvement. James Gamble followed a few years later, involving his sons, James N. and David B. Gamble.

At the time of incorporation, William A. Procter became president, with James N. Gamble and Harley Procter as vice presidents, David Gamble as secretary treasurer, and William Cooper Procter (son of William A.) as general manager. (George Procter had left the business by then.) In 1891, P&G securities were listed on the New York Stock exchange, and ownership began to diversify, especially after Harley Procter soon phased into retirement while still in his mid-forties.[2] David Gamble retired by 1906, and James N. Gamble wound down his active involvement before World War I, although he remained a vice president until his death in 1932. Thereafter, no Gambles continued in senior executive positions, although a family member served on the board of directors until 1971. The last Procter in executive leadership was William Cooper Procter, who retired as president in 1930 and remained chairman of the board until his death four years later. His cousin William (Harley's son), who died in 1951 while a director, was the last Procter on the board. Another Procter descendant, Samuel Benedict (grandson of William A. Procter and nephew of William Cooper Procter), served as corporate secretary in the 1950s and 1960s.

Since 1890, P&G has been led by a single individual bearing the title of "president" until 1971 when the title changed to "chief executive." Whatever the title, the top executive has often doubled as chairman of the board since 1930, when the position was designated, although at times the positions have been divided.

Procter & Gamble Leaders Since 1890

William A. Procter, President, 1890–1907

William Cooper Procter, President, 1907–1930,
Chairman, 1930–1934

Richard R. Deupree, President, 1930–1948,
Chairman, 1948–1959

Neil H. McElroy, President, 1948–1957,
Chairman, 1959–1971

Howard J. Morgens, President, 1957–1971,
Chairman and Chief Executive, 1971–1974

Edward G. Harness, Chairman and Chief Executive, 1974–1981

John G. Smale, President and Chief Executive, 1981–1986,
Chairman and Chief Executive, 1986–1990
(Owen B. Butler, Chairman, 1981–1986)

Edwin L. Artzt, Chairman and Chief Executive, 1990–1995

John E. Pepper, Chairman and Chief Executive, 1995–1998,
Chairman, 1999 and 2000–2002

Durk I. Jager, President and Chief Executive, 1999,
President, Chief Executive, and Chairman, 1999–2000

Alan G. Lafley, President and Chief Executive, 2000–2002,
Chairman, President, and Chief Executive, 2002–

NOTES

Prologue

1. See, for example, annual rankings of most admired companies in *Fortune* since 1985.

2. David Swanson to Ed Rider, 5 December 2002, Procter & Gamble Corporate Archives, P&G Corporate Headquarters, Cincinnati, OH (hereafter cited as P&G Archives). Many senior executives came to admire the management best-seller *Built to Last,* by James C. Collins and Jerry I. Porras (New York: HarperBusiness, 1994) who studied pairs of long-lived companies in various industries—including P&G and Colgate in consumer products. Collins and Porras sought to understand why some companies prospered and led consistently over the long term. They concluded that the winners succeeded through an ability to distinguish between their abiding and their transient characteristics. These companies hewed resolutely to core beliefs and principles but were willing to change, sometimes dramatically, everything else. These notions resonated at P&G in the 1990s because the company was in the throes of a period of dramatic change—change that ultimately would cause it to modify some long-standing policies, such as steady employment for workers, and divest some of its oldest brands, such as Crisco, Jif, and Spic and Span.

3. P&G Corporate Archetype report, 2002, P&G Archives.

Chapter One

1. *Cincinnati Daily Gazette,* 26 October 1838. This is Procter & Gamble's earliest known advertisement. For more background on the company's founding fathers (and founding father-in-law), see Alfred Lief, *It Floats: The Story of Procter & Gamble* (New York: Rinehart & Company, 1958), 14–20; and Oscar Schisgall, *Eyes on Tomorrow: The Evolution of Procter & Gamble* (Chicago: J. G. Ferguson Publishing, 1981). Both Lief and Schisgall (generally trustworthy sources) fix March 1837 as the earliest appearance of "Procter & Gamble" as a firm name and an indication that the firm was up and running, but P&G archivist Ed Rider points out that this dating is based on an evidently misdated letter (which is from James *N.* Gamble, not James *A.* Gamble, to Campbell Morfit, sent in 1857 not 1837).

2. Nancy F. Koehn, *Brand New: How Entrepreneurs Earned Consumers' Trust from Wedgwood to Dell* (Boston: Harvard Business School Press, 2001), points out that brands had been around for at least half a century by the time Procter & Gamble put its soaps and candles on the market. This early branding referred to upper- and middle-class consumption of goods made by artisans (like Wedgwood china), though, not mass-produced packaged goods.

3. Carl W. Condit, *The Railroad and the City: A Technological and Urbanistic History of Cincinnati* (Columbus: Ohio State University Press, 1977), 5–6.

4. Charles Cist, *Sketches and Statistics of Cincinnati in 1851* (Cincinnati: W. H. Moore & Co., 1851), 279 ("100,000 hogs annually"); Condit, *Railroad and the City* ("quarter of the total number of hogs slaughtered annually in the United States"); Charles Cist, *Cincinnati in 1841* (Cincinnati: W. H. Moore & Co., 1841), 54, 58 ("62 beef and pork butchers . . .").

5. Cist, *Cincinnati in 1841,* various pages.

6. See especially William Cronon, *Nature's Metropolis: Chicago and the Great West* (New York: W. W. Norton, 1992).

7. Steamboat names taken from Accounts Journal, 1852–1853, P&G Archives.

8. Procter & Gamble to A. Ives, Detroit, 17 November 1848, P&G Archives.

9. Cronon, *Nature's Metropolis.*

10. Cash Book (1849–1852), P&G Archives. On the use of soap and candles to pay expenses like wages, see also John M. Donnelly, undated statement (recording the recollections of an employee from this period), P&G Archives.

11. Cash Book (1849–1852).

12. On local banks' role, see Donnelly, undated statement. Note that this pattern of financing was common among industrial enterprises of the antebellum period.

13. Ibid.

14. Condit, *Railroad and the City,* 6–9.

15. Ledger, 1864–1866, P&G Archives.

16. James Norris Gamble, laboratory notebook, Nippert Collection, P&G Archives.

17. Lief, *It Floats,* 34–35.

18. Dunn & Bradstreet Credit Records, Baker Library, Harvard Business School, Harvard University, Cambridge, MA, 78: 302, 303, 464.

19. *Cincinnati Sun,* 22 December 1886 (clipping available at P&G Archives); the article's numbers on candle and soap production were supplied by Harley Procter.

20. Cronon, *Nature's Metropolis,* 228–230.

21. Stuart Bruchey, *Enterprise: The Dynamic Economy of a Free People* (Cambridge: Harvard University Press, 1990), 270.

22. Ibid., 308–311 (on industrialization and rising income), 263 (on urbanization).

23. The definitive source is Alfred D. Chandler, Jr., *The Visible Hand: The Managerial Revolution in American Business* (Cambridge: Harvard University Press, 1977).

24. On Heinz, see Nancy F. Koehn, "Henry Heinz and Brand Creation in the Late Nineteenth Century," *Business History Review,* autumn 1999, 349–393.

Chapter Two

1. Alfred Lief, *It Floats: The Story of Procter & Gamble* (New York: Rinehart & Company, 1958), 49; and James N. Gamble to H. J. Morrison, 3 February 1923. Manufacturing Administration Research Library, Ivorydale, Procter & Gamble. Unfortunately, the letter has not survived in the P&G Archives, although Lief transcribed a copy.

2. Lief notes, P&G Archives. For a source, Lief cites James N. Gamble to H. J. Morrison, 9 February 1923, Manufacturing Administration Research Library. Unfortunately, the letter has not survived in the P&G Archives. On the divine inspiration, see Lief, *It Floats,* 6.

3. Susan Strasser, *Satisfaction Guaranteed: The Making of the American Mass Market* (New York: Pantheon Books, 1989), 44–45. Fittingly, in 1878, just as Ivory was emerging from P&G, a group of U.S. manufacturers formed the United States Trade-Mark Association.

4. Lief, *It Floats,* 6–7.

5. Ibid., 7.

6. Ibid., 8–9.

7. For a breakdown of Ayer's clientele, see Ralph Hower, *The History of an Advertising Agency: N. W. Ayer & Son at Work, 1869–1939* (Cambridge: Harvard University Press, 1939), 638.

8. Strasser, *Satisfaction Guaranteed,* 91.

9. Ibid.

10. *Advertising Age,* 20 August 1987, 10.

11. *Independent,* 21 December 1882; and *The Century Magazine,* February 1883. The ad from *The Century Magazine* emphasized the "99 44-100%" in boldface type. The *Independent* version added this copy at the end of the advertisement: "Try it. *Sold Everywhere.*"

12. Ivory is a classic case of what Richard Tedlow, *New and Improved: The Story of Mass Marketing in America* (Boston: Harvard Business School Press, 1996), calls a stage two market.

13. On the other hand, the advertising showed Ivory as an unwrapped cake of soap, and not as a package. Throughout the nineteenth century, in fact, ads rarely depicted Ivory as a package.

14. Two small notebooks in the P&G Archives show that Harley Procter closely tracked magazine advertisements, recording fees paid to artists for drawings (Harley Procter, Account Books). The fees ran around $20 to $75 per drawing, and the company commissioned a steady stream of illustrations.

15. *Cincinnati Sun,* 22 December 1886 (clipping available at P&G Archives).

16. "A Trip to Ivorydale," undated newspaper item, c. 1886 (clipping available at P&G Archives).

17. *Cincinnati Enquirer,* July 1885; "A Trip to Ivorydale," *Moonbeams* (P&G in-house newsletter), July 1920, 4.

18. Thomas Glenn, "Reminicences [sic] of the Procter & Gamble Company's Central Avenue Plant by Mr. Thomas Glenn," typescript manuscript, n.d., P&G Archives, 2.

19. "A Trip to Ivorydale," *Moonbeams,* July 1920, 1.

20. Glenn, "Reminicences," 3.

21. "Before Ivorydale: The Central Avenue Factory," *Moonbeams,* February 1920, 2.

22. "A Trip to Ivorydale," *Moonbeams,* July 1920, 4. Wrapping machines came into use around 1905.

23. Lief, *It Floats,* 73–79.

24. Ibid., 75–76.

25. Profit and Loss Statements, Box 4, Nippert Collection, P&G Archives.

26. *Cincinnati Sun,* 22 December 1886 (clipping available at P&G Archives).

27. Profit and Loss Statements for six months, ending 1 April and 1 October 1889, Box 4, Nippert Collection, P&G Archives.

28. Handwritten circular letter, 28 November 1885, P&G Archives. How large the mass mailing was, and precisely how the company identified the "one or two good housekeepers" in a given "locality," are not clear from the surviving record.

29. Ibid.

30. Handwritten circular letter, Procter & Gamble to "Madam," 24 August 1889, P&G Archives.

31. Sales Department Notebooks: "Misc. Memorandums," nos. 1 and 2, P&G Archives.

32. Copy of boilerplate letter, undated, P&G Scrapbook, 1896–1912, P&G Archives.

33. *The Century Magazine,* July 1891, advertisement.

34. [Hastings French and Harry Brown], "Misc. Memorandums #2 Opened October 1st 1896," P&G Archives.

35. See notebooks in file: "Sales by Brand, 1888-1910, 1910-1918," Sales Box 6, P&G Archives. The totals reflect conversion of boxes of six-ounce Ivory bars into ten-ounce ones. Sales data is unavailable for the nineteenth century.

36. Ibid.

37. Hower, *History of an Advertising Agency;* and Stephen Cox, *The Mirror Makers: A History of American Advertising and Its Creators* (New York: William Morrow and Company, Inc., 1984.)

Chapter Three

1. Many U.S. companies incorporated in New Jersey in the late 1800s, as a result of the state's favorable laws structuring incorporation.

2. For background on the emergence of a market for industrial equities and modern U.S. corporations, see Thomas Navin and Marion Sears, "The Rise of a Market for Industrial Securities, 1887–1902," *Business History Review* 29 (1954): 105–138; Naomi Lamoreaux, *The Great Merger Movement in American Business, 1895–1904* (New York: Cambridge University Press, 1985).

3. See, especially, Sanford M. Jacoby, *Modern Manors: Welfare Capitalism Since the New Deal* (Princeton, NJ: Princeton University Press, 1997).

4. Quoted in Alfred Lief, *It Floats: The Story of Procter & Gamble* (New York: Rinehart & Company, 1958), 84.

5. Oscar Schisgall, *Eyes on Tomorrow: The Evolution of Procter & Gamble* (Chicago: J. G. Ferguson Publishing, 1981), 65.

6. Statistics from U.S. Bureau of the Census, *1890,* vol. 11; and *Manufacturers,* vol. 2 (1930). The 1890 figures reflect both soap and candles (and do not break out separate numbers for soap); the 1930 figure tabulates soap manufacturing only. (The figures for candle manufacturing, by this point, would be minor in comparison.)

7. Ferdinand Otter, "Two Great Soap Companies Compared," *Magazine of Wall Street,* 6 September 1930, 740–741.

8. "99 44/100% Pure Profit Record," *Fortune,* April 1939, 154.

9. A number of heavy industry enterprises were establishing labs by this point, but not firms in industries like soap.

10. "History of the Chemical Division," typewritten report, 1960, file: "History of Chemical Division," Research & Development Box 6, P&G Archives.

11. Ibid.

12. Schisgall makes this point in *Eyes on Tomorrow,* 41.

13. R. A. Duncan, "Some Items of Interest on the Record of Procter & Gamble," 24 October 1958, P&G Archives.

14. Ibid.

15. The company had marketed lard in the mid-1800s, however.

16. The best source on Crisco's marketing campaign is Strasser, *Satisfaction Guaranteed,* 3–15.

17. J. George Frederick, "Efficient Planning Before Advertising," *Printers Ink,* 9 January 1913.

18. Richard R. Deupree, "Talk Before the P&G Club," 19 September 1912, P&G Archives.

19. Procter & Gamble Distributing Co. to wholesalers, undated circular letter (circa 1905), P&G Scrapbook, 1896–1912, P&G Archives.

20. Ibid. (emphasis in original).

21. Procter & Gamble Distributing Co. to retailers, undated circular letter (circa 1903/1904), P&G Scrapbook, 1896–1915, P&G Archives.

22. Procter & Gamble Distributing Co., circular (undated, circa 1904), P&G Scrapbook, 1896–1912, P&G Archives (emphasis in original).

23. Deupree, "Talk Before the P&G Club."

24. Ibid.

25. Richard R. Deupree, "Dividend Day Talk," 13 February 1926, P&G Archives.

26. Deupree, "Talk Before the P&G Club."

27. Ibid.

28. Ibid.

29. Deupree, "Dividend Day Talk."

30. See, for example, *Interstate Grocer,* 30 June, 10 July, and 17 July 1920, clippings P&G Scrapbook, P&G Archives.

31. Deupree, "Talk Before the P&G Club."

32. Ibid.

33. Ibid.

34. William Cooper Procter to Mary E. Jonston, 6 July 1922 and 19 January 1923, *Letters of William Cooper Procter* (privately printed, 1957), P&G Archives, 136, 151.

35. D. P. Smelser and J. D. Henry, "Taped Interview Between D. P. Smelser and J. D. Henry," 29 August 1962, "MRD Talks" File, AD1, Market Research Box 1, P&G Archives.

36. "99 44/100% Pure Profit Record," 162.

37. Smelser and Henry, "Taped Interview."

38. "Outline of Market Research Department History," typed manuscript, 1 February 1962, Market Research History File, AD1, Market Research Box 1, P&G Archives.

39. Ibid.

40. Ibid.

41. D. P. Smelser, R. N. Humpheries, C. W. Knappenberger, and Ruth Mooney, "Talk on Market Research Department," October 1958, "MRD Talks" folder, AD1 Market Research Box 1, P&G Archives.

42. Ed Rider to John Smale, "Brand Management History," (letter summarizing conversations with W. R. Chase and Clint Pace) 30 June 1987, P&G Archives.

43. Neil McElroy to R. F. Rogan, 13 May 1931, P&G Archives.

44. Ibid.

45. Alfred D. Chandler, Jr., *Strategy and Structure: Chapters in the History of the American Industrial Enterprise* (Cambridge: The MIT Press, 1962).

46. Otter, "Two Great Soap Companies Compared," 740–741.

47. Lief, *It Floats,* 198.

48. Plants in Kansas City and St. Louis experienced brief cutbacks in workweeks. The Buckeye plants did resort to layoffs.

49. See data from Curtis Publishing Company, reported in "Setting the Pace," *Moonbeams* (P&G inhouse newsletter), April 1929, 10.

50. "99 44/100% Pure Profit Record," 81–82. Unfortunately, no concrete data survives giving more precise breakdowns.

51. Duncan, "Some Items of Interest."

Chapter Four

1. *Time,* 5 October 1953, 92.
2. G. Thomas Halberstadt, interview, 7–9 April 1984, P&G Archives, 34.
3. Robert A. Duncan, "P&G Develops Synthetic Detergents 1931–1946: A Short History," typewritten report, 15 July 1958, P&G Archives.
4. Ibid.
5. David "Dick" Byerly, "History of Tide," typewritten report, 15 June 1950, P&G Archives; see also G. Thomas Halberstadt to Alan Kantrow, 24 April 1984, P&G Archives.
6. Halberstadt, interview.
7. Ibid. Halberstadt's account of Tide's R&D is one of the best and closest accounts of this critical stage, and except where otherwise noted, quotes over the next few pages detailing the period from 1939 to 1946 come from this source.
8. In addition to Halberstadt, interview, see G. Thomas Halberstadt to Alan Kantrow, 24 April 1984, P&G Archives.
9. Halberstadt, interview.
10. For a detailed description of the elaborate process by which P&G traditionally developed and rolled out products during this period, see "Curtain Going Up on Brand X," *Moonbeams,* general office edition, November 1948–May 1949.
11. P&G Archives electronic database.
12. On Gerhart's central role, Don Baker entry, P&G Archives electronic database. See also Thomas Hine, *The Total Package: The Evolution and Secret Meanings of Boxes, Bottles, Cans, and Tubes* (Boston: Little, Brown and Company, 1995), 147–149, which credits Donald Deskey with the original design.
13. Gibb Carey to Ed Rider, 12 December 2002, P&G Archives.
14. Background information on towers and granulation process from James M. Ewell, Charles Fullgraf, and George Broadfoot, telephone interviews, 10 May 2001.
15. James M. Ewell, interview, 22 June 1994, P&G Archives.
16. Dean P. Fite, letter with Tide recollections, 6 January 1996, P&G Archives.
17. Ewell, interview.
18. Charles Fullgraf interview, 16 February 1995, P&G Archives.
19. Robert Lake, letter with Tide recollections, 20 December 1995, P&G Archives.
20. Ewell, interview.
21. George T. Myers, letter with Tide recollections, 21 December 1995, P&G Archives.
22. Bruce W. Price, Sr., letter with Tide recollections, 20 December 1995, P&G Archives.
23. Max B. Schmidt, letter with Tide recollections, 19 February 1996, P&G Archives.
24. George Broadfoot, telephone interview, 10 May 2001.
25. G. Thomas Halberstadt to Alan Kantrow, 24 April 1984, P&G Archives; *Consumer Reports,* August 1949, 357; February 1951, 53–54.
26. Edgar H. Lotspeich, interview, 1 March 1993, P&G Archives.
27. *Time,* 5 October 1953, 92.
28. "Synthetic Granules Production, 1941–1973" Folder, chart, P&G Archives.
29. On reformulating Oxydol as a synthetic, see *Time,* 5 October 1953, 93; Manufacturing Minutes, 7 April 1950, P&G Archives.
30. Richard R. Deupree, "President's Report to Shareholders at Annual Meeting," 8 October 1947, P&G Archives.
31. Spencer Klaw, "The Soap Wars—A Strategic Analysis," *Fortune,* June 1963, 123–125, 184–198; market and earnings data from 125."

Chapter Five

1. John Smale, letter to authors, 13 January 2003.
2. The company expressed its growth objective in terms of volume rather than revenue. The feeling was that revenues could be distorted by factors such as inflation. John Smale, interview 8 February 2001; Peter Vanderwicken, "P&G's Secret Ingredient," *Fortune,* July 1974, 75–79, 164–166.
3. Most of this section relies on Bernard Bailyn et al., *The Great Republic: A History of the American People,* 4th ed., vol. 2 (Lexington, MA: D. C. Heath and Co., 1992), and Thomas K. McCraw, *American Business, 1920–2000: How It Worked* (Wheeling, IL: Harlan Davidson, 2000).

4. Spencer Klaw, "Winner and Still Champion: P&G," *Fortune,* March 1956, 105–106.

5. Ibid.

6. "Howard Morgens to Retire After Forty-Four Years with P&G," *Moonbeams* (P&G in-house newsletter), manufacturing edition, February 1977, 2–3.

7. Howard Morgens, interview with John G. Smale and Edwin L. Artzt, 18 June 1994, P&G Archives.

8. Charles Fullgraf, interview, 16 February 1995; Howard Morgens, interview, 11–12 August 1993; Editors of Advertising Age, *Procter & Gamble: The House That Ivory Built: 150 Years of Successful Marketing* (Lincolnwood, IL: National Textbook Company Business Books, 1989), 28.

9. John Pepper, interview, 12 December 2002.

10. McCraw, *American Business, 1920–2000,* 7–8, 48–49, 209–211.

11. "Twenty Years of Effort: The Story Behind Crest," *Moonbeams,* manufacturing edition, June 1962, 3; Verling Votaw, interview, 7 April 1984.

12. Editors of Advertising Age, *The House That Ivory Built,* 24.

13. Charles Fullgraf, interview, 16 February 1995. P&G Archives.

14. Jim Monton, "Hair Care History at P&G," presentation, 1999, P&G Archives; Lief, *It Floats,* 256–257.

15. Monton, "Hair Care History at P&G."

16. Nancy Giges, "Shampoo Rivals Wonder When P&G Will Seek Old Dominance," *Advertising Age,* 23 September 1974, 3.

17. Harry Tecklenburg, speech given at Industrial Research Institute Annual Meeting, Phoenix, Arizona, 4 May 1987 (typed report), 1–2, P&G Archives.

18. Procter & Gamble, Annual Reports for 1955 and 1956; Lief, *It Floats,* 289.

19. Oscar Schisgall, *Eyes on Tomorrow: The Evolution of Procter & Gamble* (Chicago: J. G. Ferguson Publishing, 1981), 230.

20. Schisgall, *Eyes on Tomorrow,* p. 186.

21. Bailyn et al., *The Great Republic,* 485; Margaret Josten and Alan Vonderhaar, "P&G Chief Belies Grey Flannel Myth," *Cincinnati Enquirer,* 8 July 1979.

22. McCraw, *American Business, 1920–2000;* Vanderwicken, "P&G's Secret Ingredient," 75; Schisgall, *Eyes on Tomorrow,* 193.

23. G. G. Carey, letter to Ed Rider, 9 December 2002, P&G Archives.

24. McCraw, *American Business, 1920–2000,* 126.

25. Schisgall, *Eyes on Tomorrow,* 193; John Smale, "Remarks by John G. Smale, Retired Chairman and Chief Executive," P&G Operations Committee, Cincinnati, 3 November 1997, P&G Archives.

26. Schisgall, *Eyes on Tomorrow,* 160, 278; Editors of Advertising Age, *The House That Ivory Built,* 158–165.

27. See, for example, Klaw, "Winner and Still Champion: P&G," *Fortune,* March 1956, 198.

28. Warren Albright (of N. W. Ayer), interview by G. G. Carey, undated, P&G Archives.

29. Walter Lingle, interview, 27 September 1987.

30. Walter Lingle, "How P&G Entered France," typescript, 22 June 1992, P&G Archives.

31. These tacit understandings were especially prevalent in the chemical industry, although they also existed in glass, electrical equipment, and other industries.

32. Lingle, interview; National Aeronautics and Space Administration, "Biographical Sheet on Walter L. Lingle, Jr., Deputy Associate Administrator, NASA," 3 March 1964. Copy in Walter Lingle file, P&G Archives.

33. For a general account of this political history, see Michael C. Meyer and William H. Beezley, eds., *The Oxford History of Mexico* (New York: Oxford University Press, 2000), 576–587.

34. Lingle, interview.

35. Morgens, interview, 11–12 August, 1993; Tom Bower, interview, [1996?]; "P&G Makes Its Pitch in Europe," *Chemical Week,* 30 March 1963.

36. Lingle, interview; William Gurganus, interview, 27 April 1994.

37. Samih Sherif, interview, 8 September 1996.

38. Morgens, interview, 11–12 August 1993.

39. Fullgraf, interview, 16 February 1995; Gurganus, interview, 27 April 1994; Ed Artzt, interview, 6 December 2002.

40. O. B. Butler, interview, 26–27 September 1994.

41. Procter & Gamble, Annual Report, 1972, 9.

42. Ibid., 4; Procter & Gamble, Annual Report, 1971, 3.

43. Walter Lingle, quoted in Schisgall, *Eyes on Tomorrow,* 182.

44. Gurganus, interview, 27 April 1994.

45. Jim Edwards, interview, 7 February 2001.

46. Editors of Advertising Age, *The House That Ivory Built,* 32.

47. Smale, interview, 8 February 2001.

48. Ibid.; Gary M. Walton and Hugh Rockoff, *History of the American Economy,* 9th ed. (Stamford, CT: Thomson Learning, 2002), 658; McCraw, *American Business, 1920–2000,* 137; Blackford, *Rise of Modern Business,* 182. See also Neil Fligstein, *The Transformation of Corporate Control* (Cambridge: Harvard University Press, 1990).

49. Fullgraf, interview, 20 September 1995.

50. Walton and Rockoff, *History of the American Economy,* 654–655.

51. National Industrial Pollution Control Council, "Detergents: A Status Report," subcouncil report (Washington, D.C.: National Industrial Pollution Control Council, March 1971); Good Housekeeping Institute, "An Institute Report on the Detergent Dilemma" (New York: Hearst Corporation, January 1971); Procter & Gamble, Annual Report, 1971, 5; Smale, interview, 6–7 May 1997.

52. Tom Laco, "Music Hall Speech," 15 December 1972, P&G Archives.

53. Smale, interview, 6–7 May 1997.

54. Ed Harness, "Music Hall Speech," 8 December 1977, P&G Archives; Smale, interview, 6–7 May, 1997; Schisgall, *Eyes on Tomorrow,* 257.

55. Laco, "Music Hall Speech"; Harness, "Music Hall Speech."

56. "Gone Fishing: Edward Harness Retires from P&G," *Moonbeams,* manufacturing edition, March 1984, 23; Oliver M. Gale, "Edward Granville Harness," University of Cincinnati, Internet Business and Economics Library, Web site available at <http://www.libraries.uc.edu/research/subject_resources/business/book_Edward_Harness.htm> (accessed February 2003).

57. Fullgraf, interview, 20 September 1995; Vanderwicken, "P&G's Secret Ingredient," 75.

58. Schisgall, *Eyes on Tomorrow,* 248.

59. Fullgraf, interview, 20 September 1995.

60. Giges, "Shampoo Rivals Wonder When," 4.

61. Ray Bolich, interview, 14 November 2001, 72. Tobie Sullivan, "Keeping Pace with Fickle Customers," section 2, "Toiletries/Beauty Aids," *Advertising Age,* 25 February 1980, S10.

62. Cecilia Kuzma, interview, 6 April 2001.

63. Edward G. Harness, "Why I Think Procter & Gamble Is Unique: Excerpts from a talk at the recent Year-end management meetings," *Moonbeams,* manufacturing edition, February 1972, 4.

64. James K. Todd, et al., "Toxic-Shock Syndrome Associated with Phage-Group-I Staphylococci," *The Lancet 1116* (1978): 2.

65. "Warnings Fail to Halt 'Rely' Tampon Sales," *Washington Post,* 24 September 1980; "FDA Plans Warning Labels on Tampons," *Washington Post,* 26 September 1980; Dekkers L. Davidson, "Managing Product Safety: The Case of the Procter & Gamble Rely Tampon," HBS Case study no. 9-383-131, 1983; 1, 6; *Kehm vs. Procter & Gamble,* 724 F.2d 613; "A New Warning for Tampon Users," *Newsweek,* 6 October 1980.

66. Tom Laco, Comments to P&G Board of Directors, 9 September 1980, P&G Archives.

67. Chuck Fullgraf, interview, 20 September 1995; "Managing Product Safety," 7; Memo from Robert J. Miller to Ed Artzt, et al., copy in P&G Archives, 68. Jim Edwards, interview, 7 February 2001.

68. "$75 Million Reserve Set By Maker of Rely," *Washington Post,* 15 October 1980; "The Decision Was Easy," *Advertising Age,* 20 August 1987, 207; Jeffrey B. Kaufmann, et al., "The Myth of Full Disclosure: A Look at Organizational Communications During Crises," *Business Horizons,* July–August 1994, 32.

69. "The Decision Was Easy," p. 207.

70. *Advertising Age,* 20 October 1980.

71. Smale, interview, 6–7 May 1997.

Chapter Six

1. Howard Morgens, interview with John G. Smale and Edwin L. Artzt, 18 June 1994.

2. Jim Edwards, interview, 7 February 2001.

3. "Diversification Has Always Been Important and Profitable to P&G, Chairman Declares," P&G news release, 9 October 1956, P&G Archives; Neil McElroy, "Dividend Day Talk," 19 January 1957, P&G Archives; "P&G to Acquire Assets of Charmin Paper Mills," P&G news release, 20 September 1956, P&G Archives.

4. Gary Martin, interview, 31 May 2000, Dick Feldon, interview, 28 June 1994.

5. "The Tissue-Paper War," *Forbes,* 15 January 1965, 21–23.

6. "Paper," *Forbes,* 1 January 1957, 85; "P&G vs. Scott: Battle of the Century," *Forbes,* 15 June 1963, 16.

7. "Charmin Paper . . . Past . . . Present . . . and Future," *Moonbeams* (P&G in-house newsletter), manufacturing edition, April 1965, 8; Feldon, interview, 28 June 1994.

8. Morgens, interview, 11–12 August 1993; Walter Lingle, interview, 27 September 1987; Edwards, interview, 7 February 2001.

9. Ed Harness, remarks at Charmin Management Dinner, 18 February 1965, P&G Archives.

10. Schisgall, *Eyes on Tomorrow,* 213; "Interview with Victor Mills, Paper Products," 25 August 1961, P&G Archives.

11. "Interview with Victor Mills, Paper Products"; Larry Sanford, interview, 19 November 1998.

12. "Interview with Victor Mills, Paper Products."

13. Ed Artzt, interview, 6 December 2002.

14. Morgens, interview, 11–12 August 1993; "P&G vs. Scott," *Forbes,* 15 June 1963.

15. Artzt, interview, 6 December 2002.

16. Ed Harness to Bill Snow and others, P&G internal memorandum, 12 March 1964, P&G Archives; "Meet Our New Chief Executive Officer," *Moonbeams,* manufacturing edition, 1974, 16; Chuck Fullgraf, interview, 20 September 1995.

17. "The Tissue-Paper War," 22.

18. The Mehoopany plant was not completed until the early 1970s, although its first paper machine was started in May 1967. By July 1968, its pulp mill was producing a low-cost sulfite pulp for the tissue and towel products.

19. Fred M. Wells, interview, 9 June 1984. See also Jim Edwards to Ed Harness, P&G internal memorandum, February 1966, P&G Archives.

20. Ed Harness, remarks at Paper Division Management Dinner, 9 December 1965, P&G Archives; "Charmin Paper . . . Past . . . Present . . . and Future," 8; "Secret Ingredient," *Forbes,* 15 November 1962, 42–43.

21. Sanford, interview, 19 November 1998.

22. Ibid.; Artzt, interview, 6 December 2002.

23. Feldon, interview, 28 June 1994.

24. Sanford, interview, 19 November 1998; Fullgraf, interview, 20 September 1995; Jim Edwards, December Meeting Talk, 10 December 1976, P&G Archives; Martin, interview, 31 May 2000.

25. J. E. O'Brien to Ed Harness, P&G internal memorandum, 20 January 1964, P&G Archives; Edwards, interview, 7 February 2001.

26. Edwards, December Meeting Talk; Ed Artzt, interview, 25 April 2000; Sanford, interview, 19 November 1998.

27. A. J. Hayes to Ed Harness, P&G internal memorandum, 25 February 1965 (the cost of converting the mills are estimates), P&G Archives; Ed Harness to Bill Snow, P&G internal memorandum, 3 March 1965, P&G Archives.

28. A. J. Hayes to Ed Harness, 25 February 1965, P&G Archives; Martin, interview, 31 May 2000.

29. Artzt, interview, 6 December 2002.

30. Ibid.

31. Ibid.

32. Ibid.

33. Ed Harness, Taft Theater Talk, 11 December 1969, P&G Archives; Harness, Cheboygan Management Dinner Talk, 27 May 1970, P&G Archives.

34. Michael Porter, "The Disposable Diaper Industry in 1974," Case 9-380-175 (Boston: Harvard Business School, 1980), revised 24 September 1985, 4–5.

35. Kerry McLellan and Allen J. Morrison, "The Diaper War: Kimberly-Clark Versus Procter & Gamble (A) (Condensed)," Case 92-M003, version 1992-01-19 (London, Ontario: Richard Ivey School of Business, 1992), 2–3.

36. "The Story of Pampers," P&G document, 9 October 1970, P&G Archives, 4.

37. Lingle, interview, 27 September 1987.

38. Harry Tecklenburg, remarks at Industrial Research Institute Annual Meeting, Phoenix, AZ, 4 May 1987, P&G Archives, 7.

39. Ibid., 5; Harry Tecklenburg, "A Dogged Dedication to Learning," *Technology Management,* September–October 1989, 2; Bob Duncan, interview, 22–24 June 1984; Vic Mills, interview, 5–6 August 1983.

40. "The Story of Pampers," 5; Duncan, interview, 22–24 June 1984; Mills, interview, 5–6 August 1983.

41. Porter, "The Disposable Diaper Industry in 1974," 8; "The Story of Pampers," 7–9.

42. Ibid. According to Duncan, it was Bill Snow who chose the name Pampers.

43. "The Story of Pampers," 10, 14; Duncan, interview, 22–24 June 1984; Tecklenburg, "A Dogged Dedication to Learning," 3; Fred Wells, Manufacturing Meetings, December 1969, P&G Archives; Ernie Lewis, interview, undated. According to Arnie Austin, interview undated [probably late 1990s], Professional Services began marketing Pampers to hospitals because they were "calling solely on dentists and they were telling the same story all day long, it gets kind of boring. Also, in some cities on Thursdays most of the dental offices are closed. . . . Pampers was being marketed by Toilet Goods [which also marketed Crest], so it was a very natural fit."

44. "The Story of Pampers," 10; Duncan, interview, 22–24 June 1984; Porter, "The Disposable Diaper Industry in 1974," 6.

45. Tecklenburg, "A Dogged Dedication to Learning," 1, 3.

46. Ibid., 4; Duncan, interview, 22–24 June 1984.

47. "The Story of Pampers," 16; Duncan, interview, 22–24 June 1984; Feldon, interview, 28 June 1994.

48. Ibid.; Duncan, interview, 22–24 June 1984.

49. Wells, Manufacturing Meeting, 1; Harry Tecklenburg, remarks at Industrial Research Institute Annual Meeting, 5.

50. "The Story of Pampers," 17; Wells, Manufacturing Meeting, 2.

51. Porter, "The Disposable Diaper Industry in 1974," 8; Tecklenburg, "A Dogged Dedication to Learning," 4.

52. "The Great Diaper Battle," *Time,* 24 January 1969; Tecklenburg, "A Dogged Dedication to Learning," 1, 3; Ed Harness, Technical Services Dinner, 29 September 1966, P&G Archives, 10.

53. Harry Tecklenburg, remarks at Industrial Research Institute Annual Meeting, 8; Porter, "The Disposable Diaper Industry in 1974," 8.

54. Porter, "The Disposable Diaper Industry in 1974," 2.

55. Wells, Manufacturing Meeting, 12; Ed Harness, Taft Theater Talk, 11 December 1969, 8–10; Porter, "The Disposable Diaper Industry in 1974," 3; Pankaj Ghemawat and Stephen P. Bradley, "The Disposable Diaper Industry in 1984," Case 9-794-130 (Boston: Harvard Business School, 1994), 1; Tecklenburg, remarks at Industrial Research Institute Annual Meeting, 9.

56. "The Story of Pampers," 18; Wells, Manufacturing Meeting, 8.

57. McLellan and Morrison, "The Diaper War: Kimberly-Clark Versus Procter & Gamble (A) (Condensed)," 11.

58. Morgens, interview, 11–12 August 1993; Richard Feldon, Paper History Talk, 1994, 8, P&G Archives.

59. William Gurganus, interview, 27 April 1994; John Smale, interview, 8 February 2001; Harry Tecklenburg, interview, 26 April 1985.

60. Artzt, interview, 6 December 2002. According to Artzt, Harness initially asked Tom Laco to take the European job, but Laco declined, citing family reasons.

61. The Editors of Advertising Age, *Procter & Gamble: The House That Ivory Built, 150 Years of Successful Marketing* (Lincolnwood, IL: National Textbook Company Business Books, 1989), 30.

Chapter Seven

1. *Chemical & Engineering News,* 6 April 1976. The ad was reproduced in *Moonbeams* (P&G in-house newsletter), manufacturing edition, April 1977.

2. National Institutes of Health, "Oral Health in America: A Report of the Surgeon General" (executive summary) (Washington, DC: National Institutes of Health, 2000), NIH Publication Number 00-4713. Available online at <http://www.nidcr.nih.gov/sgr/execsumm> (accessed January 2002).

3. Verling Votaw, interview, 7 April 1984.

4. Ibid.

5. Division of Oral Health, National Center for Chronic Disease Prevention and Health Promotion, Centers for Disease Control and Prevention, "Achievements in Public Health, 1900–1999: Fluoridation of Drinking Water to Prevent Dental Caries," *Morbidity and Mortality Weekly Report* 48 (1999): 933–940; "Toothy," *Newsweek,* 28 July 1958; Bob Broge, interview, 22 November 1998.

6. "Twenty Years of Effort: The Story Behind Crest," *Moonbeams* (P&G in-house newletter), manufacturing edition, June 1962, 3; Votaw, interview, 7 April 1984.

7. F. S. McKay and G. V. Black, "An Investigation of Mottled Teeth: An Endemic Developmental Imperfection of the Enamel of the Teeth Heretofore Unknown in the Literature of Dentistry," *Dental Cosmos* 58 (1916): 477–484; F. S. McKay, "Relation of Mottled Enamel to Dental Caries," *Journal of the American Dental Association* 15 (1928): 1429–1437; H. V. Churchill, "Occurrence of Fluorides in Some Waters of the

United States," *Journal of Industrial Engineering Chemistry* 23 (1931): 996–998; H. Trendley Dean, "Endemic Fluorosis and Its Relation to Dental Caries," *Public Health Report* 53 (1938): 1443–1452; H. Trendley Dean, "On the Epidemiology of Fluorine and Dental Caries," in *Fluorine in Dental Public Health,* ed. W. J. Gies (New York: New York Institute of Clinical Oral Pathology, 1945), 19–30.

8. National Institutes of Health, National Institute of Dental and Craniofacial Research (division of the National Institutes of Health), "The Story of Fluoridation," available online: <http://www.nidr.nih.gov/fluoride.html> (accessed January 2001).

9. Brian Martin, *Scientific Knowledge in Controversy: The Social Dynamics of the Fluoridation Debate* (Albany: State University of New York Press, 1991), 3; National Institutes of Health, "Oral Health in America."

10. Wilfred Martin, "The Development of Crest," draft typewritten manuscript, 1986, P&G Archives, 3; A. W. Radike, "Dr. Radike Comments on Dr. Bibby's Letter," *Journal of the American Dental Association* 52 (February 1956): 243–244.

11. Votaw, interview, 7 April 1984.

12. "Crest Development," a timeline of key dates, 4 February 1987, P&G Archives, 2; Radike, "Dr. Radike Comments on Dr. Bibby's Letter," 243–244.

13. John Smale, interview, 8 February 2001.

14. John Smale, comments to authors, 4 December 2002.

15. Votaw, interview, 7 April 1984.

16. Martin, "The Development of Crest," 6; Bruce Bliven, Jr., "Annals of Business: And Now a Word from Our Sponsor," *New Yorker,* 23 March 1963, 96.

17. Bliven, "Annals of Business," 88–89; Martin, "The Development of Crest," 2; Votaw, interview, 7 April 1984.

18. Ibid.; Votaw, "Chronological Outline of Work in Crest Development," 8 September 1960, P&G Archives; Harry C. Day, "On Making Stannous Fluoride Useful," *A&S Review* (summer 1975), 10. Along with Muhler and Nebergall, Day was a principal researcher on the fluoride project.

19. Votaw, "Chronological Outline of Work in Crest Development"; Martin, "The Development of Crest," 6–7.

20. Consumer Reports, *The Medicine Show* (New York: Simon & Schuster, 1961), 32; "Crest Historical Roundtable," 1990 (videotape), P&G Archives.

21. *Advertising Age,* 8 February 1954, quoted in Lief, *The House That Ivory Built,* 24; Smale, interview, 8 February 2001.

22. Bliven, "Annals of Business," 95.

23. Ibid., 86; Votaw, interview, 7 April 1984.

24. Broge, interview, 22 November 1998.

25. "Fluoride Dentifrices Appear on the Market," *Journal of the American Dental Association* 50 (April 1955): 472; "Fluoride Dentifrice Sale Premature, Association Says," *Journal of the American Dental Association* 52 (March 1956): 368. Procter & Gamble later ran tests that determined that fluoride levels in urine were not significantly affected by the ingestion of fluoridated water (Arnie Austin, interview, undated [but probably late 1990s]).

26. "Crest Historical Roundtable"; Bliven, "Annals of Business," 100, 102, 105–106, 108.

27. Oscar Schisgall, *Eyes on Tomorrow: The Evolution of Procter & Gamble* (Chicago: J. G. Ferguson Publishing, 1981), 206; Judy Jakush, "ADA Evaluation Programs: A Proud History of Public Service," *Journal of the American Dental Association* 114, (April 1987): 446–452; Council on Dental Therapeutics, "Cod Liver Oil/Accepted Nonofficial Dental Remedies," *Journal of the American Dental Association* 17 (October 1930): 1941–1943. For the Colgate advertisements, see *Journal of the American Dental Association* 18 (April 1931): A–2, and 18 (January 1931): A–2.

28. Smale, interview, 6–7 May 1997.

29. Martin, "The Development of Crest," 9.

30. Ernie Lewis, interview, undated.

31. Ibid.; Votaw, interview, 7 April 1984.

32. Smale, interview, 6–7 May 1997; Consumer Reports, *The Medicine Show,* 31.

33. Schisgall, *Eyes on Tomorrow,* 207; Bliven, "Annals of Business," 112, 115–116.

34. Bliven, "Annals of Business," 112, 115–116.

35. Ibid., 118; "Historical Dentifrice Share Data (Yearly Averages)," 1954–1967, 8 December 1967, P&G Archives.

36. Broge, interview, 22 November 1998.

37. "First Anti-Decay Dentifrice Approved by American Dental Association," ADA news release, 1 August 1960, P&G Archives. See also Council on Dental Therapeutics, "Evaluation of Crest Toothpaste,"

Journal of the American Dental Association 61 (August 1960): 272–274; Council on Dental Therapeutics, *Accepted Dental Remedies,* 26th ed. (Chicago: American Dental Association, 1961), i–xii.

38. Lewis, interview.

39. Smale, interview, 6–7 May 1997; "Crest Historical Roundtable."

40. Martin, "The Development of Crest." According to John Smale, comments to authors, 4 December 2002, "the brand had developed great momentum behind the 'Look, Mom' campaign and would have continued to grow until Colgate moved its brand to an anti-cavity formula."

41. "Crest Historical Market Share," 1955–1985, P&G Archives; Consumer Reports, *The Medicine Show,* 29.

42. Bliven, "Annals of Business," 122, 128, 130.

43. Lewis, interview.

44. Smale, interview, 6–7 May 1997.

45. Paul H. Jeserich, "Report of President," American Dental Association, October 1960, P&G Archives, 1205; "ADA Head Insists Crest Endorsement Will Spur Truth in All Toothpaste Ads," *Advertising Age,* 24 October 1960, 1, 110.

46. "Flack Ack-Ack," *Newsweek,* 30 October 1961, no page available; "Will Crest Gain or Lose from Rival's Stealthy Tactics?" *Advertising Age, Printer's Ink,* June 1961, no page available. For the ADA's censure of Colgate, see Board of Trustees, "Report 6 of Board of Trustees to House of Delegates," *Transactions of the ADA,* 1961, 204–212.

47. Lewis, interview.

48. Schisgall, *Eyes on Tomorrow,* 204.

Chapter Eight

1. The quotation from Richard Deupree is used widely at P&G, including in training programs for supervisors and managers. Brad Butler recalls hearing the remark in a speech to company management that probably took place in the 1940s, but we've been unable to locate an original source. See Oscar Schisgall, *Eyes on Tomorrow: The Evolution of Procter & Gamble* (Chicago: J. G. Ferguson Publishing, 1981), 262.

2. David Swanson, interview, 11 April 2001; David Swanson to Ed Rider, 5 December 2002, P&G Archives; Stona Fitch, interview, 2 December 2002.

3. Historical Background for HPWS [High Performance Work Systems], Supplemental Text, 12. P&G document furnished by Mary Anne Gale, Procter & Gamble, Cincinnati, OH.

4. Swanson, interview 11 April 2001; Douglas McGregor, *The Human Side of Enterprise* (New York: McGraw-Hill, 1960), passim; Robert H. Waterman, Jr., *What America Does Right: Learning from Companies That Put People First* (New York: W. W. Norton, 1994), 36–39.

5. Swanson, interview; Waterman, *What America Does Right,* 39–41.

6. Historical Background for HPO [High Performance Organization], 12. Document furnished by Mary Anne Gale.

7. David Swanson, Untitled Speech, 24 October 1990; Historical Background for HPWS, Supplemental Text, 12; Waterman, *What America Does Right,* 40.

8. Swanson to Rider, 5 December 2002.

9. The Oxnard plant was acquired from International Paper Company.

10. Swanson to Rider, 5 December 2002.

11. "How P&G Selects New Plant Sites," *Moonbeams* (P&G's in-house newsletter), manufacturing edition, April 1968; Bob Seitz, interview, 5 July 2001.

12. *Moonbeams,* manufacturing edition, January 1985; Seitz, interview with author; Art Kleiner, *The Age of Heretics: Heroes, Outlaws, and the Forerunners of Corporate Change* (New York: Doubleday Currency, 1996), 66–74; Charles Krone, "Open Systems Redesign," in *Contemporary OD: Conceptual Orientations and Interventions,* ed. W. Warner Burke (La Jolla, CA: University Associates, 1975); David Jenkins, *Job Power: Blue and White Collar Democracy* (Garden City, NJ: Doubleday, 1973), 231–235.

13. Robert Seitz, letter to the authors, 14 February 2003.

14. Seitz, interview.

15. Dick Antoine, interview, Cincinnati, OH, 11 November 1999.

16. Seitz, interview.

17. Quoted by Price M. Cobbs, "Report of Pacific Training Associates Consultation Activities through 30 September 1973," typescript, 5 March 1974, 1–2 (copy at P&G facility in Albany, GA).

18. Price M. Cobbs and Ronald B. Brown, "Evaluation Report of the First Two-Day Management Awareness Workshop for Charmin, Albany held in Atlanta, Georgia on August 16–17," typescript, 14 September 1972 (copy at P&G facility in Albany, GA).

19. Swanson, interview.

20. H. E. Stokes, "Organizational Planning and Design: The Albany Approach," typescript, 19 April 1972 (copy at P&G facility in Albany, GA).

21. Ibid., 16, 26.

22. William H. Grier and Price M. Cobbs, *Black Rage* (New York: Basic Books, 1969); Jarrow Merenivitch, interview, 12 December 2001. Cobbs defined and explained ethnotherapy for P&G in Cobbs, "Report of Pacific Training Associates," 20–21.

23. Cobbs and Brown, "Evaluation Report."

24. Ibid.; Swanson, interview; Merenivitch, interview.

25. Cobbs, "Report of Pacific Training Associates," 21–22.

26. Merenivitch, interview.

27. Nancy L. Brown to Jarrow Merenivitch, 31 January 1973; "Review of Female Awareness Training Sessions Held with Converting Managers and Female Technicians Between November, 1973 and February, 1974," typescript (n.d.), copy at P&G facility, Albany, GA, 2.

28. "Female Awareness Training Sessions," 4.

29. Merenivitch, interview.

30. Ibid.

31. Bob White, "Leveraging the Legacy," talk delivered at Twenty-Fifth Anniversary of the Start-Up, 7 August 1997 (copy at P&G facility in Albany, GA); Al Collins, interview, 12 December 2001; Mary Anne Gale, interview, 4 March 2002.

32. M. J. Gowin and R. H. Beacham, "Review of New Plant Characteristics and Key Learnings Reapplicable," typescript, 9 December 1980 (copy at P&G facility in Albany, GA).

33. Gale, interview; David S. Swanson, "High Commitment Work Systems," talk delivered at the MIT Sloan School on 12 April 1984, at Harvard Business School on 4 May 1984, and at Yale School of Management on 29 January 1987, P&G Archives.

34. Antoine, interview.

Chapter Nine

1. John Smale, interview, 8 February 2001.

2. Ibid.; *Advertising Age*, 28 December 1987, 26–27.

3. *Wall Street Journal*, 26 January 1982; *New York Times*, 20 February 1982; "Why P&G Wants a Mellower Image," *BusinessWeek*, 7 June 1982.

4. *Wall Street Transcript*, 11 April 1983, 6.

5. Tom Laco, interview, February 6, 2001.

6. "Why Procter & Gamble Is Playing It Even Tougher," *BusinessWeek*, 18 July 1983, 176–178; *Adweek*, 12 September 1983; *Wall Street Journal*, 30 March 1983; A.

7. *Wall Street Journal*, 11 August 1987; for Smale's views on teams, see Priscilla Hayes Petty, "Behind the Brands at P&G: An Interview with John Smale," *Harvard Business Review*, November–December 1985, 78–90.

8. Wahib Zaki, interview, 17 July 2000.

9. *Wall Street Journal*, 12 September 1983; Zaki, interview, 17 July 2000.

10. *Washington Post*, 13 September 1989.

11. *The Globe and Mail*, 16 January 1985; *Los Angeles Times*, 6 July 1987; Lawrence D. "Mike" Milligan, interview, 15 May 2000.

12. *Los Angeles Times*, 6 July 1987; Milligan, interview, 15 May 2000.

13. Victor Mills, interview, P&G Archives.

14. Mills, interview; F. J. Baur, interview, P&G Archives; F. J. Baur, Development Record, 12 March 1957, P&G Archives.

15. Ed Artzt, speech, 14 December 1973; Robert Gill, interview, 4 December 2000; "Pringles History," copy in Pringles file, P&G Archives.

16. *Wall Street Journal*, 28 March 1974.

17. "Pringles History," 5.

18. Robert Gill, interview, 4 December 2000.

19. Ibid.

20. "Pringles Wins Worldwide with One Message," *Advertising Age*, international edition, 11 January 1999; Pringles promotional video, undated, copy furnished by Robert Gill; Shawn Tully, "Teens: The Most Global Market of All," *Fortune*, 16 May 1994; Gill interview, 4 December 2000.

21. *New York Times*, 12 June 1986; *Washington Post*, 13 September 1989.

22. *BusinessWeek,* 15 April 1985, 90; *Advertising Age,* 7 February 1983; Dick Feldon, interview, 28 June 1994; Richard Feldon, Paper History Talk, 1994, P&G Archives; David J. Arnold, "Procter & Gamble: Always Russia," Case 9-599-050 (Boston: Harvard Business School, 1998), 7.

23. Marsden, "The Always Story," 9 January 1985, 7, typescript at P&G Archives; Feldon, Paper History Talk, 10; Durk Jager, interview, 1 June 2000.

24. P&G Web site, June 2002; "P&G Readies Test," *Advertising Age,* 7 February 1983; *BusinessWeek,* 15 April 1985, 90.

25. *Wall Street Journal,* 11 May 1984; *BusinessWeek,* 15 April 1985, 90; Feldon, interview, 42–43; Feldon, Paper History Talk, 11.

26. *Moonbeams* (P&G in-house newsletter), manufacturing edition, July 1986, 18–19.

27. Marsden, "The Always Story," 9; Ed Artzt, interview, 25 April 2000.

28. John Smale, interview, 6 and 7 May 1997; Margaret Wyant files, P&G Archives.

29. Procter & Gamble, Annual Report for 1980; *The (Toronto) Globe and Mail,* 13 June 1980; *BusinessWeek,* 9 June 1980; "A Superpower Enters the Soft-Drink Wars," *Fortune,* 30 June 1980, 76–77; Dow Jones News Service, 20 January 1983. The acquisition price of Crush Canada Inc. was $13.3 million. The deal was closed on 1 March 1984 (*Wall Street Journal,* 1 March 1984).

30. Dow Jones News Service, 18 August 1981. When Beatrice was broken up in the mid-1980s, Seagram's acquired Tropicana for $1.2 billion.

31. *Wall Street Journal,* 9 September and 8 October 1982; 20 January and 25 May 1983; "Procter & Gamble's Comeback Plan," *Fortune,* 4 February 1985, 30–35.

32. John Smale, comments to P&G Board of Directors, February 1982, P&G Archives; *Wall Street Journal,* 18 March 1982; "Rx for Building Business," *Moonbeams,* 1982/83.

33. "Rx for Building Business."

34. Ibid.

35. Smale, comments to P&G Board of Directors, February 1982; Smale, interview, 6 and 7 May 1997.

36. Tom Blinn, interview, 20 November 2001.

37. "P&G to Acquire Richardson Vicks," *Moonbeams,* special edition, October 1985; "New to the Family," *Moonbeams,* December 1985.

38. John Smale to P&G Board of Directors, 28 September 1985, P&G Archives; Smale, Year-End Meeting Speech, 7 November 1985, P&G Archives.

39. *New York Times,* 18 April 1982; *Wall Street Journal,* 10 June 1985.

40. *Advertising Age,* 29 July 1985; *Financial Times,* 24 September 1985.

41. "The King of Suds Reigns Again," *Fortune,* 4 August 1986, 130–134.

42. *New York Times,* 12 June 1987.

43. David Swanson to Ed Rider, 5 December 2002, P&G Archives. Swanson regarded the end of steady employment as "arguably one of the most dramatic, controversial, sensitive, and important issues that has faced Procter and Gamble in the last 50 years—perhaps in its entire history."

44. "The Move to Category Teams," *Moonbeams,* November 1987, 3–5; "The Marketing Revolution at Procter & Gamble," *BusinessWeek,* 25 July 1988, 72–74; "P&G Rewrites the Marketing Rules," *Fortune,* 6 November 1989, 34.

45. Procter & Gamble, Annual Report for 1988; David Swanson, interview, 11 April 2001; Gary Martin, interview, 31 May 2000; *Wall Street Journal,* 12 October 1987; "P&G Rewrites the Marketing Rules."

46. Procter & Gamble, "Purpose, Values, and Principles," 1987, P&G Archives.

47. Martin, interview.

48. *Wall Street Journal,* 23 May 1989.

49. Jurgen Hintz, presentation to P&G Board of Directors, 14 March 1989, P&G Archives.

50. Based on information found at <http://www.olean.com> (accessed May 2002); *Wall Street Journal,* 11 May 1987.

51. *Wall Street Journal,* 11 May 1987; <http://www.fda.gov/opacom/backgrounders/Olestra.html> (accessed May 2002).

52. *Washington Post,* 26 July 1987.

53. *Wall Street Journal,* 11 May 1987 and 24 April 1989; *BusinessWeek,* 11 January 1988; <http://www.olean.com> (accessed May 2002). The Center for Science in the Public Interest, an advocacy organization, maintains a Web site of critical information about olestra and its regulation at <http://www.cspinet.org/Olestra/> (accessed May 2002).

54. Procter & Gamble, Annual Reports for 1980 and 1989.

55. Harald Einsmann to Ed Rider, 20 December 2002, P&G Archives; Wolfgang Berndt to Ed Rider, 16 November 2002, P&G Archives; Christopher A. Bartlett and Sumantra Ghoshal, *Managing Across Borders: The Transnational Solution* (Boston: Harvard Business School Press, 1989), especially 93–94 and 144–151.

See also Christopher Bartlett, "Procter & Gamble Europe: Vizir Launch," Case 9-384-139 (Boston: Harvard Business School, 1986).

56. Einsmann to Rider, 20 December 2002.

57. Harald Einsmann, interview, 5 December 2000; *Wall Street Journal,* 5 August 1987.

58. Ed Artzt to Board of Directors, 10 April 1990, P&G Archives; Jorge Montoya to Board of Directors, 13 November 1990, P&G Archives.

59. Samih Sherif, interview; Fouad Kraytem, interview, 3 April 2002.

Chapter Ten

1. "Very Clean People, the Japanese," *Economist,* 2 August 1997.

2. Michael Y. Yoshino and Paul H. Stoneham, "Procter & Gamble Japan (A)," Case 9-391-003 (Boston: Harvard Business School, 1990).

3. "Clean Competition in Japan," *U.S. News and World Report,* 29 July 1968; "Procter & Gamble Invades Japan," *Daily News Kashu Mainechi* (Los Angeles), 9 July 1968.

4. "P&G Trys [sic] for a Soft Landing in Japan," typescript translation of article appearing in *Nihon Keizai Shimbun,* 17 October 1970.

5. The following account of P&G in Japan in the 1970s and 1980s is based on Yoshino and Stoneham, "Procter & Gamble Japan," revisions A through D, Cases 9-391-003, -004, -005, and -054 (Boston: Harvard Business School, 1990–1994), and O. B. Butler, interview, 26–27 September, 1994.

6. William Gurganus, interview, 27 April 1994; Howard Morgens, interview, 18 June 1994; Butler, interview.

7. Butler, interview.

8. Yoshino and Stoneham, "Procter & Gamble Japan (A)," 8–9.

9. Butler, interview.

10. Ibid.

11. Ibid.; F. W. Caswell, speech to Board of Directors, 8 June 1987, P&G Archives.

12. Butler, interview.

13. Quoted in Yoshino and Stoneham, "Procter & Gamble Japan (C)," 1.

14. Ed Artzt, "Winning in Japan," speech to Pacific CEO Conference, 4 November 1988, P&G Archives.

15. Yoshino and Stoneham, "Procter & Gamble Japan (B)," 1.

16. Ed Artzt, comments to Board of Directors, 11 June 1985, P&G Archives. In retrospect, Butler believed that P&G spent too much time seeking government intervention and that its competition viewed the effort as a sign of weakness (Butler, interview).

17. *Tokyo Sekken Shoho* (weekly trade publication), quoted in Yoshino and Stoneham, "Procter & Gamble Japan (B)."

18. Yoshino and Stoneham, "Procter & Gamble Japan (C)."

19. Andrew Tanzer, "They Didn't Listen to Anybody," *Forbes,* 15 December 1986.

20. Durk Jager, presentation to Board of Directors, 1987, P&G Archives; Yoshino and Stoneham, "Procter & Gamble Japan (C)," 8.

21. Dennis Chase, "Massive Losses Resulting from Mistakes Near End; In Japan, It's 'Learn the Hard Way'," *Advertising Age,* 20 August 1987.

22. Hiroko Wada, quoted in Artzt, "Winning in Japan"; Bob McDonald, interview, 11 April 2000.

23. T. Miyanoiri, speech to Board of Directors, 8 June 1987, P&G Archives; Yoshino and Stoneham, "Procter & Gamble Japan (C)," 5.

24. Yoshino and Stoneham, "Procter & Gamble Japan (C)," 6; Jager, presentation to Board of Directors, 8 July 1986, P&G Archives; Jager, "Japan Organization Change 80s," memorandum to file, 17 September 1998, P&G Archives.

25. Yoshino and Stoneham, "Procter & Gamble Japan (C)," 7.

26. A. G. Lafley, "Board of Directors Asia Presentation," 14 January 1997, P&G Archives; *Business Tokyo,* November 1988, quoted in Yoshino and Stoneham, "Procter & Gamble Japan (C)," 8.

27. Jager, "Japan Organization Change 80s."

28. "Procter & Gamble Japan (D)."

29. Lafley, "Board of Directors Asia Presentation"; McDonald, interview.

30. McDonald, interview.

31. McDonald, presentation for P&G Board of Directors, April 2000, P&G Archives; McDonald, interview.

32. Larry Allgaier and [unidentified colleague, MJG], "The Japanese Recipe for Higher Order Innovation," Presentation to Global Leadership Council, June 1999, P&G Archives.

33. Lafley, "Board of Directors Asia Presentation."

34. McDonald, presentation for P&G Board of Directors.

35. Norihiko Shirouzu, "P&G's Joy Makes a Splash in Japan's Dish Soap Market," *Wall Street Journal,* 10 December 1997.

36. McDonald, presentation to P&G Board of Directors.

37. Ibid.; Bob McDonald, e-mail to author, 3 November 2000.

Chapter Eleven

1. "What Makes Luvs Different?" *Moonbeams* (P&G in-house newsletter), manufacturing edition, November 1980, 6–7; Pankaj Ghemawat and Stephen P. Bradley, "The Disposable Diaper Industry in 1984," Case 9-794-130 (Boston: Harvard Business School, 1994), 1.

2. "What Makes Luvs Different?" 6–7.

3. Ed Artzt, interview, 25 April 2000; "What Makes Luvs Different?" 7.

4. "The Great Diaper Race," P&G Corporate Recruiting Presentation, P&G Archives, 6.

5. Howard Morgens, interview with John G. Smale and Edwin L. Artzt, 18 June 1994.

6. Mark Ketchum, interview, 25 April 2002.

7. Kerry McLellan and Allen J. Morrison, "The Diaper War: Kimberly-Clark Versus Procter & Gamble (A) (Condensed)," Case 92-M003, version 1992-01-19 (London, Ontario: Richard Ivey School of Business, 1992), 4.

8. Ibid., 7–8.

9. Ibid., 5; "The Great Diaper Race," 9.

10. *Advertising Age,* 14 February 1985; "The Great Diaper Race," 6–8; McLellan and Morrison, "The Diaper War," 5.

11. "A Change for the Better: New Pampers with Gathers," *Moonbeams,* manufacturing edition, February 1983, 9.

12. "P&G's Diaper Offensive Takes Shape," *Moonbeams,* manufacturing edition, February 1985, 3; "The Great Diaper Race," 10; Mark Ketchum, interview, 27 June 2001.

13. "A Change for the Better," 10.

14. This and the following two paragraphs rely heavily on Jim Edwards, letter to Ed Rider, 5 December 2002, copy at P&G Archives.

15. Ibid.

16. Ghemawat and Bradley, "The Disposable Diaper Industry in 1984," 2; "A Change for the Better," 9; McLellan and Morrison, "The Diaper War," 4; Sandy Weiner, "Disposable Diaper Business, Year-End Meeting," 5 November 1985, P&G Archives, 4.

17. Dick Andre, "Disposable Diaper Business, Year-End Meeting," 5 November 1985, P&G Archives, 7–8.

18. Harry Tecklenburg, interview, 26 April 1985.

19. "Ultra Pampers: A Revolution in Disposable Diapers," *Moonbeams,* manufacturing edition, March 1986, 4; "New Weapons in Diaper War," *New York Times,* 25 November 1986; Artzt, interview, 25 April 2000; McLellan and Morrison, "The Diaper War," 5.

20. "The Great Diaper Race," 20–21, 23.

21. Ibid., 24, 25, 28.

22. Ketchum, interview, 25 April 2002.

23. Ketchum, interview, 27 June 2001.

24. John Pepper, interview, 20 December 2002; Ketchum interview, 27 June 2001.

25. Ed Artzt, "Brand Strategies," P&G College Cornerstone Talk, P&G Archives, 12; Weiner, "Disposable Diaper Business," 4.

26. Ketchum, interviews, 27 June 2001 and 25 April 2002.

27. John Smale, interview, 8 February 2001.

28. John Smale, "Remarks by John G. Smale, Retired Chairman and Chief Executive," P&G Operations Committee, Cincinnati, 3 November 1997, 5, P&G Archives.

29. Ed Artzt, interview, 6 December 2002.

30. Artzt, "Brand Strategies,"18; Artzt, interview, 6 December 2002.

Chapter Twelve

1. Claude Salomon, interview, 11–12 June 2001.

2. Kingston Fletcher, interview, 12 November 2001; Walter Lingle, interview, 29 September 1987.

3. Salomon, interview; Procter & Gamble, *Procter & Gamble de Mexico, 50 Aniversario* (Mexico City, Mexico: privately printed, 1998).

4. Fletcher, interview.

5. Salomon, interview; Manuel Reyes, interview, 11 June 2001; and Miguel Garcia Morenos and Enrique Valdez Serrano, interview, 13 June 2001, P&G Archives.

6. Salomon, interview.

7. Ibid., Manuel Reyes and Enrique Valdez Serrano, interview, 11 and 13 June 2001; Lucio Arguello, "Procter & Gamble of Mexico: A History of the 20th Century," *Luna y Estrellas* [the Mexican edition of P&G's in-house publication *Moonbeams*], October 1969.

8. Salomon, interview.

9. Arguello, "Procter & Gamble of Mexico."

10. Fletcher, interview.

11. Ibid.

12. Ibid.

13. Salomon, interview; Manuel Reyes, interview.

14. Fletcher, interview.

15. Ibid.

16. Miguel Garcia and Enrique Valdez Serrano, interview; "Why Senoras Buy a P&G Product," *Printers' Ink*, 8 December 1961, 44–45.

17. "Why Senoras Buy a P&G Product"; "Rapido Brand History" Folder, Box 243, chart, P&G Archives.

18. "Rapido Brand History" Folder, chart.

19. William O. Coleman, "Music Hall Talk," 19 November 1981, Speeches File, P&G Archives; Lombera, interview, Mexico City, 12 June 2001.

20. On Ariel's pricing compared with Rapido, see "Rapido Brand History," chart.

21. Ibid. (for share data); Coleman, "Music Hall Talk," Lombera, interview; *Procter & Gamble de Mexico: 50 Aniversario*, 68–69.

22. Lombera, interview.

23. "Ariel Brand History of Formulation Changes," Box 243, P&G Archives; Lombera, interview; Jaime Davila, "1982/83 State of the Business Speech," Speeches File, P&G Archives.

24. Chart: "Latin America P&G Consumer Business," prepared for Ed Artzt, "Board Comments, December 1989: International Share Progress," Board Meeting Notebooks, P&G Legal Division (for share data); Chart: "1987–88 Sales and Earnings Breakdown," from Board Meeting Notebooks for 12 July 1988, Legal Division.

25. John Pepper, "Board Comments, International Business Discussion," 11 May 1993, Board Meeting Notebooks, Legal Division.

26. T. Fealy, "Latin American Growth Plan," Year-End Talk, 8 December 1981, P&G Archives.

27. Claude Salomon, "Latin America Laundry/Paper Presentation," 13 November 1990, Board Meeting Notebooks, Legal Division.

28. Claude Salomon, "Increasing Profit Through Productivity," 7 December 1981, Speeches File, P&G Archives.

29. Lombera, interview, here and in following paragraphs.

30. Salomon, "Increasing Profit Through Productivity."

31. Lombera, interview.

32. Ibid.

33. Jaime Davila, "How Mexico Managed Through Economic Turmoil," Year-End Talk, 1984, P&G Archives.

34. For an overview of local handling of the crisis, see especially Davila, "How Mexico Managed," and Davila, "Talk to Employees of P&G de Mexico," November 1983, both in P&G Archives.

35. Salomon, interview.

36. Davila, "How Mexico Managed."

37. Ibid.

38. Ibid.; Jim Monton, interview, 14 November 2001.

39. Davila, "How Mexico Managed."

40. Ibid.

41. Salomon, interview; Lombera, interview; Reyes, interview.

42. Salomon, interview; Lombera, interview.

43. On Zest's margins, see Davila, "How Mexico Managed." On earnings impact, see Lombera and Salomon Oral Histories. See also *Procter & Gamble de Mexico: 50 Aniversario*, 71 ("Zest *te vuelve a la vida!*").

44. John Pepper, telephone interview, 20 December 2002.

45. Ed Artzt, "Board Comments, December 1989: International Share Progress," Exhibit 4, Board Notebooks, Legal.

46. "1987–88 Sales and Earnings Breakdown," International Division, 12 July 1988, Board Notebooks, Legal Division. The net sales figure does not include RVI Mexico results, moreover, which amounted to an additional $61 million.

47. Salomon, "P&G Mexico Is on the Fast Track," *Moonbeams,* February 1991, 7.

48. Claude Salomon, "Latin American Laundry / Paper," presentation to Board of Directors, 13 November 1990, P&G Archives.

49. Jorge Montoya, "Sector-Geography Partnership: A Must to Win," 4 June 1993, P&G Archives.

50. Jorge Montoya, "Latin American-Multinational Perspective," talk delivered to MIT-Sloan Business School, 8 March 1997, Speeches File, P&G Archives.

Chapter Thirteen

1. "Shampoo Rivals Wonder When P&G Will Seek Old Dominance," *Advertising Age,* 23 September 1974, 3.

2. Joanne Cleaver, "Awash in a New Wave of Haircare," *Advertising Age,* 28 February 1983, in "Special Report: Toiletries and Beauty Aids Marketing," M-24.

3. Tobie Sullivan, "Keeping Pace with Fickle Customer," section 2, "Toiletries / Beauty Aids," *Advertising Age,* 25 February 1980, S10.

4. Cecilia Kuzma, interview, 6 April 2001; Jim Monton, "Hair Care History at P&G," presentation, 1999, P&G Archives, lists Pert launch year as 1976. The 1979 figure is from Sullivan, "Keeping Pace."

5. Kuzma, interview.

6. Ray Bolich, interview, 14 November 2001. The technical and historical background that follows draws primarily on Bolich's account.

7. Jim Monton, interview, 14 November 2001.

8. Bolich, interview, with additional account provided by Ray Bolich, telephone interview, 25 July 2002.

9. Kuzma, interview.

10. John Pepper, "Presentation to U.S. Advertising Group: Pert / Rejoy / Sassoon Wash & Go Case Study," 30 March 1993, P&G Archives.

11. From the boxes Ray Bolich supplied to the P&G Archives. A post-it label attached to the Silk Blossom package reads: "Original BC-18B Bases product. This was with the betaine surfactant base. BC-18B had a safety issue. So was replaced with BC-18S & used in 'Pert Plus.'"

12. Kuzma, interview.

13. Actually, P&G had test marketed a shampoo called Pert in 1961—a pearly pink cream, similar in composition to Head & Shoulders. This early version, unrelated in formulation to the Pert of the 1980s, apparently never made it out of test market (George Holman, "History of the Drug Products Division," typewritten manuscript, 28 May 1987, P&G Archives; and Monton, "Hair Care History").

14. Kuzma, interview. See also Cecilia Kuzma, "Presentation to U.S. Advertising Group: Pert / Rejoy / Sassoon Wash & Go Case Study," 30 March 1990, P&G Archives.

15. Pepper, "Pert / Rejoy / Sassoon Wash & Go Case Study." See also *Advertising Age,* 20 August 1987, 110.

16. The marketing strategy is spelled out in Procter & Gamble, "Brand Franchise Measurement Summary," 1991–1992 Budget, P&G Archives.

17. Kuzma, "Pert / Rejoy / Sassoon Wash & Go Case Study," 30 March 1990.

18. Share and earnings information from 1991–1992 budget. Long term goal from 1989–1990 budget preface. On the role of sampling in driving early brand growth, see also Rob Matteucci, interview, 24 January 2002.

19. *Consumer Reports,* February 1987, 97.

20. On the impact of independent third-party endorsement, see Kuzma, interview. On share leadership in dollar terms, see Bill Connell, "Operations Committee Meeting Panel Discussion—Global Expansion of Two-in-One Hair Care Strategy," 12 March 1990, P&G Archives.

21. See, for example, Pepper, "Pert / Rejoy / Sassoon Wash & Go Case Study."

22. Martin Neuchtern, interview, 13 November 2001.

23. Procter & Gamble, "1991–1992 Budget," preface, P&G Archives.

24. On "year of reckoning" and share and sales data, see Procter & Gamble, "1992–1993 Budget," preface, P&G Archives. On the "executional shift" in the "Lockers" campaign, see Procter & Gamble,

"1991–1992 Budget," preface, P&G Archives. See also Jennifer Lawrence, "P&G to Unveil Pert Plus Ads as Two-in-One Shampoos Expand," *Advertising Age,* 6 July 1972.

25. Matteucci, interview.

26. For background on P&G in Taiwan, see John Kennedy, "The Global Introduction of the 'New' Pantene Shampoo: Success in Taiwan," Case 9A99A038 (London, Ontario: University of Western Ontario, Richard Ivey School of Business, 1999); James Wei, telephone interview, 16 December 2001.

27. Wei, interview.

28. Market data from P&G's habits and usage study, summarized in Kennedy, "Success in Taiwan."

29. Kuzma, interview.

30. Richardson Vicks, "A Special Report on Hair Care," promotional brochure, circa 1983, P&G Archives. For background on Pantene's development and early history, see Kennedy, "Success in Taiwan."

31. Wei, interview.

32. Ibid.

33. Quoted in Kennedy, "Success in Taiwan," 5.

34. Ibid., 5–6.

35. Wei, interview.

36. Kennedy, "Success in Taiwan," 6–7; Wei, interview.

37. Wei, interview.

38. Kennedy, "Success in Taiwan."

39. This version of events is from Wei, interview. Kuzma, interview, and others confirm central roles played by Blanchard, and above all Artzt.

40. Matteucci, interview.

41. Jim Monton, interview.

42. Jim Monton, telephone conversation with author.

43. *Wall Street Journal,* 19 November 1992.

44. Neuchtern, interview.

Chapter Fourteen

1. *Wall Street Journal,* 11 October 1989.

2. Procter & Gamble, Annual Report for 1990; Hintz left P&G in 1991 while Jager, like Pepper, eventually became chairman and chief executive.

3. Ed Artzt, interviews, 25 April and 3 October 2000.

4. Quoted in Procter & Gamble, Annual Report for 1993; Fouad Kraytem, interview, 3 April 2002.

5. *Wall Street Journal,* 5 March 1991.

6. Ed Artzt, Remarks to Financial Analysts, Cincinnati, 15 July 1993, P&G Archives; Procter & Gamble, Annual Reports for 1989–1994. Procter & Gamble phased out the Clarion brand, a small, unprofitable line, in 1994.

7. Quoted in *Wall Street Journal,* 25 and 16 March 1992; Procter & Gamble, Annual Reports for 1992 and 1993; Gary Martin, interview, 31 May 2000.

8. *Wall Street Journal,* 10 and 11 June 1991. Although Artzt vigorously denied the rumors, the episode led to an embarrassing moment for him and the company. At about the time the rumors leaked, P&G was in fact privately discussing selling off underperforming brands in its food and beverage business. *Wall Street Journal* reporter Alecia Swasy somehow learned of these discussions and reported them. Artzt was infuriated by the leaks, and P&G arranged to review Swasy's phone records under the authority of an Ohio statute outlawing conversion of trade secrets. Once discovered, this act opened P&G to a firestorm of public criticism. On August 13, editorial writers at the *Wall Street Journal* scolded the company and suggested that it ought to "be grown-up enough to recognize that there's something sinister in pawing around in other people's phone records, and in suborning law-enforcement powers to pursue petty disputes." Although Artzt acknowledged the mistake and expressed regret, Swasy went on to write a book, *Soap Opera: The Inside Story of Procter & Gamble* (New York: Times Books, 1993), which recounted the episode, attacked Artzt, and portrayed P&G in unflattering terms.

9. *Wall Street Journal,* 25 April 1991; S. P. Donovan, Project Joe Board Presentation, 8 September 1992, P&G Archives; *Wall Street Journal,* 29 November 1996; Board Presentation on Fisher Nuts, 1995, P&G Archives.

10. *Wall Street Journal,* 17 July 1991; *Cincinnati Post,* 30 June 1995.

11. Procter & Gamble, "Manufacturing Competitiveness and Strengthening Global Effectiveness at Procter & Gamble," Media Backgrounder (n.d. [July 1993]).

12. Ibid.

13. Ibid.

14. Michael Hammer and James Champy, *Reengineering the Corporation* (New York: Harper Collins, 1993); George Stalk and Thomas Hout, *Competing Against Time: How Time-Based Competition Is Reshaping Global Markets* (New York: The Free Press, 1990).

15. "Behind the Tumult at P&G," *Fortune,* March 1994.

16. Artzt, Remarks to Financial Analysts, 15 July 1993, P&G Archives, 7–8; Media Backgrounder (see note 11).

17. Procter & Gamble, Annual Report for 1993; *Cincinnati Enquirer,* 16 July 1993.

18. Information in this and the next paragraph comes from Teresa Amabile and Dean Whitney, *Corporate New Ventures at Procter & Gamble* (Boston: Harvard Business School) Case 9-897-0881997, 3–4.

19. Ibid., 6–7.

20. "No More Mr. Nice Guy at P&G—Not by a Long Shot," *BusinessWeek,* 3 February 1992, 54–56; Artzt, interview, 3 October 2000.

21. John Pepper, interview, 8 December 1999.

22. See, for example, "Characteristics of Successful P&G Managers," 8 December 1980; "Let Us Never Forget," 15 June 1998; "Building the Future: The Evolution of Procter & Gamble," 20 August 1998; and "Essence of P&G," 20 July 1999. All speeches given on multiple occasions and locations by John Pepper, copies available at P&G Archives. Pepper is completing a book drawing on these and other sources to highlight principles and lessons learned in his career at the company.

23. *Cincinnati Post,* 30 June 1995; "Make It Simple," *BusinessWeek,* 9 September 1996, 96–103; "P&G: New and Improved!" *Fortune,* 14 October 1996, 151–160; "Death of the Proctoids," *Financial Times,* 21 May 1998.

24. "Make It Simple"; "P&G: New and Improved!"; Pepper, interview, 8 December 1999 and 20 April 2000.

25. "Make It Simple"; "P&G, No. 1 Again, Aims to Reinvent Marketing," *Advertising Age,* 30 September 1996.

26. Procter & Gamble and Tambrands had some earlier connections. In 1981, Tambrands had recruited its chief executive, Edwin Shutt, Jr., from P&G. Shutt, who had helped launch P&G in Japan, led Tambrands until 1989.

27. "P&G Will Buy Tambrands for $2 Billion," *Wall Street Journal,* 9 April 1997.

28. John Pepper, "Overview of the Evolution of Procter & Gamble Structure," 7 June 1998, copy at P&G Archives.

29. Procter & Gamble, Annual Report for 1995.

30. Procter & Gamble, Organization 2005 Overview, P&G Archives.

31. Kerry Clark, interview, 1 October 2002.

32. Procter & Gamble, Organization 2005 Overview; Procter & Gamble, News Release, 9 September 1998, P&G Archives.

33. Procter & Gamble, Organization 2005 Overview.

34. Ibid.

35. Procter & Gamble, News Release, 8 September 1998, P&G Archives.

36. Steve David, interview, 30 September 2002; Procter & Gamble, News Release, 13 September 1999.

37. Procter & Gamble, News Release, 26 August 1999.

38. Procter & Gamble, News Release, 11 August, 1999; *Wall Street Journal,* 12 August 1999; <http://www.iams.com>; Jeff Ansell, e-mail to Charlotte Otto, 9 March 2002.

39. John Pepper to Jeff Ansell, April 5, 2003.

40. Jeff Ansell e-mail to Charlotte Otto and Ed Rider, October 7, 2003. Subsequent quotations from Ansell in this sidebar are also from this source.

41. David S. Hilzenrath, "P&G Ends Effort to Buy Drug Companies; Price Slide Thwarts Plan to Use Stock," *Washington Post,* 25 January 2000.

42. Procter & Gamble, News Release, 7 March 2000.

43. Clark, interview.

44. Elizabeth Olson, "Strangers in a Strange Workplace," *New York Times,* 30 November 2000.

45. Pepper, interview, 20 December 2002; A. G. Lafley, interview, 13 and 14 December 2001; Emily Nelson, "Rallying the Troops at P&G," *Wall Street Journal,* 31 August 2000; Clark, interview.

46. A. G. Lafley, speech at Annual Meeting, October 2000, P&G Archives.

47. A. G. Lafley, Remarks at Rotman School (University of Toronto) Integrative Thinking Series, 21 April 2003, P&G Archives; A. G. Lafley, interview, 9 July 2003.

48. Lafley, interview, 9 July 2003.

49. Procter & Gamble, Annual Report for 2002; Clark, interview.

50. Lafley, interview, 13 and 14 December 2001; Procter & Gamble, Annual Report for 2002.

51. Lafley, interview, 9 July 2003; Lafley, Remarks at Rotman School; Robert Berner, "P&G: New and Improved," *BusinessWeek,* 7 July 2003, 52–63.

52. Norman R. Augustine to Ed Rider, 27 June 2003.

53. Procter & Gamble, Annual Report for 2002; Katrina Brooker, "The Un-CEO," *Fortune,* 16 September 2002; "Why P&G's Smile Is So Bright," *BusinessWeek,* 12 August 2002; *Wall Street Journal,* 19 March 2003.

54. Lafley, Remarks at Rotman School; "P&G: New and Improved"; *Wall Street Journal,* 23 March 2001 and 14 June 2002.

Chapter Fifteen

1. Lou Pritchett, interview, 13 August 1989.

2. James L. McKenney and Theodore H. Clark, "Procter & Gamble: Improving Consumer Value through Process Redesign," Case 9-195-126 (Boston: Harvard Business School, 1995), 3; Bill Saporito, "Behind the Tumult at P&G," *Fortune,* 7 March 1994, unpaginated reprint; Lawrence D. "Mike" Milligan, "'Keeping It Simple': The Evolution of Customer Business Development at Procter & Gamble," speech to American Marketing Association Doctoral Symposium, Cincinnati, OH, 31 July 1997, 2; Tom Muccio to Ed Rider, 12 December 2002, P&G Archives.

3. Milligan, "'Keeping It Simple'," 2.

4. David S. Swanson to Gibby Carey, undated letter, mid-1990s, copy in P&G Archives. Carey's personal collection, Cincinnati, OH; David Swanson, interview, 11 April 2001.

5. Swanson to Carey, undated letter.

6. This and the following paragraph are based on "Why P&G Wants a Mellower Image," *BusinessWeek,* 7 June 1982; Bill Saporito, "Procter & Gamble's Comeback Plan," *Fortune,* 4 February 1985; Chuck Downton, interview, 10 May 2001; and comments of an anonymous reviewer to Harvard Business School Press, November 2002.

7. Sam Walton with John Huey, *Made in America: My Story* (New York: Doubleday, 1992).

8. Pritchett gives his account of what happened next in Lou Pritchett, *Stop Paddling & Start Rocking the Boat: Business Lessons from the School of Hard Knocks* (New York: HarperBusiness, 1995), chapter 3.

9. Tom Muccio, interview, 21 June 2000; Milligan, interview, 15 May 2000; Mike Graen, "Technology in Manufacturer/Retailer Integration: Wal-Mart and Procter & Gamble," *Velocity* (spring 1999).

10. This paragraph and the following are based on Lou Pritchett to J. E. Pepper, T. Laco, and W. W. Abbott, 22 July 1987; and Lou Pritchett to Sam Walton, 24 July 1987, all in P&G Archives. See also Pritchett, *Stop Paddling,* 26–31; and Muccio, interview.

11. Tom Laco, interview, 6 February 2001.

12. Milligan, interview.

13. Muccio, interview.

14. Quoted in Graen, "Technology in Manufacturer/Retailer Integration," 13.

15. Tom Muccio, "Procter & Gamble/Wal-Mart Value-Added Relationship—Background." Copy furnished by Muccio.

16. Tom Muccio to Ed Rider, 12 December 2002; Mike Graen, interview, 21 June 2000.

17. Graen, "Technology in Manufacturer/Retailer Integration," 15–16.

18. Wal-Mart/P&G Team, Business Results/Strategic Review, 7 March 1990, P&G Archives.

19. Muccio, interview.

20. Milligan, "Memorandum on Customer Development, Status Report," 20 June 1989, P&G Archives.

21. Milligan, "'Keeping It Simple'," 4; Paul S. Beck, Coliseum Talk, 4 November 1996, P&G Archives.

22. Milligan, "'Keeping It Simple'," 4; Milligan, interview.

23. Rajiv Lal and Mitchell Kristofferson, "Value Pricing at Procter & Gamble (A)," Case M284B, (Boston: Harvard Business School, 1996), 5.

24. The authors thank an anonymous reviewer for this information.

25. Lal and Kristofferson, "Value Pricing at Procter & Gamble (B)," Case M284B (Stanford Business School, 1996), 7.

26. Quoted in *Advertising Age,* 22 June 1992. See also Lal and Kristofferson, "Value Pricing at Procter & Gamble (B)," 8.

27. McKenney and Clark, "Procter & Gamble: Improving Consumer Value through Process Redesign," 3

28. Milligan, "'Keeping It Simple'," 5. The authors also thank an anonymous reviewer for this information.

29. Milligan, "Keeping It Simple," 5.

30. Durk Jager, interview by Koji Yamasaki and Ralph Drayer, 23–31 March 1998, copy at P&G Archives; McKenney and Clark, "Procter & Gamble: Improving Consumer Value through Process Redesign," 9–10. In 1994, P&G sold its software development operations to IBM. According to Chuck Downton, P&G's move to category management inspired key officials at the Food Marketing Institute to urge member retailers to reorganize purchasing and merchandising activities around categories (Downton, interview).

31. Milligan, "'Keeping It Simple'," 9–10.

32. Tom Muccio to Ed Rider, 12 December 2002.

Chapter Sixteen

1. Information in this and the following paragraph is based on Wolfgang Berndt, Procter & Gamble Eastern Europe, undated presentation [1997?], P&G Archives; Herbert Schmitz, interview, 18 November 1997.

2. Schmitz, interview; Berndt, Procter & Gamble Eastern Europe.

3. Berndt, Procter & Gamble Eastern Europe.

4. Jeffrey Gandz, Maurice Smith, Asad Wali, and David W. Conklin, "Procter & Gamble in Eastern Europe (B)," Case 97H002 (London, Ontario: University of Western Ontario, Richard Ivey School of Business, 1997), 6–7; Berndt, Procter & Gamble Eastern Europe.

5. Schmitz, interview.

6. Ibid.

7. Gandz, Smith, Wali, and Conklin, "Procter & Gamble in Eastern Europe (B)," 5.

8. Berndt, Procter & Gamble Eastern Europe.

9. Ibid.

10. Kevin Edwards, interview, 29 October 1997, P&G Archives.

11. David J. Arnold, "Procter & Gamble: Always Russia," Case 9-599-050 (Boston: Harvard Business School, 1998), 10–11.

12. Information in this and the following paragraph is based on Otto Hausknecht, interview 1997; Ben and Valia Bethell, interview, [undated, 1997?]; Schmitz, interview; P&G Central and Eastern Europe, Legal Department, Novomoskovsk Calendar of Events, P&G Archives.

13. G. L. Sobel and A. O. Andreev to S. Anastassov, "Head & Shoulders—Russian Success Factors," 4 October 1996, P&G Archives; "Blend-a-Med Eastern Europe—Turn-around," n.d., P&G Archives.

14. Edwards, interview; Arnold: "Procter & Gamble: Always Russia," 6; Berndt, Procter & Gamble Eastern Europe, 15.

15. Laurent Philippe, interview, 27 February 2001.

16. Ibid.

17. Ludmila Biriukova, interview; Natasha Glazova, interview; Ruslan Giniyatov, interview, all November 1997.

18. Alexander Filatov, interview, November 1997.

19. Luba Pelikhova, interview, 3 March 2001.

20. Philippe, interview.

21. Procter & Gamble, Russia: January–June 1999 Business Plan, 7 December 1998, P&G Archives.

22. Philippe, interview.

23. Angelike Gaedtke, interview, 1 March 2001.

24. Ibid.

25. Ibid.

26. Henry Karamanoukian, interview, 1 March 2001; Procter & Gamble, Eastern Europe Subsidiary (Russia-Ukraine-Belarus), presentation slides, n.d. [2001?].

27. Philippe, interview.

28. Ibid.; Pelikhova, interview; Andy Peterson and Shannan Stevenson, interview, 2 March 2001. The loans proved hard to collect, and P&G expects to write them off eventually as bad debts.

29. Phillip Wellens, interview, 28 February 2001.

30. Ibid.; Pelikhova, interview.

31. Philippe, interview.

32. Peterson and Stevenson, interview.
33. Anton Andreev, interview, 1 March 2001; Vitalius Paulus, interview, 1 March 2001.
34. Robertson and Stevenson, interview, 2 March 2001; Andreev, interview; Paulus, interview.
35. Schmitz, interview.
36. Peterson and Stevenson, interview.

Chapter Seventeen

1. Alfred Lief, *It Floats: The Story of Procter & Gamble* (New York: Rinehart & Company, Inc., 1958), 296.
2. Mary Carethers to Ed Rider, 28 April 2003, P&G Archives.
3. Gina Drosos, interview, 20 May 2003.
4. "P&G Struggles to Regain Crest's Toothpaste Lead," *Cincinnati Enquirer,* 7 April 2001; *Business and Industry,* 1998.
5. *Advertising Age,* 29 July 1985; *Financial Times,* 24 September 1985; Michael Kehoe, interview, 25 June 2002.
6. Zachary Schiller, "The Sound and the Fluoride," *BusinessWeek,* 14 August 1995.
7. Dana Canedy, "P&G Seeks to Stem Loss of Smile Share," *New York Times,* 20 June 1997.
8. Paul Sagel, interview, May 2002.
9. Andrea M. Grossman, "Merchandising Strategies Challenged by Premium Specialty Toothpastes," *Drug Store News,* 22 June 1998.
10. Michael Kehoe, interview, 25 June 2002.
11. Schiller, "The Sound and the Fluoride"; Canedy, "P&G Seeks to Stem Loss of Smile Share."
12. Grossman, "Merchandising Strategies Challenged"; Tara Parker-Pope, "Colgate Total(ly) Set for Teeth Tiff," *Pittsburgh Post-Gazette,* 30 December 1997; Marilyn Much, "How Terrific Ads Propelled Colgate, Dethroned Longtime Leader P&G," *Investor's Business Daily,* 20 April 2001.
13. Kehoe, interview.
14. Blendax had a number of brands, including shampoos, shower gels, and deodorants, but the oral care business was the most attractive to P&G. Blendax had a very strong share in the German-speaking countries in oral care products, including manual and electric toothbrushes, and had an infrastructure for visiting and selling to dentists (Kehoe, interview).
15. John Smale, interview, 8 February 2001.
16. Grossman, "Merchandising Strategies Challenged."
17. Ibid.; "Whiteners Still Creating All the Excitement," *MMR,* 24 November 1997.
18. Much of this section was based on Sagel, interview.
19. Ameet Sachdeve, "Whiteners Clean Up in Oral Care," *Chicago Tribune,* 23 April 2002.
20. Bruce Byrnes, interview, June 2001.
21. Kehoe, interview. Thanks also to his comments on a draft.
22. Sachdeve, "Whiteners Clean Up."
23. *BusinessWeek,* 12 August 2002; Shekhar Mitra, interview, 30 November 2002.
24. Kehoe, interview.
25. Byrnes interview; Kehoe interview; *BusinessWeek,* 12 August 2002.
26. Kehoe interview; Cliff Peale, "Brighter Outlook for P&G," *Cincinnati Enquirer,* 2 December 2001.
27. Paul Cootes, interview, 30 May 2002.
28. G. R. Dennis, "1986 Annual Report" memo, 22 July 1986, Box 109, P&G Archives.
29. Susan Arnold, Presentation to Analysts, December 2002, Seattle, WA, P&G Archives. In the years just prior to acquisition, RVI had launched several line extensions, including an Oil of Olay beauty cleanser and cream.
30. "Oil of Olay Brand Organizer, 1991–1992," Box 270, P&G Archives.
31. Drosos, interview.
32. R. T. Blanchard, "Executive Committee Share Report, U.S. Beauty Care," 12 February 1996, Speech File, P&G Archives.
33. Drosos, interview.
34. Specifically, the formulation blended vitamin E, pro-vitamin B5 (panthenol), and niaminicide (vitamin B3).
35. Quoted in *Cosmetic World,* 21 February 2000, 72.
36. Drosos, interview.
37. Jim Stengel, interview, 19 May 2003.
38. Kehoe, interview.

Chapter Eighteen

1. Harry Tecklenburg to Board of Directors, 8 September 1981, P&G Archives.

2. Marion David Francis, Oral History, 24 January 1997, Chemical Heritage Foundation, Cincinnati; "The Calcium Connection," *Moonbeams* (P&G in-house newsletter), 6 February 1989, 6–7.

3. Francis, Oral History.

4. Ibid. See also "1996 Perkin Medal Awarded to M. David Francis of Procter & Gamble," *Chemical & Engineering News,* 11 March 1996, 34–35.

5. Francis, Oral History.

6. Alfonso Gambardella, *Science and Innovation: The US Pharmaceutical Industry During the 1980s* (New York: Cambridge University Press, 1995), 18–21.

7. Mark A. Collar, "Emergence of P&G in the Pharmaceutical Industry," speech to Allicense '98, San Francisco, 1 April 1998; G. Place to W. N. Zaki, 10 February 1982, G. Place File, P&G Archives; Tecklenburg to Board, 8 September 1981.

8. *Wall Street Journal,* 18 March 1982; Tecklenburg to Board, 8 September 1981; Kay Napier, interview, 26 October 2001.

9. Tecklenburg to Board, 8 September 1981.

10. Ibid.

11. The best overviews of the evolution of the pharmaceutical industry are Basil Achilladelis, "Innovation in the Pharmaceutical Industry," in *Pharmaceutical Innovation: Revolutionizing Human Health,* ed. Ralph Landau, Basil Achilladelis, and Alexander Scriabine (Philadelphia: Chemical Heritage Press, 1999), 1–147; and Alfred D. Chandler, Jr., *Shaping the Industrial Century: The Creation and Evolution of the Chemical and Pharmaceutical Industries* (Cambridge: Harvard University Press, forthcoming, 2005). We are grateful to Professor Chandler for showing us this work in advance of publication.

12. Achilladelis, "Innovation in the Pharmaceutical Industry," 113–130; Gambardella, *Science and Innovation,* 104.

13. John Smale to Ed Rider, 4 December 2002, P&G Archives.

14. Tom Blinn, interview, 20 November 2001; "Norwich Sells Four Brands," *Moonbeams,* January 1985.

15. Blinn, interview.

16. "P&G to Acquire Richardson Vicks," *Moonbeams,* special edition, October 1985; "New to the Family," *Moonbeams,* December 1985.

17. P&G recouped some of the investment by selling unwanted parts of the Norwich Eaton, Searle, and RVI portfolios. Within a year of closing on RVI, for example, P&G sold RVI's businesses in furniture stains and finishes for $66 million (*Moonbeams,* July 1986). Obviously, the RVI acquisition included businesses unrelated to health care.

18. Achilladelis, "Innovation in the Pharmaceutical Industry," 138.

19. Blinn, interview; *Wall Street Journal,* 3 June 1993; Gambardella, *Science and Innovation,* 99.

20. John Smale, interviews, 6 and 7 May 1997.

21. *Wall Street Journal,* 18 March 1982.

22. G. Place to C. D. Broaddus et al., "Memo on Health Care Focus Areas," 21 December 1983, P&G Archives.

23. G. Place to John Smale via W. N. Zaki, 29 October 1984, P&G Archives.

24. Procter & Gamble Pharmaceuticals, *Research and Product Development* (undated brochure [2000?], P&G Archives.

25. Place to Smale via Zaki, 29 January 1986.

26. G. Place to M. Jozoff, "Project Magnum," 21 December 1988, P&G Archives.

27. T. A. Moore, Year-End Talk, 11 March 1992, P&G Archives.

28. John Pepper, videotaped speech, 1995, quoted in Collar, "Emergence of P&G in the Pharmaceutical Industry"; "Procter & Gamble Heads for the Medicine Cabinet," *BusinessWeek,* 7 August 1995.

29. "P&G Acquisitions/Joint Ventures/Divestitures/Agreements Since 1980," List maintained in P&G Archives; Moore, Year-End Talk, 1992.

30. *Wall Street Journal Europe,* 11 May 1992.

31. Achilladelis, "Innovation in the Pharmaceutical Industry," 131–138.

32. Bruce Byrnes, "U.S. Health Care Update for WCB's GM Meeting," 29 August 1996, P&G Archives.

33. Mark Collar, interview, 25 October 2001.

34. Procter & Gamble, News Release, 5 May 1997, P&G Archives.

35. Blinn, interview.

36. Byrnes, "U.S. Health Care Update."

37. Procter & Gamble, News Release, 5 May 1997.

38. Procter & Gamble Pharmaceuticals, Research and Product Development, undated brochure, P&G Archives; "P&G's Pharmaceutical Plan," *Cincinnati Enquirer,* 4 February 2001. According to P&G Pharmaceutical's Web site <http://www.pgpharma.com> (accessed February 2002), the Aventis deal on Actonel applies everywhere except Japan.

39. "P&G's Pharmaceutical Plan," *Cincinnati Enquirer,* 4 February 2001.

40. Collar, "Emergence of P&G in the Pharmaceutical Industry," 1 April 1998; <http://www.pgpharma.com>; <http://www.regeneron.com>; <http://www.genelogic.com>; <http://www.alexionpharm.com>; <http://www.inpharm.com/intelligence> (all accessed 10 January 2002).

41. Procter & Gamble Pharmaceuticals, Research and Product Development, undated brochure; Blinn, interview.

42. Blinn, interview.

43. Ibid.

44. Ibid.

45. Ibid.; Blinn, Speech at Euro Conference, 18 May 2001, P&G Archives.

46. Blinn, interview; and two brief documents furnished by Tom Blinn: "Global Personal Health Care Leadership" and "PHC Abbreviated History."

47. Achilladelis, "Innovation in the Pharmaceutical Industry," 140.

48. Collar, interview; Blinn, interview.

Chapter Nineteen

1. Berenike Ullmann to Jack Borcherding, 28 April 1992, Ullmann Files, P&G China Headquarters, Guangzhou.

2. Ed Artzt, interview, 25 April 2000, P&G Archives.

3. Ullmann to Borcherding, 28 April 1992.

4. James Wei, interview, 28 May 2002, P&G Archives.

5. Yvonne Pei, interview, 29 May 2002.

6. Dimitri Panayotopoulos, "Gray Asia Pacific Regional Conference," 10 June 1996, Beijing, copy in P&G Archives. See also Ullmann, interview, 28 May 2002.

7. Ullmann, interview.

8. John Pepper to Board, 13 June 1989, Legal Department, P&G.

9. John Pepper to Board, 10 September 1991 (referring to results for FY 1990–1991), Legal Department, P&G Archives.

10. Dimitri Panayotopoulos, interview, 3 April 2002.

11. Kenneth Zhu, interview, 27 May 2002.

12. Panayotopoulos, interview.

13. Dimitri Panayotopoulos, "Gray Asia Pacific Regional Conference."

14. Dimitri Panayotopoulos, "Board Meeting Speech," 1995, P&G Archives.

15. Sandra Bereti, "MBA Talk," draft, 24 May 2000, Ullmann Files, P&G Headquarters, Guangzhou.

16. Raymond Co, interview, 28 May 2002.

17. Pepper to Board, 10 September 1991, copy in P&G Archives.

18. Winfried Kastner to Board, November 1991, Board Notebooks, Legal Department, P&G Archives.

19. Ullmann, interview, 28 May 2002; Austin Lally, interview, 27 May 2002; *South China Morning Post,* 17 April 2001.

20. Ullmann, interview.

21. Pei, interview.

22. *Wall Street Journal,* 12 September 1995.

23. Panayotopoulos, presentation to Board of Directors, 12 June 1995, Board Notebooks, Legal Department, P&G.

24. Ibid.

25. Ibid.

26. Tide's leading share reflected its relatively high price and wide proportional representation: The brand did not lead in any given region, but held the lead nationally because it was available in more regions than any other brand.

27. Dimitri Panayotopoulos to P&G Headquarters, monthly letter, February 1999, P&G Archives.

28. Debra Caswell, interview, 30 May 2002.

29. Ibid.; Lally, interview; Bonnie Curtis, interview, 29 May 2002.

30. *South China Morning Post,* 17 April 2001.
31. Lally, interview.
32. Ibid.
33. Ibid.
34. Shekhar Mitra, telephone interview with authors, 20 November 2003.
35. Caswell, interview.
36. Shekhar Mitra, interview, January 2003.
37. Chris Buckley, interview, 30 May 2002.
38. Mitra, interview.
39. Buckley, interview.
40. Ibid. Other savings were found in formula components such as locally sourced flavors.
41. Ibid.; Mitra, telephone interview, 20 November 2002.
42. Charles Yang, interview, 30 May 2002.

Epilogue

1. Alfred Lief, *It Floats: The Story of Procter & Gamble* (New York: Rinehart & Company, Inc., 1958); Oscar Schisgall, *Eyes on Tomorrow: The Evolution of Procter & Gamble* (Chicago: J. G. Ferguson Publishing, 1981).

2. Hence, again, a reason why so many P&G senior executives admire James Collins and Jerry Porras, *Built to Last*. See above, Prologue, n. 2.

3. Procter & Gamble, Annual Report for 2002.

4. In the 1980s and 1990s, Ed Artzt frequently delivered a speech on this theme called "A Company of Individuals." He also used that title on his retirement book, a tradition at P&G in which outgoing chief executives publish collections of their major speeches, presentations, and writings for limited distribution.

Appendix Four

1. P&G was incorporated in Ohio, its present legal home, in 1905.

2. P&G was delisted by the New York Stock Exchange in 1903 because it declined to comply with recent rules for disclosure of financial information. The company's stock continued to trade on other stock markets, however, and after P&G revised its disclosure policies it eventually returned to listing on the NYSE in 1929.

INDEX

ABOUT THE AUTHORS

DAVIS DYER is president and a founding director of The Winthrop Group, Inc., a Cambridge, Massachusetts–based firm specializing in the documentation and use of organizational experience, and a faculty member at Monitor University, part of the Monitor Group. He is author or coauthor of many publications, including *Changing Fortunes: Remaking the Industrial Corporation* (2002, with Nitin Nohria and Frederick Dalzell) and *The Generations of Corning: The Life and Times of a Global Corporation* (2001, with Daniel Gross).

FREDERICK DALZELL is a history partner with The Winthrop Group. He holds a Ph.D. in American Civilization from Harvard University and is coauthor (with Nitin Nohria and Davis Dyer) of *Changing Fortunes: Remaking the Industrial Corporation* (2002). He is currently completing a biography of electrical inventor Frank J. Sprague (with John Sprague) and investigating the history of mortgage financing.

ROWENA OLEGARIO is Assistant Professor of History at Vanderbilt University, where she teaches courses in the history of business. She received a B.A. in history from Yale University and a Ph.D. in the same subject from Harvard University. She is currently completing a book on credit and business culture in the United States from 1830 to 1920.